MONTANA PAY DIRT

GUIDE TO THE MINING CAMPS OF THE TREASURE STATE

"THE HILL," BUTTE, FROM MEADERVILLE

MONTANA PAY DIRT

A Guide to the Mining Camps
of the Treasure State

MURIEL SIBELL WOLLE

SAGE BOOKS

First Edition
Third Printing, 1982
First Paperback Edition 1983

Sage/Swallow Press Books
are published by
Ohio University Press
Athens Ohio 45701

Library of Congress Catalog Card Number 63-14650
ISBN 0-8040-0210-X (cloth bound)
ISBN 0-8040-0722-5 (paper bound)

To Anne McDonnell
and Virginia Walton,
devoted librarians,
who unlocked Montana's
treasure chest for me.

CONTENTS

MAPS

ILLUSTRATIONS

ACKNOWLEDGMENTS

Only an author knows how completely dependent he is upon the gracious people who take time to answer questions or verify from the original sources the facts he has accumulated.

To the many persons who helped me, my sincere thanks, not only to those whose names I know, but also to those whom I met in passing — the countless number of filling station attendants and garage men who serviced my car and provided local information on road conditions; the truck drivers, ranchers, storekeepers, waitresses, forest rangers, people on the street and those at whose doors I knocked. Each added something that is imbedded in this book.

People like the three ladies in the county clerk's office at Thompson Falls, who supplied information on short notice about mines I wanted to visit, and the proprietor of the Ox-Bow Bar at Bannack who handed me a pamphlet describing dredge operations in Grasshopper Creek, or the Albrights of Helena whom we met in Confederate Gulch and who cautioned us about the roadbed. When we failed to reach a designated spot within a reasonable time, they hunted us up to see if we were all right.

Each of the following contributed to my stock of information: Mrs. Anne Mulvey of Anaconda; Mrs. Gwen Vaughn Rhys of Barker; Mr. and Mrs. Howard Place of Missoula; Mrs. Ann Rogers of Clinton; Harry Bouton of Garnet; Dan Cushman of Great Falls; Miss Bernice Boone, Mrs. Stella H. Denial, Miss Susan Eaker, John C. Moore and Dee Scott of Helena; Mrs. Olga W. Johnson, Russell Littell, Len Olson, Oliver Phillips, Joe Pondelick of Libby, and H. B. Smith, a geologist from Salt Lake City, who was in Libby at the time of my visit; Katherine Sullivan of Marysville; Mr. Sutton of Neihart; Mr. and Mrs. John Judge of Polaris; Alex Eklund and Mrs. McGill of Rimini; Father Martin Florian of Stevensville; Mr. McDonnell and Fred Mayo of Superior; Gene and Ruth Grush of Sylvanite; Mr. Pitcher of Twin Bridges; Mark Sherman of Unionville; the late Houston Clay Groff of Victor; the late Peter A. Dawson of Whitehall and his daughter; Mr. and Mrs. John Reilly of Wickes; and Mr. Kellerman and his daughter of Zortman.

J. H. Vanderbeck, Secretary of the Vigilance Club of Virginia City, Evans G. Imes, of the Beaverhead Museum and Dillon Chamber of Commerce, and Harold A. McGrath of the Butte Chamber of Commerce, all provided answers to my many questions. Miss Dorothy R. Woods, County Clerk's Office at the Courthouse, Lewistown, found the townsite plat of Kendall and Miss Dorothy Dodson, County Clerk and Recorder of Thompson Falls, not only provided data, but interested Neil Fullerton, a retired Forest Service man, who wrote accurate descriptions of mountain passes and copied maps to accompany his directions.

Two unexpected windfalls were contacts with Mrs. Althea B. Seirer, niece of James Parfet, Superintendent at Hecla, and Mrs. Leah Morris Mendenhall, daughter of William W. Morris, mining expert and banker of Pony. Both ladies were most generous with letters and information. J. Allan Norton, photographer and lecturer from Flint, Michigan, loaned me kodachromes which acquainted me with Jardine; Nathan B. Blumberg, Dean of the School of Journalism of Montana State University, Missoula, put me on the track of certain authors; Richard G. Magnuson, District Attorney, Wallace, Idaho, loaned be a rare letter from his private collection and Willard Fraser of Billings, a friend of many years, opened many leads which I could not have found for myself.

At places where I knew no one, I wrote to the postmaster requesting information. I am grateful for answers from Julian Robe of Sheridan, J. C. Emerson of Stevensville, E. R. Bennett of Superior, J. E. Bobbitt of Victor, and David C. Bryan of Whitehall, as well as

9

to the postmasters of Melrose and Norris who replied but failed to sign their names, and to the postmistress of Hilger who sent us to Joe Jost, railroad station agent, for directions to Kendall. The postmistress at Emigrant not only gave us information about Chico, but added a touch of local color by mentioning that while her daughter was driving, a buffalo jumped over the front of the car and put a hoof through the windshield.

Authors are especially indebted to librarians and I was unusually fortunate to find Mrs. Anne McDonnell in the Montana State Historical Library when I started my research in 1951. It was she who introduced me to the history and romance of Montana's rich mining lore. On my next visit to the state, I found Virginia Walton carrying on the competent and helpful tradition set by Mrs. McDonnell. Miss Marguerite McDonald and Miss Mary K. Dempsey from the same library have since provided me with much needed assistance. At the State School of Mines in Butte, librarian Mrs. Loretta B. Peck and her assistant, Mrs. Lois Fordmeier, produced an abundance of technical material. For information about the northwestern corner of the state, I depended upon Mrs. Inez Herrig, librarian of the Libby Public Library. Not only did she put at my disposal the collections of the library, but she arranged to have the old files of the Libby newspapers brought over from the *Western News* office, that I might use them more conveniently. In Colorado, I always turn to the Western History Collection of the Denver Public Library when I need specific material, confident that Mrs. Alys Freeze and Mrs. Opal Harber will furnish me with what I am after. At the University of Colorado, Miss Virginia Holbert and Miss Ellen Jackson of the Government Documents division and her assistants found obscure bulletins and professional papers full of statistics. Don Wolf, who is in charge of the Geology Map Room at the University, showed me a drawerful of Geologic Survey maps. To Mrs. Dorothy Lewis, Mrs. Hazel Potts, Miss Mary Lou Lyda and Miss Elizabeth Mowrey who kindly spent hours reading proof with me, and to Mrs. Carletta McKee and Mrs. Eloise Pearson, who typed my voluminous manuscript, my sincere thanks.

I am especially grateful to Hazel Potts of Boulder and to my husband for driving me throughout Montana, and to Howard and Arline Cook of Anaconda for serving as guides to several of the more remote camps, and for sharing with me their detailed notes on the mines.

But it is the encouragement and help of my husband, Francis Wolle, that has made this volume possible. He has been driver, interviewer of oldtimers, critic, proofreader, and general booster of morale over the eleven-year period in which this book has been jelling. Without his support, it would not have been written.

MURIEL SIBELL WOLLE

CHAPTER I

THE TREASURE STATE

You are coming into the heart of the West where you will cut a lot of mighty interesting old time trails. Just turn your fancy loose to range the coulees, gulches, prairies, and mountains, and if your imagination isn't hobbled you can people them with picturesque phantoms of the past.

Robert H. Fletcher,
Montana Highway Historical Markers

Montana is a big state. It is possible to spend two or more weeks just driving up one valley and down another and crossing range upon range of mountains, stopping often to explore side roads that lead to old camps, and still at the end of a labyrinthine itinerary to have covered only half of its surface. The eastern portion, consisting of range land and wheat farms deserves a separate trip.

Montana is a mining state. Except for the Indians whose home it was and the solitary mountain men who trapped in its wildernesses, prospectors were the ones who pushed up its streams, searching for the elusive "colors" and nuggets that promised richer yields of ore when the mother lode should be located. A number of its discoveries were accidental and were made by men, who, while hurrying across the land to the Salmon gold fields in Idaho in 1861, panned the streams along the way and, finding gold in them, stayed to wash a fortune from the gravel.

At the close of the Civil War hundreds of footloose men went west to make a living, and their presence accounts not only for several of the early camps, but also for such names as Confederate Gulch and Jeff Davis Gulch. Even Virginia City is a compromise to the southern faction who proposed that it be called Varina City, honoring Jefferson Davis' wife. The Union judge refused to record the name and substituted "Virginia."

Some gold was found in Montana in the 1850's, but it was the great strikes of the 1860's — at Bannack in 1862, at Virginia City in 1863, at Last Chance Gulch in 1864, and in many other portions of the mountains within the decade — that started the mining boom. The camps were built along the sides of the streams, whose beds yielded gold when placered or worked by hydraulics. Water was all essential. When the placer gold, which in some areas seemed inexhaustible, petered out, lode mines were discovered and the gold was recovered from within the mountains. Some mines produced silver rather than gold, and in such places the camps flourished only until 1893, when the government demonetized silver. A third wave of mineral discovery centered around the copper deposits found in or near Butte. More recent strikes have been built on zinc, manganese, and phosphate deposits.

Actually, the first mining camps weren't even in Montana; for no such place existed until 1864, when it was established as a Territory carved from the vast spaces that comprised Idaho and Dakota territories. Idaho itself was at that time only one year old, as it had been created on March 3, 1863, from portions of Washington, Dakota, and Nebraska territories. In July of that year, President Lincoln made William H. Wallace governor of Idaho Territory, and named Sidney Edgerton of Ohio, chief justice. Governor Wallace then divided the huge area into three judicial districts and assigned one federal judge to each. Edgerton was placed over the third district, which included Missoula County and the wilderness area east of the Divide. Since Bannack was the largest town of the district, he and his family settled there late in 1863.

The new territory was completely isolated, especially that portion east of the Continental Divide. Miners' courts and Vigilante committees did much to maintain order, but the need for recognized law was apparent, and Idaho's capital at Lewiston was 800 miles away over roads that were completely snowlocked much of the year. The indignant miners and merchants, therefore, felt that Washington was neglecting this portion of the frontier and that a new territory should be cut from eastern Idaho.

Through the efforts of Colonel Wilbur F. Sanders, Sam Hauser, and a few others, the sum of $2,500 in dust and nuggets was raised, and Chief Justice Sidney Edgerton was asked to journey to Washington and present the case of the people to Congress and to the President. He accepted the mission and left for the States in January, 1864. His pleading was so effective that on May 26, 1864, the President signed the act which created Montana Territory, a vast area with its western boundary the Bitterroot Mountains. On June 22, President Lincoln appointed Edgerton the first territorial governor. Upon his return he named Bannack the temporary territorial capital.

Both men whom the President appointed to be secretary of the Territory declined the honor, and the office was vacant when Lincoln was assassinated. President Andrew Johnson, therefore, filled the post by the appointment of Thomas Francis Meagher on August 4, 1865. Soon after Meagher reached Bannack, late in September, Governor Edgerton took his family back to Ohio to put the children in school and then hurried to Washington to devote himself to territorial business. By this time, the Alder Gulch discoveries had so drained away most of Bannack's population that Virginia City was the larger town, and with little difficulty, because of Edgerton's absence, Acting-Governor Meagher "put the official papers of state in his pocket," and took them to Virginia City, where he installed the executive offices in the best hotel. The legislature officially recognized Virginia City as the territorial capital.

MINING CAMPS AND MINERS

Montana's mining areas reveal great contrasts. Bannack, the earliest camp of any size, is still in existence and is preserved as a state monument. Butte, with its mines and Anaconda with its smelter, are bustling industrial cities. Helena, the capital, started as a placer camp — Last Chance Gulch — and today, modern though it is, its main street is called by its original name. To reach these and other outposts in the wilderness took courage and stamina, and, I suspect, the very lack of information about the hardships ahead was a blessing in disguise, as it kept weary, disillusioned individuals rolling west, blinded to discomforts by the glittering mirage before them.

Nothing but the lure of gold made the prospector willing to face and surmount incalculable difficulties to achieve his goal. Excerpts from a letter written in 1866 to the *Montana Post* bear this out:

Bannack, Jauary 17, 1866
A few days ago another party, with hand sleds, started for Lemhi. Each man took a sack of flour besides his blankets and the necessary cooking utensils. It was a novel sight. The old proverb is still true, "Money makes the mare go." The first day out was cold and stormy; but now, as the weather is pleasant, they will make the trip without danger. The former party that went out have not yet been heard from; but it is generally believed that good "diggings" will be developed in that vicinity. It is wonderful to witness the energy displayed by some prospectors to uncover the hidden treasures of Montana. They face every danger; endure every privation. Tired, hungry and cold, they wrap themselves in their blankets and sleep upon the snow; and not infrequently the result is frozen feet, amputation and death; wives and children too, perhaps in the States, dependent upon their labor for support; and it is doubtful if one miner in ten ever makes more than a support for himself and family.   S.F.D.

Even as late as 1895, the Libby *Silver Standard* described the typical prospector as he penetrated the wilderness area in the northwestern corner of the state:

In early days prospectors had to pack in from Horse Plains, 135 miles; or from Thompson Falls, 65 miles over a very rough trail; or from Bonner's Ferry 65 miles by boat and make a portage at Kootenai Falls, and all pronounce the latter route a "holy terror." . . . A man had hard knocks at every mark in the road . . . and under such conditions who but a prospector would go on (with) bloodthirsty Kootenai all around him, a trusty rifle always in his hand, his noble dog trotting along in front, his nose in the air at the first scent of danger and his patient horse walking behind with all his worldly possessions; plodding, plodding over high mountains; places inaccessible to all others than the prospector or a wild goat; down, down into the dismal depths of a canyon, aye, into a dense jungle, the home of the grizzly and more savage silver top; in search of gold and silver.
                    July 13, 1895

If the white intruders had been satisfied to stay in barren, eroded country, the Indians would probably have ignored them, but when the invaders appropriated fertile range land, polluted streams with tailings, cut down forests, and shot game, the redmen fought for subsistence and to preserve their rightful homeland.

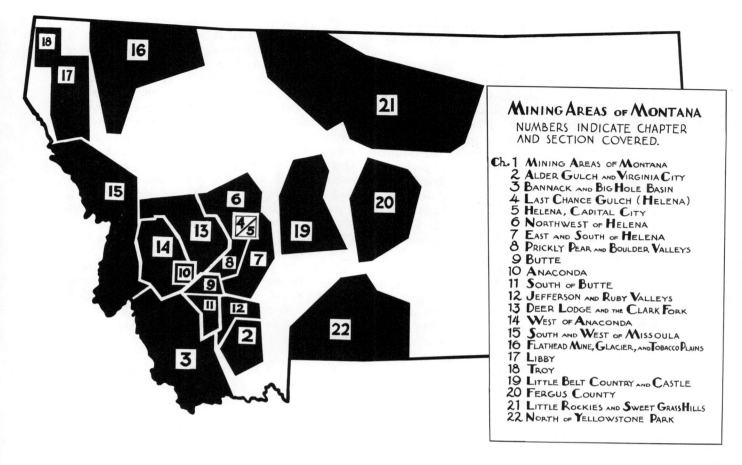

MINING AREAS OF MONTANA

NUMBERS INDICATE CHAPTER AND SECTION COVERED.

Ch. 1 MINING AREAS OF MONTANA
2 ALDER GULCH AND VIRGINIA CITY
3 BANNACK AND BIG HOLE BASIN
4 LAST CHANCE GULCH (HELENA)
5 HELENA, CAPITAL CITY
6 NORTHWEST OF HELENA
7 EAST AND SOUTH OF HELENA
8 PRICKLY PEAR AND BOULDER VALLEYS
9 BUTTE
10 ANACONDA
11 SOUTH OF BUTTE
12 JEFFERSON AND RUBY VALLEYS
13 DEER LODGE AND THE CLARK FORK
14 WEST OF ANACONDA
15 SOUTH AND WEST OF MISSOULA
16 FLATHEAD MINE, GLACIER, AND TOBACCO PLAINS
17 LIBBY
18 TROY
19 LITTLE BELT COUNTRY AND CASTLE
20 FERGUS COUNTY
21 LITTLE ROCKIES AND SWEET GRASS HILLS
22 NORTH OF YELLOWSTONE PARK

Each side hated the other and looked upon any intrusions as just cause for extermination. The Indian was fighting for survival, the white for land and wealth, to be obtained only by staking off portions as his own.

COMMUNICATION AND TRANSPORTATION

The small camps that were established here and there on the prairie or in the mountains, were completely isolated from each other as well as from the rest of the country. Before telegraph linked the frontier with the States, news traveled slowly. Robert Vickers was in Salt Lake City when he heard of Lincoln's assassination on April 15, 1865. The Salt Lake City newspaper printed an extra carrying an account of the tragedy. Vickers bought a copy of the paper and took it with him when he left by stage for Virginia City on the morning of the sixteenth. Since none of the passengers had a copy of the paper, he read the news to them as they traveled. Wherever the stage stopped long enough, he read the item to the startled crowd which gathered around the vehicle. They were nine days on the road to Bannack, and, while stopping there, a man asked Vickers to lend him the paper. Instead of returning it, he jumped on his horse and rode as fast as he could to Virginia City to break the news. The following day the stagecoach was met by a crowd of people two miles before it reached the mining camp, so eager were they to hear further particulars from Vickers.

STEAMBOATS

There was no easy way to reach the gold fields. Many prospectors and "pilgrims" — inexperienced newcomers — came up the Missouri River by boat as far as Fort Benton. For a number of years, the steamboat pilots who ran the tricky stream, following its shifting channels through shallow water, between sandbars and around submerged logs and other snags, deposited load after load of eager gold-seekers on the muddy banks of the river port. Captain LaBarge, one of the most experienced of these pilots often said he could name a hundred places along the banks where passengers or members of his crew were buried.

Mrs. Julian M. Knight left Independence, Missouri, on the steamer *Tacoma*, on April 9, 1867, bound for Virginia City, where she was to join her husband who had gone to the gold fields the previous year. Her account of the journey mentions dangers from hostile Indians when the boat was passing through the Dakotas. For safety, several boats "landed near each other at night." By the time that the boat's larder was getting low and the passengers were living on beans and crackers, a band of buffalo swam across the river in front of the boat. One was shot for food and was pulled aboard, but since it had only been wounded, it charged the length of the vessel and plunged back into the river. Mrs. Knight writes that the ladies passed the time by reading, sewing and writing letters. The passengers often held sings, which on Sundays consisted of hymns. Three days before reaching Fort Benton, a boat bound for St. Louis signaled the *Tacoma* to drop anchor. As a rowboat with three men in it approached the *Tacoma*, Mrs. Knight recognized her husband who, impatient at the delayed arrival of the steamboat, had come downriver to meet her.

STAGE AND FREIGHT LINES

Even when men reached frontier outposts like Fort Benton, M. T., the remainder of the trip to the remote mining camps was difficult and dangerous. Indians often attacked wagon trains and freight outfits, and road agents ambushed coaches to rob the passengers and steal the treasure chest bolted to the floor of the vehicle. It was not unusual for a traveler to seek protection by paying ten dollars — as did E. McSorley in 1867 — for the privilege of walking beside a wagon from Fort Benton to Helena.

All supplies were brought into the camps by freight teams, until the coming of the railroads in the eighties. Freight wagons followed the streams wherever they could in order to avoid steep grades. A freight outfit consisted of three covered wagons, coupled together, each one smaller than the one in front. The three were drawn by twelve to sixteen horses, mules or oxen. It took a skillful driver or "muleskinner" to handle such a train. A muleskinner from Gilt Edge, Montana, went back east and told a friend how he used twelve horses to pull his wagons. "I'm no fool," the man replied. "There's no wagon tongue long enough for six

teams of horses." This man, of course, knew nothing of the way in which the teams were hitched to the lead wagon. The animals were driven by a jerk line, which the driver, who rode the left hand pointer (or horse nearest the wagon), used to signal to the lead horse. This animal was trained to turn left at one jerk and right at two jerks. The teams between the leaders and pointers were called swing teams. The trip from Helena to Salt Lake took three months. On one such journey, a freighter brought back a load of green and dried fruits and sold it for $2,100. X. Beidler of Helena, a messenger for Wells Fargo & Company, rode the trail between Helena and Corinne, Utah — a distance of 500 miles. Of the run, he wrote, "we went down one week and back the next. The heavier the treasure, the thicker the road agents. It got so dangerous that express companies put on more messengers and guards." With the coming of the railroads, travel became easier and safer and the road agent disappeared.

MY SEARCH FOR MINING CAMPS — LIVE AND GHOST

For thirty-five years, I have been absorbed in visiting mining camps, first in Colorado and later throughout the other eleven states that fill the western portion of the United States. The western half of Montana is full of such camps, in all degrees of decay, preservation or activity. Most of them can be reached fairly easily by car or by trail.

Even on my first trip through the state I was drawn to it and determined to return and make a thorough study of its mining history, to sketch the camps and to learn as much as I could about them from oldtimers. For five summers, I pursued this self-appointed project and most absorbing hobby, and for eight years I have spent all my spare time in research concerning Montana's mining history. In this book, I share with you my discoveries. In it you will find a digest of the facts, legends, mining statistics, adventures, and human contacts that I have encountered. It should appeal to the tourist, the historian, the mineral geologist, the ghost town hunter, as well as to the armchair traveler. The illustrations were made on the spot.

On each of my trips to Montana, I had a companion who did the driving in order to leave me free to look, and sketch, and read. Mrs. Hazel Potts, a friend of long standing, drove me all over the state on my first two visits. We made a fine team. Whenever we

GHOST HOTEL, ROCHESTER

stopped, I sketched while she talked to old-timers or explored buildings and reported what she had found. No road fazed her; so we reached places far back from main highways. My husband, Francis, a retired English professor, was my other companion. He got me to every place that I had missed on previous trips, even when it meant finding someone to take us by jeep or to go along as guide. In the weeks that I spent in Helena and in other places, poring over books and newspaper files, he patiently waited or did writing of his own. These two made it possible for me to devote my whole attention to intineraries, sketching, and research.

Mining statistics quoted in this book have been obtained from five major sources. In 1885, a history of Montana was published — a huge volume crammed with information and edited by Michael A. Leeson. This book (which is referred to in the text as "Leeson") Mrs. Anne McDonnell put into my hands as soon as I started to delve into Montana's history, and to it I turned more frequently than to any other single source. Rossiter Raymond's reports on mining in the Western states; the U. S. Geological Survey reports and special papers; and the mineral surveys of Montana by both Uuno

M. Sahinen and Oren Sassman have been studied and quoted.

The material in each chapter covers a limited area and is accompanied by a map, which, when used in connection with a modern road map, should enable the traveler to find desired locations with comparative ease. Those who are curious about the names and locations of mines in a given area will find this information in small type, usually at the end of the mining data in each chapter.

When I started my search for the old mining camps of the West, I knew nothing about mining methods. For the benefit of others like myself, I have tried to describe the basic mining procedures in simple terms.

MINING METHODS

Each camp started as the result of a strike — a discovery made by a party of men or by a lone prospector. If alone, his burro carried his pick, pan, and grub, and he wandered over the hills, panning gravel in streambeds or pecking at outcrops of rock in his endless and optimistic search for gold. He examined every streambed for "colors" and when he found them, he washed the gravel hoping to find gold dust, flakes, or nuggets in the bottom of his pan. As soon as he found placer gold, he staked a claim which permitted him, as discoverer, to dig and wash the earth within the limits of his allotted land. Then, for fear that others might "jump" his claim, he recorded it at the first opportunity.

Panning was slow work, so the prospector next constructed rockers — long cradles in which the dirt was "rocked," the gold sinking to the bottom and the waste washing away. Or he might construct sluice-boxes, several long troughs connected end to end and provided with cleated bottoms. The dirt was shoveled into the upper boxes and water was run though the troughs. The cleats or "riffles" caught the gold particles, which sank to the bottom, and prevented them from washing away. At stated intervals, usually once a week, the water was turned off and a cleanup was made. The gold was scraped from the bottom and placed in buckskin pokes or other containers.

Since gold is heavy, the auriferous grains were often distributed throughout a stratum of sand or gravel many feet thick. Often the richest particles lay at the bottom of the streambed on bedrock. If this was deep below the channel, a drain ditch was built to divert the water, and a shaft was sunk in the gravel to bedrock, so that the miner might shovel the rich sand into a bucket to be lifted by an elevator or by a windlass to the surface and there be sluiced and cleaned.

Drift mining meant digging a tunnel into the bank of a gulch to reach pay gravel and bring it out to be sluiced. This was ticklish work; for, unless the dirt was kept from sluffing off into the tunnel, it might cave in on the men at work. It was therefore necessary to timber the drift, and timbers cost fifteen to twenty cents each!

Oftentimes the gold lay in bars, benches, and ledges alongside and above the level of the stream. To reach this ground, hydraulics were employed — hoses with large nozzles mounted on a swivel standard (called a monitor), and supplied with water under high pressure, obtained from reservoirs. The nozzles or "giants" were directed against a hillside and the terrific force of the water cut down the bank. The loosened earth was then washed for gold in the regular way. The gold found in placers

was "oxidized" and free-milling; that is, easily recoverable by relatively simple processes.

When the placers were exhausted, the miners worked their way upstream searching for the source of the gold and thereby discovering lodes in the hills. This gold lay in veins, pockets, and chimneys within the earth and was often mixed with other rock. Sometimes the gold- or silver-laden rock protruded above the surface of the ground as an "outcrop" and was thus easily located. Upon finding an outcrop which he wished to explore, the prospector staked off a claim, wrote a statement describing its location, which he placed in a "monument" of stones, and trudged off to the nearest courthouse to record his discovery.

Returning to his ground, he dug a prospect hole and, as it grew deeper, he timbered its sides. When it was so deep that he could not climb out of it, he erected a windlass over the shaft so that the dirt and ore could be hauled to the surface in a bucket. By now, he usually had one or more partners to assist him. One stayed at the bottom of the shaft to shovel the broken rock into the bucket. The windlass, which was operated by manpower or by a horse whim, raised the load to the surface.

Gold from lode mines was usually recovered by grinding or stamping, both of which operations pulverized the rock and released the gold. The simplest device was an arrastre, a primitive mill of Spanish invention in which ore was dumped into a shallow stone basin. In this hollow, one or more heavy stones or wheels, propelled by a horizontal beam which turned about a vertical axis, were drawn or pushed by horsepower. Water flowing through the basin washed away the ground-up waste rock, but the heavier mineral residue was retained.

Larger quantities of ore were handled in a stamp mill, which contained one or more batteries of heavy weights or "stamps," which were raised by water power or steam pressure and released to fall repeatedly and pound the rock into powder. The gold could then be recovered by mixing it with quicksilver to which it adhered. In a further process, the quicksilver was removed by evaporation, leaving only the gold.

The character of the ore changed often with depth; that is, gold or silver was found in threads or small particles imbedded in other rock. The miners described such ore as "refractory," because the precious metals could not be released by crushing, but only by treatment with chemi-

MILL AT STERLING

BIG-SCALE HYDRAULICKING, GERMAN GULCH

cals or by roasting. For the latter, smelters were required.

The initial methods of recovering gold and silver were crude and inefficient, and large percentages of high-grade metal were washed away or lost in tailings or were thrown with waste rock on dumps. Constant experimentation and technical improvements have resulted in appreciable savings of precious metals. Today scarcely any values are lost.

In the 1890's, dredges were built or assembled on ground where gold-bearing gravel was known to exist (usually at considerable depths below the ground). These dredge boats were floated on artificial ponds, made by damming or diverting a stream. An endless chain of steel buckets, propelled by electric power, gouged out the gravels below the surface of the streambed and brought up dripping loads of pay dirt. A gold-washing machine and recovery plant was part of each dredge. The waste rock was spewed from the "stacker," which was at the opposite end of the boat from the bucket line, and was deposited in ricks or dumps that still cover hundreds of acres of ground.

Today, the dragline has succeeded the dredge, especially where the "field is not large or rich enough for the installation of million dollar" boats. The dragline is a combination of a steam shovel which lifts dirt and a washing plant which extracts the gold.

Processes for recovering copper ore, the deposits of which are found mainly in the Butte area, are mentioned in the chapter on Butte.

Through this book, I share with you my hobby — the exciting rediscovery of old camps and the imaginative recreating of how active camps and towns looked in their initial boom days. Montana is full of adventure for anyone who knows its history and relives it. If you find things which I have missed, share them with me, for I shall never be through hunting ghosts.

SUNRISE, EMPTY TOWN EXCEPT
FOR CARETAKER

CASTLE RESIDENCES

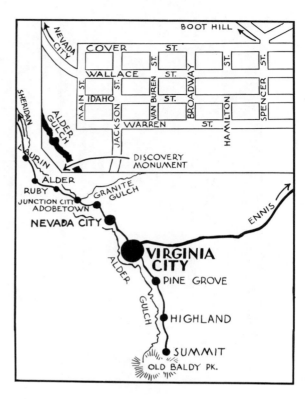

CHAPTER 2

ALDER GULCH and VIRGINIA CITY

The rain slashed against the car, and curtains of low-hanging clouds obliterated all but occasional glimpses of the Madison Range of mountains which hem in the eastern side of the wide Madison valley. The drive from West Yellowstone, past Hebgen Lake and through Hebgen Canyon, pinched in between steep mountain slopes, had been a fitting introduction to Montana's scenery. This was the summer of 1950, and as we drove through the heavy mountain shower toward Ennis, our excitement grew, for our destination that night was to be Virginia City, one of Montana's oldest mining camps and the scene of much of its pioneer history. It was still raining at Ennis, but shortly after we left that active agricultural town and started to climb the mountain road to Virginia City, the sun broke through the clouds and flooded the Madison Valley with late afternoon light.

From the top of the grade we saw below, to the west, the twisting road to Virginia City. The town itself is situated in a hollow surrounded by rolling slopes of the Tobacco Root mountains, and is well hidden until one passes the cemetery, high above the roadway, and starts to roll down the main street. Virginia City consists of two parts: the older residential section flanking Wallace Street, and the restored business section closer to Alder Gulch. In the latter, authentic old buildings have been preserved or reproduced, and false-fronted frame stores have been moved in from abandoned towns to augment the look of early

boom days. Charley Bovey, a Montana state senator from Cascade County, is responsible for this restoration. Keenly aware that the West's early camps are fast disappearing, he has endeavored to preserve as much as possible the look and feel of Montana's early mining days. His absorbing hobby began in 1946 when, on a visit to Virginia City, he saw one of its historic landmarks being demolished. He bought the relic and, after he had restored it, found another one and another, and moved them in until his purchases lined one end of Wallace Street. He and his wife, Sue, like living in the present as much as they enjoy recreating the past for the benefit of the thousands who never knew the West when it was frontier wilderness.

Drive into Virginia City if possible in the late afternoon, when sunlight mellows the wooden sidewalks and stains the weathered boards of the shops a tawny hue. Lights begin to glow in shops and, except for the crowds of tourists that mill about the street and park Cadillacs and trailers by hitching racks, Virginia City takes on life and sounds reminiscent of the days when the Virginia Inn was the leading hostelry and stagecoaches rolled to a stop in front of the Wells Fargo office across from the hotel.

STORES ON WALLACE STREET, VIRGINIA CITY

WOODEN SIDEWALKS, VIRGINIA CITY

By the time it is dark, the sidewalks are illuminated by a soft glow from the old street lamps and from the pools of light that spill from store windows. Tinkling music draws crowds to the Bale of Hay Saloon, where music boxes and Wurlitzer hand organs clang and bleat and jingle when fed the appropriate coins. In the soft light, Wallace Street with its stores and displays — the tiny barber shop with the Swan barber chair, the Chinese laundry, even the mannequins in the Wells Fargo office and the Oriental beauty peeping from an upstairs window — takes one back nearly one hundred years to when the camp was new.

At the lower end of Wallace Street is a stone barn which once had stalls for thirty horses. In the days when Boyd & Smith leased it as a livery stable from R. T. Cook and stocked it with a variety of vehicles, the miners hired rigs to make frequent trips to Summit, at the head of Alder Gulch, or to Central City, Nevada City, Adobetown and Junction City, the smaller settlements that bordered the stream all the way to its mouth. Today the barn is a theater where melodramas and olios are presented nightly to audiences who are encouraged to hiss the villain — a milder form of disapproval than was common in the 1860's when southern sympathies were strong. Whenever "Dixie" was played at a show, the northerners present would fire their guns at the ceiling, but if "Yankee Doodle" was the selection, the southern supporters did the shooting.

A little farther up the street is C. F. Sauerbier's blacksmith shop. The yard behind it is empty, unlike the days when restless mules and oxen crowded it, waiting to be shod. The *Montana Post* building on the corner of Wallace and Jackson Streets was recently rebuilt by public subscription, through the efforts of the Historical Landmarks Society of Montana. This was the first full-fledged newspaper in the territory. Its history is imposing and exciting. During the years when the paper's hand-press was turning out tri-weekly editions, the *Montana Post* office occupied the rear and a bookstore the front of the building.

The Territorial Capitol that was used from 1865 to 1875 and the Madison County Courthouse, an imposing stone and brick structure built in 1875, are both on Wallace Street.

On the opposite side of Wallace Street adjoining buildings, which date from the City's earliest years, contain Rank's drug store and the Masonic Temple. The ground floor of the store, whose walls of rock and adobe were built in 1863, served as a gathering place when the Vigilantes held their organizational meeting. The basement of the drugstore is fitted up as an old-time apothecary shop, but of chief interest to visitors are two signs which read:

December 23, 1863
A group of 47 men barred the door of this store and held a Vigilante Organization meeting in the basement and signed the Vigilante oath.

Capt. Jack Slade was arrested in this store March 10, 1864 and hanged on the corral gate back of the store.

The second floor of the building was built in 1865 and was used as a lodge room by the Masonic fraternity. In fact, the first Grand Lodge A. F. & A. M. of Masons held its convocation in this upper room on Jan. 24, 1866.

In 1867, a fine stone structure, costing $35,-000 — the new Masonic Temple — was built adjoining the older building (that containing the drug store) and was dedicated December 27, 1867.

Another handsome granite building on Wallace Street houses the Thompson-Hickman Museum, given by William Boyce Thompson, a native of Virginia City, in honor of William Thompson and Richard O. Hickman. Its two floors are filled with priceless relics, mementos, and pictures, as well as with many volumes belonging to the Madison County library.

Near the museum is the present schoolhouse, a two-story structure surrounded by a terraced lawn. The territory's first governor, Sidney Edgerton, provided for education as early as 1864, by appointing Professor Thomas J. Dimsdale as Superintendent of Public Instruction. Dimsdale is credited with opening the first school in the city in August of that year and teaching its classes. The first public school was held in the Union church on Idaho Street (where, at a later date, the Methodist church with built) with Mrs. Sarah H. Herndon as teacher and eighty-one pupils enrolled. A new two-room log schoolhouse served for a time, and then in 1876 a four-room brick building (which was later enlarged by two rooms) was erected in which classes were conducted by the Reverend H. H. Prout and his daughter.

Almost opposite the Thompson-Hickman Museum, in Daylight Gulch, is the Gilbert Brewery, the oldest in the state and a show place in itself. Overlooking the town is Boot Hill with the graves of the five road agents who were hanged in the city.

Shortly after the major gold strikes in the territory, the Historical Society of Montana was organized by a number of farsighted citizens for the purpose of collecting and preserving material of historical value. A meeting for the purpose of incorporating was held shortly afterwards at the office of Messrs. Dance and Stuart in Virginia City and by March, 1865, the Society was in existence. According to Leeson, between 1865 and 1873 "the organization slept soundly," but in October, 1873, it roused itself and met at Deer Lodge. In recent years it has become increasingly active, and its headquarters in Helena contains a remarkable library, museum, and art galleries. The organization also maintains a fine publications program.

Many mining camps owe their existence to some harrassed prospector who started to heave a stone at a wandering burro, only to find that the rock contained gold and came from the type of outcrop for which he had been searching. But Indians, not ornery creatures, were responsible for the discoveries at Alder Gulch, turning what seemed like a rout into a lucky break for the party of six men, scurrying back to Bannack as fast as their jaded mounts could carry them.

Early in February, 1863, these gold-seekers — Thomas W. Cover, Henry Edgar, William Fairweather, Barney Hughes, Harry Rodgers, and Michael Sweeney, with two others, George Orr and Lewis Simmons — had left Bannack, where they had been mining since the preceding fall, for the Sun River, but in traveling through Deer Lodge Valley (where they went to get the horses that would be needed) they learned that James Stuart was also about to set out on a prospecting trip. He was going to the Big Horn and Yellowstone country in the hope of discovering gold and establishing townsites, and his plans were so appealing that the eight decided to join his company. Stuart, however, had gone to Bannack to round up his men and equip them. George Orr decided to stay in the Deer Lodge Valley, but the others planned to meet Stuart's party of fifteen at a pre-arranged rendezvous after it left Bannack.

Fairweather and his partners reached Mill Creek, near the present town of Sheridan, and waited for Stuart, but since they were a few days ahead of schedule, they camped in the foothills to hunt and prospect and kept a watch out for his party. Stuart had expected to see them at the mouth of the Stinking Water (Ruby) River and when, on April 12 (the agreed upon date), he saw no signs of them, he passed through undetected. On April 15, Fairweather and Edgar discovered the prints of

shod horses at the river's edge and realized that Stuart must have gone on. They immediately broke camp and followed his trail with Simmons, who had been a trapper, as their guide. They were well on their way to the Big Horn Mountains when, on May 2, a war party of Crow Indians swooped down upon them, captured them, and took them into camp. Let Henry Edgar tell the rest of the story:

It was jointly through Bill Fairweather and Lewis Simmons that we were saved. I don't know how it was, but a rattlesnake would never bite Bill. When he saw one he would always grab it up and carry it along with him a ways. They never seemed to resent anything he would do to them and he never killed one. As we were going toward this Indian village he picked up a rattlesnake and just at the outskirts of the village he picked up another. When the Indians saw him come in with a rattlesnake on each arm, they were awed. He put the snakes in his shirt bosom and Simmons told the Indians he was the great medicine man of the whites.

They took us into the medicine lodge, where there was a big bush in the center. They marched us around that bush several times and finally Bill said if they marched him around again he would pull up the sacred medicine bush. They marched us around again and Bill pulled up the bush and walloped the medicine man on the head with it. We then formed three to three, back to back. We had refused all along to give up our guns and revolvers. The old chief drove the other Indians back with a whip. They had a council which lasted from noon until midnight. In the morning we got our sentence. If we went on they would kill us. If we went back and would give up our horses we would not be harmed. It was Hobson's choice. I got for my three horses an old horse, blind in one eye, and a yearling colt. For my three pairs of Oregon blankets I got a buffalo robe and a half, and for my grub, consisting of flour, bacon, coffee, beans, etc., I got a dozen dried buffalo tongues. Simmons was left as hostage.

We came on the north side of the Yellowstone one day's travel. Wet met an old squaw woman, who warned us not to cross the river, and we didn't. Instead, we took up into the mountains and camped there until morning, fearful of the Indians. In the morning we saw thirty or forty of them looking for our trail. We camped until night and then crossed to the south side of the river . . . We found the Indians were ahead of us and had taken over the hills toward the West Gallatin. We came on over the pass where the city of Bozeman now lies, and saw the Indians coming up the valley. We concealed ourselves in the brush along the creek and exchanged shots with them. There was a parley. They agreed that if we came out they would not harm us, but we wouldn't trust them. We waited until dark and then struck out for the Madison river, . . . and went into the hills between the Gallatin and the Madison. The next day we crossed the Madison river and came up what is now known as the head of Wigwam gulch. We camped beside a lake at the foot of Bald Mountain.

The next day we came down by the lake and over the ridge to Alder Gulch. That was May 26, 1863, about four o'clock in the afternoon.

The men made camp by the side of the stream on a level stretch between two bars. While Fairweather and Edgar stood guard, the others started up the gulch to prospect. When Fairweather crossed to the west side of the creek to picket the horses for the night, he noticed some exposed rimrock jutting into the stream.

"What do you think of that?" he called to Edgar, who replied, "I'll get the tools and we'll see."

As Fairweather started to dig and Edgar to wash the dirt, Fairweather said, "I hope we can get enough dust to buy some tobacco in Bannack"; for the Indians had stripped them of their supply as well as of everything else of value at the time of their capture. The two men worked quietly searching for colors until Fairweather shouted, "I've found a scad," to which Edgar replied, "If you have one, I have a thousand." The gold in the first pan was worth, some say thirty cents, and others $1.25, and the scad or nugget, $4.80. The second pan of gravel yielded $1.75, and the third $4.40. When the men got back to camp, they showed their scads and dust. Early morning found the miners working in pairs — Hughes and Cover, Sweeney and Rodgers, Fairweather and Edgar. That day the six panned out $180.00.

By this time their provisions were exhausted, with only antelope left for supper, so the men knew that they must go to Bannack for supplies if they were to hold and work the ground that they had discovered. Each man had staked two claims 100 feet wide and extending from rim to rim of the gulch, one by right of discovery and one by pre-emption, and Edgar was asked to write up the notices of the claims and of the water rights. In his report he had to identify the gulch, so he named it "Alder" because it was solidly lined with that type of tree.

With their twelve claims properly posted, the six set out on May 28 for Bannack, sixty-five miles west of the gulch, and two days later were in the bustling camp, stocking up for the return trip. Although they tried to keep their strike a secret, when they started back on June 2, they were followed by at least 200 men. Realizing what this would mean when they reached the diggings, they stopped at Beaverhead Rock and confronted the horde, demanding that their discovery rights, which entitled each of them to two claims and to water rights, be honored and that unless this was agreed to they would not show the crowd the way. With this and other rules established, they continued, but that night, while the prospectors slept, Barney Hughes tipped off his friends and led them in the dark to the diggings so as to give them time to make locations before the milling mob arrived.

The Fairweather District was organized on June 6, 1863, the day the stampede arrived. A second miners' meeting was called the following day and a committee appointed to draft mining rules and laws. On June 9, with men swarming all over the gulch, a third meeting was held, at which time definite mining laws were adopted. Dr. Wm. L. Steele was elected president of the district and Henry Edgar recorder. Dr. G. G. Bissel was made judge of the Miners' Court, and shortly afterwards Richard Todd was appointed sheriff.

Within a year of the discovery, Alder Gulch was staked with claims from top to bottom and bordered with tents, brush wickiups, rock shelters, and mud-chinked cabins so that it formed one continuous straggling street locally known as Fourteen-mile City. In its center was the discovery site in the Fairweather District. Above discovery was the Highland District, and above it was Pine Grove, with Summit at the very head of the gulch. Below discovery was Nevada District and then Junction. Brown's District embraced the gulch of that name south of Nevada City, while Granite District was approximately two miles northwest of that camp on Granite Creek. While all the districts were organized by the placer miners who opened them up, lode mines were soon discovered within their boundaries and these remained active long after the placers had played out.

With Alder Gulch crowded with claims and crude shelters for the miners, it was natural that enterprising companies laid out townsites at intervals along the stream, and that merchants set up shop in tents and shacks at these places. On June 16, 1863, the Varina Town Company recorded its claim to 320 acres in the Fairweather District. The first settlement was called Varina in honor of the wife of Jefferson Davis, and since there were more Confederate sympathizers in the gulch, no one protested the name until G. G. Bissel, the ardently pro-Union district judge, refused to write it in his court records and substituted Virginia City instead. Since the name "Virginia" was also agreeable to the southerners, the town was thereafter officially called by that name. Nevada City stretched along the gulch until it joined Virginia City's western boundary; Adobetown and Junction City were further downstream. Central was over the hill between Virginia and Nevada, and Highland, Pine Grove, and Summit were above Virginia near the head of the gulch.

Most of the substantial buildings in each settlement were one-room log cabins with roofs made of poles covered with dirt or sod and with packed earth floors covered with cow or buffalo hides. In one such cabin Gohn and Kohrs ran a butcher shop where the "beef was well-seasoned with alkali dust" which could not be kept from sifting through the chinks in the walls and roof. Bunks two tiers high were built along the walls of most of the cabins, and fireplaces were made of boulders.

The miners, many of whom came from the California, Colorado, and Idaho gold fields, were hardy, roughly dressed men with long hair and beards, who worked killing hours under the most trying and unhealthy conditions in their frenzied search for the elusive colors which would make them rich. The first placering was done with pick and pan or with rockers, which caught the golden particles in the riffles of the boxes, but when bedrock was found to be too deep below the surface to be reached by these primitive methods, many prospectors left. Their superficial panning of surface dirt had convinced them that the diggings were lean.

The determined companies of men who remained sank shafts by drifting (or tunneling) the creek bed in an effort to reach bedrock. This meant timbering the excavated area to prevent cave-ins which were all too frequent, as water undermined supports and trapped men in the deep pits. Before long it was found that not only the channel but also the bars and benches bordering the stream contained rich dirt, for all were part of an ancient river bed and were filled with auriferous gravel. The staking of bar and hill claims brought still more prospectors to the overcrowded area.

The bench or ledge claims, high above the channel of the gulch, needed flumes to bring water close enough for sluicing away the banks. For larger scale operations additional flumes and pipes were laid to bring water from great distances to wash down the benches and cut away the worthless rock and sand so that the pay gravel could be caught and refined. Fortunately for the miners, the first two winters were not too severe and much work was carried on. As drifting and stripping increased, miles of ditches were dug to drain the hundreds of properties throughout the long, twisting gulch. It has been estimated that $30,000,000 was recovered from placers alone in the first three years.

The Boyer brothers came to the gulch from Denver in October, 1863, by wagon train, camping below the site of Virginia City. Their reminiscences offer first-hand reporting on conditions. Upon their arrival they were

astonished at the intense activity. Myriads of tents dotted the sides of the gulch and hundreds of buildings were erected or in the course of construction. Many of these were in the then embryo hamlets of Adobetown, Nevada and Centerville, while in the gulch itself, thanks to 100-foot claims, and two-tiers of them at that, for miles below, Virginia was a busy hive of industry. Most claim owners employed six to eight men and while some were running drains to their claims, others were stripping where it was shallow, to bed rock. Some were drifting where it was deeper and many were sluicing out gold galore.

There was some very good ground near Nevada. Men made from $6-9 a day, the latter for drifting, and as high as $12 for wet drifts — tempting bait. On the way up to Summit, the diggings were deeper and drifting was more generally resorted to.

Boyer Bros., Pony, Mont., March 31, 1897
The Madisonian, April 10, 1897

Henry Plummer appeared in Bannack in March, 1862, where his charm and powers of leadership quickly made him an important and respected member of that community. No one knew his criminal background; nor that many of his henchmen had followed him to the Grasshopper Diggings from Nevada, California, and Idaho to form a desperate and clever band of highwaymen whose sole object was to separate the miners from their wealth. When Bannack needed a sheriff, Plummer's many friends saw that he was elected and when the rich placers of Alder Gulch produced fabulous amounts of gold dust, Plummer forcibly persuaded the sheriff of Virginia City to turn over that office to him by default. Before the end of the year, handsome, personable Henry Plummer was duly elected law-enforcement officer of both camps. Masking his true character with dignified respectability, he and his gang terrorized the mining towns for more than a year before the frantic citizens took matters into their own hands and hunted down the criminals.

Wearing distinctive knots in their neckerchiefs and calling themselves "The Innocents," this desperate group held up stages, stalked solitary travelers and murdered any who resisted them. While Plummer directed the forays, his blackguard followers, led by Boone Helm, Cyrus Skinner, George Shears, Whiskey Bill Graves, George Ives, Red Yeager, Buck Stinson and Ned Ray, followed up tips reported to them by spies who were stationed throughout both mining camps, and split the loot taken ruthlessly from stage strong boxes or passengers' purses. The i n f o r m e r s were planted in stores and stage stations where they marked coaches and men for robbery and signaled ahead to members of the gang, waiting in ambush on the trail. Their headquarters were Rattlesnake Ranch, fifteen miles east of Bannack, although it is believed that some of their plots were hatched over bad whiskey in Pete Daly's Place, a stage-stop known as Robber's Roost, near the present town of Sheridan. This two-story building, which is still standing, is a much visited tourist attraction. It is made of square-hewn logs, with a porch and second-story veranda across the entire front and contained one large room with a bar downstairs and a dance hall above.

Most of the holdups occurred on the ninety-mile stretch of road between Alder Gulch and Bannack, although at times the robbers, working in pairs, trailed their prey greater distances. The unfortunate traveler who, upon leaving for "the States," confided to Plummer, as sheriff, that he carried gold upon his person, was sure to be waylaid by masked riders whose horses were blanketed to escape detection. If he handed over his gold without argument he might escape injury; if he hesitated or refused he was shot. If Plummer wished to supervise a robbery, he had one of his men summon him, saying as he left Bannack that he was going to examine a silver deposit that had just been found. Upon his return he did not mention the discovery.

The crimes committed by the Innocents were many and brutal. One young man left the mining camp by Concord Coach for Salt Lake City, taking with him money for his mother, who was ill. For safety, he carried the gold dust in small sacks sewed inside his underwear. The coach was held up by eight masked men and when the driver was told to throw down the strong box he told the robbers he wasn't carrying one. Although this was true, they killed him and then searched the passengers. When the young man was forced to reveal where he carried his gold, they stripped him, ripped out the pokes of dust, and left him naked. Six days later he got back to Virginia City. Before his departure he had asked Plummer if it was safe to travel with treasure and had been assured that it was!

"Bummer Dan," whose real name was Daniel McFadden, sold out his claims in Alder Gulch in the fall of 1863 and started for the States. When he first reached Virginia City, he was shiftless and evaded work. This so irritated the hard-working miners that one day, when he was caught stealing a pie, they gave him a set of tools and took him to an unclaimed portion of the gulch below the city and told him to dig. He pecked at the ground in a superficial way while they watched him and would have quit but for their threats to return and inspect his work. Hours later, when they came back, he was digging feverishly in gravel which was filled with dust and nuggets. The neglected bar which he had opened was full of gold, and its location still bears his name. From it and other prospects he amassed a small fortune, and it was this money which he was carrying in sacks strapped to his body when he left Alder Gulch by coach for the East. Before reaching Bannack, two horsemen with shotguns held up the stage and ordered Rumsey, the driver, to disarm and search the passengers. Rumsey thoughtfully overlooked some of the money until commanded to make a second search, after one passenger had admitted at gunpoint that he still had a little on him. "Get the big sack from Bummer Dan. He's the one we want to strip," snapped the road agent, and Dan unwillingly loosened the sacks and delivered them to Rumsey. Even though he hid one, he lost $7,000. When he reached Bannack, Plummer said to him, "Never mind, when I get my cut, I'll return your money." Stunned by this revelation and sure that he knew the names of the men who had fleeced him, Dan was afraid to expose Plummer and shortly thereafter left Virginia City for good.

Toward the end of 1863, Henry Tilden, who worked for Chief Justice Edgerton, was held up by masked men while looking for some horses which he was to drive into town. One of the men's masks slipped, and the frightened boy recognized the sheriff. Although he was threatened with his life to keep still, he told the astonishing news to Edgerton. Another

MONTANA POST BUILDING, VIRGINIA CITY

MASONIC HALL, VIRGINIA CITY

story of a holdup says that the bandit's hands were recognized as those of Plummer.

The murder of Nicholas Thiebalt for a mere $200.00 in gold dust shocked the leading citizens of the camps into unified action against further lawlessness. Thiebalt sold a span of mules and, with the money from the sale in his pocket, set out to deliver them to their new owners. Everyone was surprised when he failed to return, for he was an honest fellow who would not steal away with the animals for which he had been well paid. Ten days later, William Palmer, in crossing the Stinking Water Valley, shot a grouse which fell in a thicket, and when Palmer found it he also discovered the frozen body of Thiebalt, hidden in the sagebrush. That it had been dragged there was evident, for marks of a lariat could be seen on the wrists and neck of the corpse. In the head was a bullet hole.

Palmer went a short distance down the road to the "wackiup" of Long John Franck and George Hilderman and asked them to help him put the body into his wagon, but they refused to have anything to do with it. Palmer therefore took the remains into Nevada City where they were buried. Although shootings were commonplace occurrences at the time, the infuriated residents decided to act. A posse of twenty-five men left the city at ten that evening and rode quietly along back trails to the valley where the murder had been committed. Crossing icy creeks through which their horses floundered, they approached the shebang about three a.m. Encased in frozen garments, they circled the building, and their leader called out, "Is Long John here?" When he came out, he was hurried to the scene of the murder and charged with it. Although he protested that he was innocent, one of Thiebalt's mules was spotted on a hillside; so Long John admitted that "Nick" had ridden it down there, and that one of his cabin mates, George Ives, was the killer.

Ives, Franck and Hilderman were then arrested, and the posse with its prisoners started back toward Nevada City. On the way, Ives joshed with the men and proposed a race between his horse and theirs. The men foolishly accepted the idea and soon realized that Ives was streaking ahead toward Daly's Ranch and a fresh mount. The race then became a pursuit, until Ives' horse foundered. He ducked into a ravine but was captured and brought to Nevada City on the evening of December 18. There was some discussion as to whether to conduct the trial in Nevada City or in Virginia City, but for a variety of reasons, the former place was selected. During the night, "Club Foot" George Lane, one of the "Innocents," galloped to Bannack to tell Plummer what was going on and to get him to come to Nevada and demand a civil trial which would permit him to stack the jury, but Plummer, fearing his own discovery, prudently stayed away.

All through December 19, miners and Ives' many friends from the surrounding camps streamed into Nevada City, until it was choked with milling, argumentative, armed men. Messrs. Smith, Ritchie, Thurmond, and Colonel Wood were Ives' lawyers. Dr. Don L. Byam of Nevada was judge, and Colonel W. F. Sanders conducted the prosecution. The incensed miners insisted that the trial be held in the presence of all the citizens and that the ultimate decision be left to them on all questions, although a jury of twenty-four — twelve from Nevada and twelve from Junction — would give its verdict at the conclusion of the testimony. The trial began late in the afternoon and continued into the night. It was resumed the next morning and continued with few interruptions until three p.m. on December 21.

During the trial the three prisoners, George Ives, George Hilderman, and John Franck were fettered with logging chains securely padlocked around their legs. The judge and the witnesses occupied wagon beds which set them above the heads of the crowd. At the examination, Long John admitted that he had not seen Ives shoot Thiebalt, but he saw "Nick" arriving with the mules and Ives riding to meet him. After a short while Ives appeared with the mules and said that the Dutchman wouldn't trouble anyone again. The jury deliberated less than half an hour and, with one dissenting vote, pronounced Ives guilty. As soon as a motion that the jury's report "be adopted and accepted as the judgment of the people there assembled" was formally passed, Colonel Sanders announced that Ives be hanged by the neck until he was dead. A strong pole resting across a beam of an unfinished building supported the noose, and a packing case served as a platform. Fear that an attempt to rescue Ives might be made by his desperate friends caused the miners to hurry him to the gallows immediately after his conviction. After several pleas of his to delay the hanging were refused, he said, "I am innocent of this crime — Aleck Carter killed the Dutchman."

All being ready, the word was given to the guard, "Men, do your duty." The click of the locks rang sharply, and the pieces flashed in the moonlight as they came to the "aim." The box flew from under the murderer's feet with a crash, and George Ives swung in the night breeze, facing the pale moon that lighted up the scene of retributive justice. As the vengeful click! click! of the locks sounded their note of deadly warning to the intended rescuers, the crowd stampeded in wild affright, rolling over one another in heaps, shrieking and howling with terror.

When the drop fell, the judge, who was standing close beside Ives called out, "His neck is broken; he is dead."

P. 114, Thomas Dimsdale
The Vigilantes of Montana

The other prisoners, George Hilderman and Long John, were banished.

To put an end to such organized crime as the "Innocents" were constantly carrying on, a small group of grim and determined men — five from Virginia City, one from Nevada City, and the rest from Bannack — working simultaneously but independently, took steps immediately after Ives' execution to organize a Vigilance Committee patterned after those which had effectively policed the mining camps of California. Within two days the groups combined forces and thereafter held secret meetings in Virginia City in the basement room of a drugstore.

Mrs. (M. H.) Melvina J. Lott, county historian, who with the assistance of pioneer women throughout the immediate vicinity prepared *The History of Madison County, Montana*, states in Chapter VI: "Every man in Montana then was either a 'tough' or a member of the Vigilantes. Several hundred whose names were never known to the public signed the oath. John Creighton and W. H. Sanders are said to have been the real organizers. John S. Lott of Nevada City drafted the Vigilante's oath . . . but never signed it. His reasons as given to his relatives when he sent the document to the State Historical Society for preservation in 1900 were that 'The oath was signed in the back room of our store in Nevada City, and as host, I passed it my guests first, and thus overlooked it at the time. I met with the Vigilance Committee at Virginia City and with others took the oath orally; and didn't need to sign it.'

"3-7-77, the sign used by the Vigilantes . . . marked the Vigilante Trail leading through Madison County from Yellowstone Park . . . through Ennis, Virginia City, Sheridan, Twin

TERRITORIAL OFFICE BUILDING, WALLACE STREET, VIRGINIA CITY

Bridges, Silver Star and on to Butte . . . John Lott is the authority for saying, 'It worked very effectively, since no man was known to tarry when this sign appeared on his door overnight.' James Williams, Capt., Judge Wilbur F. Sanders, prosecutor, John S. Lott, Sec.-treas., were the big three of the Vigilance Committee."

Working swiftly during the next few weeks, the organization hunted down the road agents, one or two at a time, and brought them to trial. Some they banished, but men like Red Yeager and George Brown they hanged. Yeager, in a futile attempt to save his own life, named all the outlaws and confessed that Plummer was their leader. Early in January, 1864, the Vigilantes closed in on Plummer and his two deputies, Buck Stinson and Ned Ray. Plummer's true identity was still unknown to most people, for only a few weeks earlier he had given a dinner party in his home to several prominent persons, including the governor of the territory and certain of the Vigilantes. For this occasion he had obtained by stage, from Salt Lake City, a forty-pound turkey which cost him about fifty dollars in dust. But his time was running out, and on January 10 he was hanged in Bannack from a gallows which he had ordered raised for another criminal. His two deputies swung beside him.

From the time that Ives was hanged, many threats of vengeance were made against the Vigilantes and to prevent wilful murders of their members, the group stepped up its pursuit of the outlaws. On January 13, six of the remaining criminals from Virginia City were named for capture. One of them, Bill

Hunter, suspected that he would be next and managed to escape, but was later strung up in Gallatin Valley. Let Dimsdale describe the arrest of the five men:

Frank Parish was brought in first. He was arrested without trouble, in a store, and seemed not to expect death. . . . Club-Foot George (George Lane) was arrested at Dance & Stuart's. . . . Boone Helm was brought in next. He had been arrested in front of the Virginia Hotel. . . . He quietly sat down on a bench, and on being made acquainted with his doom, he declared his entire innocence. . . . Helm was the most hardened, cool and deliberate scoundrel of the whole band and murder was a mere pastime with him. . . . He called repeatedly for whiskey, and had to be reprimanded several times for his unseemly conduct.

Jack Gallagher was found, in a gambling room, rolled up in bedding, with his shot-gun and revolver beside him. . . . Haze Lyon . . . had come back . . . to a miner's cabin on the west side of the gulch, above town. . . . The leader threw open the door, and bringing down his revolver to a present, said, "Throw up your hands." Lyons had a piece of hot slapjack on his fork; but he dropped it instantly and obeyed the order.

All five men protested their innocence, but overwhelming evidence determined their fate.

After all was arranged for hanging them, the prisoners were ordered to stand in a row facing the guard; . . . The criminals were marched into the center of a hollow square, which was flanked by four ranks of Vigilantes, and a column in front and rear, armed with shot-guns and rifles carried at a half-present, ready to fire at a moment's warning, completed the array.

Vigilantes, with pistols, were stationed throughout the crowd to see that the "roughs" did not kidnap the prisoners. As soon as the ropes were secured to the roof beam of an unfinished house on Wallace Street at Van Buren, and a box placed beneath each, the men, whose arms were bound, were ordered to mount the platforms. The guards adjusted the nooses and, at a signal, knocked the supports out from under the road agents' feet. Each met death in his own way with Helm shouting at the last, "Every man for his principles. Hurrah for Jeff Davis! Let her rip." The bodies were later cut down and laid in the street in front of the building where they were claimed by friends and buried on a hill above the city.

One more hanging had a sobering effect upon the lawless element of the town. Joseph A. (Jack) Slade, a former division agent of the Overland Stage Company — a killer with many notches on his gun, but on the side of the law — came to Virginia City in the spring of 1863. Slade immediately made many friends, not only among the business men and miners, but also with the tough characters who admired his reckless, braggadocio ways. He even joined the Vigilantes. When sober Slade was a likeable and useful citizen, but when drunk he was ugly, noisy, and dangerous. At such times he would shoot up the town, galloping through the streets, yelling and cursing and even riding into stores and breaking up bars, until the merchants, aware that he was on a spree, hastily closed their shops and put out all the lights. Mary C. Ronan, who grew up in Virginia City, in her *Memoirs of a Frontier Woman* recalls "an evening when I was sent on an errand to a store and barely escaped being shot by Slade, who was indulging in the pleasant pastime of shooting up and down the main street of Virginia, regardless of whom might receive one of his playful bullets." Slade always paid for the damage he did when he sobered up, but as the outbreaks became more frequent, the merchants tired of his actions.

After they had eliminated the road agents, the Vigilantes were instrumental in setting up a Peoples' Court where offenders were tried by a judge and jury. More than once Slade had been arraigned for his destructiveness and had paid fines to this body. On March 9, while on one of his customary sprees, he again smashed property on Wallace Street, including the house of Moll Featherlegs, who reported the damage to Sheriff J. M. Fox. Next morning Fox took Slade before Judge Alexander Davis of the Peoples' Court and read a warrant for his arrest. Furious at the accusation and still drunk, he tore the paper in shreds and stamped on it. One of the committee urged him to get out of town and go home, but instead of heeding this warning, he threatened Judge Davis with his derringer.

Even before this drunken action, the Committee had met and agreed to arrest him. When the men in Nevada City were informed by messenger of what was happening, some six-hundred of them marched in a body to Virginia City. Their leader reported that they meant business and were prepared to see that Joseph Slade was hanged. When Slade saw the tenor of the mob, he went to Judge Davis and apologized, but it was too late. He was arrested, and while preparations for his execution were made, regardless of his pleas to be spared, a friend rode twelve miles to his ranch on Trail Creek in the Madison Valley to notify his wife. Upon hearing the ominous news, she jumped on her horse and galloped to Virginia City in hopes that her arrival would stop the execution. Such an interruption was just what the exasperated miners feared, so Slade was hanged without delay from a corral gate behind a stone store building on Wallace Street. When he realized that there was no escape, he crumpled, crying, "My God! Must I die? Oh, my dear wife."

Before Virginia Slade reached the city, her husband's body had been cut down and laid out in the Virginia Hotel. "Cowards," she screamed at the men who still crowded the street. "He died like a dog. Why didn't you shoot him and not let him die by a hangman's rope?" She stayed in Virginia City and had the body placed in a metal coffin filled with alcohol. Three months later she left by coach for Salt Lake City, taking the sloshing coffin with her. There Joseph Slade was buried in the City Cemetery on July 20, 1864.

Mrs. Peter Ronan, whose memoirs were later printed in a pamphlet issued by the Great Northern Railroad, witnessed the execution. "On a still afternoon," she writes, "as I came out of the log school-house, I saw before me hundreds of men with guns in their hands, and coming down the gulch was Slade bareheaded and clothed in buckskin. . . . His arms were bound to his body above his elbows; up and down he moved his hands as he pleaded, 'For God's sake, let me see my dear, beloved wife.' Twice I heard him utter the same words, then the square-looking man with a broad black hat, standing beside him, kicked the box from under his feet. . . . When the crowds dispersed I started home; on the way I looked into a small room, and there, alone, sat Mrs. Slade weeping over the dead body of her husband. I did not know the woman, but felt sorry for her and tiptoed into the room to tell her so; the scene was so terrible I could not speak, so I left the room as quickly as I had entered, but when outside the door I ran as fast as I could to my home."

Virginia City was laid out in June, 1863, and within eight months 500 dwellings and stores lined its streets and nearby Alder Gulch. The first building to be constructed was a "mechanical" bakery erected by T. L. Luce on Wallace Street; the second was a saloon. Lumber freighted in from Bannack sold for $250 gold per thousand feet until February, 1864, when Thomas W. Cover and Perry W. McAdoo built their sawmill on Granite Creek, four miles above the Junction. By spring of that year the population of the city reached 7,000. By fall it was estimated at 18,000, with a total of 20,000 in the gulch. The better homes and business blocks, such as the Elling State Bank and the Masonic Temple, were of stone from a nearby quarry, operated by Joseph Griffith and William Thompson.

Recollections of the city in its infancy, as recalled by Mrs. Ronan (believed to be the first white child to reach the gulch), begin: "Above all else my mental vision rests upon the long rows of sluice boxes into which, as a little girl, I used to watch the miners shovel the gold-laden soil."

Many of the miners were married and had left their wives and babies in the east, and although robbing a sluice box was a shooting offense for an adult, children could scrape gold from the riffles and buy candy with the dust. Mrs. Ronan adds: "After the sluices were cleaned, at supper time, we'd go to them with our blowers and hair brushes and gather up the fine gold . . . it amused the miners to have us girls clean up after them." Before banks were set up, there was no completely safe place for the men to keep their dust except to give it to young girls whom they trusted. One of them hid the purses entrusted to her care in the mattress, and, as the number of pokes increased, her bed became uncomfortably lumpy.

Wells were the sole water supply of the growing city, but as the population mushroomed they failed to supply the demands. When an epidemic of "mountain fever" (believed to be typhoid) broke out in the sewerless community, Anton M. Holter, N. Cornelius, and J. P. Olison obtained a charter from the first territorial legislature, which entitled them to bring water from a large spring a mile east of the town for the use of the entire city. Since no iron pipes were to be had, logs with a three-inch bore were fastened end to end, and through these the water ran for many, many years.

The earliest stage connection with the States was established in 1863 by A. J. Oliver & Company, whose coaches ran between Bannack and Salt Lake City, where they connected with Ben Holladay's Overland Stage Lines. By August, 1864, Holladay ran triweekly stages, which carried the United States mail between Salt Lake City and Virginia City by way of Bannack. To travel by coach was both uncomfortable and dangerous, for bad roads, Indians, and road agents guaranteed that any trip would provide some unforeseen excitement. Take, for instance, a prosaic journey on one of Oliver's coaches when

eighty miles east of Virginia City, the coach upset and a double-barreled shotgun was caused to go off, two balls entering the driver's thigh, and one ball going through a passenger's arm and entering his left breast. Our informant further states that he could not say whether the wounds were mortal or not, until a physician could be procured.

Montana Post, Sept. 24, 1864

Heavy snows in the spring of 1865 prevented freighters from getting through from Salt Lake City to the camps with trains of foodstuffs. When local stocks of flour were almost gone, certain Virginia City merchants jumped prices from $25.00 to $150.00 gold per 100 pounds. After unsuccessful attempts had been made to reach the stalled trains, a meeting was held at Leviathan Hall at which the indignant citizens decided that flour prices must be reduced. When the merchants stood pat, the miners raided their stores and took the flour in wagons to the Hall. Neil Howie, one of the Vigilantes, was assigned to protect store property. To the angry crowd outside he said: "Gentlemen, this uprising is to get flour and pay a reasonable price for it; it is not to sack the town. The first man that steals from a store or a saloon will be shot or hanged. The same men that fought for law and order a few months ago are prepared to fight for it now." The storekeepers were paid what the committee felt was a fair price and the flour sold in small amounts to those in greatest need of it. When the snows melted sufficiently for oxen to plough through the heavy drifts, the flour train arrived and the famine was over.

Robert L. Housman, in his *Beginnings of Journalism in Frontier Montana* (1936) credits a short-lived sheet known as either the Beaverhead or Bannack *News Letter,* as the first on Montana soil. Wilbur F. Sanders of Virginia City appears to have edited the first news sheet to appear in Virginia City, in January, 1864, several months before the appearance of the *Montana Post.* (This possibly was a later version of the *News Letter,* moved from Bannack, but the name has been lost to history.) Ben R. Dittes furnished the press for Sanders, and John A. Creighton, the leading merchant, assisted by a printer whose name has been forgotten, set up the forms and did the actual work. When all was ready, the men celebrated by drinking six bottles of champagne, provided by Creighton, and toasting the future of journalism in the Territory. The publication was short-lived, for nothing more is heard of it. The only known copy of the *News Letter* is in the Beaverhead County Museum at Dillon.

On August 27, 1864, the officially recognized *Montana Post* made its first appearance with John Buchanan publisher, and Professor Thomas J. Dimsdale, editor. John Buchanan and M. M. Manner, printer-journalists, came west by steamboat up the Missouri River. Eighty miles below Fort Benton their steamer, *Yellowstone,* ran aground on a sand bar and had to be unloaded. Mules and oxen hauled passenger and freight on up to the river town, where the two men joined a large wagon train bound for Virginia City and other gold camps. At the end of the slow, dusty journey, the men set up their hand press and stowed away their ten bundles of precious paper in an empty cellar of a log cabin. There the first issue of the *Montana Post* — 960 copies, which were immediately bought at fifty cents a copy — was printed.

The six-column paper was full of news as the following excerpts show:

Virginia City is not a myth, a paper town, but a reality . . . The placer diggings will require years to work out . . . Many persons are taking out $150 per day to the hand . . . Wages are high $6-$12 per day. Old miners have the preference as they are worth much more than green hands . . . An ordinary laborer can get $6 per day, and this in gold, making it equal to $12 in greenbacks per day . . . The abundance of gold makes everything high.

Arrival of the Governor   Serenade — His Speech

Gov. Edgerton paid our place his first visit last week . . . On Friday evening his honor was given a serenade. He remarked . . . on the growth of our beautiful city . . . beckoning the emigrant to the "Switzerland" of America. His remarks were conservative, no political harangue was indulged in. This was right. Saturday he returned to Bannack.

The second issue of the paper, which appeared on September 3, carried a column headed "News From America," which indicates the sense of isolation felt by the citizens. One item of concern reads:

Lost. Wm. Fairweather, lost last week in Virginia City a valuable nugget of gold, being the first taken out of Virginia Gulch. Finder amply rewarded.

Advertisements provide information concerning business establishments:

Ice Cream Saloon. We call attention of our citizens to the preparation made for their entertainment at

"The Counts." A fine lunch is provided in the evening for the benefit of frequenters of the saloon. That rarest of stimulants, a good cup of coffee, is there to be had, in perfection. A trial will convince the most skeptical.

Count Henri Murat, said to have been the nephew of Joachim Murat, King of Naples, ran this saloon for a short time during 1864. Then he and his German wife left for Colorado where he became a barber. The most select gambling house in the area was the "Senate." Only the best whiskey was sold, ivory chips were used in the games, and the clientele was limited to gentlemen. The average miner got his rot-gut in the cheap bars and hurdy-gurdy houses, the latter providing refreshment, gambling, and dancing partners. All such places paid quarterly license fees, the wholesale liquor dealers $25.00, the saloon proprietors $37.50, and the auctioneers $25.00. Gambling houses were taxed $75.00, and dance and hurdy-gurdy houses $150.00.

Fire protection, which was of paramount importance to everyone, was a subject of frequent discussion in the *Post*.

Fire! Fire!

It appears to us that a night watch should be instituted. One good, sober, vigilant man could be found to patrol from sun to sun, over all the town, and to give the alarm of fire.

As we like to see such matters arranged in a business like manner, we have thought over a plan, which should prove very simple; more so than a patrol. Let a watch box be built high on Cemetery Hill, furnished with a window divided into three compartments facing the town. Let one compartment be painted blue, another red and one left plain, representing Cover, Main and Idaho street districts. A light placed east, west or in the middle of the proper compartment, would at once specify the locality of the fire, and five shots in quick succession followed by blasts from a horn, or the roll of a drum, would be a certain and easy alarm.

Montana Post, Oct. 29, 1864

As a result of this crusade, money for a patrolman was raised, and the editor proposed the next step for the protection of "our city of wood."

Let someone look to the *Water*. Without it, buckets are as useful as thimbles to thirsty men . . . A few reservoirs could be made along the branch so that water could be had at once . . . Most important additions to the tools of a fire company without an engine, are two or three troughs, holding about a barrel of water each. Such a trough laid on the ground and worked by a stout fellow throwing up

MADISON COUNTY COURTHOUSE, VIRGINIA CITY

water with a large wooden shovel, can do more than 12 bucket men . . . A good man can throw water with it on top of almost any house in town, except the two-story buildings, and the side walls of these can be kept safe by water thrown from the ground where no man can stand the heat and smoke on a ladder.

Montana Post, Nov. 12, 1864

When strikes in other sections of the Territory skimmed away part of the city's population, advertisements calculated to lure the discontented or surfeited "pilgrim" home appeared in the paper:

HO! FOR THE STATES
20th of September, 1865
600 Passengers Wanted

A fleet of Mackinaw boats will leave the mouth of the Yellowstone Cañon for the States. The boats are from thirty to thirty-five feet long; sharp at both ends, and built so as to be proof against all injury from obstructions to river navigation.

FARE — From Virginia City to St. Joseph, Mo. $40.00, from the place of embarkation, $30.00.

Experienced navigators of the Yellowstone and Missouri will act as pilots, and the whole will be in charge of a man well acquainted with Indian affairs.

TERMS — Ten dollars in advance, the balance on embarkation.

R. C. Knox & Co., Proprietors
Montana Post, Aug. 26, 1865

Editor John Buchanan sold the *Post* to D. W. Tilton, proprietor of the City Bookstore, before the third issue was printed. Tilton published the paper until 1867, when it was moved to the growing town of Helena. This, however, did not leave Virginia City without a paper; for the *Montana Democrat,* with John P. Bruce and E. S. Wilkinton as editors, had been established in the fall of 1865. The *Montana Daily,* which began to circulate in 1870, was merged with the *Madisonian* in 1873. The *Weekly Madisonian* is still published.

Frontier communities have to provide their own amusements or import whatever entertainers are in the vicinity, and Virginia City, realizing this, provided a theater and a Lyceum Hall for such programs. As early as December 10, 1864, the *Post* announced that

The New Montana Theater will open this evening. The scenery is all new and was painted by DeWitt Waugh. The opening bill, "Faint Heart Never Won Fair Lady" contains comic and sentimental songs and a grand overture by the Orchestra. It will conclude with the roaring farce, "The Spectre Bridegroom." An efficient police will be on hand to enforce order.

Little more than a month later the Lyceum opened:

Virginia City is a young city of the mountains; with her churches, her schools, her waterworks, her fire companies, her stately buildings, her theatre and . . . the best among them all, her lyceum and reading room.

The woodwork is richly grained, the floor has been smoothly planed and the ceiling is to be frescoed.
Montana Post, Jan. 28, 1865

Jack Langrishe and his celebrated theatrical troupe made regular appearances in the camp, as did other companies. Various musicians and brass bands also gave performances, and, if professional talent was lacking, the miners themselves put on concerts.

A few evenings ago we were gratified by hearing the most artistically executed music we have listened to for many a day. Four newly arrived Pilgrims sat upon a log, by the wayside, and sang "Faded Flowers," and "Maggie by my Side" for their own gratification.
Montana Post, Aug. 26, 1865

In 1867, A. K. McClure made a trip to the West and, in the course of his travels, vis-

WALLACE STREET RESIDENCES

ited Virginia City. In his "letters," written on the spot and later published under the title, *Three Thousand Miles Through the Rocky Mountains,* he mentions that

Pretty much everyone goes to the theatre; and the "Pony" just opposite, clears the cobwebs out of the throats of the people between the acts . . . When the curtain falls the glasses rise, and are emptied between social greetings and commercial contracts.

Christmas Ball in Virginia City
Tickets were $20 each . . . A second floor over one of the large store-rooms was fitted up most tastefully for the occasion. Evergreens and flowers were festooned around the walls, and the Stars and Stripes hung in graceful folds over the orchestra . . . Supper came with midnight: Oyster soup opened the course, (followed by) elegant salads, delicious jellies, game of all kinds, candies manufactured here into temples and monuments, almost every variety of fruits, and sparkling wines.

On New Year's Day, McClure and his friends made calls, having imbibed egg nog which he describes as a blend of "three gallons of whisky, one egg and a little cream." He continues:

We did not get over half of the city until the walking became very hard for our party, owing to the condition of the streets, and other causes; and it was found impossible to conclude the calls on foot.
Letter XLIV, Virginia City
Mont. Terr., Dec. 6, 1867

Sports attracted a different type of audience but were quite as popular:

Prize Fight. Between Riley of Virginia City and Foster of Bannack to be held on Sept. 17. Both men are under heavy training. We see by the cards of admission that no weapons of any kind are allowed around or outside the enclosure.

Montana Post, Sept. 3, 1864

Horse-Race

On the 2th inst. the sporting fraternity, on excited cayuses of different patterns, rode up the mountain road to the Madison to see the race between Monte's Wild Charley and Foster's Crepin Horse. A tent was provided for "Lightning," John Bull's champagne, or, in short metre, "(H)ale" and "Sudden Death," a liquid intended to resemble cider, and sometimes facetiously called by that name in the mountains. As, however, the liquor was better than common in Virginia, we revert to our main proposition, the races.

Montana Post, Aug. 26, 1865

The real race covered a distance of six hundred yards on Monte's track for a purse of "$250.00 a side."

There was always some excitement on crowded streets:

This has been a runaway week. At Nevada the animals knocked down a large pole in their course. Between Nevada and Central, Gray's hack horses ran off, and the passengers jumped out behind. At the narrow part of the road, the vehicle passed within a few inches of the perpendicular descent into the gulch. In our own town, a span of horses, with half a wagon behind them came dashing through Jackson street, from up the gulch and running foul of the posts supporting the sign at Hitchins' store, broke them, and smashed the contents of a box of glass, before they were stopped.

Montana Post, Aug. 26, 1865

Direct communication with Salt Lake City by wire was established November 2, 1866, by the Western Union Telegraph Company. Ed Creighton of Virginia City sent the first dispatch to the people of Montana:

Allow me to greet you. It gives me great pleasure to connect your city by lightning. Gov. Green Clay Smith will send the first message free to Andrew Johnson, Pres. of the U.S.

The Governor's wire reads:

Montana sends greetings. We are this day brought in hourly communication with the United States and the world. God save the Union. Smith.

According to Mrs. Peter Ronan's reminiscences, "Divine service was held for the first time in Alder Gulch in the fall of 1863 by the Rev. Joseph Giorda, S.J. The cabin in which the holy sacrifice of the mass was celebrated was crowded with miners, and a few women and children. During the time of prayer, all knelt on the dirt floor." Some sheets laid

over rough-hewn boards provided the altar. Toward the end of the service "a tinkling sound of large tin cups, passed from one man to another" was heard. "Each poured a trickle of gold dust from his buckskin pouch into the cup and then the gold dust from all the cups was poured into a yellow buckskin purse and laid on the altar. When Father Giorda went to the stable where he had left his team and asked for his bill, he was told that it was $40.00 for the two days. He said he didn't have that much. Mr. Ronan asked if he knew how much was in the buckskin purse. He said 'No.' When he looked he found it contained several hundred dollars!"

A theatre building on Jackson Street was bought by his congregation, was remodeled so as to serve as All Saints church, and was dedicated on Christmas, 1865. Father Giorda remained in Alder Gulch until February, 1866. Later that year Father A. Grassi, who replaced Father Giorda as head of the Missions in the Rocky Mountains, sent Father James A. Vanzina to Virginia City. He remained there with Father Van Gorp, who occasionally held services in the camp until the fall of 1867, when he was replaced by Father J. D'Aste from Helena. From the summer of 1869 until December, 1873, Virginia City had no resident priest. Then the Reverend Frank J. Kelleher arrived, and for eleven years was in charge of that Mission where he "labored with zeal and devotion, endearing himself to all classes of people, Catholics and Non-Catholics alike." The church on Jackson Street served the community until 1930 when it was razed. Since then, its members attend the stone church at Laurin, which was built in 1902.

The first Protestant clergyman to preach regularly in the Territory was the Reverend A. M. Torbett, a Baptist minister. Through his efforts, a society was formed that built a Union church on Idaho Street in 1864, near the present Methodist Episcopal church. This structure was dedicated, January 22, 1865. A notice in an August, 1864, issue of the *Post* mentions "preaching every Sabbath by the Rev. A. M. Torbett at 11 A.M. at the Court House. Sabbath School at 2 P.M. All are invited to attend."

A local preacher and miner, Reverend Hugh Duncan, who reached Alder Gulch in 1863, preached the first Methodist sermon in Virginia City. The following September the first Methodist missionary to Montana, Reverend A. M. Hough, arrived with his wife. During his two years' stay, aided by George Forbes, who made his fortune in Alder Gulch, the Methodists built, in 1864, a log chapel at the corner of Jackson and Cover Streets. When, in 1865, Brother Hough saw that Last Chance needed a preacher, he hurried over the hills to the new diggings, leaving Reverend King to carry on the work in Virginia City. Brother King stayed but one year during which a frame Methodist Episcopal church was begun; but the $3,000 raised for its construction was not enough to complete it.

The first Protestant Episcopal service was held on Christmas Day, 1865, in Judge Lovell's office, with Thomas J. Dimsdale the lay reader. Later gatherings were held in the Young Men's Literary Hall, the schoolhouse, and the Council Chambers, until on March 17, 1867, a meeting for the formation of St. Paul's parish was held in the home of Judge H. L. Hosmer. At that time, the church which the Methodists had started to build was unfinished, so, with the approval of Bishop Tuttle, the Episcopalians bought it and in 1868 completed it. When the first service was held in this structure, the walls were still unpainted, no pews had been installed, and no glass was in the windows, only muslin stretched across the openings to temper the light. This frame church was razed in 1902 to make way for the present grey stone structure. The new St. Paul's — the Elling Memorial Episcopal Church — was given by Mrs. Henry Elling and her children in memory of her husband.

Grace Methodist Episcopal church, a stone building on the corner of Idaho and Van Buren Streets, was built in 1875 and cost $4,-100. William Fairweather's funeral was the first service held in it on August 28, 1875. Reverend W. C. Shippen was the pastor.

With so many churchgoers in the town it is not surprising to find the following notice, signed by thirty-four merchants, in an issue of the *Montana Post in* 1866.

NOTICE

We, the undersigned, merchants and business men of Virginia City, thinking it is our duty, to ourselves and to those in our employ to observe the Sabbath Day: Therefore, we do hereby agree to close our respective places of business on that day of each week, from and after, January 1st, 1866.

John S. Rockfellow
Nowland & Weary
Etc.

Two miles below Virginia City, skirting the gulch, is Nevada City, recently restored by the Boveys, but in the 1940's and '50's, scarcely more than a site with only two or three false-fronted buildings or barns weathering beside the highway. Both it and Virginia City sprang up at the same time and were for several years the largest towns in Alder Gulch. The editor of the *Montana Post* mentions Nevada City, the Junction, and Centerville as "enterprising and flourishing cities" and devotes considerable space in the second issue of the paper (Sept. 3, 1864) to Nevada City.

Last Sabbath we closed our office and started out to take a walk. Passing down Wallace St. which was jammed with people, we saw the neat and thriving village of *Centerville*. We say village, it is more classic . . . a large number of neat buildings being erected and the place having the appearance of thrift. Stopping with our friend Chamberlain opposite the half-way house, we talked of America over a bottle of sparkling champaign-cider.

Soon we entered *Nevada*, which contains clean streets, neat and substantial business houses, thronged with customers. The city does not present the hustle and bustle of Virginia though it is growing in importance.

Our omnibuses between Virginia and Nevada cities . . . are doing a heavy business. By all means take a buss and avoid being squeezed.

Joseph Cruwit
French Baker, Nevada City, Mont. Terr., . . . would say to his numerous customers that he is always on hand to stuff the mouths of the hungry. Give him a call.

Star Bakery & Saloon
Nevada City . . . . Here is the place to get an honest loaf, a cake or pie, and . . . something to wash it down.

At the first Territorial election, Nevada City cast 1806 votes, and its Masonic Temple antedated the one in Virginia City. Adelphi Hall, which housed Nevada Lodge No. 4 A. F. & A. M., was the popular gathering place for all sorts of meetings and for dances:

Ball at Nevada
On Tuesday evening last, the citizens of Nevada held a reunion of the happiest and, indeed, most joyous kind, at the Adelphi Hall. The proceeds of the ball were devoted to the benefit of the Vigilante Committee. The supper at J. M. Closser's was all that could be desired; and the attendance on the guests, by the Nevada gentlemen, was both prompt and courteous. We thought we had lit upon an oyster bed in Nevada.

Nothing but the approach of daylight could have broken up that party. We are happy to hear that, through the able management of our friend Joe Taggart, quite a respectable sum was realized from the proceeds of the tickets sold.

Montana Post, Jan. 20, 1866

When the gulch was stripped of its best gold, the mining population left for richer diggings. By 1868, J. Ross Browne described Nevada City by saying:

At present it shows signs of decay. In the winter the people of the inhabited parts of the town make use of the uninhabited houses for firewood. If a bed-rock flume is put in the gulch, Nevada will probably regain in some degree its former life and activity.

J. Ross Browne, "Report on the Mineral Resources of the States and Territories of the Rocky Mountains, 1868".

Some of the best mineral deposits lay in Brown's Gulch, just south of Nevada. One company of five men took $30,000 in nuggets from it in eleven working days, each nugget averaging three to four ounces in weight. Both the Easton and Pacific mines, whose ore shoots were on one vein, were important producers for many years and were still being worked in the early twentieth century by lessees. Thereafter Nevada City became a ghost until restored by Charles Bovey in 1960-61.

As one drives through Nevada City today, one wonders where the execution of John Dolan took place. It was probably in the vicinity of the Jackson House. The event is graphically described in the *Montana Post* issue of September 24, 1864:

Sat. evening, Sept. 17, John Dolan, *alias* Coyle, *alias* The Hat, paid the penalty of his crimes at Nevada.

Shortly after sundown, a strong body of armed citizens marched from Highland, Pine Grove, Junction and Virginia, and joining the force already on the ground, formed on each side of the entrance to the ball-room next to the Jackson House where the prisoner was confined. In a few minutes the culprit, pinioned and guarded, made his appearance, when the procession moved in military array to the place of execution. The prisoner . . . was in the center. At the ground, a circle was instantly formed and the prisoner standing on a board supposed . . . that a touch of the hand only was required to convert it into a drop. The citizens' guard, revolvers ready for instant use, faced outwards, and confronted the crowds, 4000-5000 individuals.

The prisoner admitted he had committed the crime . . . but was drunk when he did it. He requested that some of his friends would bury his body . . . The plank fell and in a moment, the prisoner was

GILBERT BREWERY, DAYLIGHT GULCH, VIRGINIA CITY

swaying in the night wind. He died without a struggle.

A stern order to fall back, enforced by the click of 500 revolvers, startled the dense crowd, and a stampede of the wildest description took place . . . After ascertaining that life was extinct, the body was delivered to Dolan's friends.

ADOBETOWN

A mile below Nevada was Adobetown, the third oldest placer camp in the gulch whose claims were worked almost wholly by flume companies. During 1864, Adobetown was the center of a very rich section of the gulch, from which $350,000 is said to have been taken. Although it was never a large place — its population in 1872 was only 150 — it has the distinction of having had for many years the oldest existing school building in the territory. The first postoffice, authorized by President Andrew Johnson to serve Nevada, Junction, and the upper Ruby (or Stinking Water) Valley, was located here in 1865. Sylvan Hughes, the first young man from Montana to enter West Point, left Adobetown for the States in 1870. At its height the camp had one store, a blacksmith shop, two hotels, and two halls. In 1879, its population was 175 whites and 250 Chinese.

JUNCTION CITY

One mile farther down stream was Junction City on Granite Creek. It was laid out in January, 1865, by the Junction City Town Company and was spoken of during its first two or three years as "one of the sprightly mining towns of the gulch." It contained stores, boarding houses, a schoolhouse, a public hall, and a meat market. Junction City Lodge No. 15 I. O. G. T. was organized July 21, 1869, with thirteen members. As a camp it began to fade in 1868-69. Its population in 1872 was one hundred.

VIRGINIA CITY (Continued)

Virginia City, like other western camps, had its Chinese population. It was fortunate for the prospectors that the Orientals, most of whom had drifted east from California, followed the stampede to the gulch as soon as they did, for the miners were too busy staking claims and shoveling dirt to bother with creature comforts and were glad enough to get the Chinese to do their laundry and some of their cooking. Most of those who opened restaurants were well patronized, but it was the laundries which really paid off, for the sands of Alder Gulch clung to the miners' clothes and the thrifty laundrymen panned the wash water and pocketed the accumulation of dust.

About 1870, after the white placer miners had stripped the gulches of the richest gold and had moved on to new diggings, several companies of Chinese bought the right to rework the ground. These companies brought with them several hundred native laborers, who swarmed into the gully and from it picked gold which had eluded the prospectors. For twenty-five years, by dint of exhausting, backbreaking work, these blue-smocked, tireless little men lifted boulders and shoveled dirt into wheelbarrows, pushing them over precarious plank catwalks to be washed, trotting back and forth all day, and receiving for their labors a pittance in wages and food and lodging of a sort. Many raised part of their food, such as pigs, chickens and ducks, and grew native plants in their tiny truck gardens. They diligently worked the gulch from its head to the mouth of the canyon, and when they could no longer find colors they left.

The history of mining in the West is full of injustices and violence practiced against the Chinese, especially those who mined. High taxes, fees and exorbitant rentals failed to dislodge them, and only threats of bodily harm caused them hurriedly to leave the ground that they were legally working. Rossiter W. Raymond, U.S. Commissioner of Mining Statistics, states in his Sixth Annual Report (1874)

his views on the situation, and in what must have been an extremely unpopular point of view:

CHINESE

The legislature of Montana is reported to have passed a bill prohibiting aliens from acquiring or maintaining any titles. Whether this sort of law is constitutional or not, it is certainly destructive of the interests of the community, as may be shown in numerous instances where the Chinese have purchased, for cash, claims which white men could no longer afford to work, and have proceeded to make them productive, at a smaller profit to themselves than to the Territory. Besides being bad policy, this course toward the Chinese is rank dishonesty. The men who are glad enough to sell their old and worn-out diggings to these patient and frugal strangers join in the cry that the Chinese will overrun the land, and propose to eject them from the property they have paid for. It seems to me there is no harm to society in that kind of ursupation of soil which consists of buying it and paying for it; and, at all events, those who, by virtue of laws of their own manufacture, excluding foreigners from right of original location, get the land in the beginning for nothing, and then, after having skimmed it of its richest treasure, sell it at their own price, and pocket the money of the purchase, are no better than highway robbers, if they conspire thereafter against the title they have transferred.

During their many years stay in Virginia City, the Orientals, possibly 500 in all, occupied a large Chinatown made up of nondescript hovels, stores, laundries, restaurants, opium dens, and some rather elaborate saloons and gambling houses which sprawled beside the gulch at the foot of Main Street. Most impressive in this jumble of buildings was a two-story Joss House with a curved roof and porch. It stood on a rise of land where the stage road entered town at the lower end of Wallace Street. Built of logs, its upper story housed the Joss and a beautifully decorated altar. For many years this temple served as the religious and social headquarters for the seven to eight hundred Chinese in the city and the surrounding camps, as well as a meeting place for the Chinese Masonic Fraternity. It is a pity that this historic landmark was razed some years ago. Some of the relics of the Chinese have been preserved in the two museums at Virginia City, by Charles Bovey at Nevada City and Virginia City, and in the State Historical Museum at Helena.

Alder Gulch was the scene of a war between the Chinese in which all the members of the six companies that worked the gulch

NEVADA CITY (1950's). *Reproduced courtesy of Senator and Mrs. Charles Bovey*

KEARSARGE PROPERTY, SUMMIT,
ALDER GULCH

participated. The headman of each had absolute authority over his men and gave orders that were obeyed without hesitation. When arguments over leases or water rights arose between the companies, the head men settled the disputes among themselves. But in time two factions developed, with four of the companies aligned against the other two. When the Two Company, as the smaller group was called by the white residents of Virginia City, got control of an especially good piece of ground for which the Four Company had been negotiating, the heads of that group issued an ultimatum that the Two Company give up their lease or fight. All members of the two companies which legally held the ground were armed and ordered to entrench themselves upon their land. The four opposing companies also armed their men. The battle, which lasted for two days until all the ammunition in the area was exhausted, was noisy, but none of the six hundred warriors was killed.

The four companies then decided to try weapons which they understood better than firearms. Reverting to Chinese practice, they made stink pots and sharpened shovels, pitchforks, and pikes. Armed with these and wearing hideous masks, the yelling Four Company aggressors charged the Two Company defenders and routed them. Two of the latter were killed, one of whom stumbled as he fled down the gulch and was decapitated with a shovel by a Four Company man who took the gory trophy back to his ranks in triumph. The sheriff of Madison County and his posse finally felt that matters had gone far enough and arrested forty chattering contestants, including two members of Four Company — Ah Wah and Ah Yen — who were charged with murder.

Interpreters for the Chinese realized that the witnesses would more readily testify truthfully if sworn in on the blood of a freshly killed rooster rather than on a Bible. Therefore, when the hearings were about to open, the jail yard was filled with crates of birds, and each witness was taken into the enclosure and sworn in as the bloody head of a cock was severed for him. At the close of the hearing, Ah Wah and Ah Yen were bound over to the Grand Jury.

During the trial a juror became ill and left; but the judge proceeded with only eleven present, over the protests of the defendants' counsel. The verdict of the eleven was "guilty of murder in the first degree" and Ah Wah and Ah Yen were sentenced to death. Because of the irregularity of a conviction by eleven jurors, the case went to the Supreme Court, and a new trial was ordered. Ah Wah and Ah Yen were returned to jail. About a year later the case was called. In the meantime, an election had been held and a new sheriff, prosecuting attorney, and district judge had taken office. As the trial commenced, one of the attorneys for the defense addressed the judge:

"Your honor, when a man is on trial for his life he must be present."

"Are these two men not Ah Wah and Ah Yen?" asked the astonished judge.

"They are not our clients," replied the attorneys for the Chinese prisoners. Since the new officers had never seen the condemned men before, they were powerless to prove or disprove their identity, and the two were released. During the year between the arrests and the trial, the warring Chinese companies had settled their differences and had agreed to save the lives of the men awaiting trial. Visitors were free to come and go at the jail and toward the last, two friends of the condemned men had changed clothes with them and remained in the cell while Ah Wah and Ah Yen returned to the gulch. Strangely enough, the men could never be found!

Chinese miners are thorough and when they could no longer reap a living from the much-turned sands, it was to be expected that no one else would try, and that the mounds of boulders, the crooked ditches and tunnels, and the tortuous plank runways to and from the bed of the creek would be lasting monmuents to a great era of placering. What man could do was finished; what machinery could accomplish was soon to be seen.

RUBY AND THE DREDGING ERA

Anyone who has driven into Virginia City or Nevada City for the first time from Sheridan may be as disappointed as my husband was, for the approach is through an open valley, past miles of dredge dumps, whose barrenness is only partly hidden by clumps of alders and hardy sagebrush whose roots have fought their way into the scanty soil caught between the boulders. We were prepared for the debris left by hand placering and hydraulicking, but not for pasture land turned inside out so that hidden gold could be sucked from its soil.

The German Bar Placer Mining Company

introduced dredging machinery into the area when it built and operated a dredge in Alder Gulch, four miles below Virginia City in 1896-97. But its recovery of gold was small as compared to the large-scale operation which commenced in 1898 upon the advice of Dr. N. S. Shaler, a geologist from Harvard University. Shaler interested Gordon McKay, a shoe manufacturer from Boston, in organizing the Conrey Placer Mining Company and in acquiring the necessary placer ground for the enterprise. Dr. Shaler assured Mr. McKay that sufficient gold still lay caught in the deep gravels of the gulch and the adjoining meadowland to warrant washing away the waste dirt to bedrock to recover the dust. Upon his advice, McKay purchased the Phillip Conrey ranch, one mile below the mouth of Alder Gulch, for $30,000 and built his first gold boat on the property. McKay, who held a controlling interest in the company, was also its first president. He guided its development for several years, and upon his death, by the terms of his will, Harvard University assumed control of the company. From this legacy Harvard received a large income for many years. Dr. Shaler succeeded McKay as president of the organization.

A steam dredge, the Gordon, built by the Vulcan iron works of Toledo, was ready to start digging by the fall of 1899, but its machinery was not heavy enough to work the gravel beds and new equipment was installed. The boat was dismantled in 1907. The Maggie A. Gibson, another steam dredge, built and operated at Bannack for several years, was brought to the Ruby Valley and rebuilt during 1897-1898. It operated satisfactorily in its new setting for five years, using sixteen to twenty cords of wood a day for fuel.

As work progressed, the company bought up more placer ground in Alder Gulch as far upstream as it could get colors. It also bought ranches on both sides of the creek below the mouth of the gulch, and, as the dredges bit into larger areas of auriferous gravel, the company continued to build additional boats.

A steam dredge, built in 1901, was equipped with machinery hauled from Twin Bridges. One portion of the machinery required sixteen horses to move it, and as the heavy load crawled along the roadway, six men watched over it, walking beside the animals. Oldtimers tell how it took a whole day to move it ten miles from Twin Bridges to Sheridan and another day to make the next mile, as the load bogged down

in alkali dust and had to be dug out by hand. The third day, the machinery rolled into Ruby and installation was started. This dredge was in operation in 1902 and was not dismantled until 1907. Two electric stacker dredges, built between 1904 and 1908, continued eating their way through the gulch.

So that even more efficient dredges might be constructed, President McKay sent Julius Baier, one of the company specialists, to California to study current placer mining methods. While he was gone, a third boat was built and put into operation. Upon his return he supervised the construction, in 1910, of a mammoth electric dredge — the largest in the world — which is said to have cost close to half a million dollars. This boat was capable of digging 10,000 cubic yards per day from a strip of ground 300 feet wide and fifty feet below the surface of the water. It was also equipped to handle gravel that carried as little as eight cents in gold to the cubic yard and to crush and treat quartz ore, for it was both dredge and mill. At the weekly cleanup, the gold that had been recovered was melted in coke furnaces in fireproof pots and then poured into moulds, to make gold bricks.

As the number of employees of the Conrey Company increased, the town of Ruby was built near the mouth of Alder Gulch, to provide homes for the men and their families. Although it is little but a site today, in the early 1900's Ruby had a population of 500, a postoffice, three hotels, three stores, a meat market, a three-room schoolhouse, a church, and a town hall. As soon as a power line was strung from the Madison Electric plant to Ruby, in 1906, and a sub-station built in the town, both dredges and homes were furnished with electricity. At night the boats were brightly lighted and gave a festive air to the barren gulch. When all the dredges and machine shops and the sub-station were operating, the company's monthly electric bill ran between $10,000 and $11,000. When the Northern Pacific built a branch road up the Ruby Valley to Alder, one mile below the Conrey ranch, in 1901, supplies and freight were more easily handled, and curious tourists flocked into the diminutive settlement of Ruby to board the dredges and ride on their drifting hulls.

For twenty years the dredges slowly ate their way through the soil and gravel of lower Alder Gulch and the meadowland bordering the Ruby River until seven miles of ground, or 1,000 acres, was laid bare to bedrock. The undertaking was a profitable one, as during that period $9,000,000 in gold was recovered by the greedy maws of the huge boats.

At one narrow place in Alder Gulch, a rocky spine blocked the path of the dredge and, since the boat was too big to slide past it, the company decided to cut through it. The character of the soil and gravel was such that little fine gold was saved, so the engineer was told to stop work. Upon examination, the water tables were found to be so choked with heavy gold that the finer particles had been washed away with other debris. In its gouging, the dredge had cut into a ledge of gold-bearing gravel for some reason overlooked by the placer miners. During its first day's work on this ledge, the dredge took out $40,-000 in gold.

When the ground was worked out, the dredges were dismantled one by one until only the biggest of the group continued working. It ceased operations in 1922, and the gutted gulch became silent for the first time in many years. The only tangible sign left of the gigantic operation was miles of naked gravel and boulders, heaped in sinuous mounds between the banks of the creek. The dredge machinery and the company shops were loaded on cars at the Alder station and shipped to Seattle and, as Leslie Gilman, an employee of the Conrey Company for more than twenty years, put it: "The once beautiful valley, once filled with grain, alfalfa and stock is now a mound of gravel."

With the cessation of dredging, Alder Gulch lay ripped inside out, its fourteen miles of grey denuded boulders only partly hidden by new thickets of alders which line its barren bars. Virginia City has dwindled, too, from 10,000 fanatical miners in 1863-1864 to a stable population of slightly more than 300 in 1960. But one night during 1959, the city came alive in a way that made old-timers recall the good days when everyone worked together and the gulch ran with gold. The cause of this excitement was the earthquake that tossed a mountainside into Hebgen Lake and buried campers and dammed a river. Virginia City was on the fringe of the quake area, but as the land heaved, the citizens ran into the streets to stand in frightened groups waiting for new shocks. The rumor that Ennis would be evacuated for fear of flood, gave the people something concrete to do, as they made hasty preparations to care for refugees from the Madison Valley. Therefore, hotels, restaurants, and taverns kept open all night, and housewives prepared coffee and food. The dreaded flood did not materialize, and Virginia City returned to its normal routine after a sleepless night.

UPPER ALDER GULCH

On my last visit to Virginia City I took the road to the head of Alder Gulch to Summit, a deserted camp high in the hills. The first point of interest is the historic marker, one-half mile south of Virginia City, which indicates the site of Fairweather's strike. It is close to the stream and is inscribed:

ON THIS SPOT MAY 26, 1863, GOLD
WAS DISCOVERED BY
WILLIAM H. FAIRWEATHER
HENRY EDGAR   THOMAS W. COVER
MICHAEL SWEENEY   HARRY RODGERS
BARNEY HUGHES

THE GULCH WAS NAMED ALDER
THE MINING DISTRICT FAIRWEATHER
MAY 26, 1864, MONTANA TERRITORY
WAS CREATED BY ACT OF CONGRESS
APPROVED BY ABRAHAM LINCOLN

ALDER GULCH HAS PRODUCED OVER ONE
HUNDRED MILLION DOLLARS IN GOLD

SIZE AND PRODUCTION CONSIDERED
IT RANKS AS THE
WORLD'S RICHEST PLACER GULCH

At the base is the dedication: "To the Pioneers of Montana, in honor of Andrew J. Davis, Pioneer, by his nephew Andrew J. Davis, of Butte, Montana." Judge Andrew Jackson Davis came to Montana by wagon train in 1863 and was among the first to find gold in the rich gulch, but he was not a member of the Henry Edgar party. Following the discoveries in the gulch, he engaged in merchandising and then in banking.

From this historic bar, overgrown with alders, just as it was in Fairweather's time, the discovery of gold started a chain reaction which extended the entire length of the gulch and into the surrounding hills. So many prospectors jammed both sides of the stream that six distinct mining districts had to be set up along Alder Creek or its tributaries. Four of these lay above Virginia City, beginning with the

Fairweather District which absorbed the town. The Highland District was two miles above the city, with Pine Grove above it, and Summit District, where the largest settlement was built, six to seven miles upstream at the head of Alder Gulch, below Old Baldy Peak.

The present shelf road up the gulch is narrow and skirts the creek all the way. A heavy rain the preceding night had left deep puddles across the road and had softened shoulders or washed them away in more than one spot, making me recall a manuscript in the Montana State Historical Library at Helena which mentions that a road between Virginia City and Summit was built in the middle 1860's but that it was a failure structurally and financially. The document presents the case of "The People of the Territory of Montana... vs. The Virginia City and Summit City Wagon Road Company," in which the attorney for the people claims that the company permitted the road "to fall into such a state that it was rendered dangerous and inconvenient to travelers passing over the same." Part of the fault lay with the miners themselves who, by their sluicing, "washed it out every day or every week" so that after trying to maintain it for a year, the road company abandoned it. The first two miles up the gulch were through open country with sagebrush and shrubbery covering benches and bars, both below and above the level of the road. A scant mile above the Fairweather monument, on the west side of the gulch, were the first mine buildings and dump and the foundations of a good-sized mill, and a short distance beyond was another property with dumps, higher on the hillside. These were the U. S. Grant and Fairweather mines in the Highland District. Both are said to have been located in 1881 by John M. King and were part of a group of claims on a single vein from which high-grade ore was profitably shipped during the 1890's. Other mines in the Highland District included the Eagle, Bell, Sonoma, St. John, Valley View, and Winnetka.

I am not sure when we passed through Pine Grove, or just where the St. John property, described as four miles from Virginia City, lay. In 1901, the lessees, Davis and Gray, opened a rich lead and shipped ore which netted them $100.00 to $150.00 a ton.

Farther up the gulch, we left the sagebrush and were surrounded by trees, which permitted only occasional glimpses of the streambed far below. By now the creek was on our left. With the exception of one flat, large enough to have accommodated a small settlement, the gulch was narrow and the road clung to the side of it, winding with the stream and climbing steadily toward a distant peak which blocked the head of the valley. At four different locations were the remains of solitary, chinked cabins or clusters of rotting sheds, and at one point, on the north bank of the gulch, were a number of copper-colored dumps and some ruined mine buildings below them. Farther on, two cabins on a bench above the water had stone steps leading down to the streambed.

By now the gulch had narrowed to a deep-cut channel, choked with debris left from placer operations, and as the road rose toward the head of the valley, it left the streambed farther and farther below it. Above the road, against the mountain, were tunnel entrances boarded up or caved in and occasionally a loading platform. At one place was the skeleton of a large stone building, roofless and perforated with gaping windows.

SUMMIT

A curve revealed a large flat below and to the left of the road, on which stood cabins and other large and small buildings in various states of decay. Beyond and above the level of the road were several big dumps, and at the head of the flat, beside the road, were the stone foundations and the charred remains of stamps from a mill. Placer dumps throughout this townsite restricted the stream to a narrow channel.

The road swept on beyond this flat around the shoulder of the mountain toward the bare peak, whose summit was gouged with a glacial cirque. After ascending a steep pitch it leveled out on a high clearing where big red dumps and a shaft house stood at the edge of a stand of timber. Beyond this point the road narrowed still more, and since it had recently been dug out by a bulldozer, its bed was soft as sand. While we were debating whether to go on or not, we heard the whine of a motor and then saw a truck among the trees. We backed into a new access road slashed through the forest and returned to the clearing. When the truck reached us, I hailed it to ask the driver if we had reached Summit.

"Sure, lady, you passed it down below on the flat where the buildings were. The Kearsarge property was there, too," he shouted over the noise of the gears.

The Summit Mining District, which was organized in July, 1863, embraced both Bachelder and Alder Gulches from their heads to the Pine Grove District, a mile below the junction of the two. A placer camp called Summit was platted at the mouth of Bachelder Creek and was soon covered with tents and cabins. It was a lively, noisy place with the usual saloons and hurdy-gurdy houses. After the first boom was over, the Chinese who stayed on bought the privilege of ripping up the board floors of the saloons and washing the dirt underneath, from which they recovered appreciable amounts of gold dust. All provisions were packed in from Virginia City, and the cost of even staple produce was exorbitant. Butter was $1.50 a pound, onions forty-five cents a pound, syrup $9.00 a gallon. Five potatoes brought $1.25.

But the gold was there, so that from the start Summit was an important camp which attracted men to the area. The gold in the gulches was coarse and as plentiful as at other diggings, and nuggets valued at from one to one hundred dollars were more commonly found at bedrock than at other locations downstream. One, taken from a claim above Summit, was valued at $600.00. Another, which was found near the Lucas lode in 1864, was said to be "worth $715.00 in coin and over $1700 in currency."

Not satisfied with placer gold, men like F. R. Steele began searching for the quartz veins from which the glittering particles came. In January, 1864, Steele located the Mountain Sheep — the first quartz lode in the district — named for an animal he had attempted to shoot. The Oro Cache and the Lucas lodes were also uncovered in 1864, and soon afterwards the Kearsarge, Nelson, Polar Star, and Excelsior were located. During the summer of 1865, a crude stamp mill run by waterpower was built in Bachelder Gulch to handle Oro Cache ore. Within the next three years, seven steam stamp mills were crushing ore from the district's deep mines.

The Oro Cache mine, which was half a mile from Summit on Spring Gulch, was one of the most important producers of the district. It was operated for a time by Colonel A. K. McLure of Philadelphia, who built a large mill on the property and ran it successfully, only to sell out to Charles D. McLure of St. Louis. Between 1864 and 1880 the mine is said to have produced $500,000 in gold; by 1901 the estimated output was $1,000,000. The richest

gold mine in the area, however, in its early days was the Lucas; but after its lead faulted and could not be rediscovered, it shut down. During the peak of its productive period, its valuable ore was protected by guards with shotguns.

A partial picture of Summit as it appeared in November, 1865, is given by a reporter from the *Montana Post,* who describes a visit to the lofty camp:

The snowline is a little above Highland, at this time, the road being very slippery and even dangerous to any but a sharp shod beast. Arrived at Summit, I talked with Hank Haines, who lives in the neighborhood of his great discovery, the Yankee Blade, which he visits occasionally and breaks off a piece of quartz, with a smile to pan out the gold as a relaxation in the evening. I left him smoking his calumet with the air of a convinced Washoe man.

Nov. 25, 1865

Another account, written more than a year later, further describes what Summit and its mines were like:

We went about half a mile up the gulch to the Lucas mill, which we found pounding away. It is a twenty-four stamp mill. Mr. Countryman designed it and superintended the construction work. The building is of stone, 62 feet by 72 feet. The company . . . is now only saving free gold. The last run of six days was satisfactory.

Nearly opposite to the Lucas, on the west side of the Gulch, Messrs. Messler & Co. are running a tunnel, which is 190 feet long now. They propose striking the Butler lode, 180 feet below the surface. The mountain rock is very hard and every foot has to be blasted.

Just at the mouth of Batchelor's gulch is Col. W. H. Postlewait's stone building and 15-stamp mill. The next mill up the gulch is the Seneca Falls mill, purchased by a New York company who propose enlarging it and putting in improved machinery.

A short distance up the gulch we come to the sawmill . . . The town is rather dull. The Summit dancing club has a grand time once a week, at other times the inhabitants manage to while away the time Micawber like "waiting for something to turn up."

Yours,
PETE
Summit, Jan. 18, 1867

A year later, J. Ross Browne in his *Report on the Mineral Resources of the States and Territories of the Rocky Mountains* (1868) mentions Summit City as

substantially built of logs, but in building this town the streets appear to have been forgotten at first and put in afterwards. In the case of fire the whole town would burn with as much facility as a single house. It seems strange, after so many mining towns have been utterly destroyed by fire, that in laying out a new one, where the ground costs nothing, the streets should not be left sufficiently wide to form a barrier to the progress of fire, as well as a means of communication. With a sufficient width, a fire could be confined to one square.

The rich and extensive quartz veins in this vicinity will probably render Summit City permanently prosperous.

By 1868, quartz mining began to diminish and, by 1871, scarcely any of the properties were being worked. In 1876, the Oro Cache was the only active mine in the district. Unsuccessful attempts to revive lode mining were made throughout the 1880's and considerable prospecting was carried on, but the Summit District remained quiet until 1901, when W. B. Millard began a systematic development of the quartz veins from which so much gold had already been extracted. With the leasing of the Kearsarge mine, a heavy gold producer in earlier days, a new era began for Summit. The Alder Company, organized by Millard and C. Damours, obtained fourteen quartz and two placer claims, bonded the Kearsarge mine and hired a crew of eighteen men to explore its abandoned workings, from which $150,000 in gold had already been recovered. The exploratory work uncovered two veins which contained large bodies of low-grade sulphide ore, carrying coarse gold with values of $20.00 to $25.00 a ton. To handle this mass of valuable rock, the company was fortunate in finding a sixty-stamp mill, equipped for amalgamation concentration and cyanidation at the Kennett mine, four miles from Virginia City. This mill, which was built in 1897, was moved to the Kearsarge property and began to operate in 1903.

To accommodate the increased population at Summit resulting from the boom, new buildings were needed for the company's officials, employees, and laborers. Old cabins were remodeled and new buildings, such as a two-story boarding house with ten sleeping rooms, a two-story bunkhouse with accommodations for seventy-two men, a stable, "double boarded and papered the same as a dwelling house," were made available. Even the old Masonic Temple was pressed into service as a bunkhouse for forty men. Mr. Millard and the company officials lived in a fine mansion high on the wooded hillside overlooking the town and the mill. The building was three stories high with a fireplace in the main room made of boulders from the gulch, inlaid with specimens of ore from the Kearsarge mine. I did not find Millard's dwelling nor the mill when I visited Summit in 1956.

During our last minutes in Summit the sky had darkened and thunder grumbled through the hills. The road back to Virginia City was not one on which to be caught in a downpour, so we hurriedly left the scene of so much former activity and rolled down Alder Gulch on grades so steep that even low gear only partly checked our speed. As we drew into Virginia City the first big drops began to spatter the ground, and the sky behind us was inky black.

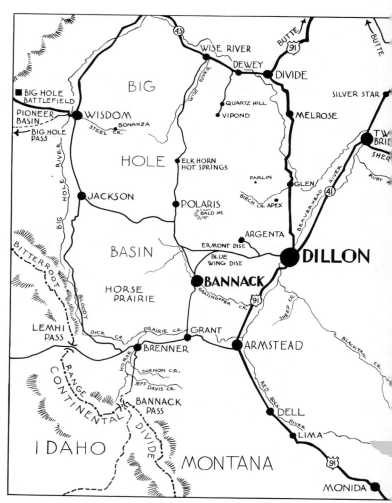

CHAPTER 3

GRASSHOPPER CREEK and BIG HOLE BASIN

"Have you been to Bannack?" people in Virginia City asked when they saw me sketching old buildings. "It's the oldest camp in Montana and it's pretty much the way it was in the early days." With anticipation I planned a trip that included Bannack. It seemed a good idea to start from Dillon, drive west into the Big Hole Basin, detouring to Bannack and other small camps on the way, then swing north to Wisdom and the Big Hole placers and from there to continue on the main highway to Divide.

DILLON

Dillon, the seat of Beaverhead county, did not exist until 1880. In fact, the land where it stands was merely part of Richard Deacon's ranch until the Utah and Northern railroad laid its track north to that point and steam locomotives chuffed into the work camp, whose canvas tents stood beside the rails. One account mentions that the tracklayers were temporarily hampered by a rancher who refused to give them the right of way across his land. Since everyone else was impatiently waiting for the road, a group of far-sighted men bought the ranch, gave the railroad permission to cross it, and then formed a town company which by December, 1880, was ready to sell lots at public auction. Next, the place was surveyed and a few log and frame shacks were hurriedly thrown together, but even so few people had an idea that the town would be permanent, the prevailing opinion being that while the railroad remained, and while the place continued to be a shipping point for Helena, Bozeman, Butte and Virginia City, some business would be done, but as soon as the road moved on, the town would move with it.

from Mr. Wilson's *Wayside Gleanings* (Leeson, 1885)

When the railroad was completed to Butte, Dillon's boosters applauded the sentiments of the *Glendale Atlantis*, which prophesied:

The Salmon River country, situated in the adjacent county (Lemhi, Idaho), will replenish its supplies here. The tourists for Yellowstone National Park will all debark here. Montana so far has no metropolis; she should have one; she will have one; and Dillon City is to be that one.

Sept. 22, 1880

The next excitement was over the county seat — Dillon wanted it and Bannack had it. Moreover, Bannack had just completed a new two-story brick courthouse and could see no reason for abandoning it. The Dillon Townsite Company countered with an offer of a "suitable building rent free for five years" and agreed to pay for the removal of the records and office fixtures from Bannack. Feeling was strong throughout the county as the 1881 election day approached. The returns favored Dillon and, in a short time, the county officials were installed on the main floor of its newly built, frame schoolhouse. The school occupied the second story except when court was in session. At such times classes were dismissed and cases were tried in the large upstairs room.

Two fires in 1882, which destroyed many of the canvas-roofed cabins, did little to dampen the enthusiasm of the residents. With a population of 1600, Dillon in 1883 is described as having "streets full of bustle and people well charged with energy, snap and ambition."

Most of the mining in the region was carried on west of Dillon, but smaller districts lay north and south of the present city.

The mines on Carter and Hoffman Creeks were 10 miles southeast of Dillon. The Jake Creek district, 18 miles southeast of Dillon produced some lead ore. The Blacktail district, at the head of Sheep Canyon, a tributary of Blacktail Deer Creek, 15 miles south of Dillon, showed activity in 1934 when gold was recovered from drag boulders or fault blocks. Placer gold was reported from the Frying Pan Basin, north of Dillon in 1932. Farlin was a camp in the Mt. Torry district, 14 miles west of Glen and north of Dillon. An old photograph shows several mine buildings, a shaft house and big dump silhouetted against a background of high peaks.

More important than these was the Birch Creek district, 12 miles northwest of Dillon and 6 miles west of Apex, a station on the railroad. The district was discovered soon after the Bannack and Virginia City diggings but did not develop rapidly, due to its lack of "attractive gold placers" and its distance from smelters and markets for copper ore. In 1883, one company which discovered several large veins of magnetic iron, was able to sell the ore as flux to the smelters at Glendale and Butte at a profit of $1800 a month. In the late 1890's, the Indian Queen mine was opened. Other claims were the Greenwich, Treasure, Greenstone and Fairview.

Dillon today is a bustling place — a shipping and ranch center and the home of Western Montana College of Education. Its excellent Beaverhead Museum is filled with regional relics and documents, some of great value. It is there that I found old photographs of Bannack and Argenta, the camps that I was about to visit.

ARGENTA

Leaving the Museum in Dillon, my friend and I drove to the end of the street which flanks the railroad, crossed the tracks and the Beaverhead River, and climbed to the top of a bluff. As far as one could see sagebrush covered the rolling prairie. At the end of eight miles we turned north on a side road and drove five miles to Argenta.

I knew that the town, which was originally called Montana, had been chartered on January 6, 1865, and had been laid out at the mouth of Rattlesnake Canyon on the south side of the stream. Within two years its name was changed to Argenta. During the 1860's, when it flourished because of its gold placers and silver quartz lodes, it had a population of 1,500 and an estimated 3,000 claimants to mineral rights in the vicinity. At that time Argenta supported 3 hotels, 6 saloons, 2 grocery stores, 1 drygoods store, 2 butcher shops, 2 blacksmith shops, 1 bakery, 1 tailor shop and 1 dancehall. Argenta Lodge No. 29 I. O. G. T. was established June 7, 1871, and its charter was forfeited in 1874, by which date the camp was nearly deserted. Argenta had no church — only occasional services when some preacher rode over from Sheridan or from some other camp. During the winter of 1882, a snowslide five miles above town buried the entire Taggart family. All seven bodies — parents and five children — were recovered in March of the same year and dragged on rawhides into camp.

In 1954, when I first saw Argenta, most of its old houses had been remodeled and repainted. A few log cabins were canopied by big trees which pressed against them. In a few places even the cabin had disappeared, but a grove of trees indicated the site of the forgotten homestead. From a sod-covered house children and dogs rushed out to charge upon the car and peer in its windows. A little girl offered us a string of rainbow trout which she said her daddy had caught and told her to give to us. The low hills behind the town were full of prospect holes. On one hill, a new outfit was fixing up an old property.

Next to Bannack, the Argenta district is the oldest quartz camp in Montana. Although the placers discovered in 1862 were unimportant, lode mines, opened up shortly afterwards in the hills north of Argenta, on Rattlesnake Creek, caused great activity in the district. The initial silver discovery is credited to William Beeken, Charles S. Ream, and J. A. Brown, who located six lodes on June 25, 1864, staked the Montana lode the following day, and named the area the Montana Mining District. The richest lode, the Legal Tender, was found on July 3, 1865, by A. M. Esler. Other discoveries were made until, before long, ore from the district was being shipped to Swansea, Wales, for smelting.

The first smelter to be built in the Territory of Montana, was erected in 1866 by the St. Louis & Montana Gold & Silver Mining Company with capital obtained through the efforts of Samuel T. Hauser of Helena. The plant consisted of a German double-cupola furnace and a large cupelling furnace. Charcoal for the smelter was burned on upper Rattlesnake Creek. Fire bricks for the furnace lining were shipped from St. Louis up the Missouri River to Fort Benton and hauled by ox-team to Argenta. Besides silver from the six mines owned by Hauser and James Stuart, considerable high-grade ore from Esler's Legal Tender mine was run through the furnaces.

Early in the 1870's, S. H. Bohm & Company of Helena remodeled the St. Louis smelter, making of it the largest plant at Argenta, capable of handling custom ore as well as silver from the local mines. Smith (E. S.) Ball acquired the smelter in 1879 and ran it successfully until 1885. He bought his ore from the Blue Wing District, fluxed it with Argenta lead deposits, and sent the bullion to a refinery for treatment. The St. Louis Company had unsuccessfully attempted to cupel the metals so as to destroy the lead they contained but such treatment only caused a loss of values, as the metal often boiled over the cupels and was lost. Under Mr. Ball's management the ground where the cupel furnace had stood was dug up and was found to contain $8,000 of almost pure silver.

The second smelter was erected in 1867 by Esler at a cost of $4,000-$5,000. It is said that he made $8,000 from silver bullion run through it. By 1886, A. J. Schumacher had acquired the Esler furnace and was producing "tons of silver-lead base bullion" from high-grade ore obtained from the Dexter mine and the Legal Tender. Only the walls of this smelter, which was located a little below the present concrete bridge west of Argenta, are still visible.

The third smelter, one mile up the creek, was built in 1868 by Tootle, Leach & Company of St. Louis. G. W. Stapleton was manager. It was spoken of as the "Tootle-Leach," "Stapleton" and "Tuscarora Smelter," the latter name because ore from the Tuscarora mine was handled by it. This plant was finally operated by W. A. Clark's Tuscarora Company, but low prices of silver forced it to shut down in 1893.

A fourth smelter, under the supervision of P. F. Rompf, made a few shipments and then closed down. The last furnace to be built was a complete failure for it operated but one day. It was located a short way above the Tuscarora smelter.

By 1882, smelters in Glendale and East Helena, Montana Territory, were operating, as well as some in Utah, and much of the ore produced in the Argenta district was sent to these larger and more efficient plants. All during the 1870's new mines, such as the Iron Mountain and Midnight, were opened. As late as 1895, W. A. Clark bought the Alice, Copper King, Hillside, Silver Rule, and Mayflower claims — silver properties six miles northwest of Argenta.

In spite of extensive silver activity, it was gold placers that first attracted prospectors to the district. In the early 1870's, Jack Kingsley built a four-mile ditch to placer ground across the creek from the town and worked the banks with hydraulics. From this enterprise four men recovered $40 in gold dust per day. After they quit the diggings, a Chinese miner washed $3 a day from their abandoned ground.

Productive placers were found in 1882 below Argenta by P. J. Kelly, L. Scott and W. Ravenscroft. Other paying properties were located on French Creek and Watson Creek, north of Argenta, where Charles Watson took out $100,000 in gold. A total of $600,000 is estimated to have been produced from these two creeks.

During the 1880's, large bodies of low-grade smelting ore were recovered from a number of properties. High prices for lead and silver caused a brief revival in the district from 1906-1909. Total production up to 1930 is estimated at $1,500,000, mostly in lead, silver and gold. Due to higher silver prices, the district was active again in 1934. Short spurts of lode mining have kept the camp alive.

Oren Sassman, *Metal Mining in Historic Beaverhead (1862-1940)*

As we left the silver camp where so few people live today, I told my companion about the horse race in which John Stone bet Bill

BANNACK, MAIN STREET LOOKING WEST.
(right) 1876 COURTHOUSE; BECAME *HOTEL
MEADE. (left)* MASONIC HALL AND SCHOOL-
HOUSE WITH CUPOLA

MAIN STREET, ARGENTA

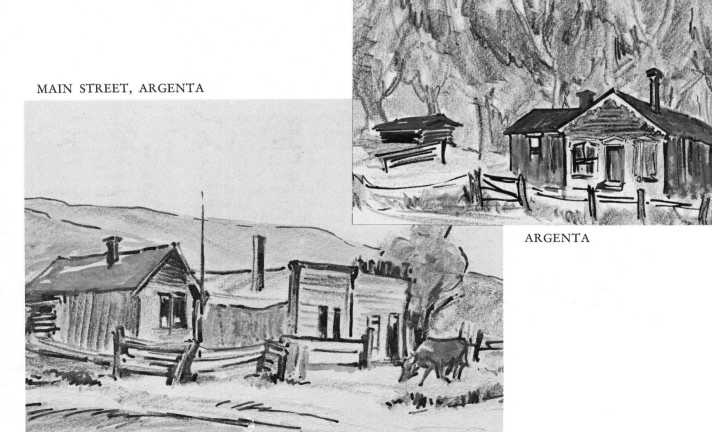

ARGENTA

Bivens that he could ride his mare "Nellie" to Bannack and back in two hours. The race was held on the Fourth of July, 1867, with a wager of $2,000. Stone lost by eight minutes, but, when two weeks later the race was repeated, he won by the same amount of time!

ERMONT MINES

Two miles farther west of the highway from its junction with the Argenta road is the turn-off to the Ermont mines. These mines were located in 1926 by D. V. Erwin and W. J. Corbett. Oren Sassman, in his treatise *Metal Mining in Historic Beaverhead (1862-1940)* gives the best description of them. According to Sassman, these two men "prospected the ground until the property was bonded by them to the Standard Silver & Lead Co. of Spokane."

The company further explored the area and sank a 110-foot shaft on the claim . . . The discovery of gold ore in the region, coupled with the inflated price of gold, aroused interest in the Ermont area and started a rush to it during 1932. Before long, most of the area was staked out. The next owners of the Ermont mines were R. B. Caswell, J. R. Bowles and F. C. Gram, who obtained thirty-three unpatented claims. They worked their holdings until 1933 and reopened the properties in 1936, at which time they erected a 100-ton cyanide mill, which refined an average of 90 tons of ore every twenty-four hours. Water for the mill was piped four miles from Rattlesnake Creek. Electric power was obtained by extending the line originally built to supply the Golden Leaf mill at Bannack. The mill ran three shifts and employed 60 men. During this prosperous period, the monthly output of the mine was $22,000.

BLUE WING DISTRICT

When we swung south off the highway west of Badger Pass on the way to Bannack, the Blue Wing Mining District was on our left. It was tucked into a rough and hilly section on the divide between Rattlesnake and Grasshopper Creeks with its center about one mile north of Bannack. Silver mines, including the famed Blue Wing, were discovered in this area in 1864, and a few of them have been worked more or less continuously until well into the twentieth century. The native silver ore was rich and, although high-grade specimens assayed $200-$700 a ton, it was not free-milling. Within ten years of its discovery, the district produced $200,000 worth of ore; by 1910 it is estimated to have yielded $7,000,000, of which $2,000,000 was silver and the rest gold, lead, and copper. As soon as the smelter at Argenta was blown in, ore from the district was sent to it for treatment. After it closed, ore was sent to Swansea, Wales, until later when smelters in Utah and in East Helena provided shorter hauls and lowered costs.

BANNACK

Bannack is the scene of Montana's first significant gold rush. The first time that I saw the town was in 1951. The twenty-one mile drive from Dillon was across lonely, rolling prairie which concealed the hollow in which Bannack lay. The only clues to its whereabouts were several small signs tacked to fenceposts which read "Ox Bow Cafe, Bannack." The last eight miles was a winding, downhill drive between barren hills to the bottom of a gulch. At the western approach to the town was a cemetery which contained a few granite and marble markers and many weathered picket fences surrounding individual plots. The grease wood and sagebrush through which we had been driving for miles grew as luxuriously within the town as on the prairie. Clumps of the pungent shrubs had rooted along the main street and had completely choked deserted front yards, while their spiny twigs scraped fence palings and shuttered windows. In this trough in the hills through which Grasshopper Creek twists, big cottonwood trees shade many of the old cabins whose square-hewn, mortised logs and lime-chinked walls pronouce their age. A few of these older homes were whitewashed and all were only one-story high. A number of false-fronted stores stood at intervals along the thoroughfare, with gaps between them indicating where other buildings once stood. A frame church, built in 1870, stood on the north side of the street. It was padlocked, and its Gothic ribbed window was too high from the ground to permit me to peep inside.

Everyone who visits Bannack investigates the dark interior of Montana's first jail, built in 1862 by the infamous sheriff Henry Plummer. Its thick, log walls and timbered, sod-covered roof and its tiny barred windows are still formidable. Inside, bolted into the rock, are the original leg irons. The one small cell was probably kept for men awaiting a swift miner's trial which often resulted in a hanging. Fortunately, when dredges were chewing at the banks behind the town, the historic jail

GOLDEN LEAF PROPERTY BEYOND GRASS-
HOPPER CREEK, BANNACK
METHODIST CHURCH BUILT IN 1870,
BANNACK

escaped their greedy jaws. Another of the famous old buildings is Skinner's Saloon, a one-story frame store with pilastered front and bits of dentil trim on the cornice.

The most impressive building in Bannack is the two-story, brick courthouse, erected in 1875 and used until 1881, when Dillon succeeded in wresting the county seat from Bannack by the slender majority of 170 votes. Upon the removal of the records to the new location, the building was abandoned until 1890 or 1891, when Dr. Christian Meade turned it into a hotel. For years now the Meade Hotel has been vacant; even its name below the eaves is dim. Its windows are broken and the porch sags, but when Bannack's population shrank so sharply that the postoffice was officially closed, the hotel came alive again. The remaining residents drove nails into the wall of the building and hung sacks of all sorts from them. When the mail was delivered, each person would dive into his own sack to see if it contained any letters or packages. The sacks served as private mailboxes in lieu of a regular postoffice.

Almost across the street from the old hotel is another historic two-story structure with a cupola — the weatherbeaten Masonic Hall, erected in 1874. The main floor of this frame building, in which Bannack Lodge No. 16 A. F. & A. M. met, was used for some years as the town schoolhouse. As early as the winter of 1862-1863 a group of four Master Masons met in Bannack for the purpose of organizing a lodge. Authorities differ as to where this first meeting in the Territory was held. One of the four, N. P. Langford of the Fisk train, wrote that they climbed to the top of a hill and "there in imitation of our ancient brethren, opened and closed an informal Lodge of Master Masons." Another writer mentions a log cabin on Grasshopper Creek "just back of Jack Oliver's express office." At any rate, they applied to the Grand Lodge of A. F. & A. M. of Nebraska for a charter on April 27, 1863, but before the dispensation was received, a majority of the Bannack Masons had left for other diggings and the Lodge was not regularly organized until October, 1877. Where in this silent town did Bannack Chief Lodge I. O. G. T. and Hope Lodge No. 19 I. O. G. T. hold their meetings? The former was founded January 3, 1870, and the latter on November 12, 1877. No meetings seem to have been held after 1879.

The only building that was open on my first visit to Bannack — prior to its being made officially a Montana State Park — was the Ox Bow Bar. Inside, as we drank our beer, its affable and well-versed proprietor chatted about Bannack's early history, its electric dredges, and his views on the Democratic party. He pulled a U. S. Government bulletin on dredge mining from under the counter and gave it to me to read. All the time I was taking notes from it he was busily telling us about the five dredges that worked the channel of Grasshopper Creek and recovered quantities of gold dust, left from earlier operations. He mentioned a forty-four mile, hand-dug ditch, built in 1866 to bring water from Horse Prairie to the placers, and explained that "it was all pick and shovel work." He pointed out the big gold mill across the creek and added that the Maggie Gibson dredge had worked the channel below the mill and the Græter boat had operated above it. He insisted that we walk up Hangman's Gulch before we left to see a replica of the gallows which mark the spot where Henry Plummer was hanged. He also pointed out the old cemetery close by on the hillside, where one of the oldest markers is inscribed:

Nellie Paget, aged 22, shot, April 22, 1864.

We appreciated his directions and set off down the straggling street with its fragmentary original board sidewalks. On our way to the gallows and Boothill cemetery, which is distinctly separate from the burying ground where Nellie rests, we were accompanied by a friendly collie who joined us outside the cafe and demanded much scratching. As we looked at the overgrown graves, I wondered if one of them belonged to Copley, the deputy sheriff who was killed in 1863 while trying to arrest a Spaniard for murder. The miners lost no time in tightening a rope around the killer's neck and dragging him over the rough streets until he was dead.

The first known white men to see the Beaverhead Valley were the Lewis and Clark expedition which, in 1805, came up the river by canoe. The next whites were the early fur trappers. Finally came the prospectors who settled beside Willard Creek (later known as Grasshopper) in 1862, and laid out a camp which they called Bannack, after the Indians of the region. Into this country came John White and John McGavin, members of a party from the Salmon River mines of Idaho, which set out for Deer Lodge Valley in the early summer of 1862, crossed Lemhi Pass, and trudged east down to Horse Prairie Creek. In an attempt to find an old trail from Salt Lake City to Deer Lodge Valley, they tried a short cut, and, near where Willard Creek enters the Beaverhead River, they made camp on July 28, 1862. From force of habit, White panned the gravel of the streambed and found colors. This spot, where Montana's first major placer diggings were discovered, is close to U. S. Highway No. 91, about half way between Armstead and Dillon. McGavin and White, unaware that the creek had already been named "Willard" by the Lewis and Clark expedition, called it "Grasshopper," because of the hordes of insects that infested its banks. The men working the sandbar made from $5 to $15 a day "to the hand."

The discovery of the Grasshopper placers brought swarms of prospectors to the area, many of them from Colorado. As winter approached, these miners, who had been living in the crudest of dugouts and flimsy shacks, built log cabins in the newly laid out townsite of Bannack. Among the 400 men in camp were James and Granville Stuart, who had been digging for gold around Gold Creek and Cottonwood for some time. They drove a herd of cattle from the Deer Lodge Valley to the diggings and remained there until the following April.

In the photograph file of the State Historical Library at Helena is a reproduction of a drawing which shows Bannack in its infancy. The original was drawn by an Englishman, Robert Holiday, for James Fergus, who at that time was living in Bannack. Fergus wrote on the sheet:

I enclose a pencil sketch of part of the first mining camp at Bannack and the first in Montana, taken by an Englishman who crossed the plains in the James L. Fisk party when I did in '62. The writing on the back of it by me is explanatory.

The paper is not large enough for the whole village. One-third of it lies to the left of the picture. . . . Nearly all the diggings are down in the canyon, the creek and bar diggings commence here and run down creek and are worked as far as four miles below. There are two small villages down the canyon on bars. The dry diggings are immediately behind you as you look at the picture. Two Indian lodges to the right in front are the ones the Indians were killed in. Our cabin is on the right in front of the picture near the lodges. It is improperly drawn as it is double-roofed and the chimney is in the centre. On the extreme left is Aults Hall, larger than it looks, nearly in the middle of town . . . To the right of our cabin stand our wagons and McIntires. Behind the cabin and between you and it is a hay yard.

James Fergus' notes on Holiday's sketch mention two Indian lodges which were fired upon. An outlaw named Reeves was responsible for the attack. Shortly before the shooting, Reeves bought a Sheep Eater Indian squaw and brought her to Bannack, but his treatment of her was so inhuman that she ran away and took refuge in the tepee of an old chief whose lodge stood on the fringe of the settlement. Reeves went after her but was driven off. He returned with Augustus Moore and the two shot up the lodge, killing the old man, a lame Indian boy, and a papoose. The ruffians of Bannack so intimidated the jury at the trial that it voted for banishment of the murderers instead of hanging. The decision elated the rough element who thereafter took things in their own hands and terrorized the solid citizenry for over a year.

While both Holiday's sketch and Fergus' description are fragmentary, they give some idea of Bannack's initial appearance. Fergus' notes also mention smaller camps downstream. The extensively worked placer ground extended from Bannack down through the canyon of the creek and for four or five miles below it to the mouth of Spring Gulch. One mile below Bannack was Centerville, renamed Marysville in honor of Mrs. Mary Jane Wadams, the first woman resident. Jim's Bar, named for Jim Griffith or "Adobe Jim," a plasterer, was near White's Bar. The small group of buildings in this vicinity was called Jerusalem.

Throughout 1862 and 1863 small parties of men and large wagon trains of miners from the states and other western mining areas poured into Bannack, swelling its constantly growing population to 3,000 or more. The first sermon heard in the camp was given by an itinerant Negro preacher who came to the settlement with a wagon train in April, 1863. Supply trains also arrived from time to time, coming by way of South Pass, Wyoming, or Fort Hall, Idaho. Best of all, by July, 1863, the homesick miners could get mail by Pony Express from Fort Bridger, Wyoming. Letters came through in a week and cost four bits (fifty cents) each.

By the time travelers reached Bannack their funds were sometimes gone. The story is told of two men whose money was spent before they reached their destination. One sold his pistol, and by combining the proceeds from it with the little money that the other still had, they reached Bannack with a total of six cents. A jeweler bought the pennies for seventy-five cents each to use for alloy, and the delighted pilgrims took their profits and hurried across the mountains to Virginia City.

When Henry Plummer arrived in Bannack on December 25, 1862, no one knew any more about him than that he was a well-educated, agreeable, and sociable fellow. As such, he was quickly accepted by the community. It was not healthy in those days to inquire into a man's past; each was accepted at face value until subsequent actions altered his status.

Soon after Plummer's arrival, a friend of his, Jack Cleveland, showed up in Bannack. He, too, was accepted until he killed a man and committed other crimes that marked him as a desperado, but no more violent than others in the rough and tumble camp. Finally, Cleveland picked a fight with a stranger in Goodrich's saloon and Plummer stopped it, telling Jack to behave himself. When Cleveland bragged that he wasn't afraid of any of the men present, Plummer replied, "This has gone far enough" and shot the bully below the belt. "Would you shoot a man when he's down?" Cleveland cried as he crumpled to his knees. "No, get up," snapped Plummer and shot him twice as he rose. Bannack's first sheriff, Hank Crawford, assisted the wounded man to his home and cared for him until he died a few hours later. Although Plummer was tried and acquitted on a plea of shooting in self-defense, he feared that Crawford's suspicions as to his own true identity might have been aroused by dying statements made by Cleveland. He therefore determined to get rid of the sheriff. Crawford realized this and kept out of sight for two days. Finally, he crossed the street to a restaurant; but when he saw Plummer waiting for him to come out, he borrowed a rifle and fired through a window, shooting Plummer in the right arm. After his recovery, Plummer learned to draw with his left hand. By then Crawford was on his way to the States.

The episode left Bannack without a sheriff. Plummer's qualities of leadership and his personal charm made him a favored candidate for the office. When he was elected in April, 1863, he bought a fine home to which he brought his bride from Sun River, and he became one of Bannack's most respected and popular citizens. But, simultaneously with his election, Bannack entered upon a period of violence which lasted as long as he was in office. Most of the crimes were committed on the road between Bannack and Virginia City. After George Ives, one of Plummer's henchmen, was hanged in December, 1863, by the

OLD COURTHOUSE, BANNACK. HANGMAN'S GULCH AND GALLOWS IN BACKGROUND

Vigilantes, other arrests and convictions followed in rapid succession.

On January 9, 1864, the Vigilantes rode to Bannack late in the evening, broke into Plummer's home, and seized him. All his arrogance and poise disappeared. He begged for mercy, pleading with them to banish him, cut off his ears, turn him out naked in the snow, but spare him. His captors were not impressed. One Sunday morning, January 10, 1864, Henry Plummer and two of his bloodiest agents, Ned Ray and Buck Stinson, were hanged from the gallows which, ironically enough, Plummer had ordered built for the execution of a horse-thief. Following these deaths, the Vigilantes systematically rounded up the rest of the road agents and got rid of them by banishment or by means of a noose. As soon as law and order were restored, Bannack regained its place of commercial importance in the Territory.

The discovey of gold-bearing quartz mines in the hills near the town, shortly after the locating of placer ground, had brought many prospectors to the settlement. The first lode claim to be recorded proved unimportant. The second claim was the Minnesota, located in November, 1862, by James Fergus. The first lode to be worked consistently was the Dakota, also located in November of the same year by Charles Benson, H. Porter, E. Porter, and C. W. Place. It and other properties such as the Wadams, Excelsior, and Wallace, were recorded according to local mining laws, which limited the length of a claim to one hundred feet. Three years later, when Montana Territory's second legislature met, it changed this ruling and defined a claim as "200 feet along the lode, with all the dips, spurs, and angles and 50 feet on each side of the lode for working purposes, but 1000 feet of ground may be taken in each direction along the lode for the same uses."

During the first winter, the owners of lode mines dragged sacks of ore to their cabins and crushed the rock in stone mortars, making from $10.00 to $20.00 a day. The first stamp mill on Montana soil known as the Bannack City Quartz Mill was built during the winter of 1862-1863 by Allen and Arnold in their blacksmith shop to treat ore from the Dakota lode. This mill, whose six stamps weighed 400 pounds each, was hand-made by its owners, who utilized iron tires and lumber from discarded freight wagons and refashioned these materials into the necessary machinery. The mill stood below the Dakota mine and pounded out $1,500 worth of gold per week with the help of a water wheel which supplied the power. It was so successful that the following year a steam-operated mill with twenty-four stamps was built above Bannack by Butterfield and Hopkins, at a cost of $25,000. Three more mills, including the Shenon, located on the site of the present Golden Leaf property, were erected before 1870. These mills made it possible to treat ore for as little as $4.00 a ton.

Although Bannack's population and that of the rest of the Grasshopper diggings during the first two years is given as between 500 and 5,000, depending upon the enthusiasm of the informant, the discoveries at Alder Gulch in 1863 and in Last Chance (Helena) in 1864 drained the restless population away and left the camp nearly deserted for a couple of years; not that its gold had given out, but simply that new diggings produce headlong stampedes.

A crowd of optimistic miners who assembled in a Bannack saloon in 1863 framed a petition to Congress, requesting that a new territory called "Montana" be cut from Idaho. Signatures from men in all the gold camps were obtained and, as soon as sufficient money was raised to finance the journey, Sidney D. Edgerton started for Washington, D. C., to present the document. As a result of this campaign, the Territory of Montana was established on May 26, 1864, with Bannack as capital. Edgerton was made governor, and the first legislature convened on December 20th. The buildings where the legislative council and house met have long been razed, but a letter written in 1908 by the late Judge Francis M.

Thompson of Greenfield, Massachusetts, who was a member of that council, describes them:

When Gov. Edgerton decided to call the legislature at Bannack we found a vacant store that we thought would do for the house and hired it. No place could be found for the council. Before the stampede to Alder Gulch, some person had started to build a log hotel at Bannack, and had the first story walls erected, but he joined the stampede and abandoned it. The governor had no funds at his command, and I went to Virginia City and purchased the premises, returned to Bannack, and taking down what had been commenced on the second story, I roofed in the first story and put it into comfortable condition for use of the council.

I rented it to the territory, but for how much I do not remember . . . we had a big stove in the front room occupied by the council. The rear was occupied by the . . . clerks. I think their room was heated by a fireplace.

The building used by the house was a two-story log building about twenty rods west of my building, used by the council, on the northerly side of the street. If I remember correctly, C. D. French, who made Plummer's coffin for me, had his carpenter shop in the upper room when Governor Edgerton hired it for the legislature's use.

Cascade Courier, by Warren W. Moses
Letter in Library, State Historical
Society, Helena

Shortly after the discovery of the bars on Grasshopper Creek, the need for additional water to work them caused Henry Morley and Jule Pitcher to dig the first ditch in the district, which they completed in May, 1863. The Bannack Mining & Ditch Company also constructed one the same year on the south side of the creek for the sole purpose of selling water to the miners. Their charge of seventy-five cents a day per miner's inch of water was excessive, but the fifteen-mile ditch carried an adequate supply of water. It was built by hand labor with the help of oxen, it cost $15,000, and the men who constructed it received half an ounce of gold dust per day for their labors. To serve another part of the diggings, M. J. McDonald, James Doty, and H. M. Mandeville built the North Side ditch in 1865.

By the time hydraulics were in use, Grasshopper Creek could not furnish sufficient water to work the bench gravels. Therefore, the Bannack Mining & Ditch Company built a second flume in 1867, at a cost of $35,000. This ditch, which tapped Coyote and Painter Creeks as well as tributaries of Horse Prairie Creek, was thirty miles long and carried 1,000 inches of water to the bars south and west of the camp. When Græter and Graves gained control of this company, they used the water from the ditch to operate six "Little Giants" which worked their bars in Humbug and Buffalo Gulches. During the fall of 1868, Pioneer Ditch, ten miles long, was constructed to serve the bench gravels north and west of Bannack. By 1870, two more ditches were completed — White's and Canyon. White's took water from Grasshopper Creek one mile below town and "crossed and recrossed the stream for three-and-a-half miles." Canyon Ditch also tapped Gasshopper Creek, cost $7,-000, and was built to work the Bon Accord placers near the mouth of Spring Gulch. These several ditches renewed men's interest in placer mining and enabled much of the abandoned ground to be reworked.

Bannack had a major Indian scare in August, 1877, when word reached camp that Chief Joseph and his Nez Percé Indians had defeated General John Gibbon in battle in the Big Hole Basin and were moving in the general direction of the town. The inhabitants prepared for an attack and fortified their homes as best they could, for it was feared that the Indians would murder any whites whom they encountered on their determined march toward freedom. A barricade was built to the town well so as to protect the water supply in case of seige; but Joseph and his harrassed people slipped across Montana farther to the north and Bannack was unmolested.

By 1880, when the population had dwindled to 232, Bannack's business men included a carpenter, a blacksmith, an attorney, a banker, a wagon-maker, an assayer, and several merchants who operated stores devoted to hardware, drugs, general merchandise, meats, and liquors. Still active were a quartz mill, brewery, hotel, several saloons, and mining and milling companies. For the ladies, there was one dressmaker, who was undoubtedly extremely busy toward the end of the year when a Masquerade Ball was held on Christmas Eve at the courthouse, followed by supper at the Bannack Hotel, all for $3.00! The *Glendale Atlantis* reported the event under the caption:

THAT MASQUERADE AT BANNACK
At about 8 o'clock . . . the ball opened to the music of Clark Smith's band . . . Mrs. Basette, in selecting her costume made a choice of the emblem of liberty. Like every true American she wore it to her heart, encircling her sylph-like form with its majestic folds . . . At precisely 12 o'clock the dancers unmasked,

and much was the surprise manifested by nearly everyone, so complete had been the deception.
January 5, 1881

Dancing continued until five in the morning.

Mining and milling operations continued sporadically in the area between 1875 and 1896. In the latter year, dredging began.

The Excelsior mine, located in 1872 by W. L. Farlin and Philip Shenon, was soon bought by Shenon from his partner for $250. The mine lay east of the Golden Leaf and its lead extended into Grasshopper Creek. When dredges gouged out the streambed, some of the richest ground was recovered from this lead. Late in 1884, the Shenon tunnel, which was planned to tap both the Golden Leaf and Bannack lodes, was commenced. At about the same time Graves and Græter were working their diggings across the creek from Bannack, getting water from the old canal of the Bannack Ditch and Mining Company.

The best results, however, were obtained by hydraulics. The Bon Accord Placer Mining Company, organized in the summer of 1885 to work the bed of Grasshopper Creek in the vicinity of Spring Gulch below Jerusalem, dug a pit to bedrock and uncovered pay dirt. The company diverted the creek by cutting a 1500-foot channel in the gravel and then built a 500-foot flume to carry the dirt to their plant. In winter the men tunneled the ground, which was kept dry by means of pumps. This was dangerous work, for at depths of thirty-five feet or more, the loose ground tended to cave in. The company's waterwheel provided power for the hoists which brought the dirt from bedrock to the flume.

In 1890, Philip Shenon sold his holdings, which included a mill along with the Wadams, Wallace, Golden Leaf, French Excelsior and other mines, to an English company — the Golden Leaf Mining Company, Limited. This company employed fifty to sixty men, built a new mill at a cost of more than $50,000 on the site of the old Shenon plant, ran a store, and worked the Golden Leaf placers.

By 1891, the population of Bannack had dropped noticeably, yet the town insisted that all the houses were occupied and that nearly every man who wanted work had it. Even Miss May Call, the schoolteacher, was busy with an average attendance of fifty-two children a day.

The year 1895 marked another important "first" for Bannack, for it introduced dredging to the Territory. Between 1895 and 1904, several dredging operations were carried on along Grasshopper Creek and at nearby Horse Prairie, with most of the activity centered at Bannack where five boats were built. A sixth sucked up the gravel of Jeff Davis Creek at Horse Prairie. Since bedrock was known to be deep in Grasshopper Gulch, no one was sure that even a dredge could reach it, until H. J. Reiling of Chicago and others organized the Gold Dredging Company and built the first boat. The "Fielding L. Graves," the first successful, electric, bucketlift dredge in the country was launched "near the old Wilson House in the lower part of Bannack." According to the *Dillon Examiner*:

In the presence of a large concourse of people . . . the dredging boat . . . was successfully launched, Wednesday, May 15, 1895 at 2:45 p.m.

A large number of invited guests, including many ladies, witnessed the ceremonies from the boat. When the time arrived, Mrs. H. J. Reiling, of Chicago, the wife of the president of the company, broke the customary bottle of champagne and christened the boat the "Fielding L. Graves," in honor of one of Bannack's well known pioneer merchants. Cheers rent the air as the boat slid gracefully from its ways and floated on the waters of Grasshopper Creek . . . After navigating the waters of the river for half an hour, during which time the visitors sampled a basket of champagne donated by the Hon. F. L. Graves and toasted the success of the new hydraulic mining enterprise, the boat was tied close to the shore and the visitors landed.

Mr. F. L. Graves was presented with a gold-headed ebony cane, upon which was engraved the names of the officers of the Gold Dredging Co. He was also presented with a gold watch, which had "F. Louis Graves" around the dial instead of the customary numerals. The "F" served as the numeral twelve.

May 22, 1895

As originally constructed, the dredge was unsatisfactory and had to be remodeled. Its capacity was increased to 2,000 yards of gravel per day and its total cost exceeded $35,000; yet, even with these additional expenses, it was reported to be more economical to operate than a steam dredge. The boat worked about a mile of stream to bedrock, thirty feet below the surface. The recovery of gold exceeded the company's expectations, with cleanups averaging from $800 to $7,000. On two successive weeks, when the boat was clawing at the richest ground, the totals ran $22,000 and $38,000 respectively. The gold dust was run into bars and shipped east. In July, 1896, the company workmen struck for higher wages.

During the trouble, one of the ditch flumes was blown up and its supports cut. The company, however, continued their dredging with other laborers. The "F. L. Graves" operated profitably until 1902, when "it ran out of auriferous gravel."

The second dredge, known as the "Gilman-Smith Co." boat, was launched in July, 1896, under the supervision of Edward L. Smith, general manager of the Chicago Mining & Development Company, which built it at the Golden Leaf placers. The following spring, when it was remodeled and equipped with buckets, it seems to have been renamed, for the *Dillon Tribune* of May 28, 1897, mentions the

christening of the dredge boat the "Maggie A. Gibson," owned and operated by the Chicago Mining & Development Co., of whom C. C. Gilman of Marshaltown, Iowa is president.

The exercises were begun by Mrs. Maggie A. Gibson, in whose honor the boat was named, who stepped to the bow of the boat and with one blow smashed the ribbon-bedecked bottle of champagne against it, the steam whistle was turned loose, the band played, the people cheered, and the boat was named.

The third dredge, the "A. F. Græter," was launched in June, 1897. Its owners, the Bannack Dredging Company, contracted with H. J. Reiling to let the contract for its construction. The dredge paid both for itself and the ground in which it worked during its first year of operation, recovering $200,000 in gold dust from the gravels. This dredge dug its way upstream to Bannack and then reworked ground previously cleaned by the Graves boat. In 1902, it ceased to operate and was finally dismantled west of Bannack. An interesting sidelight on its findings is reported as follows:

A great many relics of the days when Bannack was in its infancy are constantly brought to light and saved in the sluice boxes . . . Only a few days ago, a heavy 18K gold ring was dug up . . . a cabinet in the company's office is filled with these relics, and they consist of coins, cartridges of all kinds, medals, a part of an old pistol, nuggets, belt buckles . . . At one point, which is said to have been the site of Henry Plummer's cabin, a cache was evidently uncovered as the buckets brought up ten $1 gold pieces, nine $2.50 gold pieces, one five-dollar gold piece and three fifty-cent silver pieces, dated '58 to '61, although there are a few of recent years.

Dillon Examiner, Oct. 2, 1901

The fourth boat was built in 1898 by the Bon Accord Company, an English corporation, which had already scraped a small area of streambed by sinking shafts and diverting the creek from its pits. From these operations it recovered about $4.00 in gold from each square foot of cleaned bedrock. The company's dredge, which was similar in construction to other boats, was built three to four miles below the town. Its buckets were unusually large and reached from its prow to the tip of its sluice line. Its activity was short-lived, for only a few days after its launching it sank. The accident occurred on a Sunday, shortly after midnight and was attributed to its top-heavy bucket line which caused it to settle and list. "Within fifteen minutes it lay at the bottom of the creek with one side and the hull partially above the water." It was raised and remodeled, but the expense incurred forced the company to suspend work before the end of the season. Its machinery found its way in 1901 to the John Day country in Oregon, but its hull was left in Grasshopper Creek.

The fifth dredge, the "Cope" boat, was built during the summer of 1898 to work placer ground sold by its owner, George F. Cope, to the Montana Gold Dredging Company for $150,000. The area which the company worked until 1902 was near Spring Gulch, a mile below the Bon Accord dredge.

From 1895 throug 1902 — the years when the dredges were reclaiming dust from bedrock in Grasshopper Creek — the town revived only to decline again as, one by one, the auriferous deposits were cleaned out. Years later, prohibition cut off another source of income to its merchants:

Closing of Last Saloon Recalls Placer Camp's Glory

King Alcohol, after a reign of fifty-five years in Bannack has abdicated. The last saloon closed a few days ago because the authorities refused to reissue a license which had expired. Bannack is dry six months in advance of the time fixed by law when selling liquor will be a crime.
Plains Plainsman, July 8, 1918

For a number of years, little mining has been done around Bannack except by lessees.

Hydraulic mining was resumed on a small scale in 1939 when F. M. Miles of Tacoma, Washington, began to work a bar southwest of Bannack, near the Armstead road. Grasshopper Creek was again tapped to provide water, which was carried to the placer ground through an iron pipe. Returns averaged thirty-five cents to $3.50 in dust per cubic yard.

Total production from the Bannack area up to 1930 was estimated at $12,000,000, of which the first $600,000 was recovered from placers in 1862. The deposits in the area were not particularly large in size, but they were nearly all high-grade.

The last time I saw Bannack was in 1955. This time I was showing it to my husband and as the camp was completely deserted it was fortunate that I knew where the chief landmarks were located. The cemetery on the hill looked much as it had, except that a few of the stones had been toppled over by cattle. The church on the main street was wide open and its interior was empty, save where plaster from the blue, peeling walls had fallen on the littered floor.

"This was built as a community church," I said as we peered into the forlorn and dusty building, "but I was told that at the dedication, Brother W. W. Van Orsdel, a beloved frontier Methodist minister, was present and thereafter that sect claimed it."

As we walked up Hangman's Gulch to the gallows, I told my husband of the cache of gold dust and nuggets, done up in buckskin pokes and valued at $8,000, that Tom Underwood, an old prospector, had found in the middle 1930's while repairing a chimney in an old cabin, near the spot where we stood. At the time of the discovery it was thought that it might have been secreted by Plummer or by one of his victims.

Bannack is now a Montana State Park, and as such it will be preserved as a monument to Montana's initial gold rush. It was never completely deserted until 1953, when the I. B. Mining Company, which had owned most of the town for the thirty years preceding, failed. Needing to sell out, the company negotiated with C. W. Stallings, the sole resident, and agreed to sell its holdings to him for $1,400. A few citizens of Dillon heard of the transaction. They talked with Stallings and asked if he would sell them the town that it might become a state historic landmark. He agreed, provided he could keep his home and one or two buildings; the rest he released to Dillon for $1,000. The several county organizations that had started a movement to preserve historic Bannack, as far back as 1947, now joined in a drive to raise the needed money. With the help of the Beaverhead Post of the American Legion, the Beaverhead Museum Association, the Beaverhead Chapter of the D. A. R., the Dillon Chamber of Commerce, and the Beaverhead Mining Association, coupled to a newspaper fund-raising campaign, Bannack was officially presented to the State of Montana on August 15, 1954. Stallings remained in his own house, as caretaker.

HORSE PRAIRIE

To the south and west of Bannack lay another pioneer mining district, Horse Prairie, a once trackless area from which prospectors skimmed high-grade gold. The placers were located on the headwaters of Shenon and Jeff Davis Creeks and on Horse Prairie Creek. As soon as dust was washed from these creeks and from Colorado Gulch and Solomon's Bar in the summer of 1863, a mining district was organized on July 4 by a party of eleven men, one of whom, named Graham, presided. When thirteen articles were drawn up and voted upon, the miners demanded that they be recorded in a book:

Blank books were very scarce but Graham remembered that he had an old hotel register down at the cabin, which he had brought with him when he closed his hotel back in the States, because it contained the names of men who had stopped at his hotel and hadn't paid him.

Flaxville Democrat, June 10, 1918

This book, in which the mining laws of Jeff Davis Gulch were recorded, was later deposited in the vault of the Beaverhead county courthouse.

The gold which these early prospectors failed to extract was later recovered by hydraulics. William A. Clark, the man who became a Montana mining magnate, mined briefly at Horse Prairie diggings. When he became ill, he temporarily abandoned mining, went to Bannack, sold his ground, and became a merchant. The first settler to live in the valley is said to have been Charles Fortier, a French Canadian who arrived in 1862. The first permanent residents, Barrett and Stineberger, came some time later and began to farm the land, although they had to be on the alert for Indians, who were especially troublesome in 1877. By that year, there were sufficient people in the valley to warrant the establishment of the postoffice called Horse Prairie.

In the early 1890's a few mineral locations were worked by white miners and some Chinese. The district has been generally inactive for some time.

Directly west of Bannack and north of Brenner, a station on the Gilmore & Pittsburg Railroad, is the Bloody Dick District, never an important area, but one that has been worked intermittently.

BALD MOUNTAIN, LOST CLOUD, POLARIS, ELKHORN DISTRICTS

From Bannack we drove eight miles back to the highway and turned west, as our next objective was Polaris, some twenty miles distant. From the crest of the next hill, a huge valley opened out before us. It was rolling land thatched with sagebrush and with no signs of life except a few cattle so tiny against the immensity of the land that they looked like toys. In the distance were a couple of ranch-houses surrounded by hay fields.

From the time we reached the top of the bluff above the Beaverhead River at Dillon and could look out over the vast prairie that stretched to the west, we had noticed a bare, rock-tipped mountain, miles away to the north. As we drove across the sage-covered hills we drew closer to it and finally circled its southern and western faces. This was Bald Mountain, about five miles southeast of Polaris, the peak from which the Bald Mountain Mining District takes its name. Adjoining this district is Polaris or Lost Cloud District. The latter was named for the Lost Cloud mine, once owned by Cochrane & Company and worked by lessees in 1891. Next to it was the Silver Key mine. Placer mining in this area began in 1869 and was soon supplanted by lode mining which, between 1876 and 1885, produced moderate amounts of silver ore. The chief mines in the Lost Cloud or Polaris District were the Silver Fissure, which produced $60,000 in silver in 1886, and the Dakota. Four blast furnaces and a 100-ton smelter were erected near the mine in 1907 but ran only one year. Uuno Mathias Sahinen of the Montana School of Mines wrote in 1935: "the region has not been thoroughly prospected and it is unlikely its gold resources have been exhausted. The Elkhorn district, also called Beaverhead district, is north of Polaris. Its mines, discovered in 1874, carried copper-silver ore."

POLARIS

Mile after mile of sagebrush slipped by, cut only by the ribbon of road that swung north toward Polaris. We crossed Grasshopper Creek. In a few more miles we left the highway where it veered toward Jackson and continued north on a less-traveled road past the Tash ranch, a well-kept, prosperous layout where men were haying. Five miles farther were a shed, a small roadside tavern called the Polar Bar, and a big two-story log house with a porch. These three buildings comprised Polaris in 1955. The largest was both store and postoffice. Inside we met the postmistress, Mrs. John Judge, and her husband. Both knew the area well and helpfully directed us to the site of the old camp.

"Drive up the lane, north of the store for two miles, until you come to a cabin," said Mrs. Judge. "That's where the town stood. This store used to be a boarding or bunk house up there. It was moved down here when the camp died. There was a smelter, too, but it's gone, and so are all the miners' cabins."

We took the country lane, opened a pasture gate, and climbed over rolling, treeless hills until the narrow dirt track led into an aspen grove. There I found two cabins, one of which was built into the barren hillside and that was all.

The Polaris mine, the most important silver property in this region, was located on January 31, 1885, by a group of men — John Chase, John S. Meade, Wm. Bevon, Charles Chase, Henry Meade, and W. M. Servis, although one source mentions that the mine was worked intermittently much earlier — "shortly after the establishment of Bannack." It lay on the south side of Billings Creek and its discoverers found in it a vein of high-grade ore fifteen inches in thickness at a depth of one hundred feet. By 1886, the mine belonged to B. F. White, Phil Shenon, L. C. Fyhrie, and J. S. Meade, who hired twenty men to work it and equipped the shaft with a steam hoist and a Knowles pump. The mine was a steady producer through 1891, shipping ore "sampling 75-400 oz. per ton in car lots," by team to Dillon.

J. S. Meade sold the mine in 1892 to the Polaris Mining Company, a New York syndicate which reportedly took out $250,000 before financial problems forced the property into litigation. In an effort to recoup its losses, the company erected a cyanide reduction plant at the mine. Through its leaching tanks, several thousand tons of ore from the dump were run, but since the mine produced chiefly silver, the entire value of the ore was lost. This threw the company deeper into debt and further litigation followed. After years of legal controversy, J. E. Morse obtained a sheriff's deed to the property.

In 1900, J. J. Cusick and others leased the Polaris workings from Morse for $25,000, and once more six-horse teams hauled ore to Dillon for shipment. The Silver Fissure Mining Company, organized in 1905 with Harry H. Armstead in charge, bought the mine and immediately planned extensive improvements, which ran up to three-quarters of a million dollars. In order to deliver new machinery and equipment to the mine from Armstead, a new town on the Oregon Short Line, forty miles of road had to be built. During the next six years, this stretch of road was in constant use as steam traction engines, pulling specially constructed iron-wheeled cars, hauled ore over it. For years after the mine closed down, two of the cars and part of one of the engines lay beside the Polaris-Armstead road.

The camp at the mine contained a boarding house, bunkhouses, cabins, sheds, a 100-ton smelter, and four blast furnaces, all of which were completed and in use by 1907. The following year the plant shut down because of insufficient ore, leaving valuable property which was gradually stolen or wrecked by vandals. As a final blow, the smelter was destroyed by fire on October 12, 1922. Since then, little has been done in the area. In 1939, only $296.00 was produced in the entire district.

We stopped at the tavern before leaving Polaris to see the bar which Mr. Judge said came from a Bannack saloon — "the very bar where Plummer took his last drink."

From Polaris we drove back to the Tash ranch and turned west across the valley to Jackson. We were now in the heart of the lush Big Hole Basin, an area sixty miles long and from three to twenty wide. This is cow country, sometimes called the valley of Ten Thousand Haystacks.

PIONEER BASIN

It was news of the gold placers, found by John J. Healy and George Grigsby, in 1861, on the Salmon River near Florence, Idaho Territory, that caused men to hurry to these new diggings. By the spring of 1862, word of the discoveries had reached Denver, and Samuel McLean, impatient to start for the Salmon mines, organized a party of men and set off for Idaho by way of the Overland Trail and Fort Hall. At about the same time, another party left Denver under the leadership of Captain Jack Russell. Somewhere on the trail this group met Michael LeClair, a French fur trader who knew the Salmon country and attempted to discourage them from going to it. He told Russell in confidence, that gold had been found at Deer Lodge and on the Beaverhead and hinted

POSTOFFICE AND STORE, POLARIS

that they might find what they wanted in those localities.

Russell's party and McLean's met unexpectedly at Fort Hall, and the two went on together, ultimately reaching Fort Lemhi, Idaho Territory. They were still more than one hundred and twenty-five miles from Florence and, to their distress, they found that it was impossible to go downstream on the wild Salmon River to the mines. Other companies of miners — nearly 1,000 men in all — were marooned in the Lemhi Valley and equally unwilling to spend the winter there. Among these was another Colorado party led by Mortimer H. Lott. Captain Russell's disclosure of LeClair's secret caused the Colorado parties to cross the mountains and search for gold in the Deer Lodge and Beaverhead country. Of this part of the journey Mortimer Lott writes:

We went down the Salmon River and up the North Fork getting indications of quartz, and some small prospects. We got the idea that the east side of the mountains would be the best place, so six of us packed ourselves with grub, picks, pans, and shovels, and walked up a very steep Indian trail and on to the eastern slope. About a mile from the main range we found a small stream, a tributary of the Big Hole river, with a few paying claims, about six feet to bedrock at discovery and called it Pioneer, supposing it to be the first discovery of gold, in paying quantities found in the county.

Leaving one of our party to dig a drain ditch, the rest of us went to Lemhi for our wagon. From Lemhi there was a very large Indian trail crossing the main range of mountains east to Horse Prairie. Knowing that the Indians took the lowest passes, I thought we had better follow their trail. We put both hind wheels on one side of the wagon, and in that way kept from upsetting. At last we got to the Horse Prairie side. Crossing over a low range from Grasshopper to Big Hole, we found the remains of a wagon, showing that we were not the first people to take wagons into that section. We reached our claims as near as I can recollect, about noon July 12, 1862.

We worked the claim out, taking out several hundred dollars.

— *Mortimer Lott Diary*

61

These gulch claims which Lott and his party discovered were near the head of Ruby Creek. The foot trail across the mountains was probably Big Hole Pass, which is reached today from Gibbonsville, Idaho, on the west and from Wisdom, Montana, on the east. Henry Morley, a miner from Gold Creek, wrote in his diary, in August, 1862, that he had visited the mines, which were in wild country, covered with fallen timber, and had found thirty miners at work — mostly men from Colorado territory. Each was making $4.00 to $8.00 per day. When news of the Grasshopper diggings reached the Pioneer miners, most of them left, and by some time in 1863 the district was deserted.

No one investigated the area again until the middle 1880's, when gold was found on Trail Creek, about five miles north of Lott's diggings and about three miles from the site of the Big Hole battleground. By 1886, one hundred and twenty-three claims were recorded at these Big Hole Placers, as they were called, and the Salt Lake & Big Hole Mining and Placer Company had completed a seven-mile ditch, which cost $1,400 per mile, to work their ground. According to W. L. Wunderlich, placers on Cow Creek were located in 1898 by W. P. Nelson, but as soon as the ground was washed out, the white population left and Chinese miners reworked the gravels. Since the gold was close to bedrock and not evenly distributed, dredging was not attempted.

WISDOM

Wisdom is a typical Montana cow town with plenty of room on all sides to swing a rope.

It is also a supply point for the mines in that portion of the Basin. The Ajax mine, fourteen miles southwest of Wisdom, is in the Beaverhead Range at the head of Swamp Creek. The Wisdom or Big Hole mining district is five miles east of Wisdom. Placers were located on Steele Creek during the late sixties or middle seventies by Mike Steele, but they were not rich enough to attract much attention.

The Bonanza mines, ten miles east of Wisdom on Steele Creek, are described in the *Big Hole Breezes* of September 5, 1902:

The newest mining camp in Beaverhead county is Bonanza, at the head of the east fork of Steele creek, a tributary of the Big Hole river . . . a group of mines has recently been bonded for $60,000 to a company represented by W. E. Sanders, a young mining engineer from Helena. The group consists of six claims — Bonanza, Mountain View, Sanders, Clifford, Sentinel and Maynard. They were discovered by Harry Clifford and Louis and Charles Maynard.

The first work done in the district was in 1895 on the Phoenix group, one mile below the Bonanza camp . . . The country was nearly inaccessible, and after almost endless toil and expense, an arrastre was built directly below the mouth of the Phoenix tunnel . . . Considerable ore was milled by this method, the ore yielding $10 a ton average, and concentrates having a value of $300 in gold. The arrastre ran every summer for three years.

But the ore milled did not pay expenses . . . In 1899, operations at the arrastre and on the Ibex mine were suspended and the partners moved up to the Bonanza group. Here . . . ore from 18 inches to 4 feet was encountered. This ore carries considerable gold — $40, and from two to three ounces of silver to the ton.

From Wisdom, the highway skirts the Big Hole River for fifty-two miles all the way to Divide, first across prairie and, toward the end, cutting through a steep-walled canyon. Six miles west of Divide is Dewey, a once-active mining settlement. Above it in the mountains is the historic Vipond Mining District.

VIPOND

The road to Vipond leaves the highway, about one half mile west of Dewey. A U.S. Forest Service marker identifies it as the Quartz Canyon Creek road, and gives the distance to the Quartz Hill mines as six miles and to Vipond Park as eleven. The dirt road climbs beside the creek the entire way to the mines and its surface is rocky and full of ruts. By the end of five miles we had driven through a wooded canyon with high, jagged walls and saw ahead on our left some large dumps — the first signs of mining activity. As we drove higher we noticed more dumps and a large, ruined mill with a settling pond. A short distance ahead was a group of buildings, not too old — typical company houses — evidently occupied, for cars stood in front of a few and washing flapped from lines stretched between pine trees. There was no one in sight and after a careful inspection of a shaft with a headframe and a windlass, we drove back to Dewey. At the foot of the last grade the late afternoon sun picked out the white stones of the Dewey cemetery, which lies east of the creek road on a small flat.

The Vipond District is named for John Vipond who, in April, 1868, discovered its first

QUARTZ HILL, VIPOND

DEWEY

lode, the Mewonitoc. He immediately interested his brothers, Joseph and William, and other prospectors in the area where, by January, 1869, William Vipond had located the Grey Jockey mine. These discoveries led to further prospecting by other parties during 1870 and 1871, though development of the district was slow. The mines were found in Vipond Park, at an elevation of 8,000 feet, and at Quartz Hill. The richest lodes were in this area. When discovered, the mines were isolated from any main trail through Deer Lodge Pass, so, in order to get their ore to the smelters, the miners built a road, in 1872, from the mines to Dewey and then alongside the Big Hole River to Divide. Colonel Washington Black is reported to have discovered the Quartz Hill silver mine and to have hauled the first ore from the area by mule team to the railroad at Corinne, Utah. From there it was shipped to Swansea for refining.

Vipond was primarily a silver district, although certain ore carried considerable lead, zinc, and some copper. One of the best properties, the Lone Pine, was operated by the Partridge Brothers for five years and then sold in 1891 to the Jay Hawk Company, an English syndicate which paid $725,000 for the mine and other holdings. Under the management of Captain Prideaux, the mines produced $33,000 in silver each month. With returns such as these, the stockholders agreed to spend $50,000 for further development of the property. The fifteen-stamp mill at Dewey was moved up to the mines and ten additional stamps added, and a concentrating plant was erected near the property. Only a decrease in the price of silver forced the company in 1895 to shut down its mill, "one of the best equipped plants in the west for treatment of free-milling ores." Several of the properties changed hands or were worked by lessees in the early twentieth century. According to a man with whom we talked in Dewey, the Vipond mines have worked very little since 1949.

DEWEY

The town of Dewey is named for D. S. Dewey, an early rancher who is said to have built the first cabin in the area. The original townsite was south of the Big Hole River, and above the present location. Lumbering was the first industry in the camp, carried on in the late 1860's; mining was the second. As soon as the lodes on Quartz Hill were opened, Dewey became a supply point for the properties, as well as a likely site for their arrastres and ore mills, which utilized waterpower from the Big Hole River.

An astute business man, Peter Dolman, foresaw that the mining boom would make Dewey grow. He therefore staked placer claims on the flat beside the river and worked the diggings just enough to hold his title to the claims. The fact that he found no gold did not matter, for his scheme was to sell the placer ground for a townsite, with lots purchased from the Carroll Placer Company, which he organized.

The town's best years were between 1877 and 1895. The first arrastre for the Vipond district, built by D. S. Dewey, was later sold to John A. Leggat who converted it into a two-stamp mill. This mill, which was below the present town of Dewey, was built to handle custom ore. By 1885, the town had three mills — one with fifteen stamps owned by the Monroe Company, Leggat's mill enlarged to five stamps, and a two-stamper belonging to Allen Hay. In addition, there were several arrastres, several charcoal kilns, a hotel, a saloon, a slaughter house, and a postoffice with C. R. Hay as postmaster. As soon as a narrow gauge railroad was completed from Divide through Big Hole Canyon to Elkhorn, near Polaris, the shipment of ore from the Dewey mills and the Vipond district was simplified.

Francis and I drove into Dewey just at sundown when the last glow on the hills tinged the weathered cabins and remodeled log houses with a warm patina. Two big log barns beside the highway were silver grey with age, a couple of false-fronted stores had boards across their windows. Against the hillside, swamped in weeds and brush, were stone foundations of old mills and arrastres. A log schoolhouse stood back from the road on a side street which I discovered was called Mountain Lane — the only street in town to bear any designation — and although the walls looked old, a big picture window on the east and a freshly painted porch suggested recent improvements. It dates from 1890 and was built on land given by Peter Dolman, the pioneer placer-real estate tycoon. The first school was set up in the 1870's in Quartz Hill Gulch in a private home. Later on, school was held in another house near the Quartz Hill mill. Still later, classes were taught at Dewey Flats in a small building. In 1890, when the present building was erected, there were thirty-three pupils. In 1952 the enrollment was two, and in 1955, Jimmy Sims, age ten, was the sole student. Thanks to his teacher, Mrs. Elizabeth Long, the ladies of the Dewey School and Community Club took as their project during 1954 the history of Dewey, and much of the data about the town I gleaned from their research.

The lighted windows of the false-fronted cafe-and-hotel lured us inside, where the proprietor told us yarns of Dewey's earlier days. One was about Harrison Churchill, who carried the mail between Dewey and Wisdom. During the winter he made the trip on snowshoes; at other seasons he traveled by boat on the Big Hole River. Another story described the Fourth of July celebrations. Hundreds of people from Butte came annually to enjoy the varied sports — the square dancing and the horse races. Seats surrounding the race course were beer kegs.

"Are you driving toward Divide?" the proprietor asked as we got back into our car. "If you are, you'll go right by the old powerhouse and dam. You've probably heard about the man who registered placer claims along the river and then sold them as town lots? Later, when the Montana Power Company put in the powerhouse and dam, farther down the canyon, the water backed up so high it flooded the river lots. This fellow who owned the land was crazy mad and sued the power company for $36,000. I don't know whether he got it

RUINED POWERHOUSE AND DAM, BIG HOLE RIVER BELOW DEWEY

or not. Years later, the dam broke and washed out the railroad track between it and Divide. You'll see all that's left of the dam, but it's not as high as it was when it was built. The stone powerhouse was a beauty — the walls are as good as new, but the building's a wreck."

It was dark when we pulled out of Dewey, away from the twinkling lights that marked the homes of the fifteen to twenty families who made up the population in 1956. At its peak, the town had a population of five hundred.

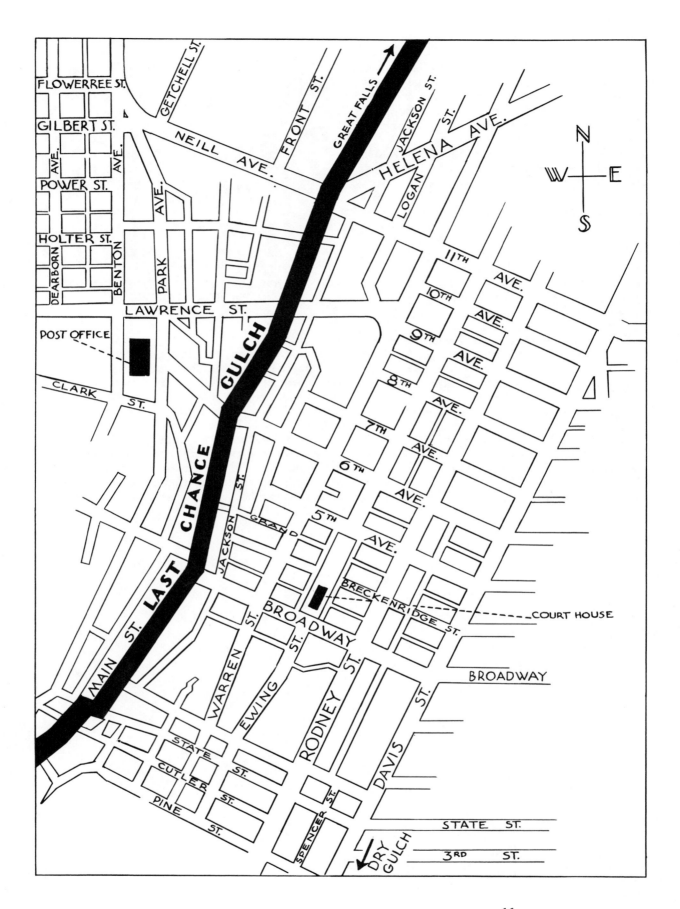

FLOWERREE ST.

GILBERT ST.

POWER ST.

HOLTER ST.

GETCHELL ST.

NEILL AVE.

FRONT ST.

GREAT FALLS

JACKSON ST.

LOGAN ST.

HELENA AVE.

N
W E
S

DEARBORN

BENTON AVE.

AVE.

PARK AVE.

LAWRENCE ST.

POST OFFICE

CLARK ST.

LAST CHANCE GULCH

11TH AVE.

10TH AVE.

9TH AVE.

8TH AVE.

7TH AVE.

6TH AVE.

5TH AVE.

JACKSON ST.

GRAND

BRECKENRIDGE ST.

COURT HOUSE

MAIN ST.

WARREN ST.

EWING ST.

RODNEY ST.

DAVIS ST.

BROADWAY

BROADWAY

STATE ST.

CUTLER ST.

PINE ST.

SPENCER ST.

STATE ST.

3RD ST.

DRY GULCH

CHAPTER 4

LAST CHANCE GULCH: The Heart of Helena

Bannack, Alder Gulch, Last Chance Gulch— the first three gold discoveries in Montana Territory! I had seen two. Now, as we neared Helena and caught a glimpse of the Capitol dome above the rolling prairie, we were about to visit the third. Entering from the east gives little idea of the layout of the city and of its famous gulch. The Capitol and the group of State buildings that surround it are still on one edge of the town, with prairie to the east. A gridiron of streets lined with private homes stretches north, west, and as far south as the rising hills permit.

Helena welcomed us with a gully-washer. On my first afternoon there I hurried to the quarters of the Historical Society of Montana then housed in the basement of the State Capitol, to start reading the old newspapers filed in its library. Whenever I glanced up from my work, sheets of rain sluiced the windowpanes, but I thought nothing of it — it was just a heavy shower. By five, when the library closed, the storm had passed, but the streets were wet and those that were unpaved were sticky with mud. When Hazel and I drove downtown to look for a restaurant, the car ploughed through shallow lakes at intersections. At the foot of the hill we entered Main Street, or Last Chance Gulch, as it is still called. Here a portion of the thoroughfare was roped off where paving had been undermined by the rush of water and had caved in, trapping a car. As we looked curiously into the hole, an old man who had

also stopped to investigate pointed to the broken surface and said, "There's still gold down there. Some of us pan a little of the dirt after a gully-washer like this. You're standing in Last Chance Gulch, you know. They built the street right over it. Go up to the Montana Club and read the plaque on the Fuller Avenue side of the building. That's the site where they found the first gold. The best placers were farther up the gulch, between Broadway and State Street. They say the miners couldn't get down to bedrock there and that the gravel under the old buildings was never worked out."

This was exciting! Here we stood where a few men took a "last chance" and struck a bonanza. I knew their story.

It was the Kootenai mines of Canada that sent the party of four streaking north from Alder Gulch across the Deer Lodge Valley in the spring of 1864, in an attempt to reach the strike before all the best claims were staked. The group, known as "the Georgians," consisted of John Cowan, D. J. Miller, John Crab and Reginald (or Robert) Stanley. While they were working their way down the Hell Gate River, they met James Coleman returning from the Kootenai and so pessimistic about its mines that he convinced them that their trip into Canada was not worth the effort.

After the party decided to change its itinerary, Stanley, who had been with one of the James L. Fisk expeditions in the summer of 1863, told of finding colors in the bed of the Little Blackfoot River and suggested that they begin by prospecting its bars. They traced the river to its source and even followed side creeks, but when systematic panning of its gravels failed to yield gold in paying amounts, they turned south and made camp near the summit of the Rockies. One of the men climbed to a high point where he looked down on the wide Prickly Pear Valley, which was cut by several streams. The next morning the party started down the steep east face of the mountains where, according to one of the group, the "pine brush stood up so thick in places you couldn't stick a butcher knife to the handle in it." The descent was easier after they found a game trail which led into the valley. At each stream they stopped to pan gravel, but the inevitable "colors" were their only reward.

At the end of another disillusioning day, they made camp on the bank of what is now Last Chance Gulch. That evening they discussed their situation and decided to go north along the range, trying their luck in every mountain stream. If nothing turned up, they would return to the gulch where they were camped and prospect it thoroughly. Half-heartedly they even panned some dirt, but again found only colors.

For six weeks they trudged north as far as the headwaters of the Teton and Marias Rivers, "digging innumerable holes and not finding anything." In fact, the farther north they went, the less likely the land became. By then their provisions were running low, and the only game they saw was grizzlies. Completely discouraged, they turned south and started the long trek back to Alder Gulch. Each day someone would say, "When we get back to the Prickly Pear Valley, there's that little gulch. It's our last chance."

The weary men reached the spot July 14, 1864, and made their camp farther up the gulch than on their previous visit. Without delay, Cowan, Crab, and Miller dug holes to bedrock on opposite sides of the stream near the lower end of the gulch. The hole on the north side yielded several flat nuggets weighing about fifty cents in value. Stanley went half-a-mile farther upstream. A letter of his, written in 1909, describes the discovery:

I commenced a hole on the bar and put it down to bedrock some six to seven feet deep. I then panned the gravel. Three or four little flat, smooth nuggets and some fine gold was the result; nuggets that made the pan ring when dropped into it — and a very refreshing sound it was.

Convinced that this was the strike for which they had been searching, the men fell to work feverishly, their fatigue forgotten. Cowan and Crab soon set out for Alder Gulch for provisions and while there kept their secret from all but a few close friends; but as their purchases and actions aroused curiosity, they were followed back to the gulch. Not that any single stampede took place, but a succession of small rushes which brought parties of a dozen or more at a time to the diggings.

Stanley and Miller, anticipating such arrivals, drew up a set of regulations, limiting claims to 200 feet up and down the gulch and across it from rim to rim, and also insisting that all claims be recorded within three days of location. In addition, no single person could hold more than one claim by pre-emption and another by purchase, except members of the discovery party. Discoverers were also given the initial use of water in the gulch. On July 20, 1864, at a miner's meeting where Stanley acted as Recorder, the rules were voted upon, the

gulch was named Last Chance, and the district, which extended "down three miles and up to the mouth of the canon, and across from summit to summit," was called Rattlesnake.

Last Chance was not the first discovery in the area. Eighteen months earlier Montana City had sprung up in the Prickly Pear Valley several miles to the east, and in May, 1864, Silver City, some fourteen miles north of the diggings, became the center of the Silver Creek placers. But Last Chance was the newest and biggest attraction, and the gulch soon swarmed with miners. Some prospectors left shortly after their arrival because of the small amount of water. Stanley mentions this in his letter, and continues:

Indians visited us, but besides stealing our horses they did not interfere with us. They would perch on the bank of the gulch opposite us, and watch us for an hour at a time, toiling in the hot sun, no doubt thinking what fools we were to do so.

John Cowan built the first house, I (Bob Stanley) the second. . . . By October 1 there were five houses in the gulch and many more building. Wild meat was plentiful. All camps had men who hunted wild meat for marketing, so the first winter no one suffered for food . . . The winter of 1864-65 was mild and nearly all of us lived in tents or out in the open.

Captain George J. Wood arrived in Last Chance about the time that the discovery party was making its first cleanup and was so impressed with what he saw that he decided to stay, although the Georgians assured him that there was no gold in the gulch above them. Nevertheless, he built a cabin next to theirs. In it, on October 30, 1864, a miners' meeting was held to appoint commissioners and lay out a town. A request to give the camp a more suitable name was also proposed. Out of several suggestions — Pumkinville, Squashtown, Cowan, Stanley, Wood, Tomahawk, Tomah, and St. Helena — only the last two were considered. Tomah was the name of a friendly Indian, and St. Helena, proposed by John Somerville, was the town in Minnesota from which he came. Somerville harangued enthusiastically for its adoption. When the vote was cast, Helena won, with the "St." dropped as unnecessary. The Minnesota town was called HeLENA. To the miners, HEL spelled "hell." Last Chance, therefore, became HELena.

The "Georgians" worked their gulch ground until the summer of 1867. Then they sold out and went back East, packing a large amount of dust with them. Bob Stanley describes their departure in one of his letters:

WATCHTOWER HILL ABOVE LAST CHANCE GULCH

THE "CASTLE"
AND THE
WATCHTOWER

To leave the mountains with such a quantity of dust was perilous. A wagon was engaged and a start made under cover of darkness. The gold was packed in boxes, on which the owners and some trusty friends took their seats, shotguns loaded with buckshot, hanging out on either side to instant readiness. A . . . flatboat was bought and on it the ex-goldseekers floated and rowed back to civilization.

Throughout the 1860s, the placer ground in Last Chance and the surrounding gulches was explored and worked with great success. According to *The Statistical Almanac for 1869 and Year Book of Facts, Showing the Mineral Resources of Montana,*

In Last Chance gulch . . . a great deal of ground which was deemed worthless, is still being profitably worked by Chinese. The upper part of the gulch, near the canyon, and thence to the forks of Grizzly and Oro Fino, owing to its greater depth and the necessity of bed-rock drainage, has been worked slowly, and still contains much ground that was very profitably worked last season by drifting.

About half a mile above Helena, Last Chance forks, and from there up is known as Grizzly, the left hand tributary being Oro Fino. In the latter gulch placer mining has thus far been almost unremunerative, though gold has been found its entire length. Grizzly gulch has been profitably worked for the past four years, and several claims are still yielding handsomely.

Dry Gulch, which enters Prickly Pear Valley just east of Helena, has been productive of gold for 3 miles . . . Nelson gulch, a tributary of Ten Mile, lies immediately west from Grizzly, and has been worked almost continuously since the spring of 1865.

Reprinted in the *Montana Magazine of History*, April, 1951

Up to 1869, the approximate aggregate yield of the placers in Last Chance Gulch was $7,-000,000; in Grizzly $5,000,000; in Dry and Tucker $3,000,000; and in Nelson $2,500,000. Thereafter, the yield dwindled as claim after claim was worked out. By 1875 the placers seemed almost exhausted. Most of the miners who had saved money and bought land in Helena, or in the surrounding country, turned to new enterprises. These paid off at a later date — in fact, many of Helena's millionaires got their start through such ventures.

One of the clearest pictures of what Last Chance Gulch was like is given by William M. Sprague, one of the earliest settlers, in his speech before the National Mining Congress at Helena on July 12, 1892:

I came from Alder gulch here in May 1864, and bought out the bar and ditch belonging at that time to the Buchanan boys and Jim Gourley on Prickly Pear. There was a grove and a creek right where Main St. is now . . . The mountains were covered with timber which they cut for lumber for buildings. Mt. Helena and others hills were overgrown with large trees. There were probably 1,000 here by the first of March 1865.

In 1866 there was a great stampede from the states. During 1865 they made some big strikes. The first ditch brought in that year was by Chessman & Cowan and a few others. The upper ditch was brought in in 1866 by Plaisted, an old California miner. The men worked for $6 and $7 a day.

There was considerable difficulty getting supplies. There were no potatoes. When some were brought in they cost 65 cents a pound. Flour was $1 a pound. A good-sized cabbage cost $10.00. Everything was paid for in gold dust. Everybody had lots of money. Miners were paid $10 a day, top hands $7 . . . There was a good deal of shooting and hanging. The shooting was most all done by the gamblers, other people having very little trouble.

The Mines of Montana, Their History and Development to Date, James Arthur MacKnight

Fortunately for Helena, lode mines were discovered almost simultaneously with the placers. The gold veins lay above Last Chance, on the divide between Oro Fino and Grizzly Gulches, four miles south of Helena. James Whitlatch uncovered the first of these in September, 1864 — a lode which became the famous Whitlatch-Union mine. His discovery sparked others to search the hills, so that by the close of the year, a number of gold and silver-lead deposits had been located. Most of the gold and silver lay near the surface and was free-milling. It responded to amalgamation, and with the development of the several properties, small mills were erected to crush and treat the ore. Around these mines camps grew up — Unionville, Park City, Dry Gas, and Springville — but their story will be told later.

At first the miners in Last Chance lived in makeshift shelters — wickiups, tents, and dugouts gouged into the banks of the gulch. During the first winter many cabins were erected of logs or whipsawed lumber, for it was spring before Sanders and Rockwell set up their steam sawmill. With a townsite laid out, buildings began to line Main Street at the bottom of the gulch, and Bridge Street (later renamed State Street), which ran at right angles to it. Judge J. B. Stuart of the Probate Court built the first hotel, the International, in November, 1864, on the corner of the two main thoroughfares. By January, 1865, the camp contained forty-five food stores, twenty drygoods and clothing emporiums, fifteen corrals and feed stables, seven carpenter and furniture stores, fourteen saloons, seven restaurants, eleven blacksmiths, ten doctors, and sixteen attorneys. Venison sold for ten cents a pound; eggs were $2.00 a dozen.

By midsummer 1865, three thousand people crowded the gulch and the streets were choked with men, animals, and piles of merchandise. The twisting trail was far too narrow to accommodate the amout of traffic that fought a way through it; consequently, many ox-trains and pack trains camped outside the town, waiting for a chance to snake their way up the gulch so as to unload their stock. Connection with Diamond City and other thriving mining camps east of the Missouri River was made that summer when Chivers & Company put on a line of coaches to Confederate and White Gulches. For those anxious to return to the States, Sprague & Company provided six boats, each capable of carrying 150 passengers, which left Fort Benton in August, promising a safe passage down the river.

Life in the camp during its first year is recorded in the *Montana Post* which, although published in Virginia City until 1867 (when the editor moved his press to Last Chance), ran a regular column devoted to "Helena Items," from which we quote:

The water in our gulch is not fit to drink, after the early hours of the morning, it is so much disturbed. A supply is brought around by teams. Cattle are a source of constant trouble to their owners. It is the custom to turn them out at night and fetch them in soon after daylight . . . (a man) may hunt two or three days to find them.
Montana Post, April 22, 1865

An abundance of hay, grain and garden vegetables are being hauled in every day . . . Travis still persists in selling wild "broncos," to the infinite amusement of the large crowds, attracted by his noisy and humorous descriptions of the merits of the animals auctioned.

The writer of this article also mentions many saloon signs that advertise drinks, but concludes:

The inspiring effect of the artistic labels . . . is considerably dampened by the prominent and large lettered announcement of NO CREDIT. The crowded bars, however, prove both that the money is in the country, and that whiskey can bring it out.
Montana Post, Sept. 23, 1865

From time to time Indians visited the camp:

On Wednesday the streets of our city were overrun by "red brethren" of the Pen d'Oreilles, Flat Heads, Nez Percés from the Hell Gate country. The abo-rigines are camped about three miles from town, on Ten Mile creek and number over 1000 warriors on 3000 ponies. They state that they are going on a buffalo hunt. A good deal of trading has been done with them, and that without the assistance of Webster's dictionary. Several of our citizens have paid their respects to the "lords of the soil" at their camp.
Montana Post, Oct. 14, 1865

Throughout 1865, while the gulch was one long series of claims, men and animals had to walk warily for fear of falling into prospect holes and shafts dug to bedrock, which in some places was thirty to fifty feet below the surface of the stream. Such excavations were seldom filled in, when abandoned, and, worse still, new diggings might appear where only a few hours before there had been solid earth. Buildings that were secure one day might be supported on stilts the next, as the earth underneath them was dug away and washed for the gold it contained. A dancehall girl at the Gayety Saloon, newly arrived in town, stepped to the back of the hall where she worked to get a breath of air between whirls. She opened the door and stepped off into space, landing shaken and bruised on bedrock, ten feet below. Only that day the ground under the building had been excavated and the hall propped up. Not until the summer of 1866, when much of the placer ground on Main Street was worked out, were bridges put across intersections, making travel less precarious.

When A. K. McClure called "a truce with politics and law for a season" and set out in 1867 "to see the Great West, to gaze upon its virgin beauties, learn its gigantic progress and mingle with the sturdy pioneers who are laying the foundations for future empires," he wrote a series of letters that two years later were published in book form. They were written on the spot and "often in the midst of annoyances not favorable to epistolary perfection." This very directness makes them alive. In Letter XXVIII he describes his arrival:

Helena Hot Springs, Mont. Terr., Aug. 23, 1867
When we reached the summit of the divide northwest of Hoggum, the Prickly Pear Valley was presented in all its beauty. We dined sumptuously at a two-story ranch on savory elk-steak and the finest vegetables, and had an hour of rest among the latest Eastern periodicals.

When within five miles of the city, we saw a cloud of dust rise ahead of us, looking as if a troop of Indians were upon our trail; but, as we met it, my old friend and companion through the perilous Indian troubles of Bridger, Dr. Cass, surrounded us with a mounted escort of twenty-five men, and bid us welcome to the city of Helena . . . We all dismounted in obedience to orders from Dr. Cass . . . He had a buggy, and from under the seat a willow basket temptingly projected. In its capacious quarters were many bottles, tumblers, and blocks of crystal ice; and he insisted that all must partake.

McClure's companions thought it was water.

"Water," responded the genial doctor . . . "Water is all very well in its place, very good for baptizing infants . . . and excellent for sluicing out gulches; but it don't go for a steady beverage up here, where the air is so thin." . . . corks flew in every direction . . . I could not deny the theory that sparkling wine refreshes the horses, when imbibed by the driver or rider.

Helena has all the vim, recklessness, extravagance, and jolly progress of a new camp. It is but little over two years old, but it boasts a population of 7,500, and more solid men, more capital, more handsome and well-filled stores, more fast boys and frail women, more substance and pretense, more virtue and vice, more preachers and groggeries, and more go-ahead activeness generally, than any other city in the mountain mining region.

The only tree in the city is a short, thick pine, known as the "Hangman's tree" on which many a desperado has yielded his life to the terrible judgment of the Vigilantes.

Three Thousands Miles Through the Rocky Mountains, A. K. McClure

The famed Hangman's Tree in Dry Gulch was indeed a symbol of law and order. At least thirteen men were hanged from its branches between 1865 and 1870. John Keene, a gambler and gunman, is credited with having committed the first murder in the gulch on June 5, 1865, by shooting Harry Slater as he stood in the doorway of Sam Greer's saloon. Keene was arrested by Sheriff Wood and tried by the citizens in a lumberyard, in lieu of a courtroom. After his hanging in Dry Gulch the same day, the Vigilance Committee of Helena was organized to deal with future crimes.

In 1870, the body of an Oriental swung from the tree, and, according to local reports, "was left on the rope all morning." The *Helena Daily Herald* describes the incident:

The Vigilantes at Work
The Capture and Execution of Ah Chow
The Body of the Murderer of Bitzer Swinging on
Hangman's Tree

At last the murderer is caught. The miserable, abandoned wretch, who had killed three human beings during his hardened existence, has, at last, been brought to a dreadful accountability, and the scriptural injunction that "he who sheds man's blood, by man shall his blood be shed," has been faithfully carried out. His worthless body now dangles in the air.

. . . That his awful fate is a just one none can deny. It is a fate which many others should have met long ago, and thus avoided thousands of dollars of unnecessary expense to the Territory.

A placard pinned to his back (reads) "Ah Chow, the murderer of John R. Bitzer. Beware! The Vigilantes still live." It is reported that he was found and arrested at ten o'clock last night, about six miles "down the gulch."

Jan. 25, 1870

The following day an article signed 'citizen' took an opposite view of the incident. It included the following paragraph:

I knew neither the Chinaman nor the man whom he shot; but . . . the facts of the case go to show that Ah Chow was justified in the shooting. He was a cripple, having the use of his left hand only; had been sick for two preceding months and was in his own house at the time of the affray, ten to eleven p.m. Bitzer had no business at the Chinaman's house that late in the evening.

On May 17, 1876, the Hangman's Tree was chopped down by a Methodist minister, Reverend W. C. Shippen, on whose ground it stood. The residents of Helena were indignant, for to them the stocky tree on the corner of Hillsdale and Blake Streets was a symbol of law enforcement. The clergyman, however, considered it a poor landmark to perpetuate.

As the city grew, the need for a Vigilance Committee disappeared. Criminals, when arrested by appointed officers, were imprisoned until tried. The city jail, in use as late as 1884, was described as "a poor, thin, insecure building no stronger than a pidgeon box, with only a watchman on guard." On the night of July 24, even the watchman was off the premises for an hour and a half, "looking at the Prize Fight at the Academy of Music." During his absence, one of the prisoners, Con Murphy, road agent and horse-thief, broke out of the jail and made his getaway. The *Herald* reported the jail break and concluded: "The shaky condition of the city jail was known to everybody. A hole overhead showed where he made his escape."

* * *

Helena never lacked newspapers. The *Radiator* appeared briefly from December 17, 1865, until July, 1866, when it was bought by the three Fisk brothers — R. E., D. W., and A. J. They called their paper the *Weekly Herald* and put out the first issue on November 15, 1866. Since no white newsprint was on hand, the first number was printed on brown manila paper. Subscription rates were $10.00 a year in gold.

OLD SECTION OF HELENA, LOOKING WEST TO MT. HELENA

OLD QUARTER, HELENA

The *Herald's* politics were solidly Republican. Within the first six months of operation, the brothers spent over $6,000, much of which went into the purchase of paper brought from Salt Lake City by stagecoach at a cost of $125.00 for a bundle of 1,000 sheets. The *Daily Herald* appeared on August 1, 1867; rates were $1.00 a week in gold. During 1867, the *Montana Post* was moved from Virginia City to Helena. A third paper, the *Rocky Mountain Gazette,* was published from 1866 to 1874. The *Independent,* a Democratic paper, established at Deer Lodge as early as 1866, was moved to Helena in 1874. During the 1880's, the *Daily Journal* was added to the impressive list of publications. Telegraph connections had put Helena in communication with the outside world in 1867.

Helena's business district filled Main Street, south from Broadway and then spread up the steep side streets east of that thoroughfare. As the population increased, buildings were crowded into upper Last Chance as far as the forks of the gulch. In a short time, new streets were laid out farther north than the original cluster of gulch trails, but still east of Main Street. Each street that paralleled the gulch stood at a higher level than the one below it, and the cross streets climbed from bench to bench until the rim of the north gulch was reached. There the Prickly Pear Valley prairie began.

Despite fires, depressions, earthquakes, and new enterprises that have razed landmarks and built on old sites, Helena today contains many buildings that date from its earliest past and are well worth searching for. One unque monument is the watchtower on Fire Tower Hill. This wooden structure, on the summit of a conical knoll, dates back to the days when Helena had no fire protection other than volunteer fighters who responded to an alarm.

At first, when a fire occurred, someone would race to the top of the tower and shout and point toward the flames to show the volunteer brigade where to go. Next a triangle was hung from a building on the corner of Bridge and Water Streets and struck until the din attracted attention and sent men running with their buckets. Every cabin had a fire bucket hanging outside so as to be handy if high winds carried blazing shingles and sparks beyond the range of the firefighters. When the triangle fire alarm was moved to the structure on Tower Hill and suspended from the wooden framework, a watchman was hired to stay on

guard day and night. When he tapped out an alarm in the daytime, he ran outside and waved a red flag on a long pole, pointing with it toward the smoke and flames. If the alarm came at night, he waved a lantern.

Inspectors made the rounds of the town and checked all flues and stovepipes in an effort to reduce fire risks, but little was accomplished by such visits. Chinatown was a constant threat and was actually the district in which two of Helena's worst fires originated. The first broke out in a gambling house on the corner of West Main and Bridge Streets, on April 28, 1869, and before it was extinguished, most of the business section was destroyed. The *Herald* office was gutted by the fire and its entire stock of paper ruined. The editors immediately sent a messenger to Corinne, Utah, with orders to return by fast coach with enough paper for an edition.

Nine Husky Porkers that were lying in back of Travis & Bro.'s stables when the fire overtook them, rushed frantically into the basement of Mather & Crocker's Billiard rooms, or rather into the Mammoth Concert Saloon, and there perished a few minutes after, in the flames. One or two of them, very nice shoats, were roasted just enough for the table, and we learn that a squad of hungry boarders who had just been burned out, feasted heartily upon the ready cooked swine.

Helena Weekly Herald, May 6, 1869

After this fire, it was suggested that one long stone building be erected on Main Street, from Bridge to Broadway, in the hope that it would serve as a "break" and withstand future blazes.

Dr. Frank, who ran a bathhouse equipped with a steam engine, offered to lend his machine to fight fire whenever it was needed. It was used several times and was especially helpful on March 24, 1870, when another blaze broke out. Unfortunately, the available hose was too short to throw water on all the burning buildings. The Helena brewery was beyond the range of the water, and its frantic owners, determined to save their plant, carried kegs of beer to the roof and spurted streams of the foaming liquid over the walls and on adjacent buildings that were also threatened, keeping the surfaces damp enough to withstand the heat. When the flames were out, the other town breweries treated the fire fighters, of which there were more than one hundred.

In October, 1870, after fire had again destroyed considerable property, it was pointed out that with Dr. Frank's engine and a new one, recently installed in the *Rocky Mountain*

Gazette office, plus sufficient hose, there would be sufficient pressure to sluice out every building in town, provided that the city had iron pipes to carry the water. Prodded by public opinion, the Water Company replaced the log pipes with iron ones.

Several bad fires in 1871, coupled with the division of the city into six fire districts, prompted Colonel C. A. Broadwater, owner of the "Diamond 'R'" freighting outfit, to offer to haul a fire engine to Helena from Corinne or Fort Benton free of charge. On December 29, 1872, the Helena Fire Department was organized with three companies, represented by Helena Engine No. 1, Tiger Engine No. 2, and Hook & Ladder Company No. 1.

At three p.m. on August 3, 1872, fire, which broke out in the rear of the North Pacific Hotel on Main Street, leveled six blocks and part of a seventh one, including much of the residential district. After this fire, $5,-907.50 was subscribed for a fire engine, and hand equipment, such as hooks, ropes, and axes, was recommended for purchase.

The third great fire occurred on January 4, 1874, starting, as had the first one, in a Chinese restaurant behind a gambling house. In minutes Chinatown was engulfed in flames. According to the *Herald,* the blaze was caused by a Chinese lighting a fire with coal oil. When he poured too great a quantity on the coals, an explosion blew down the stovepipe and scattered the fire against the flimsy wall of the room. In panic, the Oriental grabbed a bucket of liquid and doused the flames, thinking it contained water. Instead it was filled with oil! In this holocaust 150 buildings were reduced to ashes and Conrad Knipper burned to death while attempting to escape from the International Hotel. Losses were set at $850,000 and irreplaceable records, like those of the Masonic Grand Lodge and the Historical Society were destroyed. Both the *Gazette* and the *Herald* were burned out for the second time. Although the latter published an account of the disaster the following day, the description was contained on a half-sheet of paper. The staff admitted they were to exhausted to put out a bigger sheet.

Help came from many quarters. The people of Diamond City sent over a big wagonload of food and clothing, and a fund for the purchase of a bell for Helena's Roman Catholic church was allocated instead to the use of the needy. Finally, in 1875, the city bought a steam fire engine.

In 1878, when telephones were installed within the city, one was placed in the watchtower. A large bell, weighing 2,200 pounds and costing $535.00, was ordered hung in the tower in 1886. This necessitated bracing the structure against additional stress and weight. Mechanism to ring the bell was installed in the tiny room on top of the structure. Here the watchman lived in a glass-enclosed ærie, sitting from five p.m. to eight a.m. in a swivel chair watching for unexplained smoke or flame. His salary was $75.00 a month. The alarm system was used until January, 1931, when the mechanism controlling its ringing froze up. Today the tower is only a historic landmark.

The Helena Directory of 1868 lists the embryo city's many establishments, some of which were operated by men who became civic leaders. J. H. Ming stocked books, stationery, and the "leading newspapers and periodicals of the world." Cannon's Steam Bakery is praised for "the rapidity with which it turns out crackers, pies, bread and cakes." Holter & Anderson ran a distillery on West Main Street which turned out "an immense quantity of whiskey." Nick Kessler's Brewery, two miles west of the city, and Binzel & Hamper's Union Brewery and Bakery were both advertised. The Occidental Billiard Hall is said to be "the only house of any description in the Territory illuminated with gas." Fraternal organizations include Helena Lodge No. 3 A. F. & A. M.; Montana Lodge No. 1, I. O. O. F.; Helena Royal Arch Chapter U. D., and the Helena Typographical Union No. 95. In the 1870 Directory, the census for Helena covers six pages, with the most common occupation that of miner.

Almost as soon as gulch mining started, Last Chance had its Chinatown, a colorful, if ramshackle, section of the camp near the head of South Main Street. Incidents connected with the Orientals were always noticed in the papers, like the murder of Chinese Mary in 1867, killed for her gold, or the unexpected deaths of four Chinese:

The first fatal effects of the present cold weather, we learn, was the freezing of four Chinamen on lower Last Chance. It appears they came to town Tuesday morning with the intention of celebrating one of their innumerable holidays, and enjoyed themselves with their Celestial friends during the day, with never a though of the cold bed and chilly pillow in store for them that bleak winter's night . . .

After celebrating . . . the Chinamen got kegs, filled with whisky, which they carried in their hands. It was taking cold chances to venture out that evening but the Chinamen had imbibed considerable fluid, and felt warm and brave . . . So at four o'clock in the afternoon they bid their friends goodbye and started on their journey home. They only got about half a mile below town . . . Their comrades on the claims below, had kept the fires burning in their cabins during the night . . . Morning came, but no Chinamen. Becoming alarmed, they started out to search for their missing friends . . . and discovered them on the road, lying close together, cold and stiff. their little kegs of whisky beside them, the contents also frozen . . . We understand the unfortunate men belonged to the See Yup Co.

Helena Independent, Jan. 15, 1875

Sometimes a funeral was deferred until ceremonies for several of the deceased could be held at one time. In June, 1884, when two Chinese were drowned in a flood, a joint funeral of this sort was conducted. Two large tables laden with roast pig and a variety of sweets were set up in the street near the hovels where the deceased had lived. Around this repast marched some thirty Chinese dressed in white and carrying banners and transparencies and throwing strips of perforated paper into the air to confuse evil spirits who might follow the souls of the dead men. The hearse bearing the two coffins was preceded by the Turnverein Band. Behind it came a wagon filled with tea, rice, and other foods to be placed on the graves. Back of the vehicles walked friends and the members of the secret society to which the deceased belonged.

Saloons, gambling joints, dancehalls and theatres jockeyed for good locations as soon as stores began to line Last Chance Gulch and adjacent streets.

The gambling business is as openly conducted as the dry goods store, in fact more so, since the stores do close up once in a while — which is more than can be said of the "tiger dens" . . . There are twelve or fifteen places . . . all run in connection with saloons. Most of the tables are on the first floor; some few have an upstairs apartment, a little more exclusive and more handsomely furnished which it seems to be the fashion to call "reading rooms." Faro, roulette and poker are the most popular games . . . Everyone plays . . . To the man who is poverty stricken today and possibly a wealthy man next week, any ordinary amusement is entirely too tame. Then there are men here who have made fortunes at gambling, but they are the dealers.

History of Montana, Leeson

Helena's first theatre was Leviathan Hall on Bridge Street. This entertainment center was destroyed by fire on November 7, 1869.

The alarm was given from the bell of the Catholic church and district school house . . . The wind was blowing a hurricane . . . The loss fell heavily upon Mr. Boulon and the theatrical corps, just arrived from San Francisco, who had commenced a successful engagement. The members of the company lost everything — clothing and wardrobe, worth $2,000. The musical instruments of the band were entirely consumed. The total theater loss was $9,000 . . . Katie Buchanan's house was torn down to stop the spread of the fire.

Rocky Mountain Gazette, Nov. 9, 1869

The second theatre was established in 1865 by Jack S. Langrishe, in the C. C. Huntley building on Wood Street. Langrishe, who was well known in all the major mining camps of the West, fitted his theatre with two proscenium boxes and lighted it with "scores of coal oil lamps." His programs satisfied the people, for the 1868 Directory stated:

He is constantly serving up to the public a variety of plays and adding to his troupe new faces of acknowledged merit. Prominent among his troupe are Mr. and Mrs. Langrishe, Mrs. Fitzwilliams, Mrs. Shields, Mrs. Waldron, Messrs. Pauncefort, Mortimer, Martin, Griffith, Shields and Waldron.

His popular opera house burned in 1874. When Captain Parkinson built a concert hall on South Main Street, opposite the International Hotel, in 1889, Langrishe and his troupe (which included several stars "brought from San Francisco and the States") gave the opening performance. During the summer months, a tour of other camps was made:

The Langrishe theatrical troupe leaves tomorrow for Deer Lodge, Blackfoot and other prominent camps over the range and will give a series of performances at each one of them. Mr. Langrishe will also visit Cedar Creek before he returns to Helena, and give the people of Louisville the benefit of a week's entertainment. The troupe will be absent several weeks.

Helena Daily Herald, July 20, 1870

The Broadway Theater, later known as Harmonia Hall, was built in the fall of 1878 by J. Al. Sawtelle. But not until Ming's Opera House on Jackson Street was opened in 1880, did Helena have a first-class theatre. John H. Ming came to Montana in 1863 to open a stationery store in Virginia City. Two years later he moved to Helena where he ran a similar store. His fortune, however, was obtained through investments in real estate, livestock, and mining. When his splendid Opera House, which stood where the Consistory Shrine Temple now stands, was nearing completion, he advertised that the four stage boxes could be reserved. Nate Vestal, wealthy owner of the

Penobscot mine near Marysville, took one at $10.00 a night for the entire season.

For the grand opening on September 2, Ming engaged Katie Putnam and her company, featuring the leading lady in sketches from Charles Dickens' *Old Curiosity Shop*. Miss Putnam and company came up the Missouri by steamboat to Fort Benton, where they gave a performance in a wool warehouse. They then traveled by stage to Helena, reaching that city ten days before the building which they were to open was completed. The company therefore accepted a week's engagement at Fort Shaw, playing to big audiences of soldiers for small cash receipts. It was the custom for the first sergeant of each company to list the names of the men from his unit who attended the show. When the army paymaster came around a few months later, the admission price was deducted from each man's pay and sent to the theatrical manager of the traveling company.

In addition to professional performances, Ming's Opera House was used for local benefits and musicals, such as Ye Olde Folkes Concerte given in February, 1884, by the Fifth Avenue Presbyterian church. John Ming died on December 27, 1887, at the age of fifty-six. He was buried from St. Peter's Episcopal church.

Recreation other than the theatre took many forms. In winter sleighing was popular, with even a 200-mile drive from Helena to Missoula attracting enthusiasts who reported that

with the exception of the first five miles out, it was fine sleighing, the snow lying well packed on the road, at an average depth of about six inches.
Helena Weekly Herald, Feb. 4, 1869

Hunting and horse-racing attracted other sportsmen.

The Antelope Hunt of yesterday, in which a score of our most dashing equestrians participated, resulted in an exhilarating "chase of the antelope o'er the plain" and in bagging one, which was brought to town.
Helena Weekly Herald, Feb. 18, 1869

In the 1870's, the Hunters & Fishermen's Club, the Pastime Baseball Club, the Helena Literary and Social Society, the Pioneer Dancing Club, and other private social organizations attracted a select membership. During the 1880's, lawn tennis and croquet clubs were organized and a Bicycle Club of seven hardy members practiced by riding up Mount Helena.

The first Masquerade Ball was held on March 1, 1870, with W. A. Clark, the future copper magnate, chairman of arrangements.

The dance, which was held at the courthouse under the auspices of the Helena Library Association and included a midnight supper served at the Magnolia Hotel, was publicized in the papers by a notice signed by Clark, according to which "no gentleman will be permitted to appear in female attire." A list of the guests and their costumes shows great originality. Two well-known figures who attended were Henry Parchen as Othello and A. M. Holter as St. Valentine. The ball netted the library fund $300.00.

* * *

The best way to see Helena today is to walk its winding streets, neighborhood by neighborhood, to discover the old buildings tucked in between the new, and the sections that represent different eras of the city's progress.

The sides of Last Chance were built up first. Then followed the cross streets to the east that sloped up hill to the crown of the prairie. Streets paralleling the gulch had to be cut in rock terraces along the eastern side, one above the other. These soon became the first residential section, extending from Eleventh Avenue to Broadway and from Warren to Davis Streets. At the south end of this area stands the old stone successor to the original courthouse. In this neighborhood Helena's first schools, churches, and hospitals were built. As the city continued to expand, the west side of the gulch was developed, and a second more fashionable residential section filled the higher streets which overlooked Last Chance Gulch. By the late eighties and nineties the city had stretched out in all directions, barred only on the west by the slopes of Mt. Helena and on the southwest by the hills that formed rugged Grizzly, Oro Fino, and Dry Gulches.

My favorite method of exploration was to park on some street and stroll up one block and down another, sketching as I went. In this way I discovered many residences, churches, and some business blocks that I recognized from old photographs or newspaper cuts. In certain cases the buildings had been greatly remodeled, in others little change was evident. As I covered more and more of the city in this way, I began to sort out types of buildings and trace their progress through the years.

The first time I drove up Main Street, I noticed a big red brick brewery, built close to the limestone cliffs of the upper gulch. Next day I hunted in old newspapers at the library to find out something about it. It was one of several in the city. John Horsky had started a brewery in a log cabin in 1865. Nicholas

Kessler founded another one the same year on a ten-acre tract two miles west of the camp. Kessler had an eye for the needs of the new community, for he shrewdly located his brewery on ground that contained excellent clay deposits. His brickyard was soon employing thirty-five to seventy men and turning out 8,000,000 bricks a year. The Western Clay Manufacturing Company, which until recently occupied the same ground, was the outgrowth of Kessler's small beginning. The Kessler Brewery, whose brick buildings loom up near the entrance to the Green Meadow Golf Course, was incorporated in 1901, and was capable of turning out 30,000 barrels a year.

The Union Brewery, located at the junction of Grizzly and Oro Fino Gulches, was another early enterprise. I am not sure when it started, but in July, 1867, it was "reopened by Messrs. B. Zinzel and J. W. Hamper, a new firm."

The Capital City Brewing Company, in the southern part of the city on West Main Street, occupied a four-acre tract and was in operation by the 1870's. It changed hands several times, was enlarged and shut down more than once. The brewery was turning out 25,000 barrels a year in 1903, although a 1904 account mentions a capacity of 100,000 barrels. After its final shutdown, it stood empty until the Helena Chamber of Commerce reopened it in June, 1954, as a tourist attraction — the Last Chance Gulch Theater. This was part of its "Helena Unlimited" program, of which the theatre was but one project.

Religion came to the gulch about the same time as beer. When the Reverend A. M. Hough, a Methodist minister stationed in Virginia City, learned of the stampede to Last Chance, he, as the first Methodist missionary to Montana, felt it his duty to send E. T. McLaughlin there to hold services. Reverend McLaughlin preached the first sermon in the gulch, standing on a pile of logs.

The first church in the city, organized through his efforts, was the Methodist Episcopal, founded in 1865, with services held in a log cabin on Cutler Street, between Wood and Bridge Streets. Reverend Hough moved to Helena in 1866, remaining for two years. During his stay, the log meeting place was replaced by a new building at Ewing Street and Broadway, whose cornerstone was laid in September, 1867. It was probably for this church that the concert mentioned by George Comfort, the Methodist minister, was held.

The following is an exact exhibit of the net proceeds, in currency, of the concert on Oct. 20, 1868:

	Net proceeds	$280.50
Bought	17 yds. carpeting	$ 53.25
	9 bracketts	75.62
	1 communion table	37.50
	1 pulpit chair	18.00
	2 stand lamps	25.00
	2 altar chairs	37.50
	4 chairs for choir	30.00
	sewing carpet	3.63
	Total	$280.50

The above named articles, purchased by a Committee of ladies, have been received by the Church, which we appreciate, and for which we are truly grateful.
Geo. Comfort, Pastor
Helena Weekly Herald, Nov. 19, 1868

The Roman Catholics were the second denomination to build. Reverend Francis Kuppens, S. J., established the Church of the Sacred Heart during the summer of 1866, although even earlier than his visit Reverend Joseph Giorda held a service in a gulch cabin. An old photo shows the first small church on Ewing Street north of St. John's Hospital, the latter a three-story mansard building administered by Roman Catholic Sisters. On May 2, 1884, Bishop Brondell "received from Rome the papers creating the 'See of Helena'" and making him Bishop of Montana, the limits of the diocese to be "the civil limits of the Territory of Montana." St. Helena's cathedral, which dominates the city's skyline, is a relatively new building, not dedicated until Christmas Day, 1914. Thomas Cruse donated the site. His fortune, made in the Drumlummon mine in Marysville, provided most of the funds for its erection, although additional gifts were made by his heirs and by other members of the rich parish. The cathedral, built in German Gothic style of the fourteenth century, cost $1,000,000.

The Rt. Rev. Daniel S. Tuttle, Episcopal Bishop, reached Virginia City on July 17, 1867, having been consecrated only three months before. He was assigned to the Territory of Montana with the missionary districts of Nevada, Utah, and Idaho also under his jurisdiction. His brother-in-law, Reverend George Goddard, accompanied him to Virginia City. Less than a month after their arrival the two traveled by coach the 125 miles to Helena, where the bishop held his first service on August 11th. The collection consisted entirely of gold dust and nuggets. Leaving Goddard in charge, Tuttle returned to Virginia City. Later the bishop moved to Helena with his wife and son, arriv-

DOWNTOWN, HELENA, LOOKING UP LAST CHANCE GULCH

CAPITAL BREWERY, HELENA, RECENTLY THE BREWERY THEATRE

ing in December, 1868, and assumed the work of the church there. The Tuttles occupied a five-room house on Jackson Street, a thoroughfare called by the miners "Pig Alley."

Church services were held in an old schoolhouse on Rodney Street, until the county commissioners offered the use of the courthouse on Sundays. From August, 1869, until St. Peter's church was built, services were held regularly in the courthouse with only Mrs. A. M. Holter's melodeon, which she graciously loaned, providing a churchly atmosphere. By January, 1869, there were but fourteen communicants, although people of other denominations attended and helped with church work. Bishop Tuttle took an active and genuine interest in the life of the growing city and was always ready to offer his services when needed.

Through his tireless work with the bucket brigade at a fire in 1869 Bishop Tuttle won the lasting respect of the entire community. According to the *Herald*:

He was everywhere in the midst of the many heroic and tireless workers, braving the heat, lifting and tugging like a Trojan. Had the scores and hundreds who stood by with idle hands but busy mouths, giving orders, opinions and commands, followed the example of that worthy man, much might have been saved that was lost, and the fiery element sooner arrested in its progress.

Feb. 18, 1869

St. Peter's stone church, founded by Bishop Tuttle, stood on the corner of Grand and Warren Streets. The first service was held October 26, 1879. The Episcopalians maintained a small hospital in the old Holter residence for some years. Then Mrs. Brewer, wife of the Bishop, visited eastern cities to raise funds for a larger building and was so successful in her mission that in 1887 the church was able to buy several lots on Eleventh Avenue and build a brick hospital. On June 22, 1887, Bishop Brewer and Reverend Webb presided as the cornerstone was laid, "amid the tailing banks on the rough remains of early day placer mining on the hill east of North Main Street." The present Episcopal church, St. Peter's Pro-Cathedral, stands on Park Avenue on the west bank of the gulch.

The Presbyterians built on Courthouse Square in 1872; the Baptists started a building fund in December, 1881, initiated with an oyster supper, held at the Merchant's Hotel on Warren Street. Both the Congregational and Christian churches, erected in 1883, were on the west side of Helena, "surrounded by the

handsomest private residences in the city." A successful social at the Christian church was in the form of a

Pink Tea

given by the young ladies of the Church . . . at Harmonia Hall. Everything was pink from lamp shades and Chinese lanterns to the blushing cheeks of the ladies . . . By ten o'clock the abundant supply of refreshments was exhausted, and by the time the participators at the Skating Amphitheater got to the hall there was not a saucer of the luscious ice cream left for their parched lips.

Helena Weekly Herald, April 10, 1884

The Baptists, Lutherans, and other denominations built at later dates.

One of the first fraternal groups to organize in Helena was the Masons, who were granted a dispensation by the Grand Lodge of Colorado during the summer of 1865. The first regular meeting was held on August 17 in the second story of a log building at 53 South Main Street.

According to an article on Helena's Masonic history, published in the *Herald* in 1885, this first meeting "was held in a room over the Perkins and Hughes store, occupying the site of the Gans and Klein building on upper Main Street, now the I.X.L. Hotel. The room they met in had rough logs for sides, with no ceiling, and only the rough shakes that served for shingles in those days; and for a carpet, and to deaden the sound, as there was only a single floor and no ceiling under that, the floor was covered with six inches of sawdust. The furniture was crude and homemade, but served the purpose just as well as the most elegant and expensive."

From the Quarries of Last Chance Gulch,
William C. Campbell

The second meeting place was at 38 South Main Street on the second floor of the E. M. Dunphy Block. In November, 1866, they moved into a two-story frame hall they had built at 106 Broadway near the Merchant's Hotel. This served them until 1872. The first Masonic Temple was built at the corner of Main and Edwards Streets during 1872 and was occupied from January, 1873, until December, 1885. Needing larger quarters, the Masons then bought land on Broadway at the corner of Jackson Street and built a Temple which still stands, although it is now occupied by the State Publishing Company. The present Consistory adjoins the back of the building on Jackson Street.

In wandering through Helena's old residential streets, I noticed a brick building of substantial and distinguished design, set back from the sidewalk and surrounded with an iron fence. This was the U. S. Assay Office, established by Act of Congress, October 14, 1874, designed by A. B. Mullet, the architect for the Treasury Department building in Washington, D. C., and completed by W. A. Potter, Mullet's successor. The building was begun in 1875 and completed one year later. Prior to 1879, the government kept $100,500 on hand for the purchase of gold and silver. By 1885, this amount had been increased to $250,000. It is estimated that over $2,000,000 in gold passed through this office officially, most of it recovered from nearby placers and free-milling ores.

Just east of the Assay Office, but with its back to Broadway, the present Lewis and Clark County Courthouse occupies a city block, surrounded with landscaped grounds and green lawns. It was built in 1885 at a cost of $200,-000, a massive, gray granite structure trimmed in red sandstone. Originally a tall clock tower ornamented the facade of the building, but after the earthquake of 1935 this feature and the heavy stone copings were removed. The first courthouse, a small, two-story building, stood directly north of the present one and was razed only after the newer building was completed. In the new structure, all the county courts and offices were accommodated, as well as the Montana Law Library and the Historical Society. Space was rented to the territory for the use of the governor, secretary, auditor, treasurer, and legislative bodies. Thus, the building served as capitol as well as courthouse.

A statue of George Washington stands in front of the main entrance. When the county commissioners bought it from California in 1888 for $250.00, plus freight charges, and placed it on its granite pedestal, the purchase drew considerable criticism from the press. According to the *Herald*, it was "hideous" and showed "wear and tear and long and disrespectful use." Its only worth was said to be the value of the marble from which it was carved.

East of the courthouse is the jail, another stone building, built in 1891 at a cost of $38,-000. Like the courthouse, it was shorn of its battlements as a safety measure after damage that it suffered in the same earthquake.

In 1889, when Montana became a state, the sentiments of its citizens were voiced in the annual report of the Board of Trade:

The formalities are few and easily complied with, but the difference they make to this community can scarcely be computed . . . We are no longer an unknown, ignored Territory, but, clothed in dignity and power of a State, challenge the attention of the world . . . The year 1889 will be a red-letter day in the history of Montana.

Statehood will give Montana 5,000,000 acres of school lands, the sale of which will yield an endowment that will relieve the second and succeeding generations from the burdens the first generation has had to bear to educate its children.

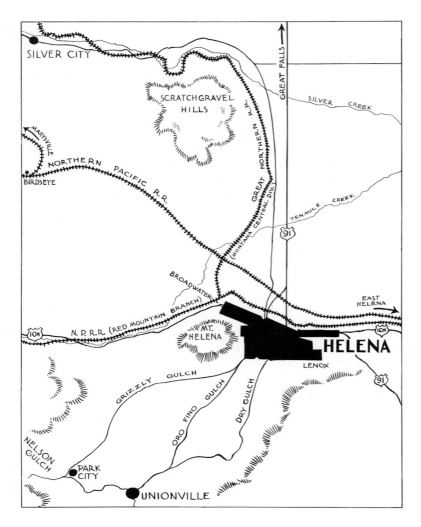

CHAPTER 5

HELENA,
The CAPITAL

On November 8, 1889, Montana became a state. Almost immediately the question arose as to where the permanent capital should be located, for in territorial days Bannack, Virginia City, and Helena had all served in that capacity. Bannack was the first location. Then, in 1865, the legislators whisked the seat of government to Virginia City. To further confuse the issue, the first Constitutional Convention met in Helena in March, 1866. In September, 1867, the voters of the territory had a chance to decide whether they wanted Virginia City or Helena as capital. They chose Virginia City. But Helena did not give up easily, and in 1869 she reopened the debate, placarding her houses with posters which read:

Lost, Strayed or Stolen! The Seat of Government. A liberal reward will be paid for its return to Helena. No questions asked.

LAST CHANCE

This brought no action, so, in 1874, the issue was pressed again. By vote of the people on February 11 the removal of the capital to Helena was authorized. When official ratification was received, Helena went wild and, on August 8, 1874, celebrated with speeches, music, fireworks, and a torchlight procession.

As soon as possible, Territorial Secretary James E. Callaway, made arrangements with Colonel C. A. Broadwater, owner of the "Diamond 'R'" freighting company (whose bull trains had for years hauled merchandise into Helena from Fort Benton), to come to Virginia City and get the records, furniture, and other property belonging to the government. So, on April 2, 1875, "the 'Capitol' of Montana Territory was loaded on the Diamond 'R' wagons at Virginia City and hauled through Alder Gulch to Helena," where it arrived on April 15. The entire second floor of the Blake

Block at 105 Broadway had been secured for territorial headquarters at an annual rental of $650.00. There the records and other property were unloaded and stored. With the completion of the Lewis & Clark County Courthouse in 1885, territorial headquarters were moved to it. With the change to statehood in 1889, these headquarters automatically became those of the state, and the Courthouse became the Capitol.

As Butte and Anaconda rose in industrial and economic prominence, Helena's suitability as permanent capital was questioned by certain factions, and the old issue of its location was reopened in 1894. This time, two of Montana's copper magnates directed the power plays. Each was determined to win. Marcus Daly wanted his growing smelter city of Anaconda to be the permanent seat of government. William A. Clark, of Butte, insisted that Helena be retained. The two cities were nearly equal in size, with the population of Helena listed as 27,028 and that of Anaconda as 25,118.

Butte backed Daly's choice of Anaconda at the same time that Clark's newspaper, the *Butte Miner,* led the fight for Helena. News items and brochures, published by each side, attempted to inflame the prospective voters and to sell them on the respective merits of the contested sites. Excerpts from one of Helena's pamphlets stated:

Helena has no pedigree. She was neither sired by a millionaire nor born of a corporation. No townsite company in her case staked off a few barren acres of sagebrush and peopled it afterwards. The people came first and laid out the town afterwards. No unworthy spite against a sister town attended her birth. The manicured hand of wealth did not grade her first street nor erect her first building. It was the weatherbeaten hand of toil, the brawny arm of labor, which blazed the trail to her virgin soil and planted the first log cabins upon her sightly hillsides . . . Helena is the easiest to reach of any city in the State.

Come to Helena to live

Helena is a City.	Anaconda is a Village.
Helena is everybody's town.	Anaconda is one man's town.
In Helena the people rule.	In Anaconda a corporation rules.
Helena wants the capital for the Capital.	Daly wants the capital to boom real estate.
Everybody has a show in Helena to make money.	Nobody but a Dalyite has a show in Anaconda.

The people are the same in both towns but Helena has more of them with no strings to their collars.
Helena is governed by whichever political party the people choose.

Anaconda is governed by the same old party and always will be — the Daly party.
This fight for the capital is not Helena vs. Anaconda, but the State of Montana vs. Marcus Daly.

When the election was over, Helena had won, and the capital fight was over.

One may have to hunt for the courthouse and assay office in the midst of the city's many streets, but the State Capitol rises above the rooftops and stands at one corner of Helena, waiting for the rest of the town to finally enclose it. Ground for the building was broken on October 1, 1898, just four years after the permanent location was settled. The cornerstone was laid the following Fourth of July. The three-story, sandstone structure, faced with Montana granite, cost $2,000,000 and its copper dome — Montana would not have dared to use gold-leaf — is surmounted with a small replica of the Statue of Liberty. On July 4, 1902, the building was dedicated.

Helena has excellent libraries, one near the Capitol in the Veterans' and Pioneers' State Museum on Roberts Street, and the other downtown. The latter, the Public Library on Park Avenue at Lawrence Street, was originally a church and was given to the city in 1933 by the Unitarians. Both the original library association, which was formed in 1866, and the Historical Society, of which William F. Wheeler was librarian for many years, assembled and preserved many valuable publications and original manuscripts, so that today their collections are treasure houses of Western lore. During the 1880's, the Y. M. C. A. maintained a public reading room, as did the W. C. T. U. ladies. The latter group ran an "inexpensive eating establishment," or coffee house, opposite the International Hotel where, in addition to providing magazines, books, and newspapers, "every man can be made comfortable away from the temptations of the saloon."

Schoolhouses in different portions of the city show by their architecture approximately when they were built. The older ones are sturdy brick and stone structures dating from the eighties and nineties. Crowning a hill in the northern part of the city is Carroll College, a Roman Catholic institution. North of the Capitol on Eleventh Avenue is the Montana Deaconess School, a haven for homeless children.

Helena has a number of hotels, both old and new. At the corner of Main and Grand Streets stands the Placer Hotel. Built in the twentieth century, right in the gulch, it is said to have been partially financed by the gold washed from the earth excavated from its basement. But while the Placer is the leading hotel of the city, persons interested in the earlier days of Last Chance search for the site of the first hotel, built by J. B. Stuart "on Lissner's corner," or go to the site of the International Hotel, also built in the middle sixties, on the corner of State and Main Streets. This three-story building with a broad piazza was convenient to the theatres and stagecoach offices, and, although destroyed three times by fire, in 1869, 1873 and 1874, it was always rebuilt. In 1878, it was enlarged and advertised as a "comfortable summer resort," which provided a "table liberally spread and the cooking delicate." Terms were $2.00 to $2.50 a day.

Part of the big four-story building which stands on the corner of Main and State Streets today was used at one time as the International Annex and was connected with the hotel proper by an enclosed, second-story bridge across State Street. The main floor of the building was occupied during the 1880's by the New York Dry Goods Store, later known as Fligelman's.

The four-story, eighty-room Cosmopolitan Hotel stood two blocks away on Main Street, and the Grand Central, another four-story structure, stood on the west side, a few doors north of Edwards Street. It was built in 1884 and opened in May, 1885. Its sixty rooms were "neatly furnished, carpeted with brussels carpet and supplied with gas and steam heaters. . . . Every floor is connected with the office by means of speaking tubes, while an elevator affords ready travel."

The Merchant's Hotel at Broadway and Warren Street stands just west of the Assay Office. According to the souvenir issue of the *Helena Journal*, of July, 1891, the four-story brick building with its mansard roof was closed in July, 1890, to permit extensive remodeling for the new lessee, the Merchant Hotel Company of Helena. "The top story was razed and two stories built on with forty-four rooms for guests. The first story, fronting on Broadway, contains the most elaborate barber shop in the state of Montana, in two departments, for ladies and gentlemen, each department having large bath rooms containing commodious porcelain tubs."

Helena's economic development was slow, due to its isolation. Throughout the 1860's, the main route to the territory was the Missouri River and the head of navigation was Fort Benton. During the high water season, which lasted only four to six weeks, all steamers landed their passengers and cargoes on the sloping banks, below the shacks and warehouses of the river port. At other times, steamers were forced to tie up at Fort Union at the mouth of the Yellowstone, which means that passengers and freight were landed much farther from their destination than had been anticipated.

From Fort Benton it was a rough 150 miles to Helena. Swaying coaches filled with passengers rolled into Helena and returned to Benton loaded with men and dust headed for the States. Bull trains hauled supplies and machinery to the mining camps and pulled heavily loaded wagons full of ore and concentrates over the dusty road back to the waiting river boats and barges which floated the valuable cargoes downstream to eastern smelters.

Upon the completion of the Union Pacific Railroad to Corinne, Utah, in 1869, a second route was opened up. Corinne immediately became the transfer point for rail freight to and from Montana Territory. As long as free-milling ore was abundant, it was possible to ship gold 450 miles by ox-team to Corinne, transfer it to the railroad to be hauled to San Francisco, and from there ship it to Swansea, Wales, for treatment, and still make a profit. Since many of the lode deposits required expensive metallurgical treatment before the ore could be shipped for further processing, only the richest specimens were sent out.

When the placer mines began to play out, many men left the area. The rush to the Black Hills in the middle seventies drained away many more, so that for a time Helena's very existence seemed doomed. Real estate could be given away but no one wanted it; so the owners hung on to their land. Later, when Helena's economic status improved, these men found themselves rich.

In 1878 men began to drift back from the Black Hills to resume mining. Their operations, however, were on a small scale, for they were awaiting the arrival of a railroad that would furnish reduced freight rates so that low-grade ore might be profitably handled. With the extension of the Northern Pacific to Helena in 1883, the growth of the district and of the city appeared assured. On June 12, 1883, there was great excitement when:

The first whistle from a locomotive that ever wakened the echoes in the canyons of Last Chance and Grizzly Gulches, and cheered the hopes of the people of

HELENA HILLS. GRANDON HOTEL AT LEFT

HELENA ARCHITECTURE

Helena, sounded at precisely 11 o'clock . . . as the construction train of Winston Bros. pulled into place where the station will soon be erected. A great concourse of people on foot, on horseback, and in all sorts of vehicles, was at the depot to welcome and cheer the iron horse . . . The track-laying was participated in by one of the ladies present, Mrs. D. Eckler, who wielded a great sledge hammer until she drove home a large spike.

Helena Herald, June 12, 1883

To celebrate the official arrival of the railroad, printed invitations were sent out which read:

Helena, Mont., June 15, 1883

You are respectfully invited to attend a celbration at Helena, Mont., Wednesday, July 4, 1883, commemorative of the one hundred and seventh anniversary of American Independence and the completion of the Northern Pacific Railroad to the Capital of the Territory.

Signed,   A. J. Davidson, Pres. Board of Trade
T. H. Kleinschmidt, Mayor of Helena
D. H. Wade, chief justice of Montana
(and 13 citizens)

The festivities on the Fourth began with a procession led by the Helena Silver Cornet Band. The city's two steam fire engines — *Rescue* and *City of Helena* — gaily decorated, paraded behind the band. The mayor and aldermen rode in "Zeigler's four-horse open omnibus," followed by floats representing the city's industries: George E. Boos with his "printing press in operation throwing off dodgers and advertisements," Horsky and Kenck's brewery wagon loaded with cases and barrels of beer, and drawn by a span of matched Percherons. Even Cowden's bull train plodded along the line of march.

A significant part of the publicity was the sending east of a freight train made up of thirty-six box cars loaded with silver bullion. Two engines decorated with bunting pulled the heavy train, which rolled out to the accompaniment of cannon, the whistles of fire engines, blasts from bands and shouts from the crowd.

On August 7, the first train crossed the Continental Divide west of Helena, and a month later the golden spike, which joined the East and West gap of the road, was driven near Garrison. Passenger service was then established between Helena and Deer Lodge by means of connections with the Utah and Northern at Garrison.

Quick Time
Under the new schedule . . . a person leaving Helena in the evening after supper can be in Butte the next morning for breakfast, having a whole day there for business, and return to Helena, all in 34 hours.

Helena Herald, July 10, 1884

The same year (1883), the Helena & Jefferson railroad, later a part of the Great Northern system, connected Helena and Wickes and enabled ore from the Wickes smelter to be economically shipped.

In 1887, Colonel Charles A. Broadwater, president of the Montana Central, brought his railroad into Helena. By the first of November, thirty teams were grading ground for a depot and freight house in lower Last Chance Gulch. By the middle of the month the tracklayers were at Silver City. When word was circulated that the tracks would reach Helena the following day, horses and buggies jammed the wagon road between the city and Scratch Gravel, as hordes of citizens drove out to await the arrival of the work train with the final rails. At one point, the Montana Central had to cross the Northern Pacific tracks, and there the established road placed a locomotive blocking the right of way. Both roads had attorneys on the spot, but not until a telegram was received from Northern Pacific headquarters in St. Paul, ordering the removal of the locomotive, could the Montana Central resume work. At noon on November 19, the tracklayers entered Last Chance Gulch.

A formal welcome took place on Monday, November 21. On the day of the celebration it snowed, but despite the storm, a parade, said to have been two miles long, formed on Jackson Street and moved down Main and Lawrence to the new Montana Central depot. A triumphal arch at Main and Edwards Streets bore the inscriptions, "Manitoba-Montana," "J. J. Hill and C. A. Broadwater" and "Hail to the Chiefs." After the parade, the dignitaries assembled on the stage of Ming's Opera House for speeches and a suitable ceremony. Even one of the churches welcomed the new road when the Methodist minister, Reverend A. D. Raleigh, preached on the text "Make Straight in the Desert a Highway." The year 1887 brought other railroads to Helena, and by mid-September, trains were operating between the city and Boulder on the Helena, Boulder & Butte line; and on October 22 the Helena & Northern, a branch of the Northern Pacific, "made its maiden run from Helena to Marysville in a blinding snowstorm" with two carloads of Helena's leading citizens aboard.

"Let us suppose," as the Helena Board of

Trade Report for 1887 states, "that you arrive in Helena on the train from the East just at the close of a summer day":

The bustle at the station, the long line of freight cars, the array of hacks, and hotel omnibuses, all suggest a large and busy place . . . a brightly painted street car . . . takes you "up town" for ten cents, and glancing around at the warehouses, lumber-yards, taverns and saloons which gather about the station, (you) discover that this is a new suburb, created by the railroad and that the city proper is more than a mile away . . . You pass heaps of boulders and gravel, beds of old ditches and huge excavations . . . the remains of abandoned gold diggings . . . All this debris gives to the city a singularly ragged and uncouth look and makes the contrast a striking one, when the car turning and descending a little hill, suddenly brings you into a long, narrow, winding street, full of vehicles and people and bordered with a picturesque variety of buildings, ranging in size from the log huts to the four-story brick hotel and the cut-stone palace of a bank . . . Leaving your grip at one of the hotels . . . you determine to . . . walk about the place. The stores strike you as surprisingly large for a town so remote from the East . . .

Turning up a broad street that climbs a hill on a grade that makes you stop to get your breath . . . you pass the offices of the daily newspapers . . . A street of pleasant homes, with green dooryards, poplar trees, and flowers attracts your steps . . .

As you descend to the business quarter, the electric lights are blazing and the night life of the city has begun . . . Bands are playing in the music halls. The clinking glasses in the saloons and the jingle of coins in a gaming house mingle with the tone of a bell from a church on the hill calling the pious to the weekly prayer meeting. A dusty four-horse stage comes rattling in from some mining camp; a six-mule team goes down the street with loud cracking of a blacksnake whip and sundry emphatic words of encouragement from the driver, who gives scant room for passing to a barouche full of merry-makers from the Hot Springs. The lobbies of the hotels are thronged with people and in each of them is a big cabinet full of specimens of gold and silver ores from the neighboring mines . . . Helena is a rich, prosperous, growing place, with solid, well-established business relations and an active, intelligent population drawn from all part of the world, eager to make money and free to spend it.

The decade between 1883 and 1893 was that of peak production for the rich silver-lead mines of the area, and as mining continued to develop so did Helena. When the Helena and Livingston Smelting & Reduction Company built a lead smelter at East Helena in 1888 and commenced to treat ore from all sections of the Territory, its operation further boosted the city's economic status.

CANNON HOUSE, HELENA

Helena already had electric lights, the first city in the territory to be so illuminated. When the Brush Electric Light & Power Company installed them, late in August of 1882

Miss Stella Knight, the little daughter of Mayor Knight, president of the company, had the honor of setting free, by the delicate touch of her little hand upon the lever of the dynamo machine, the mighty electric current which in a moment flashed along the wire and blazed forth in brilliant light from every lamp upon the uptown current.

Helena Herald, Aug. 28, 1882

One day in 1951, after I had studied many illustrated pamphlets which showed the city's larger buildings and had read something of their history, Mrs. Anne McDonnell, who was then the librarian of the State Historical Society, said to me "You've read enough for a while. How much of the city have you really seen and how many of its buildings that date from the peak years of the mining era have you found? They were built in the eighties and nineties and the majority are made of stone. A good number of the business blocks on Main Street and Broadway belong to that period. You've probably seen the residences on the East side of the city, but you may have missed the West side. Why not take this afternoon off and drive all over the city?"

What an afternoon that turned out to be! Beginning at Sixth Street, I walked slowly along Main to State Street, studying each building and trying to date it by its architecture. On Broadway, I noticed buildings I had overlooked on a previous tour of that street. West of Main Street I discovered Park Avenue and beyond it, a whole area of fine residences, set along tree-bordered streets.

The architect, Henry Hobson Richardson, never visited Helena to my knowledge, but his style, as reflected in the work of his followers, is evident in most of the larger commercial buildings and residences. These massive structures, often trimmed with stone of contrasting color, have round-arched windows and entrances. One of the first that I noticed was the Novelty Building on Main Street, with its twin bay windows, balconies, and stone cupolas. Even stranger was the three-story Atlas Block, built in 1889 by Francis D. Jones. A trip east took Mr. Jones from the city while the building was under construction, but since he left detailed plans with a stone mason he had no misgivings as to how it would turn out. Ornamentation on the facade called for a figure of Aetna. When Jones returned, he found that a statue of Atlas, not Aetna, supported the central ornamental pilaster. He insisted that the carving be changed and that the word "Atlas" be cut in stone underneath the base of the flagstaff that surmounts the cornice. This pole itself is unique, for descending the staff toward a stone bowl is a salamander, and supporting the bowl on either side are winged griffins.

The old high school on Ewing Street opposite St. Helena's Cathedral, the already mentioned courthouse and jail, the old Masonic Temple on Broadway at Jackson are all built of rusticated stone and some, like the Homer Block behind the postoffice on Park Avenue at Clark Street, are trimmed with slabs of contrasting color. Stone for many of the large buildings came from granite and limestone quarries located but a short distance from the city. Pine lumber was cut in nearby forests and planed in local mills. Cedar, hardwood, and redwood were brought in by rail from both East and West coasts. Brick, from which many of Helena's residences were constructed, was a local product, much of it made in Kessler's yard from clay deposits found within three miles of the city. The iron in the clay produced hard, durable bricks of a bright cherry red, "when properly burned."

The older houses of wood or brick on the east side of the gulch that line the shaded streets from St. Helena's Cathedral to the courthouse, as well as those found west of Benton Avenue on the opposite side of the gulch, are often adorned with cupolas, broad piazzas, bay windows, and round towers with curved plate glass windowpanes. Many have mansard roofs, like the Holter home on South Rodney Street, and others, like the Chessman Apartments and the Porter Flats, look as dignified and substantial as the day they were built. One of the oldest houses is a gracious Gothic home, the Cannon residence, which dates from the 1870's and stands on a terraced lawn at the corner of Broadway and Warren Streets.

The west side of the city contains even larger and more pretentious mansions than those on the east side. A few of these homes, complete with stable and conservatory, fill a city block and are surrounded with gardens and fenced with ornamental retaining walls. They are architectural triumphs of their day and represent the diversity of styles that flourished toward the end of the century. Some are English half-timber and stucco; others are brick, and the rest are massive stone.

One of the most impressive granite mansions belonged to the Honorable T. C. Power, one of Helena's fifty millionaires, who amassed a fortune through establishing the largest mercantile business in the state. Power, who came to the territory as a pioneer, started in business by running a steamboat line on the Missouri and handling merchandise and supplies for the mining camps. His store in Fort Benton was the first of many which eventually served all the largest cities in the state. His palatial Helena home is now the residence of the bishop of the Roman Catholic church of Helena. A much simpler residence is that which belonged to Thomas Cruse, another millionaire, whose fortune was made from the Drumlummon mine in Marysville. Built of brick, and surrounded by an iron fence, the house stands on the corner of Benton Avenue and Lawrence Street.

During this prosperous period there was an orgy of display on the part of Helena's wealthy citizens. Men who had been prospectors and had made millions from their mines, built lavishly and lived extravagantly, perhaps to make up for many years of precarious existence.

Sure that the city's growth would continue indefinitely, they platted lots several miles out in the valley and even built a streetcar line to serve these "outskirts." While waiting for the city to catch up with its transportation system, they lived in pretentious mansions on the West Side and in the suburbs of Kenwood and Lennox, and rode about town, first in coaches driven by top-hatted and swallow-tailed coachmen, and later in electric coupes that moved at a dogtrot on the level and stalled on the hills. A small army of maids, butlers, and other servants waited on them, and served them foods and wines as different as possible from the sour-dough, beans and raw firewater of their prospecting days. The houses they built were ornate affairs in a variety of designs . . . with iron deer on the lawns and stone lions or other figures at the entrances. Some lawns were further adorned with fountains, lead statuary, granite mounting blocks, and carved stone hitching posts.

Montana, A State Guide Book, Federal Writers' Project of the Works Project Administration for the State of Montana

Some idea of life in the 1880's is also shown in the account of an elaborate gathering held at the home of John H. Ming:

The wealth, the beauty, the fashion of the capital were assembled there, with many other good and proper persons whose modest ambition led to less exalted pretensions. At the hour of nine o'clock the greater part of the 300 invited guests had arrived . . . and dancing after the superb music of Hewins' string band had already commenced. The Constitutional Convention adjourning at an early hour, permitted its members to swell the number of welcomed guests crowding to the hospitable home to participate in the grand reception.

Mrs. Ming, assisted by her sister, Miss Ida Cole, received the guests with charming grace and cordiality . . .

The furnishings of the delightful house were viewed and admired by scores of guests . . . The size and sweep of the spacious apartments; their fine appointments and costly belongings; the rich furniture, expensive paintings, engravings, and other adornment attracted general attention and elicited unlimited admiration . . .

Supper was served, commencing about eleven o'clock on the third floor. Here in a commodious apartment were tables spread for a hundred guests at a single sitting. The repast was elaborate and elegant. While a third of the guests were at table, the others held to the dancing floor and went on with their quadrilles and promenades.

Helena Weekly Herald, Feb. 7, 1884

Some three miles west of the city near Ten Mile Creek are hot springs which, until the mid-eighties, were protected only by a rustic shed. Late in July, 1888, Colonel C. A. Broadwater announced that he had bought land and water rights in the vicinity of the springs and that architects were already planning a large resort hotel to be built on the site. Ground was broken in August, and one year later the hotel and natatorium were ready for use. The hotel, which was three stories high, was built on the "cottage plan with broad verandas" and was furnished with "the most sumptuous private bath houses in the world — finer than Cæsar gave to Rome." The hotel alone cost between $60,000 and $75,000.

HOLTER HOUSE, 15 SOUTH RODNEY ST.

There is also a great pool made bright with gold fish. The Acquatic theater of Moorish design is 150 feet by 350 feet. The Swimming Pool is 100 feet by 300 feet.   *Souvenir Journal*, 1891

For this plunge and for an artificial lake and fountain, the Colonel piped water from the hot springs. By the time Broadwater built additional attractions which included "miles of macadamized road" leading to the resort, he had spent half a million dollars.

On the evening of August 26, 1889, the hotel was thrown open to the public and "about 400 citizens of Helena went out for dinner by motor car, while at least another 100 came in their own carriages." Talks by Mayor Fuller, Tom Carter, Colonel Sanders, and R. C. Walker were interspersed with music by the Capital City band. Colonel Broadwater was not present, for business had taken him to Anaconda, but in his absence, Mrs. Broadwater, Mrs. Chumasero and Miss Chumasero received the guests.

As long as the hotel and natatorium flourished, an electric trolley line connected them with the city.

The passenger that in the evening lands in Helena, and is quickly transported to the neighborhood of the Hot Springs, some three miles distant, beholds a mirage that does not pass away . . . Suddenly after the darkness blaze twenty acres of electric lights, a fountain playing at his feet, grand castles stand out under the strange light, stained glass windows reflect back the sheen and he rubs his eyes and wonders if all is not enchantment.

Helena Journal, Souvenir of Montana*
July, 1891*

The motorist driving Highway No. 10N west from Helena sees none of this illusion as he passes the old hotel. For years it has been empty and neglected, with dust-smeared windows and weed-choked grounds. Even the steepled tower over the main entrance has disappeared. The Moorish Natatorium has been razed, leaving only an excavation where the plunge stood and an artificial cliff of rocks at one end.

Many of the patrons of the Broadwater Hotel were also members of the Montana Club whose six-story building stands on the discovery site in Last Chance. A bronze plaque on the Fuller Avenue side of the building marks the event and reads:

Discovery of Gold
In Last Chance Gulch
On this placer mining claim gold
was discovered on July 14, 1864
by John Cowan and John Crab of
Georgia, Bob Stanley of London,
England, and D. J. Miller of California, known as "The Georgians",
who were returning from an unsuccessful prospecting expedition
to the Kootenai country. This discovery was called Last Chance
Gulch until Ocober 30, 1864,
when it was named Helena.
This memorial of the Achievement of These Pioneers
Is Enacted by the Historical Society of Montana and
the Society of Montana Pioneers
"Si Monumentum Requiris Circumspice"

The location was established as accurately as possible by T. C. Power, Mrs. C. B. Nolan, John Shober, and Maurice S. Weiss, who reported that it was difficult to determine the exact site, since Main Street was "a little east of the thread of the gulch" and that the latter had been filled in "from twenty to thirty feet from its original bed, and the hills to the east and west cut down to the present street grades."

The Montana Club, the successor of the Rocky Mountain Club which had functioned for some years, was organized in 1885 by a group of wealthy cattlemen and miners, with a membership of 130. Its first meeting place was the Parchen Block; its second, the top floor of the Gold Block, which it occupied until July 1892. From the first it had exchange privileges with the Union, Harvard, and Lotus Clubs in the East. On its guest list are the names of Mark Twain, Theodore Roosevelt, Prince Albert of Belgium, and other notables.

During its first seven years the membership grew so rapidly that larger quarters became obligatory. The property at Sixth and Fuller Avenues was obtained in 1890 and a five-story brick and granite building was erected and made ready for occupancy in 1893. On April 27, 1903, fire destroyed both building and contents, but before the smoking debris was cold, the Board of Directors met and leased the residence of the late Samuel Word on Madison Avenue as a temporary meeting place. Within a week the members voted unanimously to rebuild on the original site and engaged Cass Gilbert, noted eastern architect and designer of New York's Woolworth Building, to draw up plans for the new structure. The Club, which resembles an Italian Renaissance palace, is made of glazed brick and native granite. The basement contains a rathskeller, the second floor a bar and ballroom, the next three floors living quarters for members, and the top floor the dining room. On June 24, 1905, the club moved into its present home.

During the first quarter of the twentieth century, despite its fine building, the club failed to flourish. Members moved away and the automobile made distant places so much more accessible for both business meetings and recreation that the club was used less than in former years. During the 1930's, the board of directors, with the approval of the members, made drastic changes in certain of the organization's policies. For the first time women were allowed to use the building. Previously, they were permitted only to inspect the club rooms during morning hours, while escorted by a member. The new ruling "marked the end of an era but also the revitalization of the club." By 1950, the Montana Club listed 900 resident, 400 non-resident, and 150 associate members.

In 1954 — its sixtieth anniversary — the club bought Green Meadow Farm, west of the city, and within four months converted it into a country club and golf course. Since then, the Montana Club and Green Meadow Country Club have been affiliated.

An earlier sixtieth anniversary, that of the discovery of gold in the gulch, had been celebrated on July 14, 1924, with a dinner honoring Helena's pioneers. Norman B. Holter presided and John H. Shober, the only living person who had attended the gulch meeting in October, 1864, was also present. Printed

CORNER,
RODNEY ST.
AND BROADWAY

THOMAS CRUSE
MANSION,
BENTON AVE.
AND LAWRENCE ST.

418 LAWRENCE ST.

28 SOUTH RODNEY ST.

on the back of the program for the evening were the words:

From these gulches alone was taken twice as much as the United States paid Napoleon for the entire Louisiana purchase.

During the weeks that I spent in the State Historical Society's library studying Helena's past, one thing perplexed me. Nearly all of the photographs of the city's buildings showed ornate decoration that was no longer a part of their facades. What had happened? And why were so many gravestones toppled from their pedestals and still lying awry in the cemeteries? A description of Helena's worst earthquake, written in 1936 by C. R. Anderson and M. P. Martinson, provided the answer. The towers, cupolas, chimneys, and cornices that I missed had either crashed to the street during the upheaval or had been loosened and cracked and were removed for safety. The grave markers had been dashed to the ground during the 1935 quake.

Not that this earthquake was Helena's first. On December 10, 1872, a shock was sufficiently heavy to "startle people in their houses and cause them to seek safety in the streets" and again on July 5, 1879, the *Herald* reported

Those who were still celebrating this morning, and those who were up for the early worm, felt the distinct shock of a lively earthquake at six o'clock. It was perceptible on the hill and the dwellers on the upper end of Rodney St. heard and saw the dance of pitchers and wash bowls on marble stands.

The series of earthquakes in 1935, however, were by far the most disastrous.

The first tremor occurred on October 3 and was followed by a more violent one a week later, and fifty-seven additional vibrations within the next few days. Then, on the evening of October 18, shortly after eight o'clock, a "sudden and prolonged trembling . . . came like an explosion, continued for a few minutes and went rumbling away." At 9:47 a severe quake struck suddenly. City lights went out, and the only illumination was from car headlights and flashlights. The tremors continued for a while, and then the lights came on again and the swinging ceased. In the morning the damage could be seen. The west end of town lost only a few chimneys; a falling wall on South Main Street killed a Negro; some coping stones were loosened, and some ornamental marble trim on St. Helena's Cathedral fell, but all of the city's spires and towers were intact, including the minaret on the Shrine Temple. The State Arsenal on Helena Avenue lost a section of wall; the Capitol suffered only minor cracks. Hardest hit was the newly completed high school, which showed bad cracks and a large hole in one wall.

For the next few days everyone was jittery. When a week went by and nothing happened, repairs began. A few minor tremors were felt on October 29 and 30 but so slight as to be disregarded. On October 31, just before noon, a third temblor "rocked the city and countryside." Beginning with a trembling, accompanied by a roar, the motion increased until whole buildings shook and walls, loosened by the first quake, toppled to the ground. Terrified people awaited the end of the shock, but instead of subsiding, it increased in violence. After twenty seconds, the "shaking ceased and the rumbling died away." Although the duration of this earthquake was shorter than the earlier one, the havoc resulting from it was much greater.

Two men who were repairing a chimney at Kessler's Brewery, which had been damaged by the first upheaval, were killed when the shock jolted them off the stack and dashed them to the ground. As building after building was inspected, weakened portions were removed. The courthouse and the old high school, opposite the Catholic cathedral, were shorn of their towers, and the castellated coping on the jail disappeared, to mention but three changes. Until the new high school was again ready for occupancy, the Helena Board of Education gladly accepted the offer of the Northern Pacific and Great Northern railroads' loan of eighteen coaches for use as classrooms.

I was sorry when my stay in Helena was over, for not only is the city a fascinating one, but also the library in the Veterans' and Pioneers' Memorial Museum contains one of the best research collections in the country, and its quarters are remarkably comfortable. To rest my eyes from hours of reading faded, fine type in old papers, I had only to look out the windows to the Bear's Tooth in the north or to the Belt Range beyond the Missouri River. At regular intervals the "Last Chancer" stopped in front of the building, and I liked to watch the loads of tourists alight from the tiny, gasoline-powered "train" which trundled them around the city streets from one landmark to another. From another window I could see one of the museum's newer possessions — a 66-foot long keel boat such as was used on the Missouri during fur trading days. It was built for the movie *The Big Sky*, which was adapted from the book of the same name by Montana's author, A. B. Guthrie, Jr. The boat, named the *Mandan*, was given to the state of Montana by the film company after the completion of the picture. If I needed a longer break, I could slip downstairs to the galleries of the museum to see the natural history exhibits, the displays of Montana's industries, and the hall devoted to the work of the state's cowboy artist, Charles M. Russell.

On my last day in Helena I drove about the city for a final look at its landmarks. A panoramic view from a hill on the south side, high above Last Chance, revealed Main Street, following the crooked channel of the gulch and curving as it stretched north to be lost in the Prickly Pear Valley. North of the business section the Moorish minaret of the Shrine Temple stood like a gleaming white lead pencil above all other buildings. This ornate lodge hall on Neil Avenue, built in 1920 for the Shriners, is the present Civic Center. On the hill east of the gulch, the spires of St. Helena's cathedral rose above the trees that hid the residences in that portion of the city. Farther east, I could see the Capitol, surrounded with state office buildings. Below me was the old part of Helena — State, Cutler, Pine and Wood Streets, whose brick homes and stone warehouses are crowded between vacant stores, and whose frame houses perch one below the other, on a series of terraces all the way down to the gulch. At the foot of Fire Tower Hill is the Castle, a stone mansion with bay window and cupola. Governor Toole's modest home still stands on State Street. Davis Street runs south from State for several blocks, until it merges with the road up Dry Gulch. Somewhere among the old houses that cover the rounded hilltop at the mouth of that gulch stood the Hangman's Tree.

Across Last Chance to the west is Reeder's Alley, a narrow, winding street little more than a block long, lined with small one-story brick and frame dwellings. Named for Louie Reeder, a Quaker and a bacheor who came to Helena in 1867, the upper exit of the alley joins the end of the old Benton stage road which followed the western rim of the gulch. Reeder, who was a stonemason, did some of the work on the courthouse. When he died in 1884, as the result of a fall from a scaffold, he owned valuable property in the city and was said to be worth $25,000 to $30,000.

LIME KILN, GRIZZLY GULCH

Mt. Helena forms the western boundary of the older portion of the city, and is girdled with the LeGrand Cannon Boulevard, a drive built by Charles W. Cannon as a memorial to his son. Cannon agreed to construct it around the base of the mountain within the city, if the county would build the section from the city limits to the Broadwater.

Just north of the city dredge dumps are visible from the Great Falls highway, or from the Municipal golf links. These date from the 1930's and 1940's when Porter Brothers built a gold dredge with a capacity of 5,000 cubic yards a day and began working the lower end of Last Chance Gulch from the Great Northern railroad tracks for a considerable distance out into the Prickly Pear Valley. The company was enthusiastic over its project, and tried to obtain more land so as to take the dredge right up Main Street, but the idea received no encouragement from the city officials.

That last evening we had dinner with Anne McDonnell, Bernice Boone, Virginia Walton, and Susan Eaker, the Helena friends who had opened so many doors for me in my fevered search for the state's mining history. Just before dark we drove out to see the pottery works at the Archie Bray Foundation. Here in the old Kessler brickyard is a modern plant where fine ceramics are being made by Helena's gifted potters.

"There's one more thing you must do before you leave this area," my friends told me on the way back to town. "Drive out West Main Street past the Capital Brewery to where the canyon forks and make the loop up Oro Fino Gulch to Unionville and back down Grizzly. These two canyons were developed simultaneously with Last Chance, and the Whitlatch-Union mine at the head of the gulches was the biggest lode mine around here in the sixties."

UNIONVILLE

Next morning we started for Unionville. Last Chance Gulch narrows south of the city, and its limestone cliffs rise abruptly behind the single row of houses that line both sides of the roadway. The forks of the gulch are only a short distance from town, and turning to the left, we started up Oro Fino. Except for a kiln or two, a few houses, and some debris left from mining, the gulch is deserted until the outskirts of Unionville are reached.

Helena's first gold came from the placer mines of Last Chance Gulch, but the gold that sustained it after the placers were worked out came from the lode mines that were found in the hills on three sides of the city. The Whitlatch-Union, the oldest quartz discovery in the region, lay on the summit of a low divide between Oro Fino and Grizzly Gulches, four miles south of Helena. It was located in September, 1864, by James W. Whitlatch and recorded February 28, 1865. The vein, which ran at right angles to the placer gulches, averaged $20.00 to $25.00 a ton.

Whitlatch had made and lost fortunes through mining in Colorado and Nevada before wandering across Idaho to the placer fields of Montana. The placers of Last Chance paid so well that Whitlatch decided to stay in the area and to search for the mother lode or vein from which the decomposed gold came. For weeks he wandered up and down the gulches, returning empty-handed to his cabin at night, but starting out again each morning for another day's digging. His companions were not so optimistic as he and made him agree to quit if, by the close of a certain day, he had not found the lode. The day arrived and was nearly gone before he uncovered a fragment of quartz which, when broken open, contained free gold. Further digging uncovered the gold-bearing ledge for which he had been searching.

The lode was developed by several companies, each of which owned but a limited amount of ground.

Roosevelt
Mr. James W. Whitlatch and owners of the "Union," "Owyhee" and "D. R. Biggars" lodes with the other settlers at the head of Oro Fino gulch, near Helena, have given the name of Roosevelt to their settlement, which promises to be a place of importance in the Territory. The name is given in compliment to

Theodore and James A. Roosevelt, Esq. of New York City.
Montana Post, Oct. 28, 1865

The frame house which Whitlatch built in 1865 housed mine superintendents for many years and is still standing in a grove of aspen trees. It is easily identified by its porch, carved barge boards, and picket fence.

In 1866, the Whitlatch-Union and Turnley stamp mills were erected to crush ore, and as the number of men employed by the several companies increased, a settlement grew up around the mills. The name Roosevelt, previously proposed, seems to have been forgotten, for the *Post* describes the Whitlatch mine and adds that close to the Whitlatch-Sensendorfer mill in Oro Fino Gulch

a village of twenty-six whitewashed houses has sprung up, inhabited principally by employees of the Company . . . in neat and tidy surroundings. A billiard saloon is in construction. The only thing wanting is a name for the place — but this suggests itself and Unionville, should it be. Seventy-five pairs of hands are now busily engaged in finishing the mill and taking out ore.

Fleetwing
Montana Post, Aug. 10, 1867

In 1867 James Whitlatch disposed of his holdings in the mine, from which $3,663,000 had already been taken, to

J. H. Hubbell of the North West Fur Co., Gen. Sol Meredith, Surveyor General of Montana, and Pinney & Trumbull, bankers of Helena, for the sum of $250,000 . . . the sum is small, the sale can only be accounted for on charitable grounds, that the owner wished to withdraw himself from the excitement and turmoil incident to a miner's life and retire on a handsome competence.
Montana Post, Sept. 21, 1867

This last statement was not true, for upon selling the Whitlatch-Union, he plunged into other mining ventures in which he was successful. As late as 1887 he was spoken of as "Col. Whitlatch, The Quartz King" and the "Luckiest Man in America." Three years later he committed suicide in a San Francisco hotel. His death was due to illness and financial reverses.

The new owners of the Whitlatch properties and the companies which were already operating portions of the vein, continued the successful development of their mines. The IXL, one of the oldest and most successful mines at Unionville, with seventy men on its payroll, continued to run its 24-stamp mill under the expert direction of Superintendent J. C. Ricker.

WHITLATCH MILL, UNIONVILLE

STAMPMILL, UNIONVILLE

By 1870 Charles Hendrie's twenty-stamp quartz mill was also pounding away on the district's ore. The mill was begun in the summer and completed in September, "showing the go-ahead-a-tiveness of those concerned in this new enterprise."

Chas. Hendrie invested his capital without stint and has contributed more to the development of our great mineral resources than any man in the Territory — $150,000 at least.
Helena Daily Herald, Jan. 26, 1870

The Whitlatch-Union remained the most productive property in the district and was worked for a greater number of years than others by a succession of owners and lessees. Unfortunately, sometime in the early 1880's, miners lost the vein when they ran into a fault or slip and could not relocate the lead on its dip. When all attempts to rediscover it failed, the Company operating it allowed the mine slowly to fill with water.

In 1957, I looked up Mark Sherman, caretaker for the Whitlatch-Union property, who lives in one of the town's older cabins with his two dogs, and occupies himself with his garden and greenhouse. Mr. Sherman, who has spent many years in Unionville, showed me old photos of the camp taken in 1904, when it contained more buildings than now, and when its mills were in good condition. We walked together to a vantage point from which to look over the town, and he pointed out many buildings which still belong to the Whitlatch property — a stone warehouse, a powder house, the assay office, the superintendent's office and home, and the ruined stamp mill on the west side of the road. Farther down the hill on the east side of the highway are the remains of the two cyanide plants which belonged to the company. The frame schoolhouse on the hill is also old, but the addition to it is more recent.

"The discovery of the Whitlatch lode in 1864 started men looking for quartz leads all over Montana," Mr. Sherman told me. "Besides Whitlatch's frame house down the road, the mine boardinghouse that he built was about the first place built here. It burned in 1876. There were three hundred people living in Unionville in 1879, I'm told, and there was quite a little going on in 1904, the year those photographs were taken. One of them shows the stamp mill and the cyanide plants with their tanks and settling pond. Only lessees work the mines nowadays. This Whitlatch-Union lode is the biggest thing in the district.

The vein can be traced for five miles on the surface, and even though there's no work going on now, they've taken out between five and six million in gold from it."

PARK CITY

Above Unionville the road winds through woods and bears west toward the head of Grizzly Gulch. I was glad it was summer, for I remembered reading in an early copy of the *Helena Herald*, "At the head of Grizzly Gulch, yesterday morning, we are informed that the thermometer stood at thirty-eight degrees below zero. Tolerably cool that." (Jan. 18, 1870). Before we had driven far, I began to look for the site of the IXL mill, said to have been half-a-mile west of Unionville in Grizzly Gulch, but I could not locate it.

I knew, however, that west of the Union mine was the "Owyhee or Whitlatch and Parkinson Mining Company's ground," and that still farther west and across Grizzly Gulch opposite the IXL had been the "new" Whitlatch mill, which handled ore from the Park lead. This lode, one-half miles west of the mill, Whitlatch had owned and worked with a crew of seventy-five men. The quartz averaged $20.00 a ton, but the ore was different from that of the Union, for it contained mineral "charged with copper pyrites." From the Park Lode, the best property in that vicinity, an estimated $1,500,000 was taken.

The first stamp mill to operate in the district was built in Grizzly Park in 1865 by Lilbourn G. Turnley. Some idea of the difficulties attending the transportation of machinery into the Territory is given in a manuscript written by Turnley and preserved in the library of the State Historical Society in Helena:

I bought a ten-stamp quartz mill, made by Dowdal & Co., of St. Louis, Mo., and a sixteen-H.P. Boiler, engine etc. . . . in the summer of 1864, with the view of their being erected and operated on a group of gold bearing quartz lodes . . . in Colorado. It was shipped from St. Louis for St. Joseph, Mo., via the Hanibal & St. Joseph railroad from which place it was to be hauled across the plains to its destination. But, in transit, the railroad train bearing it was burned by the notorious "Bill Anderson's Guerrillas," where it remained until the following spring (1865) when the wreck was collected and shipped to St. Joseph, the damaged parts repaired, and then shipped by steamboat for Fort Benton, Montana Terr.

The steamer was so delayed by a broken shaft, Indian trouble, low water, etc., that it got only to Cow Island, where it dumped its entire load out on the prairie. Late in the fall, Richardson & Walters' ox-train hauled it to the site already prepared for it on Grizzly Gulch in Grizzly Park . . . where it was erected with all possible dispatch.

It started crushing ore . . . on the 14th day of December, 1865, under the management of Richard Fisher, to whom I had conditionally sold it.

The first "clean-up" was made the following Christmas eve, an 8½ days' run, which at $18.00 per oz. which was then the selling value of retorted gold, was worth nine thousand three hundred and twelve dollars and sixty cents ($9,312.60).

The mill then ran on ore from the Park Lode, until the fall of 1866, when the undersigned having resumed control, contracted with James W. Whitlatch, to haul and crush one thousand tons of ore, from the "Whitlatch Union" mine, at $18.00 (gold) per ton. After which, additional contracts were made at fifteen dollars ($15.00) per ton until a total of twenty-seven hundred and fifty tons was crushed and amalgamated from the Whitlatch Lode, which yielded an average of $63.90 per ton, gold.

This was the first ore milled from that mine. There were other mills in the territory before the Turnley mill commenced crushing, but none had been started up, so, that little Ten-Stamp Park mill is entitled to the honor, if there is any, of being the first steam mill to crush quartz in the Montana Territory.

The boiler in this mill was first used in the St. Louis Republican printing office. I believe the first printing office so equipped in that city.

It cost for freight from St. Louis, Mo. to Cow Island, ten cents per pound in currency . . . and thence to Grizzly Park seven cents per pound in "dust," equivalent at that time to 8¾ cents in currency, making the cost for freight 18¾ cents per pound.

It did not take us long to reach the head of Grizzly Gulch where the highway left the timber and emerged onto a meadow. So as not to miss out destination, I flagged down an approaching car to ask the driver how to reach Park City.

"There's nothing there, woman," he replied, as children's heads popped out of every window to look at the strangers. "I've got the only place that's still standing. Everything else has been carted off. What are you looking for? Just riding around to see things? Turn left at the fork ahead. That's the road to where Park City was and to Nelson Gulch, too, but there is nothing to see," and he drove on.

We took the lefthand fork and drove across a meadow to a gate which led only to a ranch. Retracing our way to the main road, we noticed a few foundations and some placer debris but nothing else; yet in 1879 Park City had a population of 300.

With the exception of a few lodes that were developed, it was the placer ground in this area from which thousands of dollars were cleaned up daily during the sixties. At that time, Grizzly Park was full of big trees. To-day, except for second growth spruce, it is a sandy waste filled with debris left from sluicing operations. In addition to Park City, two other camps once occupied the gulch — Dry Gas and Springtown. Both Park City and Dry Gas have disappeared completely.

Notwithstanding the immense amount of gold that has been extracted from the rich gravel streak in Grizzly Gulch, there is no doubt that the half is not yet reached. For the greater portion of the distance down from where once stood the euphoniously denominated village of Dry Gas the bed-rock was never touched, while on No. 5 below Wright's district, which was originally worked by Doctors Steele and Six, and which at a depth of twenty-five feet froze so hard in the drifts last winter that it did not thaw out all last summer, the parties who now hold it have been able to make $6 a day to the hand working frozen ground beneath what had been originally worked to as the bed-rock, and there has been no effort made as yet to see how deep this character of dirt extends. In the flat above, what is known as "Pilgrim's Bar," just above Springtown, they are now running a drain ditch in the deep channel of the gulch . . . and are working through gravel that pays from $1.00 to $2.50 to the pan.
                    Rocky Mountain Gazette, Feb. 23, 1867

Springtown is mentioned as early as 1867 and was in the vicinity of Spring Hill mine. This important property, originally located in 1868, lay on the east side of Grizzly Gulch on the opposite side of the divide from the Whitlatch-Union, and three miles above the junction of Grizzly and Oro Fino Gulches. When fully developed, it covered 400 acres in what was known as the Owyhee Park district. Exploration of the ground revealed a dike more than a mile long which contained gold ore on which twenty-four patented claims were staked. These, when combined, comprised the Spring Hill mine.

This gold property was worked during the 1880's largely for pyrrhotite, which averaged only $5.34 a ton in gold, but contained iron which was needed for flux at the smelters. Between 1885 and 1890, 23,000 tons of this ore is said to have been sent to the smelter at Wickes. Around 1900 the property was worked for a year or two and produced a limited tonnage of low-grade ore that was treated at the Whitlatch mill, but the results proved disappointing and the property was abandoned. For a time the mine was extensively developed by W. C. Conrad, a stockman, banker, and capitalist, or by lessees under contract. During these intermittent spurts of activity, large amounts of low-grade ore were blocked out, and some new mineral bodies uncovered.

The year 1928 marks the beginning of full scale production. By then the mine had been bought by the Montana-Idaho Mines Corporation of Idaho. This investment proved a bonanza to the new owners, who for years·had suffered from a series of unsuccessful ventures. Using what little stock was left in the treasury, the company bought two mines near Winston, Montana — the East Pacific in 1926, and the Kleinschmidt in 1927, and began operations at once.

At the same time, the company took a lease and bond on the Spring Hill mine, built a cyanide mill, and were soon processing 100 to 150 tons of crude ore a day. The cyanide process, however, was not successful, so, early in 1929, the mill was rebuilt as a flotation plant, which was so efficient that before long a steady tonnage of concentrates was being shipped to the smelter at East Helena. The gold content of the ore processed during this period ranged from $3.00 to $20.00 a ton, with an average of $6.00 to $7.00.

The Montana Consolidated Mines Corporation succeeded the Montana-Idaho Corporation in September, 1929. Improvements made by the new organization included a large ball mill, blacksmith shop, warehouse, timber shed and ore bin, a new road up to the mill, a long trestle and a snowshed from the mine portal to the crushing plant. Work was carried on by a force of fifty men through a large open pit and three adit tunnels. By 1930, the Spring Hill property was the foremost gold mine in the state, "producing approximately 38,000 ounces of metal."

Early in 1931, fire destroyed the milling plant, which caused a shut down for two years. In 1934, the flotation plant was reconstructed, only to shut down three months later. During this short period of operation, concentrates containing over 1,000 ounces of gold were shipped to the East Helena plant and netted returns of $31,202.59. The *Mining Review of the Greater Helena Region* (July, 1935) contains a photograph of the Spring Hill property with its dozen or more buildings, and a long belt conveyor to carry the ore from the crushing plant on one side of the gulch to the mill on the other side. During the latter part of the 1930's, 300 tons a day of gold ore carrying some silver, lead, and copper were milled in the flotation plant, and flotation concentrates were cyanided in the 25-ton treatment plant. The total production from 1928 to 1940, when the company went into receivership, is estimated at two millions.

The Spring Hill mine to the east of the road, and the remains of its big plant on the west side of the gulch, are easily spotted. The superintendent's house is high up on the east side of the gulch. Close to the streambed, which is almost overgrown by bushes and underbrush, are a loading station, stone foundations, and a few sheds. In 1928, about twenty mines were operating in the vicinity of the Spring Hill lode. "Mining has been carried on intermittently in this area since 1900," one mining man told me. "Some new ore bodies have been opened up, but the main operation has been hauling off old slag dumps for resmelting and reworking piles of tailings from several idle properties."

As we neared the mouth of Grizzly Gulch on our return to Helena, we passed two large stone furnaces which were probably kilns. Back at the edge of the city, the extension of West Main Street contains many old houses, including the Pioneer Cabin, built in 1865 and preserved as a historic landmark. It is almost completely hidden by big trees that are said to have been brought across the prairies by a bride when they were saplings and planted in her front yard. When we passed the Capital Brewery, the first building that had excited my curiosity, I felt that the cycle was complete and I could now leave Helena and explore other mining camps of this big state. Having seen the gulches from which the city's wealth originated, I would next visit the camps northwest of the Capital City.

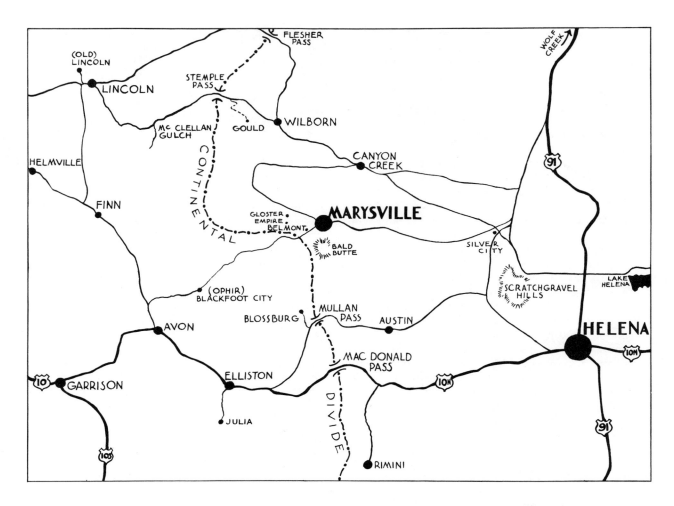

CHAPTER 6

From SCRATCH GRAVEL to RIMINI

Helena is the hub of a mining district from which radiate roads to its many camps — some large and some small — that surround it on all sides. To the north of the city are diggings which antedate Last Chance by a few months, and in the hills are ghost towns and live towns, all of which began as placer camps. Only when the gravels ceased to yield gold did the settlements crumble away or become centers for other industries such as ranching, timbering, and agriculture.

SCRATCH GRAVEL HILLS

Three miles north and west of Helena are the Scratch Gravel Hills, pitted with prospect holes and tunnel openings, and rising 1,500 feet above Prickly Pear Valley. This area is nearly two miles square and extends from the northern outskirts of Helena to the Iowa and Silver Creek mining districts and on the west to Seven-Mile Creek. In Iowa Gulch, in the northern part of these hills, placer gold was discovered shortly before any was uncovered in Last Chance Gulch, but the gravel deposits were scattered over a wide area and brought only moderate returns. Years after the gold was washed away, nuggets could be found in Butcher Knife Gulch after a heavy downpour. In the southern portion of the hills, the gold lay in a sheet of gravel close to the surface of the ground and was so easily removed that after E. R. Tandy ploughed up several acres of land so as to have it ready for spring planting, and found a gold nugget in the soil that "weighed 27 ounces," others ploughed the ground and then raked the surface to find the nuggets which it contained — hence the name Scratch Gravel.

Lode mining, which began in the 1870's, followed placer activity and paid well. The Lexington, the first paying quartz mine in the district, shipped silver-lead ore profitably to Swansea, Wales, for smelting. The Franklin, worked by Thomas Cruse until his death, yielded $500,000 within a four year period. Scratch Gravel Gold Mines was another strong producer. After World War I, however, increased labor costs forced both the Franklin and Scratch Gravel Gold Mines to close down.

Even before I reached Montana I had heard about these mines from Mr. Dee Scott of Helena, who on more than one occasion leased properties in the Hills. Scratch Gravel Gold was a stock company which owned a good piece of earth adjoining the Franklin in which lay a blanket of ore, not far from the surface. In time, all but two of its directors died. Scott tried to lease the land, but the remaining two officers refused to consider any deal. Then one of them died. Scott tried again but was refused by the sole survivor, only to find that a Swede named Victor Hegman had obtained a lease. Hegman with one helper cleaned up, according to Scott, $47,000 in seventeen months. At another mine Scott had a contract to rework the dump for flux. The previous owner had already made $900,000 from shipments to the smelter. When Scott began to demolish the dump, he discovered that the valuable white quartz which contained arsenical iron mixed with gold lay only on the surface of the waste rock pile!

If one drives to Marysville, twenty-one miles northwest of Helena, the Scratch Gravel Hills will be on the left of the road.

SILVER CITY

One August morning in 1956, my husband and I left Helena and drove nearly ten miles north of the city on Highway No. 91, to a road which angled westerly toward the mountains. As we were about to leave Prickly Pear Valley and climb deeper into the hills, we noticed a crudely lettered board which read:

"Marysville, next road." In a short distance we came to the turnoff, but before starting the six-mile climb to the mining town, we looked to the north across the sagebrush to the site of Silver City.

When William Mayer (Mayger) discovered gold in 1862 in the bed of Silver Creek, a stream which rises in the vicinity of Marysville, he touched off a stampede which soon clogged the stream with placer claims for a distance of over four miles. When even richer bars were discovered in 1864, a lively camp, called Silver City, sprang up on the flat near the lower end of the diggings. By 1865, Silver City and Helena had become rivals, and both wanted the county seat. The dispute was settled only when Colonel W. F. Sanders of Last Chance rode horseback to Silver, stole the records, and galloped back to Helena, where he delivered the valuable books. Thereafter, Helena was the county seat, and Silver City remained little more than a supply point and stage station for the Marysville district.

Thomas Cruse was another who worked in the Silver Creek placer mines before he got restless and started looking for quartz in the hills at the head of the stream, in 1868. His creek diggings paid him well, sometimes as much as $100.00 a day, but he was not satisfied with panning gold. It was the lodes from which the colors came that drew him deeper into the mountains where he found his bonanza, in the Drumlummon mine.

The gold in Silver Creek was not so fine as that found in Last Chance and brought only $14.00 an ounce, yet, although it contained a considerable amount of silver, the gravels produced a total of $3,000,000. As soon as the placers began to play out, the men began to leave.

Today, the site of Silver City is part of a ranch and lies about half a mile from the highway. The old roadhouse with its wattled walls and the schoolhouse where twenty-five children studied are things of the past.

MARYSVILLE

The road to Marysville, which parallels Silver Creek for several miles, climbs past deserted mines, dumps, old dams, and settling ponds. Just before it swings into town, it passes below the Drumlummon property, the mine which made Marysville.

Thomas Cruse, whose name is inseparable

MARYSVILLE. *Reproduced courtesy of* THE BONANZA TRAIL, *Indiana University Press*

SALOONS, MARYSVILLE. *Reproduced courtesy of Senator and Mrs. Charles Bovey*

from the Drumlummon mine, came to Montant from California in 1868, a disappointed prospector, and drifted to Silver Creek. There he met William Brown, who had been stripping the gulch for gold since 1864, and who offered him a placer claim if he would stay and work it. This he did. Cruse was curious as to the source of a kind of quartz that often stuck to the gold in his pan, and, believing that the mother lode from which it came **must** be in the vicinity, he suggested that Brown join him in searching for it, but Brown was only interested in placers and refused the offer. Certain that he was on the right track, Cruse began prospecting on what was later known as Marysville Mountain and even started work on a tunnel. Only when he needed money for powder or grub did he work his placer claim. When he struck hard rock in his tunnel, he started a second adit in the hope that it would tap the vein he had uncovered in his prospect hole. In this he was successful and cut the vein below the discovery shaft.

Another version of the discovery of this famous lode describes how George Detweiler, William Mayger, and William Brown came to the gulch, some time before the discoveries in Last Chance, and Detweiler staked a claim and did some development work, but not enough to hold the property. He disregarded warnings from his friends that his claim might be jumped, and it was, by Cruse, who filed on it after the first of January, 1876. According to another account, Detweiler arranged for Cruse to do the necessary work on the claim while he went to the Centennial Exposition in Philadelphia. Cruse did nothing while he was gone, but after January 1st, when Detweiler had not returned and the title had legally lapsed, he filed on the claim and thereby obtained a valuable property.

Cruse named his mine the Drumlummon after the parish in Ireland where he was born. The district and the mining camp was called Marysville, in honor of Mrs. Mary Ralston, a pioneer of the vicinity. As soon as he uncovered high-grade ore in his workings, Cruse looked up Nate Vestal, the successful owner of the Snowdrift mine, and drove a bargain with him by which he obtained a five-stamp mill in Marysville in which to treat his ore. For six years he worked the mine with its shallow prospect holes, its tunnel only 200 feet long, its vein cut only to a depth of 140 feet, yet from the 6,000-7,000 tons of ore which were reduced in arrastres and the small stamp mill, he recovered $144,539 in bullion. In 1882, he sold it to an English syndicate for $1,500,000.

After Cruse sold the Drumlummon, his whole life changed. He married and lived in a fine house in Helena. His wife died and left him with a small daughter. He founded a savings bank in Helena and another in Marysville and became a small banker. When Montana's capitol building bonds went begging, he bought up the entire issue. Although he was illiterate and couldn't sign his name until his wife taught him how, he enjoyed attending board meetings and being driven to work behind fast horses with a coachman on the box. But his wealth only made his days empty, so he returned to his mine, to sit for hours at a time in front of a tunnel or near a shaft. Finally, he acquired some property on Bald Mountain and, by returning to the life that he knew, he recaptured some of his former contentment. He died in 1914 and is buried in Resurrection Cemetery in Helena. His red brick home on Benton Avenue is still occupied; while St. Helena's Roman Catholic cathedral, which dominates a hilltop in the heart of the city, is a lasting monument to his generosity. Yet, like all of us, he had his idiosyncracies.

In the years prior to his strike, he barely made a living. At one time his five pinto ponies were about to be seized for taxes. Cruse went to Sam Ashby, a Helena banker, and tried to borrow the necessary amout of money but was unsuccessful. He then went to a friend, an old prospector, and obtained $9.00 in gold dust with which to pay his tax. Shortly afterwards, the prospector died and was buried in Mt. Helena cemetery. Every afternoon during the summer, Cruse walked out to the plot and placed a flower on his friend's grave. Years later, when he had his own savings bank in Helena, Sam Ashby requested a loan. He was refused. When the citizens of Marysville were raising funds for a schoolhouse in the rapidly growing town, Cruse showed no interest in the undertaking. When he was asked to donate two lots for a community church, he grudgingly gave only one. Unaccountably, when the building was completed, it occupied both lots!

Raleigh Wilkinson in the *Roosevelt County Independent* (Nov. 12, 1921) tells how the Drumlummon mine came to the attention of the English company. Chadbourne & Richardson, the London firm for which Am Mallory was the Montana representative, was not interested in the silver mine he was attempting to sell them, but agreed to consider a gold mine if it was a sound investment and one which they could inspect. Mallory, at the suggestion of Wilkinson, visited Marysville, met Thomas Cruse, and after examining the Drumlummon, began an intensive correspondence with the London firm. He also interested several Americans, including Henry Bratnober, a mining expert, Hugh McQuade, and Sam Wood in the proposition. After many cablegrams, further investigation, and a final report by John Darlington, an English engineer, the mine was sold and became the Drumlummon Ltd. Mining Corporation.

Some time later, Bratnober learned that the property was not producing as expected and discovered the reason. The rich ore was being placed on the dump, and the low-grade ore run through the mill. He notified the owners and went to London to meet with the directors. They sent him back to Marysville with authority to manage both mine and mill. Under his administration the Drumlummon became the biggest producer in Montana, paying $15,000,000 in dividends to stockholders.

The English company found abundant ore reserves in the upper workings. Additional stamps were added to the mill and two amalgamating pans and a settler put in operation. By 1884, a 50-stamp mill was completed and Frue vanners were installed to extract sulphides. Two years later, a 60-stamp mill was built to handle an increased output of ore. During the peak of production, one ton of concentrates was procured from 135 tons of ore, and company profits ran between $40,000 and $50,000 per month.

Had every year's output equalled that of 1887, during which eight dividends amounting to nearly $920,000 were paid, the stockholders would have had no complaints, but the deeper the mine was driven, the poorer the quality of the ore, and as lower levels were developed, underground water was a major problem. By 1890, when a new portion of the property was opened up, a pumping plant became a necessity.

The stone pump station was built and is said to have resembled a Gothic chapel. A Cornish pump, costing $55,000, plus $25,000 more for transportation costs, was bought to replace the pumps then in use. A large chamber was excavated and timbered and made ready to receive it. With the pump came an ex-

SCHOOLHOUSE, MARYSVILLE

pert from London, to install it. Unfortunately, when he examined the deep workings, the flow of water in the lower levels, which drained downwards, was lower than usual. He reported an insufficient amount of water to even prime the pump and returned to London in disgust. While all this was going on, freight wagons were hauling the heavy pump up Silver Creek Canyon. Just below the town they broke down, the pump was abandoned, and left to rust away in the gulch. In 1895 a Riedler pump with a capacity of 400 gallons a minute was installed in No. 1 shaft and so greatly reduced draining costs that a second Riedler was installed at a later date.

The year 1892 was full of misfortunes. In May a fire in No. 1 shaft destroyed 800 feet of timbering. A flood, a cave-in and expensive litigation forced the company to reorganize as the Montana Mining Company, Ltd. After two years of operation, the vein was worked out.

In 1896, C. W. Merrill ran a series of tests which proved the advisability of working the tailings from the mills by cyanide treatment. A $66,000 cyanide plant was therefore built the following year with a capacity of 400 tons a day. Since the tailings were held behind five dams below the mine on Silver Creek for a distance of several miles, rails had to be laid to these settling ponds so that ore trains could haul the dirt to the plant. From this venture $1,500,00 was realized. Later on, the St. Louis Company worked the tailings a second time and recovered more gold.

When Cruse uncovered the Drumlummon lode in 1876, he assumed that it and another mineral outcrop 200 feet away were both on one vein and recorded his claim accordingly. As the Drumlummon mine was developed, it was soon evident that the second outcrop was on another property, and that any expansion of the Drumlummon in that direction would cross into adjoining territory. To avoid litigation over Apex rights, the Drumlummon company bought the adjoining claims on both sides of their land.

The St. Louis Mining Company, which also operated an adjoining property, discovered, in 1889, that the Drumlummon miners, in following a vein, had crossed onto St. Louis land and were taking out ore below their tunnels. St. Louis miners were also driving toward the Drumlummon, close enough for both crews to hear blasts set off by the other. A breakthrough was imminent. To prevent entrance into their mine, the Drumlummon men erected a bulkhead in their tunnel and placed in front of it stink pots which, when ignited, would smoke out the intruders. The fumes drove back the St. Louis men, but did not rout them, for the determined miners then bulkheaded *their* drift and drove another which broke into the Drumlummon workings on a different level. While this was going on, Drumlummon workers pulled or blasted out all stulls, except enough to hold up the ground. The remaining stulls were wired for simultaneous blasting. The explosion shook Marysville and caused a cave-in and slide of major proportions. These shenanigans precipitated a lawsuit which lasted twenty-one years. When the case was finally decided in favor of the St. Louis Company, the Drumlummon company, aware that they had already taken the best ore from their property, did not contest the decision. The St. Louis Company absorbed everything, but due to litigation, it was unable to do much with the property for some years.

Nate Vestal reached the district with $12,-000 of dust from Alder Gulch and began hunting for a quartz claim. Some say that he located the Penobscot in 1872, and others are equally sure that he did not discover it but bought it in the fall of 1876 from its original locators, J. E. Murphy, W. H. Murphy, Wm. Rader, and H. C. Nash, who took up their claims December 1, 1874. At first Vestal merely worked the ore already on the the dumps in a small stamp-mill and found that it paid well enough to warrant further development of the property. But, by August, 1877, when all the ore from the dumps had been run through the mill, Vestal and a man named Captain Sears negotiated a division of the property, Sears taking the Emma mine and arrastre and Vestal the Penobscot.

With limited finances, Vestal and a small force of men began taking out ore from Discovery and shaft No. 2, crushing it in an arrastre. During the season of 1878, Vestal found 160 tons of ore in the Snowdrift, a property he had already acquired and worked in a small way, believed to be the east extension of the Penobscot. This provided some cash, but not enough to buy a ten-horsepower steam engine. Through a friend, John Whitehead, who endorsed his note, he got the engine and hired men to cut and haul cordwood to feed it. He bought more equipment for the mine and ran up a $7,000 debt. Though he couldn't pay his men for several months, they stuck with him. With several months of wages owing them, they started to sink a third shaft. This time luck was with him, for at grassroots he uncovered a wide vein of good ore between well-defined granite walls. The ore grew richer with depth, until a 15-foot body of choice quartz was uncovered. Vestal now realized that he must begin to work the mine on a larger scale. Still without funds, he made a contract with a Mr. Courtwright of Helena, the owner of a five-stamp quartz mill which was idle, to crush 500 or more tons of ore. The mill was brought from Helena and set up at Silver City, and the high-grade Penobscot ore was hauled to it.

With both mill and arrastre running, the Penobscot began to show a profit at last. The first cleanup produced a gold bar worth $20,-000! On February 14, 1878, which was his birthday, Nathan Vestal went to Helena with sufficient gold bullion to cancel all his debts and leave him $13,000 in the clear. The next four cleanups were held back and then cast into one gold brick weighing 242 pounds and valued at $54,262.62 — one month's output. This famous Penobscot brick was exhibited in Helena in the window of L. H. Hershfield & Bros., bankers.

The following summer, after taking out more than $80,000 — some say $150,000 — he sold the mine to Wm. B. Frue (the inventor of the Frue Vanner) for $350,000 or $400,-000, and left Helena for the east, where he played the stock market and succeeded in spending $20,000 in three weeks. A whirl through Europe ate up the rest of his fortune and brought him back to New York broke. He would have not been able to return to Helena if friends had not sent him train fare. Shortly after his return, he went to work for $3.50 a day, in his own stamp-mill and then moved on to placer diggings near Jefferson City. He even joined the rush to Alaska. In 1919 he died in Oakland, California. Always generous and easy-going, he staked many prospectors and helped open properties that in time paid dividends. His money enabled Thomas Cruse to start production in the Drumlummon; his backing opened the Belmont and Whippoor-will mines at Empire. During the latter 1870's, when the Black Hills gold rush was draining men from the camps, Vestal kept on working the Penobscot and urged others to stay where they were and develop their properties in and around Marysville.

Under new management the Penobscot became one of the leading producers of the district, especially after a new 40-horsepower stamp-mill was erected at Belmont, near Marysville, to treat its ores. Mining and milling costs ran $10.00 a ton. For a time the daily output was several thousand dollars, but values decreased with depth, and the ore was described as "erratic and pockety." By January, 1880, the mine showed a deficit of $15,852. Not long afterwards it was closed down. In 1885 it was sold to John Longmaid who, surprisingly, took out $65,000. His son, the next owner, took out $215,000. Total production is estimated at $1,230,000.

Tucked away, behind the folds of hills, Marysville needed a railroad which would ship its ore and bring in supplies faster than crawling ox-teams and horse-drawn freight wagons could move. In 1887 two railroads started to race toward the camp. Both ran surveys and began grading operations between Helena and Marysville, which at that time was at its prime.

The Northern Pacific Railroad wound through the hills and kept above the gulches to swing into town across Sawmill Gulch on a long trestle. It won the race at the head of the canyon, which provides the only entry into the Marysville valley, and built its station in a convenient location. The Great Northern kept east of the Scratch Gravel Hills and ran a steep grade all the way up Silver Creek. It laid track to the head of the gulch, where it was stopped by the Northern Pacific, which refused to grant a right of way under its trestle. This kept the Great Northern outside the camp, and it was compelled to erect its station one-quarter of a mile below the town. After two years of daily train service the road quit, for passengers preferred the

road that took them into Marysville, besides the fact that it was safer, the extreme grades in Silver Creek Canyon having caused several wrecks. In 1925, the Railroad Commission authorized the Northern Pacific to tear up its tracks, and since then Marysville has been without rail connections, though it is the Great Northern grade that is the present automobile road into the town.

With the opening of the Drumlummon and other rich lodes, Marysville blossomed into a properous settlement with a population of 5,-000. In its heyday it supported four churches, of which two — the Catholic and the Methodist — are still standing, and two newspapers, one Republican and the other Democratic. When Annie Dillon, who ran a boardinghouse, felt that Marysville should have a Catholic church, she stood at the mouth of the Drumlummon and other mine tunnels just as each shift emerged and asked each man to donate a day's pay for the building. It was then that she asked Thomas Cruse to donate two lots for the edifice and he gave only one. The completed church occupied both and Cruse gave in rather than fight Annie.

The hills surrounding Marysville are riddled with mines. Around the larger properties small mining camps grew up.

GLOSTER

Three miles northwest of Marysville is the Piegan group of claims and the Gloster mine, the latter discovered in 1880 and actively operated during that decade. Between 1884 and 1885 a small settlement, consisting of several stores and hotels, two saloons, a blacksmith shop, and a Chinese laundry, was built near the 60-stamp mill of the Gloster Mining Company. Annual production was $600,000.

BELMONT

The Belmont mine, west of Marysville, was active in 1880, running ore througt its 30-stamp mill which averaged $8.00 to $20.00 per ton. At one period, William Frue of Detroit owned the mine. Fire in the underground workings on February 11, 1881, exploded a magazine of Hercules powder, which killed six men.

EMPIRE

On the west side of Belmont Mountain and one-half mile south of the Gloster property is the Empire mine whose owners, Hickey & Cotter, sold out in 1886 to the Empire Mining Company, Ltd. of London. Daily stage service from Marysville brought passengers, mail, and freight to Empire, a camp which flourished for eight to ten years, close to the mines.

Both the Empire and the Drumlummon mines had several of the same Englishmen as directors; so, when the Montana Company, Ltd. of Marysville completed a 60-stamp mill, these same men agreed to erect a similar mill on the Empire property. The mill was completed in January, 1888. Many owners have operated the property at various times.

BELL BOY

Bill Murray owned a quarter interest in the Bell Boy, an undeveloped property which was discovered in 1888 at the head of Townsley Gulch. When no ore was uncovered in its 65-foot tunnel, Murray tried to sell his interest to a muleskinner in exchange for a mule, but without success. Murray and the other owners were also unable to interest the Montana Company in the mine, even after their representative, C. H. Robinson, inspected it and took from it several ore samples. Robinson left the samples in his cabin, where they were examined by John Gleason, owner of a sawmill, and taken by him to be assayed in Helena. The assay ran $165.00 to the ton in gold, and Gleason lost no time in staking the adjoining claim, which he called Gleason's Fraction. His mine more than paid for itself. The Bell Boy yielded $500,000.

BALD BUTTE

Several Helena businessmen owned the Bald Butte property south of Marysville, but when it failed to produce, they sold out to an English company. One of the former owners, B. T. Tatem, owned 70,000 shares of Bald Butte stock. He went bankrupt, and this stock was considered so worthless that it was not even listed among his assets.

The English company kept one man at work on the property for nearly three years, and still no ore was discovered. The company never paid the man, but he was confident that the mine would ultimately produce. One day, while he was pushing the ore car, he tripped and uncovered some dirt in which he saw traces of gold. He toted enough of the pay gravel to Helena to pay his back wages, and

then he reported his discovery to the company. The mine is said to have yielded $3,000,000 and Tatem cashed in on his 70,000 shares.

MARYSVILLE (Continued)

But to return to Marysville. Even today, with its small population, the place contains many buildings, brick business blocks, a Masonic lodge, false-fronted stores, a huge, drab, two-story schoolhouse isolated in a marshy meadow, and a shed which shelters a hand-drawn hosecart. Most of the residents live in small frame houses, scattered on either side of the several streets that climb beyond the business section toward the hills.

The town is so quiet these days that it takes imagination to see it as it was when the Drumlummon Company Ltd. gave a certain air to the camp. Its company officers were usually close relatives of the aristocratic stockholders and, although they knew nothing about mining, it was believed that this business experience would turn them into engineering experts. At times there were more of these young officials on the payrolls than miners, and their high salaries enabled them to live extravagantly. In this they were encouraged by the company, which provided excellent housing for its staff, with electricity, steam heat, hot and cold water, and expensive furnishings taken for granted. Even the grounds of the manager's house were artistically landscaped. Although unions were not allowed, the company paid union wages.

At one end of town, among empty barns and weathered houses, stood two large, false-fronted sentinels. When I showed a sketch I had made of these windswept husks to a woman downtown, she identified them as saloons. "A woman lived in rooms above one of them. She was the only woman in Marysville who drank. She never did till she lived there, and then the saloon was just downstairs. Women didn't go into bars in those days. She was a disgrace, and no one had anything to do with her or her children. The other building was a saloon too — the Mountaineer.

"You should have been here when the mines ran three shifts and the Cornishmen would sing as they went back and forth to work," she continued. "There were lots of Cornishmen here and they had the fine voices. To look around you'd never think that they took $40,-000,000 in gold out of these hills, would you? After the St. Louis Company pulled the pumps

CHURCHES AND SCHOOL, MARYSVILLE

DRUMLUMMON MINE, MARYSVILLE

in the Drumlummon in 1910, the town went down fast." We thanked her for her help and started to drive away, but she called us back.

"Did you hear about the time that Bob Riding bet Jim McDougal that he'd see snow on Bald Mountain on the Fourth of July? By the end of June the snow had all melted away and the boys who'd taken the bets were ready to collect. As soon as it was light on the morning of the Fourth, all the betters rushed out to look up at the mountain. There was a patch of snow up there, all right, just as Bob said there'd be, and he won his bet, but he and his friends were pretty fagged out from hauling it up there in the night.

"The men were that starved for sport they'd bet on anything, like whether an ore car from the Belmont mine would ride the tram to the mill or tip over on the way. One day Lily Jones, a girl from the 'row,' jumped into a mill pond just when a shift was changing and the men bet '$500.00 she drowns, take you up, she doesn't.' One of the boys waded in to rescue her, and the bets went up. He saved her, but both sides had their fun."

We were anxious to reach the town of Lincoln, so, with a last look at the big Drumlummon mill and its dumps, which cover most of the mountainside, we crept around the shoulder of a hill at the upper end of town and wound between pastures and thickets of trees until we reached the next valley. At a tiny settlement known as Canyon Creek, which is little more than a filling station and a few ranches, we checked directions before climbing up a gulch through which Canyon Creek has cut a gorge. During placer days low terraces or bars yielded moderately rich gold from this streambed for a distance of four to five miles.

"Where are we?" I asked of two men who were repairing a roof when we next reached a group of cabins and a schoolhouse. "This is Wilborn," they answered. "The road ahead goes to Lincoln over Flesher Pass, and the one to the left goes over Stemple Pass. It's twenty-six miles if you go that way." We chose to climb up a narrow wooded gulch toward Stemple Pass. Had we gone over Flesher Pass, we would have been close to the Heddleston mining district.

HEDDLESTON (BIG BLACKFOOT, SILVER DISTRICT)

Thirty-three miles northwest of Helena. District discovered in 1889 at the head of Big Blackfoot River. District is reached by Helena-Lincoln highway through Wilborn and over Flesher Pass, then several miles west and north.

It is named for Wm. Heddleston who, with George Padbury, discovered the Calliope lode. The men built an arrastre on Pass Creek, treated ore from the Calliope and recovered $11,000 in gold. In a few years the ore body was worked out. Later, lead was found in the district. . . . In 1919 . . . a concentrating mill was built at the Mike Horse mine. Since then . . . ore has been shipped to smelters. . . . Total production for the district is $120,000, of which lead accounts for half, and silver, gold, and some copper the remainder.

GOULD

About four miles below Stemple Summit, a lefthand fork in the road led into a deep, heavily wooded side gulch, at whose mouth stood a battered sign which read "Gould Creek." The mine was several miles from the highway, and, having been warned that the road was not recommended for modern cars, I drove on reluctantly. Farther on was the entrance to the "Gould Trail." It showed no signs of recent travel.

The Jay Gould, one of the biggest mines in the district, was discovered in 1884 and was worked intermittently until the middle 1930's. Its high-grade surface ores were easily milled in a ten-stamp mill until 1890. Then the property was closed down. The mine was subsequently opened, and considerable milling was done between 1903 and 1907, and again from 1910 to 1914, except when heavy flows of underground water suspended work. A drainage tunnel on the Fool Hen Creek side of the mountain was started, but lack of capital soon stopped work on the project.

In 1922, State Senator Owen Byrnes acquired the property and resumed work on the Fool Hen tunnel until it reached one mile and 600 feet into the mountain. The tunnel partially drained the old workings and permitted the resumption of mining. After Byrnes' death, the property changed hands and became the Standard Silver Lead Company. An old photograph of the Jay Gould shows a good-sized mill, surrounded by several sheds and shops, and a dozen smaller buildings or miners' cabins above the mill on the mountainside. High-grade ore from the mine ran 95 per cent gold and the rest silver. Estimated total production up to 1915 was mostly from gold found in a vein of limestone, and totaled $2,500,000. Additional returns after 1922 ran at times as high as $40,000 a month.

The higher we drove, the denser the forest became. Virginia Creek and the highway run parallel for some distance below the top of the divide. At many places the streambed was clogged with mounds of stones left from placer workings. The banks, too, contained dumps and scattered stone foundations, partly covered by dense underbrush. Could these be the remains of Stemple?

In less than a mile we saw a cabin in the trees and beyond it a larger building and some cyanide tanks. On the hillside was a big mill. We drove up to the cabin, just as an old lady stepped out on the porch. "Are you fishermen? Are you interested in mining?" she asked, pointing to a collection of ore specimens displayed on window ledges and on an oilcloth-covered table. "No," she replied to our question, "you haven't gotten to Stemple yet. It's up at the top of the grade. There's not much left of it but an old stage station. This property here is the Bachelor. Me and my son bought it and worked it for a spell. Then we had to quit. The big mine is up on the hill. You can see the dumps and the mill from here. The tailings you passed below here were from the mine. The cyanide plant was put in about 1915. The biggest producer around here was the Homestake near the head of Virginia Creek. John Stemple discovered it in 1878. Folks say they took out $420,000 from this district — all gold."

STEMPLE

From the Bachelor property to the top of the pass the climb is steep and the road full of curves. In a small moraine below the summit stood several sagging log cabins, weathered to a silver sheen. One of these was the stage station. Mine roads took off in all directions between dense stands of young lodgepole pines. Dumps scarred the hillsides. Another steep pull brought us to Stemple Pass, elevation 6,373 feet.

Virginia Creek rises on the eastern side of the Divide. Its bed, from which $600,000 in gold has been taken, has been mined its entire eight-mile length, from Stemple to its mouth. On the western slope of the pass were additional auriferous gulches.

SEVEN-UP-PETE GULCH

Five miles north of Stemple in a deep valley west of the Divide, which leads into the Blackfoot Valley above Lincoln. Lodes were discovered in 1886 by W. F. Howe, but they proved to be low-grade ore. Twelve tons of ore were shipped out by pack train between 1923 and 1933.

McCLELLAN GULCH

The long descent on the west side of the Divide cuts through the forest with only an occasional deserted cabin to suggest earlier days of activity. Signs of mining increased as we dropped steadily down the mountain — overgrown placer diggings and a series of quiet stagnant ponds completely surrounded by dumps.

At McClellan Gulch the road crosses the mouth of the creek, which at this point joins Poorman Creek. McClellan and its side gulch, called Crevice, were the richest diggings in the area. The main gulch is two miles long; Crevice, at its head, is only half a mile long.

Placer deposits were mined from 1864 to 1875 and were so rich that at times a single pan of gravel yielded $500.00. One account describes men "hooking up nuggets out of the crevices in which they had lodged" and another mentions a nugget worth $945.80. During boom years, in Pacific City, as the gulch was first called, "$150-$200 to the hand" was often taken out in a day, and $65.00 in a pan from the discovery claim is also recorded. One prospector recalls that $8,000 was divided after a week's work from "Claim No. 8 below discovery." In all, $7,000,000 was taken from the relatively small area of rich gravels.

Although the men usually left their diggings during the winter when no water was available to wash the dirt, W. S. Barrett wrote in November, 1868, that

Some 70 men are at work there and fair pay is being obtained. Much of the ground that has once been mined is again taken up and the dirt washed a second time. The yield . . . on the old claims, averages ½ an ounce per day to the man.
Helena Weekly Herald, Nov. 19, 1868

Since 1875 the gulch properties have been profitably reworked two or three times. In the spring of 1927 a nugget weighing 57 ounces was found, valued at $1,026 — the largest nugget found in the gulch.

Looking up McClellan Gulch, huge cones of waste gravel — the remains of placering and dredging — almost fill the creek bed as far as one can see. These pyramids of clean-washed pebbles and boulders are stacked twice the height of a car. Beyond Poorman Gulch we caught one glimpse of a ranchhouse across the stream, reached only by a road cut between stacks of boulders. Then we were on flat meadowland where we passed a few ranches before diving into another stand of timber, from which we emerged on the outskirts of the town of Lincoln.

LINCOLN

This was not the old mining camp, but a new Lincoln, a settlement where ranchers, cowboys, and tourists have built rustic homes among the trees and where the main street is also part of Highway No. 20, which runs between Great Falls and Missoula. At the general store I learned where Lincoln Gulch lay. "Drive two and a half miles west of the highway till you see the Gulch sign. Then turn right and drive two miles in," said the busy storekeeper between customers. The narrow road to the gulch led across pasture land and through trees. Soon signs of placering were discernible — overgrown dumps and rotting cabins deep in the forest. A few cabins faced with tarpaper were of newer construction. Beside the road was a sign: "Go Beyond Here at Your Own Risk. Lincoln Placers, Inc. Lincoln Assoc. Inc."

We drove on a short distance to the edge of the gulch. It was twenty to thirty feet deep and all dredged out, a wide gouge cut for miles through the timber. Rusted machinery and fragments of crumbling buildings stood here and there, back from the eroded banks. Some of the gravel dumps were hidden by bushes and small trees, while others stood naked — masses of yellowish dirt rimming the stained ponds which once floated the dredges.

Lincoln Gulch is ten miles long and the site of the original discovery is three and a half miles from its mouth. Except for occasional fur traders in the early part of the nineteenth century, and the surveying party of the Pacific Railway Survey in 1853, the gulch was unknown except to Indians. In the summer of 1865 a party of prospectors with difficulty sank a shaft in an attempt to reach bedrock. They found enough colors in the gravel to encourage further exploration, and on August 31 they held a meeting and drew up the following document:

Abe Lincoln Gulch, Andy Johnson District, Aug. 31, 1865 on this day at 2 o'clock,

Thomas J. Patterson
D. W. Culp
Jack Lewis
John Lawdell
James Giles,

Located ten claims five by preemption and five by right of discovering gold in paying quantities in the Gulch. Making in all (2,000) feet in length commencing at a tree with a notice upon it at the lower end of said claims and extending to a corresponding one above.

D. W. Culp,
Recorder.

Records of Lincoln Gulch 1865-1879;
(original handwritten Recorder's Journal of Lincoln Gulch) Library, Montana Historical Society Library, Helena

The gold lay hidden in a dry gulch which, for lack of water, could not be worked successfully that fall or winter; so it was the following spring before men swarmed to the new diggings and staked off claims both above and below the discovery claim — 110 locations in all. The men hastily put up cabins and shacks near their properties and waited impatiently for the spring runoff of snow to provide the necessary water for sluicing. To insure an adequate, year-round flow, an eight-mile canal from Beaver Creek to the gulch was constructed by the miners and called Discovery Ditch. The gold from Lincoln Gulch, which was unusually pure, was worth $19.00 an ounce. Men averaged from $1.00 to $5.00 a pan, and in some cases got $15.00 to $20.00.

The gold was recovered by drift mining, by open pits and ground placering. By 1867 drift miners had recovered $7,000,000 from 7,400 feet of gulch. The pay streak was fifty to three hundred feet wide and "arasted $375 a set," a "set" being a block of ground four feet wide, four feet high, and ten feet long. After three drain ditches were hand dug in the lower part of the gulch so that shafts could be sunk to bedrock without being flooded, new properties were opened up.

According to one account, the camp was first called Springfield. As more and more men crowded into the gulch, the first-comers moved farther upstream and when they found that the dirt there was as rich as that in the lower diggings, they built a new camp and called it Lincoln. In time both camps were known by this name — the first camp was called Lower Lincoln and the second Upper Lincoln. With 400 men at work, merchants opened stores, so

REMAINS OF PLACERING, McCLELLAN GULCH

BLACKFOOT CITY, OPHIR GULCH

that by May, 1867, the camp had a butcher shop and a bakery, a general store, and two saloons, one of which served as a general meeting place.

Lincoln Gulch was hard to reach, for it was flanked by dense forests and was surrounded by mountains. Furthermore, the Blackfoot River was often difficult to ford. To facilitate transportation, Kennedy, Rose & Company decided to build a toll road from Blackfoot City (Ophir) to Lincoln. This road, which was completed by April, 1868, was literally hacked through the timber and scraped through the meadows. It was steep and rough even for pack trains, and packers were glad to have merchants and miners order supplies sent in during the summer when the road was passable. Winter trips were avoided. The road did, however, enable passengers from Blackfoot City to travel by coach all the way to Lincoln without changing to saddle horses at Jefferson Gulch for the final climb over the mountains.

Soon after its completion, a second toll road was built to Lincoln by a Mr. Negus, beginning at Silver City (a stage station on the Fort Benton and Helena road) by way of Canyon Creek and over Flesher Pass. It was shorter, and coaches made the 65-mile trp to Helena in ten to twelve hours, with a dinner stop at Negus' stage station.

Even the Indians, who resented the encroachment of whites on their hunting land, seldom made trouble for the miners except to steal horses. Whenever there was something to do, everyone pitched in and did his share, and when there was something to celebrate, like a barn-raising or the Fourth of July, everyone was there too. One such holiday is described by the *Helena Weekly Herald*:

Letter from "The Old Man,"
Lincoln Gulch, July 5, 1869
There was at least *one* truly patriotic, generous and public-spirited camp in Montana. A flagpole nearly 100 feet in height was raised, in front of the postoffice and a $100.00 flag was provided. A salute of 100 guns was fired, between daylight and sunrise, and by nine, hundreds of miners and ranchmen and citizens of Lincoln in general, as well as numbers from McClellan and other neighboring camps, gathered and assembled . . . in front of "Uncle Bob's," beneath the old flag — men of all shades of political and religious belief, yet all united as with one heart in the true and all-inspiring impulse of the occasion — to mingle their voices in song, and cheers and warm greetings of the day . . . . The Glee Clubs of Lincoln and McClellan Gulches united for this occasion . . . . Then came the booming of loud guns.

Perhaps a story told by Jean Moore best describes the community spirit. A small child became lost in the dense woods surrounding the camp. Search parties scoured the area without success and decided that some wild animal had attacked the child and dragged it away. The parents were distraught, especially since no Christian burial was possible. The citizens of Lincoln met, and word got around the next day that the body had been found and placed in a pine casket in the schoolhouse. The miners conducted a funeral service, the parents were comforted and never knew that the box that was buried was empty.

The years 1869 and 1870 were boomers. A sawmill was in operation, the Springfield Hotel and Kelley & Company's Livery Stable did a brisk business, mail service from Helena kept the camp in touch with the outside world, and the population rose to over 800. Some say that in 1871 the population reached 3,000, but that during the year news of new strikes caused the miners to stampede to richer diggings. By 1872 only 100 remained. By the following year, only sixty people were left in the once teeming gulch. These eked out a living by panning an ounce of gold per day.

Some of the undrained gravel near the mouth of the gulch was worked through shafts and tunnels in 1904 by Dr. O. M. Lanstrum and his company. By 1926, the gulch was deserted. In 1931, a dredge was brought in and the mounds of gravel seen today are the refuse spumed from its stacker. Old Lincoln camp has virtually vanished. Its site is hard to determine, and even its cemetery is choked by hardy lodgepole pines.

From Lincoln Gulch we returned to the highway and continued west a short distance. "Take the road that runs south through a pasture. Cross a cattleguard and a bridge and then go on," the storekeeper had told us. We found the road and drove for miles over Dalton Mountain and down into the next valley. It was a lonely, rutted and narrow track, and we met but one car. We passed few ranches until we were off the mountain and approaching Jefferson Gulch. There we saw many signs of hydraulicking and a few miles farther on, at Finn, we crossed Washington Gulch, another formerly rich area.

FINN (WASHINGTON GULCH)

Washington J. Stapleton and two other prospectors were tramping from one mining camp to another during the summer of 1866 when their rations gave out. To replenish them, Stapleton set out to hunt some game. He soon jumped a deer and chased it two miles up a creek where he killed it. In dressing it he discovered a nugget. As he washed it in the stream he noticed glittering particles on the creek bottom. Thus he found a new gold bar which he named Stapleton Bar; the creek he called Washington.

Stapleton Bar was rich, and from it many men, including its discoverer, made fortunes and hurried back to the States. Adjoining gulches were also explored by the horde of miners who rushed to the area, and as each stream yielded pay dirt, camps sprang up along their banks — one in Jefferson in 1867, and others in Nevada, Madison, Buffalo, American, and California gulches. Washington Gulch, which was torn up for a distance of six miles, paid on some claims $13.00 to the pan. The gold was described as found in scale form, resembling parsnip seed, only irregular in shape and deep yellow in color. It was all washed down by hydraulics and required quantities of water.

When a bigger head of water was needed at Stapleton Bar, a company of miners dug a thirteen-mile ditch from Nevada Creek to the Bar with pick and shovel. Upon its completion the controlling company boosted the rates for its use to such an extent that many of the men refused to pay the price. Consequently, without water, little mining was done, and disappointed men drifted away to better prospects. Others turned to homesteading and stockraising or ran sawmills.

For some years, Dr. Remington, a one-armed physician who lived at Washington Gulch, cared for the whole area, which included Helmsville, Lincoln, McClellan Gulch, and Blackfoot City. A twenty-mile horseback ride over mountain trails to set a bone or extract a bullet was not at all unusual. On one occasion the brother of a seriously injured man had to make a fifty-mile horseback ride to bring the doctor to the patient!

When a postoffice was opened at Stapleton Bar in 1866, the name was changed to Washington Gulch. Later on, the postoffice was changed to its present location, and the camp was renamed Finn, the name of a pioneer rancher. By 1893, the camp contained one hotel, one store, two saloons, two livery stables, two houses, and a stage station. Today, most of these structures are deserted or demolished,

and little is left except a well-kept ranch and a modern schoolhouse.

HELMVILLE

Placers in Nevada Gulch were discovered in the 1860's. Some say that the first settlers came into the valley in 1867, having left exhausted diggings in Washington Gulch. Production from the bars was intermittent, averaging between $1000 and $2000 annually. The gold was recovered by sluicing and hydraulicking. Helmville, a ranch settlement on Nevada Creek, fifteen miles northwest of Finn, did not exist until Henry Helm wrote to Washington, D. C., for a postoffice name. Helmville was selected.

OPHIR GULCH

The drive from Finn to Blackfoot City and Ophir Gulch was through rolling ranch country. After some miles we saw a narrow trail and a sign: "Blackfoot City 2 miles, Ophir Gulch, 3 miles." This road climbed and twisted across an open valley toward wooded hills. Beyond a branch of Ophir Creek, we saw the first placer dumps. On ahead was Ophir Gulch. To the right, or east, and over a low hill lay Carpenter Gulch, and on the marshy meadow in front of us was what was left of Blackfoot City.

Placer deposits were discovered in Ophir Gulch on January 12, 1865, by Nagle, Pemberton, and others. As usual, lack of sufficient water for sluicing hindered production until Bratton and Pemberton built a ditch into the gulch that same year. As word of the strike became known, men hurried to the diggings, until by 1868 there were over 1,200 men in Ophir, Carpenter, and Snowshoe Gulches.

Toward the head of the gulches the gold was coarse; near the mouth it was fine and nuggets were "common as dust." Jean Moore, an early resident, wrote: "I noticed a miner tossing and catching a big nugget worth $1,880, taken from No. 11 above Pence's discovery in Ophir Gulch. It made a nice handball." No records of early placer production are available, but it is estimated that at least $3,500,-000 was taken from these workings. Ophir Gulch was mined for eight miles from its head to a point in the valley four miles below the foot of the mountains. Carpenter and Snowshoe Gulches were each worked for several miles. Mining operations also flourished on Nelson Hill, and in Eureka and Tiger Gulches.

Ophir Bar had a number of claim holders in 1879, including Quigley & Quigley, William Pearl, and Bratton & Pemberton, but the principal claim holders at that time were Chinese. Little gulch mining has been done in recent years, although a dredge was placed on Ophir Creek in 1932. Lode mines containing gold, silver, and copper ores have been worked at various times, with a total production since 1900 of $225,000.

Carpenter's Bar, which in itself attracted over 600 miners, was a real bonanza. It lay two miles east of Blackfoot City (Ophir) beyond a low divide on high, rolling prairie. The large auriferous belt covered twenty square miles, with the rich leads running south as far as Snowshoe Gulch. The gold lay so close to the surface that the hardy miners had only to lay their sluice boxes on the ground, dig up the earth beside them, shake out the grass and shovel the dirt into the boxes. Bedrock was only two and a half to four feet below the surface of the prairie, and by working steadily one could take out "$15-$20 to the hand at a cleanup." In summer, when there was plenty of water, one man could pan three ounces of gold per day. Jean Moore tells of one miner who "scrubbed down three lengths and gathered a pile of amalgam about the size of a dairy roll of fresh butter."

Men worked around the clock on Carpenter's Bar and kept guards on duty to prevent claim jumping. To rob a sluice box was as serious a crime as murder. When the miners working for McDonald & Company found that the riffles had been removed from one of their boxes, they set a trap to catch the thief. The next evening the water was turned off at the usual time, and the men left the claim unguarded and presumably went to dinner. Instead, they hid near the property. Before long, they saw a man slip up to their sluice boxes and examine them. When he lifted the upper riffle, McDonald fired at him and ordered him to "Stand still." The thief fled and was never seen again, although the next day Dr. Glick told of being wakened to treat a gunshot wound by a man who threatened him if he mentioned it.

Snowshoe and Deadwood Gulches, which run parallel to Carpenter Gulch, also contained rich auriferous leads. According to one account the diggings were discovered by Bell and Newell in 1865. By 1868 Rufus Johnson, a California freighter, and E. W. Pryor owned 7,000 feet of bar and gulch property which paid $10.00

a day. It was from Deadwood Gulch in 1865 that a party of men which included Edward M. Rising (or Risson) in sinking a prospect hole on the McKay claim found a nugget worth $3,280.

During the early 1870's, a freighter bought three or four camels to use as pack animals and grazed them near Johnson's Lake. One was accidentally shot by a hunter who took it for a moose. He proudly staggered into camp with it and was promptly fined $300.00, his watch, and his gun.

BLACKFOOT CITY (OPHIR)

Blackfoot City (also called Ophir) was located May 16, 1865, "where Ophir gulch widens into meadowland," at the foot of a wooded mountain. An old photograph shows about one hundred buildings arranged along one long street and a shorter street parallel to it with cross streets connecting the two. Almost all the buildings were one-story cabins. House lots sold for $125.00; corner lots brought $150.00. Within a year the population included seven storekeepers or traders (whose most popular commodities were whiskey, candles, flour, and boots), two blacksmiths, two doctors, a carpenter and coffin maker, and several liquor dealers. The one hotel is described as having a restaurant and bar on the main floor and "a few dark cubby holes for lodgers," on the second story.

In 1867, A. K. McClure visited Blackfoot City as part of his western tour and describes it graphically in one of his many letters:

After crossing the divide, we landed in this city . . . . Half the cabins are groggeries, about one-fifth are gambling saloons, and a large percentage are occupied by the fair but frail ones who ever follow the miner's camp . . . . I am placarded to speak Saturday evening; . . . Balls soaked in kerosene were suspended from a post, which brightly illuminated the crowd and streets. I stood on a box in front of the hotel, with a bar doing a brisk business behind me. Immediately on my left, with double doors and windows open, was a gambling-saloon, in full blast, with a faro-bank, three or four poker tables, a billiard table, a bar, all liberally patronized . . . . I left the famous city of Blackfoot with few regrets. A Sunday there is anything but pleasant to one who don't gamble, race horses, or buy at street-auctions.
Three Thousand Miles Through the Rocky Mountains, A. K. McClure

Blackfoot City's first fire, which occurred on June 29, 1869, caused a loss of $35,000. When fire struck again, on July 3, 1882, only four able-bodied men were in town to fight it. Many homes were lost, as well as the Globe Hotel, and the damage amounted to $15,500.

Each year when the streams froze and snow blanketed the claims, many miners left the gulches and went to Deer Lodge for the winter. Mary C. Ronan and her husband spent the winter in their gulch cabin:

When freezing weather put a stop to work in the mines, Mr. Ronan was at home most of the time. He read "Josephus" aloud to me and all of Shakespeare's plays; we had papers and magazines, for once a week he would tramp out on snowshoes to Blackfoot City for mail. We also had horses and a sleigh.
Memoirs of a Frontier Woman, Mary C. Ronan

During the years when placer mining was successfully carried on in Ophir, Carpenter, and Snowshoe Gulches, Blackfoot City boomed. From *The New Northwest* we get a picture of Blackfoot's many activities:

Blackfoot City, March 5, 1876
This place, like many others at this time of year is somewhat dull. The monotony is broken occasionally by sociables where we trip the light fantastic toe until the early dawn, which, in the absence of sleighing, is the only amusement indulged in to any extent.
Mrs. Thos. E. Pounds has a class of young ladies to whom she is teaching vocal and instrumental music.

April 11, 1876
There has not been any gambling allowed in the saloons this winter, which speaks well for the morals of our thriving city.
"Tom Cat"

April 25, 1876
Water was turned into Ohio, Tiger, Ophir Bar, Nelson Hill and Ballarat ditches about the first of May — two weeks sooner than usual.

All merchandise had to be brought in by freighters until the coming of the railroad in 1882. At one time as many as 500 Chinese were working the mines, and one of them ran a grocery store in Blackfoot and received large shipments of rice direct from China. These were brought in from Helena by ox-team over the Dog Creek Hills. There was no bridge at Avon, so the teams forded the Little Blackfoot River. One spring, the stream was unusually high and so deep that rice in the three wagons got well soaked. By the time it reached Blackfoot City it was swollen and bursting out of the straw sacks in which it was packed. The freighter almost lost money on that shipment.

Butcher Ridge cemetery occupies a steep hill south of town well beyond any possible encroachments from placering. It was never fenced, because the ground was never bought from the owner. For some years Chinese miners were buried on the north side of the cemetery, but prior to 1880, their remains were disinterred and sent back to China. When Allen Davis drove one of the wagons which carried the barrels of bones to Helena for shipment, two Chinese rode with him, throwing perforated red streamers into the air at intervals to keep evil spirits from the deceased Celestials.

At the entrance to the townsite of Blackfoot City there stands today a government marker which states that Blackfoot once had a population of 1,500 (although old timers claim 2,000) and that after the fire of 1882, it was renamed Ophir. Visitors to the site are indebted to J. Clay Moore of Helena, who has identified and labeled the remaining, crumbling cabins, thus enabling strangers partially to visualize the city in its heyday. These signs indicate the location of the brewery, the stage barn, Pat Raferty's cabin, and of his Chinese partner known as Raferty No. 2, Chinatown, and the names of at least thirty of its residents. China Mary's house is marked and mention is made of her many kind deeds and of her burial in Helena. At the mouth of Ophir Gulch is the cabin of Grandmother Arina "Irene" Davis, who "knew as high as 300 men to come down this gulch on Saturday nights to Blackfoot City." Another sign commemorates a patriotic gathering.

CELEBRATION — 4TH JULY, 1876
AT THIS SPOT ON THE 4TH OF JULY, 1876, THE CENTENNIAL OF THE SIGNING OF THE DECLARATION OF INDEPENDENCE WAS CELEBRATED. 4000 PEOPLE FROM FAR AND NEAR TOOK PART. THE INDIAN AND THE CHINAMAN WERE THERE TOO. THE OPENING ADDRESS WAS GIVEN BY ASIA BROWN, BLACKFOOT CITY'S FAMOUS LAWYER. A SPLENDID ORATION WAS SPOKEN BY JOHN C. MOORE, STATESMAN, LAWYER, CIVIL ENGINEER, WHO ALSO READ THE DECLARATION OF INDEPENDENCE. THEY DINED AND DANCED FROM DAY TO DAWN. LIQUID REFRESHMENTS FLOWED LIKE WATER. THE FIREWORKS CAME FROM CHINA (BUT NOT THE FIREWATER). TWO ANVILS, TWO PLAYING CARDS, SOME BLACK POWDER AND A HOT ROD WAS THE PRINCIPAL NOISE MAKER. A LOT OF 4TH OF JULY'S HAVE PASSED IN THIS CITY OF GOLD SINCE THEN, BUT THAT DAY WILL NEVER BE FORGOTTEN. THANK GOD FOR AMERICA. "OUR AMERICA."
JOHN C. MOORE

We walked upstream to the mouth of Ophir Gulch. As far as one can see, the bed of the creek is full of gravel dumps left from placer activities, while the banks are covered with trees and underbrush. Blackfoot City is a true ghost town and it is difficult to see it through the eyes of the prospector who wrote: "Blackfoot City will soon be unsurpassed as a mining town . . . The country is full of game — mountain buffalo, bison, elk, black and brown bear, black and white-tailed deer, prairie chickens, grouse and quail . . ."

AVON

From Blackfoot City we drove back to the dirt road that led to Avon, a small settlement established by the Northern Pacific railroad in 1900. Avon is a distributing center for the immediate area, but in mining days it was the shipping point for ore from Blackfoot, Finn, and nearby gulches, with gold dust a common medium of exchange in the local stores. After mining dwindled, two new industries were developed — stockraising and lumbering, the latter providing raw material for sawmills and tie camps.

Prior to the completion of the Northern Pacific R.R. in 1883, the roads of the region were hardly more than trails, over which stages from Deer Lodge and Helena swayed and creaked in good weather and crawled during blizzards. At the beginning of the winter storms, passengers assisted the driver by planting willow poles, which he gave them, in the snow at intervals beside the road to guide him on his return run.

When the railroad survey crew came through the valley, William Cramer built a log house farther upstream than his homestead to serve as a boardinghouse for the work crew. The Cramer House was the scene of many dances and festivities and, since it was the original house on the Avon townsite, it was regarded as a landmark. In 1910 it burned down. In 1882, rails were laid through Avon and a large tent was erected beside the tracks to serve as a station. The following year a depot was built opposite the Cramer House. The first freight delivered by train is said to have been four barrels of whiskey.

Heavy rains during June, 1908, plus the spring run-off of melting snow, washed out a dam on Little Blackfoot River above the town and flooded the business portion for two weeks. Water stood more than a foot deep in the stores, railroad tracks were washed out, and Avon was cut off from mail and supplies for nearly a month. Men worked day and night during the peak of the flood, dyking the river so as to save the residential section of town. Refugees were cared for in the schoolhouse. When the shortage of food became critical, men drove teams to Helena and returned with provisions.

Operation of the Gravely and Luke phosphate mines six miles northwest of Avon proved to be the leading industry during the 1940's. The mines employed 120 men and averaged a daily output of eight cars, each with 54 tons capacity.

As we left Avon and turned east on the main highway toward Helena, I tried to imagine the excitement in town when a trained bear, belonging to an Italian showman, broke loose after a performance in front of the Cramer House. No one ventured out during the two days that the animal roamed the streets. Finally his master was able to coax him close enough to hand him a bottle of whiskey. As he drank it he was captured.

ELLISTON

Nine miles east of Avon the highway passes through Elliston, no longer as lively a town as it was in the 1890's when thirteen saloons catered to woodcutters and railroad men employed by the Anaconda Copper Mining Company. Marcus Daly's Fluming Company, which provided cord wood for the smelter at Anaconda, was the town's main industry from 1889 to 1894. A nine-mile flume carried a quarter of a million cords of wood from the forests to a dump east of town where they were stacked and then loaded on railway cars to be shipped to the smelter. The work was done during the winter and spring by more than one hundred cutters, and to ensure the wood moving down the flume men on horseback rode the length of the trough to break up any jams that occurred.

Elliston's two fires, one in 1894 and the second in 1895, completely destroyed the town, so that today none of the original buildings remains. According to one story the settlement was christened Alicetown for the daughter of an early resident, but through usage it soon became Elliston.

Mining properties in the Elliston district are both north and south of the Little Blackfoot River. From the Julia mine, eight miles south of Elliston on the south side of Telegraph Creek, gold was obtained from surface ore. Several log buildings, including a bunkhouse and a large dump, remain — perhaps in use in 1913 when the property was operated by the Montana-Clinton Copper Mining Company. Two other mines in the district were the Twin City Mining & Milling Company's property, also eight miles south of town on the east side of Telegraph Creek, and the Ontario, still farther south near the same stream. The upper part of the Gold Canyon district, five miles north of the town, was placered as late as 1911.

Two small formerly active mining camps lie northeast of Elliston. Little of either remains. One of these is Blossburg, nine miles northeast of Elliston on Dog Creek. The second is Austin (or Greenhorn).

AUSTIN (GREENHORN)

The town of Austin, which is thirteen miles northeast of Elliston, east of the Divide, is a flag station on the Northern Pacific railroad. The original settlement, called Greenhorn Gulch, was a placer camp. The area is drained by Seven-mile Creek, along which placers have been worked for a distance of twelve miles. Total placer production is estimated at $1,200,000. In 1883 the postal authorities in Washington, D. C., were startled to receive a communication from the territorial governor which read: "Vigilantes at Greenhorn, Montana, have removed postmaster by hanging. . . . Office . . . now vacant." In the rugged mountainous region surrounding the town were lode mines. Those, worked between 1880 and 1935, have yielded $300,000 in silver, copper, lead, and gold. The ore was valuable for fluxing because of the amount of iron it contained.

RIMINI

From Elliston it is only a few miles to the crest of the Continental Divide at MacDonald Pass (elevation 6,323 feet). About two miles east of the foot of the pass a graded road, which forks south from the highway, leads to Rimini, once a trade center for a mining district which produced gold, silver, and lead. Originally known as Young Ireland, it was renamed Rimini in the 1880's by the citizens after they had witnessed the drama, *Francesca da Rimini*, performed by a traveling road company. Their pronunciation, which is still used, was Rim'-in-eye.

The eight-mile drive from the highway skirts Ten Mile Creek, which cuts through a narrow wooded gulch. The town, to which a branch of the Northern Pacific railroad was built between 1885 and 1900, consists of one long street lined with many false-fronted frame buildings, and a second street parallel to and behind it, also filled with houses and cabins, except where mine dumps crowd close against them. One or more loading stations crumble beside the main thoroughfare. At the far end of the street Red Mountain, which rises to a height of 8,802 feet, seems to block the gulch.

This place is probably one of the oldest lead-zinc camps in Montana, for patent surveys Nos. 3, 4, and 5 were designated as being on Red Mountain, and survey No. 13 included Lee Mountain directly west of the townsite. The Nelly Grant, General Grant, Good Friday, and Little Jenny lodes were on Red Mountain. The claim for the Lee Mountain mine, which was discovered in 1864 by John Caplice, was staked under the old Montana law which allowed the preemption of a claim 2,200 feet long and 100 feet wide. Lode mining began before 1870 and was most actively pursued between 1885 and 1900. A total of $7,000,000 is estimated to have been produced from the various mines by the end of 1928. Certain properties were explored by lessees as late as 1930.

Placers above Rimini were worked during the 1870's, 1880's, and from 1900 to 1903. More recently, placer ground four and a half miles south of Rimini on Try Again Creek was equipped for hydraulicking with a pipe line and a reservoir. The property, which extended more than a mile along the stream, was owned by the N. J. Gould estate.

When James J. Hill, president of the Great Northern Railroad, founded the Red Mountain Consolidated Mining Company in the early 1880's with capital provided by European financiers, he hoped to build a branch of his road into Rimini so that shipments from the mines could be sent direct to the Helena & Livingston Smelting & Reduction Company's smelter, but when the plan failed he abandoned his mining project also. He had expected to drive a cross-cut tunnel into Red Mountain above the town, but only after his death, when the property became the Montana Lead Company and was administered by his estate, was this project begun. The tunnel was bored 4,000 feet into the mountain. The refusal of the City of Helena Water Department, which has a reservoir near Rimini, to permit the erection of a concentrating plant near the mine, further curtailed big scale development.

I have been twice to Rimini, once in the early morning, when the sun was slowly creeping down the dark canyon wall, the clean, sharp light emphasizing each tree and mine dump and setting them aside from the shadowy depths of the gulch, and once in the late afternoon when even the trees on the summit of Red Mountain caught the rosy stain of the afterglow.

On that afternoon trip in 1951, we nearly ran over a beaver. He was a huge old fellow and was dragging a heavy aspen bough toward the beaver dam in the stream. On that trip I saw but one resident, a man who told me that the camp had been virtually deserted since the late 1920's. "It's not what it used to be," he added. "Most of the old timers have gone over the divide."

On my second trip to Rimini, in 1956, my husband drove past the last houses and up beyond the town to the Helena Waterworks control gate. There were mine buildings, foundations, shafts, and dumps all over the hillsides.

In walking about town we noticed thin threads of smoke from two cabin chimneys, and as we approached one house, out rushed three frisky dogs. While they sniffed at us, a woman opened the door to call them back and I asked her if she could identify the mines for me. Two mine dumps, spilling onto the street near her home, she called the Susie dump and the Minnie Lee dump. When she saw me drawing, she shyly brought out a sketchbook, filled with pastels of animals sensitively rendered, and told us that her husband was a professional wrestler and that they'd lived in many places, including New Zealand and Australia, but they'd come back to Rimini because they liked it.

As we walked toward our car, a man came from the other cabin where we'd seen smoke and introduced himself as Alex Eklund, a resident of Rimini for forty years. He had covered his house with tin sheeting for fire protection as Rimini no longer has any fire company.

"The Valley Forge is the big mine over the hill to the east," Eklund explained. "It operated between 1906 and 1920. Its ore bins from the mouth of the lowest tunnel were connected with the loading station by an aerial tram. They took $200,000 out of it. Funny thing — the ore contained more gold than silver values.

"Some of the mines, such as the Lee Mountain which produced $1,500,000, the Valley Forge and the Porphyry Dike, were finally controlled by the Montana Lead Company. I used to work in the Porphyry Dike. It's eight miles farther up the gulch near the summit of Red Mountain. Rhyolite flows held plenty of low-grade ore, but only large scale milling paid. My wife used to keep the boardinghouse up there. It was only a half-mile trail from the mine to the top of Red Mountain. You ought to see the view from there. Red Mountain's 8,800 feet above sea level, you know. There's lots of mines all through these hills. The Armstrong in Minnehaha Gulch reopened with Seattle capital. The Monte Cristo is between the Montana Lead and the Porphyry Dike, but they're all idle now."

RIMINI AND RED MOUNTAIN

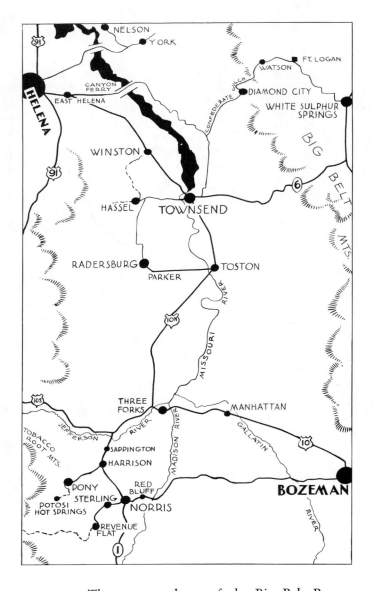

CHAPTER 7

BIG BELT CAMPS and TOBACCO ROOT TOWNS

The western slopes of the Big Belt Range, which barricade the eastern side of the Missouri Valley near Helena, are split by many narrow mountain valleys or gulches to a depth of from 1,000 to 2,000 feet. Seven of the creeks which gouged out these deep cuts carried gold in their beds or deposited it on terraces and bars on their way to the Missouri River. York and Trout Gulches were the most northerly of these; then came Oregon, Cave, Magpie, Avalanche, Hellgate, and White. Confederate Gulch at the southern end was the richest of all. Confederate and its trbutaries produced $12,000,000, the Missouri River bars $2,000,000, and the rest $3,500,000 in placer gold.

YORK

The earliest claims were worked for free gold, found in small stringers and veinlets in shale formations. These responded to treatment by crushing in small mills or arrastres. Placer ground along Trout and York creeks attracted hundreds to the diggings in the spring of 1866. By the following summer a townsite, at the junction of Trout Creek and York Gulch, had been surveyed and named New York. A smaller settlement across the stream was called Brooklyn. The population of Trout Creek between 1866 and 1869, while the placers yielded freely, reached several thousand. Some of the men who prospected the ridges found quartz

120

outcrops, but because of primitive reduction processes, they were able to recover little gold. According to the *Helena Weekly Herald* of January 24, 1867:

The starting of the new 24-stamp Hendrie mill at New York, on Thursday last, was the occasion of a jolly and spirited blow out by "the boys" . . . A splendid supper was gotten up and partaken of, while champagne and speeches flowed in sparkling plenitude. The new mill is not yet entirely completed; they have, however, twelve stamps now running, and the others will be ready in the spring.

Lumber used for sluices, flumes and timbering was provided by Sutton and Marshall, who ran a steam sawmill in York Gulch. After the placer deposits were washed away, the population dropped to a mere handful, mostly families who lived by stock raising or ranching. By 1880 the population had dwindled to forty-nine.

Lode mines were opened during the 1880's. The Old Amber (Golden Cloud), a gold-quartz lode on the south side of York Gulch, three miles above its mouth, must have been discovered shortly after placer mining began, for before 1870 a small mill at the mouth of Rattlesnake Gulch was crushing its ore. In 1899, a larger mill was built which ran successfully for nearly five years. The property's next owner, a stock company, only succeeded in piling up debts, and before long the mine was shut down. By 1927, it was in a state of dilapidation.

The richest lode mine, the Little Dandy, was located in 1883, and shortly afterwards the Golden Messenger was uncovered. The prospector who pounded out $8.00 in gold from a piece of float quartz found in outcrops of shale on a dike on north Trout Creek is credited with its discovery.

The Golden Messenger mine, situated a short distance above York on Dry Gulch, has been worked during every cycle of mining since its location in the early 1880's. On the same ridge as the Little Dandy, but one-half miles west of that property, it was found to contain immense bodies of low-grade ore in ladder veins. Early attempts to extract the gold by amalgamation recovered only thirty-five per cent of the values. A succession of operators subsequently worked the property — La Casse Bros., the French Bar Mining Company, and in 1913, the York Mining Company, whose new cyanide mill recovered ninety-two per cent of the gold. In 1927-1928 the property was acquired by the Golden Messenger Corporation, whose holding included the Faith lode and the Little Dandy mine. In January, 1934, United Gold, Inc., of Duluth reopened the mine and reconditioned the cyanide plant erected in 1917. Under their supervision, shipments of bullion were sent to the Denver mint.

One summer afternoon, when lengthening shadows on the Big Belt Mountains picked out the series of gulches which once held fabulous amounts of placer gold, I drove northeast from Helena, past Lake Hauser and along the west side of the Missouri River to the three-span steel bridge. Across the river the road enters Trout Creek Canyon and winds for five miles between high cliffs, rosy-hued near the mouth of the gulch and tan and white in the upper section. Finally I came to all that is left of the mining camp of New York. Signs of early placering filled the gulch beside the road the entire distance from the river to the townsite. Most of the mounds of discarded gravel were overgrown with vegetation and even good-sized trees; only the more recent stacks were clean-washed stones. As I approached York, as it is now called, the number of old diggings increased until the streambed was nearly lost among them. Except for a few old cabins, one of which is dug into the hillside, and the placer dumps, little of its early appearance remains.

York is now a small summer resort, with a couple of stores and a sawmill. From the center of town, the main road continues north to Nelson and Eldorado Bar where, they say, sapphires can still be found in the gravels beside the river. In one of the stores a man described each mine location to me as well as the site of a big log building that had served as store, saloon, and dancehall. Finally, it was used as a schoolhouse.

"I taught there," writes L. A. Osborn in the *Glasgow Courier* in December, 1923. "Every Friday night I turned the old log schoolhouse loose for debating and recitations. Nearly everyone took part along with the children. One old forty-niner . . . would bob up on the platform at every meeting and spout forth 'I am dying, Egypt, dying' — he did it well, too.

"An outfit a good many years ago excavated a bed-rock flume from the Missouri river eight miles to New York Gulch, and worked it all out. They washed out a pit fifty feet deep. I don't know whether it paid or not but my old log schoolhouse had to give up the ghost during the proceedings."

As I drove back to Helena down the darkening canyon, it seemed a pity that the region east of the river should be so empty. As Mr. Osborn said: "They're nearly all gone now — even the gulches, but they sound familiar to me yet — Johnny's gulch, German gulch, Kingsbury gulch, Cave gulch, Jimtown and York. There's little left of them."

ELDORADO BAR

Eldorado Bar, one of the smaller placer camps of the late 1860's, from which several thousands of dollars worth of gem sapphires were mined, as well as gold, was located on a terrace close to the Missouri River, a few miles northwest of York. No better picture of its placer days exists than these excerpts from a newspaper:

"Tailings from El Dorado"
This camp, as well as the whole county, was terribly Democratic before Grant's election. Everybody I meet now-a-days is *Union*, and "allers was." Full-fledged Republicans are springing up on Democratic stubble. These changes are, I suppose, owing to the very mild winter we have enjoyed thus far.

————

Our indomitable ferryman [Rube Shroyer] has, by care, perseverance and the sunny smiles of Providence, succeeded in making regular trips with his largest ferryboat from shore to shore on the Missouri at this point, up to within the last ten days — a thing unprecedented almost anywhere on the whole river.

————

Our population this winter consists of three families and about fifty men. Some are and have been since winter set in, out hunting and supplying the camp with an abundance of choice, wild game; some are setting around, reading a little, dozing a good deal, taking their regular toddies at Capt. Stout's and the old Major's.
Helena Weekly Herald, Jan. 24, 1869

Cave Gulch, in the Kingsbury region south of York and close to Canyon Ferry, contained several rich mines near its mouth, close to the bar diggings which lay just east of the Missouri River. Some of the mines were worked "to some distance below the water level of the river and would not have been abandoned but for want of power to keep the water down." Activity in the gulch as of May, 1874, is described in the *Helena Weekly Independent* as follows:

May 29, 1874
Springtown, in Cave gulch . . . is a trading center of a mining section embracing an area of one-hundred square miles . . . There are two excellent boarding houses, the first under Capt. Stafford, the second under Mr. Al Spencer. The place supports two billiard halls.

Besides a white residing population of 150, various gulches contain nearly one hundred Chinese, under Mr. Pie, an intelligent, celestial laundryman.

Miners are working in the beds of Cave, Oregon, New York, Magpie and Avalanche gulches, and on the bars and in the hills adjacent to nearly all of them. The most extensive bar mines are adjoining the lower end of Cave. Warner & Stafford and Hornbuckle & Marshall are running their hydraulics and doing well. The mines pay $5-$40 per day to the hand, and wages are $4 a day.

Cave Gulch was the scene of a fight between organized claim jumpers and mine owners in 1865, before official United States laws protected Montana Territory. This party of men came from Idaho and Nevada, attracted by the wealth of Confederate Gulch and well aware that as yet no laws existed which could touch them. Their headquarters was Cave Gulch, satisfactorily inaccessible yet close to good prospects. After they ordered two miners to leave their diggings by the following day, the lawful owners enlisted the aid of twenty prospectors from five nearby camps. These men, well supplied with provisions and ammunition, holed up in a cabin near the disputed claim and waited for the jumpers to reappear. At dusk a dozen of the thieves showed up, ready to take possession of the seemingly abandoned property. As soon as their leader stepped up to the flume, a shot from the cabin killed him. His henchmen opened fire and for a few minutes the sniping continued from both sides. Finally the miners burst from the cabin and fought in the open, killing three of the jumpers. The rest hit for the timber and got away.

Near the close of the nineteenth century, the placer gravels of Magpie Gulch were worked by drift mining. Even as late as 1928 some work was carried on in the district — one from which an estimated $280,000 in placer gold was recovered.

In the early days a little placer gold was also found near the head of Hellgate Canyon, and two companies working two and a half miles above its mouth, in 1874, worked pay gravel. The Argo and other lode mines, which operated prior to 1918, produced about 3,000,-000 pounds of copper, valued at $500,000.

White's Gulch, the most southerly of the streambeds with the exception of Confederate Gulch, was discovered May 2, 1865, by Mr. White. It held one of the best placer fields in Montana, with gravels that paid as late as

1885, considerably longer than those in Confederate Gulch and its branches. S. E. Stager ran a general store at the tiny settlement five miles up the canyon and "enjoyed the entire trade of the camp." A wagon road the length of the gulch, built by Capt. Stafford in 1873, served the six families and the few miners who worked the area. In the fall of 1878 the gulch contained but thirty voters. By November, 1882, there were only nineteen.

CONFEDERATE GULCH

Confederate Gulch can be reached from Helena by way of Canyon Ferry, or from Townsend, but if approached from White Sulphur Springs, one sees its entire length and comprehends the immensity of the gold deposits that made it the richest of them all.

Some say that the Civil War is responsible for the discovery of the gulch, for the first prospectors to sample its gravels were Confederate soldiers, men who had served in the army of Stirling Price. When his forces were captured by Union troops, the men were given a choice of surrendering and returning to their homes, or of being sent to Montana Territory and released. Many of the soldiers preferred the latter option and were shipped up the Missouri River to the head of navigation and turned loose in Montana's badlands and trackless prairies. While at Fort Benton these men learned that gold had been discovered at Last Chance, and although the gulch was two hundred miles away, they started on foot toward it. Some took the overland stage road to the diggings and others followed the river, prospecting the bars as they went. Late fall of 1864 found three of the men, Jack Thompson, Washington Baker, and Pomp Dennis, camped near the mouth of a gulch. Thompson followed the usual procedure and sank a prospect hole in the sand from which he washed out ten cents worth of gold dust from a single pan of dirt. Encouraged by this discovery, the party began to test the gravels as they traveled up the gulch, and the higher they climbed, the richer the ground became. Others followed them and uncovered more rich ground. News of the discovery reached Last Chance and other diggings, and within a few weeks a straggling camp, called Diamond City, stretched along the edge of the gulch where five hundred prospectors were already washing the auriferous dirt. The naming of the gulch is explained by an item in the *Montana Post*, June 8, 1867:

Little was known of the rich deposits of gold in gulches and bars east of Last Chance across the Missouri river . . . until the winter of '64 when Jack Thompson and party struck what was by him instinctively but inappropriately, under the fallacious impression of the eventual success of the Confederate States of America, named Confederate Gulch.

During 1865, a party of Germans found excellent pay dirt farther upstream in the gulch channel. Their discoveries of Montana and Cement Gulches started a rush to that area.

One of these properties, the Shinneman mine, employed nearly one hundred shovelers. Thomas M. Brown was one of them, and in a letter, written in 1866, he tells how at the end of the day

the signal gun was fired for dinner, [and] I was told to pitch up an empty powder keg. I was given a tin plate, iron knife, fork, tea and tablespoon and a place was made for me at the table.

It was a rough board trestle about one hundred feet long and was set under a shed that was covered with sweet, fragrant spruce boughs. On the table was salt, pepper, vinegar and brown sugar . . . Very soon they began digging in the ground at the end of the table and brought out three large dutch ovens with smoking hot beans, another with hot corn bread, coffee and tea . . . Sunday forenoon was the week's cleanup of gold. Perhaps $25,000-$50,000 was recovered in gold of fine quality . . . the gold was put in pans and set out on the table during the Sunday dinner hour for admiration and inspection.

New discoveries of increasing importance were made throughout 1865. Boulder Bar, from which $2,000,000 was taken, was at the junction of Montana Gulch and Confederate Gulch. Greenhorn Gulch, Gold Hill, and Diamond Bar were upstream from the original townsite. At the foot of Gold Hill was Montana Bar.

This fabulous bench — two acres of pay dirt, two to three hundred feet deep at some points, stood seventy to eighty feet above the level of Confederate Gulch. The pay dirt ran in depth "from nothing, where it was windswept on the rim to forty feet deep on the back of the bar against Gold Hill." Reports from the claim owners were staggering. The first cleanup clogged the flumes with gold "by the hundredweight." Worcester Fox, who reached Confederate in 1865 and stayed in the gulch for thirty-five years, told a reporter:

I saw seven pans of clean gold taken out at one cleanup. Twenty men had been working one day . . . I lifted each one of the pans myself because I wanted to have the satisfaction of handling the gold. There was 700 pounds of it and the cleanup was worth $114,800.

Even when the Bar was said to be exhausted, Fox obtained a claim and washed out several thousand more dollars.

During the winter and spring of 1866, a ditch was built on the north side of the gulch to facilitate sluicing. All through the spring and summer Montana Bar crawled with miners, feverishly cutting away the terraces where the richest deposits were trapped. The incredible wealth of Montana Bar made all other claims seem insignificant, for even when the bar was nearly washed away, men obtained $1,000 a pan from dirt at bedrock. And then, only a few months after its discovery, the bar, from which one million dollars had been recovered, was worked out.

Sometime late in 1866 after the flume water gave out and Montana Bar was nearly stripped to bedrock, a company of Germans — John Schonneman, Alex Campbell, Charles Fredericks, and Judson, who owned a claim on the bar — made a cleanup and prepared to ship their gold back to the States. They could haul it to Helena and send it by stage express with charges totaling twenty per cent of its value, or they could freight it to Fort Benton and ship it by boat down the Missouri. Either way was dangerous on account of road agents, for only while the gold remained in the Gulch was it protected by the Vigilante Committee.

After some discussion, the partners decided to ship their treasure by boat, and accordingly packed the dust in buckskin bags of five pounds each and then in watertight boxes which held ten sacks. They hired men and teams to haul the gold to the river and deputies to ride the wagons to protect it. Thus they saved the exorbitant express charges. On September first, the freight outfit left Diamond City, loaded with two and one half tons of gold, valued at between $900,000 and $1,000,000 — their cleanup from one season's work on Montana Bar. Accounts differ as to how the dust was shipped from Fort Benton. Some say on the steamer "Luella" which was chartered for the trip, and others that, since no steamers were operating just then, it was floated down the Missouri in Mackinaws. At any rate, the gold ultimately reached New York, where each man deposited his share with a private banking firm on Wall Street. Fredericks then left for Germany, where he was questioned about his wealth. When he told his friends where it was deposited, he was advised to return to New York and get it, which he did. While there, he urged his three partners to withdraw their money

also, and the group hurried to the bank, only to find that it had closed! Sometime later, a settlement was arranged by which they received about half of their deposit.

The collapse of Montana Bar in 1866 did not end mining in Confederate Gulch. Even before the famous bar was scraped clean, the Boulder Ditch Company was constructing a four and a half mile flume on the south side of the gulch, using Boulder Creek water and diverting it to a point one mile above Diamond City so as to supply the higher benches, such as Diamond Bar. The hand-dug ditch was five feet wide and two and a half feet deep, and it was capable of carrying 2,000 miners' inches of water. At one point, the water was siphoned across the gulch through an iron pipe twenty-two inches in diameter and 1,800 feet long, and by thus conducting it from hill to hill, "several additional miles of ditching" was avoided. The ditch was in use by the spring of 1868. That it and other bedrock flumes were used for hydraulicking is shown by the following item from the *Montana Post* of June 8, 1867:

On Diamond Bar, directly above and north of the city, fourteen two-and-a-half inch nozzles eject a stream of water day and night, washing the immense banks of loam away from the rich pay ore by the acre. Six pipes play on Slaughterhouse bar, one-quarter of a mile below town; one on Wood's bar and, as soon as the Duck creek ditch is completed, the Boulder Bars will be piped.

DIAMOND CITY

The tremendous activity of the gulch almost swamped the struggling settlement which tenaciously clung to the rim of the gorge. Diamond City consisted of one long street, built "on uncertain foundations and surrounded by piles of tailings and streams of water." The original townsite was in the bed of Confederate Gulch, but when the bars were sluiced away, the buildings had to be raised on stilts to escape being washed away also, or buried in tailings. "Hydraulic mining is 'playing Hob' with some of the business houses and offices," wrote a reporter from the *Rocky Mountain Gazette*; and continued:

A small mountain has "reared its diminished crest" in front of the Court House. They have raised that Bldg. twenty feet and still the gravel keeps piling up. They have given it up and the building subsides as the mountain rises. Dick Richardson, the Recorder and our friend Mulk stood the raise twice, but the

REMAINS OF DIAMOND CITY

CONFEDERATE GULCH, DIAMOND CITY

third time they couldn't stand it, so they moved to new quarters. We overheard Mulk grumbling as he carried his traps away from the muddy deluge that had filled his room. We stepped to the back of a saloon to look at water and gravel that was pouring from a high flume.   July 6, 1867

As the volume of placering and hydraulicking increased, the flimsy shacks were moved to higher ground on the bar, well above the mutilated streambed. This new location, beginning at the lower end of Montana Bar and extending down the gulch, was the second townsite of which but one cabin remains today.

Diamond City cannot boast of beauty in architecture, or convenience of access, being surrounded on all sides with immense piles of tailings . . . On entering the town, the usual great number of loungers and idlers, which often give a dull camp the appearance of a lively place, are not seen here . . . The German element predominates in the population and the leading spirits of the camp are self-made, industrious, go-ahead fellows of the pure Saxon race.
Montana Post, June 8, 1867

The years 1865-1868 covered Diamond City's boom. During this period, roads were built to the camp from all directions, and daily stage service was established with Last Chance by way of Canyon Ferry. The up coach and the down coach met at the Canyon Ferry House where passengers were served dinner. When cold weather froze the streams and curtailed sluicing, the miners got ready to "hole up" until spring.

Last week a pack train of ninety animals arrived from the west, bringing clothing and groceries of a superior quality. The supplies from that direction are beginning to make themselves felt in our market . . . The more the better . . . Flour has been up to $36 per sack and tobacco $6.50 per lb.
Montana Post, Nov. 4, 1865

As Christmas approached the diggings were forlorn. No merchandise was available in the stores, only wild meat was plentiful, and the best that the miners could do to provide gifts for the few women in camp was to fashion ornaments from gulch gold.

In December of 1865, there was talk of organizing a Masonic lodge. A letter dated 1866 and written by Thomas H. Brown indicates that such a lodge existed as well as another important organization. Mr. Brown writes:

There was a Masonic Lodge meeting the evening we arrived at Confederate Gulch and quite a number of us attended. After the meeting we were called into a room and informed that all good Masons were members of the Vigilante committee. Of course we joined. We were then told to observe the wooden boot sign on the street in front of a cobbler's shop. If a pair of children's shoes were hanging on the heel of the boot, all was quiet, if on the instep, that was notice of a regular meeting, but if the shoes were on the toe of the boot, we were to strap on our gun and get to the meeting place as soon as possible.

The following shows that the Vigilantes had not been idle:

A man by the name of Jack Howard was found dangling from a limb of a tree in town. His face was turned toward the east and a paper was pinned upon a leg having a significant inscription, 'Robber.' He was left dangling nearly all day.
Montana Post, Sept. 30, 1865

Diamond City was made up of both Union and Confederate sympathizers, and on occasion tension between the two factions ran high. Yet when the Union men organized as the Union League of America and raised the stars and stripes in front of their hall, the *Montana Post* of April 20, 1867, reported it as follows:

Yesterday, the American flag, for the first time since the existence of this place, under the auspices of the U.L.A. was made to float over Diamond City . . . It is well known to every one that the 9th of April was the second anniversary of the surrender of Gen. R. E. Lee to Gen. Grant, and it was thought a very appropriate day for the hoisting of the first flag over the place. A very neat octagonal pole, thirty feet long, was prepared and raised over the U.L.A. hall . . . Later in the day there was a dance . . . by four o'clock the hall was crowded by all parties, none were excluded . . . champagne, wine and beer were there in abundance, furnished by the U.L.A.

The whole thing was a grand success, and be it known from this time forward that, if we are cursed with the name of Confederate gulch, there are Union men here, and lots of them, too, and the day *has* come when it is safe to hoist the American flag over Diamond City.

In lighter vein, the press reported:

One evening last week Messrs. T. Collins, Charley Smith and W. C. Landers fell down a shaft twenty feet long. The evening was very dark, and all three were walking arm-in-arm . . . when Smith suddenly lost his footing and did not regain it until he had fallen to the bottom of the shaft. Collins followed him, ditto Landers — the latter landing on the "sanctum" of Collins. In going down each one would grab at everything that was in reach consequently a lot of cribbing went along with them. Smith, reaching the bottom, cut his boots severly on a whisky bottle . . . They were soon released by a passer-by . . . The mystery is how a whisky bottle ever came into the shaft just when these Good Templars fell in.
Helena Weekly Herald, Sept. 16, 1869

All through the early 1870's, the gulches continued to produce gold, although in smaller amounts than previously. Still the camp flourished. According to the *Helena Weekly Independent* of May 29, 1874, Diamond had

much the same appearance as in 1870, except that the gulch opposite from the town has been filled up with tailings nearly to the level of the townsite.

A Good Templars Lodge is in flourishing condition with a membership of 70. Mr. Kelley . . . is teaching a select school in the public schoolhouse.

On November 25, 1875, R. N. Sutherlin began publication of the *Rocky Mountain Husbandman*, a newspaper which he printed at Diamond City during his residence there. Upon moving to White Sulphur Springs, he continued the publication for twenty-five years. Toward the end of the seventies, Diamond City was rapidly fading, although it was still the seat of Meagher County.

By 1880 the population had dropped to sixty, and when Judge Cornelius Hedges visited the camp in 1883 he wrote:

Diamond City is desolate, deserted and dreary . . . Its very site will soon go down the flume, which is already within the borders of the old town and gleaning a rich harvest — probably the last. There are only four families left of all the hundreds that have dwelt here since the glorious days of '66. If the goose that laid the nestful of golden eggs can only be found in the shape of a prolific mother vein of gold-bearing quartz, the days of Diamond's departing glory may return, otherwise it will disappear utterly with another season.

Fairfield Times, Feb. 14, 1921

Although gold-bearing lodes were discovered soon after the placers, they did not pay off nearly so well. Lode mines were operated, however, from time to time in certain parts of the gulch and are said to have yielded a total of around $800,000. During 1896, considerable activity in quartz mining was carried on around the site of old Diamond City and above it, on the divide at the head of Montana, Cement, Benton, and Johnny gulches.

The early prospectors left some gold in the poorer and less accessible portions of their claims much of which was recovered, first by Chinese, who reworked the tailings of abandoned properties, and later by companies which reopened a stretch on the main gulch below the original site of the city. Since then the much-washed gulch has been deserted except when optimistic leasers have reworked once profitable claims.

So as to see the entire area from which such quantities of gold streamed, my husband and I drove from Helena to Townsend one summer morning in 1956. We crossed the Big Belt Range and reached White Sulphur Springs, where we received explicit directions as to how to reach Confederate Gulch. About sixteen miles northwest of the Springs we found the site of Fort Logan, of which nothing remains but a blockhouse in a meadow. Beyond the fort the road climbed gently through ranch country. Farther on, in a hollow, in the midst of a grove of trees, were two buildings — a barn on the left of the road and a white-washed log house marked "Watson P.O." on the right. Just beyond was a long line of dredge dumps, the first signs of mining that we'd seen. Again we climbed through timber until we reached a forestry sign which read "Belt Mt. Divide Trail." A short distance from it the road forked, and the sign to the right read "White's Gulch, Benton Ranger Station, Canyon Ferry." The left hand fork, which had no sign, was a much poorer road but, by deduction, we believed it to be the head of Confederate Gulch. It was narrow and rough and took careful driving all the way. After dropping down a particularly abrupt pitch, we met a station wagon. The driver reassured us that this was Confederate Gulch and warned us to "look sharp" so we wouldn't miss Diamond City. We continued down terrific grades and still saw no signs of mining. The next forestry sign read "Cement Gulch." Nearby was a mine shaft hidden by trees and a man's shirt hanging from a branch. Next we found Black Tail Creek. Not far away were stone foundations, stone walls, part of an old stove, and several hollows indicating where cabins had stood.

Some distance below was Montana Gulch. Here there were many signs of early placering with large trees growing in between the mounds. A side gulch on the north was all washed away, and its bed was carpeted with coarse grass and trees. The gulch below us, to the left, had seen big operations. It was cut deep and from its bed rose fantastic columns and dikes of earth. Below Montana Gulch were more signs of tremendous workings at many levels. The ground was a solid mass of mounds, boulders, stones of all sizes stacked up and washed clean, leaving little space where anything could grow except a few trees crammed into crevices between the rocks. From the scale of the workings and the amount of tailings, we agreed that this must have been the base of Gold Hill or part of Montana Bar.

Another stretch of trees and overgrown dumps brought us to a curve beyond which was a deep gash which the road straddled on a narrow dike. A marker identified this spot as "Greenhorn Gulch." This portion of Confederate had seen big-scale hydraulicking. The bed of the gulch was forty to fifty feet below the road. Both sides of the gorge showed the height to which the giants had been directed to claw away the gravel benches. Beside the highway stood three weathered cabins and next to them a new trailer. On the sagging porch of one of the cabins stood an old man with a long beard. We talked to him and learned that he was R. L. Robertson and that he had lived in Diamond City for forty years. He seemed pleased when I took a snapshot of him and said that his picture was all over Montana. As we left him I looked into the gulch, where, far below in the bed of the stream, three men were at work. I presume they were leasers and I'm sure that they owned the shiny trailer that we'd seen. Below Diamond City, the gulch gradually widens and the hills decrease in height. At the mouth of Confederate Gulch was a dragline and dumps from recent operations.

From the mouth of the gulch we drove toward Canyon Ferry and Helena. After several miles, a road joined ours from the east, marked "White's Gulch, Watson." We'd seen the upper end of it when we bypassed it to enter Confederate Gulch. In a few more miles we reached Canyon Ferry and the big plant of the Montana Power Company. From Canyon Ferry it was only sixteen miles to Helena.

EAST HELENA

Five miles east of Helena is the industrial town of East Helena, whose life revolves around the American Smelting & Refining Company's lead smelter and zinc recovery plant. To these furnaces, which have operated since 1889, ore from many mines in Montana and Idaho is sent for treatment. The great stack and the slag heaps loom above the stores and private homes of the mill and smelter workers, whose tiny front-yard gardens lend color to the busy gray town.

WINSTON

As one drives southeast from East Helena through Winston, Townsend, and Toston on U. S. Highway 10 N., there is nothing to suggest their connection with mining activity, yet each owes its existence to the many placers and lodes hidden in the mountainous area to their west. That Winston was originally dependent upon mining is shown by the name of its newspaper, *The Prospector*. Although the first lode was staked in 1867, most of the mines, which lie eight miles back in the hills, were discovered in the 1890's. Dumps dot the hillsides west of the town, but few of them mark rich properties.

Billy Slater worked his claim, seven miles southwest of Winston, single-handed until old age slowed him down. Whenever he needed money for powder or grub, he rustled a job at some other mine, and as soon as he could hustled back to his tunnel. In spite of all his years of labor, he never shipped a ton of ore. Dave and Charlie Gonan worked the Strayhorse mine in 1896, although they presumably were not the original locators. The mine was at the summit of a hill and when, in 1897, they sank a shaft and struck rich gold ore, they built a road up to the tunnel mouth so as to haul the ore by wagon to the railroad at Winston. In time they disposed of the mine for more than $70,000. Dave went into stockraising in the Boulder Valley, but Charlie remained a prospector. Robert A. Bell also came to Winston in the 1890's. When he stumbled onto the East Pacific prospect hole, six miles southwest of Winston, it looked so promising that he used up all his money to buy it. In developing it, he opened three rich ore bodies of lead and silver and some small pockets of gold. For twelve years the mine produced lavishly and from it Bell made a fortune. When the ore began to pinch out, he quit. In Texas he lost his wealth playing the oil business.

The entire district, which was active into the twentieth century, is credited with a total of $3,000,000. With the gradual reduction of mining, Winston developed its ranching and agricultural interests and has become the quiet cluster of buildings one sees today. It was named for P. B. Winston Bros., railroad contractors and one-time owners of the East Pacific mine.

TOWNSEND AND HASSEL

Townsend, the seat of Broadwater County, is bigger than Winston and is also the gateway to two ghost towns, Diamond City and Hassel. For three summers I passed through Townsend, and each time I looked up Indian

BED OF INDIAN CREEK, HASSEL
FLUME, INDIAN CREEK BELOW HASSEL

Creek, west of the town, and stopped to inquire how much was left of Hassel, or St. Louis, to use its original name. The answers were discouraging: "It's all dredged out." "Only one house standing." "Not much of a road." On my last trip I decided to go and see for myself.

As early as 1866, placer ground was discovered on Indian Creek where, for more than twenty years, it disgorged nearly $5,000,000 in gold. A placer camp called St. Louis grew up on upper Indian Creek and, by 1875, was described by the *Helena Independent* as

a live little place and a good winter camp for all who have employment . . . Some 35-40 men (are) at work. Mr. John Murray is keeping a boarding house at Cheatem, two miles above town and feeding more than half the camp with the best the market affords.
June 3, 1875

That same year the St. Louis Lodge No. 49 I. O. G. T. was chartered on March 8 with eighteen members. Between 100 and 300 men were scattered through the district, all of whom "lived and all had silver." The camp prospered up to 1879, and then, with most of the ledges and terraces worked to bedrock, bar-washing virtually ceased.

The Jawbone gold property, which lay at the head of the right hand branch of Indian Creek, was one of the earliest quartz mines to be developed. Tom Reece owned the mine in 1870, and when he needed a stamp mill to crush the gold, he arranged with Henry Sieben, a freighter, to haul one to his ground. The mill which Reece bought came originally by steamer up the Missouri to Fort Benton and was hauled by ox-team across the prairie and the hills to Gold Creek, where it was installed. Reece bought this mill from Charles W. Cannon and gave Sieben a freighting contract to bring it from Gold Creek, across the Continental Divide over MacDonald Pass, through Helena, and up the Missouri Valley to his property. It took ten days and two trips to bring all of the machinery the 130 miles. Gold from the Jawbone mill netted Reece a clear $50,000. In later years his wealth was considerable, and the story is told that he once loaned $1,000,000 to F. Augustus Heinze.

A new wave of mining swept the district in the mid-1890's and revived St. Louis. This period of the camp's growth is characterized by a reporter from the *Helena Weekly Herald* of July 9, 1896:

There is a vast change since my last visit . . . At that time . . . a few of the pioneer placer miners, Wm. Rick, Joe Hassel, Geo. Weston, Charlie Moffit and Frank Lewery were "sniping" around the gulch making a good living and wondering if the palmy days of '66 would ever return.

After a twenty year sleep, rich quartz mines are being discovered, hundreds of busy prospectors swarm through the hills and the old gulch has taken on life anew.

The quartz mines lay in the hills directly above St. Louis in what was called the Park Mining District. The sales of the New Era mine to F. Longmaid of Marysville for $25,000 and of the Silver Wave to an Omaha company, brought the area to the attention of the public. Diamond Hill, "a great mountain of ore," about half a mile above St. Louis, was called the backbone of the district. Since no placer ground had been found above Diamond Hill in any of the gulches, it was also called the mother lode. To crush the "two million tons of ore in sight, a mill began in May, 1895, to drop its forty-stamps on the oxidized ore."

Sometime during the 1890's, the name St. Louis was dropped in favor of Hassel, honoring Joseph E. Hassel, a pioneer miner. In September, 1895, the Hassel Miner's Union, a branch of the Western Federation of Miners, was organized. On September 17, 1896, the non-partisan Hassel Independent Silver Club was founded "in the interest of silver and the election of Bryan and Hartman." A month later the paper comments that "the Hassel Ladies are showing their good sense and patriotism by joining the silver club."

On the summer afternoon in 1955 when my husband and I went to Hassel, we followed the directions of a man whom we hailed in front of a store in Townsend. "Drive north on the highway until you cross the Missouri River, then turn left and cross the railroad track. Take the road that bears west up the gulch."

As we climbed up out of the valley placer ground lay on both sides of the road. Some of the mounds were overgrown, and some were stacked ricks of waste rock left by dredges. This large auriferous plateau was worked systematically for twenty-five years and intermittently in more recent times. After a five-mile climb, the road entered a gulch whose bed was filled with more dredge dumps. The canyon narrowed to a gorge whose high white walls of fantastic rock shapes cut out the sunlight. For more than a mile the narrow road hugged the bottom and twisted through alder and willow thickets. High on the side of the cliff clung the weathered splinters of a wooden flume. At the head of the gorge we climbed again into sunlight and skirted the gulch the rest of the way. Where the canyon widened the Radersburg road joined ours. At this junction a battered signpost listed: Hassel 1 mile, Radersburg 9, Cow Creek 6, and Townsend 9 miles.

There was some water in Indian Creek and much debris from old workings, such as bits of flume, pipes, and broken rockers. Cattle grazed on the grass-grown placer dumps. The gulch was an appalling sight, for it had obviously been torn apart until its bed was many feet below the original level of the land. At one place a ladder was attached to this wall of eroded earth. Nearby, on a small meadow, stood a two-story house, completely isolated by the high gulch walls. Just ahead, where the deep dredging stopped, was another house shaded by big trees. The road crossed Indian Creek at this point and ran beside it out of sight. A signpost pointed left to the Eagle Ranger Station and the Blacksmith mine, and right to the Park Mines, six miles northwest of Hassel. This group of mines included the New Era, Lone Star, Big Hill, and Bunker Hill.

It was now late in the day and shadows were making strange patterns on the gulch walls, so we turned back toward Townsend. All the way downstream we talked of the mines — the Little Giant from which William Roberts took $2,500 in six months single-handed, and the Ajax, whose ore was so similar to that in the Diamond Hill that it was believed to be an extension of that lead. As we neared Townsend we mentioned the Sunday group, two miles from that town on the Crow Creek Divide. From it gold averaging from $27.00 to $466.00 a ton was found in a shaft only 110 feet deep. We now knew that the placer land in the Hassel area lay in two locations both above and below the narrow gorge of Indian Creek and that the original settlement of St. Louis is a lonely and forgotten site.

TOSTON

Two big red silos were the landmarks by which I recognized Toston, a small farm center, eleven miles southeast of Townsend, on the bank of the Missouri River. Surrounded by irrigated fields of alfalfa and by fertile pasture-land, I failed to discover the site of the small blast furnace which was built in mining boom

RADERSBURG

days to treat the sulphide ores from nearby Radersburg.

RADERSBURG

A paved road at right angles to the highway near the railroad station at Toston leads straight west for nearly twelve miles into Radersburg, a once active mining center. Where the old Bozeman stage road crosses Crow Creek, the mining camp sprang up in 1866 as soon as John A. Keating opened his rich quartz lode.

James Waters, who built his cabin in these hills during the early 1860's, is credited with finding the first lump of free-milling gold ore in the area, on the very land where Keating later located his famous mine. The Keating, which became the most important property in the district, was discovered in 1866 and was worked constantly until 1877. During the earlier part of this period, Keating and his partners, Blacker and Oldman, located and developed other properties — the Leviathan, Ohio-Keating, and Congress mines, and constructed the Keating and Blacker stamp mills which they equipped with amalgamating plates. A short-lived camp called Keatingsville was laid out less than half a mile from the mine. Many years later George G. Griswold, a metallurgist from Butte, leased the mine and designed an electrically equipped mill to handle its unique type of ore.

The discovery of placer gold started a fresh stampede. Most of the ground lay west of the camp for a distance of a mile and eastward for several miles down Crow Creek. Those whose claims were away from the stream packed dirt half a mile to the water until William Quinn and his company dug, with pick and shovel, a five-mile ditch, which was gouged from the shoulders of hills and flumed across ravines.

131

Placers on three other gulches — Faith, Hope, and Charity — were supplied by Payton & Company's ditch, which enabled such properties as Rabbit, Greyhound, Badger, and Bay Horse bars to operate. The miners would pay almost any sum for water, for with good pressure, a six-inch hose, and a two-and-a-half inch nozzle, they were able to cut down the banks and wash the dirt into their sluice boxes. Although no accurate count was kept, the placers are believed to have yielded over $500,000 in gold. When the water froze late in the fall, the men searched the hillsides for gold-bearing quartz lodes.

The Radersburg area was good country for mining; Rattlesnake Butte, Slim Sam Basin, and the foothills of the Elkhorn mountains to the west contained lodes and Crow Creek provided convenient water for sluicing. Named for Ruben Rader, who donated the townsite from his large tract of farmland, Radersburg contained two streets — Front Street and Back Street. It is also the birthplace of Myrna Williams, known to movie fame as Myrna Loy.

Thomas R. Moore, who came to Radersburg as a small child, states in his reminiscences that the camp had an exceptionally domestic atmosphere, perhaps because it contained more women than any other place of its size. It was an all night stopover station for the Concord coaches which carried passengers, mail, and express on the Bozeman Trail between Bozeman and Helena. Freighters took four to six months to make the trip from the nearest railroad at Corinne, Utah, hence prices were high — 25 cents for an apple, 25 cents for a bar of soap, $1.00 for a pound of flour.

Joe Poe hauled water to town from Crow Creek during the winter months and sold it to each household. The only other source of drinking water at such times was melted snow which had to stand until the dirt in it settled. The slaughter house was only a quarter of a mile from the butcher shop, behind which was a livery barn. Mosquito netting protected the fresh meat from a few of the hungry flies! Moore also recalls how the miners amused themselves by scattering gold nuggets on the ground to watch the children scramble for them.

By 1868, Radersburg had a population of 600. Of its growth a correspondent to the *Montana Post* writes:

April 25, 1868

Radersburg has improved more in the last three months than any other camp in the Territory. It has two first-class hotels, the Tremont House . . . and the Planters House . . . The Quartz Hotel is doing a fair business. The mines are worked advantageously, "Charity" and "Hope" gulches, the best paying in the district.

Bay Horse Bar and several other bar and hill diggings are turning out the ore as a reward for the toil in the mines. I was present at a clean up after a twelve-hour run on a claim on Hope gulch. It paid $24 to the hand after the expenses for water were paid.

T. F. Bramhall, D. R. W., for the I. O. G. T. has paid a visit and organized a Lodge at this place. We have thirty-six charter members who contemplate erecting a Temple for Lodge purposes. Although bar rooms are very plentiful here, we have a very orderly community.

Yours,
Observer

Mount Hope Lodge No. 4, I. O. G. T., mentioned by "Observer," was organized April 12, 1868, and reorganized in September, 1869, with twelve members and H. C. Powers the lodge deputy. Its two-story hall is still standing.

Quartz mining began in 1870 with recovery of the oxidized gold ores accomplished by amalgamation or by crushing in small stamp mills or arrastres. Any attempt to work the sulphides which were encountered 100 feet below the surface proved unsuccessful. By 1878, when oxidized ores were exhausted, most of the mines shut down, although a few new properties such as the Deer Lode and Bonanza Chief were discovered at that time by Boyd and Rader. As soon as the Northern Pacific railroad laid its tracks through Toston, a blast furnace was built near that station to treat the refractory sulphide ores. When the large smelters at East Helena and Butte were blown in, and sulphide ores were in demand, the Radersburg output was shipped to them and the Toston furnace shut down. As late as 1910 certain properties, including the Black Friday, continued to operate. The total production from the area through 1928 is estimated at $6,130,000. In 1933, rising metal prices brought a brief revival of mining to the district.

Many stories about Radersburg graphically describe its boom days when "what with lawsuits, horseracing, pugilistic encounters and gambling of every description, life is manifesting itself in quite a lively manner."

Grace Stone Coates records incidents told to her by Thomas R. Moore, who spent the greater part of his life in the once busy camp.

Miss Mary Gilman, the first schoolteacher, taught as best she could in a dirt-roofed, two-room log cabin. Such tiny children were sent to school that the teacher had to bundle them up on benches for their afternoon nap. The school term was during the three winter months. In 1872 a new schoolhouse was built and a summer term held with sixty-two children enrolled. No credentials were required for teachers, and often most unsuitable men applied for the job. One was a politician who spent his weekends gambling and drinking and often sobered up during Monday's classes.

A cross beside a road near Radersburg marks the grave of Charity Jane Dillon, who ran an inn at the Crow Creek crossing below the town. She was well-liked but kept to herself, and she never married. While still a young woman, she was found dead in bed by a neighbor. Under her bed were a trunk and a demijohn. The trunk, which was believed to have contained money, was open and its contents strewn about; the demijohn was half empty. The hired man whom she had employed was gone. Little was known about her except that she was from the East and that she was engaged to a young man who came west and forgot her. She decided to search for him and found him in Radersburg, married. She kept his identity secret and filled her brief life with her work.

For years Radersburg (now in Broadwater County) was the seat of Jefferson County with a courthouse and jail that cost $26,000. As the mines played out, the major part of the population drifted away, and those who stayed turned to agriculture and stockraising. The population in 1879 is given as 250. The following year it was sixty-nine. In 1883, Radersburg lost the county seat to Boulder, a growing community west of the Elkhorn mountains. Today it is a pleasant small town with shaded streets lined with residences and an occasional square-hewn log cabin. Nothing suggests that it once boasted of "fourteen places where scorpion juice brandy, acidulated gin, and tangle leg whisky is freely dealt out."

PARKER

Eight miles west of Toston and close to the Radersburg road is the site of Parker. Only traces of placering mark its location. John Parker, for whom the camp was named, had mines and a mill in the hills on Johnny Creek, eight miles west of Radersburg.

SAND CREEK

On my way to Pony I had to pass through Sappington (on Highway No. 1) near which in the 1890's, the new gold field of Sand Creek was opened up. The *Belt Mountain Miner* of June 8, 1892, calls Sand Creek "The Creede of Montana" and mentions that "about fifty men are on the grounds prospecting and making locations." John A. Pashley discovered the lead "which is easily traced on the surface for a distance of five miles" in a granite formation, and staked the Good Friday, the first mine to be located. A short time later he recorded three more strikes. In 1897, free-milling gold from the Chile mine was treated in a five-stamp mill. Another property, the Whipporwill, ran for about two years. The mines of the district were active intermittently, but the total production from the area was slight.

PONY

At Harrison, six miles south of Sappington, the road to Pony swings west toward the Tobacco Range. A six-and-a-half mile drive brings one to the outskirts of Pony, a trade center for a large mineral and farming area which includes the mining districts of Potosi, Mammoth, Sand Creek, Norwegian Gulch, Norris, Red Bluff, Richmond Flats, Revenue, Meadow Creek, and Sterling.

"Pony" Smith, for whom the town is named, was a restless prospector who left booming Alder Gulch and Virginia City in 1866 or 1867 and started to hunt for gold along the eastern side of the Tobacco Root Range of mountains. In a creek bottom, a little above the present town of Pony, he found the colors for which he was searching and staked a claim, but he did not work it at that time. In 1868, he and a partner returned to the location and began to wash the placer ground that he had previously staked. The streambed yielded coarse gold and a few nuggets, and for a time he was satisfied, but like most prospectors he became restless again and wandered off to search for richer diggings.

His real name was Tecumseh Smith or Smith McCumpsey, but he was such a little runt that everyone called him "Pony." When asked the whereabouts of his diggings, men would reply, "They're on Pony's gulch," or "Go up to Pony's creek," and so his nickname was given to a gulch, a stream, and finally a town.

A number of placer mines were worked in the gulch, especially after George Hadzor and J. C. Hawkins provided additional water for sluicing by bringing a ditch from Cataract Creek down into Pony Gulch in 1870. But when the placers gave out the claims were abandoned. Lode mining began in the summer of 1875.

Gold-bearing quartz was first found about two miles above the present town of Pony by George Moreland. His mine, which he named the Strawberry, because the outcrop lay in a patch of wild berries, was considered the mother lode of the placer ground which Pony had uncovered. At a depth of fourteen feet Moreland uncovered a lead ten feet wide which contained free gold worth from $20.00 to $100.00 a ton. Sometime during the summer or fall of 1875, Albert Mason, Thomas Carmin, Alex Lefler, William Robson and Albert Dinnock located the Boss Tweed. Another famous lead, the Clipper, was staked out by W. V. Ryan, Jesse Barker, and W. H. Metcalf. The Clipper, Belle, and Boss Tweed properties were later known as the Boss Tweed group. Within a year, Jerome W. Boles and George A. Kendall located the Ned and the Willow Creek. Walters and Reynolds held ground just below the Strawberry which contained float quartz so full of free gold that it could be pounded out with mortar and pestle. McCoy and Edmindson uncovered a two-foot crevice of pay rock in the Crystal lode and William Robson located the Keystone.

STRAWBERRY

News of these strikes started a stampede to the district and caused a camp called Strawberry, with a population of 400, to spring up close to the mines. At its peak it contained a store, a postoffice, and a mill, the latter built on Crevice property, another of Moreland's productive claims, from which he cleared $10,000.

PONY (Continued)

During the winter of 1875-1876, A. H. and James A. Mallory built the first quartz mill in the embryo' camp of Pony. This five-stamp mill was moved from Sterling and ran by waterpower. An additional five stamps, obtained from the Rising Sun mill at Norwegian Gulch, were soon added. During its installation one of the Mallory brothers was killed when he fell on ice while carrying timbers. Mrs. Leah Morris Mendenhall, daughter of one of Pony's most influential citizens, William Wardner Morris, wrote to me recently and recalled girlhood recollections of this mill:

Ore was hauled from the mine to the Mallory Mill with six yoke of oxen to each wagon. The scales for weighing the ore were at the end of the trestle. Ore was unloaded on a platform and then conveyed to the top of the mill and crushed just enough to feed the stamps. At the sound of Swiss bells worn by the long-horned oxen which were coming around the bend, my brother and I would bound up to the scales, intrigued beyond words to watch "Biddy," the Swiss, guide them by "gee" and "haw." And when they had to be shod, we found a high place of safety to watch them suspended on leather belting as the little half-pieces were nailed on in place of the familiar horseshoe. Coming down one day, with a heavy load of ore, the "rough-lock" broke, and six of them were dashed down the steep mountain to their death. After that, horses were used. Later trucks came in.

Pony camp, which immediately overshadowed Strawberry, obtained a postoffice in 1876. The postmaster, N. J. Isdell, also ran a store, as did a "Mr. Cramer" who scurried over from Sheridan so as to get in at the start of things. Michael Hauley and Pattee opened a butchershop; Hauley, Paul Taft and Potter had a livery barn, and Pony Gilbert ran a saloon. Since there was no schoolhouse, Mrs. Marsh held classes in a store which also served as a church.

The spring of 1877 brought a second stampede to the district. Nearly 1,000 men from all over the territory swarmed into the hills to scratch for gold. But prospectors are notoriously fickle, and when, after several months, new strikes were reported in Glendale, Phillipsburg, Butte, and other locations, Pony was emptied almost overnight. Although a log schoolhouse and forty log cabins were completed by 1878, as well as two hotels, a blacksmith shop, a billiard saloon, and a public hall, the population had dwindled to a mere hundred.

Two influential citizens who did much to shape the growth and stability of Pony were Henry Elling and William W. Morris. The latter was formerly a druggist in Virginia City and was constructing his store at the time that the Vigilantes did away with five of Plummer's road agents. A beam in Morris' unfinished store served as the gallows! Somewhat later, Morris settled in Pony where, in 1880, he and Elling bought the Boss Tweed-Clipper

PONY. MORRIS STATE BANK AT LEFT: MORRIS-ELLING MILL
AND OLD HOLLOWTOP MT. IN DISTANCE

mines, the most famous and valuable properties in the district from which $5,000,000 was recovered.

Active mining was resumed during the 1880's and additional mills were needed to crush rock from the many leads which produced hundreds of thousands of dollars of gold —the richest of which lay in pockets and chimneys. During this period Mineral Hill properties above the town were developed. The twenty-stamp Elling and Morris stone mill ran to capacity on ore from the Boss Tweed and Keystone mines. No ore which ran less than $25.00 a ton was handled. The fifteen-stamp Morain mill ran by steam, the ten-stamp Getchell used waterpower. Three arrastres also ground large quantities of rock with varying success. The purchase of the Strawberry-Keystone group of mines by A. M. Holter, head of a Helena syndicate — the Pony Mining Company — attracted further attention to the district.

Both the Boss Tweed and the Clipper mines were active throughout the nineties. Elling died in 1900, and the same year the properties were sold outright in combination with the Bell, Eclipse, Charity, and Summit, to a Boston syndicate for $600,000. This transaction stimulated further development of the entire district, and the following decade saw renewed activity in many properties. Experts who examined the property at the time of the sale reported $10,000,000 worth of ore in sight. Consequently, the syndicate bought the electric, 100-stamp mill, formerly erected at Hassel by the Diamond Hill Mining Company, and installed it at Pony, three miles from the mine, adding cyanide tanks to treat the tailings. The mill never dropped a stamp, for the enormous body of quartz proved to be only low-grade smelter ore. William Morris was in California when this project blew up, but upon his return to Pony he leased the property and, with

135

his knowledge of metallurgy, treated the ore in his twenty-stamp mill with profit, until his death in 1904. He even tried to buy the mill for $50,000 but was refused. It was finally sold to a wrecking company for $15,000, and most of its lumber turned up in sheep sheds on nearby ranches. Still later, in 1927, it was sold for taxes and leased to a company of Japanese. They knew nothing about mining and pulled out, leaving the property heavily in debt.

Increased mining operations during the 1930's kept the town lively and proved the importance of the mineral deposits. Even as late as 1948, Pony's population was close to 1,000.

Early one July morning in 1951, I drove into Pony. The wide main street ran straight toward the foothills of the Tobacco Roots above which rose a majestic peak — said to be an extinct crater, Hollow Top (Mt. Jefferson on maps). The thoroughfare was lined with buildings — weathered false-fronts elbowing brick business blocks, and small homes smothered by shrubbery. At the far end of town a road entered a canyon, at whose mouth stood the imposing skeleton of a stone stamp mill, roofless but still containing a few heavy timbers. "What mill is this?" I called to an old man who buzzed past in a Jeep. "The Elling," he shouted as he disappeared up the road.

As I wandered around the streets, I looked for the lodge of the Ancient Order of United Workmen, which was chartered in 1885, and for the meeting place of the Pony Womens' Club, organized in 1902 for the purpose of studying current events and literature. I did discover the Morris State Bank, a two-story brick structure which, when built, was arranged to accommodate, on its upper floor, the Pony Commercial Club, consisting of fifty members. William Morris, bank president for many years, died of a heart attack while inspecting mining properties in Reveille, Nevada, in August, 1904. His funeral, which was held in the Presbyterian church in Pony, was attended, in addition to family and friends, by 150 members of Virginia City's Elks Lodge to which he belonged. His obituary in the *Pony Sentinel* of August 26, 1904, states that he was born in 1840, came to Montana in 1864, and lived his last twenty-two years in Pony. Through his death Pony lost one of her foremost citizens. Another source reports that every child in the town laid a small bouquet on his grave.

Several large homes in Pony and a big red brick-and-stone schoolhouse stand on a rise of land in a side gulch. By the time that the $12,000 school was built, Pony had "churches, newspapers and other trimmings." The Episcopalians built in 1908 with the Rev. Lewis performing services "whenever weather permitted, usually twice a month." The Catholics also had a small building and held occasional services. The Presbyterians, under the Reverend J. L. Marquis, built in 1894. Their church ultimately became the community church.

In 1911, the Madison County Publicity Club and the county commissioners published a descriptive pamphlet which stated that two electric plants furnished power for mining operations and light for the town, and that "hospital service was furnished by one of the local physicians where frail humanity is skillfully repaired in case of accidents and the necessity for surgical operations."

While in Helena I read the *History of Madison County*, prepared by Mrs. Melvina J. Lott and others, and from stories contained in it gained a clearer picture of life in Pony in early days. The two given here are concerned with illness and ingenuity.

It was three o'clock one afternoon when Dr. Harvey Foster Smith learned that William Beckwith had accidentally shot his nephew while working at a mine three miles up in the hills above Pony. The doctor hurriedly loaded a bed into a wagon and drove to the mine, where he treated the patient and brought him back to town, taking him to his sister's house while he telegraphed to a Bozeman surgeon to come as quickly as he could. While waiting for him to arrive, Smith wired his sister's house and installed electric lights, so that when Dr. Blair, who had to drive sixty-five miles, arrived he could see to perform the operation.

The second story is about homesteaders. When Hanson knew that his wife was about to give birth, he went for help. It was a June evening in 1866, when he left to fetch the Indian woman midwife who lived seventeen miles away. While he was gone a spring blizzard struck and slowed his progress, so that he was still fighting the storm at the time that his daughter was born. Meanwhile, his wife, left alone in a draughty cabin through which the snow sifted, crawled to the fireplace to get hot water to bathe the baby. The following morning when Hanson returned with the nurse, his wife handed him his child.

POTOSI

At the head of North and South Willow Creeks, eight to ten miles from Pony in the Tobacco Root Range, were the mines of the Potosi district. The earliest settlement of the area dates from 1864 when placers in Norwegian Gulch were discovered, but the mining district was not organized until 1874 when Hughes and Howe located the Bullion lode. A silver camp called Potosi was laid out at the head of South Willow Creek to accommodate the miners. An eight-mile climb through Potosi Canyon to the Hot Springs, which lie in a natural park at the base of the range, brings one fairly close to the site of the old camp and its mines. The mineral deposits of North Willow Creek were not developed until the Strawberry was located by L. C. Moreland.

NORRIS

Norris, ten miles south of Harrison on Hot Springs Creek, is a business center for four mining districts — Lower Hot Springs, Upper Hot Springs, Washington and Meadow Creek, and Norwegian Gulch. While some of the properties were placer claims, lode mines were discovered by the late 1860's and were active for many years. Production figures from 1864 to 1930 inclusive, including the Washington district, are given as $3,964,500, mostly in gold.

RED BLUFF

Lower Hot Springs District is east from Norris and extends six miles to the Madison River. It includes Hot Springs Creek below Norris, Cottonwood and Burnt Creeks, and the area around the old town of Red Bluff. The hard-surfaced Norris-Bozeman cutoff passes through the townsite, which can be identified by a three-story stone house to the north of the road and a tunnel to the Gold Cup mine to the south of it. Red Bluff, which dates from 1864, was once a lively camp, and the big stone building was Scanlan's boarding house. It was later used as a residence and a hotel and at one time was owned by A. W. Tanner, who discovered garnets in the vicinity.

Tanner often appeared in Bozeman with a bagful of gems which jewelers eagerly bought and polished. The Boaz and Josephine were the most valuable mines near Red Bluff, the former producing $200,000 in gold and silver,

chiefly between 1870 and 1880. The Grubstake was the most developed property and yielded free-milling ore that ran from $60.00 to $80.00 a ton. The Red Bluff, an important producer during the 70's and 80's, was reopened in 1901

by the Elling estate and operated by the Red Bluff Mining Co. Ltd. . . . When the present company took charge, the property had produced $300,000 above the 130-foot level and was stoped clear to the surface. It was left a total wreck as the result of neglect and difficulties of retimbering and of putting a drowned mine in operation . . . It is in fine condition now . . . the ore yields $14 a ton. The company expects to erect a 100-ton concentrating plant to cost $30,000.

Western Mining World, Nov. 2, 1901

Upper Hot Springs District is six miles southwest of Norris in the hills. Its chief mines during the 1890's were the Revenue and the Monitor. These properties were combined in 1903 and controlled by the Montana Revenue Gold Mining Company. The Revenue, which became inactive in 1921, yielded $2,000,000 in gold. The Red Rose claim was nearby.

Washington and Meadow Creek District is farther away. The Washington district is twelve miles southwest of Norris between North and South Meadow Creeks. Placers on South Meadow Creek were discovered in 1864. The area also contains quartz mines. The southern portion of the district, sometimes called Bald Mountain, was the most important discovery made since 1900. Placer ground was reworked by a dredge prior to World War I. The Meadow Creek district is fifteen miles southwest of Norris, and at one time is said to have contained two sawmills, one quartz mill, a church, and a school. The Frisbie mine was on North Meadow Creek.

Norwegian Gulch District is seven miles northwest of Norris. Its placers were discovered in 1864 and were worked successfully for ten years with a total recovery of $150,000 in gold. A ditch built in 1865, which carried 300 inches of water from South Willow Creek, served the mines until 1875, when it was enlarged. A dredge constructed in 1932 has operated intermittently. As early as the summer of 1864, the Reverend L. B. Stateler, a Methodist preacher, assisted by the Reverend Hargrove, pitched his tent in the gulch and preached to the three hundred placer miners who were washing gravel. He reported that "attendance was good and the singing was especially enjoyed."

STERLING

STERLING

It was a hot morning when we drove into a filling station at Norris to inquire the way to Sterling and other camps in that vicinity, and the two ranchers drinking 7-Up and waiting for their truck to be serviced, gave us just the information we needed. Sterling, they said, was three miles west of Norris, and Revenue Flat (or Richmond Flat, as it was also called) was three miles beyond the first stone mill, if one followed the left fork of the road from that point. Washington Bar and North Meadow Creek were never more than gold placers. Both places could be reached from Revenue Flat by driving for several more miles across the rolling hills. Just as we turned onto the dirt road leading to Sterling, an old battered truck full of children and driven by a man with his arm in a cast pulled into the gas station and was hailed by the men to whom we had been talking. After nearly three miles, we approached a ruined stone mill, similar to the one at Pony. Here the road split three ways: the left fork passed the side of the mill and wound up a steep hill; the right fork led to a ranchhouse beyond which stood sheds and a mine shafthouse; the road straight ahead was barred by a gate.

To get our bearings, we drove to the ranch, where we found a Sunday family picnic in full swing. From one of the older men we learned that Sterling had stood right where we were. The rest of the townsite was only a quarter of a mile away, beyond the gate on the other road. The mine just behind the ranch house was the Billie.

We returned to the mill and drove beyond it through the gate, only to enter a rocky gorge which climbed over a low saddle and then dropped rapidly to a small meadow in which stood a number of old buildings. Just beyond the saddle stood a second mill, similar

REVENUE FLAT AND ROAD TO MEADOW AND WASHINGTON CREEKS

to the first, with thick stone walls pierced by empty window and door openings. The meadow at the foot of the hill, which contained low cabins, barns, sheds, and one long ranchhouse with a porch, was hemmed in on all sides by steep cliffs and odd rock formations. As we approached the buildings a dog came wiggling toward us followed by a young chap who said he was hired by the ranch. He spoke of the Galena mine, which was active in 1874 and which produced $150,000 in gold and silver during one ten-year period, and of other properties farther up the canyon, all of which were long shut down because the low-grade ore failed to bring a profit. "Every now and then some fellow takes a lease on the mine," he said, "and makes it pay off, but you never know."

Sterling at its peak contained three saloons, two hotels, a livery stable, and other business houses. Bill Reel, the son of a Montana prospector, came to the camp with his parents at the peak of the boom and stayed on after the population of 600 dwindled to zero. He bought up claims and land, including the townsite of Sterling, which he turned into a farm, and

on which he built his ranchhouse. He also acquired a second townsite, a diminutive rival about 200 yards south of Sterling, which had sprung up around the property of the Midas Company. The ninety or more men who worked for this company refused to be absorbed by the larger settlement and called their collection of cabins and tents, grouped around the $80,000 Midas mill, Midasburg.

Miners rushed to the district in 1867 when

REVENUE FLAT

promising prospects were opened in the Tobacco Root Mountains. The first of five stamp mills was built shortly afterwards to refine the ore from the several properties. Machinery for these mills was freighted in from Bozeman, one hundred miles distant. Over $1,000,00 was spent in developing lodes and building mills, some of which ran sporadically as late as 1913, and although profits were realized, especially after 1872, the bulk of the ore remained low-grade and averaged only $9.00 to $12.00 per ton. By 1880, the miners from Sterling were hurrying over the hills to the new camp of Richmond Flat, a few miles away. Thereafter, the once prosperous gold camp of Sterling, hidden in its lonely ravine on Hot Springs Creek, lay forgotten. When its buildings were demolished, two prospectors found it profitable to pan the dirt under the saloon floors.

REVENUE FLAT

We drove back past the first stone mill, the Midas, to the road fork and turned south at the second mill, the Sterling, to begin the climb to Richmond or Revenue Flat. It was a long, slow pull up a narrow winding road all the way to the deserted camp.

The men at the gas station warned us to watch for rocks and it was good advice, for the roadbed had a high center and was full of sharp, loose stones. In some places the surface was down to slick rock. Near the end of the climb it passed between sentinel-like black bluffs. Ahead, at the top of the hill, on a flat stood mine dumps and shafthouses. Below the road was an old settling pond. The countryside in all directions was pitted with prospect holes and location stakes. As we pulled up the last grade, the road grazed a big mine dump and then fanned out at the top into several grass-grown trails which straggled toward the scattered properties on the high wind-swept flat. While we were exploring the principal ones — the Revenue, the Idaho, the Arkansas, and the Treasurer — we heard a car

motor and around the big dump came the truck full of children that we had seen in Norris. It did not stop but ground on to the west toward Washington Bar. We watched it wind across the hilltops until it disappeared down the far side.

The mines at Revenue Flat were discovered in the middle eighties. According to Colonel J. H. Johnson, general manager of the Revenue company, 8,000 tons of ore were in sight in June 1885 and the mine was considered a number one property. The Arkansas lode, whose shaft was down 35 feet, reported 18 inches of $250.00 ore in sight, and the Idaho revealed a "splendid crevice." The first issue of the *Madison County Monitor*, which appeared April 1, 1892, contains the following item concerning Richmond Flat:

Revenue to the Front
First Mill in the State Using the Cyanide of Potassium Process

The Revenue mine well known for the last four years, is a good producer with $500,000 of ore in sight. Because of the refractory nature of the ore, the owners, up till last September were unable to catch the gold. The new cyanide process, put in operation March 2, has proved a complete success. On the first run of 100 tons, a saving of 80% was made. This run was on the tailings of an old stamp mill.

That this process continued to be satisfactory is shown by a later report made by the *Western Mining World* in 1896. According to it

the mine has been running steadily for the past year and a half, reducing 25-30 tons of gold ore a day, averaging $30 a ton . . . The past season high-grade ore was struck, in which the gold was so coarse and free that the cyanide process had to be abandoned for a time . . . The Monitor, near the Revenue, carries similar ore.

As we left Revenue Flat and looked out over the bare, moraine-like hills, it was difficult to picture them as they must have looked in the spring of 1892 when, according to a newspaper item: "The boys of the Revenue are beginning to move out of the boarding house for the summer and the surrounding country resembles a soldier's camp."

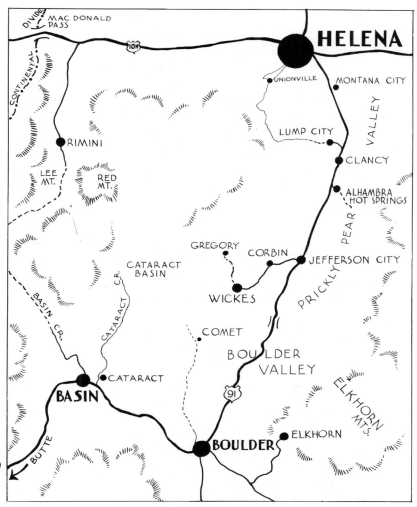

CHAPTER 8

PRICKLY PEAR
and BOULDER
VALLEY CAMPS

MONTANA CITY

Highway No. 91, between Helena and Butte, passes through several small towns, all of which started either as stage stops on the Virginia City-Helena road or as mining camps. Just east of the capital city the road veers south and skirts Prickly Pear Creek to the head of the valley. About ten miles from Helena in the midst of weed-covered tailings is the site of Montana City, an early mining camp. Only the historic marker beside the road indicates where the short-lived placer camp stood.

The Fisk, or Northern Overland Expedition, stumbled onto the gold-bearing gravels in the summer of 1862 while crossing the valley in order to open a wagon route to Fort Benton, the eastern terminus of the Mullan Road. Captain James L. Fisk led this party of 125 emigrants from St. Paul and en route to Fort Benton camped on the future site of Montana City.

Although his train was not made up of miners, when it found Gold Tom, one of the territory's first prospectors, panning gravel on Prickly Pear Creek, a number of men caught gold fever and stayed in the valley to try their luck with the elusive sands. Two other early arrivals at the diggings were a man named Harlbert and his Negro partner, part of a party which came up the Missouri River and found colors in the gulch.

Montana City, the name given to the scattering of cabins in September, 1864, was never a big camp, although at one time several hundred miners worked the placers extensively. G. O. Vineyard, one of the first commissioners of Jefferson County, wrote from his home in Anaconda, in 1903, of Montana City as he remembered it:

Jefferson county was not on the maps until the winter of 1864 and 1865 when the first Legislature met at Bannack City in what is now Beaverhead county. That legislature created the counties of Beaverhead, Madison, Gallatin, Jefferson and Choteau. Afterwards the county seat of Jefferson was located in Montana City . . . and consisted of fifteen to twenty cabins, the most prominent of which was Charley Hollenback's store which was of logs. Bill Whetstone had a small place lower down the gulch where he parted with wet goods at 25 cents a smile. On the opposite side of the street, next to the gulch, was a butcher shop. . . . I was county committioner of Jefferson county with George Case of Boulder Valley and Mr. McFarland. Frank Wells was clerk of the board. This was in 1866. At the next election the county seat was moved to Radersburg.

LUMP CITY

"Let's see if there's anything left of Lump City," I said when Montana City townsite was behind us. "It's said to be less than two miles west of this highway before we reach Clancy, and the schoolhouse should still be standing."

"What do you know about the place?" asked Francis, as we drove south between the railroad and Prickly Pear Creek.

"A copy of the *Western Mining World* published in the middle 1890's said that when the price of silver was lowest, production from high-grade ore deposits in the Lump Gulch district began and continued for a number of years. The area in which silver was found covered a tract eight miles long by four wide and included Lump, Clancy, Strawberry, Shingle, and Warm Springs Gulches. For two or three years, before the railroad was built through this valley, ore was shipped by wagon to Corinne, Utah, and then by rail to the coast and sent by ship to Swansea, Wales, for treatment. After the railroad was completed, ore was shipped from the Hartford and Clancy stations and sent to the custom smelters in East Helena.

"Lump Gulch was prospected for placer gold in the early days, and exaggerated reports of its richness brought a stampede to the diggings. When they failed to yield heavily, the gulch was quickly deserted. In later years, quartz lodes were discovered in the coarse-grained micaceous granite, and Lump and other nearby gulches were worked with considerable success.

"Thomas G. Merrill is probably responsible for the successful development of the district. He was in the first disappointing stampede, but he must have stayed around, for in 1866 he located a quartz claim on ground which was later part of the Liverpool property. It wasn't much good either and he abandoned it.

But like most prospectors, he returned to the gulch and in the early 1880's relocated the ground, calling his claim the Liverpool. Other prospectors who had located quartz lodes had already left the gulch, as their discoveries had shown only lean surface veins. Since Merrill lacked capital, he was unable to develop his property until after 1890, when he interested John S. Miller of Helena in associating with him in the enterprise. To the surprise of the men, Merrill found that the mineral-bearing ledges of Lump Gulch were inverted — that is, small near the surface and widening with depth and that they needed only moderate development to open up rich deposits of silver ore. A few weeks work put the mine on a paying basis, and eighteen months later, it paid $200,000 in dividends. The Liverpool, which produced $1,500,000 by the later 1890's, was on the north side of Lump Gulch near its mouth, three-quarters of a mile from Hartford railroad station. During its peak of production it employed forty-five men. The success of the mine encouraged other claim owners to develop their prospects until two dozen mines were actively producing in the district."

We had no trouble in finding the Lump Gulch road, and after driving a scant two miles along it, past a ranchhouse and one or two old cabins, we stopped at another ranch where a man was shoeing a horse. He was too busy to talk and waved me toward the house, where his wife stood in the doorway. "Ask my missus. She can tell you what you want to know. You're in what was Lump City right now," he said, turning back to his work.

"Where's the schoolhouse?" I asked his wife.

"Right across the road," she replied. "That pile of lumber is where it stood. We just tore it down."

I looked at the heap of weathered boards which lay on the plank floor and thought, "Another landmark gone."

Had we approached Lump City directly from Helena by the mountain road that crosses the hills above Unionville and drops down to Prickly Pear Creek, we would have passed other mines. Later, in Helena, I found copies of the *Lump City Miner* and from it learned more about the vanished camp.

Vol. I, No. I, Jan. 5, 1895
Lump City itself, while not boasting of quite so many or so pretentious a class of buildings as either Helena or Butte, is perhaps as handsome in general appearance as was either of those cities in their infant days. There is, at this writing, some sixty buildings in the

camp, and more are being erected every day. When spring opens a building boom will set in.

The early life of the camp was far from dull. By February, 1895, the 400 to 500 men in the town were clamoring for a postoffice. In March, "the Citizens of Lump City and Vicinity" protested against the employment of Chinese and "circulated a paper up and down the gulch" which read:

Lump City, March 26, 1895

We, the undersigned citizens of Lump City and vicinity, discountenance the employment of Chinese labor in any manner, and pledge ourselves to support all white labor in preference.

We think in particular, there being a number of white cooks seeking employment, that the Chinese now employed should be discharged and that their places be filled by white labor.

"Citizens of the United States"

It was signed by more than one hundred and fifty men. Less than two weeks later (April 6) the "Clancy Miners' Union in a Body visit the Non-Union Miners of the District." According to the paper, "The result of the night's catch was 16 members, with more to come."

That spring, Lump City had a Cornet Band and a Base Ball Club. In July the First Annual Ball of the Lump City Lodge, A. O. U. W., No. 61 was held with "thirty-five couples present in addition to a number without partners." Although I find no mention of a church, by November the paper states that the Lump City Sunday School showed a marked increase in attendance. By fall, weekly cleanups from the mines produced ore shipments totaling five carloads — three from the Liverpool and one each from the Little Nell and Little Alma. According to the newspaper reports, Lump City and its mines during the initial year of great activity played an important part in the economy of the district.

CLANCY

We had no sooner driven back onto Highway No. 91 from Lump City than we reached Clancy, a once busy trade center and silver camp whose estimated production up to 1928 totaled $3,500,000 from silver, gold, lead, and copper. It is a small quiet town fourteen miles southeast of Helena. Placer deposits drew prospectors to its streambeds in 1865 and caused the camp to be built. Placers at Buffalo, eight miles to the west, contributed to its wealth.

CLANCY

The discovery of lode mines in the nearby hills helped it grow, until by 1879, when its population reached 200, it contained a general merchandise store run by H. M. Hill, a drug and a hardware store, as well as a postoffice, a machine and blacksmith shop, an assay office and a butcher shop.

Clancy's greatest activity was prior to 1890, when its Legal Tender mine, situated one quarter of a mile from town on the east side of Prickly Pear Creek, was most productive. This pioneer property is credited with an output of one million dollars in silver. The best ore ran 10,000 ounces of silver to the ton. Ore that carried less than 200 ounces of silver was left in the mine.

A fire in 1902 razed most of the business section. Caused by an overheated stove in Saevy Hall, a frame building in which a "hard times" dance had just been held, it was discovered in the early morning hours; but since Clancy was without fire fighting equipment, it gained headway and spread rapidly. Wet blankets protected a few buildings, but since it was bitterly cold and the thermometer registered fifteen degrees below zero, water froze immediately. There was no loss of life, but the guests in the Albany Hotel, next to the burning hall, lost all their possessions. A second fire a few years later burned the roundhouse of the Montana Central railroad and destroyed what was left of the business blocks. It is therefore hard to imagine where the Star of the West Lodge No. 46 I. O. G. T., founded in 1874, was located, or where the Jefferson Valley Woolen Mill (erected in 1879) — the pioneer woolen manufacturing industry in Montana — stood.

ALHAMBRA HOT SPRINGS

Alhambra Hot Springs, a mile south of

Clancy, still has an outdoor plunge. This was a popular resort as long ago as 1875, when it was managed by the Messrs. Niedenhoffen & Co. and when its patrons not only enjoyed vapor baths and the mineral water which flowed underground from Mt. Lava, above the spa, but also received their "mail every day and read the daily papers almost as soon as if they were in the city."

JEFFERSON CITY

Jefferson City, four miles south of the Hot Springs, dates from 1864 when a stage station on the Virginia City-Fort Benton road was built at the junction of Comet and Prickly Pear Creeks. The same year, a party of men from Alder Gulch settled there after Allen T. Axe, one of their number, discovered the Gregory lode west of the present town.

The following year the Jefferson Town Company was incorporated on January 11, a postoffice was established, and the Territorial Legislature made Jefferson the county seat. As the town grew, a school was opened (in 1866) and a hotel, replaced in later years by the Emerson House, provided lodging for the many arrivals to the mining camp. William Whitstone ran one saloon and billiard hall, and Kessler & Winters ran a rival one. Jefferson Lodge No. 14, I. O. G. T. was organized May 6, 1869, followed by Lodge No. 33 on August 10, 1872. The 1879 Directory lists the population as 500.

Placer gold discoveries along Golconda Gulch and Prickly Pear Creek attracted prospectors to the area, and lode mines, such as the Mount Washington, brought a later wave of miners to the hills. The Big Chief, at the mouth of Golconda Gulch, east of the town, and the Buckeye mine, several miles up Golconda Creek, were both worked intensively. For many years part of an old Spanish-type arrastre, used by the Buckeye's first owners, could be seen on the property. As mining increased, William Nolan built a smelter one mile from the city. During the first part of the twentieth century mining activity slowed down; but when Winston Bros. Company of Minneapolis, in 1939, obtained a lease on many acres of gold-bearing placer ground along Prickly Pear Creek and employed thirty men to operate its equipment, the enterprise brought new life to Jefferson City.

The dredge handled 6,000 cubic yards of gravel every twenty-four hours, burying top-soil and stacking gravel as it progressed. This mining operation, when completed, left not only the dredge floating in its man-made pond, but also miles of dumps between Alhambra Hot Springs and Jefferson City. A few false-fronts along the highway and some log cabins and other old buildings bordering the road to Corbin and Wickes constitute Jefferson City today.

CORBIN

Two miles west of Jefferson City are the remains of the mining and smelting camp of Corbin, named for D. C. Corbin, owner and builder of the Spokane & Northern Railroad. Some false-fronted frame buildings and one log house date from days earlier than the rest of the buildings. Corbin stands on a flat, surrounded by rolling hills riddled with prospect holes. In the distance one mountain is checkered with mine trails. Dredge dumps border Comet Creek all the way from the highway to the town. A railroad trestle crosses a road near the concrete foundations of a concentrator. Opposite it, across the road, is a settling pond and the remains of another concentrator. Most of the tailings from the pond were shipped to the East Helena smelter years ago, and part of them came from the Peck mill, the first to be built for the Alta mine.

WICKES and GREGORY

Another two or three miles through a fertile valley where men were haying brought us to Wickes, slightly larger than Corbin, but a mere ghost of its former self. The first signs of the town are three big smokestacks and the stone foundations of a smelter. Across the road is a row of conical charcoal kilns, all but one of which is partially demolished.

Wickes was settled in 1877 and flourished until two major fires leveled the greater portion of it at the beginning of the twentieth century. It was named for W. W. Wickes, engineer and promoter of the Alta Mining Company.

On my first visit to the camp in 1951 I talked to a man working in a false-fronted store now used as a garage. "You should have seen this place before the big fire in 1902. There used to be fifteen hundred people here. Now there's only twenty-five. The mines around here were all silver and lead until you sank below the silver belt. When

CONCENTRATOR FOUNDATIONS, CORBIN

SMELTER STACKS, WICKES. *Reproduced courtesy of* THE BONANZA TRAIL, *Indiana University Press*

the first miners struck copper, they didn't know how to treat it so they quit. The lodes here carry silver, gold, lead, copper, and zinc. In fact, all the elements needed in smelting are found in the ores of this district, and in the right proportions, too. That's why there were so many reduction works here and in Corbin and Gregory. There are plenty of good properties near here. The Mount Washington, just a mile south of Corbin, produced $1,000,000. The Gregory, northwest of here, is another old property that paid off by $9,000,000, they say. It claims to be the second quartz lode discovery in the greater Helena district. The Ninah, a mile and a half northwest of Wickes, was another of the paying mines. J. O. Briscoe, the first operator in the district, developed it and took out between $2,000,000 and $5,000,000. The Alta, up on the hill, is still being worked. There's men up there now with bulldozers and steam shovels cutting the hill down.

"It and the Alta South, the Rumley, the Custer, the Comet, and the Gregory were the mines that made a name for this place. Including the Comet mine, total production is quoted at $59,500,000. You see, this area has been worked a long time. Lode mining began here in 1864 and has been carried on more or less ever since.

GREGORY

"While you're here run up to Gregory. There's nothing left, but you ought to see the place where the first smelter stood. The second one was built here at Wickes and the third at East Helena."

I didn't go to Gregory, but I read what notes I had about the camp. Under the ownership of W. C. Child and L. R. Nettre of Helena and others, the Gregory Consolidated Mining Company erected a concentrator in 1884, capable of treating thirty to sixty tons a day. One 550-foot flue furnished the draft! The bullion produced by the smelter assayed at $350.00 a ton.

WICKES (Continued)

Before returning to the dark interior of his shed, the garage man at Wickes pointed out a mountain north of the town and said: "That's the Alta mine on Alta mountain where you see the trucks on the dump. It's two and a half miles from here and you passed what's

left of its old concentrator in Corbin. Some time back they found big blocks of carbonate ore full of silver, lead, and gold on the surface of the mountain, not far from the main vein. For nearly thirty years more than three hundred miners worked in that hill. They tell me there's thirty miles of tunnels in it and that they took $32,000,000 out of it."

I'd read that the Alta Montana Mining Company had spent a fortune trying to develop the Alta lode but had had hard luck. In 1882, their mill produced $64,113.56 in fine silver and $325,000 in lead bullion, but there was no cheap way to haul the ore from the mine to a smelter. After their concentrator at Wickes burned, the company was forced to sell out as soon as possible. According to Leeson, the new owners, the Helena Mining & Reduction Company, bought the Alta property in 1883, subject to $250,000 in liens and mortgages, and since they too lacked shipping facilities, they, in collaboration with Mr. Seligman of the Gregory mine, induced the Northern Pacific Railroad Company to lay a line from Helena to Wickes. This branch, known as the Helena and Jefferson County, was completed in December, 1883. With transportation assured, the company spent $190,-667 in rebuilding the entire plant, which when complete included two new concentrators — one for the Comet at Wickes and the other for the Alta mine at Corbin — as well as six kilns capable of producing 25,000 bushels of charcoal per month. With these improvements, 350 tons of ore could be hauled the three miles from the mine to the Corbin concentrator each day on a narrow-gauge road and the concentrates shipped by rail to the smelter. By January, 1885, the company had taken 21,000 tons of ore from the Comet, 13,000 tons from the Alta, and 4,197 tons from the Rumley mines and had declared dividends amounting to $72,000.

In 1955 I visited Wickes a second time and drove the length of the main street past the school to the farthest house which was marked "Postoffice." As I returned through the town, I noticed a woman at the back door of a frame dwelling hidden by trees. I hurried into the yard, full of questions which I hoped she could answer. Calling her husband, who was over eighty years of age, the couple introduced themselves as Mr. and Mrs. John Reilly, and while the three of us sat on a bench in the shade, they told me something of Wickes' boom days.

I knew that two Reilly boys left Fort Leavenworth with their father in 1880 and came up the Missouri River on the steamboat "C. R. Peck" and that they had settled in the new camp of Wickes, where William Reilly carried the mail and his brother John ran a livery barn with thirty head of horses. And here I sat talking to John, who had lived in Wickes most of his life, and to his wife who came from Leadville, Colorado!

The Reillys pointed out mines that clung to the hillsides above the valley floor and identified a tipsy shafthouse behind and above their home as belonging to the Atlas property. They also mentioned the principal mines of the district — the Comet, Piñon, Bluebird, Mount Washington, Ninah, Gregory, and Steamboat. The Presbyterian church, they told me, was completed in December, 1882. It cost $2,750, the Alta Montana company making the final payment and presenting the deed for the land on which it stood. The Reverend T. A. Wickes and his wife were largely responsible for the success of the church. In 1880, the year that the Reilly boys arrived, the Eureka Lodge No. 13 I. O. G. T. was organized. By 1883 the camp had several business establishments and two hotels, one run by Dean & Street and the other by C. F. Parker. In 1884, a forty-ton water jacket smelter was completed and blown in on May 1st. Both it and an older smelter ran for several months on accumu-

ATLAS MINE AND RAILROAD GRADE, WICKES

lated ore from the Alta and Comet properties. Custom smelting was also done by these works, and as long as belching smoke rolled from the several stacks, Wickes prospered. During this period, the town not only extended a mile and a half along the main street but also up Finn Gulch, so called because Finnish families lived there. The gulch was also known as "Kiddville" after three sets of twins arrived.

Wickes reached its peak when the railroad was built. It took months to grade the right of way and lay the tracks, and even more time

STORES, WICKES

to cut a mile and a quarter tunnel through the mountains. All the work on the tunnel was done with hand drills, and waste rock and dirt were hauled away in horse-drawn carts. All during the construction period, crews of workmen poured into the smelter town to relax and celebrate, for it was the nearest lively camp that they could reach. It was at this time, according to Mrs. Reilly, that the population reached 1,500, and that Wickes had nineteen saloons (but only sixteen according to her husband) and five dancehalls that ran day and night. Fights were so common that no one bothered to watch them. Playing cards lay so thick on the main street each morning that a man with a team was hired to sweep them up. William Litton and his wife arrived in the camp four years before the railroad was built. On the day that the first passenger train chuffed around the curve above the camp and headed for the tunnel, the Littons gladly paid an extra dollar to ride through the bore to the county seat at Boulder.

"I've seen lots of changes here," said Mr. Reilly as I prepared to leave. "When I came, there wasn't even a telephone line between Wickes and Helena. When Dad and my brother and I came up the Missouri in 1880, we reached Fort Benton the first of April. We'd anchored on sandbars more than once to let herds of buffalo cross the river. It was the only thing to do. We brought a wagon and four horses with us and drove them here from Fort Benton. There weren't any roads then and it took us six days. Fires have been hard on Wickes. First the Alta-Montana Company's reduction works burned, and then, in 1900, fire nearly wiped out the town, but we rebuilt right away. Then in 1902 it burned again. The smelter here was one of the first lead-silver reduction plants in Montana. It ran until 1889 when they moved the machinery to East Helena."

I hated to leave the Reillys, for with their wealth of information and their vivid descriptions, they had made Wickes live again.

BOULDER

The drive back to Jefferson City seemed short, and as we turned south on Highway No. 91 and started to climb toward the divide that separates Prickly Pear from the Boulder Valley, I looked in vain for Beavertown, whose population, one year after the opening of lode mines in the vicinity, was fourteen.

From the crest of the divide the highway loops down into the next valley toward the county seat at Boulder. This well-situated town, which started in the early 1860's as a stage station on the Virginia City-Fort Benton road, added its first settlers in July, 1862, when a rush of prospectors left Gold Creek and started placer operations along the Boulder River. The town was incorporated in February, 1865, but after a flurry of placering, it slipped back into a quiet existence until the valley became an agricultural area. Then Boulder became the trade center and ultimately, in 1883, the seat of Jefferson County, although the town proper had a population of only 150. Its $18,000 courthouse and $8,000 jail are still the most imposing buildings in the town.

A late as 1884 a stagecoach bound for Boulder was held up at the summit of Prickly Pear Pass by six armed men. Among its passengers were "Judge Wade, Prosecuting Attorney Johnston, and Mr. Toole, Mr. Cullen, Mr. Carter, Mr. Chumasero and Mr. Bullard of the Helena Bar." They had taken the train that morning from Helena and at Jefferson City "took passage on the stagecoach for Boulder City, twelve miles away." All of them were on their way to the county court.

Roads fan out in all directions from Boulder, leading to Butte, to Whitehall, to Three Forks, and across the hills west to Deer Lodge. Mines in the vicinity include the Australian, Belle of Boulder, Wall Street, Amazon, and the Comet, around which a small settlement grew up dating from 1869, when its population is given as 300. This famous mine is credited with a production record of $13,000,-000. Nowadays Boulder is best known for its Hot Springs, and as the home of Montana's State School for the Feeble-minded.

ELKHORN

During the summer of 1951, my chauffeur-friend Hazel and I drove into Boulder, looked with interest at its French-chateau type courthouse, and from a group of men on a corner asked directions to Elkhorn. Following their suggestions, we drove ten miles southeast of Boulder on a paved county road, being sure to "turn left at every fork." Their last warning was to "cross a red bridge and then we'd know we were on our way." We found the road well marked with signs, but the red bridge was a dusty brown. It was quite a

BACK STREET, ELKHORN

ELKHORN MILL

climb up the valley, first through ranch country where cattle grazed and a bunch of mares with four skittish colts pounded away from the pasture fence as we passed, and then, as the road narrowed and ducked through groves of willows and evergreens, up a steep pitch, past dams and settling ponds and into Elkhorn. The well-preserved camp stands on a high sloping meadow surrounded by timbered mountains on whose slopes are mine dumps. Its several streets and main thoroughfare are lined with wooden buildings — log cabins and frame houses and stores, some painted and some weathered a silvery gray or a deep brown. Tall grass and weeds edge the streets and grow around the untended buildings. The Elkhorn mill, at the head of the gulch, is a big sagging structure, set amidst dumps. In 1951 it was being worked by lessees. The engineer running the hoist shouted in answer to my question that the mine had shut down in 1912 and had just been reopened. The children and dogs we had seen belonged to the four families whose men were working the property.

A number of quartz locations were made in the vicinity prior to 1870, one of which, the Elkhorn, discovered by Peter Wys (Wyes), a Swiss, proved to be the richest. Wys died in 1872, and the property was acquired by Anton M. Holter, a Helena banker, who reached Alder Gulch in 1863 and who was one of the few men attacked by Plummer's road agents who lived to tell of the encounter. As soon as the A. M. Holter lode (or the Elkhorn, as it was also called) became productive, the district began to attract attention.

In 1872, after Holter had organized the Elkhorn Mining Company with his brother M. M. Holter, J. H. Shober, John Kinna, and Neil Vawter as fellow officers and had built the first mill in the area, a town called Elkhorn was laid out close to the mine. The Elkhorn, which has been worked from time to time ever since its discovery until the present, is one of the prominent silver deposits of the county, and, as one authority states it, "the history of the district is that of the Elkhorn mine." It is "on a silver-bearing calcite ore shoot between a hornstone hanging wall and a dolomite footwall."

The first owners had erected a five-stamp, wet-crushing, free-milling plant which was suitable to handle the surface ores by amalgamation, but in 1881, when the mine was developed to a depth of 300 feet, refractory ores were encountered, and this process recovered only fifty per cent of the silver values. A new mill to treat ore by chloridization was needed, but because of disagreement among the owners, the property lay idle during most of 1882. The following year, after company reorganization, the Elkhorn Mining Company installed a ten-stamp chloridizing plant which proved highly successful, since it saved ninety per cent of the values and produced bullion aggregating $188,375 in silver and $2,320 in gold during its first ten months of operation. The company worked the mine down to the 800-foot level where the ore appeared to pinch out.

In 1888 or 1889 the Elkhorn was sold to an English syndicate for more than half a million dollars. The company remodeled the mill and further developed the mine, paying dividends amounting to $200,000 in 1890 and $328,125 in 1891. The collapse of silver prices ended this prosperous enterprise, and the English company withdrew after selling the property.

When Walter S. Kelley was general manager in 1896, so little ore was visible that the mine was believed to be exhausted and plans for its abandonment were made. Kelley, however, found deposits that had been overlooked, which resulted in further operations. In the fall of 1899, pumping costs and fuel bills, tallied against the small amount of low-grade ore in sight, forced a shut down.

The mine was reopened in 1901 by John, Henry, and Frank Longmaid of Helena who, after spending $60,000 to $80,000 in unwatering the property and building a new mill, reworked the dumps with considerable profit. Since then it has changed hands frequently. During World War II the tailings of the old stamp mill were worked for lead, silver, and zinc.

While the Elkhorn was the principal mine of the district, a number of other properties produced smelting and milling ore. The C.&D., a mile north of Elkhorn, even built a small smelter in 1886 and processed its own ore. When the tunnels in the Golden Curry, northwest of the town, caved in, the mine was worked by the open-pit method. In July, 1910, an average of twenty tons of ore a day was shipped from it to the East Helena smelter for flux. This mine was discovered by John Rothfus, who also located the Dolcoath. The queen, three miles south of Elkhorn, a silver-lead property, is said to have been the initial discovery in the area.

ELKHORN

HOTEL AND FRATERNITY HALL, ELKHORN.
Reproduced courtesy of THE BONANZA TRAIL,
Indiana University Press

After we had inspected the mill and its hoist house with the three water barrels on the roof — reservoirs in case of fire — we explored the town. It had been built to house 2,500, and of the fifty or more buildings still standing, most are homes; for the majority of the mine and mill workers were married men who had their families with them. These houses stood on the four side streets which were named Boulder, Kilbourne, Holter, and Wye (for Wys the Swiss, I presume). Another part of the camp housed nearly 500 woodchoppers, for hundreds of cords of wood were needed as fuel for the mine engines and for heating private dwellings. French and Norwegian choppers cut this wood in the hills and brought it into town on a narrow-gauge road. A horse-drawn cart delivered water from a barrel to the housewives.

The Elkhon Mining Company ran a boarding house near the mine for the nearly 300 Swedes, Danes, Norwegians, Irish, French, Dutch, and Germans whom it employed. It is said that the camp had fourteen saloons. The bawdy houses were in the gulch. The two-story building beside the Fraternity Hall was a hotel, but whether the Metropolitan operated by James Quay, or the one run by James Mitchell, I had no way of telling. The log schoolhouse faced with siding and the post-office, with its dusty pigeonholes for the mail that arrived first by stage and later by rail from Boulder, have withstood the ravages of years. But the most imposing and astonishing architectural triumph was the Fraternity Hall, with its castellated cornice and suspended balcony over the doorway. As we approached it, two small boys dashed out of the building and raced across the street, but as soon as we went inside they slipped in behind us and showed us around.

The main floor was one big hall without any furnishings but with a stage at the far end. On it stood some painted panels representing a drawing room or palace interior. While I was taking a time exposure of the scenery, I felt a tug at my skirt, and a small voice asked, "Do you want to see the trap door?" and without waiting for an answer, one of the urchins disappeared between some loose boards in front of the platform and emerged on the stage. Inside the vestibule at the main entrance was a staircase to the second story, which contained another big room with a low platform at one end and a stove at the other. At the head of the stairs was

a door opening onto the none-too-sturdy balcony. "Ma won't let me go out there," cautioned the second boy, as I steadied my camera on the rickety railing and snapped a panorama of the street.

Frank Quinn, whose feature article on "Elkhorn" appeared September 26, 1954, in the *Montana Standard,* gives considerable local color about the town as he knows it and as told to him by several of its earlier residents. Of the Fraternity Hall he explains that you danced upstairs and ate downstais, and he describes the tragedy that occurred one night when one dancer asked the orchestra to play a square dance and another wanted a waltz. The two men argued the point until the square dancer shot and killed the other. The killer was hanged in Boulder. The Fraternity Hall was also used by the Cornish Glee Club and by the several lodges — the Masons, Knights of Pythias, I. O. O. F., and I. O. G. T. On other occasions, prize fights and boxing matches took place there. Until recently, each of the meeting rooms contained a piano, and in one a set of band instruments was left to collect cobwebs.

Amusements were not limited to affairs in the Hall. The Elkhorn Baseball Club played on the flat below the town. Rock drilling contests were always well attended. Hank Blevins' and Fred Bell's Livery Stable provided horses, buggies, and sleighs for all occasions. Dr. William H. Dudley, physician and surgeon for the C.&D. Mining Company, probably rented from the livery barn the sleigh in which he drove back from Butte with his wife after their marriage on Christmas Day, 1886.

After 1889, the Northern Pacific built a branch line through the Boulder Valley with a spur to the Elkhorn mine. The grade up Elkhorn gorge was steep and so full of sharp curves that only short trains could make it. Tri-weekly passenger and freight services connected the camp with the county seat at Boulder and permitted the bringing in of merchandise, equipment, and salt for fluxing ore. When mining began to taper off, the Northern Pacific cut its service and in 1931 removed its tracks. For years the old water tank stood at the head of the gulch near the depot. When the mines closed, not only the town but also the valley was affected, for the ranchers and farmers lost their steady customers.

As we left Elkhorn, I looked up at Cemetery Ridge and wondered how many children had died when a diphtheria epidemic struck the camp. I had read that one family lost five children and their mother. A little below the town stands a modern home. As there was a mill nearby, I stopped and asked the name of it. "It's just another Elkhorn mill," said the lady who answered my knock. "It's sort of sad to see Elkhorn today and realize that the monthly payroll at the mine was more than $15,000 and that $14,000,000 in silver was taken out of these properties."

The return drive to Boulder seemed short, and since we hoped to reach Butte that day, we drove straight through the county seat and up the Boulder River canyon to Basin.

CATARACT

"When I'm in Basin I must find out more about the camp called Cataract," I said as we left Boulder and entered the gorge of the Bouler River, west of town. "As early as June, 1862, a party of prospectors found gold near the mouth of Cataract Creek at a spot which became known as Old Bar. These men worked the sands until they were out of provisions and then hurried to Grasshopper Diggings which had been discovered just prior to their strike. Soon afterwards these claims became the property of Granville and James Stuart and of Reece Anderson who, having built cabins at the mouth of the creek, brought their families to stay at the diggings while the men washed gold."

The McIrwin brothers, while prospecting two and a half miles up the creek in 1864, found ore that was rich but too difficult to work, and therefore abandoned their claim. The next important strikes were made in 1873 by Zach Thompson's Company, which located the Big Medicine, Susie Brown, and Mount Thompson leads. The Mantle lode was uncovered in 1879. Many of the mines located in 1880 and in later years became the leading producers of the district. The best of them, including the Eva May, were up Cataract Creek. The ore in many of these changed with depth from iron to copper pyrites.

Between Boulder and Basin are many gulches — Watson, Kilbourn, Little Galena, Big Galena, and, opposite the latter gulch, Boomerang. Just before reaching Basin, the highway crosses Cataract Creek. I looked everywhere for signs of the old camp, but not even foundation stones or rubble heaps mar the lush green meadowland at the creek's mouth. In Basin I learned that the placer camp had occupied the flat through which the creek flows. Then, as the town of Basin grew in size and

importance, the older camp moved its buildings up the river to the newer settlement and was absorbed by it, and that was the end of Cataract.

BASIN

Basin, like Boulder and Cataract, dates from the 1860's, and its first cabins were those of miners who built at the mouth of Basin Creek, beside the Boulder River. As soon as the rich placers played out, the miners searched for the source of the gold and around 1870 found outcroppings on the surrounding mountain slopes. From these the lode mines of the district were developed. With the Butte-Boulder stage road running through the canyon past the mouth of the creek, and with prospectors exploring the forested hillsides in the upper portion of Basin Gulch, the small cluster of log cabins at the stream's mouth became the nucleus of a new town named Basin City, founded in 1880 by Lawson and Allport, who had mining interests in the vicinity.

The town grew slowly, for although the hills were full of prospectors, the men were without capital and could not launch big scale operations. It did, however, become the rival of Cataract and in time absorbed it. Between 1870 and 1890 Basin was an active camp with plenty going on but toward the end of the century, high smelting charges and the low price of silver forced even the large operators to shut down. Between 1897 and 1917 many of the mines were idle, though the estimated production of the district, prior to 1904, was $8,000,000.

When the Eva May, one of the district's oldest mines, was equipped with a concentrator in 1905, a brief boom followed. Mines were reopened and only a scarcity of wagons in which to haul ore to the plant kept the concentrator from running to capacity. The Bullion mine of the Cataract Mining Company, which paid $17,000 in wages in a single month, shipped one or more cars of concentrates daily to the M. O. P. and Washoe smelters in Butte.

During this flurry of prosperity, water mains were laid throughout Basin's several streets and a 30-inch flume was constructed, which brought water from Basin and Cataract Creeks to a storage reservoir in the hills above the settlement. The overflow was utilized in the concentrator of the reduction plant.

The town had several bad fires, the last one occurring in 1893. Each time it rebuilt more substantially than before, so that in 1905

153

it contained four rooming houses, one exclusive butcher shop, one millinery shop, one painter and paper hanger, one plumber, two confectionery stores, and a bowling alley. There was also a drug store owned by Dr. Rainville, who was the physician and surgeon; and there was one dentist. Three hotels, and one bath house, three grocery stores, one shoe shop, one cigar shop, two blacksmith shops, one bank, and one newspaper — the *Basin Progress and Mining Review* — catered to the population of 1,-500. John Baskier, livery stable owner, was chief of the Volunteer Fire Department. The town had no theatre but used the Eagles' Hall for road shows. It was short on churches, too, with the Presbyterians the only denomination owning a building. Secret societies were represented by Masons, Odd Fellows, Woodmen, and Eagles. The Basin Brewery, which was pround of its ten-ton ice machine, produced fifty barrels of beer a day and boasted that its product was sold in Butte, Meaderville, Anaconda, Jefferson Island, and Boulder, as well as in Basin's twelve saloons. J. P. Mulcahy, one of the saloon proprietors, a busy and versatile man, also took "photographs and operated the Helper mine." The 1905 article, from which the above data was obtained, mentions that "Basin people want a new depot and want it bad . . . Basin shipped $40,000 of freight last month, yet the railway won't put in a telephone even."

Two prominent mines, the Katy and the Hope, contributed greatly to the growth and economic status of Basin. The Glass Brothers were the first to work these properties. During the winter of 1892 they and B. R. Young erected a mill at the Hope mine and started operations the following spring. In 1893, the brothers commenced work on the Katy, the adjoining property, and , after a year's development of the mine, they organized the Basin & Bay State Mining Company in which they retained a controlling interest. The Katy mill ran successfully until a heavy flow of underground water drowned the mine. Time and money spent in draining the workings convinced the company that the mill's capacity should be increased from 150 to 350 tons per day. The enlarged mill had made but one successful run of ore when, on August 13, 1895, it, together with the hoisting plant and the shaft, was destroyed by fire. Through quick action by those in charge, no men were trapped underground and no lives were lost. Perhaps the only objects saved from the holocaust were

two iron cuspidors which were carefully carried from the burning building by one of the most conservative of the office force and safely deposited a quarter of a mile from the flames. Through this catastrophe, the Glass brothers lost control of the property.

For several years the plant was idle, until in 1905 the M. O. P. concentrator in Meaderville burned down, and its owners came to Basin and as the Basin Reduction Company took over the smelter and concentrator. The new owners spent $500,000 enlarging the plant to a 1500-ton capacity and equipping it with 94 jigs and 110 tables, chiefly Wilfley. The tailings were run, dried, and shipped out by rail. The *Butte Evening News* commented on this enterprise: "The grind of the jigs and the swish of the Wilfleys sent a new thrill through the old camp. During the past month the payroll of the territory immediately tributary to Basin footed up a total of more than $50,000. There is only one vacant house in town and it is located in the river and is not tenable."

The Hope gold mine, which adjoined the Katy, was active until April, 1896, when its concentrator caught fire. In the conflagration, seven miners died of suffocation, including the foreman Martin Buckley, who went down the shaft to rescue those trapped below ground. After the fire the mine closed down and its shaft and workings filled with water. The property was idle for nearly twenty-two years.

A story of high-grading at the Hope mine is told in the *Anaconda Standard* of January 26, 1902, and is as elusive and improbable a tale as any connected with lost mines. It begins: "Somewhere near the village of Basin, near the Hope mine, lies a powder can full of gold. It was cached more than five years ago among the rocks." Apparently, a rich strike was made in the Hope mine and a streak of almost pure gold found at the 200-foot level. "No word of its discovery got to the office of the owners and the miners each day brought up sacks of ore which contained nuggets of gold, almost pure. . . . Some say the miners who knew of the streak carried sacks of the ore up among the hills and in huge mortars beat the gold from the rock. An accident revealed all.

"One day, a little girl, picking raspberries in the hills, discovered a mortar and pestle and by its side, a powder can filled with yellow sand, hidden securely among the rocks." It was too heavy for her to lift but she "played with the implements and went home and for-

JIB MILL, BASIN

MAIN STREET AND FIRE STATION, BASIN

got the incident." Her father, needing a mortar, said in her presence that he would have to buy one, whereupon she told him she knew of one and that near it stood "a big can full of pretty yellow sand. . . . The next day he went to the spot she had described and found the mortar and pestle but the can was not there. A huge mass of rock farther up the hill had been loosened during the night and had crashed down" covering part of the ground. Although he hunted for days, he never found the gold dust.

The most conspicuous ghost of big mining in Basin is the empty, argus-eyed Jib mill across the Boulder River from the town. The 300-ton mill which dates back to the 1900's, stands on the site of the Katy concentrator. The Butte and Superior Mining Company made use of the buildings and some of the machinery between 1909 and 1912, treating zinc ore from their Black Rock mine by the froth flotation process. This method was new to the western mining world, so when E. H. Nutter, chief engineer for Minerals Separation, Ltd., of London, visited the plant in 1910 he was insistent upon seeing the mill. Upon his return, he reported to his company that their patent to the process was being infringed upon. A lawsuit, which involved several western mining companies affiliated with the D. C. Jackling interests, followed and was not settled until 1922 by each company's payment of $5,000,000 to the English firm. In 1912, the Butte & Superior Company closed the Basin mill and moved their operations to Butte.

In 1917 Marcus L. Hewitt, a former banker and merchant in Basin, and A. E. Spriggs, former lieutenant governor of Montana, with their associates, incorporated the Jib Mining Company and at the same time leased the Hope property, with the intention of unwatering the shaft and cleaning up the mill.

The Jib Mining Company was later re-incorporated as the Jib Consolidated Mining Company, and under the new management several of the old mines, such as the Hope and the Katy were reopened. By May, 1924, quantities of high-grade gold had been encountered and reserve bodies of ore blocked out "in excess of $9,000,000." During this prosperous period the company worked three shifts and employed 175 men.

Within two years gold ore totaling $1,700,000 was recovered from the Hope, Katy, and White Elephant, and as production grew, Basin's population rose from a mere handful to a thousand. Both the Miners' and the Smelter-mens' Unions were strong, and the town felt assured of a stability it had never known. Then stock market manipulations and mismanagement caused the Jib property to shut down and the boom was over.

Basin is still marking time awaiting a new strike of major proportions. In the meantime, more than 200 people live in comfortable homes that were built years ago.

As I drove away toward Butte I took one last look at the gaunt Jib mill where I had been told by an enthusiastic old-timer, "it was a common occurrence for a foreman to put his hand into a jig and pull out a handful of gold nuggets."

The highway to Butte follows Bison Creek much of the way. The Continental Divide, which is only 6,354 feet in elevation at this point, is crossed with scarcely a glance at the marker. The approach to the big city of mines is through a bare canyon. Suddenly, Butte sprawls over the barren hills directly ahead — a tangle of headframes and stacks, shafthouses and dumps, and miles of tightly-packed houses.

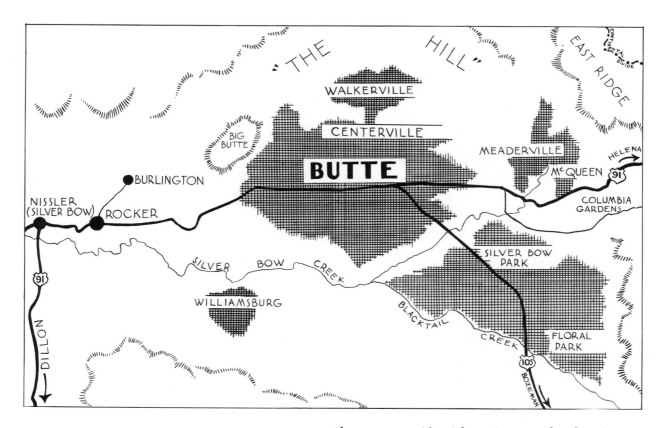

CHAPTER 9

BUTTE--the
COPPER GIANT

The first glimpse of Butte is always start-ling. From Harding Way, the southeast ap-proach, the distant city seems a gigantic, gray mirage floating between barren earth and dis-tant mountain peaks, and if a curve on the highway reveals the city at night, its lights glow and twinkle like a many-faceted jewel surrounded by black vetlvet. This approach re-veals a mosaic of headframes and shafthouses, ore dumps and ore trains, steep streets and weathered homes, crammed together or over-shadowed by mine properties, whose buildings rise tier on tier above the rest of the city. Entering from the south, the highway bisects the newer residential section on the flat, but where it swings west into industrial Butte, it skirts McQueen and Meaderville, both made up of miners' homes. McQueen is to the right of the highway. Meaderville is closer to the great honeycombed hill whose sides and summit are hidden by mine workings. Here live the Ital-ians and here, too, are many popular restau-rants and nightclubs.

The highway swings into Park Street to cut through the business portion of the city, where stores and high buildings hide the mines, unless one looks to the north at each cross street and sees dumps and gallows frames crowning "The Hill," as the mineral-packed land is called which forms the northern boundary of the city and contains the major mines. Some of these properties lie in Centerville or Walker-ville, both of which cling to the steep slopes above the city. At the west end of Park Street is the Montana School of Mines, at whose en-trance stands the statue of Marcus Daly sur-veying the city which he helped to create. In every direction — up and down hills and out on the flats below Silver Bow Creek — is a gridiron of streets lined with homes, rooming houses, hotels, stores, churches, and schools. Here the 56,000 workers and their families live.

157

In the older residential sections, trees shade the substantial and even pretentious homes, and in the newer developments lawns and flower gardens and recently planted saplings lend color to the scene. At the foot of "The Hill," in the midst of a tangle of railroad tracks where smelters and roasters once stood, is a no-man's land of crumbling slag heaps and denuded earth through which Silver Bow cuts a twisting channel. This narrow stream is hard to find in the midst of the throbbing industrial city, yet on its banks prospectors panned the first gold found in the immediate region.

SILVER BOW

During the summer and early fall of 1864, prospectors found placer gold in the bend of a stream whose winding course and shimmering surface suggested to Pete McMahon, one of their number, the name of Silver Bow Creek. One party was from Virginia City and consisted of Budd Parker (Barker or Baker), William Allison, Joseph and James Esler (Heister), who, after making their discovery, sent Allison back to the city for supplies. On the return trip G. O. Humphrey accompanied him. Another group of prospectors included Frank Riff, Peter Slater, and Pete McMahon. As soon as these discoveries were known, the gulches teemed with men, many of whom were experienced miners back from the Comstock lode in Nevada. The Summit Mountain mining district was organized with W. R. Coggswell as recorder, and before long tents and shacks lined the creek.

Early in 1865, a commission which included Granville Stuart was instructed to lay out the townsite of Silver Bow, which by the middle of February contained forty to fifty houses. Later in the year, with a population of 1,000, the camp was designated the first seat of Deer Lodge County. There in July the first court session was held. The construction of a courthouse was soon begun, but before its completion J. F. Beck loaded all the records in his wagon and when questioned as to what he was doing, replied that he was moving the county seat to Deer Lodge village!

ROCKER

The richest placer ground on Silver Bow Creek was at Rocker, a lively, short-lived camp. Here Robert McMinn found gold in a bar, but before its value was realized he sold his claim for $200.00. From this property $250,-000 was cleaned up within the next four or five years. Shoalwater Bros., who had a claim close by, averaged $1,000 a day for a limited time. Another company of men uncovered a nugget that was valued at $1,000. During the spring and summer months when water was available, the men washed out the rich dust. Those who stayed in the placer camp during the winter lived well on game which they hunted, topped off occasionally with high-priced groceries, such as fifty cent apples, grapes costing $10.00 a pound, and eggs at a dollar apiece. For relaxation, in addition to the saloons, Rocker offered a dancing club organized by a group of "the boys" and conducted by a half-breed known as Black Hawk, who was both fiddler and caller. Since no women attended the dances, a bit of rope or a bandana tied around a husky arm served to designate a lady partner.

BUTTE

William Allison and G. O. Humphrey are credited with uncovering the first quartz lode in the vicinity in May, 1864. Having worked their way upstream on Silver Bow Creek, they made camp in Baboon Gulch (on land now included in the city of Butte) and stumbled onto an old prospect hole four or five feet deep, near which lay elk antlers which had undoubtedly been used years before as crude tools by some unknown miner. Close by they staked their Original claim which they worked for a month before hurrying to Virginia City for needed provisions. Dr. Warwick, a druggist in that city, assayed their ore samples and, realizing that they had found a good thing, told Dennis Leary to trail the men on their return trip and find where their diggings lay. Leary, accompanied by Henry Porter and Herbert Madison, was able to follow their wagon tracks and discovered the two running a tunnel on the Missoula lode, which was close to the Original. Humphrey and Allison soon formed the Missoula Lead Mining Company with H. A. Hawley, E. W. Madison, F. R. Madison, William Ward, and R. W. Donnell as associates. In August the two discoverers located the Buffalo Placer, northeast of the present city, to which came Dennis Leary, Henry Porter, and others. The *Montana Post* lost no time in reporting subsequent discoveries:

We have at our office, through the kindness of Mr. R. B. Parrott, a specimen of metal, silver and copper, smelted in a common blacksmith's fire, out of some ore from the Original lode, the first discovered at Silver Bow. . . . The Original is about the richest ledge in Deer Lodge county, and promises to outstrip any other in that country.

February 18, 1865

Such news brought more men to the region, until not only the banks of Silver Bow Creek but also nearby gulches — Baboon, Buffalo, and Town — were staked and dotted with prospectors' tents and cabins. With the exception of a barren butte to the west, the district was heavily timbered.

Long ago, this isolated upthrust of rock, according to Indian legend, was the highest part of the main range of the Rockies and was believed to provide protection in warfare to Indian chieftains. When, however, a young leader was killed in battle on the mountain, the tribal medicine man cursed the peak and banished it to the valley below. That night the massive rockpile was torn loose from the range and hurtled toward the west. Its base formed the now famous "Hill" and its crest became the barren pile of rock known as Big Butte.

By the summer of 1865, in addition to the placer miners, a few families had settled in Town Gulch and cattle grazed on the hill above a new settlement called Butte, but its growth was slow. Even in 1866, when buildings first dotted Main Street and saloons and hurdy-gurdy houses ran night and day, the camp contained only 200 people. During 1867, a townsite was surveyed and a school opened by Colonel Woods, a prospector who was a more successful teacher and musician than miner. In addition to his classes he conducted a weekly singing school, and during the winter months, when the placer ground was frozen and men were marking time until the first spring thaw, he and his violin were in great demand for dances. During 1868 a postoffice was established in Dublin Gulch with Dr. Anson Ford, a druggist, serving unofficially as postmaster. The twenty to forty letters which arrived weekly were sorted by him and placed in pigeonholes above the prescription counter, awaiting delivery as road conditions permitted.

Lack of water for the placers caused Humphrey and Allison to build the first ditch to the district in 1866, bringing water from the head of Silver Bow Creek (near present Meaderville). As more ditches were constructed, placering flourished for four years and then, in 1869, which unfortunately was a dry year, the shallow deposits from which $1,500,-000 had been washed were worked out, and Butte's miners began to drift away. The few who remained worked only during the season when hydraulic gulch mining was possible. By 1874, Butte had but two saloons and no store.

The placers nearest Butte were not so rich as those at Silver Bow, and the gold from them brought no more than $14.00 an ounce. Each 200-foot claim was worked by a company of four or more men who made $6.00 to $7.00 a day and who spent Sundays — the only time that digging was suspended — in Butte or Silver Bow.

SILVER BOW (Concluded)

These two camps — Silver Bow and Butte — seven miles apart, were rivals from the start. Both depended on the placers for their prosperity, and whichever camp produced the most gold boasted the larger population. When pay dirt ran thin in one camp, the miners hustled to the other diggings, tearing down their cabins and shacks and rebuilding them in the more prosperous settlement. The following year the process might be reversed.

Christmas Week, 1866, found most of Butte's miners mingling with the 2,500 residents of Silver Bow. On Christmas Day many of the men drifted into Price's restaurant for a dinner which included all varieties of game "from rabbit to elk" for $2.50, with extras such as sauerkraut for $1.00 a plate or a boiled onion for 25 cents. As the week progressed, the temperature dropped steadily, until on New Year's morning thermometers burst when the mercury reached forty degrees below zero. The cold lasted more than a month, and it is said that the only reason that Jack Eddy and Jim McMahon did not open their saloon on March 15 was that all their whiskey was frozen. Even on June 1st, snow lay in twelve-foot drifts near Silver Bow.

When a new ditch, which furnished water for the camp's hundred placer claims, was completed in 1868-1869, another exodus from Butte took place. This was the last migration, for when silver was struck at Butte the camp of Silver Bow began to decline. By 1880 it was considered so unimportant that no mention of it is made in the census. In the jumble of buildings that sprawl westward from Butte today, were it not for highway signs, one might fail to identify the ghost of Silver Bow. Somewhere near Silver Bow Junction, or Nissler as it is now called, is the site of the first gold panning in Silver Bow Creek.

Although vestiges of silver and copper were discovered and worked during the 1860's in arrastres and primitive funaces, the miners continued to look primarily for free gold or to experiment with ways of refining the copper which they encountered, ignoring the large percentage of silver that refused to respond to their methods of reduction. When A. J. Davis bought the Lexington group of mines near Walkerville from General Charles S. Warren for, as the story goes, $20.00 and a white horse, he also acquired a small quartz mill built by Charles Hendrie in 1868. Davis increased its stamps to ten and equipped it with amalgamating plates, so as to treat free gold ores, but the amount of silver contained in the placer dust made the operation a failure.

Much of the first quartz mining revolves around the Parrot lode, named for attorney R. B. Parrot. This valuable silver-copper mine was discovered by Dennis Leary, George W. Newkirk, T. C. Porter and Henry Porter and was recorded by them on October 14, 1864. The first attempt to work Parrot ores seems to have been made by Charles L. Savage, who with some success ground out the silver in an arrastre, but after a month's run was forced to quit through lack of funds. William J. Parks owned a claim on the Parrot lode which he worked all by himself, finding both silver and traces of copper in the ore and striking pay dirt at 155 feet. Joseph Ramsdell, who also struck ore in the Parrot lode, immediately formed a company composed of himself, W. J. Parks, Dennis Leary, T. C. Porter, and others to work the property. This group built a small blast furnace during 1866 on the site of the Parrot lode, but it was not a success as they did not know how to flux ores. It was therefore torn down and rebuilt below the Parrot mine in Town Gulch. In 1868 this small smelter was blown in. Soon afterwards Park sold his Parrot No. 1 claim for $10,000.

At about the time that Humphrey and Allison staked the Original and Missoula lodes in 1864, William L. Farlin located a claim which he called the Asteroid. When he left the area soon afterwards, he took with him ore samples from his prospect hole and other properties and at a later date had them assayed at Owyhee, Idaho. Learning that they contained both copper and silver, he studied reduction methods for treating those metals, planning to put this knowledge to good use upon his return to Butte. He arrived late in 1874, and since he had saved no money, he went to work in the placer mines for a time. At midnight on December 31, 1874, he legally "jumped" or relocated his old claim, the Asteroid, calling it the Travona (Travonia). On his "black-stained quartz reef" which proved to be rich in silver, he worked by himself until he had accumulated enough money to start construction on a ten-stamp quartz mill, later known as the Dexter. Before its completion he had exhausted his funds and was forced to borrow $30,000 from the Deer Lodge bank, of which William A. Clark was president. His note fell due before he could meet it, so he surrendered his mining properties as securities with the agreement that Clark should manage them until Farlin's debt was canceled out. Clark was willing to handle the properties, but as they showed no profits, the bank foreclosed. Larabie, the other owner of the bank, had no faith in mining and sold his share of Farlin's claim to Clark, who thereby became sole owner of the Travona mine and the Dexter mill. Strangely enough the mine at once began to produce heavily, and the mill to handle the ore with profit. This Dexter mill was the first in the district to treat silver successfully.

With the discovery of pay rock in the Travona, many abandoned claims were relocated, and Butte entered its silver era.

William Andrew Clark, former trader and successful Deer Lodge banker, came to Butte in 1872. While working in the Bob Tail mine at Blackhawk, Colorado, in 1862, he heard about Montana's gold placers and was soon on his way to Bannack. His keen business sense convinced him that trading with the miners was more lucrative than digging dust, and the next few years found him making the rounds of the scattered mining camps of the territory. From this enterprise he amassed a fortune which enabled him, in 1868, to enter into partnership with Robert W. Donnell and S. E. Larabie in a wholesale mercantile business, first in Helena and then in Deer Lodge. Tiring of this, he sold his interests in 1870 and, with his partners, set up the Deer Lodge bank of which he became president in 1872. Upon his arrival in Butte he quietly bought up several claims on Butte Hill, including the Original, Colusa, Mountain Chief, and Gambetta. With samples from his properties he went to New York where he studied assaying at Columbia University. Fortified with this knowledge, he was back in Butte in 1873 and began to develop the claims which he owned. The acquisition of Farlin's holdings in 1874 merely increased his assets.

When Walker Bros., bankers of Salt Lake City, received ore from a mine in Butte and found that it ran high in silver, they became interested in the district and sent Marcus Daly, a young mining engineer in their employ, to investigate the property and to acquire a likely silver claim for them. On this trip he bought the Lexington and Alice mines, retaining a small interest in the latter for himself. As manager of the Alice he supervised the erection of a stamp mill at Walkerville in 1877 which was equipped to treat the sulphide silver ores by roasting them with salt from Great Salt Lake. No sooner had Daly acquired the Alice than Clark opened his Moulton property which adjoined it. To avoid pumping costs, he refrained from sinking a shaft on his property until the workings in the Alice were deep enough to drain the water from the Moulton.

Michael A. Hickey had noticed outcrops of green copper carbonate on Butte Hill as early as 1866, but at the time he had no interest in copper. Ten years later he and his brother, Ed Hickey, located two lodes. Ed worked one and called it the St. Lawrence and Michael the other, naming it the Anaconda. Hickey, a veteran of the Civil War, had been impressed by an editorial written by Horace Greeley which had predicted that McClellan's forces would encircle Lee's army "like a giant anaconda." Hence the name.

Somewhat later, Daly obtained a bond on the property and also on the St. Lawrence and recommended to Walker Bros. that they buy the Anaconda, but their mining experts advised against the transaction. In 1880, Daly sold his fractional interest in the Alice mine back to Walker Bros. and bought the Anaconda for $30,000. To further finance the property, he interested three Californians, George Hearst, James B. Haggin, and Lloyd Tevis, in joining him to form the Anaconda Silver Mining Company. These men held three-quarters of the shares and he the remaining fourth. Daly, as manager of the company, leased the Dexter mill from W. A. Clark and treated 8,000 tons of oxidized silver, only to find that the ore contained more copper than silver. When other silver properties shut down, so did the Anaconda. Daly, backed by Hearst, refused to believe the mine a failure and prepared to sink a new shaft. Upon the authorization of his partners, he also purchased cheaply

several surrounding claims and then reopened the Anaconda. At a depth of 300 feet a narrow seam of copper ore was uncovered which, at 340 feet, widened to reveal "needles of solid, gray-colored rock," the crown of an immense body of copper glance. With this discovery, Butte's copper era begins.

Even before the placer diggings were exhausted, attempts had been made to smelt the ore extracted from the lode mines. These met with little success. Some of the first ore shipped from William A. Clark's properties in the middle 1870's was sent to Senator Hill's Boston & Colorado Smelter at Blackhawk, Colorado, but because of the distance, reduction costs were high. Clark then sent to the same smelter, in which he had a small interest, a shipment of silver ore from his Original mine, confident that the percentage of copper in the ore would convince the Blackhawk owners that it would be profitable to establish a smelter in Butte. His strategy resulted in the forming of the Colorado & Montana Smelting Company, and the erection, in 1879, of a reduction works in Butte on the south side of Silver Bow Creek. This smelter handled ores from Clark's mines, cut production costs, and thereby enabled him to acquire additional properties in the district, until he became the leading capitalist in Montana.

Following his example, other smelters were erected in the early 1880's — the Parrot, the Montana Copper, the Colusa at Meaderville, and the Bell built by Charles T. Meader, a mining man who came to Butte in 1876. Most of these plants were south of the city in the valley beyond the creek. While these were copper smelters, several could also treat gold and silver ores. Even though the matte which each produced had to be shipped east for further refining, the local processing cut production costs appreciably.

With the development of its great mines, Butte's status as a copper camp rose. Prior to 1882 the mines bordering Lake Superior produced eighty per cent of this country's copper. Five years later Butte's output surpassed this amount. In 1898, the United States produced sixty per cent of the world's copper, of which forty-one per cent came from Butte.

During the seventies and eighties, while the lode mines were being developed and mills and reduction works employed hundreds of men, Butte grew from a village to a lusty young city which overflowed the gulches and stretched east to Meaderville, west to Big Butte, and north to Walkerville. The *Daily Miner*, Butte's first newspaper, appeared in July, 1876. The following year William A. Clark opened a branch of his Deer Lodge bank within the city limits, and in 1879 the city itself received its charter.

Religious services in the area were first held by the Reverend Joseph Giorda, a Jesuit missionary, who celebrated mass at Silver Bow in 1865, but the first attempt to found a parish and build a church in Butte was not made until 1876 under the guidance of Father Remigius DeRyckere. St. Patrick's small frame church was consecrated August 1, 1879. All the first Protestant churches — Mt. View Methodist, St. Paul's Methodist Episcopal, First Presbyterian, and St. John's Episcopal — held services in stores. Daniel S. Tuttle, the first Episcopal Bishop of Montana, wrote in his journal of his first visit to the camp accompanied by the Rev. Gilbert of Deer Lodge:

We secured the use of an unfinished new store on Main Street, fitted up a big dry goods box for a pulpit; stretched boards on carpenter's "horses" for seats and held our services in the evening. Sleeping quarters were hard to find. Someone gave us two the privilege of betaking ourselves to his cabin. There was no floor. Rolled in our blankets we went to sleep on the soft earth. And we thought ourselves alone. When we awoke next morning eleven fellow sleepers were with us, packed almost like occupants of a sardine box.

St. John's Episcopal parish was organized in 1879 and the church dedicated in 1881.

The year 1881 was marked by two important events. By act of the legislature, Silver Bow County was carved from a portion of Deer Lodge County, and on December 21st the first train of the Utah Northern Railway rolled into Butte, linking the mining city with Ogden, Utah, and providing cheaper transportation for its ores to distant markets. Two years later, on July 4th, the Northern Pacific Railroad reached Butte. During the summer of 1881 a fire, fanned by strong winds, spread through the uptown section of the city in spite of the efforts of the citizens, who fought it with bucket brigades. Although fire was an ever-present threat, a Volunteer Fire Department was not assembled until April, 1883, and six more years elapsed before a paid department was organized.

In 1882, when the camp produced 12,-093.750 oz. of gold, 2,699,296.38 fine oz. of silver, and 9,058,284 fine lbs. of copper, the Silver Bow Club was formed, with memberships limited to "millionaires, mining magnates and merchant princes." Four years later, William A. Clark started to build a $75,000 mansion in Butte for himself and family. By 1885, when Butte's population had reached 20,000, its principal mines were the Anaconda, Original, Parrot, Colusa Parrot, Ramsdell Parrot, Bell, Mt. Con, St. Lawrence, Mt. View, and Colusa, all of which produced copper, and the Alice, Lexington, and Moulton, which contained silver.

To handle this volume of ore additional plants were needed. As Boston at that time was the financial center of the copper trade in the United States, A. S. Bigelow and others formed the Boston & Montana Company and the Butte & Boston Company, each of which built works in Butte. Upon their completion, these as well as Clark's Colorado Smelting & Mining Company, the Butte Reduction Works, and Daly's smelter at Anaconda handled the increasing streams of ore which poured into them, and in turn produced $1,000,000 worth of pounds of copper a year. Men of many nationalities crowded the streets of the city at all hours — the miners and smeltermen going on or off shift and the teamsters guiding heavy ore wagons, drawn by eight or ten horses, down steep roads through the city to the reduction plants.

Excerpts from an article written for *The Northwest* of St. Paul, Minnesota, in July, 1887, give some idea of how Butte had grown since its placer days:

At one o'clock in the morning there are as many people on the streets as at one in the afternoon. There is a city beneath this city. Rents are high and many persons live in rooms because they cannot get houses.

The religious zeal of the people of the city is far more pronounced than a stranger visiting here for the first time would imagine. Numerous saloons, open gambling houses and other evidences of vice that are apparent upon an evening's stroll through the main streets are not at all indicative of the undercurrent of serious thought that pervades the community.

Military spirit is particularly ardent. Butte now has five companies, four of which are duly mustered in as territorial militia and the fifth as an independent company. As is usual the several organizations represent classes and while there is a generous rivalry between them there are no jealousies. The Union Guards is composed of Cornishmen. The Emmett Guard and the Parnell Rifles of Irishmen; the Montana Rifles of Germans; the Washington Rifles of Americans, mostly clerks and young business men.

For its size Butte has more music than any other city in the Union. All the churches have choirs, there are several glee clubs and two or three brass bands

. . . All are handsomely uniformed . . . and proficient in all the standard music.

The peak of the silver period was reached in 1887 when 290 stamps crushed 440 tons of ore per day, and the sidewalks in front of the Wells Fargo office frequently held stacks of from ten to thirty bars of silver bullion ready for shipment. Silver was mined intensively until 1893 with the Lexington and Nettie working until 1897. An estimated 300,-000,000 oz. of silver bullion and nearly 2,400,000 oz. of gold is believed to have been recovered from the many mines, as well as several billion pounds of copper.

A third railroad, the Montana Central, a part of the Great Northern system, reached Butte in 1889. In the same year William A. Clark and his brother bought the Butte Reduction Works and operated it on ore from their many mines until 1906 when the plant was destroyed by fire — but by far the most momentous event of 1889 was the arrival in the city of Fritz Augustus Heinze. This enterprising young man of twenty who was to become Butte's third copper magnate, had just received his engineering degree from Columbia University's School of Mines. In Butte he found work as a mining engineer with the Boston & Montana Consolidated Copper & Silver Mining Company, at a salary of $250.00 a month, which position permitted him to gain an intimate knowledge of the city's underground copper deposits. Within a year he knew where the richest reserves lay and the extent of the many properties owned by W. A. Clark and Marcus Daly or their associates. He was also aware that in Daly, Clark saw a dangerous rival and that a feud was developing between the two, with Clark manœuvering for a strangle hold.

Most authorities agree that the Clark-Daly war, which lasted from 1889 to 1901, began in 1882 when Clark, learning that Daly was considering a site for his smelter on Warm Springs Creek, hastily bought up the water rights and made Daly pay outrageously for them. In the ensuing years the sparring between the two centered around politics, with Clark buying his way into office on money made in his mines, and Daly pouring his growing fortune, which was also made in mining, into preventing Clark from realizing his political ambitions. Both men were leaders and each controlled a newspaper: Clark the *Butte Miner* and Daly the *Anaconda Standard*. Each had a following: Clark was respected for his wealth, education, and courage, for it is told that even during strikes and labor troubles he went about the city without a bodyguard in places where assault and murder were so common that they drew little attention, even in the press. Daly was a favorite with the people, for as a former miner he could talk their language. He was generous and sincere and his ambitions were for his mines and for the cities of Butte and Anaconda, not for his own advancement. That he amassed a fortune did not affect his unassuming nature. Where Clark spent his leisure time in Europe and surrounded himself with works of art, Daly loved sports, especially horse-racing, and this taste endeared him to the wage earners who could understand the gambling instinct and the excitement connected with it.

As a budding and ambitious politician, Heinze watched the mutual dislike between these men flare into open warfare and in time took advantage of it. This period, which embroiled not only the lives of the three millionaires but also the economic pattern of Butte has been described and analyzed in so many publications that it would be superfluous to include it here. Any reader who is not familiar with the sensational and devastating episodes that comprise it is referred to *The War of the Copper Kings* by C. B. Glasscock, and to a more recent book, *Anaconda* by Isaac F. Marcosson. Only necessary fragments of the upheaval as they affected mining will be mentioned here.

Upon the arrival of Heinze, all the important mines and reduction works in Butte were owned by Clark or by Daly. The Anaconda Mining Company, incorporated in 1891 by Hearst, Tevis, Haggin, and Daly, was made up exclusively of the latter's properties. These included the Anaconda, St. Lawrence, and Never Sweat mines, the Mt. Consolidated group of thirty-eight claims, the Union Consolidated group of silver claims, and the Anglo-Saxon group, which included the Orphan Girl mine. On June 18, 1895, all the property of the Anaconda Mining Company was transferred by the four directors to a new corporation, the Anaconda Copper Mining Company. To understand the struggle for control of The Hill, it is necessary to anticipate a little. The Amalgamated Copper Company, a trust backed by Standard Oil of New Jersey, entered the contest in 1899 and became so strong that in time even the Clark interests became a part of it. In 1915, it was dissolved and was absorbed by the Anaconda Copper Mining Company. Since then, this tremendous organization has owned and operated The Hill and has extended its interests outside the United States until it is the largest copper mining, smelting, refining, and fabricating company in the world.

But to return to F. Augustus Heinze. After a careful analysis of Butte's copper potential, Heinze was convinced that the city could support an independent smelter in addition to Clark's Colorado & Montana Smelting Company and Daly's Anaconda Smelter. To raise the necessary funds, Heinze resigned from his position and went east to interest capitalists in his plan. By 1892, after Baring Bros. of London withdrew their support, he succeeded in interesting his brothers in the project, and by the following March his Montana Ore Purchasing Company was a reality. The smelter, situated on the hillside below the Anaconda mine, began operations in 1894. From the first it reduced refining costs both for independent mine owners and for Heinze's several holdings, which included the Glengarry and Rarus. One of his many mines, the Estrella, in Centerville, was owned by James Murray.

Murray had leased it to some miners who paid him twenty-five per cent royalty on first-grade ore and fifteen per cent on second grade. Heinze offered to increase the royalty on first-grade ore to fifty per cent but to pay nothing for second-grade. Since the mine was in pay dirt, this appealed to Murray, so as soon as the lease expired he accepted Heinze's proposition. Heinze lost no time in having his men combine country rock with high-grade ore and send the mixture to the smelter. Thus, no first-grade ore was mined and Murray, becoming suspicious, sued Heinze — only to lose the case.

Heinze was a shrewd and ruthless opportunist who worked steadily toward a single goal — his own rise to power. He gambled for big stakes and beat down his opponents with noisy, libelous propaganda. He needed money to fight Clark and Daly, who controlled The Hill. Learning that a smelter was needed at Trail, Canada, to treat Rossland ores, Heinze built it, as well as a narrow-gauge railroad which connected the mines and the plant. He bought and controlled a newspaper in which he criticized the service provided by the Canadian Pacific Railroad and obtained a grant which permitted him to extend his road to Victoria, B. C. To prevent this, the Canadian

Pacific bought him out for $1,200,000. With this capital he could begin to undermine Butte's vested interests.

While Heinze was establishing himself in Butte, the silver picture changed. With Congress' repeal in 1893 of the silver-purchasing clause of the Sherman Act, the silver mines and mills ceased to function, and as chlorination and roasting plants replaced them, the big-scale copper phase of the district began. These were the years when, due to new processes of treating refractory ores, the city was enveloped in dense yellow smog and nauseous sulphur and arsenic fumes from the smelters and open "roast heaps." These latter consisted of alternate layers of cordwood and ore mixed with salt which, once set on fire, often took weeks to burn out. At times the thick pall of acrid smoke was as impenetrable as fog, while its chemical content caused bronchial irritation and killed all vegetation in the immediate area. Even the teeth of cattle grazing on tainted grass some distance away became plated with copper, according to a rancher who bought animals for slaughter. Finally, in desperation, the citizens took matters in their own hands. Armed with shovels, a determined mob attacked the heaps of smoldering ore and scattered them. Fortunately for everyone, improvements in smelting methods soon made it possible to recover tons of arsenic and sulphur, heretofore lost in the smoke from open heaps and from smelter stacks.

James Ledford stumbled onto the leaching process of recovering copper. His cabin was below the Anaconda mine dump, where tin cans and discarded iron scrap lay jumbled together. Water, which had been pumped from the mine was heavily impregnated with minerals and unfit for any use, flowed through the dump and over the discarded metal. One day Ledford discovered that instead of the junk pile only a "heavy deposit of slush" remained, which an assay revealed as almost pure copper. Saying nothing about this, he obtained a year's contract for all waste water from the Anaconda mine. He built tanks in which he placed the scrap metal and directed the water so as to run over it. At the end of a year he had cleared $90,000 from the valuable rubbish. When this was discovered, his contract was not renewed.

By 1900, Heinze was beginning to get a strangle hold on important mining properties. His acquisition of the Minnie Healy is a good example of his method of attack. Miles Fin-

MEADERVILLE

len had obtained a lease from Daly on the mine, which was less than half a mile northeast of Heinze's Rarus property. After spending $54,000 in developing the Minnie Healy and finding only low-grade ore, Finlen was discouraged. Heinze, hoping to trace the ores of the Piccolo and Gambetta claims of the Boston & Montana Company into the Healy ground, offered to take over Finlen's option and lease for the $54,000, agreeing to pay in two annual installments. In the subsequent lawsuit, Heinze testified that Finlen agreed to the offer. According to Finlen, an agreement was made giving Heinze temporary possession of the mine until Finlen could investigate the validity of his apex theory. While Finlen was east on business, Daly sent for him to return to Butte and get Heinze out of the mine. By the time that Finlen arrived, Heinze had opened a rich deposit of ore and was firmly entrenched. Finlen brought suit and demanded a cancelation of the lease, but the case was tried by

District Judge William Clancy, whose election Heinze had engineered, and the decision was in his favor.

All of Heinze's tactics centered around the Apex law — a Federal statute passed in 1866 to protect the prospector who made the original location on the outcrop or apex of a mineral vein. Such a discovery guaranteed to the owner the right to follow the vein downward, even when it led under the surface holdings of adjoining claims. Since such a vein was often broken or "faulted" by the intrusion of country or barren rock, who could prove whether the rediscovered streak of ore was a continuation of the original mineral formation or not? The usual procedure was to contest the issue in court. This resulted in litigation which often shut down both properties, sometimes delaying further operations for years until the case was decided.

After Heinze acquired the Rarus mine, he sunk a shaft and found rich ore near a vertical side-wall, through which he traced the deposit into the adjoining Michael Devitt property, which belonged to the Boston & Montana Company. When the owners found him removing pay-rock, they accused him of stealing ore, but he insisted that he was following a vein through a side-wall on his property. The Boston & Montana Company promptly filed suit but lost the case. Similarly, when he found an unrecorded and unpatented triangular fraction of forty square yards, surrounded by the Anaconda, St. Lawrence, and Never Sweat shafts, he acquired title to it and named it the Copper Trust. As soon as the ground was legally his, he announced that all three mines apexed on his fraction and slapped an injunction on the three that prevented them from operating until the title was settled. This and other procedures of a like nature, which produced hampering litigation, so enraged the rightful owners of the affected properties that they welcomed the entrance of the Amalgamated Copper Company into the fray, and were willing to merge with it.

This organization, which was formed in April, 1899, with Henry H. Rogers and William G. Rockefeller, the heads of Standard Oil of New Jersey, as its executive directors, was created, not as an operating company, but to control the holdings of the most successful mining companies, especially those of the Anaconda Copper Mining Company and the Parrot Silver & Copper Company. When the directors of the Anaconda Company were asked by Amalgamated to sell a major interest in their company to Amalgamated, Haggin refused to join and was paid $15,000,000 for his share. Daly, on the other hand, saw in the new and powerful alliance a way to consolidate the company's wealth and to protect it. He also hoped that through this merger, the legal entanglements constantly devised by Heinze might be settled. The Anaconda Company holdings were therefore transferred by Daly to Amalgamated for $39,000,000 and Daly succeeded Haggin as president of the Anaconda Copper Mining Company. In time Amalgamated acquired the Boston & Montana and the Butte & Boston interests, as well as those belonging to Clark. Only Heinze's properties remained to be dealt with. His attacks, based on the Apex law, continued and when the cases came to trial the decisions rendered by the two judges — Clancy and Harney — whom he "owned," were always in his favor.

Even before the Amalgamated Company was formed, Heinze and Clark had joined forces, and in the subsequent battle with the big company, Heinze played upon the mercurial emotions of the miners to bind them to him. When he and Clark adopted the eight-hour day for their employees and demanded that the Amalgamated do the same, they cornered three-quarters of the votes in Butte's next election. But when Clark became Senator, his long-sought goal was attained, and a new life lay before him. Without hesitation, he sold his mining interests in Butte to the Amalgamated Company for $1,000,000, leaving Heinze on his own.

During the few remaining years that Heinze spent in Butte, he used every device to swell his personal fortune. His paper, the *Reveille*, was an instrument of propaganda, and two dozen lawyers handled the many lawsuits in which he was involved. As Marcosson explains: "It cost Anaconda and the associated companies $1,000,000 a year to defend its rights and circumvent the predatory tactics of Heinze." Even legal proceedings did not stop work in his mines. When Amalgamated issued an injunction to cease work in the Nipper shaft, Heinze developed another section of the mine not specified in the order. When he lacked funds to post a bond, he sent five of his employees east to set up a fictitious organization, the Wilmington Bonding & Casualty Company, with power to issue one bond only, made out to him for $700,000.

His battles with Amalgamated over the Minnie Healy and Michael Devitt mines commenced in trickery and ended in underground warfare in which slack lime, live steam, stink pots, electrified metal plates, dynamite, and bullets all had a part. When the trouble started in the Minnie Healy, Heinze was dealing with Miles Finlen who was leasing the mine from Daly; but after Finlen was unable to oust Heinze's forces from the property, he sold his interest and rights in the suit against Heinze to Amalgamated. From there on it was war between a weasel and a giant, with Heinze winning his case after a six-year legal tussle which necessitated several trials. His victory in the first round was clouded when it was discovered that the judge had accepted a bribe.

This court decision in his favor convinced Heinze that further attacks were in order. New probings could always disgorge more ore from opponents' mines. Thus Heinze began to trace the Minnie Healy veins beyond his boundaries into the Leonard and other sections of Amalgamated ground, attempting to produce new apex litigation. Soon the crews on both sides were waging underground warfare, with Heinze's men gouging out ore as fast as they could and covering their tracks with blasts and debris. Finally, as Glasscock puts it, "Heinze engineers tapped the water column of the Minnie Healy, coupled with the city water works, and turned the flood into Boston and Montana workings. Boston and Montana engineers promptly erected a barrier and turned the flood back through a crosscut eight hundred feet into the Minnie Healy shaft. Heinze workers poured out of the lower workings of the Minnie Healy like rats out of a flooded cellar." Miraculously none was drowned, but this action so aroused each side that a truce was arranged. Again Judge Clancy upheld Heinze's case, and Amalgamated appealed to the State Supreme Court. This pattern of trial and appeal and re-trial became commonplace practice. During this period of legal turmoil it is said that Montana's courts were so swamped with cases involving mining litigation that civil suits piled up for seven years awaiting trial.

The final contest for the control of the Michael Devitt began in 1897. The Butte & Boston Company's claim that Heinze had looted thousands of tons of ore from the mine resulted in three trials, the second of which was held in Helena in 1900. Heinze's planned newspaper smear against the Amalgamated Company, which by then owned the property, swayed the jury to render a verdict in his favor, but when it was learned that he had engineered the attack, the judge ordered a third trial, which did not come up for four years. Both sides, however, were forbidden by injunction to remove ore from the disputed ground. Such restraint was against Heinze's principles, so he organized the Johnstown Mining Company, assigning his rights in the disputed mine to it, and ordering it to work in Michael Devitt ground, since the Johnstown Mining Company was not mentioned in the court order, and to bring out the ore through the Rarus shaft. The company was also to build concrete bulkheads wherever Michael Devitt and the Amalgamated's Pennsylvania mines joined.

When Amalgamated requested permission to inspect what was going on, Federal Judge Hiram Knowles granted it, whereupon Heinze accused him of prejudice and was instrumental in his ultimate removal in favor of Judge

James W. Beatty of Idaho. The Amalgamated Company also asked that Judge Knowles revoke his order preventing it from working its mine and permitting it to fight for its ore. Even with this order granted, Heinze evaded receiving the document for several days by going into hiding, so as to give his crews time to extract more stolen ore from the mine and rush it through his smelter before detection. Finally, the U. S. Circuit Court of Appeals in San Francisco examined the case and sent Judge Beatty to Montana to settle it. He fined Heinze $2,000 for contempt of court and ordered him to admit Amalgamated's engineers to inspect the workings. Before their arrival, Heinze succeeded in having his crews blast the stopes where they had been filching ore so that the amount could not be measured. The engineers' report showed a loss of 7,500 tons worth nearly $600,000. During all this time Heinze was busy tapping other mines belonging to the company in an attempt to further cripple it through false apex claims. In 1901, Judge Beatty was again called in regarding the mine, only to find that Heinze had stripped an additional million dollars' worth of ore from it. This time the judge fined him $20,000, which still netted him a good profit. The showdown came in 1903.

Heinze finagled agents into certain of Amalgamated's subsidiary companies as stockholders with instructions to bring suit against the company in the Butte courts, demanding receivership of Amalgamated on the grounds that it was an illegal trust. Judge Clancy's decision in the case was in favor of Heinze's pawns. Within hours Amalgamated closed down all of its properties in Montana and adjoining states, which threw 20,000 men out of work. For the first time feeling was strong against Heinze, yet when he addressed a crowd of more than 10,000 men from the steps of the Butte courthouse and vilified Amalgamated and all it stood for, they cheered and his oratory temporarily pacified them.

William Scallon, at that time president of the Anaconda Company, presented to Governor Joseph K. Toole a plan by which the long-waged legal battle between the giants could be solved. His proposition involved the passage of a Fair Trial Law which would provide for a change of venue wherever there was justifiable belief that the trial judge was prejudiced. A called session of the legislature met and on November 11, 1903, passed the bill, and the mines reopened.

The passage of the Fair Trial Bill effectively broke Heinze's power, as did the loss of his judges at the next election. On more than one occasion Henry H. Rogers, president of Amalgamated, made Heinze an offer for his properties, hoping to end his attacks on the company, all of which Heinze refused to consider. In 1906, John D. Ryan, managing director of Amalgamated, concluded secret negotiations whereby Heinze agreed to accept $10,500,000 for his Butte holdings. With this capital he left Montana and went to New York to invade Wall Street. Upon his departure, 110 suits which had been cluttering up the district courts were dismissed. In New York Heinze met his match, and after a disastrous partnership with Charles W. Morse, an unscrupulous speculator, he was cleaned out and broken. Morse went to Federal prison; Heinze was acquitted.

By 1900, Butte was a bustling city with police and fire departments, twenty-eight schools, a public library, and 225 active mines within its boundaries or in the immediate vicinity. Three daily newspapers, the *Inter-Mountain*, *Butte Miner*, and *Anaconda Standard*, whose headquarters had recently been moved to Butte, were widely read, as well as nine weeklies.

Butte's population of 65,000 represented a mixture of nationalities but was still noticeably "American," English, and Irish.

Miners and smeltermen numbered 13,000 in 1900, many of whom belonged to labor unions and fraternal organizations, while for the professional business man there was the Silver Bow Club. As the city stretched out in various directions, new streets were graded and quickly lined with houses west of Missoula Gulch to the foot of Big Butte and south of town in a new district called South Butte. Electric tram lines ran to these suburbs as well as to Meaderville, Centerville, West Side and Columbia Gardens, with a line promised to Walkerville in the future.

Butte never slept.

From Dublin gulch to the Boulevard at night, when Butte is supposed to be asleep, the ore car motorman guides his train bearing the fruits of miner's toil to the reduction works on the grassless banks of the muddy Silver Bow creek. . . . He must see that the ore cars do not bump into a pedestrian or leave the track and spill their contents over the ground. . . . He talks to no one between stations, and he finds it pleasant to whistle and sing as he engineers his little train down or up the hill.

One night however, a couple of hoboes got aboard at the smelter and rode uptown without aid or consent of the motorman . . . They had imbibed on Boulevard booze and were drowsy and, before the car was halfway to town, they were fast asleep in the bottom of the car. Under the ore bin chute at the mine they were trundled, and when the chute opened, and ore came crashing down into the car there were wailings and scramblings which frightened the sleepers in Dublin gulch.
Anaconda Standard, Jan. 12, 1902

The cries were investigated, and the men rescued amid curses and kicks.

Columbia Gardens, at the mouth of a canyon three miles east of the city, were opened in 1899 as the gift of W. A. Clark and were managed by the Butte Street Railway Company, which he also owned. Clark wanted above all things to be a U. S. Senator, and his gift of the Gardens made him pose as benefactor to the thousands whose votes he would need. The Gardens became a popular resort for all ages. The beautifully landscaped grounds, the flower beds, the band concerts, the large central pavilion with its cafe, banquet hall, smoking room, dancehall, wide verandas, and concession booths offered a welcome escape from the noise and dirt of The Hill and served as a picnic ground and recreation center for the city. Now that the smelter fumes no longer poisoned the air, the gardens were a green oasis.

The most dreaded sound in Butte was the persistent screech of a mine whistle, for it was a signal of underground fire or disaster.

Big Fire in Butte
The Parrot shaft house with all the surrounding buildings burned yesterday with a loss of $100,000. It is believed that a spark from a locomotive ignited a pile of shavings and rubbish near the carpenter shops and from it spread the fire, which destroyed five buildings, 12 boilers, an engine and hoist drill, a compressor, the stores in a warehouse and much machinery.
Kalispell Bee, Aug. 10, 1900

Fortunately, none of the 164 miners underground was injured. Fire swept the shafts of the Speculator and Granite Mt. mines in 1917 and trapped nearly 200 miners. Twenty-five from the Speculator were saved by Manus Duggan, who led them into a crosscut where he erected a bulkhead to shut out the fire and gases. The men were finally located and released, but Duggan died in a vain effort to locate a safe exit for the group.

From the time that Butte began to rip quartz deposits from The Hill, its growth was steady, and its population was made up chiefly of workers. Miners' days were long, and when they were off shift they wanted plenty of rec-

CENTERVILLE, LOOKING ACROSS BUTTE TO THE HIGHLANDS

reation and entertainment. As early as 1875, when the population was scarcely 300, John Maguire arrived by stage from Deer Lodge and gave a performance of recitations in brogue entitled "American Flowers and Shamrock Leaves," interspersed with concertina selections. This program, which he gave for three successive nights, crowded a small store building to capacity. When he returned in the fall, King & Lowry's saloon was available for performances, even though seats were nail kegs and candles provided the only light. The following year the Free Masons built a small hall which they occasionally rented for respectable entertainments. Loeber's Hall also served as a theatre, but its tiny stage, poor light, and lack of ventilation caused the better traveling companies to perform in Owsley Hall or in Renshaw Hall, a brick building with an auditorium on the second floor, built in 1882.

John Maguire, who established a circuit for theatrical companies throughout the territory, leased Renshaw's and served as manager until he built his own Grand Opera House, which opened on July 27, 1885. Butte audiences could then enjoy such famous performers as

Milton Nobles, Rose Eytinge, Frederick Warde, Lawrence Barrett, and Henry Ward Beecher. To this theatre came the Emma Abbott Opera Company, Fay Templeton's Opera Company, the Nellie Boyd Company, and the Haverly Dramatic Company, as well as Mme Rhea, Minnie Maddern, Helena Modjeska, Fanny Davenport, Mme. Janauschek, and Nat Goodwin. As architect for his two-story red brick building, Maguire engaged H. W. Barbour, the designer of the Tabor Opera House in Leadville, Colorado. When completed it contained 182 orchestra seats, 280 in the orchestra circle, 300 in the family circle, and four boxes. Three years later, just as a peformance was about to begin a defective gas jet in one of the borders set fire to the scenery and quickly spread to the wings. The actors and audience smelled smoke and dashed out and the theatre was reduced to ashes within an hour. Three days later Maguire reopened in a converted skating rink with scenery borrowed fom his theatre in Deer Lodge. On August 4, 1888, he was given a benefit performance at the racetrack with all the city's entertainers and the Boston & Montana, Walkerville and Emmett Guard bands providing the entertainment. The benefit, which netted around $10,000, helped build a new playhouse which he opened in 1889.

John A. Gordon and Fred Ritchie, proprietors of the Variety Theatre, built a stone structure equipped with a bar, two wine rooms, two parlors, and two tiers of boxes. "The ceiling, which is supplied with rings, bars, etc. for trapeze and aerial gymnasts, is tastefully and beautifully frescoed. Three water plugs, conveniently placed inside, each supplied with necessary hose, form a safe protection against fire."

Sports of many types were popular. Butte had two racetracks, one built by Marcus Daly, and the other a five-mile level stretch of road (now the Harrison Avenue Freeway) on the flats south of the city. Here many impromptu races were staged directly after a funeral. The mourners who had dutifully paid their respects to the deceased by driving behind the hearse to the cemetery recovered their spirits by racing each other to the Five-Mile House where they toasted the departed before returning to Butte.

A Greyhound-Coursing Park was built by the Cornish during the 1890's, next to Daly's track, and a Curling Club to which many business men belonged was opened by the English and Canadians in 1905. Prize fights always drew crowds which bet heavily on their favorites. Rivalry between racial groups fostered sports competition which was sometimes carried to extremes. The Finns were great athletes and boasted of their superiority over any other group. On more than one occasion a Finn would bet an Irishman that he could beat him swimming across Georgetown Lake with flatirons fastened to his feet. Usually he drowned. But no sport meant more to the entire community than the hard rock drilling contests.

These single-jack and double-jack demonstrations, sponsored by the Miners' Union, were held at Columbia Gardens and at Lake Avoca. The Union supplied three judges and the timers, although each team had its own timer to indicate when to change tools. Each man swung an eight-pound hammer and struck the drill, which his partner was twisting, for thirty seconds before exchanging places with him. The change was made without missing a stroke. Expert teams could strike more than sixty-four blows a minute. Water from a hose ran into the hole to clean out the powdered rock, and fresh drills were inserted as needed. For fifteen minutes each team sank steel drills into a block of hard granite, which was usually placed on a platform in view of a tense and admiring crowd. Several crack teams composed of Butte miners were in demand at regional contests, with two teams placing as World Champion double-jack drillers — Walter Bradshaw and Joe Freethy at Spokane on October 24, 1901, with a depth of fifty-five inches, and Charles and Glen Bedell at Lake Avoca on August 6, 1914, with a thirty-nine-inch hole.

Butte liked music and it was a music all its own — a mingling of sounds made up of thumping stamps and throbbing engines, steam exhaust, whining cables, rumbling ore trains, clattering hoofs, plodding feet, and the whole scale of tones that made each mine whistle distinctly different from any other. In addition there was the music produced by the people — the songs of the Cornish and Germans, the Irish and Scandinavians, the Italians and Bohemians — all of whom liked to sing and through song preserved something of their European heritage. Several of the mines had their own bands and all of the churches had choirs, but it was the spontaneous singing of the men going to and from shift or riding the cages in the shafts as they came from work that was the essence of the city's sound.

Besides its Europeans who kept clannishly together in neighborhoods, Butte also had its Chinatown, situated between Galena and Mercury Streets and Main and Colorado Streets, a colorful district in the midst of the business section of the city. The buildings were picturesque as were the inhabitants who wore native dress. A Joss House, built in 1886, was succeeded by another, a two-story balconied Temple which was not razed until 1943. The first Chinese to work the Silver Bow placers came from Bannack. Those who did not mine worked as woodchoppers until the 1880's when they were run off by French Canadians who resented any competition. The adaptable Chinese then became truck farmers, raising and selling vegetables. Others opened laundries, restaurants, and gambling establishments. During the winter months the Chinese population rose to 2,500, as many of them left their gulch placers for cosier city quarters. Today scarcely any Chinese live in Butte.

Unions have played an active part in the life of the city ever since the Butte Workingman's Union was organized in June, 1878, in Loeber's Hall with 261 charter members. By 1896, as the Butte Miners' Union, it was part of the Western Federation of Miners, an affiliate of the American Federation of Labor. When the miners in Michigan went out on strike in the fall of 1913, the Butte Union rebelled at the excessive assessments demanded of it and at the conservative policies of the A. F. of L., which forced them to pay their dues or be refused work in the mines. Led by vigorous Mucky McDonald of Butte, many members withdrew and organized an independent Butte Mine Workers' Union which soon numbered 4,000.

On June 13, 1914, which was Miner's Union Day, a mob of disgruntled men not only broke up the labor parade but led an attack on the Butte Miners' Union Hall on North Main Street, wrecking the interior and throwing typewriters and furniture out the windows. Charles Moyer, president of the Westen Federation of Miners, hurried to Butte and called a meeting in the gutted hall for June 23. On that day, a huge crowd gathered in front of the building, but the first man up the stairs fell with a bullet in his shoulder. The enraged mob scattered, as rifles and machine guns, directed by Moyer's men, raked them from the windows. Moyer and his deputies escaped before the miners returned and dynamited the Hall. This terrorism resulted in the governor placing the city under martial law. On September 9 the open shop was adopted in all of the mines.

In 1906 the zinc era of the city began when Captain A. B. Wolvin formed the Butte & Superior Copper Company to work the Black Rock mine. When the ore was found to contain zinc instead of copper, the stock dropped in value, for zinc was considered worthless; but as soon as an air-concentration process of refining it was developed, the stock rose and the company built the first successful zinc plant in Butte. Previous to this Daly had identified zinc in one of the Anaconda Company's mines in the 1890's. This heavy, black mineral, often found in silver-lead ore, was called "Black Jack" or "Rosin Jack" by miners and was extremely unpopular at the smelters, which penalized shippers whose ore contained this "worthless" and refractory metal. When this substance was encountered on the 300-foot level of the Orphan Boy, an Anaconda property, the foreman took it for high-grade copper until Daly recognized it as high-grade zinc, worthless only because no method of treating it was known. Up until 1910 only 300,000 tons of zinc had been recovered; but only three years later Clark shrewdly invested a million

dollars in a zinc-concentrator and 400-ton mill, a scant two miles south of the Butte & Superior plant, equipped to handle ore from his rich Elm Orlu mine.

Pit or strip mining began about 1912 with Captain Wolvin organizing the Butte & Duluth Company to work the Brundy group of claims southeast of the city. Upon examining the large deposits of low-grade copper ore, he decided to dig them directly out of the hillside by stripping the ground in successive tiers and then to treat the ore by leaching it. Close by was the Bullwhacker property, on the slope west of Columbia Gardens. This ore, however, was dug from the surface down, creating a terraced pit from which the ore was hauled to the company's plant which processed 500 tons a day.

Seen from the top of The Hill, the immensity of Butte is impressive. Below, the gridiron pattern of the city spreads out — line upon line of parallel streets, whose buildings seem all of one height, except a few which perforate the even crust of wood and brick. Beyond this solid mass, which contains the older portion of the city, spreads the newer part, a sea of green down on the flats, split by Highway 10S with its gaudy tavern signs and tourist motels. But beside and above are gallows frames and mills, dumps and tracks, ore trains and electric cables. In the midst of this jumble are the rest of the homes — the jaunty or rundown houses which march in rows up and down the steep hillsides or are caught between the dumps which overshadow them. Near the top of The Hill is the famous Kelley shaft.

The property is named for Cornelius F. Kelley, for many years president of the Anaconda Copper Mining Company and, since 1940, chairman of its board of directors. His vision, based on years of experience, has resulted in the Greater Butte Project, a gigantic recovery plan which employs block-caving to recover low-grade copper ore deep within the earth. Kelley described this plan at a dinner in 1947 and assured his listeners that more than 130,000,000 tons of recoverable ore could be mined above the 3,400-foot level alone. That his estimate was conservative has since been proved, for by 1954, 150,000,000 tons of ore had been removed.

Block-caving is the undercutting of sections of large ore bodies and permitting them to cave in. The crushed ore is "recovered through raises driven upwards from haulage drifts," the drifts serving as "passageways, cut between pillars of rock." As each section is cleared of ore, the cavity is filled with tailings to prevent fire and gas hazards. An estimated 9,000,-000 tons of such waste material will be used to fill the honeycombed hollows before all recoverable matter has been removed. Through block-caving, which requires tremendous tonnage to be successful, low-grade ore previously bypassed as worthless is now made profitable. The Kelley project is equipped to produce 15,-000 tons of ore daily. The great shaft has two compartments for hoisting and one mancage with a deck accommodating fifty at a time.

Anyone entering Butte from the east passes the Berkeley Pit, the first large scale open-pit mining attempted in the city. This is one of the recent developments of the Anaconda Company, begun in 1955 and expected to increase production of copper-zinc ores by 32,500 tons a day. A second involves sinking additional shafts in the Ryan and Missoula mines to permit the recovery of hitherto untouched copper-zinc ores.

In April, 1960, the Anaconda Company put into operation an electric wheel dump truck which hauls as much as seventy-six tons of material from the pit to the dumping site up a fifteen per cent grade at twelve miles an hour. Power is supplied through an overhead trolley to 400-horsepower electric motors contained in the hub of each wheel. The truck is also equipped with a diesel engine which supplies power to the wheel when it is away from the trolley power source. With this mammoth machine, open pit mining can be carried on with increased efficiency.

In driving through the city one cannot fail to see a group of buildings — the Montana School of Mines — perched on the saddle of a hill below Big Butte. At the entrance to the grounds stands Augustus St. Gaudens' bronze statue of Marcus Daly, a memorial to a man dedicated to the development of the city and its copper mines. I have spent days in the school's fine library, probing into the city's past, but always conscious of its present, pulsing vitality. The library is big and quiet, but from time to time the sound of the city creeps in. The periodic rattle of ore trains sliding down the grade from The Hill, their warning bells jangling for the crossing below the school, made me conscious that the documents I was consulting were only a key to the present productivity of the city.

At five o'clock when the library closed I always lingered on the terrace outside to look over Butte. From the data culled from mining records, I saw the city in a new light. It was more than headframes and shafthouses. Within The Hill, whose surface was so crowded with humanity, were more than 3,500 miles of passageways and it was said that one who knew the intricate underground labyrinth could enter a shaft in Walkerville and emerge at Meaderville, two miles away, without coming to the surface. Through reading I had discovered that modern metallurgical research enabled manganese as well as zinc to be recovered from The Hill's stockpile of metals and that by 1956, ninety-five per cent of this country's manganese came from the Butte mines.

The Hill provided the ore; the city was made up of the miners and of the industries and diversions connected with their lives. To complete the cycle I must see the great smelter in which the bulk of the ore was processed. Late one afternoon I left Butte and started west toward Anaconda, the town to which the heavily-loaded ore trains were headed.

ROCKER

Four miles west of Butte stands Rocker, an early placer camp on Silver Bow Creek, whose conglomeration of homes, small stores, and boarded-up buildings date from earlier times. After the placers played out, Rocker survived and even boomed because of the discovery and development of the Bluebird mine, which lay a short distance northeast of it. When the Bluebird shut down in 1893, the camp faded until the Butte Anaconda & Pacific railroad between Butte and the smelter at Anaconda chose Rocker as its division point, with all ore trains made up in its yards.

BURLINGTON

Rocker exists, but Burlington has completely disappeared. The camp grew up around the Bluebird mine, a silver property whose big mill, built in 1885, stood a mile south of the mine near the Rocker railroad station.

Burlington, whose population averaged between six and seven hundred persons, contained a postoffice, schoolhouse, church and a lodge hall, as well as stores and dwellings. The superintendent of the Bluebird, a man named Van Zandt, whose brick home stood close to the mine, started a community library

BUTTE FROM THE SCHOOL OF MINES

with both reading and writing rooms. After June, 1893, when the price of silver dropped and the mine close down, the miners and their families gradually moved away. Only the abandoned Bluebird remained. After its hoist burned in 1900 and the mill and machinery were removed, the houses and stores were also hauled away and the contents of the library taken to Butte. A few leasers worked prospects in the vicinity for a time, and then the area was put to new use. Burlington became a dairy center, providing Butte with twenty-five wagon-loads of fresh milk a day. Now even the dairy herds are gone.

NISSLER (SILVER BOW JCT.)

At Nissler, or Silver Bow Junction, one battered frame building marks the site of the original settlement of Silver Bow.

Just southwest of Nissler is the Victor Chemical Works, half shrouded in noxious clouds of heavy smoke. This company, which employs nearly 400 men, started operations in 1951 upon the completion of a $9,500,000 electric furnace, built to recover the element of phosphorus from the phosphate rock which exists in quantity in the mountains southwest of the plant.

GREGSON SPRINGS

Nine miles west of Nissler, at a little distance from the fine new highway, is Gregson Springs, a resort whose hot pool and picnic grounds were great favorites with the people of Butte and Anaconda, and to which the Butte Miner's Union came for its annual picnic on August 11, 1912. The mill and smeltermen from Anaconda also planned to hold their outing at the Springs on the same day. Trains of flatcars brought several thousands to the resort where sports events filled the afternoon. A tug-of-war between the rival factions concluded the program and resulted in defeat for the Butte team. This occasioned a free fight with beer bottles. At the end of the melee, in which many were injured and one man killed, a baggage car, provided by the railroad, took the wounded to Butte and Anaconda hospitals.

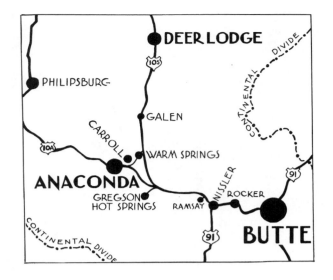

ANACONDA

Rolling hills obscure a view of the Washoe Smelter until one is fairly close to the immense plant. The first time I drove through Anaconda it was early on a Sunday morning and the place was still asleep. A thin column of smoke rose lazily from the great stack but the plant seemed nearly as quiet as the town. My second entry into Anaconda was quite different. My husband and I drove slowly through the city looking for the home of a young couple, the Howard Cooks, where we were to stay for several days. Both of them were enthusiastic about the area and its history and had offered to show us the city and some of the old mining camps that were nearby.

"We'll go down to the Montana Hotel for dinner," said our host after we had unpacked. "You must see it. It was built by Marcus Daly in 1888, and, since he hoped to make Anaconda the capital of Montana, he spared no expense to make it a first-class hotel where senators would stay and important visitors be entertained. He selected W. W. Boyinton of Chicago as his architect. Boyinton's plans for the four-story hotel called for brick trimmed with cut stone and terra cotta. Before you see it, read what the *Butte Daily Miner* said about it while it was under construction."

The style of architecture is composite . . . The interior of the first and second stories is finished in red oak and the balance of the building is eastern pine. In the basement is located a dining room for servants, the laundry, boilers and dynamos. . . . In addition to electricity, gas will also be used as an illuminant, thus insuring a constant source of light, should one or the other of these agencies fail.

In the first story, on the north side, is the main diningroom . . . with a ladies' ordinary . . . adjoining. . . . the north-east corner . . . will be occupied by a drug firm. Adjoining this is a barber shop. The rotunda is 32 feet by 44 feet. . . . A ladies' gallery surrounds the rotunda. . . . Passageways lead from the rotunda to the billiard, bar and main toilet rooms. . . . Open fireplaces with marble mantels are located in each room. . . . The main entrance on Main St. is arched . . . On the sides facing the streets the windows are French plate Cathedral glass, semi-circular in form.

On the second story . . . is a parlor. . . . Adjoining are two smaller parlors. . . . A clubroom adjoins the smaller parlor.

Thirty-three bedrooms . . . occupy the rest of the floor. The third and fourth floors are sleeping apartments; each floor has forty-four rooms. . . .

. . . For the safety of guests, a rope fire-escape will be placed in each room, besides which five regular escapes . . . have been erected . . . A hydraulic elevator, Otis Bros. patent, is provided for the convenience of those not liking the exertion required in ascending by the old fashioned method. The building is heated by steam and equipped with a complete electric service, speaking tubes, etc. . . .

. . . A promenade extends around the house on both streets. The principal stockholders . . . are Marcus Daly, W. L. Hoge and Col. S. A. Estes. The building will cost, exclusive of furniture, $135,000.
Holiday Edition 1888-89,
Butte Daily Miner

As I handed the article back, Howard continued: "After Daly's death, $96,000 more were spent in remodeling it. Then in 1949, the Charles Boveys, the state senator and his wife who rebuilt the old part of Virginia City, took the hotel in hand and restored it to its former grandeur."

When we entered the hotel I saw what he meant. Stepping into the "Red Room" lounge, we inspected the silver ceiling, the red and gray baroque wallpaper, the divans upholstered

174

in plush, the marble-topped tables, the gilt-framed mirrors which tossed reflections back and forth from side to side making the narrow place seem larger than it was, and finally the heavy, sound-muffling draperies at windows and doors. Arline Cook called my attention to the light fixtures, which were like those in the Supreme Court room in the capitol at Helena.

As we pushed through the portieres into the barroom, I saw the famous marquetry portrait of "Tammany," Daly's favorite racehorse. This handsome square of wood mosaic, consisting of more than a thousand pieces, cost $3,000 at Tiffany's. It was designed by Newcomb and inlaid in the floor by a special artisan, whose expenses were paid all the way from New York. From the time it was installed, no one has stepped on it, out of deference to the memory of the great horse.

I can't remember what I ordered from the bar, for I was too busy making a color sketch of the room, which is said to resemble as much as possible the Hoffman House Bar in New York City. The walls were deep red and the window drapes of gold brocade. The mahogany bar, on which were neatly stacked glasses and an imposing array of bottles, was backed by a huge mirror ornamented by heavy, carved columns. In a conspicuous place hung a large and elegant gilt-framed painting of four romping nudes. Light from a many-globed brass chandelier which came, I was told, from the courthouse in Great Falls threw a warm glow over the room.

What a glittering company must have assembled here on the night of July 1, 1889, when the hotel opened with a Grand Ball. On that occasion Matt Slater, the bartender, dispensed champagne as long as the supply held out. Rumor says that all the champagne in Montana was commandeered for this opening fling.

We dined that evening at the Anaconda Club. The Club, which was opened in September, 1950, at Third and Main Streets, is one of several gifts of the Anaconda Copper Mining Company to its employees, who with their wives are automatically members of the organization. Besides a snack bar and dining room, it contains an auditorium, ballroom, lounge, pool and billiard room, bar and card room, and an eight-lane bowling alley.

After dinner we walked around the city until dark. Just one square away from the Club is the "common," a city block which was cleared of trees and rocks in 1904 and graded so as to be a suitable area for sports. In summer it is a baseball park; in winter a skating rink. During the holidays, the company places in its center a large lighted Christmas tree.

At Sixth and Oak Streets is St. Ann's hospital, standing on ground secured for it by Daly. The hospital, under the management of the Sisters of Charity, was opened in July, 1889. On the western outskirts of the town is Washoe Park with lakes and a dance pavilion, another of the A. C. M. Company's gifts to the city. Finally, there is Mountain View Park, opened in 1900 and operated by the Butte Anaconda & Pacific Railway.

One of the larger public buildings is the Hearst Library, a brick and stone structure with pillared portico, the gift of Mrs. Phoebe Hearst. For three years prior to its erection she maintained a reading room in a small building at Third and Cherry Streets. The present library, which officially opened on June 10, 1898, with a reception in Mrs. Hearst's honor, was her outright gift to the city. She paid all expenses, as well as the salaries of the librarians, until someone unwittingly forwarded to Mrs. Hearst a good-sized tax bill which had been sent to the library. She then deeded the library to the city, which thereafter has had to support it.

Back of the library, close to the mountainside, is the Deer Lodge County courthouse. In 1897, the people of Deer Lodge County voted to move the county seat to Anaconda. When the courthouse was completed, it stood off by itself, blocks away from any other building. Today the city has crowded up against it and swept westwards into the valley. In 1901, the county was divided, the portion containing Deer Lodge expecting to retain that name, while the remainder was designated as Daly County. The Supreme Court, however, ruled otherwise: Since Anaconda was already the seat of Deer Lodge County, it should remain so, and the territory comprising the new county, although it contained the city of Deer Lodge, was to be named Powell, after Mount Powell. By now it was dark and further sight-seeing had to be postponed until morning. This city that I was seeing was the Anaconda of 1958. What had it been like in the beginning when it was platted?

Even before 1882, Butte faced a critical water shortage, for Silver Bow Creek and its tributaries could not furnish enough water for the many reduction plants in the area. Clark had a smelter in Butte and Daly needed one for his Anaconda properties. Two sites interested Daly — one on the Big Hole River and the other on Warm Springs Creek. The Warm Springs site, which he chose, was only twenty-six miles west from his mines and lay in a mountain valley sparsely settled by ranchers.

In the fall of 1882, Daly told Morgan Evans, a rancher, to begin to buy the land and water rights that he would need. Evans accordingly purchased the Sigsby ranch, the Gordon Vineyard ranch, the Robert Finley ground, and other acreages. The Vineyard property was set aside as company headquarters. When Clark suspected what Daly was contemplating, he bought up the water rights to Warm Springs Creek so that Daly could get no water except through him. The price he demanded was exorbitant. This action is generally conceded to have touched off the feud between the rivals.

In the spring of 1883, Daly and his family, accompanied by Morgan Evans, drove to the site of the future city of Anaconda to look at the countryside which Daly was about to develop. The mountains south of the site were thickly timbered with pine and fir trees, the meadows covered with knee-deep bunch grass, and deer, elk, mountain goats and mountain lions were so abundant that ranchers did not need to hunt for smaller animals.

The story is often told of Daly's pointing to a cow grazing on the wild hay and saying: "Main Street will run north and south in a direct line, right through that cow." Shortly after this prediction, Joseph N. Harper and his assistant, William Reed, both of whom stayed at the Vineyard ranch, surveyed the townsite. On a blustery day in 1883, Daly with a few business men from Butte visited the prairie site and negotiated the sale of the first lots. Although a gale was blowing off Mount Haggin and the party were extremely uncomfortable, Daly, ignoring the weather, strode about pointing out stakes and informing the visitors that they were at the intersection of Main and First Streets and that corner lots were $750.00 and inside lots $500.00. All four corner lots were sold at that time.

Marcus Daly wanted his town to be known as Copperopolis, but Postmaster Clinton Moore pointed out that there was already a camp of that name in Montana and suggested Anaconda instead. Daly accepted this without enthusiasm.

David Marler describes the city's first Fourth of July:

I arrived here with $2500 of goods from Butte on June 16, 1883. . . . At the corner of Main and Front Sts. James Keefe had three tents which were doing business. . . . the tents were used as saloons. One was run by the Silver Bow Brewery and the other by the Centennial Brewery. . . .

There weren't any firecrackers or fireworks but plenty of firewater. Everyone who could suspended work. . . . Having nothing else to do but drink, nearly the entire population began to tank up early and kept at it all day. . . . A tough gang had just arrived from Miles City, then the terminus of the Northern Pacific . . . Fortunately there were but few guns among them or in the camp at large. Fearing a wholesale shooting scrape, the few men who kept sober went around collecting the guns of those who were drunk.

Nearly all the citizens who had wives and children joined the ranchers at a picnic grove two miles east of the town. . . . One man got drunk and pugnacious and was promptly arrested, but what to do with him was the question. The nearest jail was at Deer Lodge. So Messrs. Jones and Crosswhite threw him down, bound him, tied him to a tree and left him till he sobered up.

Anaconda Standard, July 1, 1923

Throughout 1883, Anaconda was a city of tents, but by 1884 straggling lines of frame and brick buildings took the place of the temporary shelters. The Northern Pacific had already built a narrow-gauge road between Butte and Garrison. Anticipating brisk business if the rumored town beside Warm Springs Creek materialized, the railroad established a station called Stuart on April 10, 1883, nine miles east of the anticipated site. By June, a stage line connected Stuart and the townsite. By August 1884, the Montana Union Railway reached the city.

The history of this new town is remarkable. . . . It has over two-hundred buildings . . . among which are Christian and Methodist Episcopal (South) chapels, a . . . skating rink . . . 25 restaurants, about as many saloons, 2 hardware, 3 general merchandise, 4 clothing, 3 fruit and notion, 1 drug and 1 furniture (stores), 3 livery stables, 2 blacksmith, 1 harness and 3 barber shops, 1 planing mill, 3 lumber yards, 1 brickyard and 1 bank.

The Weekly Missoulian, Oct. 10, 1884

Construction of the Anaconda Smelting Works was begun in the spring of 1883. The plant was located on the north side of Warm Springs Creek on the Cedar Creek road. During its erection large crews of workmen lived in tents along the creek. Sawmills, set up beside every stream in the vicinity, reduced the timber, cut by French-Canadian woodchoppers, into dressed lumber. Even before the

MONTANA HOTEL, ANACONDA
BAR, MONTANA HOTEL, ANACONDA

plant was completed large quantities of logs were cut and stacked for smelter fuel or mine timbers. Hundreds of teams kicked up dust or ploughed through mud drawing to the site heavy freight wagons loaded with building materials. Every part of the plant, except the machinery and the sheet-iron siding and roofing materials, was made of wood.

The Upper Works, as they were called, over which William McCaskell was superintendent, were designed to treat 500 tons of ore per day and contained a concentrator, hand-roasters, and a small reverberatory matte furnace. The plant was in operation by September 23, 1883. Unmarried employees lived in boardinghouses and hotels in Anaconda. Certain of the boardinghouses delivered lunches across the creek to the workmen whose eleven-to-twelve-hour day prevented their return at noon.

In 1886 the capacity of the plant was doubled. The smelter as it appeared in July, 1887, is described in an issue of the *Northwest*:

a little removed from the town . . . stands the huge, many chimneyed structures of the works, panting and rumbling night and day without a moment's cessation, consuming train-loads of grey rock and producing train-loads of copper matte that goes to Swansea, Wales, for the final process of conversion into refined copper.

When the capacity of the Upper Works was inadequate for the volume of ore received, Daly built a second plant, larger than the first and equipped with the newest smelting processes. These Lower Works, one and a half miles east of the other plant, were completed in 1888 and contained an experimental electrolytic refinery.

Early on the morning of March 14, 1889, Anaconda was awakened by shrill whistles — the Lower Works were on fire. Before the flames were extinguished, the major portion of the plant was destroyed as buildings and machinery melted or were reduced to ashes. The damage was estimated at three-quarters of a million dollars and necessitated a shutdown, not only of the plant but also of the company mines. Since the fire was believed to have been of incendiary origin, Daly also placed a guard around the Anaconda property in Butte. The works were rebuilt without delay, with steel and corrugated iron replacing wood construction; and the daily capacity was increased to 3,000 tons. When the plant reopened on October 1, 1889, it was the most modern copper smelting works in existence.

The employees at the Lower Works made it known that they preferred to live near the plant, so Daly built the town of Carroll, named for Michael Carroll of Butte. In this settlement of 750 persons, sometimes called the "little red town" because nearly everything was painted red, were a postoffice, school, company store, barber shop, and a few private enterprises. Carroll was unique, for it had no saloons; but the company store stocked whiskey by the barrel.

The older residents of Anaconda remember the twenty-four houses on Carroll's main street, ten of which had porches. These were reserved for foremen and their families. The company also built two apartment houses, many small private homes, and boardinghouses for the unmarried personnel. Since employees from all departments of the plant, from laborers to superintendents, lived in Carroll, the citizens represented a mixture of nationalities and social customs. Stage service connected the town with Anaconda, but passengers had to brace themselves for the adventurous trip, as most of the stage stock were half-broken broncos which ran the stretch in record time. Individuals wishing to go to town to shop or for recreation could hire a horse and rig, but the trip was equally unpredictable, for the "spirited cayuses were brought from the hills and broken to harness in one quick lesson." Even so, whenever performances were scheduled at the Evans Opera House in Anaconda, Carroll residents were among the audience. The town had its own recreational facilities provided by the company — a park, a race track, picnic grounds, and a dance pavilion.

As Anaconda grew in size, Carroll became its fashionable suburb with much partying carried on among its congenial families. But its pleasant life cycle was short. When it was announced that a new smelter would be built across Warm Springs Creek and that Carroll would cease to exist, the people packed up and moved to Anaconda. By 1903, when the new Washoe Smelter was completed, Carroll had virtually disappeared. Most of its buildings were moved to Anaconda; and today black slag heaps and acres of tailings cover its site.

ANACONDA (Continued)

As early as 1898, Daly had made plans to enlarge his smelter, but when no economical way could be found, he scrapped the idea and built on a new site across the creek. Work on the Washoe Smelter began in 1900 and was completed in 1902. The new plant was designed to handle 4,800 tons daily in the concentrator and 1,000 tons at the blast furnaces. Fairly early in its development a plant was installed to make refractory fire brick for the furnaces. All such brick had previously been imported from Wales.

When the Montana Union Railroad, in 1891, refused to haul ore between Butte and Anaconda until a dispute over freight rates was settled, the Anaconda Company closed its mines and smelter. To avoid future shut-downs Daly built his own line, the Butte Anaconda & Pacific Railroad, to convey the company's ore direct from The Hill to the smelter. The road was in operation in 1893. For twenty years the B. A. & P. used steam locomotives and then, in 1913, the road was electrified. In 1953 diesel electric locomotives were introduced. Although the railroad was built to haul ore in its hopper-type dump cars, passenger service provided an unexpected source of revenue, necessitating, before the advent of the automobile, eight round trips each day. Passenger service was discontinued in 1955, but ore tonnage over the years has increased from 7,500 tons to 33,000 per day.

Year by year the Washoe plant continued to expand. In 1916, after Fred Laist, through intensive research which cost one million dollars, developed the electrolytic refining of zinc to a high degree of efficiency, the Anaconda Company built two zinc plants, one at Great Falls and the other two miles east of the city of Anaconda. By 1923 the Washoe Smelter's daily capacity of ore was 12,000 tons and its zinc plant was producing huge amounts of almost pure zinc each month.

Recent additions made by the company include the Phosphate plant, which manufactures phosphoric acid and Vanadium Pentoxide, the Ferromanganese plant which produces 2,500 long tons of the product per month, the Sulphuric acid plant, and the Arsenic plant which turns out 1,000 tons of white arsenic per month. The Brick plant continues to make refractory bricks for metallurgical operations.

Four months after the town was laid out, in September, 1883, Marcus Daly organized the banking firm of Hoge, Daly & Company. As bankers, the five men — Daly, W. L. Hoge, R. C. Chambers, M. B. Brownlee, and F. E. Sargeant — operated such a successful business that in April, 1889, they organized the First

HEARST LIBRARY, ANACONDA

National Bank of Anaconda, with Daly as president. There was much excitement in the city on October 19, 1895, when two young men, Arthur Firpo and William H. Darling, attempted to rob the bank. Both of them worked at the foundry and had some knowledge of explosives but were amateurs at safe-cracking. After several hours of work, their charge of powder and five pounds of nitroglycerin shattered the walls of the vault. The explosion wakened E. L. Kunkel, who slept in the building. Rushing into the street, he met Frank O'Brien, assistant chief of police, who climbed to the roof, saw the robbers, and shot at one. The other escaped only temporarily, and both were sentenced to eight years in the penitentiary.

From the first, Anaconda contained halls in which traveling vaudeville troupes and road companies performed and in which dances were held. Both the Austrian and Turner halls had dance floors, the latter provided with a balcony for spectators on three sides.

The auditorium of the Evans Opera House, which stood on the west side of Main Street, between Front and Commercial, occupied the upper story of the building and was furnished with chairs, which could be pushed back to clear the floor for other types of entertainment. Most theatrical bills were presented here until the Margaret Theater opened in September, 1897. Thereafter, performances were booked for the newer building. The programs for the opening night at the Margaret, which featured a play, "The Hoosier Doctor," were printed on yellow satin and contained, in addition to a quotation from Shakespeare, the following statement:

179

. . . By request of the directors and stockholders, Mrs. Marcus Daly graciously permitted her name to be given to the building.

Many denominations are represented among Anaconda's churches. The first to organize was the Methodist Church South in 1884. The initial group of fifteen members built a small church, but as the numbers dwindled, the church was given up. In July, 1889, when Reverend Philip Lowry was appointed to minister to Anaconda, he found no building and only seven members left. He apparently had more stamina than his predecessors, for he said to his wife as he pointed to a corner lot, "There's where the new church will stand." On December 14, 1890, a new brick church stood on the site he had chosen and was dedicated. The Christian church was the next to organize, but did not build until 1896.

The first Episcopal service was held December 12, 1886, in a room over Foskett's saloon, by the Reverend A. B. Howard, vicar of St. James' church at Deer Lodge. Besides preaching, he performed a baptism. The water used by him in the ceremony was brought to him in a beer mug! St. Mark's Episcopal church, the present stone building, was completed in 1891; its pipe organ was the gift of Mrs. Marcus Daly.

The Presbyterians under Duncan J. McMillan, D.D., and Reverend Linnel, also organized in 1886, holding their services in a small building until the present church was built in 1888. Grace Baptist Church was organized in 1887. For some time, services were held in a building shared by the Swedish Methodist, Norwegian Lutheran, and Swedish Baptist congregations. In May, 1902, the church was incorporated as the First Swedish Baptist of Anaconda. In 1934 the name was changed to First Grace Baptist Church. The First Baptist Church was incorporated in 1897. It was nearly destroyed by fire in 1928, and when it was rebuilt, a parsonage was erected also.

Father De Ryckere, of Deer Lodge, assigned Father De Siere, a Belgian, as missionary priest to Anaconda in 1887. The young priest spoke no English and upon reaching Anaconda, walked the streets, stopping each man and saying the one word he knew, which was "Catholic?" Finally someone took him to the home of George Barich, a German, and the two were able to converse. With the help of his German friend, who secured the Odd Fellows Hall, mass was celebrated the following Sunday to a congregation of twenty-five

persons of diverse nationalities. When this location was outgrown, services were held in the Evans Opera House. Finally, on November 25, 1888, St. Paul's, a new brick church, was dedicated. By 1897 there was need for a Roman Catholic church on the east side of the city where the growing Austrian population lived. The following year an Austrian priest was brought to the parish, and St. Peter's Church was dedicated.

The Norwegian Evangelical Lutheran Church was organized in 1896 and reorganized as Our Savior's Lutheran Church in 1902. After the church burned in 1927, it was immediately rebuilt and is in use today.

When Elder Lyman J. Garner was sent to Anaconda in 1906 to organize a church of Jesus Christ of Latter Day Saints, he selected Dewey Hall as a meeting place. In 1951, when the members, who numbered 500, were looking for a building site, the Anaconda Company deeded them one and a half city blocks. In 1953 the congregation assembled in a new brick building erected on the location.

The town's first newspaper, the *Anaconda Review,* appeared on May 1, 1884. L. O. Leonard and his brother Frank bought the paper in 1885, obtained a Washington hand press from Helena and shipped it to Anaconda. The two men were busily running off copies of the paper on the morning of July 23, 1885, when a telegram came through reporting the death of General Grant. They stopped the press, inserted the death notice, and finished the edition.

When Marcus Daly wanted his own paper, to offset the attacks of Clark's *Butte Miner,* he looked around for a competent and even distinguished editor. In John H. Durston of the *Syracuse Standard* he felt he had found his man. Durston came to Anaconda for a conference and to size up the community over which it was hoped the paper would exert a strong influence. As the story goes, he was unimpressed and saw little future for himself or for the town. Then he heard Daly agreeing to buy an untried colt for $4,000 for his racing stable and was so struck by the faith of a man who would take such risks in stride that he accepted the editorship. The first issue of the *Anaconda Standard* appeared on September 4, 1889. After W. A. Clark's death, the paper was moved to Butte, where it became the *Montana Standard.*

My husband and I stayed in Anaconda several days, and each evening I plied my friends with questions. "What happened to Clark's property after he died?" I asked. "We went through his mansion in Butte, and years ago, when I lived in New York, I remember that his home on Fifth Avenue was always pointed out to visitors."

"He died in 1925 at the age of eighty-six," Howard replied. "Three years later, when his estate was settled, his newspaper, the *Butte Miner,* the Butte Street Railway Company, Columbia Gardens, the Elm Orlu mine, and other holdings became the property of the A. C. M. Company. That was when a new newspaper, the *Montana Standard,* started. The *Miner* quit publication and the *Anaconda Standard* was moved to Butte to become the *Montana Standard.* The Anaconda Club where we ate dinner is the old *Anaconda Standard* building. You must have seen the Employees Club in Butte, which the A. C. M. Company opened in 1947. The building it occupies was the old Thornton Hotel."

"You say that the smeltermen represent many countries. What nationalities predominate in Anaconda?"

"Mostly Irish and Slavs. There are some Swedes, French-Canadians, and English; and a few Italians, Norwegians, and Germans, too."

"When Daly died in 1900, who succeeded him as president of the A. C. M. Company?"

"Quite a few have held that position. William Scallon succeeded Daly. John D. Ryan was made president in 1905, the same year that Cornelius Kelley was elected secretary of the company. Charles M. Brinckerhoff has been president since 1958."

"What about the operations of the A. C. M. Co. and the Washoe Smelter today?"

"To begin with, the A. C. M., which employs 4,000 men (1958), leads in the production and fabrication of non-ferrous metals and as a producer of aluminum and uranium. By the end of 1953, 24,000,000 tons of zinc had been processed and 6,000,000 tons of manganese. Ninety-five per cent of the manganese mined in the United States came from Butte in 1956. That's what we process the most of these days. The big smelterstack, which was built in 1919, is 530 feet high. Its inside diameter is 60 feet at the top and 76 feet at the base. The Hill is said to have produced three billion dollars worth of mineral wealth. Besides the Kelley shaft, the company has five hoisting shafts for copper ore, five more for zinc, and two for manganese. The deepest shaft is the Mt. Con. — 4,693 feet from collar

to sump. Each year more pit mining is carried on. The A. C. M. has two thousand, four hundred and twenty-two miles of underground workings, counting passageways and vertical shafts. The city of Anaconda, the development of the mines on The Hill, and the Washoe Smelter are as Daly dreamed they would be. Between 1883 and 1899 he controlled everying here."

In wandering around Anaconda I found several older persons who were glad to reminisce about the early days of the city. One spoke of the first schoolhouse, a brick building completed in 1886 and staffed with two teachers. Another recalled that the first high school granduating class of six held its exercises in the Miners' Union Hall. A third pointed out the site of the Margaret Theater, named for Mrs. Marcus Daly, and added that many baby girls had been named for that respected and admired lady.

There were other stories that revealed the rigors endured while the city was taking root and the ingenuity that often saved the day. During the first winter Anaconda had no minister and no one to conduct a funeral service when a death occurred. More than once the postmaster, Clinton Moore, consented to read the burial service and to accompany the procession to the new cemetery on the hill behind the present courthouse.

The Anaconda Fire Department was not organized until January, 1889. At that time, hose carts were purchased and a contract made with the city water company to supply twenty hydrants for a total of $70.00 per year. Prior to this arrangement, fires were fought with bucket brigades or with anything at hand. During the winter of 1885, when store buildings on the west side of Main Street burst into flames, the citizens fought the blaze so persistently with snowballs, dirt, and wet sacks, that it did not spread.

On our last evening in Anaconda the Cooks drove us to the west edge of the city through a new addition filled with attractive homes surrounded by gardens, but as yet unshaded by the young trees which the owners had planted.

"This section is where the old racetrack stood," Howard told us. "Wherever Daly was he built a track — he was crazy about horseracing. This one-mile course was begun in 1887 and completed the next year. Later, when it was rebuilt, stables with one hundred and thirty stalls and a grandstand seat-ing a thousand people were added. The whole set-up was owned by the Anaconda Racing Association, but Daly was back of it. The old barn was torn down only a few years ago.

"On race days his miners got a holiday with pay. So many people came over from Butte that the B. A. & P. had to run twenty-five car trains to Anaconda to accommodate them. They'd fix up some of the gondola cars with benches and pack people in them too. The trains ran within a few blocks of the racetrack. Or, if you preferred, you could ride a streetcar fom the Montana Hotel right to the gate.

"A year before the course was built a race was run two miles below the town in a field by the Warm Springs road. The racers were a black thoroughbred sprinter belonging to Daly and an old mare owned by William Hammond of Phillipsburg. The bets were an even thousand dollars on each horse. Doc Mitchell was the starter. Just as the horses were lining up he cracked a buggy whip and the mare took off, jumped a fence, and ran two miles before her jockey could stop her. The bets changed to two to one on Daly's horse. Again the mare out-ran the thoroughbred and won all the money.

"Many of Daly's horses were trained at his Bitter Root Stock Farm in Hamilton, south of Missoula. The famous Tammany raced on his Montana tracks as well as in the east. When Daly died and racing stopped, the track here was neglected. Then, in 1905, the Deer Lodge County Fair Association got possession of the property and held fairs there for several years."

We left Anaconda reluctantly, but I knew that I would return for there were many nearby camps that I still wanted to sketch.

CHAPTER 11

HIGHLANDS
GOLD and
HECLA SILVER

THE HIGHLANDS

From the top of any hill in Butte the view to the south reveals the Highlands — an isolated range of mountains fifteen miles away which rise to elevations of 10,000 feet. This mineralized area first drew miners to it in the 1860's when its camps produced purer gold than the placer diggings on Silver Bow Creek.

Placer gold was discovered in the Highlands, at the foot of Red Mountain, on July 25, 1866, on Fish Creek by E. B. and J. B. S. Coleman and William Crawford, although one account adds G. O. Humphrey to the initial party. News of this strike on the upper portion of the creek, above the junction of Wood and Highland Gulches, started the usual stampede to a new area and drained Butte of many of its miners. Among the firstcomers to the placer field were Thomas W. Rutter, Thomas Hall, Frank Beck, D. L. Parker, and J. B. Dunlap. The gold that was found was exceptionally pure and was valued at $20 an ounce. The Coleman brothers, Crawford, and possibly Dunlap, left the Highlands shortly

after their discovery, for nothing more is heard of them. Tom Rutter and Dan Parker stayed on. From his claim, Parker washed gold worth several thousands of dollars. William Owsley, Frank Beck, and Tom Hall also had a good claim from which they are said to have washed $3,100 in one day. Jim Murphy was another prospector who struck pay dirt. When he'd taken out all that he needed for a while, he'd let his friends work the claim and keep what they made. William Cooley, James McChord, and one other man had a rich claim below the townsite in a dry gulch. The partners did not trust each other and each suspected that he was being robbed. When their foreman disappeared with all the dust from a cleanup, $27,000 worth, they were sure of it.

Almost simultaneously with the Fish Creek strike, placers were found on the western slope of the mountains on Moose Creek and at the head of Basin Creek. From the latter, George Popple and his brother were reported to have made "$4 to $10 per day to the hand." As a result of these discoveries, the miners lost no time in establishing the Highland and Moose

183

mining districts, each of which had its respective camps — Highland City, near the head of Fish Creek, Red Mountain City, less than a mile to the southwest, and Moosetown, across the Divide.

RED MOUNTAIN CITY and HIGHLAND CITY

By the summer of 1867, Red Mountain City was recognized as the largest settlement in southern Deer Lodge County, which at that time included Silver Bow County and reached from the Highlands north to Canada. It and Highland City, though separate, were so close to each other that in time they were often thought of as one. Red Mountain City had a water system consisting of hydrants and pipes, made from ten-foot long green logs through which a hole was bored. It had a hotel run by Mr. and Mrs. Beden, a sawmill, a blacksmith shop, and two general stores, one operated by Charles Wunderlich and the other by Rod Leggat and E. S. Stackpole, whose two story log building housed a Masonic Lodge on the upper floor. The sick were treated by Dr. Seymour Day whenever he was sober. Quite a few of the 1,000 miners who voted in the first county election undoubtedly attended a "grand ball" which was given during the winter of 1867 under difficulties. Rod Dhu Leggat and his committee were responsible for the arrangements and when a heavy snow closed the roads two days before the event, Leggat sent men on horseback to Butte and Deer Lodge to announce that the dance would be held. While they were breaking trail to the valley, 200 men were digging out six miles of snow-packed road so that all could attend.

No sooner had placers been discovered in the gulches than lode gold was found on Nevin Hill and in other portions of the Highlands. The ore, which was free-milling, could be crushed in arrastres or stamp mills, and when the placers began to give out within two or three years, the main activity centered in these quartz properties. The oldest location was the Murphy; the richest was the Tilton (later called the Only Chance), whose lode was accidentally uncovered during road grading operations between the Murphy mine and its arrastre on Fish Creek. To mill the ore taken from its shallow fifty-foot shaft, eight arrastres were built along Fish Creek. During the life of the mine, three successive amalgamation mills were built on the property to handle its ore. The

last of these, known as Tilton's Red Mill, ran from 1912 to 1915 and was still standing in 1935.

Several companies, who worked placer claims or had arrastres, built long flumes to bring additional water to their properties, but since the entire district was on the crest of the Continental Divide, 7,000 feet or more above sea level, it was snowbound and its streams frozen for several months of every year. The spring run-off, however, brought the miners back to the diggings.

The Ballarat mine, one-half mile south of Fish Creek, above Red Mountain City, helped both to develop and to ruin the district. It was discovered in 1867 by four men who built their cabin near the property and for months took out ore and stored it. Whenever they went to town they boasted of the richness of their strike. When they finally crushed the accumulated ore in their arrastre, there was so little gold recovered that they were afraid of being joshed by the men to whom they had talked so confidently. The minute amount of dust was melted into a button of gold which they exhibited as if it were an assayer's sample. Professor George C. Swallow, of Deer Lodge, saw the gold and interested two St. Louis capitalists in the mine. A company was formed which bought it and adjoining claims for $15,000 and built a twenty-four stamp mill which cost nearly $100,000. With Prof. Swallow in charge, cabins were erected at the mine and he and his family moved onto the property. Ore from all the company claims was run through the mill for over four years, but the stockholders received no dividends. Professor Philip Knabe was sent out by the company to investigate. His brief report was discouraging — "the whole gulch isn't worth two bits." This disillusioning statement resulted in the closing of the Ballarat and other properties and the gradual vacating of much of Red Mountain City. The mill and machinery, which had been hauled all the way from Fort Benton to the site, were moved to Butte and installed in the Silver Bow mill; the whistle was utilized at the Parrot smelter.

As early as 1871, many cabins and stores on the mile-long gulch street which comprised Red Mountain City and Highland City were vacant. By 1874, both camps were virtually deserted.

Rod D. Leggat was one of the few pioneers who stayed on in Red Mountain City. He and his two brothers had started for the gold fields from St. Louis in 1866. They bought a steam-boat, loaded it with merchandise, and sold the vessel upon arrival at Fort Benton. From there they freighted their supplies to the Highlands. Leggat not only ran his gulch store until all his customers moved away, but also he built a flume and continued to work his placer ground until it was exhausted. Even then, he continued to live in the area, believing in its future and buying up claims, water rights, and hundreds of acres of placer ground along the gulches. These he proceeded to work with hydraulics, using Little Giants which "threw a six-inch stream of water with terrific force against a fifty-foot bank and cut it as though it were mist." By 1885, he owned the whole gulch, and employed a dozen men on his properties. In 1895 he sold his holdings to the Butte Water Company for $160,000.

Another oldtimer, John Kern, whose cabin is the only one left in Highland City, lived in the camp from his arrival by wagon train in 1866 until his death in 1923. Over the years he worked his placer claim and cared for the grave of his friend, a dancehall girl whom he met shortly after his arrival, and who died in 1867. She was called Lulu until she shot a man who was molesting her; thereafter she was Shotgun Liz. For a number of years he was the only resident in Highland City, and when, in February, 1923, Fred Stratton and his sons commented that they hadn't seen him lately and snowshoed from their ranch to his isolated cabin, they discovered his body, which had been dead for some time. Deep snow prevented digging a grave in the Highlands at that time of year, so his wish that he be buried beside his girl was disregarded and his remains were interred in a Butte cemetery.

A neglected grave near the head of Wood Creek is that of a cattle rustler, a young fellow named Douglas, who was hanged in the 1860's by certain members of the local Vigilante Committee. He had been accused of stealing cattle by a Helena committee and freed by them; so, when he was questioned by members of the Red Mountain group and told to move on, he refused, saying he had already been tried and exonerated. According to one story, he was asked what he would do if he were freed. "Give me a rope and I'll show you," he replied which was interpreted to mean that he would continue rustling. Another version says he was stopped on the way to Divide by one of the Vigilantes, and brought back to town where a group of men gave him a quick trial and strung him from a tree in Wood Gulch. Some of the Vigilantes did not approve of the hanging and regretted the incident.

The most important and productive mine developed during the twentieth century was the Butte Highland property on Basin Creek, three miles west of Highland City. It was opened shortly before World War I and ran almost continuously until 1942. This enterprise on Nevin Hill, the three-way divide between Fish, Moose, and Basin Creeks, comprises three old mines, the Only Chance, Murphy, and J. B. Thomson, as well as several nearby claims. From these properties, 600 tons of first-class ore were shipped in 1932. Its 100-ton cyanide mill, at the head of Basin Creek, had to be rebuilt in 1932 on the Moose Creek side of the Divide so as not to pollute Butte's water system. Both mine and mill shut down in 1942.

The Highlands never rated as a major mining region even though an estimated $1,000,-000 was recovered from it between 1866 and 1875, and an additional $1,299,533 since 1904.

Somewhere close to Red Mountain City, a fortune is believed to be buried. In the early days, a well-educated miner known as Beastly Butler, from his untidy dress and filthy appearance, worked his placers and placed his dust in tin cans which he buried near his cabin. He was killed by a cave-in on his claim, and no one has found his cache.

MOOSETOWN

The mines in the Moose Creek District were north and northwest of Moosetown, another small camp in the Highlands. The gravels of Moose Creek held placer gold, but were not so rich as those on Fish Creek. Ore from the Day and Harvey lodes, located in 1867, and the Dixie, discovered in 1870, was sent to the Ballarat mill, near Fish Creek, or to Argenta for treatment.

In the early part of the twentieth century, the Gold Hill or Free Gold property was the most important mine in that area.

SOAP GULCH DISTRICT

A few silver mines were located in the upper part of the Soap Gulch District, of which the principal properties were the Pandora and Emma Nevada, on the northwest side of the gulch, and the Old Glory, one mile north of the latter mine. Horn silver, which netted the owners $46,000, was dug from shallow workings from the Emma Nevada lode. The closing of the Hecla Consolidated Mining Company's smelter, in 1900, hastened the decline of the district for it had provided a market for the local lead and silver ores.

THE HIGHLANDS (continued)

Red Mountain City, Highland City, and Moosetown, across the Divide, are true ghosts. Highland City's three-hundred houses, ten saloons and five dancehalls have crumbled away; Red Mountain City's two cabins — a blacksmith shop and a brewery — identify it; Moosetown has only one cabin and the site where an arrastre stood. The days of freight outfits, drawn by bull-teams from Fort Benton through Toll Canyon and around Nevin Hill, are gone. Only broken flumes and dams and caved-in tunnels mark where gold was snatched from once rich ground.

In summer, one can reach these lonely campsites, a little more than twenty miles from Butte, over trails which are strictly dry-weather roads. One route from Butte to Highland City leaves U. S. Highway No. 10 one mile east of Donald, a station on the Milwaukee Railroad, and climbs through Toll Canyon to the Fish Creek road and on to the camp. Another leaves U. S. No. 10 at Roosevelt Drive, continuing on it over Lime Kiln Hill and into the Fish Creek road. Moosetown, on the western side of the Divide, may be reached by a road which angles east from Highway No. 91 at Beaudines.

Perhaps, when you are up there, you will find Bloody Bone Ridge, a section of the old Highland Trail between Alder Gulch and Silver Bow. This portion of the road was a favorite place to stage holdups. So many were robbed and murdered in this wooded pass that it was called the Bone Ridge Trail, because at times it was littered with rotting bones. The land close by was never prospected, for the miners were afraid to work in such a lonely and dangerous area. No one but Coyote Bill even set out to look it over. When he did not return, a friend rode over to Moose Creek from Highland City to inquire about him. No one had seen him and he was believed to be another casualty of the trail. His body was found the following spring by a party of miners, propped against a tree in a sitting position. As the men dug his grave, they struck gold. They staked the location,

MELROSE

which they called the Bone Ridge claim, and, in gratitude for the discovery, buried Bill in Virginia City with a marble stone over his grave. Bone Ridge Trail is a forest service road today and its only travelers are wood-haulers and hunters.

BRYANT MINING DISTRICT

One summer afternoon in 1955, while I worked at the library of the Montana School of Mines, my husband drove south from Butte to Melrose to see if he could find someone who would take us in his car or truck to the deserted camps in the Bryant Mining District. No one was interested except a man who worked mines at Hecla and went up every day to his properties. Though he refused to take us in his jeep, he said we could follow him, or go ahead if we preferred, but that he left Melrose at seven a.m. and wouldn't wait for us if we were late. The next morning we were on the road by six o'clock. At quarter-of-seven, we slid into Melrose, still hoping that we might persuade him to take us with him. While awaiting his arrival, we talked to several men in a cafe and all but one said "Sure, you can drive it yourselves!" Just at seven our friend drove up in a truck.

"Here we are," I called, getting ready to scramble into his car, which had lots of room.

"I ain't going to Hecla. I've got to help with some drilling this morning," he replied.

"How about this afternoon?" I urged.

"Nope, I don't know what I'll be doing then. I can't drive you up anyway. Lots of cars go up there. It's pretty steep in spots and it's rough, but it's only seventeen miles."

"Get in the car," said Francis to me. "We're going to Hecla."

As the miles between us and the laconic miner widened, I told my irate husband something of the history of the mining district that we were about to investigate. There are the usual disagreements as to who found the outcrop, but the discovery of the Trapper lode and the establishment of the Bryant Mining District date from July, 1873.

TRAPPER CITY

William Spurr was prospecting in the high mountains between Wise and Big Hole Rivers, in 1872, when he discovered a lode which he called the Forest Queen. Although he and James A. Bryant were partners, Spurr failed to make the location in both names and did no work on the prospect. When Bryant discovered this, he decided to relocate it for himself the following year. Early in the summer of 1873, he organized a party to go on a trapping expedition, but since his former partner's prospect was in the general area of their hunt, Bryant decided to relocate the claim first and led the men into the mountains to a spring a short distance above the presumed prospect hole. They camped for several days and, according to one account, found Spurr's location.

With this accomplished, they were impatient to get on with the trapping, only to find that their horses had wandered away. All the men searched for them but had no success. One of the group, P. J. (Jerry) Grotevant, gave up looking after some time and headed back toward camp. On the way, he sat down to rest on top of what is now known as Trapper Hill. He accidentally kicked over a small rock and saw something gleam on its underside. When he examined it, he was certain that it contained native silver. Forgetting his fatigue, he searched the ground until he found the outcrop. With several samples of the shiny rocks in his pockets, he hurried back to camp where he had little trouble in convincing his partners that they'd just struck it rich. The horses were quickly forgotten as, carrying picks and shovels, the men followed Grotevant over the hill to the newly found diggings, which they staked as the Trapper lode.

This second discovery is said to have been three-quarters of a mile northeast of the Forest Queen, "on the south side of the north fork of Willow Creek." To record the strike, Bill Hamilton, one of the party, was commissioned to pack out to Bannack at once. Even though he attempted to keep it secret, a horde of men followed him back to the hills.

Noah Armstrong, who had a group of prospectors working for him at Birch Creek in Madison County, also heard the news and promptly shifted his party to the new area, where they located the Cleve and Avon mines. All summer prospectors swarmed into the newly established Bryant Mining District, near the head of Trapper Creek, where many of them uncovered promising silver lodes. Two miners, Moffet and Maynard, staked the Minnie Gaffney. The Hecla was located by Harvey and Day. The Trapper Company, believing that the Elm-Orlu was not worth developing, disposed of it to "Messrs. Sod and Hays." Washington Stapleton and James Cameron found the Keokuk. The Franklin lay directly behind Trapper City.

Outcrops on Lion Mountain were next investigated. On its precipitous slope Noah Armstrong and Benjamin S. Harvey staked the Atlantis and Alta lodes on Sept. 4, 1873. The Ariadne, Marc Antony, and Cleopatra were discovered that fall by D. S. Dewey, McComb, Brubaker, and R. E. McConnell. The True Fissure group was found by Mulligan and Sloss.

Even before the last of these was staked, Trapper City, a single row of cabins on both sides of Trapper Creek, sprang up in the high valley. As long as silver ore was plentiful, the 100 to 200 residents lived extravagantly, patronizing the hotel, the saloons, and the hurdy-gurdy house as well as the general store and the butcher shop. James L. Hamilton, the first postmaster, was succeeded by John Canovan, a busy man, who was also proprietor of the Trapper City Hotel and owner of the livery stable.

As the various properties were developed, the men realized that they must have a road to connect the mines with the main artery of travel along the Big Hole River. This area was still wilderness; so the miners hacked their own road to the valley, sometime between 1873 and 1874. During the initial period, the Trapper mine was the only one shipping ore and no one foresaw that Noah Armstrong's Atlantis mine would in any way affect Trapper City, though the camp had already begun to decline. With the discovery of strong mineral leads on Lion Mountain and the blossoming of a new camp called Lion City at the head of a valley below the Atlantis, and other lodes, the fickle population of Trapper melted away. When the Trapper mine shut down in the summer of 1878, Mose Morrison, who alone had remained in the empty city, reluctantly shifted his possessions to the new location.

LION CITY and GLENDALE

The real development of the district centers around the mines on Lion Mountain. This amazing upthrust of bald, white rock, extending above timberline, contained most of the rich silver leads already mentioned. The mountain received its name when Joe McCready excitedly reported to Jerry Grotevant that he had been frightened away from his prospect by a mountain lion, and begged his comrades to return to the spot with him and shoot the creature. Upon investigation, the lion turned out to be an old white mule cropping bunch grass.

In the spring of 1877, Noah Armstrong, owner of the Atlantis mine, organized the Hecla Consolidated Mining Company for the purpose of working the Lion Mountain properties. He immediately bought the Cleopatra and True Fissure claims, which gave him possession of the entire face of the mountain. In subsequent transactions, the company obtained the Traper, Franklin, Cleve, Avon, Marc Antony, and Ariadne mines, as well as other valuable properties in the district.

To this beehive of mining activity, the miners gravitated to build their cabins at the head of a broad valley drained by Spring Creek. As early as 1875, Charles F. Dahler and Noah Armstrong had built a forty-ton furnace, far down the valley on Trapper Creek, to which ore from the Atlantis and other mines was packed. Around these lead-smelting works grew up a town called Glendale, its name selected by writing "Clinton" and "Glendale" on opposite sides of a chip of wood and tossing the fragment over the assay office wall.

Glendale grew rapidly, with a population of 950 in 1878, which included 262 voters and "125 school children under twenty." Although no plat of the settlement was recorded until the summer of 1879, the residents relied on possessory rather than legal rights to their lots. The town supported a paper, the *Atlantis,* in whose columns news of the district was reported.

Lion City Items
A customer in town offered a half eagle for a cigar, but the barkeeper, not having seen a $5 gold piece for so long, mistook it for a nickel, saying he had no "5 cts. cigars for sale."
Glendale Atlantis, Sept. 8, 1880

Some weeks ago we visited this little alpine city . . . where the famous Hecla mines are. It nestles down . . . with tramways running down from the mines on the cliffs and the main tramway meandering along through the vale with windings as tortuous as a gliding snake. A little above town is timberline. . . . The town has . . . one main thoroughfare. . . . One striking feature at La Marsh's Express . . . is a painting of large lions on several of the sign boards. Here is the White Lion Saloon, while yonder is the White Lion Hotel and a little further along are the Lion's Whelps.

In the summer season life is not so unbearable at such a height, but even then the rarefied air is rather rasping on the constitution and many persons cannot remain any length of time. . . . Many of the hardiest miners break down under it and are compelled to come below to the hospital at Glendale. Working in the mines is apt to overheat a person and then when he comes to the surface, his skin is quickly congested by the sudden change.
Glendale Atlantis, Nov. 10, 1880

At its peak, Lion City had a population of five to six hundred, mostly miners and merchants. Three saloons and two hurdy-gurdy houses took care of the miners' leisure hours. Noah Armstrong & Company and Thomas Armstrong ran general merchandise stores, branches of Glendale establishments. There was also a schoolhouse for the miners' children. Ore was hauled to Melrose in big-wheeled ten-ton wagons, drawn by six to eight horses. The company used 100 horses each day, working them in shifts, for the several trips.

The precipitous slopes and the absence of trees on the front of Lion Mountain gave snow little purchase so that it either blew off as soon as it fell or crashed down, past the mine tunnel mouths, burying everything in its way.

Butte Miner, May 7, 1878
Letter from Glendale
A small snowslide occurred at the Atlantis mine recently taking the stove pipe and part of the roof of the shaft house with it. John Chinaman thought his time had come and so crawled under the stove. . . . It took several hours to dig him out.

The most graphic description of the mines is given in the *Atlantis* of October 13, 1880:

MILLIONS IN SIGHT
Samuel Barbour, Supt., put us under escort of his assistant, Byron Cook who piloted us to the foot of the tramway leading to the Silver Quartz, where we took an ore boat and as the one laden with ore came, took ours containing two men up. The rope connecting the two boats is wrapped once around a wooden drum at the top of the dump, and both boats fairly fly past each other over 1,000 feet of seeming almost perpendicular track.

Right on the face of the cliffs by the side of the Silver Quartz dump, ore was being dug and sacked, that smelts nearly a thousand dollars per ton. . . .

MILL, LION CITY

LION CITY CABINS

The ores are chiefly galena, gray copper and yellow carbonates, easily fluxed with iron, lime and charcoal, a very little of them requiring roasting.

No wonder Noah Armstrong was prompted to apply to some of the mines such cognomens as Cleopatra, Marc Anthony, etc. for even the wealth of Cleopatra and that of her smitten king lover combined would make but a faint showing by the side of the untold millions that here lie embedded. This is Glendale's Treasury; and these are her bank vaults.

Noah Armstrong managed the Hecla Company until 1879, when E. C. Atkins, the founder of the Atkins Saw Works of Indianapolis, succeeded him. During Armstrong's incumbency, the mines produced 1,000,000 ounces of silver annually as well as thousands of tons of lead and copper. Two years later, in January, 1881, the Hecla Company was entirely reorganized. It bought the smelter at Glendale, made a complete change of management, and offered Henry Knippenberg, the managing director of the Atkins Saw Works, the position of general manager of the Hecla Consolidated Mining Company. Knippenberg accepted and arrived in Glendale where he set up headquarters in April, 1881. At the time of this reorganization, the company was in debt $77,785.13.

Knippenberg divided the business into three departments and appointed a superintendent for each: James Parfet, in charge of mining, with headquarters at Hecla; George G. Earles, in charge of reduction at Glendale; and John M. Parfet, in charge of the iron mines at Norwood, in Soap Gulch. George B. Conway, a former bookkeeper in the Indianapolis company, was made cashier.

HECLA

As soon as Knippenberg took over the mines, a third camp, called Hecla, was built on a bench of land one mile beyond and above Lion City, at the base of the mountain. To reach it he built an upper road which by-passed Lion City. The new community contained boardinghouses for the men and dwellings for Parfet, the superintendent, and for other officials, as well as an office, a warehouse, a stable, and a powder magazine, all provided by the company. When whiskey barrels were utilized to hold the drinking water at the mines, there were no complaints. As mining prospered, merchants opened stores on the flat directly below the benchland. Hecla was never as large as Lion City and neither place approached Glendale for size or importance.

The workings in the Cleopatra were so cold that the miners on shift wore extra heavy clothing, gum boots, and gloves. It was said that the two-men drilling teams hustled to keep warm for the man who twisted the drill was so numb by the end of the fifteen-minute period that he could hardly wait to get his circulation back by swinging the double jack. Ore from the Cleopatra came to the loading chutes at Hecla in buckets attached to a long cable, but the men had to climb up to the mine entrance along a trail so steep that a rope beside the path helped them to pull themselves up, hand over hand. A flight of stairs, built at the steepest pitch, burned and was never repaired.

GLENDALE (continued)

Knippenberg's arrival at Glendale marked the beginning of a successful, twenty-year cycle for the Hecla Company. The forty-ton smelter built by Armstrong and Dahler in 1875, and the ten-stamp mill and leaching works, which they added in 1878, ran irregularly on Hecla ore until fire razed all the buildings, except the roaster, in 1879. The plant was rebuilt and enlarged and ran until 1881, producing bullion and matte which averaged $400 a ton. During that year it was absorbed by the reorganized Hecla Consolidated Mining Company, which so expanded the plant that by 1885 it consisted of three blast furnaces, two crushers, a large roaster, a blacksmith shop, a sack house, warehouses, an iron house, a stable, two powder houses, three coal sheds, an office, an assay office, a flume ditch, a sawmill, a tramway and cars, and five private homes.

GREENWOOD

Another of Knippenberg's improvements was the erection, in 1882, of a 100-ton concentrator, between Glendale and Hecla, on a hillside at a place which he named Greenwood. In addition to the mill, the company constructed a boardinghouse, four dwellings, an office, stable, and blacksmith shop. A telephone line connected Greenwood with Glendale, seven miles below, and with Hecla, four miles above the plant. The concentrator, with its many levels, was equipped to handle low-grade ore. It was run by water power from Trapper Creek, brought to the mill by a half-mile flume with a vertical drop of 200 feet. To convey ore from Hecla to the concentrator, a four-mile narrow gauge tramway was built. Three cars, each with a brakeman, constituted a train and

"empties" were pulled back to the ore house, at the base of the mountain, by mules. The grade was steep and the heavily-loaded cars often jumped the track. The concentrator, which was a marvel of efficiency, treated (between 1882 and 1898) 177,092 tons of second-class ore.

GLENDALE (continued)

The smelting furnaces at Glendale used prodigious amounts of charcoal and coke for fuel. Coke was shipped in from Pennsylvania at a cost of $19.00 a ton. At peak production, ten tons were consumed in a day. Charcoal, which the company used in amounts up to 100,000 bushels a month, was prepared in the canyons adjacent to Glendale. Canadian and French woodcutters chopped down trees which Italian laborers burned in pits and delivered to the company at eleven cents a bushel. These workmen lived in cabins scattered through the mountains. The ruins of old kilns and burning pits may still be seen on Canyon Creek, north of Glendale. Flux for the smelters came from the company's iron mines at Norwood, in Soap Gulch, northeast of Melrose.

Though the Hecla Company was badly in debt when Knippenberg took charge, by the end of his first year as manager, it showed a profit of $237,729.76. By the middle 1880's the company was employing between 150 and 200 men and the monthly payroll averaged $50,000. For ten years stockholders received ten and a half per cent returns on capital stock. Dividends totaling $2,057,500 were distributed during a twenty-year period which ended in 1902. During the same period, an estimated $22,000,000 was recovered from the company-operated mines. As early as 1893, production began to slacken, so that only two furnaces were kept in operation at Glendale. Successive years were no better and, as the company was operating on a shoestring, the smelters were shut down on August 29, 1900. Thereafter, ore was shipped to the American Smelting & Refining Company at Omaha. That fall Knippenberg ordered the furnaces torn down. The year 1904 saw the end of operations. The company was no longer able to pay its employees; and the miners, suddenly left without work, streamed from the high camps to other districts, leaving Hecla, Lion City, and even Glendale, with a total of forty inhabitants.

191

Knippenberg, who was authorized to sell the property at Hecla, bought it up for $28,011.26, the exact amount that the company owed him. Perhaps he could have pulled it out of the red again if he had not been hampered by litigation. Finally, around 1924, a settlement was reached and the mines were sold to a Philadelphia syndicate. This new company did little with the mines, and in 1927, George B. Conway, Knippenberg's former cashier, acquired the property and shipped slag from the smelter and ore from the mine dumps for more than a year. In 1928 he sold his holdings for half a million dollars. Since then, the mines have been worked only by leasers.

Glendale in 1881 had a newspaper, thirty business establishments, and a population of 700. The following year, when the railhead of the Utah & Northern Railroad reached Melrose and the Hecla Consolidated Mining Company reorganized and expanded, Glendale's population exploded to 3,000. With rail connections close, the base silver bullion produced by the Glendale smelter could easily be hauled to the cars and shipped to Omaha to be refined. As the Hecla Company expanded its several workings, coke and mining supplies were delivered at Melrose and distributed to the various locations operated by the company. The *Dillon Tribune* describes Glendale as a "shoe-string like town of one street, a mile long on the right bank of a small creek, pure as crystal in winter but muddy and yellow in summer from concentration of the concentrator at Greenwood, six miles above town." Its lower end was called Ragtown, and its upper portion, opposite the smelter where the officials and their families lived, was known as Toney Hill. The company hospital, opened in 1881 with Dr. Schmalhausen in charge, was "kept scrupulously clean and patients received kind attention and considerate treatment." Employees paid $1.00 a month from their wages toward its support.

The Hecla Company also furnished waterworks and fire protection, and built large flue dust chambers at the smelter. The latter were a blessing to the entire community and reduced the number of cases of lead poisoning. At the insistence of the women of Glendale, the furnace stacks were built higher so as more effectively to dissipate the fumes.

Glendale's church was built by union subscription and was dedicated by the Methodists, although there seems to have also been a Baptist preacher in the town. It is described as a pretty, neatly furnished building and its board

extended "a cordial unqualified invitation to ministers of all denominations to preach the Word of God to our people." The Roman Catholics had no building and attended mass only when some priest visited the area.

That some Chinese worked in both Hecla and Glendale is shown by an item in the *Atlantis* of September 20, 1880. The article also reveals the prevalent hostility that existed against Orientals.

An interpreter was in Glendale the other day, looking up Chinese to work on the Railway grade. The very moment that a foreign corporation attempts to put Chinese coolies to work in herds in this Territory, the said peons should be treated as their kind are at Leadville, Colorado and Storey County, Nevada; just driven right back over the line and given to understand that it will be rather an unhealthy climate for them; if they attempt to return to Montana; and the contractors themselves should have a dose of welcome when they put in their first appearance.

Glendale did not lack for recreation. There was Bannack Lodge of the I. O. O. F., and for the Masons, Glendale Lodge No. 23.

A race-track was laid out on the flat behind the two-story schoolhouse, and a roller-skating rink stood two blocks east of Henry Knippenberg's residence on a hillside. Socials were held in the church hall or in private homes, and by the middle 1880's, theatrical companies performed in Glendale's Opera House. Frequently, troupes from Maguire's Opera House in Butte gave "Fanchon the Cricket" and other popular melodramas to the play-hungry miners. Such productions brought whole families down from Hecla and Lion City despite storm and bad roads, especially in the winter when entertainment was scarce. Once, when a traveling company was caught in a blizzard between Melrose and Glendale, the audience waited four hours for the curtain to go up. The performance ended long after midnight, to the complete satisfaction of the audience.

As Francis and I neared Glendale on that summer morning in 1955, I noticed across the creek on the left, the cemetery, situated on a low hill and surrounded by sagebrush, and I recalled the apocryphal story of how the pioneer settlers cleared a hilltop and then waited for someone to die. When no one accommodated, they killed a Chinaman and buried him.

We did not have time to visit the graveyard nor to search for the triple marker of Noah Armstrong's three small grandchildren who died, within a month, of diphtheria or whooping cough, nor that of his wife who lies next to them. Perhaps we should have located the grave of a doctor whose last request was to have the Glendale Silver Cornet Band play a certain march at his funeral. The musicians were willing, but no one knew the tune. Since it was winter, it seemed reasonable to pack the corpse in ice to await the arrival of the music which the band ordered. When it came and they had practiced the selection, they played it as the burial took place.

Glendale's shoe-string street is still dotted with buildings. Where, we wondered, had the Hecla Mercantile & Banking Company stood? Which pile of rubble belonged to Sam Woo Fung Gee's laundry? Which foundations supported the Glendale Brewery which, in 1881, had "just laid in a supply of 50,000 pounds of hops and a large quantity of grape sugar for the ensuing season's brewing"?

The largest ruins were skeleton stone buildings belonging to the Hecla Company and easily identified by the lone sentinel smokestack standing close to the stream. Across the road from the smelting works, crowning a low hill, stood the most amazing structure of all — Henry Knippenberg's magnificent mansion. It was large and rambling and many-gabled, with a porch across the front and a cupola on top. An open upper window, with a flapping lace curtain, suggested that part of the second floor was occupied.

As soon as Knippenberg reached Glendale, he erected this imposing residence. Those who remember it tell of its six fireplaces and sterling silver door knobs, of its Brussels carpeting and its cedar-lined closets. Some even remember Mrs. Knippenberg and her riding horse,

GLENDALE STORE

COMPANY BUILDINGS, GLENDALE

and the men always mention that she allowed no smoking except in one special room — the cupola. Probably fumes from the smelter killed any vegetation which may once have surrounded the premises, for it sat on a barren swell of ground, overlooking the bleak town.

The Knippenberg house fascinated both of us, and in the hope that the tenant might be home, we went to the front door and rang the bell. There was no response. Since our visit the mansion has been torn down.

A short distance beyond the mansion, the road forks, with the right hand branch leading up Canyon Creek, past the charcoal kilns, eventually climbing to Vipond Park and down the far side of that valley to the Big Hole River; but as our goal was Hecla, we went straight ahead on a narrow road that skirted the creek.

Bushes rubbed the sides of the car; but as soon as we had passed a white-washed, square-logged ranchhouse, we were in the open and ready to start the steady climb to the high mountain camps. The land ahead rose in a series of giant steps, each bench separated from the next by a thicket of pines or aspen. The roadbed across the open stretches was gravelly but not rough. The rises from bench to bench were badly washed out, leaving rocks for a roadbed or ruts with a high center between. In a few places, the road was a trough, walled with rocks, which we could not avoid scraping in an effort to straddle chuckholes. Over these sections the car barely crawled. The first metal signposts beside the road read "Hecla 4 mi." Another stretch of crawling and scratching brought us to the three-mile post. With each mile my excitement grew. If the road proved no worse, maybe we *would* reach Hecla.

On the next bench we found snow-crushed log cabins, dead trees, stumps, and the remains of what seemed to be a tailings pond. On the right, were the stone foundations of the Greenwood Concentrator and above it, jumbled timbers where other cabins had stood. Trails among the trees led to higher levels of the mountain or to dumps. Far below, through the bottom of a gorge, Trapper Creek twisted on its way to the valley. Just beyond the mill foundations was a steep grade, from which all semblance of surface had washed away, leaving exposed boulders with deep gullies between them. Up this rocky pitch Francis maneuvered the car, dodging from side to side to miss the worst rocks and avoid scraping the pan. At the end of a hundred yards the engine quit and no amount of coaxing could start it; by now it was overheated by its long pull from Melrose.

"We passed the three-mile marker just below the foundations. Let's hike the rest of the way," I said, impatiently gathering up sketch pads and camera. While I started ahead, Francis backed the car and left it on the Flat. From there on the trail was rough enough to make us slip on pebbles and small rocks. Although we were still climbing away from the gorge through an avenue of trees, we could hear the creek gurgling and tumbling below on our left. The wildflowers were colorful accents in the underbrush and pungent wood smells refreshed us on this hot, dusty climb. The next marker was too weathered to read. We passed an old horse trough and the remains of an ore wagon. It was so still that we were conscious of the high quiet of the mountains.

One more curve and we stopped, overwhelmed by the sight ahead. About a mile away rose a vertical slab of mountain, forming a wall across the head of the valley. It was cream-colored and perforated near its summit with many black holes from which spilled earth forming dumps on its barren face. This surprising mass of rock was the famous Lion Mountain.

A short distance ahead, a grass-grown trail dropped away from our road to cross a marshy meadow and disappear behind a low wooded hill to the south. This was, as far as I could guess, the old road to Trapper City. We made no attempt to reach Trapper for we had heard that nothing remained of it except a rotting wooden bridge across the creek, a few stone foundations, and one cabin with wooden pegged logs. Near the fork in the trail was a small dump and a crumbling shack which I believe was the Avon-Cleve mine. Ahead, on the right, and above the road, were more dumps.

HECLA, 1955

The head of the valley, which sloped up to Lion Mountain, held many cabins and a large mill. Although an old road, overgrown with grass, led into this mountain park and into Lion City, a higher road skirts the camp and climbs to the top bench of land where Hecla stands. This upper stretch of road was very narrow and badly washed away but it brought us to the very base of the cliff. On this last mile, we heard hammering and finally men's voices, which must have carried an unusual distance in the still air; for although we had been told that men were working one of the old properties, we never saw them.

To get a complete view of Hecla, I climbed to the top of a big dump which pressed against the breast of the mountain. From this vantage point I could see many mine portals, each with its dump high on the face of the cliff, and cables dangling between the tunnel mouths and the ground. One tram terminal and a big drum, entangled with rusting cable, remains below the dump over which I was picking my way.

The largest buildings still standing at Hecla are the two big cabins erected by the Hecla Mining Company. One, which contained an old safe, was obviously the mine office. The other was built for James Parfet, the superintendent of the company's operations at Hecla. Here he lived with his family and other relatives who worked under him. According to Mrs. Althea B. Seirer, Parfet's niece, the first boardinghouse at Hecla was nothing but a huge tent. The second was built close to the mine dump. A big reception was held in this building for her uncle in 1884.

From the end of the dump I looked down on a mass of flattened boards, all that is left of the original boardinghouse. On its sagging floor stood an old kitchen range. Surveying this wreckage, I tried to imagine the dances that lasted all night, to which guests rode from Glendale on horseback, to frolic to the music of accordions, fiddles, and a piano.

LION CITY, 1955

Leaving Hecla, I cut down through the trees to an old road which led to the upper end of Lion City and to the big mill and

GLENDALE WITH SMELTER STACK
KNIPPENBERG MANSION, GLENDALE (razed)

END OF TRAM, HECLA

trestle, which I had seen in the distance on our way up. The mill was a shell, without machinery or flooring, but proof that it had once worked was the tan-colored dump which sprawled below it. The sloping park, through which Spring Creek trickled, was dotted with clumps of pine trees and with cabins. The latter had evidently been built at two different periods: the older were made of chinked logs while the newer were constructed from dressed lumber. Nearly every building had managed to keep its roof, and a few of the larger dwellings had been recently occupied. One had a fence around it and a wooden walk leading to the porch, on which sat a rocking chair. Through its dusty window, I saw a few dishes and some furniture. Farther down the slope, across a marshy meadow, were two false-fronted, dilapidated stores. The faded remains of other cabins, opposite them, suggested that the grass-grown tracks between the rows of buildings were once the main thoroughfare. On the flat, below the town, was debris from a settling pond whose tailings have been salvaged. This setting of Lion City is unusually picturesque; for the valley floor is green, high mountains hem it in, and the stark white of Lion Mountain provides a dramatic backdrop.

By the time we had hiked back to the car, we were both tired and dusty. The drive down was as nerve-wracking as the ascent. Looking into the valley from this elevation, we could see how high we had climbed. Much of the way back the car crawled at ten miles an hour, bouncing and scraping against the stony roadbed. Finally we were back in the valley and running alongside the shrub-lined creek.

"Stop," I called to Francis, "I hear a car coming." Just as we squeezed against the bushes, up came a jeep driven by the Melrose man who had refused to take us to the mines. He stopped and asked, "Did you make it?"

"Not quite," Francis replied. "We got stuck on the grade above the old mill ruins."

"Yep, that's Concentrator Hill. She's a steep one. I could a told you about it. I never thought to."

"We had to hike the rest of the way in," said Francis. "Are you going up there now?"

"Yep. I go up every day."

Our car started with an abrupt jerk, and what we said between there and Glendale, I shan't repeat.

———

HECLA

CARDWELL

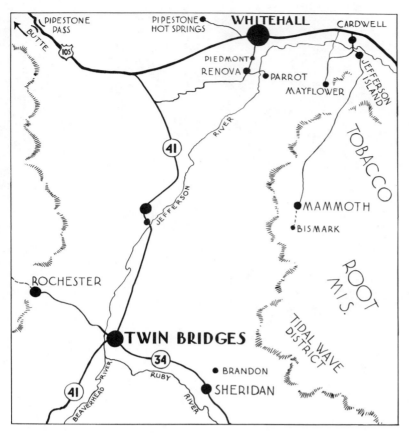

CHAPTER 12

JEFFERSON and RUBY VALLEY CAMPS

Directly west of the Tobacco Root Mountains, in the Jefferson Valley, is Twin Bridges, a small settlement which marks the head of one of Montana's majestic rivers. The Beaverhead and the Ruby mingle here to become the Jefferson. For over thirty miles this river flows north, through a wide valley, and then swings east through a canyon until it enters the Madison Valley. Here, at Three Forks, the Jefferson, Madison and Gallatin Rivers join to form the great Missouri.

Although the Jefferson Valley is luxuriously green and provides excellent grazing land and hay meadows, it was the mountains on either side that first lured men into it to search for gold in the creekbeds and in the stony ridges that rise above the river. The vestiges of mining camps lie all along the valley on both sides of the stream, or back in the foothills of the Tobacco Root Range on the east, or of the Highland Mountains on the west. One way to visit them all is to drive from Three Forks through Jefferson Canyon to Cardwell and then up the river with frequent side-trips to the several towns. The hills rise directly from the

water and the highway skirts the river the entire distance.

CARDWELL and JEFFERSON ISLAND

Cardwell and Jefferson Island, one mile apart and on opposite sides of the Jefferson River, are quiet towns today. Both are stations on railroads: Cardwell on the Northern Pacific, and Jefferson Island on the Chicago, Milwaukee & St. Paul. As long as the mining properties in the vicinity were active, each was a bustling shipping and supply center.

MAMMOTH

South from Jefferson Island a dirt road skirts South Boulder Creek, for about fifteen miles, to the deserted mining camp of Mammoth, winding by easy stages up the long, narrow valley, past ranches, between meadows, and through groves of trees, with frequent vistas of snow-capped peaks ahead. As we neared Mammoth, the valley narrowed and the mountainsides became steeper and more heavily timbered.

The camp consisted of one main street, lined on both sides with empty buildings in all stages of repair and disrepair, and with overgrown trails leading to cabins set back from the main thoroughfare. One false-fronted saloon, a big barn, a small store with a porch, a few two story houses, and scattered cabins dotted an area about one-half mile square. High up the mountain, on the east side of the valley, were big mine dumps and a mill. Broken tram-towers, set at intervals down the hillside and still supporting rusted cables, reached all the way from the mill to the street.

As we drove into the town, we found cattle grazing in what had once been front yards, or lying in the middle of the road, but no people. When we were ready to leave, however, a man came out of a house and invited us to have coffee with him. He said that he ran the store when anyone wanted anything; that the caretaker of the mine properties was away fishing, and that the night before, just at dusk, he had seen a moose and her calf come out of the woods to drink at the creek. He also identified the mine and mill on the mountainside as the Mammoth property, and he told us that the mining camp of Pony, on the Eastern slope of the Tobacco Root Mountains, was only seven miles away if one took the old trail over the divide, 1300 feet higher than the town of Mammoth.

"It's a good thing you got here when you did if you want to see what the place looked like," he said. "The town's been sold to some party that plans to tear it down next year. If you went four miles farther up the canyon to the forks of the South Boulder, you'd see more mines — the Sultana and the Mogullian and the Bismark. It was a copper property with some fair-grade ore. There's nothing left of the camp of Bismark today, but the ruins of one mill. We're 6,000 feet elevation here at Mammoth. Bismark is 2,000 feet higher."

All during this conversation, the sky was getting blacker and thunder was cracking through the mountains behind us. So, to keep ahead of the storm, we hastily gulped our coffee and said goodbye to our genial inform-ant.

The mining district was opened up about 1870 when coarse, free-milling gold ore was extracted from shallow workings in several properties and from placers four miles below the main camp; but it was a few years before five patented claims — the Mammoth, Grand Central, Leviathan, Boulder, and Ready Cash — began to attract attention.

The Mammoth, the largest producer of the camp, pierced an immense quartz dike which rose 100 feet above the face of the moun-tain near its summit, and was believed to be

MAYFLOWER MINE OFFICE AND TRAM

an extension of the Mineral Hill zone on the other side of the mountains, in which the Boss Tweed and Clipper lodes were located. The mine, which was operated by the Mammoth Mining & Power Company, was soon equipped with a 100-ton concentrator containing nine Wilfley tables and crushers, and with an aerial tram which carried the ore from the mine to the mill. By 1880, the Leviathan and Grand Central were actively producing, and the latter, which had a ten-stamp water-power mill, reported the discovery of a six-foot vein of high-grade ore. By 1926, the Liberty Montana Mines Corporation was successfully working the mine, having spent $50,000 for new equipment and development work. Production during this period averaged 1,000-3,000 tons per month. In recent years the district has lain dormant and in 1954, when I visited Mammoth, no mining was going on.

MAYFLOWER

Back at Cardwell, we stopped at a grocery store and asked the proprietor what mines were nearby. He at once mentioned the Mayflower, four miles to the west, and assured us we could drive right up to it. "You missed the Swede, two miles east of here," he said, "and that mine north of the highway with the zig-zag trail, is the Sunlight. It's a gold and silver property because it contains both oxide and sulphide ores. It was located in 1892. Back in the nineties the Golden Sunlight group of gold mines was bonded by the American Development Company. It spent $200,000 developing the property and then sold out for $500,000 to W. J. Clark of Helena. The mine's still working."

The next morning we followed his directions, driving west on Highway No. 10 until we spotted a ranch road which ran south across a fertile valley. This we took. Once across the Jefferson River, it began to climb into the foothills of the Tobacco Root Range, up a narrow rocky canyon. Within another mile or so we passed a couple of empty houses, buried in shrubbery, and then, ahead, saw tram towers, a big yellow dump, and several mine buildings. While Francis turned the car around, by the mine office, I began to sketch. At the same time a woman came out of the office and started toward him. She was badly crippled and was very lame.

"What do you folks want?" she asked, looking suspiciously at my sketch block. "This here is Anaconda-Copper-owned property and they don't allow people around. You can't take pictures either. That's company orders. I'm caretaker here and I don't want to lose my job."

While she talked, her husband limped out of the building and took down our car license number . Francis assured her that we were only interested in the history of the mine, and while he talked, I sketched as fast as I could, for I could see that this stop would be a short one. The crippled couple, who were named Stacey, had previously lived in one of the houses farther down the canyon. It had been their responsibility to carry water, several times a week, up to the caretaker at the mine. He was an old man and soon became helpless. The company then made them the caretakers. The husband was seventy-eight years old, and the former caretaker was eighty-seven. The woman took care of both of them and guarded the property. She refused to give us any information about the mine and was obviously relieved when we drove away.

No one is really certain who discovered the sensational Mayflower. Two prospectors were grubstaked by different persons, and each staked a claim. One of them is credited as the locator of the property. A few months prior to the discovery in 1895, three Butte men, S. R. Fair, Edward Clark, and Edwin Clark, grubstaked G. W. Preuitt, a former rancher from Jefferson County. Preuitt staked a few claims in a gulch southeast of Whitehall, but they proved so poor that the partners debated whether or not to sink more funds in the prospects. Before deciding, Edwin Clark, who was an assayer, went to the gulch to inspect the claims. He found tons of liver-colored rock lying on the ground, at the foot of a limestone dike, and pocketed a piece with the intention of testing it at some later date. When he did, it ran $200 in gold to the ton, and assuming that there was some mistake, he returned to the location and brought back a sackful of samples. These assayed still higher in value. With Preuitt, he returned to the gulch a third time and the men staked a claim. This was the Mayflower.

Perhaps a year before this, Frank W. Haskins, a Butte attorney, also grubstaked a prospector who located some claims in the Whitehall area. Before leaving for British Columbia and further prospecting, he left with Haskins a sackful of liver-colored rocks from his claims. Haskins never got around to having the sam-

MAMMOTH
MILL AT MAMMOTH

ples assayed until word of the Mayflower strike got out. To his surprise, he learned that the odd looking ore contained gold valued at $200 a ton. Armed with location notices, he began a hurried search for his claims, but discovered that the descriptions were so indefinite that he could not be certain his ore came from the site of the Mayflower. He frantically sent word to the miner to return to Montana and establish the exact location of his strike, but the man refused unless assured in advance of a large amount of money, which Haskins didn't have. Without further proof, Haskins was helpless to establish any priority to the discovery.

All this time, Fair and the Clark brothers were secretly sacking the rich surface rock and shipping it to the Helena smelter. After one carload of the odd looking boulders netted the owners $10,000, a man was sent from Helena to investigate the source of the ore — and the secret was out. The news started a stampede to the gulch and the surrounding hills. Men, and some women prospectors, swarmed over the area, often having risked drowning in hurried crossings of the wide Jefferson River.

By the time the owners had shipped $100,000 worth of ore, Dave Bricker, a mine operator from Butte, offered them $350,000 for the property. They accepted, but when he couldn't raise the cash, the deal was off. Senator W. A. Clark then sent his brother Joseph to examine the mine, and satisfied with his report, Clark offered the owners $250,000 for the property. The terms were $50,000 down and $50,000 every thirty days until the entire amount was paid. This offer was accepted.

Some say that Clark shipped $100,000 worth of gold ore within a month of his purchase. Others claim that he made $1,500,000 from the Mayflower. Oldtimers insist that it was at least $3,000,000. Everyone agrees it was a bonanza. Strangely enough, it was the only strike of its kind in the district. The discovery of gold in limestone-country rock caused the area to be carefully examined for other similar gold deposits. But the Mayflower ore was confined in a chimney, located in a dolomite or lime formation, and the surrounding rock was barren.

The mine produced heavily from 1896 to 1905. Since then, it has been inactive and its deep workings, 1,000 feet below the surface, have caved in and are filled with water. To treat the ore, Clark built the Parrot smelter, a couple of miles below the mine, on the river. A station on the railroad, called Renova, served as a supply and shipping center. During the heyday of the mine, a small settlement sprang up close to the workings. That it was large enough to require a school is shown by the following news item:

Whitehall parties . . . who attended a grand masquerade ball given by the ladies of Mayflower on New Year's eve, report a gloriously enjoyable time at that little town. . . . The entertainment, which was given for the Mayflower public school, netted a gratifying sum.
Jefferson Valley Zephyr, January 4, 1901

WHITEHALL

After our adventure at the Mayflower mine, we drove to Whitehall, whose long main street flanks the Northern Pacific Railroad. During the 1860's, Thomas Brooks, an Englishman, built a stage station on the Virginia City-Fort Benton road, four miles north of the present settlement, and called it Old Whitehall after his former home. When the Northern Pacific branch of the railroad between Logan, Utah, and Garrison, Montana, was completed in 1889, a new town at the present location sprang up to serve as a shipping point for the mines in the area.

Curious to learn more about the Mayflower mine, we inquired in the general store if anyone could tell us about it, and were directed to the home of Mr. Peter A. Dawson. His daughter answered our knock and called her father, who was resting. Mr. Dawson knew the mining history of the area in detail.

Mayflower ore, he assured us, ran as high as $40,000 a ton. When W. A. Clark built the smelter at Gaylord, or Parrot, as it was later called, to handle Mayflower ore, he expected it to become the Anaconda of the state. As soon as smelting operations began, he felt sure that the town of Parrot would grow to several thousand population, leaving Whitehall a mere suburb.

"What about mining in the Pipestone area?" I asked him.

"It was just placer mines," he replied. "The Big Pipestone claims were six miles west of here on Pipestone Creek. The Belcher ditch carried water from Fish Creek, seven miles to the workings. The Little Pipestone placers of Dan Stanard, Baxter, Tuttle, and some other fellows were four miles west of the Big Pipestone diggings. None of the properties have been worked for years."

Before we left Whitehall the next morning, I had learned that there were other mines

PARROT SMELTER ON JEFFERSON RIVER
MINE OFFICE AT PARROT

in the immediate vicinity. "They aren't very old," said another old gentleman whom I questioned. "They weren't located until the 1890's. Most of them are about six miles south of Whitehall and a mile or two east. The Gold Hill operated continuously until 1901, and since then there's been several outfits that have tried their hand at it. Hugh Wilson, A. J. McKay, and Tom Heinze took out the most ore. The mine paid out about $150,000. The oxidized surface ores assayed up to $100 a ton, but the sulphides that lay deep, ran only $35. The Colorado was on the same lode as the Gold Hill. The mine produced $50,000. The Bonanza Fraction also adjoined the Gold Hill and was a gold-silver property. Leasers operated it from the time it was located. There were other mines northeast of here, but most of the properties are shut down today."

RENOVA

We drove south from Whitehall, crossing both the Northern Pacific tracks and the Milwaukee tracks. The highway led through Piedmont to a larger community with a number of well-built, two story brick farmhouses surrounded by big trees. All the older buildings were of brick—the newer dwellings were frame or stucco. This was Renova, a station of the Ruby Valley branch of the Northern Pacific, six miles from Whitehall. Ranching is the industry today, but the town developed as the result of mining in the foothills of the Tobacco Root Mountains. In the Surprise and the other mines, the richest ore was close to the surface. In the Mayflower, however, it lay in a deep chimney. From 1896 until 1904, the Mayflower led all other properties. From 1905 to 1911, gold, silver, and small amounts of copper and lead were recovered from the mines of the Renova District. From then on, mining declined.

PARROT

From Renova we visited Parrot, where a smelter was located. Crossing the Jefferson River on a large steel bridge, we could see on the far bank, half a mile upstream at the water's edge, the Parrot smelter. Beyond the bridge a dirt road climbed to the top of the bluff. On the prairie stood a large, two story red brick house with castellated cornice, its porch ornamented with white latticed scrollwork. The building had been the smelter office. Across the road, surrounded by sagebrush, was a circular stone cylinder. No doubt this was the kiln which had been part of the brick plant started, in 1896, by a Butte company. From the edge of the bluff we could see the whole valley spread out like a patchwork quilt, with the river directly below us. At its edge, built against a steep bank, was the smelter.

From the *Jefferson Valley Zephyr* of January 4, 1895, I learned its history. Under a heading, "The Parrot Talks," were the following statements:

For a year or two there has been talk of the removal of the Parrot smelter from Butte to a point five miles south of Whitehall on the Jefferson river. This has all been occasioned by the fact that the Parrot works . . . lacked water.

R. D. Grant, asst. gen'l. Manager of the Parrot Co. said recently to an *Anaconda Standard* reporter: "We have been keeping very quiet and doing a little pardonable lying relative to the contemplated removal. This land is all bought and paid for now. . . . We expect to have the smelter in operation inside of a year. It will be much larger than our present plant. We will put in several lead furnaces and can handle gold, silver, lead and copper ores. The plant will employ 500 men."

The 1,000 ton plant, when completed, cost several million dollars and received its water from the eighteen-mile Jefferson River ditch which started near Silver Star. The company town, which grew up at the smelter, although usually spoken of as Parrot, was named for Jared Everett Gaylord, manager and superintendent. A paper of a later date concludes the story:

About the time the smelter was completed the Amalgamated Copper Co. was formed. The big company absorbed the majority of the Parrot Mining Co. stock, and the ores of the Parrot went to Anaconda, where the big smelting plant of the Anaconda Co. was located.

The Gaylord smelter was never operated. After a few years of idleness, its machinery, such as could not be used by the larger company, was sold for junk.

Grass Range Review, December 17, 1917

From Parrot, we drove back through Renova, past more brick homes and a brick schoolhouse, then crossed the Jefferson Valley to the highway, and turned south toward Silver Star.

SILVER STAR

This valley is wide and green, and is cut by the Jefferson River. To the east rise the Tobacco Root Mountains; the the west are the Highlands. It is easy to drive through Silver Star today without stopping or noticing a few

SILVER STAR, THE JEFFERSON VALLEY AND
TOBACCO ROOT RANGE

sod-roofed cabins, dating from the 1870's, which blend so well with the sagebrush. Age, fire and the cessation of mining have left little to testify to its prominence in 1870, when it was the only town between Virginia City and Helena. No trace of its original stores, dwellings, hotel, quartz mills, or Masonic and Temperance Lodges remain. Yet in 1870, when its population numbered 250, the Independent Order of Good Templars chartered Lodge No. 21 with a membership of fifteen, and were followed the next year by the Masons who established Lodge No. 17, A. F. & A. M.

The Silver Star Mining District is one of the oldest in the state. As early as the middle 1860's, a few quartz lodes had been located, among them the Green Campbell, the Broadway, and the Iron Rod. The first two mines were three miles west of the camp of Silver Star, which sprang up on the flat at the base of the mountains. The Iron Rod mine and its flourishing camp were three miles south of Silver Star, on the Jefferson River.

Green Campbell, who discovered the gold lode in 1867, worked his property so effectively

that by 1870, it was known as the most valuable quartz mine in the county and was one of the first quartz claims to be patented in Montana. Between 1867 and 1881, it produced $270,000, chiefly in gold.

Thomas J. Johns, the superintendent of the property in 1872, had trouble in sinking a shaft 120 feet below the tunnel level because of a "strong flow of water" which flooded the excavations. During this period, many of the old workings caved in. Next, the Green Campbell Consolidated Gold Mining Company, with stockholders from Waterbury, Connecticut, acquired the mine, the millsite, and the townsite of Silver Star, and immediately placed Bassett C. Leyson, former superintendent of the Mayflower mine, in charge of the property. Reliable sources say that the total output of the mine was $500,000.

Charles D. Everett describes boom times in Silver Star, when the Green Campbell was the bonanza. He writes in *The Madisonian* of September 1, 1899:

I reached Virginia City, June 1866. . . . I became informed of the Silver Star mining district, visited it and was enabled for the people I represented, to acquire a gold lode known as the Green Campbell. During the summer of 1868 I had erected on the bluff of the Jefferson River . . . a ten-stamp mill to reduce ores of that lead and commenced to operate the mill sometime during October. . . .

All the while the mill was thus running, I lived in the camp near the mill, around which a thriving town soon sprang up. . . . My house was the boss of them all, having siding and a shingle roof, a novelty for that part of the country . . . the house was not much for size or beauty of architecture but it was considerable for strong, and could well resist the fierce wintry blasts of the Jefferson valley. My wife was with me from the spring of 1868. We had a little garden spot, forty by forty feet — susceptible of irrigation — and upon leave from the lordly grasshopper could raise magnificent vegetables in astonishing quantities.

From the time the mill began to stamp, the retort would gradually accumulate on our hands and for safety's sake we were obliged to take it to Virginia City as often as once in two weeks on the average. We never would take it on the same day of the week twice succeeding, always leaving camp before daylight and never announcing or letting anyone know in advance when was our intention of departing, thus no scheme could be hatched to "take us in." Especially along the banks of the Jefferson, fringed by almost impenetrable jungle, were afforded places to lay ambuscades . . . we were not molested; but Wells Fargo & Co.'s express was on one occasion relieved of one of its consignments of bullion in Portneauf canyon by the road agents. . . . Some of these trips were made during the winter when it was bitter cold, and no choice was left but several times during the trip to seek the hospitable shelter of houses along the wayside and to thaw out. . . .

We had a peaceable, quiet camp, with very little quarreling and fighting. Tom Eastland lost his life by falling down a ninety-foot shaft. . . . Jimmy Farley . . . committed suicide by shooting himself with a revolver. . . . He had suicidal intent for some time prior to the act, and attempted suicide before by jumping into the Jefferson at a high stage of water, but he found the water so cold and uncomfortable that he swam out and was cured of his mania for a period.

The second big mine at Silver Star was the Broadway, a gold-bearing vein, discovered in the late 1860's, two miles west of the camp. Its first owners, Colonel N. F. Sanders, and Messrs. Daber, Lacgry, George F. Pate, N. N. Morris, and F. R. Merk, are said to have taken out more than any later operators realized, from shallow workings seventy-five feet below the surface of the ground.

When an English concern, the Broadway Gold Mining Company, Ltd., of London, bought the property, they built a forty-stamp mill on the banks of the Jefferson River, equipped with a British process for extracting gold from refractory ore. A two-mile tramway delivered the ore from the mine to the mill. But, despite a $500,000 outlay for improvements, the extraction process was a failure, and values per ton decreased sharply. By June 1884, the mill was forced to shut down.

Since the property was not patented, and title to it could not be held legally by aliens, F. R. Merk, one of the original owners, jumped the claim and relocated it as the Bowery. Under his supervision, the mine was soon producing a carload of ore a day and employing a force of twenty men. To treat the ore, which averaged $20 a ton, Merk built two mills, one on Cherry Creek and the other below Silver Star. Tailings, which were shipped to Butte and run through the smelter, averaged $10-$12 a ton.

By 1896, his son, W. W. Merk, was operating the Bowery, processing quantities of milling ore, and shipping the rest. From 1918 on, the mine has been inactive; but it is credited with production of over a million dollars.

The completion, in 1883, of the railroad to Whitehall, eighteen miles away, greatly facilitated the shipment of ore and caused a revival of mining in the district. Both Silver Star and Iron Rod camps profited from the increased activity, the former becoming a supply center for the many properties in the vicinity.

IRON ROD

From Silver Star, it is but three miles south to the site of Iron Rod, where only a stone foundation of a mill and a few houses, now used by ranchers, identify the location. The settlement which, like Silver Star, is on the west side of the Jefferson River, was never as large as its neighbor. At its peak, the business section of the town, which served its 100 residents, consisted only of one large quartz mill, a store, and a hotel. The leading mine, the Iron Rod, was located on a hill north of the camp. Its discoverers and first owners, the Messrs. Daber, Lacgry, and A. M. Porter, found the lead in the early sixties and for some time arrastred the ore. Later, a twelve-stamp mill was constructed by Stevens and Trivitt to extract the low-grade gold. The total output of the mine was estimated at $600,000.

In 1896, the Aurora-Borealis mine, northwest of the town, sent its ore to be processed in the Iron Rod mill, as did other mines in the area. On one occasion at least, the mill was forced to close temporarily, "on account of slush ice in the ditch," but arrangements were hastily made to keep the ditch open and the mill running all winter. A station on the Jefferson Valley branch of the Northern Pacific road at Iron Rod, built in 1898, facilitated shipment of ore.

TWIN BRIDGES

Close to Twin Bridges, nine miles south of Iron Rod, the Passamari, Beaverhead, and Big Hole Rivers, form the Jefferson branch of the Missouri. The town, with its many trees and shrubs, is a pleasant combination of old and new, with weathered cabins and false-fronted stores tucked in between newer buildings. Mortimer H. Lott, sometimes called the "father of Twin Bridges," died October 5, 1920, at the age of ninety-two. He was one of Montana's pioneers, who mined at Bannack and Virginia City, and ran a store at Nevada City. When he was looking for a homestead, the land that he filed on lay in this valley and Twin Bridges grew up around his acreage. Another well-known figure, of a later decade, was Noah Armstrong, superintendent of the Hecla Consolidated Mining Company during its early operations. While living at Glendale, he sponsored several horse races which were run on the Glendale track. Raising and training race-horses was his hobby, and when he bought a ranch near Twin Bridges, he built a circular barn which contained a quarter-mile track where his racers could train during the winter months. One of his three-year-olds, Spokane, won the Kentucky Derby on May 9, 1889.

ROCHESTER

I knew that the road to Rochester, a deserted camp back in the hills, ran northwest from Twin Bridges, but to get accurate directions, I stopped at a filling station to inquire of a mechanic who was tinkering with a truck. "You just go inside and talk to old man Pitcher," he said. "He knows everything around here, and before you leave I'll make you a map. You could make a couple of wrong turns." The map showed a maze of roads, most of them marked "Don't take." One scraggly line led to a dot marked "Rochester."

Mr. Pitcher was glad to talk about the old camp. "You won't find anyone up there," he said. "The town's been empty a long time except for two sisters, and they left a couple of years ago. Didn't want to go either. One went to relatives in Dillon and the other to a rest home in Alder. Said they were coming back as soon as they could; then one of them died. There used to be lots of free-milling gold near the surface in the Rochester District, but the deeper the mines went, the more complex the ore got. Then they struck water and that meant pumps. The mines are all flooded now. The country rock is porous up there; so when the pumps were working on the lower levels of the Watseca mine, they drained all the wells in town. The only water the people had for their houses had to be hauled from springs two miles away. When you're up there, look for the two story toilet and for the cemetery on the side of the hill. One of the graves is marked 'Frenchy' and some of the others just say 'Unknown.' "

It was a hot afternoon when we left Twin Bridges. For ten miles the car pulled slowly, up over dry sagebrush-covered hills, leaving a ribbon of dust behind it. Near the top of a draw, we saw the first empty houses, set well back from the road, then a few more and a mine dump or two, and, finally, a two-story frame hotel with sagging porch and gaping windows. Beyond and above the weathered building were more dumps and some mine headframes. In the distance rose the Highland Mountains. Rochester, choked by greasewood, stands high and lonely on a hilltop.

The area, known as Rabbit District, attracted prospectors in the late 1860's because of outcroppings of rich, oxidized gold ores found on Watseca Hill. By 1869, eight hundred men lived in tents and log cabins on the surrounding hills. The region was too dry for successful placer mining. Even winter snows, and the annual scanty rainfall, failed to provide sufficient water for sluicing. Arrastres, which recovered but little of the gold, were soon replaced by stamp mills. Woodsworth & Hendrie's ten-stamp mill, built in 1868 at a cost of $34,000, cleaned up $15,286 in gold in nine weeks. Encouraged by this, other plants were erected. Yet, at best, these early mills lost nearly half of the gold run through them.

The Watseca lode, which was discovered in the 1860's, was the key to the region. Dr. Getchell, W. W. Wann, and others, worked the Watseca No. 1 and No. 2, as well as other nearby properties. The Watseca was a deep mine which provided "slathers of yellow metal" until water level was reached.

With the free-milling gold nearly exhausted, and much of the refractory ore lying below water level, mining declined; so that by 1871, Rochester was nearly deserted.

The mills have been idle for a time, and the town for let; Mr. Hendrie who recently visited the place, is soon to start up his mill, giving hopes for the re-population of the town that is now deader than the deadest.

Judge.

Helena Daily Herald, June 16, 1871

Lode mining revived in 1873 with the successful operation of the Day, Julia Holmes, Poucippa, and Watseca mines. The population rose to 100; and, by 1875, a ten-stamp mill was again pounding away on pay ore.

By 1880, mining was back in full swing, with many new claims, including the Beacon Light, Champion, Bonanza, Colusa, Alameda, Gold Bug, Emma, Jack Rabbit, Ajax, Mutch, and Owsley, under development. During the summer, Henry Hawlow and a Mr. Manheim recovered, with a hand mortar, 16 ounces of gold from a washtub of quartz. The *Glendale Atlantis* of February 9, 1881, mentions that "When Columbus Ward wants money, they say he hitches up his team to his wagon and instead of going to the forest and hauling a load of wood to town, he drives around over the hills and gathers up loose quartz croppings and takes them to an arrastra."

By 1896, F. R. Merk, who already held valuable properties at Silver Star, owned by the Watseca mine, the largest property continuously operated in the district. Through lessees, free-milling gold, averaging $30-75 a ton, was recovered and processed either at the nearby Mueller mill, or at the Colorado smelter at Butte.

The Buffalo mine, which adjoined the Watseca, was also extensively developed. The Longfellow, Badger, Cooper, Shoemaker, Thistle, Concentrator, and Mutch mines all lay within a mile or two of the town. Although gold was the prevailing deposit in this area, lead and small amounts of copper were also found. To treat these varied ores, concentrators and small lead smelters were built in or near the town.

Between 1901 and 1905, the camp's population rose to 5,000, making it the largest community in Madison County. All principal mines were active and their ore was handled in stamp mills, chlorination plants, and various types of concentrators that had been built. Despite this seeming prosperity, the increased cost of labor and materials cut production profits to such an extent that by 1906, only eight mines continued to operate. Owners began to sell their properties, or to abandon them, so as to be off to new gold strikes. Even the Watseca mine shut down and in a short time with filled with water.

By 1907 the district was almost deserted and remained so until 1926. A brief boom of three years resulted from the exploitation of the Emma, Colusa, and Jack Rabbit claims, as lead-silver properties. A mill, erected at the Emma mine by the Butte Madison Mines Corporation, ran until 1932. Since then, both the town and the district have lain dormant.

Rochester's last inhabitants were two sisters who spent twenty quiet years in the deserted camp. Both were widows, and each had her own frame house. Mrs. Lucy Miller, widow of James S. Miller, a foreman and assayer, came to Rochester as a bride during its boom years and made it her home for fifty years. Mrs. Etta Fisher spent short periods of time in the town with her miner husband. After his death, she settled in Rochester to be near her sister. The two women lived a quarter of a mile apart. After Lucy Miller grew too rheumatic to get about, Etta did the visiting or sent messages by her dog, Bailey. The women raised vegetables and flowers in the summer and filled their cellars in the fall with food enough to last through the winter. After their well went dry, in 1935, they canned snow water, which they boiled and cached in cool places for future use. They gathered firewood as long as they were able. Then they bought wood, coal, and water from Twin Bridges. Since neither of them could drive a car, they seldom got down to the valley except to vote and to stock up on provisions. In winter, when snow lay two feet deep on the ground, and the temperature dipped at night to thirty degrees below zero, they were completely isolated, and for weeks at a time saw no one until the mailman or anxious friends broke trail to Watseca Ridge to see if they were all right.

When I visited Rochester in 1956, their houses were among the few still standing. They were partly obscured, however, by the shoulder-high sagebrush which is gradually creeping in over the townsite. Prominent among the draughty ghosts of Rochester was the Hardesty Hotel, a skeleton sentinel whose sightless windows surveyed the once busy district.

TIDAL WAVE DISTRICT

Back at Twin Bridges, I looked east, across the valley, to the Tidal Wave Mining District which occupied an area on the western slope

ROCHESTER AND HARDESTY HOTEL

of the Tobacco Root Mountains. It lay five miles east of Twin Bridges, and included several gulches — Dry Boulder, Coal Creek, Bear, Goodrich, and Wet and Dry Georgia Gulches.

The district was prospected as early as 1864, when the Tidal Wave and High Ridge prospects were located; but its mines were considered worthless since they did not contain free gold. In the 1870's, when interest turned to argentiferous lead ores, prospectors located several new properties. Again, in the middle 1880's, large veins of argentiferous galena were opened between Ramshorn and Georgia Gulches. These mines were successfully worked, on a small scale, by their owners or by lessees as late as 1914. The district gets its name from a mine on a ridge between Dry Georgia and Goodrich Gulches.

SHERIDAN

Ten miles south of Twin Bridges, in the heart of the Ruby Valley, is Sheridan, an unhurried but active community, whose big trees reflect the age of the town and shade the many old cabins and stone buildings which stand well back from the highway, or are caught between newer structures along the main street. Named for the Civil War general, by R. P. Bateman, who built the first cabin and took up land in the vicinity in the early 1860's, Sheridan became a supply center for the gold, silver, and lead mining operations in the Tobacco Root Mountains, and for the rich farms of the valley. Even before the mines were discovered, M. A. Hatfield built a cabin on the north side of Mill Creek. By 1866, W. Tripp and R. P. Bateman built a log store and hotel. One year later, Bateman became postmaster. The mail, which was brought over from Virginia City, was kept in a cigar box on a shelf in his store. Sarge Hall built the first flour mill in 1866, one mile east of Sheridan on Mill Creek. Charles Peitch managed the mill until 1891. A sack of flour made from wheat grown in the Ruby Valley is said to have been sent to Chicago in 1893, to the World's Fair Exposition, where it received a Gold Medal.

The town grew slowly. Oldtimers tell how, twenty years after its founding, only thirty buildings had been erected. Indians ranged the length of the Ruby Valley and the mountain slopes above it, and frequently rode into the town to trade or beg. Children often walked to school through fields of grain so as to be hidden from the Indians' sight. A number of squaws worked for the settlers, accepting trifling payment, such as a loaf of bread in return for sawing a load of wood.

Within a year of the discovery of gold in Alder Gulch, quartz veins were located in the Sheridan District, which embraced a number of smaller areas: Indian Creek, Brandon, Quartz Hill, Ramshorn, Bivin, and Wisconsin.

BRANDON

Three miles east of Sheridan, at the mouth of Mill Creek Canyon, stood the town of Brandon. Alfred Cisler, one of the first settlers, was both farmer and miner. In the 1860's, he located the Buckeye mine, and early in the next decade an even richer gold property, the Broadgauge, which produced $100,000 during the early days of its development. The *Montana Post* of January 4, 1865, describes Brandon as

a new town laid out last summer. Three months ago, the first building, a log cabin, was erected. . . . At present there are 27 good log houses and many in construction. . . . It has 2 blacksmith shops and 1 hotel, the Brandon City House. All trade now has to be done with Virginia (City). It has one quartz mill driven by waterpower.

The same article states that

All the best teams of Virginia and Nevada cities were in harness to attend a sleighing party of pretty girls and their beaux, having in view a social dance at Brandon. . . . Ensconced in innumerable wrappers with hot bricks to our feet, and as lively and ladylike bundles of muslin as any mortal might wish to be his share to sleighride with, by our side, we rode behind as fast a team as we could.

In 1874, when Virginia City and Helena were both striving to become the capital of the Territory, someone facetiously entered Brandon in the contest. Since no registration law was in force, anyone could cast as many votes as he wished by going from one precinct to another. When the ballots were counted, Brandon lost to Virginia City by a single vote. As late as 1903, when the Toledo mine, half a mile north of the town, was running rich lead and silver through its 150-ton mill, Brandon was s small but active town.

Leiterville, which was situated on the north fork of Wisconsin Creek, centered around the Leiter Company property — fourteen claims, one placer, and three mill-sites, all of which were patented. The original mine was eight miles from Sheridan and is said to have been located in the sixties or early seventies by David McCranor. During its early days, it paid well. Jerry Sullivan is believed to have discovered three other lodes (later included in the group), the Grey Eagle, Daniel, and Sheridan, in 1877, and to have developed them during the following three summers. In 1880, these, and one other claim, were sold to Hamilton and McCranor. The latter spent considerable time in Chicago, procuring capital for his mines, and upon his return, built a five-stamp mill run by waterpower. Although in operation each summer, for ten years, it was not a success. When McCranor's health failed he sold his holdings, bit by bit, until they were all owned by L. Z. Leiter of Chicago, and his nephew, T. B. Leiter. Thereafter, the mine bore the name of the new owner, and the camp, which grew up around it, was called Leiterville.

T. Benton Leiter became superintendent in 1893, and during his incumbency, miners' cabins, a boardinghouse, a manager's home, a schoolhouse, a large stamp mill with aerial tramway, and a cyanide plant for treatment of the tailings, were erected. Although production enabled the mill to run steadily on two shifts, Leiter was more interested in spending his uncle's money than in making the property pay. While he did nothing to benefit his employees, he gave elaborate dinners to his friends, whom he brought to the camp, from Sheridan, in rented livery rigs. By the winter of 1895, rumors of his mismanagement reached L. Z. Leiter, who immediately sent his son, Joseph, to Montana to investigate. Upon receiving his son's report, he fired Benton Leiter and made Captain E. A. Trevise superintendent. Under his able direction, the mine again showed a profit. The miners must have shared in this prosperity also — if one is to believe the story that, after a cleanup, when they received their pay, they would sit around the fire in the saloon and light their pipes with five-dollar bills.

CHAPTER 13

THE DEER LODGE VALLEY and the GARNET RANGE

DEER LODGE

The Deer Lodge Valley is a wide, high meadowland confined on east and west by mountain ranges in whose foothills lie isolated mineral deposits. Deer Lodge County (now Powell County), is an area "seamed with gold and silver veins," whose discovery caused camps to spring up along creeks and on the slopes of the higher peaks. The valley itself was a trading and trapping center in the 1850's, frequented by Indians and mountain men, and named by the former for a sedimentary cone built up, nearly forty feet in height, by a thermal spring from which issued volumes of vapor. From a distance, this mound resembled an Indian lodge from which smoke was issuing. The valley, in early days, was not only neutral ground for the several Indian tribes that passed through it, but was also a favorite grazing range for white-tailed deer. Hence, the name Deer Lodge.

Many of the first settlers were Spaniards, Frenchmen, and Mexicans, among whom were Thomas Lavatta, Joseph Hill, Alejo Barasta, and Joe Pizanthy. Their group of cabins and shacks, built in 1860-1861, in the center of the valley, was first called Spanish Fork and then Cottonwood. In July, 1862, Captain La Barge arrived. He and his partner, Harkness, had just opened a rival trading post at Fort Benton, called Fort La Barge, but when it was known that he planned to start a store in Cottonwood and live there, two of his friends,

John S. Pemberton and Leon Quesnell, "laid off some two or three streets and formally christened a new town 'La Barge City.'" Harkness was put in charge of the new store and stocked it with much needed miner's supplies, but he disliked the mountain country and soon left for the east.

In 1863, some of the older residents of Cottonwood organized the Deer Lodge Town Company, with James Stuart as president, and employed Colonel DeLacy to lay off a town, one-mile square. He platted a portion of the townsite and the company distributed most of the lots to "actual residents and never sold enough to get even on their survey." The settlement immediately assumed an importance beyond its size, chiefly because it was on the main traveled trail through uncharted territory. Even Captain John Mullan mentioned it in his *Miners and Travelers Guide,* saying that fresh vegetables and meats were to be had there, and that a blacksmith could repair wagons and shoe horses and oxen. When the mines in Bear Creek were draining off the population from other camps, Deer Lodge was known as "the good little town on the road to Bear." It was, therefore, natural that the first legislature, in 1865, transferred the county seat from dwindling Silver Bow to booming Deer Lodge City. The townsite company was so elated by this move that it donated the land where the courthouse and jail stand, although neither building was erected until 1868. Of the new city, the *Montana Post* of December 16, 1865, remarks:

a year ago, six cabins, some peacefully ruminating cows, a stray vaquero and a lot of half-breed papooses engaged in making mud pies, were the most startling features of the landscape. The most salient point in its history was the hanging of Bill Bunton by a scouting party of the Vigilantes.

Less than a year later, Helena's *Rocky Mountain Gazette* printed a letter from Deer Lodge which mentions that

The Bannacks are very numerous in our streets. They had a four-mile foot race on Sunday, and are having war dances every night, which are quite well attended by our young men.

September 8, 1866

As early as 1866, a subscription school, taught by the week, to which fifteen pupils came, was held by Mrs. William Hardenbrook, in one room of Granville Stuart's log home. The first district school was taught by Dallas P. Newcomer. By 1867, the city had a log schoolhouse.

The *Deer Lodge Independent*, the town's first newspaper, appeared in the fall of 1867 and was published for a few months by Frank Kenyon, a journalist-printer from Salmon City, Idaho, until it was bought by several Democrats and edited by Captain John H. Rogers. The following year, the *New North-West*, a large weekly news sheet, appeared and became one of the notable papers of the Territory, under the able leadership of Captain James H. Mills and his brother. Originally a weekly, it became a daily in 1870-1871. Chatty items from early issues mention that

On Thursday, Jan. 16, Edward Bryson, an industrious, good citizen of Bear Gulch, while running the dump car to the mouth of the shaft, pushed it a little too far, missed his footing, fell through the tramway into the shaft, and was precipitated to the bottom, a distance of 33 feet. One ankle only was fractured by the fall, but his internal injuries resulted in death on the evening of the following Sunday. Cold, terribly cold as it was, his request to be buried in Deer Lodge was fulfilled, and a dozen or more comrades mounted and escorted his remains some sixty miles to this place, arriving on Wednesday.

The Deer Lodge jail is tenantless. . . . Huntley now runs a beautiful new coach sleigh into Deer Lodge, and Brad brings up the grays smoking like locomotives.

The Reverend Daniel S. Tuttle, first Episcopal Bishop of Montana, who spent much of the 1860's in the mining camps of the Territory, tells of his first visit to the city:

I invaded Deer Lodge, July 17, 1868. Mr. Tutt and I put up at the Scott House. There was a billiard saloon next door and over it a hall used as the courthouse. In this hall on Sunday morning and evening, July 19, I held services. . . . I think mine was the second Protestant service in Deer Lodge, a Methodist South minister having preached the first one.

On the day after my arrival, Granville Stuart went around with me to select a church lot. The committee gave it to me. . . . I left $100 with Mr. Stuart to pay for fencing and holding it. The offerings Sunday morning were $46.00. There was a small Roman Catholic church in town. Father De Ryckere had been serving it for some years. I found only two communicants of our church in Deer Lodge — Dr. Rumsey and Mrs. McMurtry.

Daniel S. Tuttle, *Early History of the*
Episcopal Church in Montana, Historical
Society of Montana, Vol. 5, 1904.

The Episcopal Church, which he began, is still standing. Another structure, which visitors ask to see, is the W. A. Clark house that dates from the sixties, built when the mining magnate was a merchant and spent some time in the city.

In 1869, William A. Clark, Sam E. Larabie, and R. W. Donnell established a banking firm in Deer Lodge. Among its early transactions was the purchase of one million dollars worth of gold dust from the mines of the Bear Creek District. A grid of the townsite was completed that same year, with streets running from First to Tenth in one direction, and from "A" to "G" in the other. One year later, the penitentiary was designated to be built within the city, and its construction was begun in 1871. The many placer camps in the vicinity contributed to the city's growth and permanence, and when their deposits were worked out, lode mines in the hills produced new camps which also depended upon Deer Lodge for their sustenance. From the start, the valley attracted farmers and ranchers and some of the Territory's most successful cattle barons grazed their first herds on the fertile meadowland. When the railroad was built though the valley, Deer Lodge became a division point for the Milwaukee Road and the home of its repair shops. Deer Lodge is a good hub from which to start when visiting mining camps on the rim of the valley.

DANIELSVILLE

Several miles south of the city is a forgotten camp, high in the mountains on the west side of the Valley. Near Galen, a road runs west into the hills to Racetrack and

EMERY

Danielsville. After about twelve miles, the former site of Racetrack should be reached, and perhaps the end of the passable road. According to Forest Service maps, the old camp of Danielsville is another six or more miles.

It was a new gold camp at the beginning of the twentieth century and sprang up because of the discovery of gold outcroppings, found by an old Frenchman, several years earlier. According to the *Kendall Chronicle* of June 17, 1902: "The country was hard to get into. On one of the highest peaks, the hardy old man worked away. He found plenty of float and finally found the vein." Late in the season, he took his samples of ore and left for Deer Lodge, where he showed them around. A party of Deer Lodge and Anaconda men induced him to lead them to his discovery. In the meantime, snow had fallen, and the men tried unsuccessfully for days to reach the district. Even the old Frenchman seemed confused, and finally, when the search was called off, he went on alone and was never seen alive again. The next season his body was found in the high mountains.

In 1901, the three Daniels brothers, Frank Jones, and Dick LaCerse went to the same hills to prospect and uncovered a ledge carrying gold. The Daniels brothers and Frank Jones made the first big strike, a lead said to be eighteen feet wide. This they called the Golden Leaf. As soon as the news reached Deer Lodge, hundreds of prospectors jammed the trail to the district, near the head of Racetrack Creek, ploughing through snow that was still deep and drifted. By 1902, townsite, called Danielsville, was platted which soon contained a general store, a blacksmith shop, saloon, hotel, and a number of miners' cabins. By the time the population reached 200, stages ran twice a week between it and the valley, and freight service, once a week. Even a new wagon road was under construction. With ore on the dump of the Golden Leaf, plans were made for the erection, during the summer of 1902, of a twenty-stamp mill. But, like many camps, Danielsville rose rapidly and then faded away.

213

LOST CREEK, DRY GULCH, ANTELOPE CREEK

South of Racetrack Creek are Modesty and Lost Creeks. In the early days, placer gold was found in the foothills on the east slope of the Flint Creek Range on Modesty, Lost, and Antelope Creeks, or their tributaries. Small amounts of placer gold have been washed, annually, from Dry Gulch since 1902, but no lode mines have been active in the district since 1932, although a shipment of gold ore, from the Dark Horse in 1931, renewed interest in the area. Access to Lost and Antelope Creeks is north from Anaconda. The road to Racetrack skirts a part of Modesty Creek.

EMERY

Emery can be reached from Deer Lodge, for it lies on the west slope of the main range of the Rocky Mountains, less than ten miles east of that city, at the end of a road that climbs steadily away from the Valley. The Zosell, or Emery Mining District, which contains the deserted camp, was first discovered in 1872, and for the next twenty years, placer gold, amounting to $75,000, was washed from Rocker, Spring, and Deep Gulches, and from a tributary of Little Cottonwood Creek. The placers were shallow, rarely more than ten feet deep, and since the flow of water in the streams was slight, sluicing operations were often curtailed before all the gravel was washed.

Authorities differ as to whether Joseph Peterson or Samuel Beaumont found the first lode in the district in 1887, but all agree that it was recorded as the Hidden Hand. "The most important deposit, the Emery, was discovered by John Renault in 1888 and staked by Emery, after whom the mine was named. The original claim was called the Carbonate Hill lode."

The principal lodes were discovered during the 1890's and included the Blue Eyed Maggie, Argus, Emma Darling, and Bonanza. The Emery, Blue Eyed Maggie, and Bonanza were consistent producers with sometimes one, and sometimes another, yielding the greatest tonnage. Production increased in the 1930's, and continued uninterruptedly until about 1950, except for shutdowns during World War II.

The Emery, the most important mine in the district, is said to have produced $1,000,000 in its many years of productivity. The lode, which lies at the summit of a low peak just below the Continental Divide, and carries ga-lena, gold, and silver bearing ores, was located in 1888 by Emery and developed to a depth of 100 feet. That same year he was able to ship a little ore. In 1890, he sold the property to N. J. Bielenberg and others from Deer Lodge. The new owners patented the claim in 1893 and operated it profitably in collaboration with Powers and Harrington, lessees. During this arrangement, eighteen to twenty cars of ore a month were shipped to the East Helena smelter.

The Deer Lodge Consolidated Mines Company Ltd., or "The English Company", as it was generally called, bought the mine in 1907 and shipped concentrates totaling $15,000. Within a year the company was in debt and creditors took possession of the property.

In 1915, the Emery and Blue Eyed Maggie mines were the most productive properties in the district. Two years later, a new mill at Emery produced lead concentrates rich in silver. An electric line was brought into the district, in 1923, to provide power for a new 75-ton flotation mill on the property. In 1935, while the Tweedy Brothers Corporation was operating the Emery, nearly 12,000 tons of gold-silver ore were treated in a small flotation mill. Of this output, Coleman H. Mulcady wrote enthusiastically in the *Philipsburg Mail*:

Instead of the tink tink of single jacks and hand steel, you hear the whine of "whiggle tails" or power drills, the chug chug of compressors and the smooth whir of electric pumps and the steady strain of hoists and cables.

May 31, 1935

In 1945, John White leased the property and interested Porter Brothers in working it. A 100-ton flotation mill was built, from which $225,000 in ore was recovered, before the mine closed down in 1948.

A story is told of a French-Canadian prospector who located a fraction between Emery and another claim. When his right to the property was contested, he hired a lawyer to present his case. When asked at the trial to explain how he located the claim, he replied, to the amusement of the court, "I get the pick and shovel. I go up the hill. I find the hapex and dig the shaft."

The Blue Eyed Maggie, which, with the Emma Darling, produced lead and silver ores as early as 1910, is listed in 1932 as the largest producer in the district. All through the 1930's, it yielded a consistent tonnage of high-grade gold-silver ore, even carrying on through the years of depression when most other properties shut down. The mine was on the north side of Rocker Gulch, with its adit behind the Emery schoolhouse.

The Bonanza mine, north of Emery, "on a low ridge east of the upper course of Rocker gulch," was said to contain the largest mineralized vein in the district. It was discovered, in 1895, by William T. Zosell. The earliest recorded shipment — four and a half tons of hand-sorted ore — sent, in 1911, to the East Helena smelter, yielded "the highest per ton returns . . . ever shipped from the property." Throughout its productivity, this mine was owned, and at times leased or operated by William Zosell and his two sons.

The day we went to Emery, we pulled into Deer Lodge before the stores were open. This was unfortunate because, in the excitement of an early start, I had left the map, which showed all turns and landmarks between Deer Lodge and Emery, on the motel table. Francis discovered a cafe that was open and returned with the needed directions. "Turn east at the Montana Power Company building and take the road out to the end of Missouri Avenue and then just keep going," the man had told him. "Four miles out you'll pass the city dump. Then you'll know for sure that you're on the right road."

Missouri Avenue was wide and lined with fine homes, a school, and a church. At its end was a road in front of a big farmhouse set in a grove of trees. Should we turn right or left? Each was equally well traveled. I tried to recall the missing map. It did have a jog to the left. We turned in that direction. The gravel road soon swung east again and we passed the dump and ran across the valley to the foothills. Just before the road narrowed and began to climb out of the valley, it forked once more, but a sign to Emery pointed to the right. This was ranch country, with stock grazing on the slopes and Cottonwood Creek looping through the meadows. The higher we drove, the narrower and steeper the road became, and the rougher the surface. It threaded around the shoulders of hills, was cut by cattle guards, and entered a timbered area. Not a sign of a prospect hole or a dump on the hillsides! At the crest of a grade, we looked into a wooded cut. Still no mines, but around the next curve we found cabins, dumps, and, across the gulch, a big mill — the Emery. Beyond and above it, the road disappeared through the trees to emerge on a rise on which

stood some old buildings beside a big, gray dump — the Bonanza property.

The cabins in Emery were both old and new — the older ones built of logs and the newer ones faced with tar paper. One ruined concrete building stood in the lower end of the camp, with a wooden sidewalk, bordered with rank weeds, leading to it. Beside the mill was a large dump, and below it, a settling pond. Foundations and rotted logs marked the sites of other buildings and gave further evidence of the size of the place in more prosperous times. Emery in 1896 is described in the May 1 issue of the *New North-West*. At that time there were 100 men in the camp and application had been made for a post-office. The townsite, owned by the Carbonate Expansion Company, already had fifteen to twenty substantial buildings on it. Adjoining the Emery property on the south was the Black Rock. South of it was the Coleman group. North of the Emery was the Carbonate Expansion Company mine. Adjoining it, on the north, was the Bonanza, owned by William Zosell, but under lease to Butte men. Half a mile to the northeast was the Hidden Hand, from which about $13,000 of ore had been shipped. The Silver Queen was north of the Hidden Hand. Adjoining it was the Wake-Up Jim, with the Argus north of it. To the northeast lay the Emma Darling and the Sterrett.

Coleman H. Mulcady, in the *Philipsburg Mail* of May 31, 1935, mentions the Coleman-Caroline claims, "below Emery and adjoining the Blue Eyed Maggie on the west," as worked for nearly thirty years. Mr. Mulcady, a resident of Deer Lodge, describes some novel procedures in the Zosell District and predicts a revival of the camp:

Even the spirits are mining at Emery. Legend has it that on Cottonwood creek several men belonging to certain religious cults are haunting the pay streak in a strange manner. They first hold a seance, during which a visitation occurs to one and another. The person so favored . . . rises . . . and leads the others to a prescribed spot on the hillside, as directed. There they swing pick and shovel in the spooky quest for the yellow glitter. . . . Emery bids fair to become a roaring camp, as it was in the 1880's. The regrettable difference, of course, will be billboards and filling stations.

In 1956, when we visited Emery, we found none of the signs of progress that Mr. Mulcady had feared. It rained while we were investigating the old properties, but the storm passed over, leaving the acrid odor of a wet dump and the pungent aroma of dripping evergreens. The drive back to Deer Lodge was spectacular for, as soon as we left the timber, the whole valley spread out below us, with the city of Deer Lodge a green spot in its center. Cloud shadows drifted down the distant peaks and across the valley providing sharp contrast to the patches of sunlight that patterned the ranchlands.

"Did you know that the Zosell District has a lost mine?" I asked Francis as we rolled down to the valley floor. "It was in 1872 that an old man, named Thomas O. Spring (or Springer), used to wander into Deer Lodge from time to time with samples of rich quartz. From these he would pound out enough free gold in a hand mortar to stake him to a lengthy spree and when he sobered up, he would sheepishly ask Sam Scott, the proprietor of the Scott House, to give him a job. As soon as he got another grubstake, he'd be off to the hills again. He was very secretive about the source of his gold and refused to take anyone with him on his tramps into the hills.

"Finally, in August, 1872, he agreed to let Scott go part way with him, and on a Sunday afternoon the two drove in a buckbroad to the forks of Cottonwood Creek. While Scott fished for trout, Spring set out alone up Baggs Creek, with an old pick and shovel and two tomato cans for his ore samples. He was gone longer than Scott had expected, and just as he began to worry about the old fellow, he heard a shout and saw Spring standing on a high cliff between Baggs and Cottonwood Gulches. When Spring reached his friend, he had both tin cans filled with rotten reddish quartz, obtained, he explained, from a four-foot vein. The pick and shovel he had left in the hole. Scott asked if he had located his claim, but Spring said, 'No, it's safe enough. Nobody will ever find it.' The two men returned to Deer Lodge, and from the three ounces of gold which he pounded from the rock in the cans, he reveled in a ten-day drunk.

"Before he sobered up, two men, Major Elwell and J. W. Stearns, arrived in Deer Lodge, outfitted for a prospecting trip. Naturally, they heard about Spring's gold strike and they offered to finance his mine for a half interest in it. They signed an agreement with him and the three left the next day, with Spring carrying Scott's old shotgun, which he had borrowed to shoot grouse. The party made camp late that afternoon, somewhere near the forks of Cottonwood Creek, and Spring, with his gun, set off to get grouse for their supper. The other two made camp and when Spring failed to return, they feared he had met with an accident and searched that evening and all the next morning, but without success.

"Upon returning to Deer Lodge, they reported his disappearance and, in company with a large posse, returned to their campsite. From there the posse fanned out into the hills and in a short time found Spring sitting under a tree, with his gun across his knees. There were no signs of violence on him and it is believed that he died of a heart attack. The news of his death started a stampede to Baggs Creek, but no one, then or since, has found his claim. Perhaps Otto Engel stumbled upon it while deer hunting in 1927. He ran upon an old trapdoor and some abandoned workings from which he brought back samples of ore; but who can tell whether they were from Spring's prospect?"

CHAMPION and the ORO FINO DISTRICT

Some fourteen miles southeast of Deer Lodge, on the western slope of the Continental Divide, lies the Oro Fino Mining District, whose placers in Caribou, Oro Fino, and Dry Cottonwood Gulches were worked during the 1860's. As late as 1910, when Dry Cottonwood was dredged, it yielded sapphires as well as gold. Lode mines in the district were first operated in the 1880's and include the Champion, the most important property, and the John, Independence, Cashier, Last Resort, and St. Louis. The Champion, which was opened in 1886, operated for a few years and then lay idle until 1920-1926. Most of the ore recovered from the district — an estimated $350,-000 — came from this mine.

Uuno Sahinen, in his *Mining Districts of Montana* (1935), states that the district was active then; but the most colorful and complete description of the Champion mine and the camp that grew up around it is found in an article in the July 18, 1890, issue of the *New North-West*.

THE GROWTH OF THE FUTURE CITY
Visit Champion. . . . As you get into the mountains the stage goes slower and the road narrows and the grades are steeper. About two or three hours out of Deer Lodge the Lion shaft house is reached; then comes that of the Silver Crown and presently the hoisting works of the Champion and, in a few minutes we are driving along Main St. in the town of

Champion, at the summit of the main range of the Rocky Mountains.

About a year ago Champion had two or three houses; now in walking along Main St. one can count sixty to seventy buildings in full view, while there are buildings in the forest, in every gulch and on every hill for miles around. . . . All the buildings have the fresh smell of pine about them.

The site of the town is just south of the Champion mining claim and is on the High Tariff and East Champion mining claims. . . .

The High Tariff, to which the owners have a patent, has been platted and laid off into lots, blocks and streets, but without alleys, and the plat duly recorded. . . . East Champion or Frenchtown as they call it up there, was laid out first and the new plat was not made to correspond with it, consequently the streets running east and west have a crook in them, presenting a sort of don't care style. . . . The lots in the High Tariff site . . . are held at from $200-300. There are five or six deep wells in town but most of the water used is brought in barrels from neighboring gulches.

If saloons are an evidence of civilization, then Champion is in a high state of civilization, for she has eleven saloons with more in prospect.

There is a lumber yard. . . . a grocery store, a restaurant and lunch counter. There is also a Chinese restaurant. . . . Wm. Moltham has a post office, also a general merchandise store. . . . There are two barber shops, one run by a lady at the east end, while Ed McMahan is proprietor of the other at the west end. Also two butcher shops.

Champion has an academy of Music, which is also used for public gatherings and church services. All in Champion are pious and attend church regularly, when there is any. M. E. Pinney is the dispenser of justice, notary public and conveyancer for the camp, keeping on hand a full supply of location notices and other legal blanks.

There are now ten hoisting works in the camp. . . . As yet there is no school. Champion needs one for there are about forty children that should be corralled as soon as possible. . . .

The Champion mill shut down yesterday for lack of ore and will remain closed for ten days. The mine is all right, only money is needed.

GOLD CREEK

At the north end of the Deer Lodge Valley, the small settlement of Gold Creek dozes quietly beside the Clark Fork of the Columbia River, within sight of Highway No. 10 and its rushing traffic. Yet twice in Montana's history, it occupied a place of historic importance. On September 8, 1883, it was a center of festivity for the crowds who had gathered to see Henry Villard, president of the Northern Pacific Railroad, drive the iron spike which completed this transcontinental line, whose tracks pushed out from both the east and the west, met at this point. The earlier and more important day was the one in 1852 when Francois Finlay, a French-Canadian half-breed, known as "Benetsee", found the first float gold in what is now Montana, in a branch of the Clark Fork, later to be called Gold Creek.

Benetsee, a fur trader, had returned from California in 1850 where he had seen placer gold, and, although his interests were in trapping rather than prospecting, his discovery held a potential far beyond his realization. His findings became known to the few mountain men in the area, and the stream from which the gold came was called Benetsee's Creek. In 1853, a railroad exploring expedition, knowing nothing of his discovery, washed some flakes from it and named it Gold Creek. Their report to the government caused no stir. Angus McDonald, in charge of Fort Connah near Flathead Lake, received some dust from Benetsee. He had it assayed and reported the discovery to the Hudson's Bay Company in Victoria, B. C., but he was ordered to keep the news a secret. In the spring of 1856, a party, en route to Salt Lake from the Bitter Root Valley, stopped to prospect along the creek and found more colors than Benetsee had.

The *Montana Mining Review* of 1889 contains an article, "History of Mining in Montana," by W. H. Wheeler and A. M. Williams, which mentions Benetsee and his gold. According to Wheeler, the story was told to him by John Silverthorne, a packer who worked for Major John Owen. On one of his trips between Fort Benton and Fort Owen, Silverthorne camped at Benetsee Creek and while there visited with Finlay, who was an old friend of his. Finlay needed some tobacco and other supplies and had only dust with which to pay for his purchases, but he assured Silverthorne that a Hudson's Bay trader had told him it was gold. Silverthorne accepted the dust and, upon reaching Fort Benton, showed it to Major Culbertson, agent for the American Fur Company. He took it in exchange for $12.00 worth of goods, sent it to St. Louis to be assayed, and received $15.00 for it!

In the spring of 1857, James and Granville Stuart left Yreka, California, and with nine others started for Iowa. At the head of Malad Creek (about thirty miles north of Malad City, Utah), Granville became ill and even after ten days rest was unable to travel. The Stuart brothers and Reece (Rezin) Anderson remained behind and the rest went on. By the time the invalid had recovered, the Mormons were patrolling all the roads to the States so the Stuarts decided to winter in the Beaverhead and Big Hole Valley (near where Melrose is). The following March the three men joined others who were starting for Fort Bridger, but before long, the Stuarts and Anderson left the group and went to Deer Lodge Valley to hunt and cure meat for their trip and to investigate the rumors of gold on Benetsee Creek. On May 2, 1858, they washed a small amount of gold from the creek, having as tools only an old spade and their bread pan. They continued prospecting until June, when their provisions got so low that they went to Fort Bridger for supplies. For the time being, they abandoned mining and remained at Green River (Wyoming) as traders, until the fall of 1860, when they returned to Gold Creek.

That winter and the spring of 1861, they worked as best they could in dry gulches and along Benetsee Creek, finding colors but accomplishing little; for they lacked proper tools and had no whipsawed lumber with which to build sluiceboxes. Learning that the steamboat *Chippewa* was expected at Fort Benton, James Stuart and some others went to the fort to await its arrival, prepared to buy tools and supplies from her cargo. But the steamboat burned 400 miles below the fort when a thirsty deckhand lighted a candle in the dark hold in order to steal alcohol from a keg, and the fumes caught fire and exploded. Since there were 280 kegs of powder on board, the captain quickly ran the boat ashore, and the passengers wisely and hastily scattered into the breaks back from the river; for the violence of the explosion which followed blew a safe weighing 2,000 pounds a distance of nearly a mile. The cargo was a complete loss, and the passengers had to make their way to Fort Benton as best they could. Stuart, ignorant of the catastrophe, waited all summer for the steamer to arrive and then returned to Gold Creek.

Upon his return, the Stuarts settled down near their diggings and prospected on Gold Creek and in the nearby gulches and hills. Their findings were so encouraging that they wrote to their brother, Thomas, in Colorado, urging him to join them.

The news in their letter started a stampede, although many who came intended to push on to the Salmon River mines in Idaho, and regarded a look at the Gold Creek diggings as an interlude on the way. Some were satisfied with the placers and others stumbled into the area by mistake, while attempting to reach old Fort Lemhi. A few, upon hearing that the Salmon mines were overcrowded, decided to stay where they were and prospect an area as yet relatively unexplored. Thomas Stuart, and those with him, reached Gold Creek June 20, 1862. Only that spring, James and Granville Stuart, together with Thomas Adams, E. H. Burr, and John Powell, had obtained sawed lumber at ten cents a foot and picks and shovels which they had ordered, packed in from Walla Walla, 425 miles away. These were delivered by pack train to Worden & Higgins' trading post at Hellgate (near Missoula). With these, they were able to set up a string of sluiceboxes early in May on Pioneer Bar and systematically to work the gravels.

By 1862 a small settlement called American Fork, consisting of forty-five people, grew up at Stuart's ranch at the mouth of Gold Creek. It was never large, for the diggings were not particularly rich nor extensive, and even the Stuarts did not do too well. When word of richer strikes at Bannack, Alder Gulch, and Last Chance reached the miners, the place was almost emptied.

On July 14, 1862, James Stuart was elected sheriff of Missoula County, then a part of Idaho Territory. Later in the summer, William Arnett, C. W. Spillman, and B. F. Jernagin rode into town with six horses. A few nights later, the owners of the stolen horses, who had tracked the men to American Fork, asked the sheriff and the miners to assist in catching the thieves. Arnett and Jernagin were playing monte in a saloon when they were surrounded. Instead of throwing up his hands when ordered to, Arnett reached for his gun, and one of his pursuers shot him dead. They like to tell that his grip on the cards was so tight that they had to bury him holding a full hand. Jernagin was tried and ordered to leave the country. Spillman was hanged. In more recent years, a dredge with a daily capacity of 5,000 cubic yards, cut to bedrock along Gold Creek for a distance of more than seven miles and cleaned out the gravels.

PIONEER

I was curious to see Pioneer, for its history dated back to the sixties and was intertwined with that of Gold Creek and the Stuarts. Yet, no one encouraged me to visit the place. "Why go there? It's all dredged out."

PIONEER
BURIED TOWN, PIONEER

"There's nothing left to see." "It isn't worth your while." Being stubborn, I decided to see for myself. Leaving Highway No. 10, I turned south about thirteen miles west of Garrison, crossed the Clark Fork, drove through the diminutive village of Gold Creek, and traveled eight miles across low, rolling hills, dotted with thickets of trees. Long before the townsite was reached, great mounds of waste rock, left by the dredge, marked the bed of the creek. Soon the road ran beside and then among them so that nothing was visible but gray dykes of stones rising on either side to a height of twenty or more feet. It was like being in a trench. Suddenly, the boulders were behind me and the car rolled down a grass-grown street, toward a single line of empty buildings dwarfed by the proximity and height of the dredge dumps.

I cruised the length of the lonely street, surprised to find so many buildings still standing, especially three made of stone, whose arched windows and doors reminded me of similar ones I had seen in California's mother lode camps. In front of the one that had been both postoffice and store stood an abandoned dragline. In between these stone sentinels were old log cabins, frame sheds, and newer dwellings, all but one seemingly deserted. I knocked at the house with gay flowerbeds and wash flapping on the line, but no one was about. The road continued on beyond the street, climbing among trees toward distant hills, but it was too rough to attempt. According to a sign, Gold Hill was two and a half miles farther on.

As soon as the Stuart brothers and the other prospectors who reached Gold Creek in 1861-1862 found colors in the streambed, they began to explore the nearby creeks and gulches as well. The first group from Colorado, which arrived in June, 1862, found pay gravel on a small branch of Gold Creek and named it and their camp Pikes Peak. Another camp which sprouted in 1862 in the immediate vicinity was Yamhill, or Pilgrim Bar. The most important of all was Pioneer.

The discovery of gold on Grasshopper Creek, in the fall of 1862, drew many miners away from the area, including the Stuarts, who drove a large herd of cattle to Bannack and spent the winter there. Pioneer saw little activity from then until September, 1866, when the Pioneer Mining District was organized, with bar claims of 200 feet running back to the summit of the hill. When, in 1867, the Pioneer Company commenced using hydraulics on the banks, mining picked up, and Pioneer's population swelled to nearly one thousand. To bring sufficient water to the claims, the Rock Creek Ditch Company began to construct a thirteen-mile artery to supply the Pioneer, Willow Creek, and Pikes Peak Districts. The ditch was completed in 1868. By 1870 it is said that $20,000,000 in placer gold had been taken from the gulches and, according to the *Helena Daily Herald*:

The auriferous bar . . . worked now for the fourth year, still gives up its treasures . . . to the hardy miner. . . . The Pioneer Co. are working 25 men, both night and day shifts, and are making with pipes, uniform runs of $2000 and upwards per week. . . . In the gulches above the town at
French and Quartz
half a dozen or more companies are at work with ground sluices and hydraulics.
Pilgrim Bar
two miles west of Pioneer, over a low divide, is decidedly the liveliest camp on the West Side. The whole hillside, embracing an area of several miles of diggings . . . is covered with hydraulics, some 20 or 30 pipes, being in constant use.
July 20, 1870

All through the 1870's, Pioneer flourished, and as the population swelled, the number of business establishments kept pace. Four breweries and six saloons, in one of which six faro games ran simultaneously, and poker chips were bought with gold dust, were well patronized. Two hotels, a livery stable, four general stores, a blacksmith shop, a shoe shop, and a Chinese laundry did a brisk trade. Only one shooting is recorded, and that over a gold claim.

All this time, there were Chinese miners in the several camps. By 1871, Pikes Peak gulch was so nearly washed out that the white miners left. Fifty Chinese took their places, "using second water for which they paid ten cents an inch." The white miners received $5 a day, without board; the Chinese, $50 a month. The average mining season lasted little over six months, from April to November, even when ditches and reservoirs controlled the flow of water.

As the area was more fully prospected, new placer deposits were discovered, until, in addition to the diggings already mentioned, there were French Gulch, Squaw Gulch, Woods Flat, Wilson's Bar, and Trail Gulch, all considered part of the Pioneer District. In 1879, two hundred Chinese and between four and five hundred whites were working in the entire region and, as Leeson says: "Had the stampede of July 20, 1862, not occurred, the growth of the district would be of such a marked and permanent character that now a city would stand amid the great placers, instead of a village of 271 inhabitants."

Around 1875, Conrad Kohrs, a stockman and trader, came to Pioneer and bought up a number of mining claims and water rights, planning to leave them to his son as a legacy. He was ruthless in acquiring mineral land and froze out independent miners by cutting off their water. His plans failed to materialize, for his son died and, after some desultory placering at Pioneer, he quit mining.

Next, Tim Lee, an Oriental, brought a company of 800 Chinese to the gulch. For several years he directed these laborers, who patiently washed gold from the tailings and carried away the waste rock in baskets to restack it on new dumps. Finally, when they could no longer uncover any gold, they left. Tim Lee remained, a highly respected resident of the gulch and perhaps the only Oriental to be admitted to membership by the Masons. When he grew too feeble to look after himself, the Lodge cared for him. For a time, after the Chinese left, Pioneer was deserted.

In the early 1890's, an English syndicate, the Gold Creek Mining Company Ltd., sank test holes in the gravel and, satisfied that the streambed still held treasure, began to work the ground with a small dredge. A few of the older residents of the district, including Conrad Kohrs, resented the "foreigners," and harrassed them so persistently, by shutting off their supply of timber and water, that they reluctantly ceased work, leaving the dredge behind them. Their attorney, Charles R. Leonard, filed suit against their hecklers. The case dragged on for years and was not settled untile 1927. When Pat Wall, a mining man from Butte, offered to buy the English company's holdings, his offer was eagerly accepted.

Wall bought up the 3,200 acres held by the Kohrs-Bielenberg interests, which included water rights and the townsite of Pioneer. These two purchases, which gave him 7,000 acres of placer ground, permitted him to plan big-scale dredging on 6,500 acres and hydraulicking on 500 more. A $250,000 dredge, ordered from the Yuba Dredge Company of San Francisco, was shipped to the district on 42 freight cars, ready for assembling. A reporter for the *Montana Standard* explains the company's plans for working their ground:

An entire town . . . down in Deer Lodge valley was sold a few days ago. The purchaser is an old-time Butte man, Pat Wall. . . . With brick and stone and lumber will go apple trees brought in on pack animals and lilac bushes. Pioneer is to be fed into the maw of a huge dredge. . . .

Store and dwellings are being remodeled to form accommodations for one-hundred men who are building a new road . . . and preparing for the reception of a . . . dredge to be installed in January. The old post-office will be converted into a Bunk House. The Bank will be a restaurant, the bank vaults a pantry, for the building of dressed stone is cool enough to keep food fresh without ice. . . .

Up Pioneer Gulch the dredge will go, sluicing the territory crosswise like a loaf of bread. In time it will reach the ghost town of Pioneer. Meanwhile a new town is to be erected to house the workers. Old houses will be dynamited or moved away and the dredge will go on up the gulch, converting one of the liveliest towns to a pile of rubble.

October 27, 1929

Between December, 1933, and June, 1939, the Pioneer Placer Dredge Company, Inc., recovered a gross total of $1,374,631 from these gravels.

If Benetsee picked the first gold from this creek, as seems probable, Henry Thomas, better known as "Gold Tom," should also be remembered as having prospected near the site of Pioneer before the arrival of the Stuarts. Thomas, who drifted into the region from Lake Pend'Oreille during the summer of 1860, placered Benetsee Creek and sank a shaft on its banks from which he obtained some gold. The first wave of prospectors to explore the gulch found the remains of a crude windlass and four sluiceboxes hewed out with an axe, which it is believed he had constructed. Like most prospectors, he never stayed long in one place; so the first arrivals at Montana City found "Tom" there, washing gravel on Prickly Pear Creek.

BEARMOUTH

Within the Garnet Range of mountains (the northern boundary of the Deer Lodge Valley) quantities of gold lay hidden until swarms of prospectors picked the treasure from its gulches and slopes. The entrance to this rich area was through Bearmouth (formerly Bear's Mouth), a tiny village, eleven miles west of Drummond on Highway No. 10. Not that Bearmouth was a mining camp, but it played an important role when Bear and Elk Gulches teemed with miners.

John Lannen and his family moved from Bannack to Helena in 1865. Shortly after he obtained a mining claim, rumors of the new gold strike on Elk and Bear Creeks in the Garnet Range sent him scrambling across the Divide to the scene of activity, where he stayed throughout the winter. In the spring he returned to Helena, traded his claim for a cow, and with his wife and sons, returned to Bearmouth, where he ran a ferry across the Clark Fork (Hellgate River) to accommodate travelers on the Mullan Trail who were hell-bent to reach the mines. The ferry was just large enough for a wagon and team and was operated by a cable. Once, while the float was carrying two men and three pack mules, each loaded with 250-gallon barrels of whiskey, the cable broke and everything slid into the river. One man drowned, but the whiskey was saved. In time, Lannen built up quite a business by running a gold exchange, taking dust to Deer Lodge and returning with the equivalent amount in currency. He also had a milk route and managed a hotel.

In his log home, the Roman Catholic priest, Father Ravalli, celebrated mass for the first time in that region, probably in 1873. Thereafter, he and other priests conducted services at Lannen's for over sixty years. In the late 1870's, Father De Rycker (DeRyckere), from Deer Lodge, came over to Bear and on many of his visits was accompanied by two nuns — Sister Mary Louis and Sister Ann Joseph, the latter the first Superior of St. Joseph's hospital in Deer Lodge. They drove as far as Bearmouth in a carriage and then rode horseback up the gulch and across the divide to Elk Creek.

As the hamlet of Bearmouth grew, it became a stage stop on the Mullan Road and later a station on the Northern Pacific, whose right of way sliced through the Lannen homestead in 1883. Until a bridge was built across the Clark Fork, the mail carrier was forced to ford the river each day, protecting the mail sack by holding it above his head.

At the close of the century, the mines at Garnet were active and Bearmouth served as shipping point for the ore.

ELK CREEK and BEAR GULCH

To Ben Dittes of the *Montana Post*
from Bear Gulch, written by a responsible man.
"Friend Ben,"
You may "toot the old horn and blow the bazoo" as much as you please over Bear Gulch. It is enormously rich — claims are selling at $2000 and scarce at that. Pet Hall, Dave Thompson, L. C. May and other Virginia boys are here. The stampede is greater than ever known to any mines before.
The Elk creek mines are also thought to be big tho' not so well developed. This is reliable.
Montana Post, March 24, 1866

Late in October, 1865, a party from Last Chance Gulch, led by Jack Reynolds and composed of Bob and Joe Booth, and Charles Hickey, discovered gold placers on Elk Creek. Within a few weeks the surrounding gulches were crawling with prospectors, staking claims before winter closed in on them. Discoveries were made on Day, Deep, and Bear Gulches, and at First Chance, at the head of Bear Gulch. This last started a new rush which resulted in Bear Gulch being staked from one end to the other with most of the claims centering around its junction with Deep Creek, six miles above its mouth. Before long, the Elk Creek District had more than 6,000 men in it, some living in lean-tos and others sleeping under wagons until the first snow sent them burrowing into dugouts and hastily built cabins just big enough for a fireplace and a bunk.

REYNOLDS CITY

Most of the miners pulled out of the gulches during the winter and went to Deer Lodge to hibernate, only to hustle back in the spring, as soon as the snow began to melt. By March, 1866, the trail to Bear was again choked with prospectors of many nationalities — Spanish, French, German, and Irish — all eager to reach their claims or crazy to stake new ones. Two camps on Elk Creek — Eureka and Reynolds City — came into existence at once. Each was a mere handful of tents and log buildings which housed saloons, hurdy-gurdy houses, and a store or two. Supplies came by pack train by way of Lincoln or Helena, all the way from Fort Benton.

The pay streaks near Reynolds City were not so rich as those in other parts of Elk Creek, yet one claim is said to have produced $12,000 per running foot. The gold from Bear and Elk Creeks was deep yellow, identical in color and impossible to tell apart, except that nuggets were found in Bear Creek, and only flat flakes of gold in Elk.

Among the first arrivals at the Reynolds City Hotel were a well-dressed couple, J. B. Taylor and his wife, Letty. Taylor was a gambler, who in less than a month deserted the lady and disappeared. He had told her that if she would be a "drinking partner with the boys," while he fleeced them, he would build a cabin for the two of them when he had won enough dust. Dazed by his desertion, she went to work in a hurdy-gurdy house. Some of the "boys" felt sorry for the "sad-eyed lady," who danced with them but whose thoughts seemed far away. One evening Taylor entered the place, walked up to Letty, and looking her over said sneeringly, "Is this my wife? I suppose I have no more claim to her than the rest of you." "If we had, we wouldn't leave her to starve," replied the grizzled miner with whom she was dancing. At this, a bystander, Glen Lindsay, grabbed Taylor and knocked him down. There was a shot and a puff of smoke and Lindsay was dead. Taylor backed out of the saloon with drawn revolvers and escaped, but shortly afterward his body was found, hanged in Deep Gulch. Lindsay was buried near Reynolds City. After Taylor's death, Letty dressed in mourning and supported herself by sewing.

All mine locations had to be recorded at Deer Lodge, the county seat, and since the gulches were unmapped, the descriptions of claims were rather vague and might read: "commencing at a blazed pine about four inches in diameter, about 700 feet from the mouth of Gambler's Gulch." A Mexican, named Guayness, uncovered the first lode in the area. As Reynolds City grew and Elk Creek bristled with wooden stakes, claim jumpers made their appearance, terrorizing the area by murdering miners in their cabins for their dust or by shooting them down while at work. To put a stop to such violence, a miners' meeting was held at Reynolds City in 1865, at which an effective code was drawn up. Although the population of the camp never exceeded 500, its yield of gold, in two years, was $1,000,000.

EUREKA

Eureka (Yreka), also on Elk Creek, was a favorite spot for gamblers, who often cleaned up more gold at their games than the miners did from their claims. There were many Chinese in the camp, who came into the district with the white prospectors and stayed after they had pulled out. During the winter the camp was completely isolated:

For the last two months this quiet little camp has been almost entirely shut out from the surrounding world by the great depth of snow on the range between here and Beartown. Some articles of provisions were becoming scarce, and . . . something had to be done, so . . . every man shouldered his shovel and went to work. We opened the road to the summit,

and by the assistance of the business men of Beartown the road is now open for travel.

The New North-West, March 30, 1872

SPRINGTOWN and TOP O' DEEP

Springtown and Top O' Deep, still smaller camps on Deep Creek, were contemporary with Reynolds City. In the 1860's, William A. Clark held placer claims on the creek. All three camps were shortlived. Reynolds City, which in 1928 still contained a few skeleton cabins, Eureka, and Top O' Deep, are forgotten and inaccessible sites today, yet all three contributed to the nearly $2,500,000 in gold taken out by 6,000 miners while the district was active.

BEARTOWN

Beartown has also disappeared, but its span was longer and more colorful. The pay streak in both Bear and Deep Gulches was rich but narrow, with bedrock seventy feet below the surface. To reach it, the miners sank deep shafts from which the dirt was hoisted in buckets and then sluiced. The only available water was that from the creeks which ran full in the spring and early summer, fed by melting snows. When this water was gone, work ceased. To regulate the flow, storage reservoirs were built at the head of the stream and water was released a specified number of hours a day, with each miner using what flowed past his claim.

The gulch is said to have produced $1,-000,000 in silver and gold between 1866 and 1877. Strangely enough, only two men in the early days left the diggings with fortunes dug from their claims. Tom Keenan recovered $17,-000 from his ground by drifting, during the season of 1867, and Tom Hennessy, having amassed $25,000, went to Alaska and retired.

Beartown, at the junction of Bear and Deep Creeks, was crammed into a narrow, steep-sided gulch, with just enough space for a town plat of four blocks. No one paid any attention to the plat, however, and cabins faced in any direction, according to the miner's whim. The town proper was one-quarter of a mile long and 450 feet wide, with most of its buildings jammed against the hill on one side of its main street. Aside from dugouts and tents, it contained 17 saloons, several blacksmith shops, a brewery, livery stable, jail, slaughter house, drugstore, restaurant, Ball's Hotel, Abascal's general store, and Gee Lee's wash house. Above and below the townsite, prospectors' cabins stood at 200-foot intervals; for each man built on his own claim. Each miner kept barrels by the edge of the ditch, filling them at night so as to have water ready for the next day's sluicing. All the merchants owned claims and frequently closed their stores in order to mine.

Near the middle of the town stood the general store of the Spaniard, Joaquin Abascal, and his partner, the Frenchman, La Forcade. It was a large establishment which sold everything and to which nearly all the men in the gulch came for supplies or for a grubstake, which was never refused. Behind the store was a cellar built into the hillside where the proprietors kept their best liquors. The path between the cellar and the store was well-traveled. In addition to the wine cellar, Abascal kept a barrel of cheap whiskey in the store for free drinks. As Abascal knew no French, and La Forcade no Spanish, many of their ledger entries were unintelligible to each other. Joaquin Abascal came to the gulch with the first rush of miners and prospered until his generosity exceeded his profits and his paths to the wine cellar became too frequent. William A. Clark, who started out as a peddler, used to come to Abascal's store whenever he made the trip to Bear. Clark's sister was Abascal's wife.

The principal saloon was Pelletier's, a long, high-ceilinged, two story building with a balcony around the central room. It was elegantly furnished and well supplied with gaming tables and a mirror-backed bar.

At first, everything had to be packed into Beartown over a narrow trail. When a train arrived, the miners crowded around it, filling the dusty street with a jostling, noisy mass of men and beasts. The town had no officers; but an Irishman named McElroy was made justice of the peace by common consent after it was found that he knew legal terms and could use them fluently when he was drunk. When sober, he was tongue-tied. Whenever a case came up for trial, the "boys" saw that McElroy was well oiled and then presented their suit.

I am indebted to Mary J. Pardee, whose article about Beartown appeared in 1931 in the *Great Falls Tribune*, and contained the following stories. The first is about "Fightin' Bar," the recognized spot where men settled their arguments. When Mike Kelly tried to jump the claim of a Chinese miner, and its owner protested, the two went to Fightin' Bar

to shoot it out. Each hid behind a tree and for some minutes nothing happened. Mike got tired of waiting and cautiously peeked out. Bang, went his opponent's pistol, shooting Mike in the face. After he recovered, he claimed that he had been hit by his own bullet which struck that of the Chinaman and ricocheted.

Old Greenwood was one of the rough but good-natured characters of the town. He had no partner, so while working his deep shaft to bedrock, he talked to himself, swearing and arguing as he shoveled gravel into the ore bucket. After yelling to his imaginary partner to hoist the load, he would wait a reasonable time and then climb to the surface, curse his absent helper, and hoist the dirt himself.

Doctor Armistead H. Mitchell, who came to Deer Lodge from California in 1865, made the rounds of the mining camps and was always welcome. He was a good surgeon, especially when drunk, and performed many successful but unsanitary operations. One Saturday morning, the word spread that the doctor was seen riding up the trail. Since he always brought news from Deer Lodge and other camps, a crowd gathered outside Abascal's store, awaiting his arrival. But on this trip, "Mit," as the doctor was called, hurried inside to care for Shorty, who the night before had fallen, dead drunk, into his own fireplace and roasted his arm to a crisp. The operating table was a plank across two barrels, the anesthetic was whiskey, and with Shorty thus stupefied, the doctor sawed off the charred member and wrapped the bloody stump in a dirty cloth. When Shorty recovered sufficiently to stagger to the door, he beckoned his friends in for a round of drinks. The doctor, who was also drunk, collected the charred flesh and fragments of bone and put them in a sack, planning to take them home for further dissection and study. The afternoon was spent with Shorty, the doctor, and two cronies playing poker. In the evening a dance in honor of "Mit" was held at Pelletier's. It was planned by Madame Louise and attended by all her girls and by all the males in Beartown. When it broke up, early in the morning, the doctor mounted his horse and started down the trail, singing at the top of his voice and carrying Shorty's arm in a sack on his saddle. Somewhere along the trail, he lost the sack!

Holidays were never neglected. At Christmas, when snow blanketed their claims, the miners went to Deer Lodge, Helena, or Mis-

CENTER OF TOWN, GARNET

soula, for a bender. On the Fourth of July, someone always read the Declaration of Independence, and the miners raced their pack horses against Indian ponies on the flat at Bearmouth. For September 5th, Miners Union Day, every saloon laid in an extra amount of whiskey.

Bear Gulch was so narrow that there was no level space for a cemetery, only a steep slope above the level of the creek. This was terraced with stones so that bodies would not wash out after heavy rains or mudslides. No one thought of Beartown as a permanent place, so no attempt was made to plot a better location, and only seven persons were buried on the barren hill — two of whom were children, and one a Chinese. The rest of the bodies were taken thirty-five miles to Deer Lodge for interment. For nearly fifteen years, no road connected the two places, only a trail, down which a mule packed the body, and the mourners rode as escort, singing lustily both doleful tunes and dancehall numbers; for a trip to Deer Lodge meant both respectful concern for the

dead and a lively celebration for the living. Therefore, on such occasions, nearly all the miners trotted behind the corpse.

Before Mike Flynn died during the winter of 1870, his partner promised to give him a Christian burial. The corpse was rolled in a blanket and thrown over a saddle on a packhorse, which one of the "boys" led behind his own animal. Quite a few of Mike's friends went along with him. Near the mouth of Bear Gulch, the group divided, some of the men waiting while a man with a rip saw knocked together a coffin, and some going to Baron O'Keefe's to borrow a wagon and harness, so that two of the cayuses could be hitched up and the deceased driven the rest of the way. Since the horses were only half broken and harness-shy, the cavalcade did not get under way until the next morning and had only reached Pioneer Bar by late afternoon. Here, a stop was made for a drink. Flynn had not had a wake, so one was arranged, complete with candles and the coffin set on two beer kegs. One drink called for another, and by morning most of the boys had passed out. It was afternoon before two of them rode on to Deer Lodge to see the priest and dig the grave, and it was almost dark when the wagon and the rest of the miners arrived. One look into the wagon showed that the coffin was gone. The two drivers explained that, going down a hill, the vehicle had crowded the horses' hindquarters and, skittish as they were, they reared and bolted. The priest suggested that everyone go into Deer Lodge for the night and hunt for Flynn in the morning. By daylight, it was easy to see where the horses acted up, but it was some time before the coffin was discovered in the creekbed, standing on one end. After the water was drained from it, Mike Flynn was taken to the cemetery and buried with proper rites.

Beartown's boom years were from 1865 to 1869. By 1870 it was rumored that the gulch was worked out, and the larger part of its population left. Abascal and many others did not join the exodus, but continued to pan gold, so that, before long, a second boom brought newcomers to the district. This time, instead of being footloose prospectors, they were married men with their families.

By 1878, the need for a wagon road was so great that the following winter, which was an open one, work was begun. Everyone contributed labor or tools, and "Jimmy the Packer" loaned his string of mules. The completion of the road to Bearmouth linked it with the Mullan Road and ended the gulch's isolation. In 1881, the placer mines yielded $153,200; the following year, the output was $170,000. Even in 1893, when the gulch was believed to be completely stripped of pay gravel, $10,000 was taken out of Roger Bar, at the mouth of Deep Gulch. Probably no one can say just how much gold has been recovered from the area, but a good guess would be close to $30,000,000.

GARNET

In 1951, when I was looking for Bear Gulch, I stopped to ask directions from a woman whose house was close to the highway. "You won't have any trouble," she assured my friend Hazel and me. "The mail carrier, Mrs. McMahon, goes up every Friday. It's thirteen miles to Garnet and there's only one steep pitch at the Chinee Grade. It's only hard getting through in the winter. Sometimes even Aggie McMahon has to mush the last two or three miles on snowshoes."

Dredge dumps filled the lower end of the creek, but higher up were older mounds of discarded stones — sterile monuments to the rich placers that caused the gulch to teem with life during the frantic sixties. Occasionally, we glimpsed a broken-down cabin or shed hidden among big trees, or saw a section of rotting flume hanging above us along the face of a cliff. Where Deep Creek entered the gulch, we looked in vain for signs of Beartown. Beyond it, the steep pitch commenced, but not until we reached a series of short switchbacks, about three miles beyond the old campsite, were we sure that this was the "Chinee Grade" which freighters cursed. Somewhere nearby, one of the Chinese is said to have cached his gold, packed in five-pound baking powder tins, buried under a tree. We didn't realize how steadily we had been climbing on this hot summer morning until the car coughed and died. Vapor lock! While Hazel backed it onto a mine loading platform, I started on alone — Garnet couldn't be far away. The grade was steeper here, and the road was cut through lush green undergrowth and a dense forest of tall pine trees. I passed a mine, which I later learned was the Grant-Hartford, near which stood an old buggy whose wheels were entangled with vines, and before long I came to the first of many houses.

This was Garnet, The road swung in among the buildings, past an empty store marked "Post Office," and curved out of sight beyond the farthest shed. Several weathered stores with false fronts, a three story hotel with leaded glass windows, and a number of cabins made up the nucleus of the camp. Two or three automobiles, drawn up in front of as many cabins, and the sound of men's voices assured me that I was not alone; but nothing alive was in sight except a horse cropping mountain hay. While I sketched, a car whizzed by and, before the dust settled, a cabin door flew open, and a man called out, "Was that the McMahons?"

"I don't know, I'm a stranger here. Can you tell me something about this place?" I asked.

"Come on in. I'm batching while my wife's away. I'm Harry Bouton," he replied, leading the way into a big, clean cabin. We sat at a table and, as he talked, I wrote down what he told me.

"You probably know that placer gold was found up here in First Chance Gulch in 1865 and was recovered mostly by drift diggings.

The miners who stayed in the gulch all winter spent their time getting ready for spring work. They repaired their sluiceboxes and piled up the dirt which they dug, to have it ready for washing as soon as melting snow provided a good head of water. Did you notice how evenly the tailings were spaced down near Beartown? Each claim was two hundred feet, and a man had to dump on his own ground. The placer gravel contained some boulders too big to be moved by hand, and the water pressure wasn't strong enough to budge them; so the men made crude rollers of pine logs and worked them under the rocks by leverage. In this way they got at the dirt underneath. The Chinese were especially good at that sort of work.

"When the camps on Bear, Deep, and Elk Creeks began to play out, the miners who stayed on began to prospect for new ground and found it up here. Two new camps were built, Garnet, at the head of First Chance Creek, and Coloma, three miles north of here. Some rich gravel was also found in Williams Gulch and at the mouth of Cayuse Creek. Garnet was all placering at first. Then, about 1867, they looked for the mother lode and discovered three main veins and several pockets of rich ore. That was when the Lead King, the Grant and Hartford, and the Shamrock lodes were discovered. It was all gold around here, except for small deposits of silver, copper, and lead. Most of the mines paid for themselves from the start; for pay ore was found from the surface down. There were fifty active mines in the district at one time; the whole country is pockmarked with them.

"During the 1880's, there were a thousand men in Garnet and four thousand miners between Beartown and Coloma. The real boom came in the 1890's, whe the big outfits came in and consolidated some of the best properties. The Mussigbrod and the Mitchell is one property now and so is the Magone-Anderson. You passed the Grant-Hartford, where the buggy stood. The Nancy Hanks was one of the best producers. Sam Ritchey located it in 1873, but it wasn't developed 'till about 1896, when red ore was found in a shoot of the old shaft of the mine. That's when Garnet had seven saloons and three hotels and a daily stage between Bearmouth and Coloma. There were two mills in the district, one with ten and the other with twenty stamps, but there wasn't enough custom ore to keep them going for long. Most of the ore was trucked out

HOTEL, GARNET. *Reproduced courtesy of* THE BONANZA TRAIL, *Indiana University Press*

to Helena, Butte, or Anaconda for treatment. Between 1897 and 1917, the mines here produced $950,000, of which ninety-five per cent was gold and the rest copper and silver.

"In 1912 nearly half the town burned down and was never rebuilt. Only three hundred people lived here in 1916, although some leasing was carried on in both old and new properties. The real slump began in 1920 and lasted until the 1930's, when the price of gold rose to $35.00 an ounce. By the 1940's, most everyone had pulled out, and the district was idle until two or three years ago.

"Did you notice the schoolhouse as you came into town? Funny thing, it didn't have any windows. I've heard there were eight pupils in 1881. The town gets its name from the brown garnet rock around here. You can see a big outcrop on the hill north of the schoolhouse.

"One winter, years ago, Garnet was snowed in. When supplies got low one man, with a miner's lamp, found his way to Bearmouth by going underground through the mine tunnels. At Bearmouth, he made arrangements for supplies to be sent in as soon as packers could move their trains up the gulch. We get lots of snow each year. Last winter, thirty-two feet fell, but the greatest depth at any one time was seven feet. I had to chop steps in the snow to reach my woodshed, and my wife used to walk off the porch roof to get to the clothesline. That reminds me, she wants a screen door on this cabin and it's down at the mill where you say you left your car. Jump in my truck and I'll drive you down and pick up the door."

227

I was glad to ride and, out of curiosity, I watched the mileage to see how far I had hiked. It was 2,200 feet. I found Hazel still trying to start the Ford. With Mr. Bouton's help, she turned the wheels so that we could get a rolling start until the engine caught. Thanking him for all his information, we crept down the switchbacks and rolled to the mouth of Bear Gulch, the clutch jumping out of low gear on every steep pitch.

COLOMA

It was impossible to reach Coloma from Garnet in 1951, although the camp was but two miles away, and I did not have the time to make a second trip and approach it from the west through Potomac, so my information is gleaned from J. T. Pardee's U. S. Geological Survey reports made in 1917 and 1918.

Several mines were located, in 1886, along the main divide on Elk Creek, two miles southeast of Garnet, and these have been worked sporadically, "producing in aggregate $40,000-$50,000 in gold."

The camp of Coloma was liveliest at the turn of the century, while the Mammoth and Comet mines were in operation, and an estimated $200,000 in gold was taken from the Mammoth property. Since then, the camp has been virtually deserted.

Development of the Comet mine, three-quarters of a mile north of Coloma, in 1905, by the Quantock Mining & Milling Company, resulted in small returns in gold. In 1916 a tunnel was bored to crosscut the Mammoth and other veins.

As early as 1866, small gold-bearing quartz veins were uncovered by the placer miners and have been worked at different times to shallow depths. In recent years, most of the claims of the district have been idle due to litigation. One of these, the Pearl, situated on the divide between Deep Creek and Bilk Gulch, is reported to have once produced $20,000 in gold and copper ore.

COPPER CLIFF

Copper Cliff was another discovery of the early 1890's and caused a flurry of excitement at the time. Although only six miles airline southwest of Garnet, it was accessible only from Bonita, on a forest road up Cramer Creek, at the end of a ten-mile drive. The cliff for which the area was named was a vertical slab of rock at the foot of a slope, about one-third of the way downstream from the head of the gulch. The lower portion of the gully was narrow and the road steep. The Copper Cliff mine was toward the head of a "short steep gulch tributary to Union creek from the southwest." It was discovered in 1890 by W. P. Shipler, and was later sold to an English company that developed it extensively. Between 1905 and 1910, 310 tons of ore were shipped to Tacoma, Washington, for treatment and yielded 77,000 pounds of copper and a little gold and silver. The mine was idle for a time, but in 1916 it was leased to Bielenberg and Higgins, who further developed it.

CLINTON

The town of Clinton, seven miles west of Bonita, is completely bypassed by the present highway; so we had to hunt for an access road to reach the general store, where I hoped to gather information about the mines in the vicinity. The town is strung out along a main street which parallels the railroad, and many of its homes are hidden among shrubs and trees.

The proprietor of the general store suggested that I go see Mrs. Nettles, who lived in a yellow house at the end of a lane at the second turnoff from the main road. We found the lady, but all she could suggest was to drive about two miles up Wallace Creek, a little distance beyond the pond. We'd see the Copper Bell dump first, and then come to the Hidden Treasure. It was one of the oldest and best mines in the district. Right after it was discovered, it changed hands and before its new owners had sunk eight feet on it, they were offered $5,000 for it.

The Cinton Mining District, she told us, lies in the Garnet Range, a few mlies northeast of Clinton. Deposits were discovered in 1889 and a few mines were opened which produced small amounts of ore from time to time. The Charcoal mine, south of Clinton, yielded $15,000 in lead and silver. Between 1905 and 1912, a number of groups of claims were developed from which some copper ore was shipped, but between 1912 and 1916, the district was practically dead. Some properties have been reopened under lease since then, but no big-scale operations have resulted.

Reassured by her information, we started out, climbing beside and above the stream until we reached the pond. The road beyond the dam was narrow, and Hazel drove on to find a place to turn while I followed on foot, scanning the hills for mines and mills. After a quarter of a mile hike, I found the car by a cabin and Hazel talking to an elderly woman, Ann Rogers, who insisted we come in and sit down. Her big voice tumbled out facts about the gulch and its mines faster than I could jot them down, but from her pot-pourri of data, I learned that she had lived in Clinton from 1936 to 1939, that the Hidden Treasure was working at that time, and that she owned some claims adjoining it. She mentioned the Triangle mine and the Weston, below it, and said that the Bellevue was a mile farther up the gulch, "with switchback trails to it all over the hill." She also spoke of a big mill down by the Milwaukee tracks with salted dumps — evidently a promotion scheme. According to her, a lot of machinery, ordered for the mill, lay untouched for years in the railroad freight depot. I think she was a little disappointed that we weren't interested in dickering for a claim, although, as we left, she said, "Hell, there's not a claim to take up between here and Potomac."

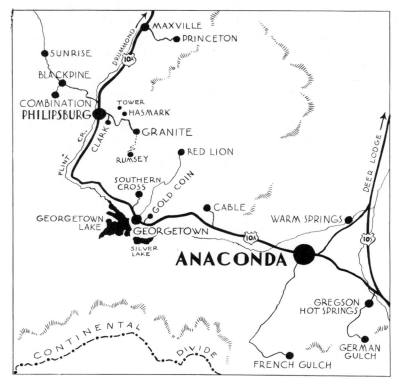

CHAPTER 14

CAMPS WEST
of ANACONDA

It was two years from the time that our friends, the Cooks, had shown my husband and me around Anaconda that I drove up to their house again. This time I had a different companion, Hazel Potts, a friend who not only likes to drive, but who also could snake a car up any roadbed without a tremor. I had told her about the Cooks and how Howard ferreted out all sorts of information about the old camps, and I assured her that the next day she would have a break from driving since we would go ghost town hunting in their car.

"How about going to French and German Gulches tomorrow?" Howard asked after dinner. "It's my day off at the smelter and we can get an early start. You'll have to take your car. We sold ours last winter."

GERMAN GULCH

The next morning, after a tremendous breakfast prepared by Arline, the four of us drove back toward Butte, across the waste-strewn flats, past Gregson Springs, to a side road marked Hi Rye Ranger Station. German Gulch lay fourteen miles south on the north end of the Fleecer Mountain Range.

For the first few miles the road twisted between hills and through a small canyon. When it ran in front of a ranchhouse and through a barnyard, we opened and closed the gates to prevent stock from escaping. Beyond the ranch were woods, and in the midst of the trees was the Rye Ranger Station. At the edge of the forest we entered a new valley, and after rolling through pastureland, dropped down to a small creek marked Beefstraight. A short distance beyond it and across a bridge, was a forestry sign pointing to a rough bench trail which rose above a stream. This was the way to German Gulch. The sign showed that it was four miles to Beale's Hill, and eight to the head of the gulch, but from the appearance of the roadbed, we were certain we wouldn't get very far. By careful driving we made it to Beale's Hill!

The creek was heaped with boulders — debris left from placering and hydraulicking. The road beside it rose steadily for four miles, in places leaving the stream far below it. It was very narrow and rocky but badly washed out in only two places. The mountainside which we were climbing was heavily timbered so that it was hard to look down into the gulch whose bottom was covered with old

230

GERMAN GULCH

workings. Finally, by rolling down a steep bank, we forded the creek. This side of the gulch was denuded of trees and showed the ravages left by big scale hydraulicking. Below the road level were pits and reservoirs rimmed with boulders in which lay rotting bits of wood and rusted pipe. Above the road, for a distance of thirty to forty feet, were ochre-colored banks of earth, gouged and runneled years ago by hydraulic Giants which, directed against the rich and sandy soil, had cut away the entire face of the hill.

The road ended abruptly in a mass of gravel and stones. Leaving the car to cool off, we started on foot to explore the empty camp. The whole gulch, from bank to bank, had been torn up. On the timbered side of the creek we could see five or six cabins in the trees and brush, and by crossing a dike, we were able to reach them. A still legible sign showed that one had been a restaurant. Another contained a sled and a couple of trunks as well as recent trash. A third yielded the lid of a chamber pot and a newspaper

dating from the 1890's. In still another, we found long underwear dangling from a peg and a sodden fur coat. Beside the dike on which we had crossed stood a barrel filled with water with a tin cup hanging from a nail near its rim.

As we retraced our way to the car, we noticed old flumes and a timbered pit, dug to bedrock, at least twenty feet below us. On the way down we spotted a broken cabin which may have been the brewery of which I had read. At the foot of the grade we read once more the forestry sign:

GERMAN GULCH
GOLD DISCOVERED 1864
PRODUCED MORE THAN $13,000,000
IN GOLD
POPULATION AT ONE TIME 1000.

"Who was Beale?" I asked Howard as we returned to Anaconda.

"Dr. George W. Beale was one of Montana's first doctors. He came to the gulch in 1865 and died in 1901. He was returning late at night from Butte, where he had gone for supplies, and just before reaching his home, his horse and wagon ran off the road, into the gulch, twenty feet below. Although miners were guarding a flume closeby, the noise of rushing water and falling rock drowned the sound of the crash. The doctor was unconscious when he was discovered in the morning, and died that afternoon. His grandson, who is now a middle-aged man, has lived in the gulch, in the old cabin known as the White House, ever since he was a baby. He has mined all these years, hoping to uncover the mother lode.

"The first arrivals in the gulch were eight men, originally from south Germany, who were returning from the Kootenay mines in British Columbia. They found the first gold in 1864. If I remember correctly, their names were Edmund Alfreildt, Fred Keis, Lewis Smidtland, John Schwartz, Fred Brown, John Sarex, Cris Meyers, and Fred Clump. They kept their discovery a secret until they were surprised, while at work, by a prospector, Charles Bass, who had followed their trail. The eight and Bass located additional claims above and below discovery for friends of theirs in Virginia City, and were ready, by February, 1865, to organize a mining district with Alfreildt as recorder. The same year, the Siberia District was laid out in the gulch, with gold yielding $15 to $18 a day, to the hand.

"Some say that the stampede which took place by the end of that month filled the gulch with a thousand men. Others believe the number was much smaller. At any rate, two camps were set up — Upper Town and Lower Town — which at their peak contained 110 houses and cabins. The trail up the gulch was a bearcat. It was not until 1870, when the trail was somewhat improved, that prices dropped. Until then, everything was sky high, with wheelbarrows selling for $25.00 and picks for $14.00. Even tobacco was $5.00 a pound.

"From the first, the camp had plenty of merchants. William Lincoln and John and William Vipond ran one grocery store and Hickman and Vance another. Charles Fitschen had a blacksmith shop and Henry Brothers opened a lumber yard. Brocky Johnson's mule trains packed in grub and packed out ore. There were two or three bakeries and the usual number of saloons. The first brewery was opened by William Rapp in Lower Town. Christian Nissler built the second one in the late 1860's. You saw the ruins of it today. A lot of men whose names were well known

in mining circles were identified with the gulch. Allen Green Campbell, for instance, and Charles S. Mussigbrod, Dennis Leary, Leo Foster, William Parks, T. N. Kleinschmidt, and the Porter brothers.

"The camp reached its peak between 1865 and the early seventies and was worked by bedrock flumes and hydraulics. During 1871, which seems to have been a good year, nine companies in the gulch were tearing off the heavy layer of topsoil with their Giants and making some good cleanups. At the same time, there were a good many Chinese in there too. They bought rights to mining ground that amounted to $61,000. That year two new claims were opened above Dr. Beale's ground — the first to be developed higher up the gulch than his property.

"Within a year or two, however, the gold began to give out and the miners left, all but the Chinese, who were content to work for smaller profits. They bought up the abandoned ground and worked it by washing and sluicing. I've heard that there were two hundred of them in the gulch at one time. Hing Lee had a store in the gulch from 1874 to 1878, when he was killed with a hatchet. Since his watch and chain and $7,000 disappeared, as well as some opium, two Chinese were suspected of the crime and arrested, but they were released for lack of evidence.

"They say that the first grave in the gulch was that of a man named Clark, a professional gambler, a big man and a bully, who enjoyed forcing a fellow named James Blake to play cards with him. Blake usually refused, until Clark grabbed him and made him play. Clark soon had all of Blake's money and Blake, frantic over his losses, shot Clark in the knee. Clark died of tetanus and, since no one knew anything of his connections, he was buried on the mountainside by the miners. Blake disappeared.

"There was also one hanging in the gulch. Sam Gowan and a man named Dowd were partners. They quarreled and Gowan stabbed Dowd with a butcher knife, wounding him seriously. Since he was expected to die, and there was no jail closer than Deer Lodge, the miners tried Gowan and sentenced him to be hanged. His only request was that he be allowed to keep his hat on. After he was dead, the hat was removed and the men discovered that he had a brand on his forehead. Dowd, the wounded man, recovered and left camp with a purse containing $1,000 which the 'boys' gave him."

FRENCH GULCH

All the way back from German Gulch, low clouds had been gathering. By the time we reached Anaconda, rain was falling steadily, making an afternoon trip to French Gulch out of the question. "You've been there. Tell me what you found and what you know about it," I asked Howard as Arline served coffee and buns to us in their cozy kitchen.

"Its history is very much like that of German Gulch," he began, "with placers discovered in 1864 and with the gulch yielding as much as a million dollars worth of gold a year up until the 1870's. The ground was then believed to be worked out, and the men left for better diggings. Even during the first few seasons, as soon as cold weather set in, the miners packed out and spent the winter in Silver Bow or Butte, returning in the spring after the first big thaw.

"From the seventies to the end of the century, the gulch was neglected. Then W. R. Allen located some valuable placer ground and by means of hydraulics made it yield good returns. He also looked for the quartz lead from which the gold must come, but I don't think he found it. By 1902 he had thirty men working for him. The three carloads of ore that he sent to the smelter averaged $15 to $36 a ton. In 1903, he went to New York to raise $100,000 for a cyaniding plant which he hoped to build in the gulch.

"Arline and I didn't find much at French Gulch when we went there last year, but it isn't hard to reach. It's only seventeen miles from Anaconda. We took Highway Number 43, southeast of the smelter, and drove along it most of the way. The last mile and a half, up the gulch, is over a good dirt road. We saw a few old cabins, and the gulch was all torn up by big-scale hydraulicking and by dredging. You've probably seen the dredge that was there, for it was dismantled and moved to the Prickly Pear Valley and reassembled at Jefferson City. Let me look in my file for a copy of a letter written from French Gulch in 1865."

Letter from Mountaineer City
French Gulch
Deer Lodge Co., M. T.,
August 31, 1865

Ed. Post:

Mountaineer City is located on a branch of the Big Hole some twelve or fifteen miles west of German Gulch. . . . The city already contains twenty or thirty homes, two or three stores, 2 blacksmiths and a shoemaker's shop, the usual proportion of whisky mills, a faro bank, and soon will have a hurdy-gurdy outfit in operation, which latter will be considered by practical miners as sufficient evidence of the richness of the gulch.

The length of the gulch is 2½ miles. About 20 claims have been located and are paying well. Some . . . yielded as much as $300 in a ten-hour's run. The gulch is shallow, not being more than 7-8 feet to the bedrock in the best paying claims, which said claims are located above discovery. The nearer the head of the gulch the further it is to bedrock. The streak is narrow which increases the difficulty of finding it. Some anticipate a big thing in the upper part of the gulch but 'gold is where you find it.'

The names of the gulches discovered and claimed are First Chance, Moose Creek, Lincoln, Oregon, California and American. Volcanic action is perceptible throughout this region, large ledges of lava being visible in many places. Many parties are actively engaged in placering.

Yours etc.
Big Medicine.
Montana Post,
September 16, 1865

On our last morning with the Cooks, we rose early, for they had planned a full day and had offered to guide us to several of the deserted camps that lay west of the city.

BLUE-EYED NELLIE

"What about the Blue Eyed Nellie mine?" I asked when we left the western limits of Anaconda and started off on the day's hunting. "All I've been able to find is that it was located in 1881 by the McCay brothers on quarry land owned by Frank Brown. The discoverers seem to have disappeared; for the next thing I found was that Marcus Daly bought the lime quarry for his company's use, and that Brown and W. A. Clark, as partners, operated the mine. When it was found to contain rich lead and silver, the owners built a small smelter on Warm Springs Creek, opposite the entrance to the quarry. They say that several hundred thousand dollars worth of silver and lead were smelted in the furnaces and shipped out before the veins petered out, about 1890. After Brown closed the mine, he went off to Alaska, looking for a new strike."

"I've seen where the smelter stood, but I didn't know what it was," Arline broke in. "They must have brought the ore down to the plant on a gravity tram. There's a black line on the hillside where the tram used to stand."

"All I can add," said Howard, "is that it

was in the Silver Lake area, a district near Brown's siding, about six miles west of Anaconda. There seem to have been a number of small silver mines and prospects in the district, of which the Blue-Eyed Nellie was the best. The only other names that I remember are the Antelope and Chain, Morgan Evans, New Year, Welcome, Silver Hill, and the Carp."

CABLE

Thirteen miles west of Anaconda we drew up beside a Montana Highway Department's roadside historical marker and read:

ATLANTIC CABLE QUARTZ LODE

This mining property was located June 15, 1867, the name commemorating the laying of the second trans-atlantic cable. The locators were Alexander Aiken, John E. Pearson and Jonas Stough. They were camped on Flint Creek and their horses drifted off. In tracking them to this vicinity the men found float that led to the discovery.

Machinery for the first mill was imported from Swansea, Wales and freighted by team from Corinne, Utah, the nearest railroad point.

The mine was operated with indifferent success until about 1880 when extremely rich ore was opened up — a 500 foot piece of ground producing $6,500,-000 in gold. W. A. Clark paid $10,000 for one chunk of ore taken from this mine in 1889 and claimed it was the largest gold nugget ever found.

Closeby, to the right of the highway was a good gravel road leading to Cable. For four miles it cut through a young forest, making a gradual ascent to a slanting meadow, where the remains of the camp stood. Three cabins, all of which were occupied, and a big barn with log sides and topped by a weathervane, constituted the town. Farther up the hill was a two-story boardinghouse, whose upstairs bedrooms still contained furniture. In the kitchen was a range, a sink, and a chair or two. Tattered wall paper above wooden wainscoting covered the walls. On higher ground stood the mill, its interior a jumble of firebricks and broken timbers, in the midst of which rested the big iron boiler. Outside were two or three tool sheds, iron balls from a ball mill, and a big settling pond.

As we walked back toward the car, a woman and two or three children came out of a cabin to meet us. She knew the Cooks, and when they told her why we were there, she said, "I wish my husband was here. He could point out a lot of things. There are two old tunnels run into the base of the hill, that were started in the seventies to cut the Cable lode at a depth of over three hundred feet. The

old toll road from Warm Springs used to run through here on its way to Southern Cross and Granite. Men used to walk over it, or pay five cents toll for a horse and buggy, and more for teams and heavy wagons. By the way, did you see the old Studebaker buggy in the barn? No telling how long it's been there.

"I've been told," she continued, "that the Cable ore averaged $18 a ton, but when they'd strike a pocket of almost pure gold, it would assay from $100 to $1,000 a ton. They sent a twenty-one pound block of it valued at $4,-000 to the New Orleans Exposition, and another collection of specimens to the Centennial Exposition. The ground was so rich that a cigar box full of samples was worth a thousand dollars. The first mill was rigged up with a steamboat whistle. A blast from it could be heard twelve miles on a clear day."

As the highway marker stated, three prospectors, Alexander Aiken, Jonas Stough, and John E. Pearson, while tracking their horses, which had wandered from camp, found float gold in June, 1867, and staked not only their original claim, but also five 200-foot claims above "discovery," and five below. The rich decomposed surface quartz was the outcrop of a great chimney of auriferous quartz in a dike of limestone. Before long, the men were positive that they had found a rich strike, for, by crushing the ore in hand mortars and hauling it nearly a mile to a stream, they could sluice out dust worth $30 a day, "to the hand." News of their strike attracted only mild attention and did not produce a stampede. Colonel James L. Fisk reported on the camp to the editor of the *Helena Weekly Herald* as follows:

Helena, M. T., February 27, 1868
. . . we drove . . . to the new . . . gold quartz and placer camps of Cable City and Georgetown, which have sprung up so rapidly as the natural consequence of the discovery and development of the famous "Atlantic Cable" lode and numerous other rich and extensive gold-bearing quartz ledges in its immediate vicinity. . . . The pioneers of this extraordinary camp . . . we found . . . to be men of intelligence, of extended experience, good hard sense and big hearts: . . . they are unassuming in their deportments, work hard, wear plain clothes and put on no airs. . . . At or near the present site of Georgetown, at the northern base of the Cable mountain they struck fair prospects for placer diggings, but, as Mr. Aiken informed us, those three men were obliged first to construct with their own labor alone, a water ditch four miles in length, which they completed in the Fall of '66, so that by the opening of the next Spring they were soon able to sluice out a moderate working capital for quartz prospecting. . . .

ORE MILL AT CABLE

BOARDING HOUSE KITCHEN, CABLE

BOARDING HOUSE, CABLE

On the 13th of June, 1867, in sinking a square perpendicular shaft in the midst of the forest and on a spot where there was not the slightest outcroppings . . . at a depth of about ten feet down through ordinary soil and pine roots, a small corner of this shaft, by the merest chance or accident, broke in upon rich looking gold quartz ore. All hands set at work for another day to strip or drift in as far as possible to prove their discovery; and striking such a mass of the richest gold ore they had ever seen, the proper locations were made, and one of the party proceeded to go immediately to Deer Lodge, about forty-five miles distant, and recorded on the 18th day of June, the "Atlantic Cable Lode."

By spring, they had made a contract with William Nowlan, a Helena banker, to erect a twenty-stamp mill, one mile down the creek from the mine, and to treat the ore they brought him for a charge of $11 a ton. In return, they agreed to supply the mill with 10,000 tons of ore. The mill, which had a capacity of forty tons, was built by Captain Plaisted and Nowlan, during the winter. The mill was not a complete success, for a large percentage of the gold was not recovered by amalgamation and "passed down the canyon." Despite this loss, $30,000 was realized within one year's time from the richest ores.

Soon after the mill was completed, Nowlan bought out the original owners and operated the property himself. He was not a practical miner and failed to properly timber the mine. In April, 1869, shortly after he sank a shaft to a depth of 148 feet and opened a drift which contained a large body of pay rock from which he was just beginning to receive a return, the whole mass, which had been supported only by stulls, caved in, completely closing the mine. During the ten months that the mine remained closed, the camp nearly died. By that time, Nowlan was in financial difficulties in Helena and, possibly as a result of accumulated reverses, he died.

In the fall of 1873, Salton Cameron, an expert millwright and blacksmith, was prospecting near the Cable lode when he struck quartz that was covered with gold. He quietly went to Helena to obtain capital with which to purchase the ground and erect a mill. A banker, L. H. Herschfield, loaned him the money, and Cameron bought the ground that he wanted, over which he held a controlling interest. His twenty-stamp Hanauer mill in which he crushed the richest of his ore was a success, a one hundred-ton lot yielding $20,-000. His ground proved to be a bonanza, for gold lay at the grass roots as well as deep in the earth. From this strike, he was able to pay all his debts and amass a fortune. Due to crude methods of mining, however, the pay shoot became lost in a wall of country rock, and, lacking ore, the mill was forced to shut down. During the early seventies, the mine worked very little; litigation, which started after Nowlan's death, prevented further exploratory work. Soon, both the Hanauer and Nowlan mills closed down. This left Cable camp with few inhabitants; so it was not surprising that a reporter, visiting it during this depression, wrote:

The first place of note is Cable, a forlorn looking town with two idle quartz mills, many deserted and torndown houses and but one solitary inhabitant. . . . The Cable mine follows the crest of the divide and stands nearly perpendicular into the earth. . . . The hillside below the discovery has been washed bare to the bed-rock, a distance of nearly 1000 feet. This alone yielded nearly $100,000. The ditch brought in for that purpose cost about $20,000 and is nearly twelve miles long.

Rocky Mountain Husbandman,
September 26, 1878.

With the arrival, the preceeding year (1877), of J. C. Savery, a brother-in-law of Nowlan, the next chapter of the Atlantic Cable began. Savery's attempt to acquire the mine resulted in the lengthy litigation already mentioned, but he ultimately secured the entire property and became superintendent.

Since Cameron had "left no ore in sight," it was necessary for the new owner to explore the working and develop whatever deposits he encountered. In 1883, he ran a long tunnel to the vein and also erected a thirty-ton mill which cost $65,000. Just as it was completed, he struck a rich body of ore from which he is said to have reimbursed his expenditures to the extent of $150,000, and all within thirty days.

High-grading was a common practice when Savery's foreman, named Jewell, was in charge. In 1883 alone, the amount of ore stolen was estimated at $60,000. Although the miners received the usual $3.00 a day wage, some seemed able to buy farms and build fine homes in the valley! Rumor also mentioned a village in Cornwall, England, which contained a street called Cable Terrace, honoring the mine whose stolen ore provided the residents with homes. To end such practices, Savery replaced Jewell with Harvey Showers. He installed a "dry" and made the men change their clothing at the beginning and end of each shift. This helped, but did not end the thefts.

During the 1880's, the mine's production was somewhat irregular. Large amounts spent in exploration might reveal nothing but barren ground, or might tap a new chute of picture rock. Toward the end of the decade, the output increased. Savery operated the property until 1891, when there was another shut down. The total production of the mine, up to 1891, was estimated at between three and four million dollars.

In 1902, two brothers, H. C. and F. W. Bacorn, signed a contract with Savery to clean out, retimber, and unwater the mine "to determine whether exploratory work was warranted." Later in the year, having organized the Cable Lease Mining Company, they began to operate the famous old property, obtaining $18,000 from their first cleanup. By 1906, the company was running three shifts a day in the mine. Eventually, the Bacorn brothers obtained the management of the property and continued developing it. The mine has been inactive since 1940.

Below the Atlantic Cable mine were placer diggings containing large amounts of float quartz. This ground, which belonged to Conrad Kohrs and Salton Cameron, was worked successfully between 1871 and 1874. During 1872, Kohrs constructed a ditch costing $10,-000 to bring water to the placers, but since it was not completed until late in the summer, his hydraulics were able to operate only for eight weeks. A snowstorm on October first put an end to further work that season. During this two-month run, however, 22,000 cubic yards of earth were washed down, yielding $18,000 or eighty-one cents per cubic yard in free gold.

The following year, the partners took out $37,000 of gold, one-quarter of which amount paid all their operating costs. In 1874, work was suspended so as to divert the water to the Georgetown placers. When they were worked out, the men returned to the Cable hillside, where they engaged in extensive hydraulicking, Cameron acting as superintendent.

Back on the highway once more, we continued west toward Georgetown Lake. As we drove, Howard briefed us on the area. "The mountains around here are full of ore and old camps," he began. "A map shows the various locations as close together, but because of ridges and gullies, roads to each mean miles of driving.

"As early as 1868, a number of tunnel companies bored into the hills, striking new

CABINS AT CABLE

lodes or extensions of those already opened. The hillsides and flats were placered with considerable success. Small stamp mills and a few arrastres were built on many of the properties by the locaters until there were mills running at all of the following mines — Southern Cross, Pyrenees, Twilight, Glenn, Gold. Coin, Red Lion, Milwaukee, Hidden Lake, and Stuart. Because of these mines, the camps of Georgetown, Southern Cross, Gold Coin, and Red Lion were born. In time, as more properties were developed, their owners clamored for custom mills for their ore, which would spare them the expense of building their own. Most of the small mills were at the diggings, while others, like the Gold Coin, were some distance from the shaft. We'll pass the Gold Coin mill on the way to Georgetown, but there's not much to see nowadays and we probably won't stop to explore it."

GEORGETOWN SENTINELS

237

GEORGETOWN

There's little left of Georgetown except two good-sized log cabins, one of which was a store, and the other a saloon and hotel. In 1900, a reporter noted that newspapers from California, pasted on the walls, dated from the early seventies. It was a placer camp and came into existence in 1868 when prospectors found nuggets in a little stream that crossed Georgetown Flats. At the news, miners from Cable stampeded to the new diggings, as well as others from more distant camps. During this excitement, placer claims were staked all the way from the Flats far up into the hills, and while the gold lasted, everyone had money and lived well. About 1872, the placers began to play out.

Some miners with money tried working down the hills with hydraulics. Then miners tried quartz mining and the camp seemed about to be revived. Good ledges were found . . . and after much expense, ore was discovered, but it was all too low grade to be worked at a profit.

Anaconda Standard, October 7, 1900

Yet mines such as the Eureka and Pyrenees were worked with some success, the latter for a period of ten years. The Pyrenees, one of the first properties owned by Salton Cameron, even warranted the building of a five-stamp mill which he operated with profit.

The first ore mill in the Georgetown area, the Stuart, is described in the October 7, 1900, issue of the *Anaconda Standard*. In it, Thomas Stuart of Deer Lodge tells the story of the mill:

The stream from which the waterpower came was a spring at the headwaters of Flint Creek. . . . Billy Wilson and John Fifer, in about 1867 or 1868, took the water right and started a sawmill there. I bought and ran it as a sawmill for a time and then, about 1875, changed it to a quartz mill to work ore from the Rosy Whitford lead. Dr. Whitford and others located the lead, a mile northeast of the mill and between it and Georgetown.

Several years before this some fellows had set up a quartz mill at Georgetown, but it failed to pay and shut down. I bought their machinery and took it to my mill. The Rosy Whitford was not a success. It ran on ore four weeks and quit. . . . The mill then ran on custom ore, the miners from Georgetown and all over bringing in ore. About 1878 I sold out the mill to Salton Cameron and Robert Kelly. They ran it for a time, then Cameron moved a portion of the machinery to a mill near Georgetown. The site on which the old mill stands is patented and it and the mill are the property of the Cameron and Kelly heirs. The last twelve-to-fourteen years it has not been operated.

The writer of the newspaper article then describes the property as it was in 1900:

The old Stuart mill . . . is a mile off the main road between Anaconda and Philipsburg. It stands on a knoll overlooking the Flats. . . . The stream that worked the mill is between weed tangled banks nearby, flowing away from the dam above. . . . The flume brought water into the mill through an entrance near the roof and dropped it upon the over-shot wheel. . . . The wheel was 21 feet in diameter and was made of fir. . . . The mill contained a battery of five stamps, each weighing 800 pounds. [There was also] a crude blacksmith shop.

By 1880, Georgetown's population had dwindled to fifty, and by 1886, the town was through. Save for the two cabins, the site is obliterated by a second growth of forest which has masked old stumps and excavations. Even the Flats are covered by an artificial storage lake, built by the Montana Water, Electric Power and Mining Company, whose plant provided power for the Bi-Metallic mines at Granite during the early 1900's. The lake covers 3,000 acres and has a twenty-mile shoreline.

SOUTHERN CROSS

"That's Southern Cross up there, isn't it?" I asked, pointing to a group of rusty buildings on top of a flat-topped hill on the right as we left Georgetown. "The first time Hazel and I were out here in 1951, we drove up there. The road was good and the view of the valley was superb. There were a number of big buildings which looked like company boarding-houses and plenty of smaller houses on several streets. One false-fronted store and a few other buildings stood in a grove of big pine trees. I remember seeing quite a few mine dumps, too.

"It was early morning and smoke was coming from the chimney of a small cottage. I went to the door and a man answered my knock. He told me I was in Southern Cross, a gold camp that dated from the seventies. It was named by a sailor. Another mine up there was called the Pleiades. The old stage road from Anaconda used to run through Cable and Georgetown to Southern Cross and on over the mountain to Philipsburg. He also said that the mines quit running about 1941 and that many of the houses had been taken away since then. Five hundred people lived there at one time; he was one of eight who remained. He added that the camp had an elevation of 7,000 feet and that it was pretty rough staying there through the winter when the snow lay

STORE, SOUTHERN CROSS. *Reproduced courtesy of* THE BONANZA TRAIL, *Indiana University Press*

COMPANY HOUSES, SOUTHERN CROSS

four feet on the level. The mine properties belong to the Anaconda Company now."

"I can't add much to that," said Howard, "except that the camp was active in the 1890's when Salton Cameron, who did a lot of mining in this district, erected his ten-stamp mill. On account of the amount of iron contained in the ore, only about fifty to sixty per cent of the flour gold was saved by the copper plates used in the mill. In 1906, the mine was producing, but by 1914, the place seems to have been almost abandoned."

His statements tallied with information which I found in the following news items:

Messrs. Cameron and Piatt . . . left on an evening train for Butte to attend a meeting of the Trustees of the Southern Cross mine. They had had a cleanup on Thursday and the retort showed 98% gold, which was made into a brick valued at $4,000. A number of car loads of ore have been shipped to Helena and Butte. A meeting of stock holders was held last night, preparatory to the establishment of a twenty-stamp mill at the mine. The new mill is to be the property of the company and run in connection with the mill now in operation, which is the exclusive property of Mr. Cameron.

The New North-West, February 21, 1890

Gold From Southern Cross

Lucien Eaves came down from the Southern Cross mine yesterday, bringing a bar of gold weighing 242 ounces, and valued at $3000. He is manager of the property and is turning out these bars quite often. He has ordered three new 30-ton cyanide tanks. . . . He has $600,000 worth of ore in sight and has only begun to open up the veins. The mill is new, and has only been in operation about two months.

Philipsburg Mail, July 13, 1906

RED LION

"It's good to have someone along who knows the way," I said when Howard pointed out a gravel road close to Georgetown and we started the seven and a half mile climb to Red Lion. This camp was not so old as the others; the first mention of it that I found spoke of a mill built by the Red Lion Company in the later 1890's. It, like so many others, was not a success, for "fifty per cent or more of the gold passed over the plates." It was therefore abandoned.

In 1906, the district was "looking up," with nearly two hundred men at work and two mills operating. At this time the Milwaukee Gold Extraction Company became extremely active. According to the *Philipsburg Mail* of March 16,

Manager Geo. H. Savage of Milwaukee was in the city yesterday on his way to the mines in the Red Lion district. His company will install machine drills and work has been commenced in a tunnel about 300 feet from the mill and this is to be driven into the mountain to open the Hannah mine at a depth of 700 feet. . . . The Hannah vein is sixty feet wide and beside gold values carries 40% iron and traces of copper.

A lot of machinery is en route from Chicago. The main water supply of the mill has been frozen up since early in the winter but there is a spring near that will furnish sufficient water for boilers to run the air compressor.

The company is putting in a stock of merchandise at Red Lion camp, for the accommodations of the men employed there.

A later notice, June 15, 1906, continues the record:

Development work will be pushed the coming season on about 15 of the 30 claims owned by the company and the tunnel that was started on the Thurston claims will be driven to the contact where it is believed large bodies of gold-copper ore exist. All minerals in this tunnel show the existence of copper veins.

. . . An aerial tramway was installed last year. Ore is now delivered to the mill, a distance of 3800 feet for less than 70 cents a ton.

. . . The Golden Eagle Co., located three miles below the Milwaukee Gold Extraction Co., resumed operations and a stamp mill will be erected this summer. John Wagner, president of the company . . . started work this past week upon bunk houses for the men.

Hazel found the winding road easy driving. Where it forked, the right branch climbed through trees and showed little travel. Some distance short of our destination, we came to an abrupt stop. Although it was the middle of June, snowbanks covered the road much too deep to drive through. Farther ahead lay a blanket of white. We could hardly believe our eyes.

"I've been here once before," said Howard when we had recovered from our surprise. "I'm sure that Red Lion is only a mile from here. You probably won't get back to these parts for years. Are you game to hike through the drifts? I'll break trail."

Leaving Hazel and Arline to visit in the car, we two fanatics started out. The farther we went, the deeper the snow became. Sometimes we were on the road and sometimes beside it, clamboring over rocks and patches of exposed grass, and, more than once, picking our way across clear mountain streams. Much of the time, we walked on the crust of the snow, only to crash through it up to our knees.

RED LION

Howard pointed out animal tracks — imprints of coyotes, rabbits, and deer. The going got harder, but we mushed on.

Finally, through the trees, we saw terraced rock foundations and a few buildings. Standing on the edge of a snowbank, I looked across a white meadow to the deserted camp. Straight ahead were the foundations of the mill, burned, Howard told me, during World War II, when men came to get its machinery for scrap metal. Higher on the hill stood what may have been a small restaurant or saloon, a blacksmith shop with an anvil, a rustic boardinghouse with overhanging eaves and an outside staircase, leading to the upper story. Behind it, a wooden catwalk led down to the stream, in the bed of which lay a "cooler," used no doubt in lieu of an icebox. Howard discovered a fire station with hose reel and hydrant, and he pointed out the most interesting ruin of all — a metal vault standing in the middle of a wooden platform — the floor of a building whose walls and roof had disappeared. Was it a bank, or was it the company office? A few tram towers were visible above the mill as well as more cabins scattered through the trees.

The sun was hot, raucous blue jays flew excitedly about, and our feet were icy cold by the time we started the long trek back to the car. Never had a Ford looked so inviting and cozy. While we wrung out our soggy socks, Howard listed the important mines of the once active camp: Red Lion, Hannah, Modoc, American Flag, Montana, Greater New York, St. Thomas, Golden Eagle, Flint Creek, Northern Cross, Yellow Metal, Nineteen-Hundred, and Robinson.

"The next town we go through is Philipsburg," said Howard as we descended Flint Creek Hill to enter a broad valley of the same name. "Philipsburg has always been a mining center and most of its buildings date from its boom days. The Kaiser Hotel is still on a corner of the main street, although it isn't a hotel any more. It's too bad the last mining company that owned the Hope mill tore it down in 1922, because they thought it was unsafe. It was a historic landmark, built the year the city was laid out."

241

PHILIPSBURG

Philipsburg is the hub of a mining district made famous by its silver deposits. Most of the camps which surround it are ghosts today, or mere sites, but during the eighties and nineties, when they were booming, they looked to the "Burg," as it was called, for their supplies, as well as for much of their gaudier recreation.

When Hector Horton, an adventurer from California, wandered alone into the Flint Creek Valley, in the fall of 1865, he was looking for gold. In his prospecting, he uncovered outcroppings of quartz and staked the Cordova lode. The following spring, he went to Silver Bow and told of his discovery. This started a stampede to the valley. The St. Louis & Montana Mining Company were, at the time, operating a small smelter at Argenta. Upon learning of Horton's strike, they investigated the area and acquired the Comanche — discovered in June, 1866 — and the Hope claims, located earlier still, near the summit of a hill, one mile north of where Philipsburg stands. In 1867, the St. Louis Company built a road to their properties and erected the first mill in the district. Some say that they brought their smelter from Argenta to the new site; others insist that the machinery for the mill was freighted from San Francisco.

Philip Deidesheimer, credited with the invention of square-set mine timbering, which was first used in the Comstock mines of Nevada, was brought to Montana by the St. Louis Company to superintend the erection of their stone mill. This $100,000 Stuart mill (named for James Stuart) was equipped with "ten 650-pound stamps, 6 one-ton pans and 3 six-foot settling tanks all driven by an 80-horse-power engine and boiler." The treatment of silver-bearing ore by pan amalgamation was successfully developed in the Washoe District of Nevada. Its use was equally successful here. From the day it started crushing silver from the Comanche lode, until its demolition in 1922, the Hope mill, as it was later called, handled large tonnages of silver. At the time of its erection, it was unique for it was the first silver amalgamation mill in the Territory and therefore attracted wide attention.

In 1867 the St. Louis Mining Company was organized as the Hope Mining Company. The Hope claim, the first to be developed by this company, was worked with moderate success until 1881, when a large body of rich ore was uncovered. That year the mine produced about $361,000, and thereafter yielded from $100,000 to $200,000 annually until 1887. When this ore body was exhausted, production fell off until another rich deposit was discovered, in 1892. Soon after the discovery of the Hope mine, other locations, including the Comanche Extension, Cliff, Franklin, Trout, Gem, Poorman's Joy, and San Francisco were made.

The development of the mines and the success of the Hope mill caused a camp, named for Philip Deidesheimer, to be laid out in June, 1867, on a small tributary of Flint Creek, south of the Hope mine. With reference to the naming of the camp, Dan Cushman of Great Falls wrote me in 1953:

At Philipsburg the mill was altered to the Washoe process by Philip Deidesheimer of Comstock fame with such great success that the new camp was named for him. I guess "Deidesheimerburg" threw them.

Perhaps the earliest account of the town is given in the *Montana Post* of August 10, 1867:

A Week in Flint Creek

Philipsburg is scarcely thirty days old and is increasing at the rate of one house per day, with tents and wagons innumerable, which give the place a business-like appearance . . . . A ten-stamp mill, belonging to the St. Louis & Montana Co., is being pushed forward . . . under the superintendence of your worthy townsman, H. Countryman. . . . It seems certain that not more than one in a hundred claims will amount to anything except to the recorder. There are a few lodes that give promise. Among the first is the Comanche lead, discovered in June, '66.

The political atmosphere of the district is rather mixed. As the fall campaign draws near the excitement increases. . . . Give us a loyal man to represent loyal Montana such as W. F. Sanders, and he may count on the support of

Old Flintlock
Philipsburg, August 5, 1867

Before the end of the year, Philipsburg contained 250 houses and boasted a population of 1,500. Everything was expensive. Lots cost $1,200 and lumber sold for $100 per thousand in gold. Colonel James L. Fisk, who toured the mining camps, visited Philipsburg in its infancy and sent his impressions of it to the *Helena Herald*, where they were printed on February 28, 1868.

A Trip to Philipsburg & Cable City

Helena, M. T.
February 25, 1868

The number of laboring and business men wintering in Philipsburg will reach as high as 600. . . . While there I counted as many as 170-odd buildings in the town proper, many of which are of the neatest and most substantial character. There are on Main St., quite a number of well-finished and commodious two-

story business houses and several hotels; buildings far superior in size, solidity and appearance to many of the tenements along the business portion of our own Helena main street.

In the town proper are to be found 6 general assortment stores; 7 saloons two of which are billiard halls; 3 first-class blacksmith shops, 2 lager-beer breweries; 3 livery sale and feed stables; 1 Masonic Hall in a second story and fully as spacious and creditable as one in Helena; 2 doctors; 1 portable steam saw mill. A large two-story hotel, recently finished, has been leased by the Helena Herald Co. for a branch newspaper and job office. There are also several restaurants and bakeries. As yet the only genuine hotel is the Dana.

The Masonic Hall, mentioned above, which cost $6,000, was the scene of festivities early in 1868:

Masonic Party at Philipsburg

It is described as a grand affair. Seventy-seven "numbers" were out, *eleven* of which were held by ladies. An elegant supper was served up at Dana's Hotel, and all was as merry as that bell which stands at the entrance of the state of matrimony.

Helena Weekly Herald, January 9, 1868

The Hope mill ran steadily until 1869 and then experienced a recession, as fewer rich pockets were found in the mines and too much silver escaped into the tailings. Milling costs continued high, since salt, which was needed in large quantities as flux, had to be brought from Utah at a cost of $120 a ton. Freight rates also absorbed the profits, especially when several shipments of refractory ore had to be hauled by wagon to distant railheads and then forwarded to Reno, to San Francisco, and even to smelters in Germany and Wales for processing. That year the young camp almost died.

A DESERTED VILLAGE

Its streets were empty, its buildings tenantless, the mines were deserted. . . . Silence and Solitude reigned almost unchallenged. Of 1500 people only three remained — Henry Imkamp, E. B. Waterbury and J. M. Merrill — and for one day Henry Imkamp was alone in the camp. . . . Alone in the little city, with its hundreds of closed doors and cheerless windows, the great mill towering like a specter of departed life, and the broad street grass-grown and deserted. . . . But

Life Came Back to the Camp

In 1870 Purvine & Schneple leased the mill and the town again picked up somewhat. In 1872 Brown & Plaisted leased it and run through a considerable amount of rock, and Col. Lyon crushed some 500 tons of Trout ore for the Imperial Co.

New North-West, August 27, 1875

The article continues with mine statistics until halted by the following editorial comment:

(The extent to which the reporter is elaborating his notes compels the managing editor to choke him off at this point until next week, when other operations and mines will receive mention.)

During this lean period, Cole Saunders organized the Cole Saunders Silver Concentrating Company to smelt ores from Poorman's Joy and other properties, and two furnaces were erected near the town only to be abandoned because of lack of suitable fluxes. The company then leased its mines and works to the Imperial Silver Mining Company, which in 1871 erected a five-stamp dry crushing mill equipped with a reverberatory roasting furnace — efficient but expensive. By 1873 the camp was returning to life as men resumed work and reopened the mines. One of these was the Speckled Trout.

When the Hon. A. B. Nettleton met James K. Pardee in Cottonwood Canyon, Utah, in 1874 he induced Pardee to go to Montana with him to look at the mining property in which he was interested. The pair arrived at Philipsburg after a 700-mile stage ride and hurried to Trout Hill where lay the Speckled Trout and other mines. Pardee's report was so satisfactory that Nettleton and his friends, who held a bond on the properties, paid off the balance due, which amounted to $151,000 and with the help of eastern capital formed the North-West Company. Pardee was made resident manager. By this transaction the North-West Company obtained the Poorman's Joy, Kitty Clyde and Pocahontas mines as well as the Speckled Trout, a valuable mine located in the late sixties and owned by Colonel W. F. Sanders. To handle the accumulated ore the North-West Company built a mill in 1875, one mile from Philipsburg. Within a year Troutville, described in the papers as "quite a little burg," grew up around the North-West mill.

TROUTVILLE and TOWER

It is a cosy, mountain-locked Y-shaped townsite, well sheltered, and has twenty or more cabins already occupied. Here live most of the miners and mill employees and soon Col. Vaill and Mr. Pardee with their families will locate there. There is a boarding house and a storehouse. No liquor is sold in the camp.
New North-West, Sept. 3, 1875

This settlement, better known as Tower, was named for Charlemagne Tower, who, with A. B. Nettleton and other Philadelphia capitalists, controlled the North-West Company.

Mines in the immediate area included the Salmon and the Gem, both on Trout Hill, the Little Emma and Osage. Ore from the Algonquin, one of the first locations in the district, and from the East Comanche mine, was worked in a ten-stamp mill erected by the Belmont Company. In 1877 the Algonquin and other mines south of the Trout were bought by a Philadelphia company and developed extensively. The Algonquin vein was four feet to six feet wide and averaged forty-five ounces of silver to the ton and from $1.50 to $3.00 in gold. As the vein widened to twenty feet, the values increased to several hundred ounces to the ton. When still richer ore bodies were tapped, a twenty-stamp mill was erected by the owners — the Algonquin Company — at Hasmark,

HASMARK

another small settlement one-half mile south of Tower. Its location and growth are described in the *New North-West* (December 5, 1879), as follows:

About one-and-a-half miles due east of Philipsburg on the north side of Frost Gulch, a rocky and precipitous ravine, resting gracefully on a permanent foundation of primal granite . . . is a new, solid structure, the Algonuin mill. . . . Up the gulch a few hundred feet south of the mill is the town of Hasmark, of contemporaneous birth. Its growth has been rapid, and its regular, wide street, lined with tasteful and well designed cottages, exhibits arrangement and detail creditable to the builder and originator of all this vast enterprise.

Quantities of mining timber and cordwood are stored about the mine and mill, and cutting the hillsides in every direction are roads leading to an inexhaustible supply for all future demands. Store houses for salt and general supplies and a large assay office are near the mill. The company boarding house in the rear is not a pretentious nor beautiful edifice, though it presumably answers the requirements of Chinamen who have it in charge.
'Sand Bar'

The Tower and Algonquin mills were both "dry crushing plants in which silver ore was treated by the Reese River Chloridizing roast and by the pan-amalgamation process." Each plant cost $150,000. The Algonquin mill's twenty stamps started to drop in February, 1880. As needed, additional stamps were added until there were eighty in all. The mill was highly successful in treating large quantities of low-grade ore. It shut down in 1883.

In scanning old papers, I found but one item of interest concerning Hasmark, other than mining news:

MINERS' UNION HALL, GRANITE

Jack Yandell shot and killed Wm. Hartly at Hasmark, near Phillipsburg last Wednesday, in a desperate fight about a town lot. Hartly knocked out teeth, split the tongue and fractured the skull of Yandell, before he was fired upon. The death shot was from a needle gun and entered the heart and passed out at the back.

The Atlantis, September 1, 1880

PHILIPSBURG (Continued)

By 1878, Philipsburg was again a thriving community with

two hotels, the Kaiser House and the Silver Lake. The Good Templars lodge . . . (with a) membership of 100 is made up of the working miners, mine owners, superintendents, their wives, sons, daughters and respectable business men of the town. The lodge has a fine organ, good furniture, a full treasury, and is about building a fine hall 22 x 80 feet.

WILL
Rocky Mountain Husbandman,
September 26, 1878

In 1881, the Good Templars Hall was completed with the first story "owned by W. T. Allison & Co., carpenters and builders." The two-story Kaiser House, already mentioned, with its porch extending halfway around the building and a fine bar and billiard room in the basement, was promised "when completed" to make "Philipsburg next to Helena in the way of fine hotels."

The city's boom years lay between 1881 and 1893. Business supported Kroegen's brewery, McDonald's Opera House, two banks — the First National and the Merchants & Miners' — and many other establishments. With the completion, in 1883, of the Northern Pacific's tracks to Drummond, the cost of ore shipments dropped appreciably, and, when in 1887, a branch line between Drummond and Philipsburg was put into operation, further cuts were made.

Although various denominations held services as early as 1875, the *Helena Weekly Herald* of January 1, 1880, points out that

Philipsburg . . . has a neat schoolhouse but *no church*. The Gospel is seldom dispensed here. Occasionally a mild-mannered, slender-waisted young man comes to see us and deliver a May morning, softly murmured, zephyr-like discourse. Miners, as a general thing, don't like things too mild or too much diluted. The waters of regeneration, dispensed as a gentle mist, will fail to penetrate the moral gum coat of the miner's conscience.

The Episcopal Bishop Tuttle, accompanied by Reverend Gilbert of Deer Lodge, visited the camp in August, 1875. Thereafter, Reverend Gilbert held services once a month, first in the Masonic Hall, next in Moore's Hall, and finally, in the schoolhouse, until St. Andrew's Church was built. The first Methodist sermon was preached in the fall of 1875, in the dining room of the Plaisted Hotel. St. Paul's Methodist Episcopal Church was built at a later date. The Presbyterians organized in 1891; the Roman Catholics were without a resident priest until 1892.

The silver crash in 1893 crippled production, although certain of the mines and mills attempted to carry on. James Patten's Sweet Home mill and the Hope operated on a limited basis, but with the majority of the miners gone from the area in search of jobs in gold and sapphire mines, Philipsburg was quiet. In 1906, a rise in silver prices permitted the milling and marketing of low-grade ore formerly considered worthless. World War I revived Philipsburg once more, as lack of ships prevented the importation of manganese from South America. When it was known that large quantities of this mineral existed in the area, the big steel companies began to buy it up. For months during the war, over 200 men were employed in mining and shipping as much as twenty to thirty carloads a day of the strategic metal. The end of the war brought another relapse, until new uses for manganese caused the concentration plants of the Trout Mining Company and the Moorhead Mining Company to manufacture manganese dioxide. This product, used in radios, flashlights, telephones, and ignition batteries, has kept production going. In 1929 it was estimated that 30,000 tons of manganese were used annually in the United States for dry batteries alone. Of this amount, ninety per cent came from Philipsburg.

GRANITE

Granite is the ghost of a great silver camp. The road to the once famous "Silver Queen City" leaves Philipsburg at its eastern boundary and immediately pulls up the mountainside, away from the Flint Creek Valley, never leveling off, but rising steadily on a shelf cut into the side of Granite Mountain. It is apt to be rough and at the end of four miles, just when you wonder if you are going to get there, the first cabins come in sight.

The great silver mine on top of the mountain, whose output in 1889 ran between $250,000 and $275,000 a month, was discovered in the autumn of 1872, but the location was allowed to lapse. There are several apocryphal stories as to how the mine was found, but all agree that the discovery occurred on July 6, 1875. The stories start with a hunting expedition in which Eli D. Holland shot at a deer near the peak of Granite Mountain. Either in its death struggles, or as it bounded away, the animal's hooves scraped bare some rock which proved to be an outcropping of silver ore. A more skeptical writer states that, "The granite fissure had an exposed outcrop and consequently had no aid from the deer. . . . Its discovery was an ordinary occurrence. . . . The act of locating it was purely perfunctory on the part of Holland."

After Holland took a sample of rock to Philipsburg to be assayed and learned its value, he and two friends, James W. Estell and Josiah M. Merrell, located a claim. This was the beginning of the Granite Mountain lode. The following year, the three owners made a deal with a miner, named McIntyre, by which, in return for a quarter of the property, he was to sink a fifty-foot shaft upon the ledge. When he reported that he was finished, the owners measured the shaft and found that it lacked one foot of the distance agreed upon. No orders to fulfill his contract could persuade McIntyre to "walk up the d----d hill again." His remarks, when the mine which he lost by his stubbornness became a bonanza, are not recorded.

The real development of the mine began in 1880, when Charles D. McLure, the superintendent of the Hope mill in Philipsburg, found a specimen of high-grade ruby silver ore on the dump of the Granite shaft. Whether he chanced upon it while roaming the hills, or visited the ledge at the request of Holland, is immaterial. The specimen, when assayed, ran 2,000 ounces of silver to the ton. McLure immediately started negotiations to secure the Granite claim. Having obtained an option from the owners, he bonded the property in his own name for $40,000 and took possession of it. Next, he and Charles Clark (not related to W. A. Clark), who was also con-

INTERIOR, MINERS' UNION HALL, GRANITE

THIRD FLOOR LODGE ROOM, MINERS' HALL

nected with the Hope Mining Company, decided to form a syndicate to develop their property. Clark left for St. Louis and succeeded, by December, 1880, in interesting capitalists in forming the Granite Mountain Mining Company. On September 3, 1881, the syndicate was incorporated with a capital stock of $10,000,000.

At the time of purchase, the property was virtually undeveloped, making extensive exploratory work necessary. After two years of development and an expenditure, on the part of the company, of over $130,000, the investors hesitated to risk further funds. Even McLure, the manager of the mine, was discouraged. Late in November, 1882, the company is said to have sent a telegram to McLure, ordering a shut down of the property. The wire, which reached Butte during a blizzard, was to be carried from there to Granite, by an express rider. Because of the severity of the storm, its delivery was delayed for more than a day.

Meanwhile, at the mine, a chute containing 406 feet of ore, averaging fifty ounces of silver to the ton, had been uncovered. This was followed by a barren strip of ground, 115 feet thick. Below it lay silver ore which assayed 1,700 ounces to the ton. This was the big strike for which McLure had been waiting. His telegram, announcing the bonanza to the stockholders, and their wire to him, are believed to have crossed. Later on, this story about the telegrams was discounted by the company and was explained as follows:

The marvelous tales arising from the telegraphic order to stop work in Nov. 1882, being crossed by a message announcing the discovery of the bonanza shoot may be set at rest by the statement that at no time during the history of the syndicate or the company have the management been either discouraged or doubtful. The order to discontinue driving tunnel No. 2 was because of lack of information at the home office regarding the development of prospects, as at that time 115 feet of barren ground had been penetrated.

Inter-Mountain, Holiday Edition, January 1, 1887

Regardless of telegrams, the boom was on, although three years would pass before the greatness of the mine would be assured. In the meantime, the company continued to pour money into the property, and miners moved to the mountaintop to be near their work. The company rented them land at $2.50 a lot, and each built his home according to his needs and tastes. In one sense, Granite was a company town; in another, it lacked the monotonous uniformity so common to most.

The camp covered the top of a ridge, its narrow streets, "only wide enough for three men to walk abreast," tilting in every direction. Board sidewalks, propped on trestles, stood high above muddy or dusty roadbeds, while buildings tucked against the steep slopes were dug into the hill behind and propped on stilts in front. These supports were not always so sturdy as they might have been, and one preacher was warned not to pound too heavily on the pulpit, as it stood at the end of the church that had but two props under it.

Old photographs show the main street flanked with frame, false-fronted stores and lined with electric light poles. One such picture must have been taken on a holiday, for the street is strung with banners and crowded with people, horses, and buggies. A parade is in progress, led by a band in fringed buckskin uniforms.

People of many nationalities worked in the Granite mines, keeping their local customs, yet living harmoniously with their Irish, Finnish, or Cornish neighbors. Each group had its own section: Donegal Row for the Irish, Finnlander Lane and Cornish Row for the others. Newcomers were called on by neighbors and usually given a "starter" of yeast sponge for making bread. During epidemics, such as the one in 1884, when more than thirty-five children and a number of adults died from black diphtheria, the women nursed the sick, even after losing members of their own families.

During the summer and autumn of 1883, nearly fifteen hundred tons of ore from the Bonanza chute were treated at the Algonquin mill at Hasmark, with a total value of $274,-000. Changes in management placed Frank L. Perkins in McLure's position as superintendent of the mine. He was succeeded by Captain John W. Plummer, who, like McLure, had faith in the property and willingly used up all the company's money, and some of his own, to make it pay off. In April, 1885, one month after his appointment, the Granite Mountain paid its first dividend of $60,000. By that December, a twenty-stamp mill was in operation. Between 1885 and 1888, the mine produced $2,500,000 and paid quarterly dividends, except during the erection of a new stamp mill.

RUMSEY

Early in 1888, the company discovered that ore production was exceeding the crushing capacity of its mill and at once began to scout for a new mill site. It selected a location on

Fred Burr Creek and began grading the ground in July. Stamps began dropping in the mill on March 15, 1889. This 100-stamp mill, known as the Rumsey, was so named in honor of Lewis R. Rumsey, president of the Granite Mountain Mining Company from December 1884 until 1898. It was built under the supervision of Angus Mackay, construction engineer for the Fraser and Chalmers Company of Chicago, who had previously supervised the erection of a thirty-stamp gold mill at Cable. Connection with the mine was provided by a 8,900-foot Bleitchard tramway, for the mill site was about two miles south from Granite and several hundred feet lower down the mountainside. Around it grew the town of Rumsey, where 500 mill workers and their families lived. The company provided a school and a "cosy reading room" for their employees, "lighted by electricity and well supplied with files of newspapers and current literature." Mill workers were paid $4.00 a day, while miners received only $3.00. Millmen and miners who disliked climbing the steep road to the mine often rode the tram buckets between Rumsey and Granite, despite the disapproval of mine officials. Occasionally a break in the cable would stop the tram and leave a man dangling in a bucket, high above the canyon — an extremely cold perch if the delay occurred at night. After such an experience, the man would swear off such rides — until the next time.

GRANITE (Continued)

Toward the end of the 1880's, Granite was a thriving community. "Many pretentious places of business are occupied by live, pushing men, most of whose names are found in our advertising columns," wrote the *Butte Miner* in 1887. The Moore House, built by T. Cumming, the first three-story structure in town, was the pride of Granite with its "first two floors furnished with hand-carved black walnut tables covered with Tennessee marble." Owned by Edward Moore, and managed in 1890 by Harry Featherman, it was considered one of the best hotels in the Territory.

Up until 1888, Granite had no town water supply. Each day, a horse-drawn cart, loaded with a heavy hogshead filled with water, made the rounds, delivering four to five gallons to each subscriber. The water came from Fred Burr Lake, four miles away, and since the lake was full of fish, many a housewife received an unexpected bonus in the form of a trout that slipped, unseen, into her container. In time a storage tank was built near the Gran-

ite Mountain mine, and water was piped and flumed to it. A story is told of two Cornish miners who fancied fish. Knowing that the tank contained fish, as well as water, they planned to stun the fish with a charge of dynamite and net them before they recovered. Their first charge was unsuccessful. When the second blew a hole in the side of the tank, the men faded away. They were caught by the deputy marshal and brought before Charles D. McLure, who insisted that putting them in jail would not repair the tank. Instead, he gave them a small lease to work, requiring them to pay off the damage costs from their proceeds. Within three weeks, they not only paid their debt, but also cleared $2,000 each from the ground.

By 1889, the little city had its own newspaper, the *Granite Mountain Star*, a folded sheet with five columns to a page. The initial issue described the town's institutions as of June 22, 1889:

Business of Granite.
The town of Granite may be said to be only in its infancy. The townsite was located in the summer of 1884 and a dreary outlook it was at that time. . . . A Presbyterian church is just completed and another — the Episcopal — will be ready for dedication in the course of a month or two. A public school has been in existence for some time, and as the attendance increased, additions were put on. . . . There are two spacious halls open for public amusements and scarcely an evening passes that some sort of entertainment is not offered to the public.

To endure the long hours and heavy labor required by their work, the miners had to have strong bodies. They were hardy men and played as vigorously as they dug. Some found relaxation in saloons, others in lodge activities, and nearly all in some type of sport. Of the town's eighteen saloons, none remain. Bon Ton Brothers, Con Peoples', and Nixon's were among the larger establishments. Penrose's was the most popular, not only because of its roulette wheels, poker tables, and well-stocked bar, but also because its lunch counter stayed open all night in August, 1893, when the order to close the mines came through. As to the lodges:

The Knights of Labor have just completed and dedicated a well-arranged and substantial hall. A project is on foot to erect an additional hall in the spring which will be for general purposes but so arranged that it can be utilized as an opera house and it will be included in the Utah-Montana circuit ,under the management of John Maguire.
Butte Daily Miner, 1887-1888

The proposed meeting place was undoubtedly

the Miners' Union Hall, which was built in 1889. In addition, there were Knights of Pythias, Masonic, and Odd Fellows Halls, as well as gathering places in each of the city's four churches.

A roller rink near the hospital was popular for masquerade and skating parties, while in winter, ice-skating could be enjoyed on Dan Bell's pond. A four-mile bob sled run to Philipsburg was always a thriller, and one could count on tying the empty sled to a stage or sleigh to return it to the mountain-top. Snow began falling in September and continued until May or early June, making a hard-packed road down which toboggans and skiers skimmed. Frank Bazinet, who lived in Granite for thirty-five years, became caretaker after the town was deserted. Even at seventy years of age, he used to ski down to Philipsburg, to visit his wife. In 1949, he remained in the valley for good. Horse races were held in Philipsburg, where land was level, but boxing matches could be held just as well in Granite, with contestants brought from Butte and other mining communities. In the early 1890's, the Rod and Gun, and Baseball clubs "trimmed their weapons" for action.

In 1881, a year after McLure acquired the Granite Mountain property, a second mine, the James G. Blaine — an extension of the Granite Mountain lode — was located by William Williams. McLure purchased it from Williams in 1882 for $1,200 and then offered it to the Granite Mountain Mining Company for the price that he paid for it. They refused to buy it. With two friends, Charles Clark and J. M. Merrell, as co-owners, to each of whom he offered a one-third interest in the mine, McLure organized the Bi-Metallic Mining Company. By 1886, when the company was incorporated, eighty per cent of its stockholders were the same persons or companies that were operating the Granite Mountain property.

KIRKVILLE (CLARK)

On the outskirts of Philipsburg, about one mile south on Douglas Creek, the Bi-Metallic Company built, in 1888, a new fifty-stamp chloridizing, dry crushing mill and a mine office. Here a small settlement called Kirkville (later known as Clark) grew up to house the 500 employees connected with the plant. This mill, the last to be built by the Bi-Metallic Company, started up about the middle of January, 1889. It was connected directly with the Blaine shaft in Granite by means of a two-

mile tramway, on which huge iron buckets moved in an endless chain, carrying fuel up the mountain and 500 pounds of ore on their return trip into the mill. Upon its completion, the mills at Hasmark and Rumsey were no longer needed and were shut down. A description of the property is given in the *Butte Daily Miner* (1889):

The mill buildings, all under one roof, are of stone, brick and wood, covering an area 150 feet wide by 367 feet in length. The mill building is large enough to admit doubling the number of stamps at any time. The present capacity of the mill is 75 tons per day. . . . A short distance from the mill, J. B. Risque has erected a two-story brick building 40 feet by 40 feet. The first floor is divided for office, drawing room, kitchen, pantry and fireproof vault. The second floor has two bedrooms, a large parlor and a library. In this building Mr. Risque will be at home to his many friends at all times.

In 1891, the mill was enlarged by fifty additional stamps, so that 200 tons of ore could be crushed every twenty-four hours. Both the Granite Mountain and Bi-Metallic mines were on the same ore shoot. Each was worked separately wtih its own reduction plants and these mills were widely known. As Dan Cushman of Great Falls wrote me in 1953:

The Granite-Bimetallic mills were the wonders of the mining world at that time. . . . At that time the engineers [at the Bi-Metallic] developed the process whereby ore and concentrates entering the top of the furnace fell against rising, combusting gasses and completed their alteration en transit, a continuous process. A rather sad thing: the engineer at the Granite had just developed a means of slow-cooling the chloridized concentrates that would have brought the recovery almost to perfection when the mine was finally forced by low silver prices to close down.

The Bi-Metallic mine provided the mineral exhibit sent by the town of Granite to the World's Fair in Chicago in 1893 — a 4,307-pound bar of silver bullion, valued at 970 ounces per ton.

GRANITE (Continued)

The silver panic of 1893 failed to touch Granite until the morning of August first, when the order came to shut down. No one quite sensed all that it implied at first, and then, with realization, a frantic exodus began. Old-timers tell how 3,000 people left within twenty-four hours, and of how the mine engineer, upon receiving word to quit, tied down the whistle and let its wail diminish as the pres-

HOSPITAL, GRANITE

BI-METALLIC HOIST HOUSE, GRANITE

GRANITE MT. MINE PROPERTY

sure dropped. When it ceased, the silence hurt. A. L. Stone (late dean of the School of Journalism, State University, Missoula, Montana) witnessed the leave-taking and described it most vividly:

It was the most complete desertion I have ever seen. . . . Down the roadway on Aug. 1 came the queerest, most incongruous procession ever seen. No one had stopped to pack. Everything was thrown in helter skelter. Dining room furniture and kitchen utensils teetered along down the hill in a lurching hayrack; while close behind followed all the china and Sunday clothes in an empty wagon. Next [came] . . . a spring buggy in the back of which was a kitchenstove. . . . Wheelbarrows, go-carts and burros had their place in the procession — the burros perhaps with trunks strapped to their sides.

Everyone was in a hurry and pushed and jostled to reach the bottom first. . . . (Some walked) carrying their hand luggage, frying pans or teakettles. Wagons that hadn't been used for ten years, creaked and screeched down the incline. Bandboxes, babies and bull dogs brought up the rear, and so it kept up all day and all night — a continual stream of almost panic-stricken people, leaving, perhaps forever, their home on the mountain.

I slept that night in a barber's chair which the barber very kindly propped up for me before he left . . . and for breakfast I feasted upon the exuberant mountain air and the bracing sunshine.

These people were mostly Cornish and Canadians and they had saved most of their money. Just a day before the report had come that a bank in Philipsburg was not reliable — the bank in which they all had their money. Indignant confusion reigned. Down they all rushed to the bank and each drew out every penny, then with that confidence characteristic of the European in his government, they invested it all in postal money orders.

The little 9 by 12 postoffice had never had such a rush of business and was unprepared to take care of so much money as was brought in every hour. Gold, silver, currency and checks lay about all over the floor in piles. Sacks of coins filled the corners and more came every minute. By night the old building was nearly full and there was no way of taking care of it, until in the morning when Granite had its one train at 8 o'clock. So Charlie Williams, the postmaster and his assistant sat guard all night over the building, guns in their hands. In the morning they sent it out and both of them left.

Edna L. Foster, *Fairfield Times*

For three years, Granite was a ghost town and then it slowly struggled back to life. In April, 1898, the two great silver properties which had lain dormant during this depression were consolidated as the Granite-Bi-Metallic Consolidated Mining Company, with Paul A. Fusz as president. This action was instigated by the directors of both companies who were also the largest stockholders in each. Production figures from 1883 to 1898 reveal that bullion ore shipped from the Granite Mountain was valued at $22,093,106.26 and from the Bi-Metallic at $7,267,813.29. The net profits to stockholders during this period was $13,770,000. From 1898 through 1904, the combined properties — the largest silver mines in the world — produced $1,000,000 a year. Ore was so rich that the pans in the mills ran red from the ruby silver.

During this prosperous period, many improvements were made by the company, certain of which enabled large quantities of low-grade ore to be processed. In 1902, a 34,000 lb. motor casting for the Bi-Metallic mine hoist was hauled up the mountain to Granite from Philipsburg. This called for expert freighting and handling of the thirty-two horses which drew the log truck to which the casting was secured. Twenty-four of the horses, hitched four abreast, were in front of the load; eight pushed behind. The four-mile trip took ten hours, with a stop at a roadhouse midway, where the horses were fed and watered and the teamsters found refreshment to their liking.

An 8,850-foot tunnel driven through the mountain and emerging on Douglas Creek, calculated to tap the Bi-Metallic mine at a depth of 1,000 feet and the Granite shaft at 1,450 feet, was also completed. It was begun prior to 1893 and had been bored to within a few hundred feet of both shafts at the time that the mines shut down. A subsidiary company, the Montana Water, Electric Power & Mining Company, transformed Georgetown Flat, near the head of Flint Creek, into a reservoir covering several square miles, the water to be used in connection with a power station which provided electricity to the company's mines and mills. The plant was later sold to the A. C. M. Company.

In 1905, reduced silver prices forced another shut down, but by the following year, one hundred men were back at work, sorting ore from the waste dumps and tramming it to the big mill. Each year, the mines produced less, and by 1913 the lower levels of both were under water. For a few more years leasers worked portions of these and other properties, but without sensational returns. The Bi-Metallic Company was succeeded in 1920 by the Philipsburg Mining Company, which reworked low-grade ores and paid dividends of ten to twelve cents a share at irregular intervals. In the late summer of 1958, the remaining Bi-Metallic buildings, which included the hoist house, compressor room, the dry, and several small sheds, were destroyed by fire. Three men who were doing exploratory work, halfway down the 1,000-foot shaft, were rescued minutes before the engine room burst into flames. The damage, as estimated by the Trout Mining Division of the American Machine & Metal Corporation, which operated the mine, was $50,000. This incident seems to have completed Granite's life cycle; but who knows — Granite has been reborn more than once.

The city of St. Louis is indebted to Granite Mountain and Bi-Metallic silver for many things. Proceeds from the Granite Mountain mines are said to have laid the foundation of the city's first big real estate boom. Several of the company directors built fine homes with their dividends. The Merchant's Bridge, the Planters Hotel, the Terminal Railway of St. Louis and the St. Louis Bank of Commerce were financed from the Montana bonanza.

It was June, 1954, when I got my first view of the ghost camp. To our right and below, in a hollow, was the Bi-Metallic property. We would investigate it later. In front of us, up against the mountain at a higher level, stood the stone foundations of the Granite Mountain mill with its row of crumbling ovens and the remains of a rail-tram, which had hauled ore from the lower shaft of the mine to the mill. The mountainside above and beside the mill was covered with second growth timber. Below the foundations were several large, tawny-hued dumps. To the left of these ruins, on Snob Hill, lived the mine officials, some of the company doctors, and certain of the office employees. Several of their homes still stand on Magnolia Avenue. Closest to the mill was the blacksmith shop with its forge and bellows. At the opposite end of the street was the stone office building of the Granite Mountain Mining Company. In between were three or four more frame homes. Magnolia Avenue, also spoken of as Silk Stocking Row, overlooks the town and has buildings only along its upper side.

The first building that Howard pointed out to me was the company hospital, operated under the supervision of Doctors Sligh and Powers, and recognized in its day as "an institution of high credit to the people." The two-story frame building stood at the base of Snob Hill, in the portion of Granite known as Sunnyside. In looking through it, Howard found a notice on the wall listing the office hours. Nearby, a small shed proved to be the fire station, with its hose reel and hydrant. On this trip, we did not discover the site of the company bathhouse with its 16-by-16 foot plunge, supplied with water that was heated in a large boiler. One dollar a month, deducted from each miner's pay, maintained the pool. In connection with the bathhouse was a reading room, and the men were encouraged to use it.

From where we stood, the main road rose steeply toward a higher ridge. Along it, partly hidden by trees, were ruins of stone buildings, fragments of walls, foundation hollows, and dry masonry terraces, which suggested Cornish workmanship. Not only were large trees growing within the excavations, but also one road, that straggled up the hillside, was nearly choked with them. At a street junction was a water hydrant.

Turning a corner, I gasped. There stood the Miners' Union Hall, the one building that I had seen pictured as still existing in Granite. Before I could reach it, Howard pulled me aside toward two cabins, one built of stone with a small vestibule entrance. "That's the vault of the Hyde Freychlag Bank," he said. "Steel rails and cement form the ceiling." While we were studying it, the wife of the caretaker of Granite stepped out of the other building and waved to us, calling to ask if we'd found any wood ticks yet. Without waiting to reply, I hurried toward the Hall.

From the day it was completed, the Miners' Union Hall became the social center for the town, the place where basket socials, concerts, operas, theatricals, and dances were held. The three-story building, with its ornate brick and wood facade and native rock side-walls, contained club and game rooms on the main floor and an auditorium, with stage at one end, on the second. A specially laid, all maple "spring floor," provided a fine surface for dances. The third story appears to have been the lodge room.

At the time of our visit, the windows were boarded up, admitting only slits of light, but sufficient to show cracked plaster walls and littered floors. Colored-glass panes enlivened the transoms above the first-floor windows and doors. After we had gone inside and gotten used to the half-light, we discovered two pool tables in one of the big rooms and a third in another. At the head of the stairs was a ticket booth and several small rooms, with papered walls. The main portion of this floor contained the auditorium. Someone who visited the building in 1941 mentions finding chandeliers still hanging, and scenery on the stage, but by 1954, the entire back end of the building had broken away. The roof was gone and sagging floorboards sloped toward a void where the stage once stood. Granite, in its prime, was on the regular theatrical circuit, and all the traveling troupes, such as the Georgia Minstrels and road companies from John Maguire's Opera House in Butte, performed here.

Before ascending to the third story, we tested the steep, narrow stairs. They led into a low-ceilinged room, directly under the roof. What light filtered in revealed stenciled walls, nondescript debris on the floor, and a desk or pulpit on its side amid the litter. We descended the creaking stairs and were just about to leave the building when Howard called our attention to a scribbled sentence on the wall which said: "Jane and Bob danced here in '89. Came back in '39."

Some months later, I found a clipping from an old newspaper from which the date was torn, which read:

Last Thursday was the anniversary of the organization of the Miners' Union in Montana. The day was celebrated in Granite in grand form . . . many of the business houses, except saloons, closed and the entire day was devoted to celebration. . . . About 400 men paraded in the line of march, headed by sweet music from the Philipsburg and Granite bands combined. The marchers proceeded to the Granite Mt. office, where a halt was made and three cheers given for Supt. Weir. The Bi-Metallic was then visited and cheered. The procession then moved to the grand stand where speeches were made. The celebration concluded with a ball.

Granite had four churches — Methodist, Presbyterian, Catholic, and Episcopal. Each had its own building, and by 1891, attendance on Sundays was reported as "progressingly large." In our wanderings around the town we found the stone foundations of one of them, probably the Episcopal. Within the excavated hollow, among debris and broken gothic window frames, strong young evergreens were growing. Balanced precariously on the stone footings was a reading desk. "This church was built in 1887 under Bishop Brewer's supervision," said Arline. "I've read that among the chief contributors toward its erection were the Charles Clarks, the McLures, and other St. Louis people, as well as Mrs. John W. Plummer, of Granite. I've heard that after this town was abandoned, the pews were taken to Philipsburg to be used in the church there."

As we started back toward our car, we detoured so as to inspect the group of buildings belonging to the Bi-Metallic property — the shafthouse and hoist, the headframe, a machine shop full of tools, and a shed or two. Inside the shafthouse the 34,000 pound motor hoist, whose transit up the mountain I had heard of, was still in place. As I took a final look around, I could hardly believe that this was the camp that in 1893 had a population of 3,000; and now, in 1954, had only two — the caretakers.

BLACK PINE and COMBINATION

On top of a mountain ridge, twelve miles northwest of Philipsburg, is the ghost town of Black Pine, contemporary with Granite. Some say that ore was discovered on the ridge in the 1870's, and that a few tons of it were packed to Philipsburg and run through the Hope mill at that time. Other authorities give the discovery date as 1882. A little superficial scratching revealed quantities of low-grade ore, but since the entire area was densely covered with timber, making access to it extremely difficult, it lay neglected for several years.

By 1885, enough assessment work had been done on several prospects to convince the owners that the ground held considerable "fair and some high-grade ore." In November of that year, a sample shipment of nearly 400 tons was run through the Hope mill in Philipsburg. Although assay values varied from twenty-five to eighty ounces of silver per ton, the ore looked good; and the mill was able to save seventy-seven per cent of the silver by its free-milling process.

Shortly after this, James A. Pack examined the property and, having secured a lease bond for $25,000 upon several claims, was instrumental in forming a syndicate to develop them. Most of this company's money was spent at first in building roads and in exploring and developing the Combination vein, "the most promising outcrop in the district." The ground proved up and by July, 1887, a mill had been built and was dropping its ten stamps on the silver ore. But the company had underestimated the excessive cost of hewing out roads through the dense woods and of clearing the ground for a mill site; so by fall, it was in debt. The disgruntled stockholders refused to advance more money. Litigation suspended further work, just when the removal of high-grade ore would have provided the needed

MAIN STREET, BLACK PINE

BOARDING HOUSE, BLACK PINE

ning, and by the end of the fiscal year, 1889, it showed a total of 9,000 dry tons crushed, with an average value of $22.76 a ton.

The mill shut down during the winter of 1890. Early in 1891, however, development of the mine caused the directors to add ten stamps to the mill. That summer with "every department of the Combination Plant reopened," and operating to capacity, the property was valued at $168,000, "including ore on the dump."

According to Frank Quinn, in the *Montana Standard* (August 18, 1957), the total production from 1900 to 1957 amounted to 39,000 tons of ore, reclaimed chiefly from dumps and tailings. The properties were last worked under the name Black Pine Mines, Incorporated. Sahinen gives a total production figure of $1,650,000.

Black Pine and Combination were company towns whose prosperity fluctuated with the output from the mines. Black Pine's boom lasted until 1897, and old photographs show a settlement with many buildings, including the big boardinghouse (which was still standing in 1957), and shafthouses, sheds, and shops on the surrounding mountain slopes. The camp was strung out along one main street, on top of the ridge, and was lined with miner's cabins and stores. More cabins were tucked away

capital. Lacking funds with which to operate, the mill was shut down in September, 1887, "by the hand of the sheriff." It and the Black Pine Company's holdings, which were also affected, were sold at public auction to satisfy the investors. A group of the original stockholders still believed in the property and bought it back. In December, 1887, they reorganized, under the name Combination Mining & Milling Company. This venture was successful, for the new owners confined their development to the Combination lode in whose hard white quartz rock lay quantities of free-milling silver ore. By June, 1888, the mill was run-

255

among the trees, or down the gulch toward Willow Creek. Burning flares, set at intervals, along the main street, illuminated the camp throughout the night.

One writer comments that Black Pine's residents were "a sober lot," because most of them were family men. Another reason may have been that the company prohibited saloons or honkytonks within the town limits. This simply produced a "suburb," known as Whiskey Hill, a place "with no churches and little law," located two miles south of Black Pine. Here, the thirsty found everything they craved in the seven or eight saloons and brothels that made up the heart of the settlement. Whiskey Hill has disappeared and only crumbling foundations and cellar hollows, in which rusted barrel hoops and broken bottles lie, mark the site of the once popular resort.

If whiskey was hard to get, so was water, and nearly as expensive. A horse-drawn cart delivered it from Willow Creek to patrons, who paid a dollar a gallon. This supply served them for drinking, bathing, and household purposes, with an extra amount allowed on wash-days. The rates were higher during the summer months, when the stream was low. In winter, many people used melted snow instead.

The company operating the mines developed four main shafts, the Barrett, Harper, Harrison, and Lewis, the latter the principal one in the region. From these approximately 2,135,-000 ounces of silver and 1,411 ounces of gold are said to have been mined between 1881 and 1897. The mill which crushed the ore was located two miles away, in the bottom of Willow Creek Canyon, close to the stream.

A second settlement, known as Combination, surrounded this mill. The road between was steep and narrow, passing through wooded Middletown Canyon. Over its rough bed, freight wagons loaded with ore were dragged by eight to sixteen teams of horses or mules. William S. Gillespie's eighteen-head string of pack mules brought in freight from Philipsburg and packed concentrates out.

Black Pine had no cemetery, for residents preferred to be buried in the "Burg." Whenever a miner died, work in the mines was suspended on the day of the funeral to allow the members of the Miners' Union to accompany the body to the interment.

The winters were severe, with snowdrifts seven to ten feet deep and temperatures dropping to sixty degrees below zero. Consequently, school was held during the summer months, when it was safe for the children to walk into Middletown Canyon, where the one-room log schoolhouse stood. The building was also the scene of many dances. Wallace Frost, who lived many years in Black Pine, recalls that it was easy to get up a dance. "All you had to do was go out in the street and holler, 'Let's dance.' "

"It isn't late. We can reach Black Pine and Combination this afternoon if we hurry," I suggested to my friends as we finished a warming lunch of coffee and chili in a little cafe in Philipsburg, after our morning visit to Granite. "According to the map, Black Pine is only twelve miles northwest of Philipsburg, on top of the John Long Mountain Range." Within a few minutes, we were going north, looking for a side road on the left which would be marked "Black Pine Lookout." The turn-off was about three miles beyond Philipsburg. This road, which leads to the mining camps, bears right after leaving the Lookout Trail and starts a long climb over rolling meadowland to the top of a ridge. Near the crest it runs through trees to emerge onto a high meadow, lined with log cabins on both sides of a grass-grown street. A third row of log dwellings stands lower on the hillside. Near the center of the camp was a two-story, frame boarding-house, facing a cross-road whose marker read "Combination, two miles." One or two ruined shafthouses, surrounded by dumps and the usual debris left from mining operations, squatted above the town, or at the head of the deep, wooded gulch. All the buildings seemed in good condition, although Black Pine was completely deserted.

After we had inspected the camp, we headed for Combination, taking the steep road through Middletown Canyon to the bottom of the gulch. The road was full of rocks and shale and the canyon was almost dark because of the dense shade cast by big pine trees. On the way down we passed miner's cabins and the schoolhouse.

Near the bottom of the two-mile hill, I caught a glimpse through the trees of a lush, green meadow cut by a stream. On the flat were the remains of a mill, several settling ponds, and a number of weathered cabins nearly choked by willows. Directly below the road was another mill in front of which was a grassy street with cabins, half hidden in shrubbery, lining the far side of it. We swung down the last fifty feet of the grade, past dumps and a high trestle which once carried

MINE OFFICE,
COMBINATION

ore cars to the upper level of the mill, and stopped the car in front of a square, two-story frame house with a porch and two big chimneys. A truck was parked by the front steps.

While Howard was inspecting the mill and the others were studying what appeared to be the remains of a flume, unsteadily supported on stilts, I started a sketch, blocking in the stone retaining wall below the mill and some big, rusted iron wheels and drums by the roadside. Just before we left Combination, a man and woman and two children came out of the two-story house.

"You interested in this place?" the man asked. "This was the mill office. There's newspapers and mine records in there dated 1936. There used to be a carved spiral staircase inside. The mill is still full of machinery. I used to work at Black Pine in 1935. That's how I know the place. I brought the family over today on a fishing trip. It's a wonder any of this place is still here. They tell me that the forest fires in the summer of 1889 were mighty bad. One of them came so close that they thought the camp was a goner. It destroyed the hoist at the mine in Black Pine and about fifty buildings. Everyone turned out to fight it, and they did manage to save the mill property. It's hard to believe, when you look around here now, that these two camps once had nearly twelve hundred people in them

and that the mines ran three shifts."

SUNRISE

It was a steep pull back to Black Pine. At the top of the hill stood a signpost, "Sunrise, 4 mi." "While we're this close, let's go there," said Arline. "We've never been up here before, so it will be new to all of us."

"Yes, let's find it," replied Howard, rapidly flipping through the pages of his notebook and adding, "It says here that while the Black Pine-Combination mines produced silver, the Henderson mines, where Sunrise is, produced gold, especially the placers in Henderson Gulch, which yielded $300,000 prior to 1870. Joe Henderson discovered the placers in 1865 and the gulch was named for him. So was Henderson, a short-lived camp in this

MILL AT COMBINATION

257

mining district not far from a camp named Emmettsburg."

Turning left at the marker, we drove the length of Black Pine's main street and entered thick woods. As soon as we left the townsite, the road began to dip into the next valley. After two miles, we saw, through a break in the pines, a zig-zag trail leading to a cluster of mine buildings high on a mountainside. If that was the Sunrise mine, we were almost at our destination. Dropping to the bottom of the hill, we followed Henderson Creek for nearly a mile before we saw the camp — just a few deserted, swaybacked cabins and sheds, a large boardinghouse, and a mill, all perched on one side of a swampy meadow. Two burros raised their heads to look at us, and then returned to cropping grass.

As soon as we shut off our motor, we heard a bulldozer, or compressor, high above us, but, although it was undoubtedly at the head of the zig-zag mine trail, we could not locate it. While I sketched the mill, Arline walked toward the boardinghouse, stopping first to peer into one of the nearer cabins. I noticed that she didn't go any farther, and that she hurried back to the others, but not until we were climbing back toward Black Pine, did we learn why.

"I was on my way to the mill," she began, "and as I passed the first cabin, I thought I'd see if it had any furniture in it. The window panes weren't broken, but they were dirty, so I had to press against the glass to look inside. Just as I took a good look, I found myself staring into the eyes of an old man who was staring back at me. That's when I started back to the car."

"He was probably the caretaker," said Howard. "I don't know much about the Sunrise property, except that it once belonged to Charles D. McLure of Philipsburg, and that he was also interested in the Black Pine mines. The twenty-stamp Sunrise mill was working successfully in 1896, on ore from large ledges of silver. I believe that this camp also went by the name of Henderson — at least it was in the Henderson Mining District."

By now it was late afternoon, and we were weary from our varied experiences and ready to return to Anaconda for the night.

GOLD COIN

It was getting dark as we drove past Gold Coin, a once-active camp, just north of the highway, near Silver Lake. The mill is set against a hillside sparsely dotted with trees. Several sheds and workshops surround the mill, as well as a few cabins. Lighted windows in one proved that Gold Coin was not utterly deserted.

The only reference I have found that mentions the place was in the *Philipsburg Mail* of July 20, 1906:

The Gold Coin mill at Silver Lake is being made ready to start and will be running within a week. Manager L. T. Ireland of the Gold Coin properties is on the ground. Water for the mine is obtained from a well and for some days pumpmen have been overhauling the pumps and getting them into shape. Quite a few men are employed there and Gold Coin camp is beginning to assume its old time activity.

MAXVILLE (FLINT)

Next morning, we left Anaconda and started northwest for Missoula. We had to watch for Maxville, a small settlement, twelve miles north of Philipsburg. Originally called Flint, only a few of the older buildings remain and most of them have been remodeled into homes. A schoolhouse, a store, and the false-fronted Silver Slipper Bar formed the nucleus of the town. Flint was renamed in honor of R. R. MacLeod, its first postmaster and merchant, and was to have been called Macville. Somehow, an "x" was substituted for the "c".

PRINCETON

From the storekeeper at Maxville, we learned that Princeton, the mining camp I was seeking, lay six miles southwest of that town, and could be reached by a good gravel road. A drive up an open valley, between timbered mountains ,revealed no signs of mining, until we were within about a mile of the camp. Then dumps near the road and a few markers pointing up side trails suggested the location of former gold-silver-lead properties. One such sign read "South Boulder, Gold Reef Mine"; another indicated that "Princeton Gulch" was to the left; a third fork led to "Maywood Ridge." After another half-mile, we rolled into Princeton — a pleasantly situated place with well-kept cabin homes, several of which were occupied. Cattle wandered on the road, and one or more dogs ran out to announce our arrival.

No one to whom we talked seemed to know the early history of the place; so I have had to depend on statements found in several

GOLD COIN MILL

PRINCETON

publications. One of these, a Souvenir Journal, printed in Helena in 1891, mentions that during the summer of 1882, a corporation known as the Princeton Mining Company was organized under the auspices of the Lexington Mining Company of Butte, to work the Princeton, Saranac, and Mediterranean mines in the Boulder or Cleek Mining District, northwest of Philipsburg. The claims included in this sale, which were discovered by the Brown Brothers some years before, consisted of "a series of parallel ledges with all the characteristics of true fissure veins. This property cost the Princeton Company about $200,000. The Princeton was the only one of the group opened up by the company." Even after the mine shut down some years ago, the company made additional profits by leasing portions of it.

According to *Leeson,* the Princeton was located at Medhurst and was owned by French capitalists, who employed fifty men and proposed, in 1885, to erect a twenty-stamp mill on the property. Ore from the rich ledge assayed $40 a ton in silver. Sahinen lists "Metals in order of importance [as] gold, silver, lead, copper. Total production to the end of 1907 was $1,250,000, the greater part from the Royal mines. The gravels of Princeton Gulch from Boulder Creek to its source are said to be gold-bearing. The pay streak is 18 inches thick and lies on bedrock. It can only be mined by drift mining, as it contains too many large boulders for dredging."

Two other mining centers in the area are:

Dunkleburg. A mining district south of Jens a station on the Northern Pacific R.R. It can be reached by road from Jens or Hall. Lode mining has been carried on intermittently in the area, which is 2 miles wide and 5 miles long, near the north end of the Flint Creek range, since the 1880's. The lodes contain lead, zinc, and silver. Prior to 1916 about $200,-000 in silver and lead was produced.

(Sahinen)

Rose Mt. (Gold Creek). Gold has been found at the headwaters of Gold Creek and its tributaries in Granite County, north of Princeton, in rugged terrain around Rose Mt. Several properties . . . were worked profitably prior to 1907. Besides these mines, McFarland's and Tibbet's Placers yielded thousands of dollars in gold from sluiced gravels which averaged 40 cents a cubic yard.

(Sahinen)

NEW CHICAGO

Beside the nine-mile stretch of highway north, between Maxville and Hall, are many vestiges of hydraulic mining. Just before reaching Drummond, a side road to the right points to New Chicago. This village, which was founded July 4, 1872, by John A. Featherstone, was on the old stage road between Deer Lodge and Missoula.

DRUMMOND

Drummond, on Highway No. 10, a station on the Northern Pacific, stands on the site of a former camp called Edwardsville, built in 1871, and named for John Edwards, a rancher. In 1883, it was renamed for Hugh Drummond. Deposits of silver, sapphires, and phosphates have been found in the Sapphire Mountains nearby.

CHAPTER 15

THE BITTERROOT
VALLEY and the
CLARK FORK CAMPS

The Bitterroot Range forms a natural boundary between western Montana and eastern Idaho, not only south of Missoula, but northwest as well, all the way to Lake Pend Oreille. Rivers cut the valley on the Montana side of this barrier — the Bitterroot, whose headwaters rise in the extreme southern tip of the range, and flow north to join the Clark Fork of the Columbia, just west of the city of Missoula; the Clark Fork itself; and the St. Regis River, which rises close to Lookout Pass and flows southeast to join the Cark Fork at the town of St. Regis. Along these waterways, trails were hacked out by the first travelers and settlers, and when gold and other precious minerals were found on the slopes of the Bitterroots and the other ranges bordering the valleys, camps materialized, to serve as supply stations and as jumping off points for the intrepid men who followed up the streams in an endless search for "colors."

Paralleling the Bitterroot Range, to the north, were two other mountain chains which also attracted gold seekers — the Ninemile Divide between the Clark Fork and the Flathead River, northwest of Missoula, and the Coeur D'Alene Mountains, south and west of Thompson Falls. This area covers many miles and includes parts of four counties — Ravalli, Missoula, Mineral, and Sanders. In it the several mountain divides and gulches which wrinkle their sides dictated the flow of streams and the placing of trails, as well as the locations for the towns.

EIGHTMILE CREEK

The area south of Missoula is ranch country, with some lumbering in the Bitterroot forests on the western side of the wide valley. The region was never a major mining area, and almost all mention of it as such dates back to the seventies and eighties. It was, therefore, difficult to learn where the placer diggings and lode mines had been located, and whether they were still accessible by road. Having studied U. S. Geological Survey contour maps, I found that Threemile Creek and Eightmile Creek, two of the mining areas mentioned, lay east of Florence. Perhaps someone there could direct me to the diggings.

My husband and I left Missoula one morning and drove south for twenty miles. From time to time, we were within sight of the Bitterroot River, a broad stream which winds through meadowland up the middle of the valley. At Florence, we stopped first at the railroad station, and then at a store, to ask the whereabouts of the placer fields. A customer, who said he knew the country round about, interrupted me when I spoke of having read of placers fifteen miles east on Ambrose Creek.

"Write that off blank," he said. "There's nothing on Ambrose or Dry Gulch either. There's a good deal on Threemile Creek and on Eightmile too. Eightmile's all tore up with placering. Threemile's a little south of here and joins the Bitterroot five miles north of Stevensville. There used to be a few lode mines in the hills on the east side of the valley, but they didn't amount to much, and nobody's worked them for years. The last time the Providence produced any ore was in 1907. The Gold Bug — that's seven miles east of Florence — was free-milling gold. Then there was the Blue Cloud and the Whaley. The White Cloud's up Eightmile Creek. Part of the mill's still standing. You'd better go see what's left. Take the road east of the railroad. It'll cross the Bitterroot River in a mile.

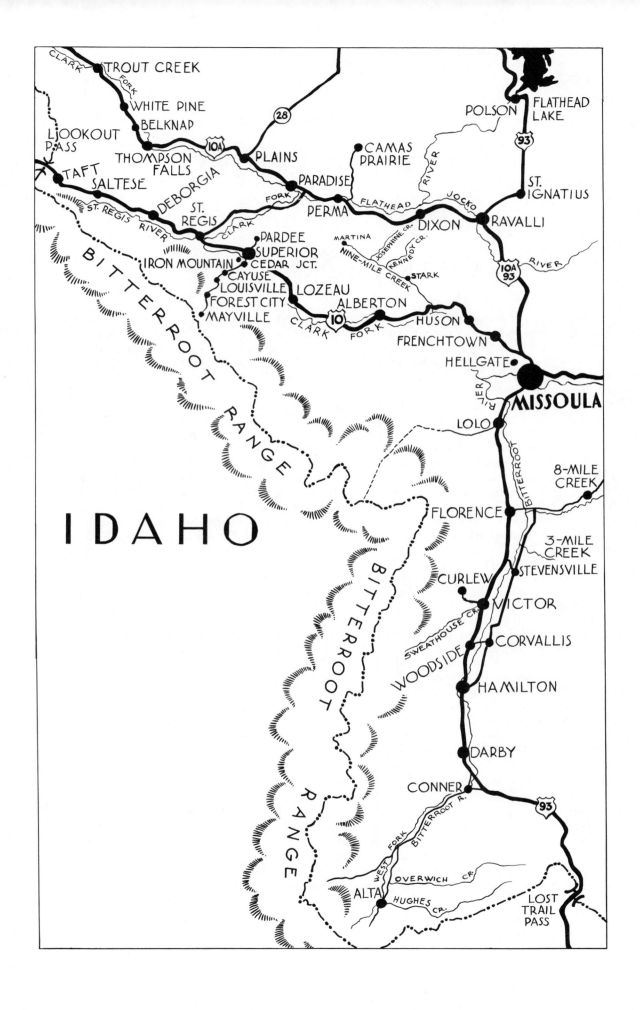

Then keep going north and east till you see diggings on the left, up a gully."

We thanked him and crossed the tracks as soon as a trainload of logs rolled by, headed for some sawmill farther up the line. Half a mile east of the Bitterroot River, the road branched. The northern fork was rough, but passable, and we followed it to the mouth of a canyon. As it left the valley to climb into the hills, it narrowed still more, but the road-bed improved. We were now almost eight miles from Florence, and as yet had seen no sign of lode mining. Suddenly I noticed yellow prospect holes among the trees, near the top of a hill. At almost the same instant, Francis pulled off the road at the mouth of a gulch in which were a large cabin, and the ruins of a mill. Upon exploring the property, we discovered several dumps, three adits, a rusted boiler, and a shaft, which was fenced off and marked "Dangerous." The five-level mill contained no machinery. As well as we could tell, this was the White Cloud mine. It was nearly a year before we were sure.

One day, my mail contained a report, issued in January, 1957, by the Montana Bureau of Mines and Geology, and written by Uuno M. Sahinen. It was devoted to the "Mines and Mineral Deposits of Missoula and Ravalli Counties," and had been sent to me by my friend, Virginia Walton, at that time librarian at the State Historical Library in Helena. In it, I found much detailed information, such as:

The mine . . . was discovered in 1866 and is said to have been worked by Marcus Daly for some time. [It was also] operated in the late 1890's. In 1898, Byrne (1898, p. 19) wrote: "The White Cloud mine . . . is owned by Jameson Bowden & Co., and operated by Clark and Wheeler . . . eight men are employed in the mine and four on the surface. The shaft is down 140 feet, and a tunnel (from the surface) connects with the shaft about midway of its depth. . . . The ore is pyritic iron and gold in combination. The mine is also equipped with a 75-ton concentrator.

1899 White Cloud mine at Pyrites was operated in the early part of the year by Clark & Wheeler, who, failing to make a success of the property, abandoned it. (Byrne 1898, p. 27)

1938 A test lot of gold ore shipped from the White Cloud mine . . . had a value of $57.00.

1953 The mine appeared to have been abandoned for many years. . . . A windlass was rigged in the shaft, which was open but partly caved.

On this trip up Eightmile Creek, we did not attempt to reach the Cleveland mine, sixteen and a half miles east of Florence, "on

WHITE CLOUD MINE, 8-MILE CANYON

the crest of the Sapphire Mts."; for the last six miles of road were said to be no more than a "poor jeep trail." Shortly after its discovery, ore from the mines was treated in an arrastra located on the hillside below the mine. Nor did we explore Threemile Creek, where gold-bearing gravels previously were found "from hillside to river." That the district once held promise is shown in a newspaper item from the *Weekly Missoulian*:

The Three-mile diggings hold a prominent position in the anticipations of many people hereabouts. The mines are not being worked at present but in a few weeks they will all be in full blast. Among the placer companies expecting soon to go to work are Messrs. Sexton & Bentley, Dobbins, Loselle & Co., Geo. Dickson & F. Harris, and Mart Slocum & Co. They all promise an abundant harvest in the near future.   July 29, 1881

VICTOR and the CURLEW MINE

From Florence, we drove south on Highway No. 93 to Victor, with the Bitterroot Range on the right. The term "bitterroot," which is given to the mountain range, the river, and the valley, describes a plant which grows abundantly in the area, whose root has a strong, rank flavor and was much favored by the Flathead Indians as a food. The blossom, which is pink at first but turns white in the sun, is the state flower. Looking past the mouth of each steep-walled canyon, we saw distant snowcapped peaks. Logging roads zig-zagged across the face of the foothills.

At Victor, we parked on the main street and separated, each going in search of information about the mines in the area. I went first to the postoffice.

"You should talk to Mr. Groff," said the postmistress. "You'll find him in the bank."

Mr. Houston Clay Groff, an elderly gentleman, invited me into his office and was good enough to answer my many questions.

"I've read about the Sweathouse Mining District near here, four miles south of Deep Canyon, and of a silver-lead vein discovered near Sweathouse Creek in 1871," I began. "According to several sources, Sweathouse was one of the old mining settlements of the county. Where was it?"

"Never heard of it. There was no such camp. My wife's in her seventies and she lived up Sweathouse Creek all her life, and if there'd been anything there, she'd have mentioned it."

"Where were quartz discoveries made in the 1870's, on the east side of the valley?"

"That would have been near Corvallis. I taught school there when I was a young man. There used to be a little gulch mining on Birch Creek, near Corvallis. There's nothing being done there now."

"Where was the Blue Bird mine?"

"It was on Bear Creek, but it didn't amount to anything. The Pleasant View was a good mine, but high up in the mountains. You couldn't get to either of them nowadays, except on foot. Lots of money was put into both properties, and little taken out. The Pleasant View was opened by a two hundred foot shaft and a three hundred foot tunnel in 1925, and one carload of silver shipped out. That was the last reported production from it. The Curlew was the big mine around here. The Curlew made Victor. There was no town until it began to produce."

Thanking Mr. Groff, I went in search of Francis. He had found a garageman and had learned from him about the Ore Finder group, a gold-silver-copper propety, five miles southwest of Victor, owned and operated in 1905 by the Ore Finder Mining Company. It was developed at that time by a steam hoisting plant, while John Hickey was general manager and superintendent. It was active as late as 1913. I had heard of this mine from an item in the *Anaconda Standard* which mentioned:

the Ore Finder Mining Co. Inc., [owned] by several Bitter Root residents who started the development of three claims. On the Ore Finder claim, men are working 100 feet below the surface. . . . Work on the claim has been done for two years.
This company, of which Frank E. Gage of Hamilton is President, has some rich ore sacked, and has spent $4000 in development work. The best ore is 600-700 oz. of silver and 2-15% in copper.
December 18, 1904

The Bitter Root Prince was another of the older mines, developed by both shaft and tunnel, but like the others, idle today and with no surface buildings standing. Even the shafts have caved in.

The Curlew mine was located near the mouth of Big Creek, four miles northwest of Victor. For statistics about it, I consulted my notes, especially those prepared by Uuno M. Sahinen in 1957, and from which I have compiled much of the following data. The mine was worked as long ago as 1887, but large-scale development began in 1891, when it was operated by the Helena Victor Company. This company employed 70 men and sank a two-compartment shaft 330 feet deep to tap four levels of the mine. It also built a 125-ton mill which shipped concentrates steadily to the East Helena smelter. By 1894, greater quantities of richer ores were found and shipped, and the mill's capacity was increased. Three years later, the Curlew was in receivership and was operated by H. P. Kenneth, the receiver, who employed "10 miners and 4 top men." An item in a paper printed in Castle, Montana, mentions this state of affairs:

The Curlew mine at Victor has shut down again. The men refused to return to work a few days ago because the receiver, acting under order of the court, was not willing to pay the excess over their current wages, received from the ore extracted, to reduce their former wage claims but wished to use it to develop the mine. Four carloads of ore have been taken out since the receiver took charge of the mine and three of them have been shipped.
It is said that the excess above mentioned amounted to 50 cents on the dollar of all labor claims. The receiver also wished the fourth car to go on the next month instead of being included in this month's returns. The receiver is trying to get other men to take the place of those who walked out.
The Whole Truth, April 3, 1897

To return to Sahinen's report:

From 1906 to 1914 it was owned and operated by A. M. Holter. He employed 20 men to work the 2 parallel veins which carried gold, silver and copper ore. The output of the mine was treated in a 120-ton concentrator on the property. . . .
The Victor Reduction Co. began operating the mine in 1915, regrinding the tailings in the mill and shipping a concentrate containing chiefly zinc with a little lead, and some gold and silver. The plant was idle in 1918.
From 1923 through 1926 the Curlew Mining Co. did development work in the shafts and drifts. By that time, the concentrating mill had a capacity of 150 tons per day. . . .
In 1937 the mine was leased by the Hamilton-Victor Reduction Co. which shipped nearly 900 tons

CURLEW MINE NEAR VICTOR

CURLEW CONCENTRATOR

of zinc concentrates to Great Falls and 800 tons of gold-silver ore to other smelters.

In 1940, 10,000 tons of old tailings were treated and yielded 491 tons of zinc concentrates and 47 tons of gold-silver ore which was shipped crude to the smelters, with a total value of $47,494. The following year the output was 12,000 tons.

The mine and mill were leased in 1943 to C. A. Tout. . . . In 1949 B. F. Tout worked the mine producing concentrates worth $28,760. From 1949 on the mine has been idle.

Uuno M. Sahinen, "Mines and Mineral Deposits, Missoula and Ravalli Counties, Montana," January, 1957

"The garageman told me how to get to the Curlew mine," said Francis when I rejoined him. "Shall we start? We take the old road out of Victor, not the highway, and drive on it to the second lane, about three miles from town. After passing a brick house, we turn left and drive another mile. At that point, we should see a big house on the side of a hill."

We followed the directions, and on the last mile saw a reassuring sign marked "Curlew," which pointed to the right. I'd been warned that the road was poor and the bridges weak. One bridge over a ditch was broken, but a dirt fill to one side permitted us to cross. A short distance ahead were a couple of cabins in a grove of trees, and beyond them, a settling pond and a mill. While I walked across the crusted tailings to make a sketch, Francis drove ahead up the road and discovered several big dumps, hidden in trees, shafts, windlasses, broken machinery, a few sheds, and the mine office. Except for the first two houses that we saw, which were tenanted, the mine property was abandoned.

As we drove back to Victor, I wondered where the placer ground lay from which "five ounces of gold worth $96," was washed in 1931. It was said to have been below the Curlew property, somewhere on Big Creek. From Victor, we drove south thirteen miles to Hamilton.

HAMILTON

Anyone driving through Hamilton sees a lively business center with a busy main street and homes bordering its cross streets. West of it rises the Bitterroot Range, with snow-capped 7,000-foot peaks, and east, across the wide valley, are the Sapphire Mountains, a secondary spine of the Rockies. If you read the Montana guidebook, you will discover that Hamiton is known as the "apple town — the land of the McIntosh Red," that is contains creamery plants, and that farmers raise sugar beets. You may also see the three-story brick administration building of the United States Public Health Service Laboratory, established for the study of Rocky Mountain spotted fever, and staffed with more than 150 scientists and their assistants. But perhaps you are chiefly interested in seeing the Marcus Daly estate, a 22,000 acre ranch two miles east of the town, or in visiting the park which covers a portion of the racetrack where his famous thoroughbreds were trained.

Daly founded the town in 1887 and named it for one of his foremen. He himself was attracted to the area because of the fine stands of trees which covered the mountainsides. As a shrewd business man, he looked upon these as valuable timber reserves. At Hamilton, he set up his Bitterroot Stock Farm. Here, between 1890 and 1900, he trained and bred the racehorses which brought him both fame and winnings, studying each thoroughbred as it went through its paces on the half-mile covered track which he built, and entering it in a race only when he was confident of its performance. He raced his horses first on local tracks at Anaconda, Butte, Helena, and Deer Lodge, well away from spying eastern scouts, and then shipped the high-strung animals as "unknowns" to the big turf events to make a cleanup. William M. Johnson, his favorite jockey, wore the Daly copper and green in many a winning race. Always on the lookout for quality, Daly hired Jim Lucas, a trainer for certain of August Belmont's horses, and watched him develop Ogden. He did not live to see Zev, from the same strain, win the Kentucky Derby in 1923. Both Ogden and Scottish Chieftain raced at Sheepshead Bay in 1896.

Montana, ridden by jockey Snapper Garrison, won a race with odds three-to-one against him. That may have been the day that Daly stopped to visit one of his mines. He changed his clothes in "the dry" before descending into the mine and left a $1,000 ticket on Montana in his pocket. When he returned to the surface, he discovered that fire had destroyed "the dry," and his clothes. Montana won the race, and had Daly had his ticket, he could have collected $40,000. Hamberg, another horse, cost Daly $41,000. He won $60,000 with him and sold him for $60,000 more. Bob Wade was one of several sprinters that the stable developed. On August 20, 1896, the four-year-old broke a world record in 21.4 on a quarter-mile track. Another of his racers, Atoka, broke another world record on September 7, 1906, with a three-furlong race in 33.5. For distance and endurance, Senator Bland, Scottish Chieftain, Ostler Joe, and Tammany Hall, son of the great Tammany, held their own.

However, it was Tammany who won all his stake races as a three-year-old, on whom Daly bet most heavily. He entered him in a $25,000 Eclipse Stakes Race at Morris Park in 1891, with betting odds 30 to 1 against him. There were few takers and the odds rose to 75 to 1. Daly bet so heavily at the last minute that the odds fell to 15 to 1. After Tammany won, Daly is said to have collected $100,000. By 1893, Tammany was recognized as the leading horse in the country. When he and Lamplighter, owned by Frederick Walbaum of New Jersey, were matched for a race, the odds were 7-10 in his favor. Tammany won by five lengths, and Daly celebrated in the Hoffman House in New York, with $27,000 cash as his take. Enroute to Montana, Tammany developed lung fever. The best veterinary care, coupled with champagne and porter, effected a cure, but depleted Daly's winnings considerably.

When Daly died, the stables were sold for $750,000. At that time, the copper magnate, who had not let money ruin him, was worth a million dollars. His friends said he would have been worth much more if he hadn't given so much away.

OVERWICH and HUGHES CREEK DISTRICT

It would be incomplete to discuss mining in Ravalli County without mentioning the Overwich-Hughes Creek District, even though returns from this remote area in the southernmost tip of the county have never been particularly important. Hughes Creek, thirty-three miles south of Darby (a supply center for the mines and farms on Highway No. 93), is a westward flowing stream which joins the headwaters of the Bitterroot River at Alta. Overwich Creek flows west into the Bitterroot three miles farther north. Placer diggings were known to exist in the area as early as 1870, according to Raymond's report which mentioned, "Chinamen working on a bar toward the head of the Bitterroot River where they earn small wages, $4 to $5 per day to

the hand, for a short time in the spring." Little else is known about the district prior to 1904, except that from time to time prospectors staked claims along the creek bottom for a distance of several miles. According to Sahinen (1958), the total gold and silver production since 1904 is valued at $260,000 and of that total, ninety-eight per cent was recovered from placers. From 1904 until 1924, the Wood Placers on Hughes Creek were the most productive.

HELL GATE RONDE and MISSOULA MILLS

One evening after dinner, I was wandering about the lobby of the Florence Hotel in Missoula, when a picture caught my eye. It was a sketch of Old Hell Gate — the settlement that preceded Missoula by several years. The drawing showed a group of log buildings, and the caption stated that Hell Gate once stood on the Frenchtown road, three and a half miles west of the present bustling city. Hell Gate had a short and lusty life. The first building was erected in 1860 and the place abandoned in 1864. It claimed the first marriage of whites and the first jury trial in Montana. Its cemetery contained road agents and other toughs who underestimated the stamina of its population. In 1863, perhaps as a symbol of sobriety, St. Michael's log church was built. Canadian trappers had already named the river which emerged from a narrow canyon east of the townsite, the Hell Gate. The large round valley at the mouth of the canyon they called Hell's Gate Ronde.

During the summer of 1860, Frank L. Worden and Christopher P. Higgins, packers, brought a train loaded with merchandise over the newly completed Mullan Road from Walla Walla, intending to trade at the Indian agency. Upon reaching the fertile valley, they changed their plans and decided to build a trading post on the flat. A log building soon housed their stock and the pair opened for business under the firm name of Worden & Company. Their store became the center of a small village called Hell Gate Ronde, to which drifted some of the roughest characters in the Territory. Because of meadowland for grazing, and the abundance of wood and water available, the settlement became an important stopover station for prospectors and travelers on the Mullan Road. Van Dorne's blacksmith shop was known as a place where broken wagons could be repaired, and animals shod, while the saloon and trading post's reputation was even greater; for where else could one find such necessities as coffee at eighty cents a pound, sugar at sixty cents, and whiskey at $8.00 a gallon? With the discovery of the Kootenay mines, and the rush to Alder Gulch in the spring and summer of 1863, steady streams of men poured through Hell Gate Ronde, replenishing supplies there or outfitting for the wilderness ahead.

Cyrus Skinner and others of Plummer's gang of road agents made Hell Gate their headquarters during the winter of 1863-1864, hanging around the post for word of treasure shipments and terrorizing the community in general. Skinner in particular liked to perch on the safe in Worden's store, well aware that the owners dared not object. They, in turn, were convinced that the gang intended to break into it and steal the $65,000 of dust that it contained. On the night of January 27, 1864, a posse of twenty-one Vigilantes, from Alder Gulch, rode silently into Hell Gate, rounded up the highwaymen, tried them in Worden's store, and sentenced six to be hanged. George Shears was strung from a beam in a barn. When all was ready, he was told to climb up a ladder. As he reached the top, he turned to his executioners and asked, "Gentlemen, I am unaccustomed to this business. Shall I jump off or slide off?" "Jump," was the reply. Another of the men, Whiskey Bill Graves, was hanged from the limb of a tree. When the lariat was adjusted around his neck, with the other end attached to the trunk, he was placed on a horse, behind a Vigilante. "Goodbye, Bill," called the rider, dashing off, leaving Bill dangling.

During the winter of 1864-1865, Worden & Higgins erected a sawmill four miles east of Hell Gate, where Missoula now stands. In the spring, they added a grist mill and a warehouse. That fall, they moved the contents of their store to the new building. As at Hell Gate, a village grew up around their property as settlers from the former community moved to the newly laid out 100-acre townsite. This settlement was called Missoula Mills. The last time I inquired as to what was left of Hell Gate, I was directed to a chicken house on a ranch, three miles west of Missoula. It is part of the original log store.

FRENCHTOWN

From Missoula, Highway No. 10 follows the Clark Fork of the Columbia in a northwesterly direction, as far at St. Regis, where the river doubles back and cuts its way through a gorge between two mountain ranges, to emerge in a new valley down which it flows into Lake Pend Oreille, and on through Idaho. Several small towns along this river show by their names something of their founders. DeSmet, closest to Missoula, was obviously named for the Jesuit priest, and Frenchtown, eighteen miles west of the city, was settled by French Canadians. As early as 1858 or 1859, two trappers, Baptiste Bucharme and Louis Brown, located in the valley and built homes on their farms, close to where Frenchtown stands. The town was laid out in 1864, and since it was on the Mullan Road, it became a shipping point and a center to which farmers brought their grain as soon as T. J. Demers built a flour mill. St. Joseph's church, with its quaint spire, is a landmark dating from the early days of the settlement.

NINEMILE DISTRICT

The Ninemile District is in the northwestern part of Missoula County, and includes that area drained by Ninemile Creek and its tributaries. Ninemile Creek is a southeastward flowing tributary of Clark Fork. Placer mines were discovered and patented ground taken up in October, 1874. Within a month men were stampeding to the rich diggings, which were said to yield as high as $100 a day to the hand, and were staking claims along the main creek and on each of its two main forks. During the peak of the excitement in 1875, about fifty claims of 300 feet each, were located in the gulch. At the junction of St. Louis and Eustache Gulches — the main forks of Ninemile — was the mining camp of Montreal, which contained a hotel, four saloons, one store, two butcher shops, two blacksmith shops, one bakery, and two Chinese washhouses. Another small camp, supplied with saloons, stores, hotels, and restaurants, was located on O'Keefe Canyon, east of Frenchtown. It, too, was an important supply center for prospectors in 1882. A third camp, called Martina, was on Ninemile Creek near the San Martina mine at the northwest end of the Ninemile Valley.

The Nine Mile and San Martina mines, adjacent properties, were eighteen miles up Ninemile Creek from Highway No. 10, and accessible by road from Huson. Gold placers also extended up the valley for sixteen miles. The Nine Mile mine was opened about 1890 and was developed by the Nine Mile Mining Company. The free-milling gold was carried by an aerial tramway, 1,100 feet from the mine to a stamp mill in the valley. The company operated the mine for nearly fifteen years. Thereafter, it was worked by lessees. Between 1912 and 1915, the Nine Mile and Martina mines produced 10,649 tons of ore and old tailings which yielded gold and silver bullion. Each property had its own mill. The total production for the district since 1908 is valued at over $480,000, almost entirely in gold.

The placer gold of the creek bed was recovered by sluicing and hydraulicking in 1908 and 1909, with some properties leased to Chinese miners. Many gold nuggets were found in the district and some were no doubt sold to jewelers and tourists. In 1911, seven placers and one deep mine produced $16,777 in gold. There has been little production since 1915.

SUPERIOR

The name Superior was originally used in 1869 to identify a settlement at the mouth of Cedar Creek, one mile east of the present town; but when the mining boom was over, and the camp disappeared, its name was taken by the newer town, which has survived.

Superior is cut in half by the Clark Fork, with the highway running through the higher side of the town and the newer homes built on the flat across the river. By the time that the Northern Pacific Railroad built along the Clark Fork to Superior, the Iron Mountain mine was producing and shipping out ore by pack train. The railroad called its station Iron Mountain, but the mining town and supply center, which antedated its arrival, continued to be known as Superior. Very few of the older buildings remain, and what few survive are at the foot of a steep hill on the north bank of the river. When I inquired where the Ordean Hotel was, I learned that it had burned down, and that the Chevrolet filling station occupies the site. In the newer part of the town, near the railroad station, stands the false-fronted Masonic and I. O. O. F. Hall.

A letter which I received from E. R. Bennett, postmaster of Superior, explains the 1960 status of the town of Iron Mountain. Mr. Bennett writes:

Iron Mountain . . . was at one time a flourishing community. Until six years ago it had its own post-office, and mail was delivered from Superior twice a day. It was also a point on the N. P. railroad. Some five or more years ago the post office was discontinued and the station was renamed "Superior." In fact, at

SUPERIOR

present Iron Mountain consists of only one building. This was formerly the postoffice, but the elderly postmistress would be out of a job if they included it in Superior. So this one building has never been admitted. It now houses a building supply business and pays a different tax than the rest of Superior and a different rate of insurance. Superior now includes everything except this one house.

CEDAR CREEK

Before we left Helena, Mrs. Ann McDonnell, former librarian at the State Historical Society, had said, "When you go through Superior, be sure to drive up Cedar Creek. The gold rush there in 1869 was a big thing. Look up by brother-in-law, too. He can tell you about the mines." In response to our inquiries, Mr. McDonneil directed us to Fred Mayo, who had lived in Cedar Creek for many years. We found Mr. Mayo and a lumberman visiting in a store, and from them learned what we needed to know.

"The road's good. I don't know if it's been dragged yet this season," they told us. "You'll see lots of mining up there, but it was all so long ago, the towns are all gone. There's a couple of newer mines that have been working recently — one's the Amador or Gildersleeve, and the other is Superior Mines. Be sure you go all the way to Mayville if you want to see the diggings."

By crossing the Clark Fork on a steel bridge and driving southeast for one mile, we reached the entrance to Cedar Creek Canyon but saw no sign of the original settlement that stood at the mouth of the creek. We turned south on a forest road and started up the canyon that beckoned to the goldseekers in 1869. It was narrow but smoother than we had anticipated, with no high centers. At first we were only a few feet above the water, but after a few miles, the road climbed away from the stream, only to cross and recross it on sturdy bridges the rest of the way.

"Just what are we looking for?" asked Francis, as we slowed up to read a sign that marked two side roads. The right hand trail was the Oregon Creek road which led to "LaCasse Camp, Oregon Creek, Big Flat, Missoula Lake, Upper St. Joe River." The arrow pointing left indicated the Upper Ada Creek road, the Superior and Gildersleeve properties, the North Fork of Trout Ceek, Hoodoo Meadow, and Cedar Range.

"From what I've been able to find out," I began, "Cedar Creek was the richest gold camp in this area during its brief boom. The estimated yield of Cedar Creek and the surrounding gulches over a fifteen year period, prior to 1885, was over a million dollars. A French Canadian, Louis A. Barrette, started it all. When he became dissatisfied with the gold diggings he found in Idaho, he crossed the mountains into Montana. He continued east on the Mullan Road until he spotted this canyon, in which he found a basin that looked promising; but, since it was too late in the season to start work, he went on and spent the winter in Frenchtown.

"In the fall of 1869, Barrette and his partner, B. Lanthier, returned to the spot that had interested him the previous season — a small tributary of Cedar Creek which he called Cayuse Creek. Here the two made camp, fifteen miles from the Clark Fork, and here, according to a story, while Lanthier cooked supper, Barrette panned out $4.00 in gold. With this beginning, the two continued to prospect and pan the gravels of the gulch, taking out $375 in a few weeks. Encouraged by this strike, they staked several claims. When their rations were nearly gone and the winter upon them, they left the gulch and went to Lozeau's ranch on the Clark Fork to stay until spring. Accounts vary as to whether Lozeau himself, or Lanthier, went to Frenchtown for provisions; but whoever went was sworn to secrecy concerning the discovery, and, of course, the news leaked out.

"Although it was the middle of January, a stampede to Cayuse Creek started, with J. R. Latimer and Hank Froach, who were in Frenchtown at the time, in the lead. These two, accompanied by a small group of men, started on horseback without stopping for provisions and rode all night, reaching Lozeau's place at four in the morning. There they found a crowd of a hundred impatient prospectors who gulped a breakfast of boiled beans and were off before daylight, fording the river and riding up the banks of Cedar Creek to the mouth of Oregon Gulch. Leaving their horses tied to trees, they struck out on foot. Latimer is said to have reached the ground first. That evening, when even the stragglers had arrived, a meeting was called and rules drawn up. By the next night, the entire gulch was staked off into 200 claims, and men were attempting to pan the stream in spite of the cold.

"By the third morning, the improvident stampeders were so hungry that they backtracked to their horses and left the gulch in search of food, returning as soon as their mounts were packed with supplies. As the winter progressed, the miners developed scurvy, so when a pack train arrived, containing a shipment of potatoes, the men gladly paid $1.00 a pound for them. A second pack train brought in nothing but whiskey.

"The news of the strike traveled so fast that three thousand men from all over Montana wintered in the gulch. It is said that ten thousand visited the placers within the first year, some to stay, and others merely to look over the gulches and move on. By the spring of 1870, the stable population had sifted down to 1500. Within three years the boom was over and the tents and cabins that littered the banks and benches above the stream were gradually deserted.

"With every new strike, the center of activity shifted up and down Cedar Creek, and at each, a camp sprang up, only to be abandoned when a richer location was uncovered at another bar. The first was Louisville, the second, Forest City, which turned out to be the biggest and most permanent, for it lasted until the winter of 1872. It had stores and a postoffice, a blacksmith shop, and a Wells Fargo express office. Sixty-mule pack trains made regular trips to the creek from Missoula, loaded with produce and supplies of all sorts.

"As soon as we come to the remains of any of these camps, stop, so I can sketch," I told Francis. "While I draw, you might like to read some first-hand accounts of what this stampede was like. I found a good many articles that were written in 1870, in old issues of the *Helena Herald*. I copied them and have them here in my notebook. They help me understand the excitement and the toughness, the faith and the stamina that made men put up voluntarily with primitive living as long as there was gold to be scooped from the beds of streams."

Helena Weekly Herald
January 18, 1870
The Cedar Creek Mines
The Richest Mines Ever Discovered, if Only One-Tenth as Good as Expected.
The Mines are located on the south branch of Cedar Creek, a tributary of the Missoula River. . . . No one, owing to heavy snows has been able to trace any of its sources, three in number, that form the creek, 21 miles from its mouth. The whole of the gulch is covered with a dense growth of timber and heavy underbrush, making the ascent over a roughly-cut trail very tedious and tiresome. . . . The width of the creek bottom varies from 50 feet to ¼ of a mile, sometimes forming a canyon and again spreading out. *There has yet no mining been done, beyond digging a few prospect holes.* On discovery there is an opening 6 x 15 feet, wherein a prospect of from seven to fifteen cents can easily be panned out, and wherefrom several hundred dollars are reported to have been washed with a pan in a few days. The pay gravel, about 14 inches thick, underlies four or five feet of coarse yellow wash and large boulders. The bed-rock is slate, but no trace of float quartz has been found yet. . . . It will be impossible to mine in the creek bottom during the high water season. . . . There is no possibility of bringing in a sawmill now and all lumber must be whip-sawed; but not a joint of sluice box is yet made or set in all these rich diggings . . . not even the rattle of a hand rocker greeted my ear. . . . There are the wildest reports of the fabulous richness of this "Second Alder" in the streets of your city, but during my short stay of twelve days I have failed to see the first ounce of Cedar dust change hands — nothing beyond a good color and fair traces of gold.

The upper or Barrette District will make . . . a well paying camp, but not extensive enough to warrant a great stampede. Every foot of ground is taken up and none as yet offered for sale.
The Tributary Gulches
Oregon Gulch, is the north fork of Cedar Creek, branching off 7 miles from the mouth of the latter. It is 18 miles long.

Cayuse, Rabbit, Spring, Boulder, Montreal, Marion, Wolverine and Illinois Gulches are all located and laid over until the fifteenth of May next — the color found in all of them.
The Towns
Eight hundred feet below the upper or Barrette discovery, a town has been laid out, christened Louisville, and a dozen houses make the city. Montroy, of the City Hotel, is building a large two-story house here. Jack Demers has an assortment of goods

also; but the town is so illy located that the only street (to give the houses room) is but ten feet wide. Lots are held high. . . . the whole town site occupying but half an acre. A plat of ground has been laid out some 600 feet above Louisville and is called Martina City. No house has been erected yet and only foundations (four sticks laid up in a square) indicate the use of this flat spot on top of a mountain.

The main town, at the present writing, is Cedar Junction, laid out in a wide bottom at the first forks of Cedar Creek. . . . Two streets forty feet wide run parallel up the gulch, divided into lots 40 x 100. Substantial log buildings are being erected and the sound of saw and axe is heard from morning until night. Chauncey Barber is the town Recorder. . . . Williams, the pioneer barber of Montana, has a barber shop in full blast, and two stores — McQuirk of Missoula and George Montgomery of Beartown, deal out the necessaries of life, and bottled *inspiration*.

There is but little sale for tools, and the high price demanded for articles is owing to the rate of freight demanded by packers to come over the bad road leading into the gulch. . . . The indomitable pioneer merchant, John H. Ming, is rushing all over the country untiring, locating on the head of the gulch, in the middle, and at the mouth — venturing in every place to be on hand, whereever the main point may be. As a sample of his enterprise, let me mention that on Christmas day he walked 16 miles, chopped a set of house logs, built a brush shanty at night, and laid his restless bones under it in the snow.

Helena Daily Herald
January 21, 1870
Cedar Creek Mines
A new town or two have been laid out during the past week, but nothing aside from the customary four sticks, called a foundation, marks the ground. One at the mouth of Illinois gulch . . . is called Jamestown and is intended as a supply point for Illinois and its small tributaries. The other intermediate between Louisville and Cedar Junction, at the point where Kyuse Gulch mingles its waters with Cedar Creek, is Mugginsville.

Building . . . is progressing rapidly at Cedar Junction and Louisville; and where two weeks ago dense forests obstructed the view heavenward, today a fine clearing offers a pleasant contrast to the surrounding sombre woods. The number of men here is 800.

Moose Creek, a tributary of Missoula, is quite a lively camp, consisting of 30 men who came over the divide at the head of Cedar on snow shoes.

One of the worst features of this whole camp is the trail following the course of the creek, and it seems an impossibility for an animal to get over the icy, precipitous ascents. . . . Let those who come bring all they want in provisions, warm clothing, plenty of greenbacks and a pair of gum boots. Then they will be equipped for this rough and wild country.

Numerous accidents by the careless handling of the axe, and some by the felling of trees, happen daily, but I forbear burdening this letter with the distressing details. . . . The boys stand out-door life well, and grow fat on bacon and molasses.

. . . There is a good deal of lot jumping going on. The weather is pleasant. Grub is scarce; whisky bad; excitement high, and — that's all.

Yours,
SIMMONS

Helena Daily Herald
January 28, 1870
The pioneers of the Walla Walla stampede have arrived, eight in number. They report that the excitement is running riot in Idaho, . . .from five to six hundred of these Idahoers will be here inside of a week, to be followed by hundreds of others. As the trail leading from the head of Cedar, *via* St. Joe mines to Lewiston, although impracticable at this season of the year, is but 168 miles to the latter city, it will be crowded with pilgrims and with pack animals as soon as it is open, . . . it will be several months ere this avenue is opened; meanwhile we depend for our supplies on Missoula. Packers have the best of it at present, receiving ten cents a pound from Frenchtown to Cedar, about 75 miles; but the depth of snow prevents animals from feeding on grass, and grain sells in the mines at 25 cents a pound. . . . The first conflagration in Cedar threatened to destroy the store of George Montgomery last Saturday. By the speedy application of snow in large quantities, and a little water, this calamity was prevented.

March 3, 1870
Louisville is improving daily. . . . On the bars below the town and above Cedar Jct. prospecting is beyond all expectations, running as high as $1.25 a pan. The Sweeney District on Lost Gulch, a tributary of Oregon, has bars prospecting 40 cents to the pan. Several drain ditches are about to be opened.

March 10, 1870
Louisville contains 680 and Cedar Junction 91 houses. All day long may be heard the merry ring of the hammer and the labored grating of the whip-saw, and the heavy thud of another monarch of the forest laid low. Wages are $4-5 a day.

Theo. A. Bailey

Helena Daily Herald
May 25, 1870
Judge Williams received last night a letter from an old miner:

Louisville, Cedar Creek, M. T.
May 21, 1870

Dear Judge;
I arrived here about two weeks ago. . . . I will state . . . my judgment of Cedar Creek, tributaries etc., backed by 21 years of experience in a gold-producing country.

First, Cedar Creek is a stream of no small importance. . . . A tourist . . . crosses the Missoula river, near the mouth of Cedar, where he finds a path or mule trail leading up the creek for a distance

of 7 miles, to a settlement called Cedar Junction, being the junction of Oregon and Cedar creeks. This settlement contains some 30 or 40 finished and unfinished buildings, claiming a population of 23 inhabitants. The creek is staked and claimed for mining purposes from the junction to Missoula [Lake]. . . .

From Cedar Creek Junction up Cedar Creek it is 4 miles to a flourishing little town called Kiyus where mining has commenced in good earnest. From Kiyus to Louisville, a distance of 4 miles further up the creek, men are at work on every claim. Louisville is the principal place of business on the creek, although there are other settlements still above, the nearest 4 miles called Forest City. There is mining on every claim between them. Discovery claim opposite Louisville, is worked by 21 men, running two strings of sluices.

My letter would be incomplete if I failed to mention the arrival of Gov. Ashley and the enthusiastic reception he received from the citizens of Louisville on the evening of the 14th. The Governor had hardly made his appearance when an impromptu meeting was arranged by the citizens in front of Montroy & Drolett's hotel, where the Governor was welcomed. . . . Gov. Ashley addressed the meeting upon the mineral and agricultural interests of this region. . . . He complimented the miner for his indefatigable trials and indomitable will in pressing his way over mountains and gorges, braving the danger and great depth of snow . . . in traveling over this rugged country in search of gold, where heretofore only the mountain sheep would dare tread. He referred to the immigrants that had been his long desire to have come and remain as permanent citizens of the Territory, what he had personally done for the same and the great usefulness of such a class of citizens. . . . The meeting adjourned with loud cheers for the Governor.

Respectfully yours,
H. L.

Helena Daily Herald
July 14, 1870
A New Free Ferry
John Kennedy has made a hide rope and crossed the Missoula three-quarters of a mile above the old ferry on the free list. The old Ferry Co. contends that all the land from rim to rim, at the mouth of Cedar is theirs by right of pre-emption and possession. A controversy ensued and the friends of both parties hauled shot-guns, rifles and pistols, and beautiful epithets passed but there was no bloodshed.

The Deroush minstrel troupe performed here two evenings with success. They are now performing at Louisville and Forest City, and living on pine bark.

The Weekly Missoulian
September 2, 1874
Cedar and Vicinity
The proper thing to do for one desiring to visit Cedar is to take passage in Robinson's little red wagon

as far as Moose creek ferry, and from there on gently persuade some equable cayuse or religiously disposed mule. The trip is not suggestive of rock-me-to-sleep-mother ruminations or dyspeptic forebodings. (Robinson) has operated this route for two years . . . and has sub-contracted for the Bitter Root route.

Mrs. McCabe still keeps the old station 13 miles below Frenchtown. . . . Superior City contains a resident population of two souls, the ferryman and George Confort in charge of Buck & Cave's store. George supplies Quartz creek miners.

Cedar Creek

The discoloration of the water shows that busy hands are rinsing the gravel above . . . Cedar Junction is 8 miles up creek, but the pay streak was never found there. . . . two miles farther up is the Cayuse Flume, which 10-15 men have worked continuously for the past four years. . . . This flume is now on bed rock.

Considerable mining is being done between Cayuse and the old town of Louisville. . . . Parties working in Rabbit gulch, a tributary of Cedar, emptying a mile below Louisville, have taken out good pay recently.

The lumber and logs of the old town of Louisville have pretty much been utilized in building flumes. There are three souls and a ghost in Louisville.

"The graves give up their sheeted dead
To walk and gibber in the streets."

There is a saloon at this place to furnish the elixir to brace the backbone for further climbing and to dispel ghostly thoughts. A half mile about Louisville have pretty much been utilized in building has paid regularly something over wages for the past two years.

The mines of the Forest Flume Co. lie 2 miles above the old town of Forest. The town of Forest has almost passed into history. One-half mile above is Mayville, the present heart of Cedar's enterprise and activity.

"One item that these clippings did not mention was that the first newspaper published in Missoula County was issued September, 1870 by Magee & Company, and was called *The Missoula & Cedar Creek Pioneer*," I said as we continued to drive up the heavily timbered gulch. "For three years this district had a paper. Then it was moved to Missoula and its name changed to the *Missoulian*.

"Another bit of pertinent information that I found was that Louis Barrette, the discoverer of the Cedar Creek mines, interested a group of men from Frenchtown — G. T. A. Lacasse, George Comfort, and Damas Asslin — in forming the Cedar Creek Placer Mining Company in 1884. This outfit, by using improved machinery, worked the gulch successfully until 1906. The ground yielded gold at the rate of thirty-six cents a cubic yard with the gold averaging $19 an ounce. The work was done from the surface down for a distance of forty feet. The paystreak in places was one thousand feet wide. According to the *Anaconda Standard* of December 18, 1904, only one-half mile of ground had been worked up and down stream in the gulch during the previous twenty years."

All the time that we were driving up Cedar Creek, we were watching the mileage in an attempt to identify the sites of the former camps. Seven miles above the Clark Fork, we had crossed Oregon Creek on a steel bridge. Cedar Junction must have been there. Four miles more and we came to Cayuse Creek. No doubt, Cayuse Camp was nearby. After another four miles, another stream flowed into Cedar Creek. On the swampy flat were a few broken down cabins. Could this have been Louisville? Three more miles and we should see the site of Forest City. By this time the road was rougher and steeper. As we climbed, along came a truck with a man and a dog. I hailed it and asked the driver how much farther Louisville was?

"You passed it back where the cabins were, just this side of where Rabbit Creek comes in. Forest City wasn't far from there. If you drive ahead a mile and a half, you'll come to the site of Mayville."

We went on until we reached a broken down frame mill with a flume and a couple of cabins. Perhaps this was Mayville, or was it the power house I had seen indicated on a forestry map? It was worth recording, and while I was sketching it, the same truck that we had seen rattled by and the driver waved. In a moment he was back again to tell us we should go on another half mile, following the left fork of the road, if we wanted to see Mayville.

"There's only a few empty cabins back in the trees now. When the boom burst, everybody got out fast and left behind everything they couldn't carry. They used to tell how you could find furniture and miners' tools just strewn around wherever they happened to be when the owners left. The billiard balls and cues were still on some of the pool tables. After the white miners pulled out, in came the Chinese. They worked the diggings for a little while, living mostly in the shacks at Louisville. There's one part of the creek still called China Gulch."

Delighted to learn more about Mayville, we drove farther up a very narrow, badly washed road until we could look across a wide meadow, filled with grass-grown placer dumps. On the far side of the clearing were the cabins. Snowy peaks in the distance rose above the heavily wooded hills.

On the way back, I looked for signs of more recent mining, and when we reached the Amador mine, we stopped to investigate it and found a bunkhouse and several smaller buildings. I had heard that the local mining excitement at the beginning of the twentieth century centered around this copper property, and that the Amador Gold & Copper Mining Company operated the mine in 1902, cutting into a large ore body 165 feet below the bed of Cedar Creek. By 1904, however, the mine was in litigation. From the *Wallace Miner* of September 19, 1907, I had learned that

Promoter Mackinnon has done much in development and equipment, and has expended $250,000. He has constructed a 10-mile railroad from the mine to Iron Mt.; erected a 60-ton test smelter, run drifts, tunnels, etc. The ore reserves of the Amador mine are unknown to the general public.

The same paper mentioned other properties that were active in 1907:

The LaCasse brothers during late years have washed from their placer areas $500,000. . . . Cedar Creek where it runs through the LaCasse placers, has exposed a number of white crystalline lodes containing high values in gold and silver and commercial values in copper and lead, the lead content in cube form.

Another paper, dated 1932, mentioned renewed activity on Cedar Creek and listed six companies as actively engaged in mining.

"We may not have seen much of the old camps that once lined this creek," I observed to Francis when we emerged from the canyon and drove back to Superior, "but we've been over rich ground from which, if we consider the entire district, $2,000,000 in gold has been recovered. Placer gold alone accounted for from $1,000 to $16,000 a year. None of the places that we'll visit west of here can equal that record."

PARDEE and the IRON MOUNTAIN MINE

"Turn north beyond the American Legion Hall in Superior, if you're looking for the Flat Creek road," Mr. McDonnell had told us, and now that we were back from Cedar Creek, our next objective was the Iron Mountain property and the long deserted camp of Pardee.

The Flat Creek trail proved to be another excellent forest road, a little steep at first, but leveling off and winding through trees. Occasionally we passed a cabin. When the road divided, we stayed with the Flat Creek branch which brought us, at the end of four miles, to a ruined mill of which nothing was left but charred wood, debris, and concrete piers. Beside it, to the left, a narrow trail disappeared up the mountainside. Close to the mill was a sign pointing to the trail and labeled "Flat Creek Trail. Next 6 miles steep and narrow with switchbacks."

Opposite the mill and to the right of the road over which we had come, was a meadow through which the creek wandered. On both sides of the stream for some distance were weathered cabins and the splintered boards and beams of others that had collapsed. This was all that remained of Pardee, the town that was named for James K. Pardee, the discoverer of the mine and the organizer of the original mining company. The property was discovered in 1888 as described here:

Last fall three prospectors, one of which was Johnson of Phillipsburg, and the others from Spokane Falls, struck a prospect on Flat Creek, a small stream emptying into the Missoula 70 miles west of this city [Missoula]. From an assay made from 10 tons of ore, $1400 was realized. . . . J. K. Pardee of Philipsburg took the train to Missoula.

As soon as he saw the prospects he decided to buy or bond it. He bonded the property for $100,000. The vein on top of the ground was 40 feet wide, with 6-feet of rich galena in the center. It is 10 miles by pack train to the N. P. R. R. near the mouth of the Jocko.

Weekly Missoulian, January, 1889

Shortly after Pardee obtained possession of the property, he erected a mill one mile from the mine on Flat Creek. Around this mill rose the town of Pardee, a prosperous gold and silver camp which flourished for several years. At first the rich surface ores were packed out of the district on mules, over the mountains north of the mine, and down to the Missoula (or Clark Fork) River. There the ore was loaded on barges and floated downstream to Paradise, the nearest railroad station, in the next valley to the north. From Paradise it was shipped by rail to various smelters.

The mine was operated by the Iron Mountain Mining Company for several years, during which period many thousands of dollars were spent on bridges, roads, and surface improvements of the property, as well as $30,000 for a concentrator, a boiler-house and other buildings. During these eight years, the Iron Mountain yielded half a million dollars in dividends and ranked as one of the best paying silver properties in the state. As soon as the Northern Pacific Railroad built its Coeur d'Alene branch through Superior in 1891, thus reducing the hauling distance to the railroad to four miles, large scale operations began, with the company building a 200-ton mill in Superior, near the station. This Iron Mountain mill was connected with the mine workings by an aerial tramway. The mine was operated between 1888 and 1896 by the Iron Mountain Mining Company, which in 1896 employed between 100 and 125 men. Later in the same year, the property was closed down by the Inspector of Mines, since, by not having two openings, it violated state law. A final shipment of twenty-seven carloads of concentrates, averaging $50 a ton, was shipped from the property in October, 1897.

In the early 1900's, the Iron Mountain Tunnel Company leased the property and planned to drill a 5,600-foot tunnel to tap the Iron Tower mine at a depth of 1,600 feet. This stock company obtained a bond and lease on a number of quartz lodes, 380 acres of placer ground, and three millsites with an option to purchase the same prior to 1910. Some work must have been done for Pardee was not abandoned until about 1930. Since then, lessees have from time to time opened the property,

with one outfit working the old diggings as recently as 1958.

ST. REGIS

A fourteen mile drive west from Superior, on Highway No. 10, brought us to St. Regis. Here the Clark Fork doubles back on itself and cuts a narrow gorge between the Ninemile Divide and the eastern end of the Coeur d'Alene Mountains. I was eager to see this portion of the river, for it was over this stretch of water that flatboats floated the Iron Mountain ore to the nearest railroad before the Coeur d'Alene branch of the Northern Pacific was built. At the east end of this canyon is Paradise; at the west end, St. Regis, a sawmill town and supply center for loggers. Like Superior, it is split by the river and connected by bridges over which run the highway and the railroad. The southeasterly flowing St. Regis River joins the Clark Fork here and gives its name to the settlement that grew up on its banks. Here, also, in early days stood Peter Rabbit's saloon and stage station, commonly called "The Kitchen." Some gold was recovered from placers in the vicinity, and at one time the St. Lawrence, Oro Fino, Amazon, Dixie, Rock Island, and Lenore lode mines were active.

"You can drive from St. Regis to Paradise

AMERICAN GOLD PROPERTY, CEDAR CREEK
NEAR MAYVILLE

MILL FOUNDATIONS, IRON MT. MINE,
PARDEE

by going down the river," Mr. Bennett, postmaster at Superior told me. "Twelve miles from St. Regis there's a ferry, but you don't need to take it for the road along the river is good for the whole twenty-three miles."

We lacked the time to make this side trip, and had to save Paradise for a later visit. Now we hurried on west to Saltese.

SALTESE

That Saltese exists is a tribute to the men who fought to save it from the consuming forest fires that raged through the entire area during the summer of 1910. There's not much of it left at that — just a scattering of stores and homes beside the present highway. The town is in the bottom of a narrow gorge. High above it, on a ledge of the canyon wall, are the tracks of the electrified Milwaukee Railroad.

The site of Saltese was first known to packers, trappers, and prospectors and was called by them Packers Meadow. Packer Creek, a tributary of the St. Regis River, joins the main stream at this point. Here, Colonel Meyers, a "veteran of several wars," built the St. Regis House, a stopping place for travelers, freighters, and stagecoaches, especially after the completion of the Mullan Road. Around his inn, a village known as Silver City grew up — a supply point for the placer mines across the pass in Idaho, and for the silver and gold mines in the immediate area, most of which were situated from two to five miles north or northwest of the townsite. The Last Chance yielded a net profit of $200,000 from silver and lead. The Ben Hur group, five miles north

of Saltese, produced both gold and silver. The Hugo contained copper. Other properties include the Bell, Tarbox, Meadow Mountain, Bryan, Silver Cable, U. S., and Hemlock.

Boot Hill Cemetery contains the graves of nine men and women who died with their boots on. Christopher Daggett, the first to be buried, froze to death on the trail to Mullan, while carrying mail. Katie Dillingham committed suicide when her love for a piano-playing traveling dentist was not returned. Frequently the graves were not dug until the coffins were deposited on the ground. Some say that it was the gravediggers who pitched pennies at the chinks between the pine boards, and that the poorest shot had to hike to town to get beer for his helper. Others say that mourners tossed coins at the casket. Either way, someone fetched a bucket of beer.

In 1891, the town received its present name — Saltese — in honor of a Nez Percé chief. When lumbering was the chief industry, eleven saloons served the lumber jacks and sawmill workers. Saltese barely survived the appalling forest fire that swept so close to it in July, 1910, the summer that the Coeur d'Alene forests exploded and sent flames leaping from ridge to ridge, blackening everything in their path. People in all the mountain towns were told to be ready to leave on a moment's warning and trains stood waiting on sidings, ready to pull away from the danger zones. Taft, on one side of Saltese, and DeBorgia, on the other, were completely wiped out. A bulletin from Montana, reporting on the fire and showing something of its extent, was printed in the

Seattle Daily Times on August 22:
Saltese is still safe, but is surrounded by walls of flame. The Northern Pacific officials' special is at Saltese, but cannot be moved as bridges are burned on every side.

St. Regis, old town, has been abandoned by the women, children and disabled, only a force of able-bodied fire fighters being retained under Supervisor Koch to make a stand against the flames which are steadily creeping on the place.

The towns of Rivulet, Superior and Iron Mountain were abandoned this morning. The Iron Mountain Tunnel Company's mining property caught fire early today and was destroyed. Some minor casualties are reported.

Frantic phone calls to headquarters from forest supervisors and their helpers were far from reassuring: "Fire all along the line. Trying to save Saltese." "This is the last call. Fire is breaking into Saltese. We'll do our best to hold it." Saltese was saved, but all over that portion of Montana and Idaho, millions of acres of forest land were destroyed.

PARADISE

The shortest way to reach Paradise and the lower Clark Fork valley from Saltese is to drive back to St. Regis and take the "cut off" road along the main stream, to its junction with the Flathead River, a few miles south of Paradise. From there, the river swings northwest and flows the length of the valley into Lake Pend Oreille, in Idaho.

Paradise was disappointing to me, partly because of the spelling of its name. I had seen it written "Paradice" and the substitution of an "s" for a "c" completely destroys the original connotation. The old Kootenai trail, a heavily traveled road between 1810 and 1883, the year that the Northern Pacific built through the lower Clark Fork Valley, followed the north bank of the river from the mouth of the Flathead River into Idaho. Along this road, on the site of the present town, stood a roadhouse called the Pair-o'-Dice. From it, the town received its name.

Nowadays, Paradise is a railroad town and division point for the Northern Pacific, with freight yards paralleling the river and no hint of its earlier importance as a shipping point for the placer and lode mines in the vicinity. Six miles south of the town, along Spring Creek, there were gold and silver-bearing copper and lead ores. The last copper shipments from the King and Queen mines, operated by the Pit Copper Mining Company, were made in 1918.

PERMA

East from Paradise, Highway No. 10A is within sight of the Flathead River much of the time. When the timbered hillsides are left behind, open prairie stretches ahead for miles on both sides of the road. This is Camas Prairie, a part of the Flathead Indian Reservation. Perma, a tiny village thirteen miles east of Paradise, squats along the shore of the Flathead River. In one of its stores, I found an old fellow just in from prospecting in the hills. "Yes," he told me, "there were mines around here, but none of them are working. There's another town, called Camas Prairie, straight north of Perma. The June Bug mine, three and a half miles northeast of it, shipped thirty tons of copper ore in 1916. The mines

SALTESE

near Perma were operating between 1912 and 1917, and they shipped out sulphide ore carrying copper and silver. The Chilson property shipped as late as 1922. Why are you so interested? Do you want to buy a claim? I know where there are a couple of good ones."

REVAIS CREEK, DIXON

Ten miles east of Perma, the highway passes the mouth of Revais Creek, a tributary of the Flathead River. On this creek, four miles south of its mouth, are mining properties. Few claims have been located, however, partly because the area lies within the Flathead Indian Reservation, which was only opened to mineral location in 1904. Active mining began in 1910, and after that occasional shipments of gold-copper ore were made until 1925. The Drake and Mayflower mines were the most important properties. Four miles beyond Revais Creek, the highway runs through Dixon, a grain and cattle shipping center, located at the junction of the Jocko and Flathead Rivers. Here we turned back and retraced our way to Paradise. From there we continued west to the Idaho line.

THOMPSON FALLS

Thompon Falls is a far more important mining center than either Perma or Revais Creek. The Falls are thirty-one miles northwest of Paradise on Highway No. 10A. During the Coeur d'Alene gold rush in the early 1880's, it was the chief outfitting point for those attempting to cross the mountains into Idaho from the Montana side.

The town won its supremacy over Belknap, six miles farther west, in 1883, the year that the railroad was completed through the valley.

The Northern Pacific trains stopped at Belknap, but not at Thompson Falls; so the enraged citizens piled logs on the tracks and, while the train crews were clearing the right of way, the zealous boosters of the neglected camp harangued the passengers and urged them to get off and look the place over. Their efforts must have been successful; for during the winter of 1883, when hordes of impatient men were flocking to the Idaho gold camps, 10,000 stayed in tents and shacks down by the river, waiting to dash over the range as soon as the weather permitted.

To handle the traffic, an Indian trail was converted into a wagon road of sorts, which connected Thompson Falls with Murray, Idaho, thirty-five miles away. This became the Thompson Falls trail, which crossed Thompson Pass at an elevation of 4,859 feet. From Neil Fullerton, a retired Forest Service man, I learned that there were two trails across the Coeur d'Alene Mountains to the mining camps. Both started at Thompson Falls and followed Prospect Creek for miles. The trail over Glidden Pass, which was the most direct route to Burke and Wallace, swung left to cross the range, while the one that led to Murray and Eagle swung right and crossed Thompson Pass.

Accounts of the scramble to the gold fields, and the equally frantic trips "outside" for supplies, include many stories of the hardships endured while traveling this most direct route from the Idaho wilderness to civilization and a railroad. A letter in the collection of Richard G. Magnuson of Wallace, Idaho, dated 1885, and written by a father to his son, mentions Thompson Falls and the trail from Murray:

Murray, Idaho, Feb. 11th 1885
to Howard Parker,
Scotland, Ill.

Dear Howard, I did not return to Colorado as first intended on account of the long journey. . . . I concluded to stay here and avoid the labor of the trip. . . . We have splendid sleighing, the road to Thompson Falls . . . is made in the snow and is as hard as ice. The sleighs make the trip in about eight hours, a distance of 40 miles over a fairly level road, crossing one range of low mountains known as the Bitter Root range, the summit being the dividing line between the territories of Idaho and Montana. The town of Thompson is located on the banks of Clark's fork of the Columbia, in Northern Montana, just above the falls of the same name and so named, they say, on account of a certain Mr. Thompson having lost his life in attempting to pass over them in a boat. I have never seen the falls but the roar of the cataract is very distinctly heard in the town. The N. P. follows its banks for a long distance and

as you look down on its rapids they appear white as snow and in calm places are the color of a Colorado sky on a clear day.

Yours truly,
Wm. Parker

Quite different is the experience of two men who left Murray in August, 1889, and did not reach Thompson Falls on schedule:

A Forest Fire Escape
Murray, Ida.

John Bloom and Louis Siff left Murray for Missoula, Monday, on July 30th with two wagons and four horses. They had been warned at Murray that the journey would be dangerous on account of forest fires raging along the line from there to Thompson. A few hours after they had started the roar of flames was heard, and they urged their teams as rapidly as possibly. The speed of the horses was slow compared with the rapidity with which the fire traveled. They were very soon overtaken and leaving their teams in a deep ravine, ran for shelter into a deserted tunnel which . . . happened to be near at hand in the dense timber. Their place of refuge was entirely surrounded by fire, and it was five days before they were able to get out. There was a small spring in the tunnel from which they obtained water, but they were without food. . . . Their horses and wagons were entirely consumed but they did not murmur at that, being too thankful that they had themselves escaped a horrible death.

Idaho Recorder, August 29, 1889

The town of Thompson Falls is named for David Thompson, a surveyor and explorer, who was the first white man to travel the length of the Columbia River, mapping the territory as he went. His journey, which covered "50,000 miles on foot, on horseback and by canoe," was made early in the nineteenth century. In 1809, he built Salish House, just east of the town which bears his name. Today, a monument erected in his memory stands nearby.

Thompson Falls is the seat of Sanders County, and as I wanted information about the district's mines, I went to the courthouse. In the County Clerk & Records Office, I found someone who not only knew the region, but willingly looked up location notices in huge tomes, which she brought from a vault. From them I learned that the Silver King and Silver Cable mines on the Thompson River, nine miles northeast of the town, were silver-lead properties. They were discovered in 1884 or 1885, and have been moderately active in this century, beginning in 1919. Shipments have averaged $1,000 a year. In addition, the Copper King, Copper Mark, and Iron Mask have yielded copper carrying some gold and silver. There were also mines and placers on Prospect Creek, about ten miles southwest of the city, but they have been idle for some time.

When I returned the huge volumes to the clerk and thanked her for her kindness in getting them out, she smiled and said, "There was a mine with a big mill about eleven miles up Prospect Creek, but the mill is gone. I don't remember what it was. It may have been the Montana Standard property. It was up there somewhere. I remember the mill, because mother used to take us girls up there picnicking."

BELKNAP

Several small towns west of Thompson Falls were more important in their youth, when mining brought men to the region, than in recent years. Each was an outfitting and shipping center, and some, like Trout Creek, even yielded placer gold.

Six miles west of the Falls is Belknap, from which another trail led across the Bitterroot Range to the gold fields of Idaho. This route was a little shorter than the Thompson Pass road, but it was a more difficult trail in winter and was therefore not so heavily traveled. Belknap, at its peak, had a population of 3,000. Today it is slightly more than 100. This settlement, as far back as 1884, had its own newspaper, the *Belknap Sun,* a paper which kept its readers informed of the latest mining developments, such as: "Saddle horses from here to the mines have been reduced to $10. John W. Miller."

Good Placer Prospects
One Gulch Turns Out Bad but Another Looms Up

The *Sun* received a letter on Thursday from a party on the Belknap trail that the long drain in the gulch opposite McKee's camp had proved a failure. . . . Some very fine . . . prospects have . . . been found in the gulch . . . east of what is known as McKee's camp. Gold as large as a kernel of wheat is reported to have been panned out there. . . . The Belknap trail passes along the creek and it therefore becomes easily accessible.

Belknap Sun, June 28, 1884

The Northern Pacific Railroad built west, through Belknap, in 1883. One year later, fire broke out in the camp and two hours later the town was a smoking ruin. With no fire department to combat the flames, only six buildings survived. One was the new depot, which was saved only by the efforts of seventy-five men who arrived from Trout Creek on a work train and promptly organized a bucket brigade. The empty hotel of the Belknap Improvement Company provided shelter for the townspeople whose homes and business establishments were in ashes. Losses were etimated at $100,000.

White Pine is the next town beyond Belknap. On Beaver Creek, west of White Pine, is the Jack Waite mine, from which some silver-lead-zinc ore has been shipped.

TROUT CREEK

Trout Creek, eight miles farther west, was another outfitting point, especially at the time of the stampede to the Libby Creek placers. Nowadays its few buildings are off the highway and across the river from it. In 1873, rich bar diggings were found on Trout Creek, and for a time the bed of that stream was worked in an effort to find further deposits. Gold was recovered from placers along the Clark Fork in 1916 and 1917, as well as from Trout Creek in 1927.

The Vermilion Creek road joins the highway from the north, almost opposite the town. Several mining properties were reached by this road, the biggest being the Silver Butte mine, which was developed prior to 1905. Although this property has been idle since 1912, the storekeeper at Trout Creek assured me that some mining is still being done higher up the creek. At one time the Vermilion Creek trail was the link between Thompson Falls, the county seat, and the Fisher River and Libby Creek mines.

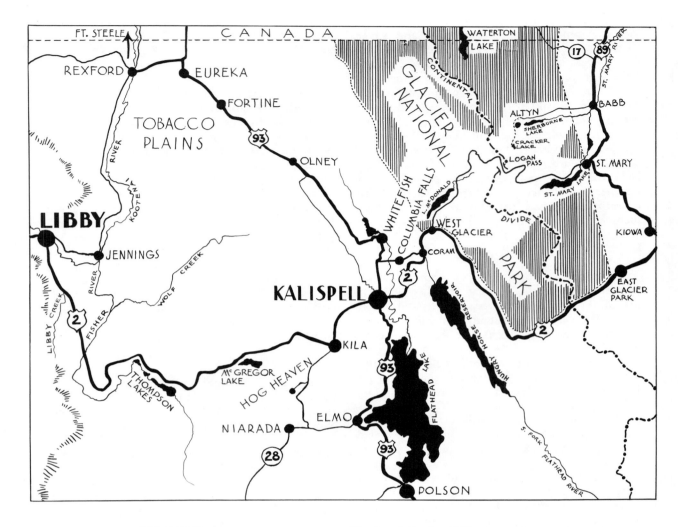

CHAPTER 16

HOG HEAVEN, SWIFT CURRENT and TOBACCO PLAINS

"This is completely new **country to me,**" I told Francis as we left Missoula and headed north on Highway No 93 **toward Glacier**

National Park. "There's a fine road the length of Flathead Lake, which everyone says is a magnificent body of water, but there's a mine back in the hills that I need to see more than I do scenery."

We hurried through St. Ignatius, located in the center of the Flathead Reservation, where a Roman Catholic mission was established as long ago as 1854 by Fathers DeSmet, Hoecken, and Menetrey, and where a mission church, school, and hospital are still maintained for the Indians. To the east rose the rugged Mission Range, above whose timbered slopes towered Mt. McDonald, topped by a glacier.

HOG HEAVEN and the
FLATHEAD MINE

At Polson, a busy trade center and county seat at the southern tip of Flathead Lake, we inquired from a mechanic, who had mining interests in the area, the way to the Flathead mine. He felt certain we could drive to it but suggested that we stop at Elmo to check with the storekeeper. The only building at Elmo was the store, and its elderly proprietor suggested that we drive to Niorada and get directions there. Fifteen miles due west brought us to Niorada, a wide spot in the road with a postoffice and a dusty store which appeared to be closed. Since it was Sunday, this did not surprise us, but when Francis tried the door, it opened. Inside was an old lady who knew every detail of the countryside.

"Of course you can drive up to the mine," she said. "It isn't working any more, but there is a watchman there. Drive back the way you came, four miles, to a gravel dump. A road runs north from there. Take it for one mile and then turn east on a ranch road. Farther along, there's a left hand fork. Take that too. I think there's a sign pointing to the mine. The Battle Butte property is up that way, also. If you get to the Flathead, you'll be almost at the top of the hill. The rest of the way is downgrade to Kila."

Following her directions, we drove north the mile from the gravel heap, and turned right onto a poorer road marked "Hill Ranch." We passed the Battle Butte schoolhouse and then climbed and wound for miles through low hills. In time we passed the gate to the Hill ranch and in the distance saw a yellow mine dump. Next, we stopped to read several signs which pointed to other mines — the Birdseye and the Rader. So far, we hadn't met a car. Perhaps we were on the wrong road. When we reached a deserted schoolhouse and a house with a garden, with clothes on the line and an empty garage, we stopped to inquire where we were. There was no one home.

Farther up the hill were yellow mine dumps and some abandoned mine workings. The road forked and we kept left, driving past more dumps on top of a hill and open trenches, apparently test holes. A short distance farther on, two dim tracks led to the left, through a gate to which was tacked a weathered, hand-lettered sign, "Crossover through Sec. 16 to Fltd. Mine Road and Gaurd Station." The trail was so overgrown that we decided against it, but watched where it went as we continued to climb. On a wooded hillside across a valley, I noticed a big dump and then lost it when our road entered a dense forest. At the top of a long grade was a sign: "Flathead Mine. Koffard Ridge Rd."

To the left was a graded road on which we drove for nearly two miles. At the next road fork, the lefthand branch led to the silver mine. There we found many old deserted cabins in among the trees on both sides of the road. They seemed to be company buildings and not too old, for many were covered with tar paper. Scrap lumber, broken tables, boxes, and general debris were scattered about. The biggest cabin had no roof and contained nothing but a sewing-machine stand. One cabin had a porch covered with trailing vines — perhaps the watchman stayed in it. Beside the road, nailed to a tree, was a sign, "Flathead Mine. Guard Station." On the way out we met a car and hailed the driver.

He told us that the mine workings we had seen several miles back, before we climbed to the top of the mountain, were silver properties that were owned by the Anaconda Copper Company, as were also the Birdseye and Rader. The area west of Flathead Lake was known locally as the Hog Heaven District, and high-grade float was found in the vicinity of the Flathead mine in 1913. This discovery interested the Anaconda Company, which sank a prospect shaft, only to have the ore pinch out with depth. When this occurred, the work was discontinued. The property lay idle until 1928, when lessees, in drifting to the north, located the ore body and shipped out several hundred tons of high grade before their lease expired in 1929. The ore was principally silver and lead and very little of the latter was saved. The Anaconda Company again took possession and began to develop the property. Between 1928 and 1930, 20,000 tons of ore were extracted, which yielded close to 1,500,000 oz. of silver. In 1930 several diamond drill holes were sunk to explore the deposit and then the company closed the mine again. The Flathead was the only productive property in the district.

Another property, the Ole, which was located in 1928, lay one mile west of the Flathead. The stockholders were Kalispell and Whitefish business men, who, shortly after the Flathead was discovered, leased 160 acres of ground surrounding the mine, from the Northern Pacific Company which owned the land. Although a 450-foot tunnel was driven on the property, development work had so far failed to show the value of the deposit.

Delighted to have met someone who knew so much about the Hog Heaven area, we drove on over the summit of the mountain and began a long, winding drop through the forest to Kila — a small community and station on the Great Northern Railroad. During this stretch of our journey, nothing but logging roads fed into ours from both sides of the mountain. From the gravel pile near Niorada to Kila was 31 miles.

From Kila, we drove east to Kalispell, a live lumber and agricultural center, where we stopped to eat lunch.

DEMERSVILLE

Kalispell, like many other towns in this northwestern corner of Montana, was the off-spring of the railroad. Prior to its founding, in 1891, as temporary railhead of the Great Northern road, Demersville, a steamboat landing, at the head of navigation on the Flathead River, four miles east of it, was the trade center of the valley. Established in 1887 by T. J. Demers, it was for several years the largest town north of Missoula. After Kalispell outstripped it and became the seat of Flathead County, Demersville moved a building at a time to the new metropolis.

ALTYN

I learned about Altyn by chance. One day while poring over bulletins in the library of the State School of Mines in Butte, the librarian, Mrs. Loretta Peck, asked if I knew that there had been a mining camp in Glacier National Park? I didn't, and she brought me an article she had written, which gave a brief summary of the camp. In 1960, I unexpectedly discovered a tattered copy of an Altyn newspaper in the Western History collection of the Denver Public Library. Upon inquiring if they had any Montana papers, the librarian replied, "Only two. One is from Virginia City and the other from Altyn." The rest of that afternoon was spent in copying portions of this long defunct publication. Excerpts from it and from Mrs. Peck's account are quoted in these pages.

The day that we reached the West entrance to Glacier National Park, Francis asked the Ranger if he knew where Altyn was, and after some searching, the man produced a map which showed its location.

"You're pretty smart," teased Francis as we entered the Park. "We're out looking for mining camps, not scenery, and here we are on our way to find a non-existent town, and where is it located? Just three-quarters of a

mile from Many Glaciers Hotel, one of the biggest and best hotels in the west."

I was too busy watching the magnificent landscape unfold to reply. Beyond Lake McDonald a fantastic sheer rock wall, thousands of feet high, shuts in the valley. Was it possible that a highway scaled its vertical face? In a few minutes we knew, for we were on the wide shelf road of Going to the Sun highway, close to the Garden Wall, and surrounded by snow-capped peaks and glittering ice fields. The descent from Logan Pass to St. Mary's Lake was equally breathtaking. By the time we turned west again, at Babb, for the final eighteen miles, I was drunk with beauty. By then, it was late afternoon and the peaks were sharp silhouettes outlined against a golden haze.

We passed Sherburne Lake and Swift Current Falls, and stopped at the enormous four-storied Swiss chalet — Many Glaciers Hotel. "Where was Altyn?" I asked the boy who took our bags. "Right out back of the hotel, on the flat, just three-quarters of a mile away," he replied. "You can drive almost all the way. Go to where the horses are stabled and ask the wranglers." We left the car at the horse corral and walked south across the flat meadow, to a thicket of trees. Below the meadow was the upper end of Lake Sherburne. In among the timber were a few broken-down cabins and some foundations. As we returned to the car, a string of horses ran by, on their way to the barns, and we waited for the dust to settle. "Where was Altyn?" I called to the wrangler who brought up the rear. "Right here, ma'am," he shouted as he loped off.

It was George Bird Grinnell, of New York, who made a hunting trip to these mountains in 1885 and was so impressed by the magnificent scenery that he determined to try to have the region set aside as a national park. His persistent efforts, coupled with his enthusiasm, resulted in its establishment in 1910. Meanwhile, much had to be arranged.

Up until 1898, the area now contained in the Park on the eastern side of the Continental Divide was part of the Blackfeet Indian Reservation, which was established in 1855. The area west of the Divide was open for settlement. The Blackfeet were not mountain Indians, but a Plains tribe, and cared little about using this section of their land; but Crees and Bloods, from the north, and Kootenais, from the west, came into it to trap beaver.

In 1892-1893, indications of copper were found in the Mineral Creek and Granite Park

FLATHEAD MINE

areas, above Lake McDonald, and a number of claims were staked. At about the same time, copper was discovered in the foothills, on Reservation land, but all such prospecting was illegal. Probably because it was forbidden ground, men were sure that it was rich in minerals, and pressure was brought on Congress to buy the strip from the Indians and open it to the whites. Mr. Grinnell, who knew the area, was appointed by the Secretary of the Interior to treat with the Blackfeet concerning such a sale, and in 1895, an act authorizing the purchase of the land from the Indians was passed, the Blackfeet receiving $1,-500,000 for the vast tract. Although this action was confirmed in 1896, the land was not thrown open until April 1898. In the intervening two years, many parties slipped into the territory, but were arrested and escorted to the border of the Reservation by Indian police.

The mining land was known as the Ceded Strip, or Swiftcurrent District. As soon as it was legally relinquished by the Blackfeet, the claims previously staked off were recorded and the miners rushed back to develop their prospects. As more of the rugged terrain was explored, copper and mineralized veins were uncovered in several locations. To provide access to this region, a wagon road was built from Babb to Altyn and extended six miles up Canyon Creek to Cracker Lake. A road also led from Altyn to mines in the Swiftcurrent Valley, and a trail over Swiftcurrent Pass to Granite Park enabled pack trains to deliver supplies to mines located there.

There is now quite a colony of prospectors camped in tents along the road at convenient places waiting for the snow to disappear and considerable prospecting has been done in the foothills, but nothing startling has yet been found.

This district being situated in Teton county, it is necessary to file the location notice in Choteau county seat, 80 miles from Blackfoot station, and this distance has to be made by team or horseback, making the total distance a prospector has to go to make his filing about 130 miles.

Swift Current Courier, September 1, 1900

Not satisfied with access to the territory, the miners were soon demanding that the land be removed from forest jurisdiction.

FARCICAL REGULATIONS.

It seems an absurdity to retain the Ceded Strip in the category of forest reserves. This district and those adjoining it are of no use whatever for . . . the maintenance of watersheds and the conservation of the present water supply; . . . for the timber hereabout can affect but little the source of that supply, inasmuch as most of the streams in this region take their rise above the actual timberline and come from glaciers whose existence promises to be perpetual. And if such were not the case, the present conditions and future necessities of the ever-extending mining oprations in this neighborhood will speedily denude the country of its forests for mine timbers, lumber and fuel. In view of such an inevitable result, — one that cannot be prevented — it is obvious that the present legal status of this part of the strip is farcical and should be abolished.

Swift Current Courier, September 1, 1900

The only settlement was Altyn, at the mouth of Canyon Creek, near Swift Current Lake. By 1899, the camp contained two saloons. Despite its promoters, who insisted that it would surpass Butte in size, it has disappeared. Its abandoned cabins and false-fronted stores stood on the flat below Mt. Altyn until a dam was built across Swift Current River to create Lake Sherburne. The lake crept in among the sagging buildings and covered many of them. Others were demolished or removed. The 1914 edition of the U. S. Geological Survey map of the Park shows a cluster of 15 buildings; the 1938 edition shows none. So, today, Altyn is merely a memory. But in 1900, it had a newspaper, the *Swift Current Courier.* The first issue contained the following:

COPPER IS KING
NO DOUBT NOW ABOUT THE PERMANENCY
AND PRODUCTIVENESS OF THE
SWIFT CURRENT MINES
NO STOCK FOR SALE.

The company operating the Cracker Mine are jubilant. $97.50 offered for $1 stock and refused.

ALTYN, MONTANA is situated about 50 miles northwest of Blackfoot and 35 miles southwest of Cardston, Alberta. It occupies a picturesque location in the center of a natural amphitheater, deeply fringed with majestic forests of pine and surrounded by titanic mountains, rugged canyons and azure lakes, the whole country being a masterpiece of beauty and sublimity.

To Mr. J. M. Harris, of Altyn . . . much credit is due for the degree of prosperity and enterprise Altyn at present enjoys. His faith in its future . . . has been backed by his means, and a large, imposing two-story store building has just been erected by him. . . .

. . . There is not a man who has investigated existing conditions in the mines . . . but is emphatic in expressing his opinion, that Altyn will be one of two things, viz: the richest and biggest camp on earth or nothing. . . .

To show that this country . . . is not half prospected the following incident will prove conclusively. Mr. Mathison, school superintendent of the Educational Department of the Reservation, with little or no knowledge of prospecting, or mining, discovered one of the most promising looking veins in the camp. Richard McCaffrey, otherwise known as Bacon Rind Dick, did the same this spring, discovering a fine lead, almost in sight of the Swift Current Falls. He and Mr. McNeil now rejoice in the ownership of mining property that will in the near future place them on easy street.

Swift Current Courier, September 1, 1900

The two best properties in the Swift Current District were the Cracker mine, at the south end of Cracker Lake, at the base of Mt. Siyeh, and the Bull's Head, on the southwest side of Mt. Wilbur, near Bullhead Lake. The Bull's Head claim, originally owned by the Stark brothers, was developed under lease and bond by A. M. Essler, of the Essler Mining & Construction Company of Helena. A small camp called Harrisville was located near the mine.

The Cracker, named by the two prospectors — L. C. Emmons and "Hank" Norris — who cached a lunch of crackers and cheese near their prospect, was owned by the Michigan & Montana Copper Mining & Smelting Company. This company, which was organized in September 1898, had a contract with A. M. Essler to mine, mill, and market 400,000 tons of ore within three and a half years. Since the last nine wagon-loads of machinery for the mill arrived late in August, 1900, the concentrator was expected to start up early in September.

Mr. Essler's death left affairs in a chaotic state and caused a setback in work but by December the concentrator was largely completed and a tunnel driven 1300 feet, including 400 feet along the vein.

CRACKER MINE pay ore has been found in the gangue and it is almost inexhaustible. We have struck the very finest kind of peacock copper ore for concentrating and as soon as a concentrator is ready we will put on more men and keep the machinery moving to its fullest capacity. . . . The blue quartz in the gangue is rich in boronite, in immense quantities. . . . T. A. Winters, one of the largest stockholders, states that as soon as sufficient tonnage is obtained, a railroad will be built from Durham to the district.

Swift Current Courier, September 1, 1900

ALTYN, GLACIER NATIONAL PARK

SITE OF ALTYN

In March, 1901, the Cracker and Bull's Head mines were consolidated, stockholders of the Essler Company receiving shares in the Michigan & Montana Company, which was capitalized at $300,000. Apparently, the concentrator at the Cracker property was still not operating, but it was promised to be ready by September. To improve the water supply for the Bull's head mine, a dam was constructed at Swift Current Falls. In December, 1901, John Longmaid, a mining expert, examined the properties to determine whether development on a larger scale was warranted. A news item, dated October 18, 1902, mentions the company's persistent efforts to open up the ore body in the Cracker mine. No further announcements appear.

At the same time that these two mines were being developed, other properties were active. One was the Josephine; another was the Ptarmigan group on Appekenny Mountain, about 8 miles from Altyn. Prospect holes covered the mountains on either side of Kennedy Creek, between Robinson and Chief Mountains.

That Altyn had grown from two saloons in 1899 to a sprouting town is shown by several items in the 1900 *Courier*:

NEWS NUGGETS

The small sea of tents is rapidly disappearing at the advance of the man with hammer and saw, and substantial houses are going up rapidly in its place. Great will be Altyn!

* * *

A first class meal can be had at Carleton and Hunter's for 50c.

* * *

Hansen's Stage is loaded down with passengers coming to camp every trip.

* * *

A water ditch is to be constructed a distance of 180 rods from Goat creek down Main St. to Swift Current Creek. It will be used for domestic purposes and also for placer gold mining, the ground on the south side of the latter named creek being rich enough to work.

* * *

The second public dance given in the camp took place a short time ago in Mr. J. M. Harris' hall and was thoroughly enjoyed by a large number of ladies and gentlemen. Those present would have graced any fashionable ball room and the gathering gave evidence of the high social standing the people of Altyn occupy.

* * *

The upper story of Mr. Harris' store building will probably be reserved for a public recreation hall.

* * *

ADVERTISEMENTS
Take Your Washing to LOUN SING, Altyn's Laundry Man.

* * *

ADLAM & THOMPSON, Pioneer Liquor Purveyors of Swift Current District.

* * *

Drugs and Medical Supplies, J. J. JOHNSTON, Cardston, Alberta, Canada.

* * *

Swift Current Pool & Billiard Hall, NEILS Y. HANSEN, All Kinds of Temperance Drinks Dispensed at the Bar, Tobacco & Cigars, Fruit & Confectionery, Stationery, etc., Altyn.

* * *

HIGH OLD TIMES
Mourning in Camp. Flag Floats at Half-Mast and Crepe Hangs on Door.

* * *

On August 14, the Stars and Stripes hung despondently over one of the largest buildings in town. The Flag was also draped in black, tar paper being used in place of crepe, and a great sheet of the same stuff was religiously and sadly hung over the handle of the front door. As early as six o'clock in the morning the mourners began to gather. . . . All conceded it to be the greatest calamity in the history of the camp. The only saloon had closed its doors pro tem.

Altyn's years were few, and despite the *Courier's* valiant efforts to publicize the camp, most of its population, which never exceeded 100, were gone by 1910, and the mining properties in the high mountains were deserted.

Having visited the site of the ephemeral mining camp and completed my sketches, I was ready the following morning to leave Many Glaciers Hotel and retrace our drive of the previous day out of the Park. From Babb, we continued south to St. Mary's, a tiny settlement at the lower end of St. Mary's Lake. At the time of the Swift Current boom, a gold rush to Divide Creek "lasted only long enough to establish the village of St. Mary's." One paragraph in the *Swift Current Courier* had mentioned this excitement:

ST. MARY'S LAKE DISTRICT
comprises all the mountains on the east side of the lake and contains a large number of promising claims. The Cracker, once more shows itself, crosses the lake and remains blind until Red Eagle creek is crossed when it again delights the vision of the fortunate prospector. Dan Doody and Jack Brice have made several locations on this apparently endless lead. The mountain on which these claims exist is known as DIVIDE. Directly west of Divide is the Kootenay Mt. which is also dotted with small piles of rock, each pile representing a mineral deposit.

September 1, 1900

As we climbed to Logan Pass, I took a last look at the mountainous terrain which had drawn so many prospectors to it. Mining experts who inspected their strikes were not optimistic and after two years of frantic work, even the most stubborn diehards admitted that high grade deposits did not exist. Scarcely any gold had been found and little copper. By 1902, the boom was over, and by 1910, the last miner had pulled out.

TOBACCO PLAINS

From West Glacier, we drove back through Coram and made a four-mile detour to see Hungry Horse Dam, completed in 1953 to impound water from the South Fork of the Flathead River.

As we left Whitefish, I pointed north and said to Francis, "Tobacco Plains are up there. It's ranch and farming country now, but at one time it had a little mining. The best source of information about the area is Olga Weydemeyer Johnson's book, *The Story of the Tobacco Plains Country.*"

No one knows when the Kootenai Indians came to the wide prairie just south of the present Canadian border and grew a wild tobacco which they used for ceremonial purposes. While the plant is no longer cultivated, a tributary of the Kootenai River, which enters the main stream at Rexford, seven miles south of the border, bears the name Tobacco River.

The British explorer, Dr. James Hector, reported in 1859 that small amounts of gold were found in the bed of the Kootenai near Fort Kootenai, but his statement went unheeded. Only when the gold strike on Wild Horse Creek, in British Columbia, sent men streaking north in the middle sixties, did prospectors discover the northern prairie. Disappointed miners, returning from Wild Horse, panned each stream from force of habit, and in a few places found small placer deposits. Some gold was washed on Grave Creek at this time, and Chinese miners sluiced Scattergravel Bar on the Kootenai, near Rexford. The Hoffman brothers placered McGuire Bar, one mile below Stonehill, and placers south of the Winkley ranch, near Fortine, were reported in 1888. Some work was done on the south side of the valley, "at Swamp Creek and as far west as Pinkham and Sutton Creeks." Lower Pinkham Creek was said by some to be the richest area in the valley. As late as 1921, placer gold was reported from the Tobacco River near Eureka.

T. C. Clark arrived from Tobacco Plains, Tuesday night and registered with two bags of gold dust.

The gold is of the fine Kootenai quality. Mr. Clark returns today to his diggings. He says that he has $10 a day and does not care who knows it.

Weekly Missoulian, October 24, 1884

Hard-rock mining was carried on in a small way in the Stillwater and Stryker area and on Deep Creek, east of Fortine. Gust Peterson held several claims on the north side of Paradise Lake, in Poorman Basin.

Ed Boyle found a good lead of ore two miles above his Indian Creek cabin in 1892. Since he made the discovery on July 4, he named the mountain and the mine the Independence. This copper and lead property lay six miles east of the Kootenai River, close to the Canadian boundary. By the summer of 1893, everyone was talking about mining and "every cabin had samples of ore from various strikes."

Tobacco Plains
July 24, 1895

Large veins of copper, silver and gold were discovered in 1892 by John Bonander and Ed. Boyle and the first claims located were the Little Willie and the Independence. These claims are on the same vein and two miles from the Plains, on the south side of the mountain. . . .

Two miles farther east over the mountain, is the Copper Glance, owned by John Bonander and William Jamieson. . . . Assays from these claims show 15% copper, 30 oz. of silver and $50 in gold at a depth of 6 feet. . . . All ores are concentrating propositions. Men with means, it is hoped, will soon be here.

Jno. Bonander
Libby Silver Standard, August 3, 1895

The Independence, with development, turned out to be the biggest mine in the district. The ore was Chalcopyrites of copper, commonly called yellow copper. The lead was large and quantities of ore, running from eight to twenty per cent in copper were extracted. Twelve men worked on the property during the summer of 1894, two cabins were built at the mine, and ore was packed out to the river bank to be shipped by boat to Jennings. Whenever capital was available, the mine was active.

In 1912, the British Columbia Copper Company, of Nelson, became interested in the Independence and several other claims in the area — the Blue Bird, Swansea Rose, Midnight, Copper Kettle, and Red Bird — and "sampled and assayed ore from their outcroppings and dumps." The results were satisfactory and the company arranged to lease the claims, but high tariffs and World War I delayed the transaction and the lease was dropped. In 1932, the Rex Copper Company of Eureka controlled the Independence property, with John L. Hartt as manager. Ed Boyle, who discovered the mine, once refused an offer of $50,000 for his claim. During the 1940's, after years of sporadic activity, the Independence was sold for taxes by Lincoln County. A part interest brought $48.00.

The Kootenai, a majestic and awesome river, which rises in Canada and flows south in a great loop through the northwest tip of Montana and Idaho, to re-enter Canada and flow north before joining the Columbia, dominates this whole area and, in early days, provided the main artery of transportation. Its loop suggested a drawn bow and the neighboring Indian tribes called the broad stream the Flatbow River and the Kootenais the Flatbows.

Steamboats on the Kootenai River were, for many years, the lifeline which transported supplies, mail, and ore, as well as passengers, to and from the isolated settlements along the banks. The boats started running between Fort Steele, Canada, and Jennings, Montana, in 1892 during the high-water season which lasted from late May until October. Each fall, when they were tied up for the winter, canoes, flatboats, and barges carried freight and passengers, as long as the river was free of ice. Passenger fare was ten cents a mile and freight $2 a ton. W. E. Doak, an experienced river man, is quoted in Mrs. Johnson's book:

At the end of the steamboat season the freight was handled by rafts and canoes down river and canoes up. This gave employment to a number of river men from both the Tobacco Plains and Libby districts, who were as hardy and happy-go-lucky a bunch of river hogs as ever climbed a boat pole. . . . The best small boat for freighting ever poled up the Kootenai was . . . the *White Swan*. . . . The end of the canoeing season for the year was when the boatmans' hands failed to keep the ice thawed from a boat pole.

The first steamboat to navigate the Kootenai River in Montana was the *Annerly*, built near the mouth of the Fisher River and launched in 1892. Thereafter a log of river traffic contains descriptions of wrecks and disasters as boat after boat cracked up or sank in the swirling eddies; for the Kootenai is a dangerous stream whose swift current and concealed rocks claimed many lives. Its most treacherous stretch was the canyon above Jennings, where high rock walls hem in tricky rapids, feared even by veteran river pilots. Naviga-

tion on the river, as one captain put it, was a fight all the way.

Found a Floater
The body of a drowned man was found floating in the Kootenai twenty miles above Jennings. He had undoubtedly been trying to run the river in a skiff which upset and caused his death by drowning.

Two men and a woman were seen to leave the Canadian boundary on a raft on the Kootenai last Thursday. Their raft has since been found bottom side up below the box canyon. None of the parties ever showed up in Jennings. . . . There is no doubt that dozens of people meet their death in this manner, without anyone knowing anything about it. These unwritten tragedies of the Kootenai would fill a large volume and the list of them is increasing every season.

The Libby News, August 11, 1898

The North Star Wrecked.
The *North Star,* one of the largest steamboats on the Upper Kootenai was in a serious accident yesterday with the loss of one life. The boat left Jennings for Ft. Steele and steamed up river five miles to what is called the Canyon. At this point the current is extremely swift, and it is hard to get the boat through it, especially when the river is on the rise. The current yesterday caught the bow of the steamer sideways, and swung her against a rock, staving a big hole in her side.

Capt. Miller allowed the boat to drift onto a bar below the canyon and lines were run out and made fast to trees on the bank. There was little excitement among the passengers, who were soon safely landed from small boats. Three deckhands were rowing ashore in a small boat, when an oar fouled in one of the lines that had been taken ashore and the boat capsized. Two of the men swam out but the third was drowned. He was a colored man about 40 years of age known by the nickname of "Ginger." The body was not recovered and probably never will be. . . . The *North Star* will be as good as new in a couple of days.

The Libby News, April 28, 1898

The most spectacular wreck occurred in 1896 when two boats, the *Ruth* and the *Gwendoline,* piled up in the canyon four miles above Jennings "on the same rock in less than one hour." The disaster, according to the captain of the *Gwendoline,* F. P. Armstrong, marked the end of a three-day race. While the *Ruth* was the faster boat, the *Gwendoline* was smaller and more easily handled in shallow and deceptive water.

Both boats left Jennings on May 5 for Fort Steele, Canada, and reached Tobacco Plains that night. The next evening they were at their destination, and on the morning of May 8 started the return run down the river. Before leaving at 8 a.m., the *Gwendoline* loaded forty tons of ore at North Star landing, but even with this delay, she hoped to overtake the *Ruth* above the canyon. Captain Armstrong did not plan to go through it, as high water made the passage extremely dangerous. At the entrance to the canyon, there was no sign of the *Ruth*, so, believing that she had made it through, the captain started down the narrow, rocky gorge, which was shaped like an elbow. The veteran pilot manœuvered the boat skillfully through the boiling rapids to the elbow, where, just ahead, he saw the *Ruth* jammed on a rock and completely blocking the channel. The eddy beside her was tricky and the remaining passageway between the rocks too narrow to permit the *Gwendoline* to slide by, and she slammed into the *Ruth* and piled up beside her. Captain Sanborn of the *Ruth,* and William Doak, the purser, directed the removal of all passengers and crew without any accident. The *Ruth* finally slipped off the rock, a total wreck. The *Gwendoline* was on the river again by May 21. Three years later, she came to her end a few miles below Libby:

Steamer Gwendoline A Ruin
Falls Fifty Feet into a Canyon and is a Total Wreck.

Captain Miller, was unfortunate in his attempt to transport the steamer *Gwendoline* around Kootenai falls and the canyon just below them. After taking the boat to the falls and getting it out of the water on skids, a spur was built and it was loaded on three flat cars. On Friday, a west bound freight train picked up the three cars on which it was loaded and in going around a curve about a mile below Kootenai Falls station, the rocks along the side of the track were a little too close and the boat had to be shifted a little to one side of the cars so she could pass. The elevation of the outer rail on the curve being pretty high, it threw too much of the weight to one side of the cars and the boat slid off, falling into a gully about fifty feet below the track. She turned over in the fall and lit on her smoke stack and is there now, not worth a bad fifty-cent piece, with her bottom up and as flat as a pancake.

The *Gwendoline* was a British bottom and had been tied up all winter and spring at Jennings from which place she had heretofore been running to Ft. Steele and other British Columbia points. Capt. Miller took a contract from the owners to take her around the falls and canyon where she was to be again put in the water and taken to Kootenai Lake. The loss will fall entirely upon Capt. Miller, as the Northern had a special contract for carrying her which relieved the R.R. of all damages in case of accident and had a bond executed for $500 for the transportation charges. The total value of the *Gwendoline* was $4000. She was 18 feet 10 inches wide.

There has been a long series of mishaps in the operation of steamboats on this end of the Kootenai River and all kinds of chances have heretofore been taken by the captains of the various crafts, running their boats over rapids and shooting dangerous canyons, and all have been rewarded for their nerve by meeting with more or less disaster at one time or another, and this last attempt to run steamboats on the R.R. offers but little encouragement for others to continue the practice.
The Libby News, June 29, 1899

With the completion of the railroad through the Tobacco Plains Valley, river traffic came to an end. One by one, the steamboats were dismantled and shipped to other bodies of water. Only the *Gwendoline* remained beside the Kootenai.

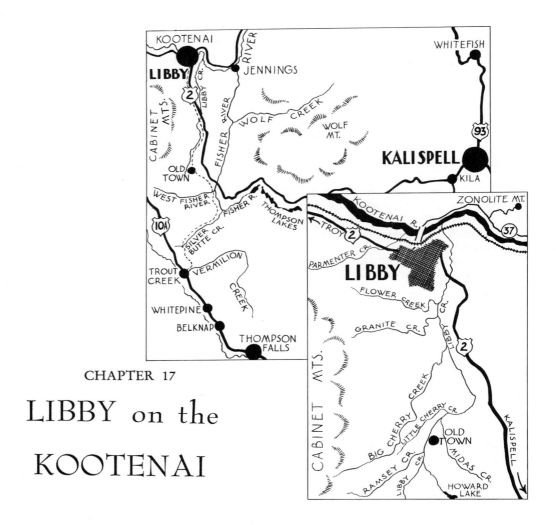

CHAPTER 17

LIBBY on the KOOTENAI

LIBBY CREEK

The eighty-nine-mile drive from Kalispell to Libby is through forests all the way. Between the trees, lakes shimmer, and at clearings glimpses of the Cabinet Range and other distant mountains are visible. When we were within twenty-six miles of our destination, narrow dirt roads, leading into the timber, bore names connected with the mining district. One led to the Silver Butte mine, a second skirted Fisher Creek, a third pointed toward Howard Lake, and a fourth was marked Libby Creek. These titles were given by prospectors who first penetrated this wilderness. The Fisher River was named for Jack Fisher, a prospector, although at one time Land Office maps designated it as Masula or Bank Creek. The Howards — B. F., Albert, and Harry — were among the first men to develop placers in the region. Libby Creek is said to have been discovered

as early as 1861, when a party that included Stephen Allen and Jack Sherry came into the country from Horse Plains. Someone suggested naming the stream for Allen, but he protested and asked that it be called "Libby," for his daughter Elizabeth. A nearby creek, named for Sherry, has since been corrupted to Cherry.

Except for a few fur trappers and missionaries, no white men penetrated these northern forest lands until 1863, when a gold strike in British Columbia, on Wild Horse Creek, started a stampede to the diggings. Impatient prospectors from California and Idaho scurried north and succeeded in crossing the wide Kootenai River on a ferry maintained by Kootenai Indians. Seeing in this location possibilities for future trade with both whites and Indians, Dr. Edwin L. Bonner, of Walla Walla, bought the ferry from the Indians and set up a post, with John Watson as factor.

The Indians in the surrounding country

290

were Kootenais. The upper villages of the tribe were in Tobacco Plains where their ancestors had raised a kind of tobacco for ceremonial use. The lower Kootenai centered around Bonner's Ferry with their chief, David. This entire section of the country was a favorite hunting ground for all the surrounding tribes, especially the Blackfeet, who, by the time that the land was thrown open for settlement, were herded onto a reservation east of the river country. These tribes, when they met, often raided one another and stole each other's ponies. The Indians also came west of the future townsite of Libby to obtain a soft white stone found in the creekbed and used for pipe bowls; hence the name of Pipe Creek, which flows into the river a short distance from the town today.

The placer mines on Libby Creek were discovered during the middle 1860's. Little is known about the discoverers, but one group of men was attacked by Kootenai Indians and three of the whites were killed. This party of four, made up of William Allen, Anthony Kavanaugh, John Moore, and Joseph Herren (Herron), were prospecting during the summer of 1866 or 1867 on what is now Libby Creek, when their provisions ran low and they went to Bonner's Ferry to restock. Returning with their pack animals well laden, the men reached a point on the north bank of the Kootenai, opposite the mouth of Libby Creek. Seeing a party of five Indians with their families camping on the opposite shore, the prospectors hailed them and asked their help in canoeing the provisions across the rapid current. With their assistance, everything was beached by later afternoon, but by the time the pack animals were reloaded, it was nearly dark and the men moved only a quarter of a mile above the Indian encampment before stopping for the night.

The squaws, who had seen the piles of provisions, urged the bucks to creep up on the white camp and run off the prospectors, believing that in their haste, the men would leave their grub and other supplies for the Indians to appropriate. That evening the braves went to the miners' camp, ostensibly to warn them of a possible attack by Blackfeet Indians, and urged them to leave immediately. William Allen, who was the leader of the white party, was used to Indians, and although he sensed a plot, he paid no attention to it. Even when one of his men suggested that they go to the main mining camp, a few miles farther

upstream, where the rest of the prospectors were, he refused to go; so the men bedded down for the night.

Before dawn, the Indians returned to the camp and found the men sleeping. Still hoping to frighten them away, the bucks fired a volley of shots. The startled prospectors, instead of fleeing, hurriedly broke camp, packing their supplies with them. Frustrated a second time by this move, the Indians fired on the men, killing all but Joseph Herren, who, though wounded, crawled into the bush. From his hiding place he watched the braves drag away the bodies of his friends, and attempt to burn them, and then steal the horses and provisions and depart. Herren, fearing that the main camp of miners upstream had also been attacked, was afraid to go in that direction; so, in spite of the bullet wound in his chest, he started along the Kootenai for the Wild Horse mining camps of British Columbia, following an obscure trail along the river bottoms. Three weeks later, having existed on wild berries, he stumbled into the northern mining camp.

His tale aroused the men, who formed a posse and started after the Indians. Some went to Bonner's Ferry and the rest to the mouth of Libby Creek. John Walton, the agent at Bonner's Ferry trading post, knew nothing of the killing, although three of the Indians who were involved had returned to the main encampment below the ferry. The other two were on the Kootenai, at the mouth of Gold Creek. Details of what happened next vary, but the result is the same.

John Walton found Old Abraham a Kootenai chief, who was friendly to the whites, and related what had occurred, warning him that unless he handed over the murderers, the miners would kill the whole tribe. If he produced the three men, "all would be well." Abraham, apparently interpreting this phrase as promise of amnesty, agreed to surrender the men, and finding them in camp, told them that if they returned to Libby Creek and showed the whites where they had cached the loot, they would not be punished, but allowed to go home. The Indians accompanied him to the agency store, where they were seized, bound, and placed under guard. The party of whites and Indians, the latter followed by a band of their relatives, started for Libby Creek. At Moyie Creek, in wading across the river, one of the Indians succeeded in breaking his fetters and was shot while trying to escape. The other two crossed the river, only to be shot on the bank and their bodies left for their relatives. When the posse reached Gold Creek, they found the other two Indians, whom they bound and took to Libby Creek and hanged.

No further mining in the region is reported until the 1880's, when prospectors from the Coeur d'Alene District, in Idaho, began to drift into the area in search of placer gold. One of these was B. F. Howard, who, having reached Thompson Falls in 1887, set out to explore Vermilion Creek. In this vicinity he met Tom Shearer, who had previously followed a party of prospectors to Libby Creek when he saw them pay for a grubstake with gold dust. Shearer, finding the placer ground unlocated, hurried back to Thompson Falls to record all the desirable claims he had located, intending to lease them to Chinese miners from Missoula. But the Orientals were not interested, and Shearer then divulged his discovery to Howard and two packers, Cooper and Decker. The four formed a company, with the packers furnishing transportation and Howard the grub and equipment.

Having mentioned their plans to the others in the Vermilion Creek camp, Shearer and Howard slipped away quietly and started for the placer ground. Upon their arrival, the men found a handful of prospectors already at work sniping or crevicing the ground, "living in tepees and eating fish and flour." Setting up a permanent camp, in which their whipsawed cabin was the first to be completed, Shearer and Howard located all the best ground and then, in subsequent trips, made sure that it was properly recorded in Missoula. Within a few days they started washing out gold dust. This district was originally called "Shearer," although the name appears on no records.

Meanwhile, their companions on Vermilion Creek discovered that the two men had gone. Determined to beat them to the diggings, and guided by Jan Eisenberg, a scout, the group, which consisted of John Leigh, George Reider, "Lawyer" Burton, Jimmy Powers, and Mart Conners, a packer, took a shortcut across the mountains. On the far side of the range, they were stopped by a forest fire and had to work their way around it. Because of the dense forests, they lost their way. Finally, a hunter whom they met told the unhappy men that they were forty miles east of the placer ground and that Shearer and Howard were already there, washing gravel; in fact, they had been there a full week. Seventeen days later, the chagrined party arrived on Libby Creek and staked their claims.

This first settlement was twenty miles up Libby Creek and one-half mile below the mouth of Ramsey Creek, the latter named for a deaf prospector who "talked" with the others by writing what he had to say. "Old Libby," as it was later called, really started in 1886, when the first prospectors whom Shearer and Howard found working the ground pitched their tents along the banks of the mountain stream. By 1887 it contained a small group of cabins, including George Good's grocery store, which was regularly supplied by a pack train of thirty-five animals.

Two of the region's pioneers, G. R. Blackwell and Martin Fields, accompanied by one or two other men, made the trip from Murray, Idaho, to Libby Creek in March, 1887. Where the snow was frozen so they could walk on it, they made good time, but where it was soft, they had trouble finding a way down the mountainsides, for they carried no snowshoes. They intended to travel down Libby Creek, but they were not certain where they were and actually followed Granite Creek instead.

"Next morning . . . we found a tree we could climb so I went to the top," wrote Blackwell.
"I said, 'I can see a glacier' which through my discovery was named Blackwell's Glacier.
"'Also I can see the Kootenai River and the mouth of Libby Creek.'"
"We are away north of where we want to go," Henniger said. . . .
We made camp and Freeman got supper.
Ben Henniger said "Do you know what creek that is?" and we said "No."
"Well," I said, "we'll call it Flower Creek."
History of Libby,
Montana Federation Woman's Club
compiled by Mrs. Maie Hillis,
Mrs. Anna G. Herbst, Mrs. John P. Wall

This party also named Granite Creek because of the heavy granite boulders in it. In their wanderings they found a man in a cabin who welcomed them and gave them supper and breakfast, telling them that they were the first white men he'd seen since the previous fall.

In the fall of 1887, Tom Shearer brought in a group of six Chinese from Missoula to work the leased ground. They whipsawed lumber and built their cabins near the camp of Oliver Woodcoe, nicknamed "Hoo Doo Joe," a member of the Howard party, who lived in a tent close to the foot of Hoo Doo Mountain. The following spring a larger party, which included A. E. Fosseum and Bill McGee, joined the Howard group.

The creek banks and gravel bars proved so rich that every patch of ground on Libby and Ramsey Creeks was staked and was soon being worked. Billy McGee's claim, above the mouth of Ramsey Creek, proved to be one of the best locations. From it, an estimated $75,-000 was washed out over a period of several years. "Doc" B. F. Howard was so well pleased with the richness of the district that in 1888 he sent for his brother, Albert V. Howard, and for his son, Harry, to join him.

The Howards and William Williams formed the Howard Placer Mining Company and, by using rockers and ground sluices, recovered coarse gold from their placer claims on Libby Creek below the mouth of Ramsey Creek. They also interested Butte investors, who formed the Libby Placer Mining Company and leased land on the Howard claims. Within a short time, the two companies controlled three miles of placer ground on Libby Creek. This company worked the bar hydraulically and from the main pit took $40,000-$50,000 in gold. Other placer deposits were discovered and worked on Little Cherry, Cherry, and Howard creeks, as well as on the West Fisher River.

Some idea of the isolation of the region is shown by the disappearance of three prospectors near Wolf Creek in 1887, whose fate was not known until the following season. According to William A. Hillis, Ben Thompkins and his partner Patterson passed the camp on Vermilion Creek — where Hillis was staying in February, 1887 — pulling a loaded toboggan and headed for the placer diggings on Libby Creek, seventy miles farther north. Although snow was six feet deep on the level and deeper on the passes, the men were confident they could make their destination. Twelve hours later, Daniel McDonald and his partner hurried by, following the first men. Three days later, McDonald's partner returned alone, heading for Thompson Falls. He and McDonald had split up, and McDonald had gone on to catch up with Thompkins and Patterson. These three men reached Libby Creek early in March and located near the mouth of Little Cherry Creek, where they prospected until summer. "Doc" Howard knew the men and gives the name of the third member of the party as John Cheley. In August, they decided to pull out and took the McMillen pack trail, by way of Wolf Creek, to return to

civilization. They made camp one evening at Little Prairie, on Wolf Creek, and, as they were finishing their meal, three Indians walked into the clearing and the miners gave them supper. Hillis says they were Flatheads.

After eating, the miners sat smoking their pipes on a log by their campfire, with Thompkins' loaded rifle resting against a nearby stump. Suddenly, one of the Indians reached for the gun and shot all three men, killing two and injuring the third, who was quickly dispatched with a second shot. The bucks then piled the bodies on the fire and burned them. When months went by and nothing was heard of the miners, they were believed to have left the country, according to their plan.

There are several versions as to how the crime was discovered. One credits an Indian with confessing the killing to a priest at a Flathead mission. A second attributes the massacre to Kootenai braves, who, having just participated in a medicine dance, were ripe for a killing of any whites within reach, and when surprised by an Indian hunter who came along, bragged of their coup. A third mentions a Kootenai pow-wow near Rexford, the following spring, at which certain braves boasted of killing three white miners. Someone present gave the information to the U. S. deputy marshal, William Ramsdell, who ran a trading post on Tobacco Plains. As soon as the weather permitted, he organized a posse and arrested four of the Indians and took them to Demersville. To verify the story, a posse went to the campsite where the men had been shot, and, in sifting the ashes from the fire, found bones, buttons, buckles, and five and twenty dollar gold pieces. The Indians were tried and hanged.

That the country was wilderness is clearly shown in John Willis' account of his first trip into Libby Creek. His hunting companion was Al Dalton, and the two went in on foot, packing their blankets and provisions on their backs.

Old man Fields, Geo. Blackwell and fifteen other men came to Thompson Falls from the Coeur d'Alene district. Hearing that Doc Howard had struck diggings on Libby Creek, and as I had a pack train, they made a deal with me to pack them and their outfits into the new camp.

This was April and streams were swollen so we had to go around by Horse Plains and up the Little Bitter Root, through Pleasant Valley and down Wolf Creek until we struck the Fisher — which was out of its banks, but our ax-men . . . cut down a big tamarack that reached across Fisher Creek, and then put stringers across, cut down pines and laid them across and put pine boughs and dirt on that. We then blindfolded our packhorses and led them across one by one.

We went on to Libby Creek and found it just as high. John Smith, our crack ax-man told me if I could swim he would throw me an ax to cut the immense tamarack that would reach across from the other side. . . . The other men took the pack ropes and went down the river one-quarter of a mile to pull me out in case I should cramp in the icy water. I went above the rapids and jumped in and went by the men like a cannon ball. I didn't land for a mile below, as it was a series of rapids and falls, I sure thought I was gone, when my knees struck a sandbar; I couldn't have held out much longer. I was naked and had to walk back through thick brush to the tree and cut it down, but when it fell, the water was so high, it sprung down and the current caught and broke it in two. That left me across the river from camp, naked and no way of getting back. John Smith yelled . . . there was a pole across the river in a gorge and that he would take my clothes up there and I might be able to coon it across. In two days we had put in a bridge here and crossed our outfit.

I stayed at the diggings four or five days until the creeks went down, as I was going back alone with thirty pack and four saddle horses. On my way I met Thompkins and another man. They wanted me to camp with them on Wolf Creek. . . . They . . . were the men the Indians killed and burned on their own camp fire.

> History of Libby,
> Montana Federation Woman's Club,
> compiled by Mrs. Maie Hillis,
> Mrs. Anna G. Herbst, Mrs. John P. Wall

To anyone driving the paved highway from Kalispell to Libby, it is difficult to imagine how the early pioneers managed to find a way through the dense uncharted wilderness. Take Patrick Dolan, for instance. He set out on foot from Bonner's Ferry in September, 1890, carrying a pack and picking his way along the north side of the Kootenai River, where there was a suggestion of a trail, until he found himself opposite the mouth of Flower Creek — a fifty-four mile trek. He liked the looks of that location and decided to file on it, but first he had to find a way to cross the river, which is all of 600-feet wide, and swift besides. Using a long rope, he tied one end to a tree and the other to a log which he rode to the opposite bank. Having looked over the site that he wished to secure, he hiked to Missoula, 200 miles away, to file his claim for a homestead, then rode the Northern Pacific to Kootenai Station, near Sand Point, Idaho, where he bought his outfit and supplies and had them freighted by wagon team to Bonner's Ferry. From there, they were carried on pack horses, guided by two Kootenai Indian youths, up the river to a point opposite his newly acquired land. Here he built a raft on which he ferried his gear across to the south side of the river and at last was able to settle on his tract.

Even after the Great Northern road was built through Libby in 1898, floods washed out roads and bridges and periodically isolated the new settlement:

Libby Creek is a rushing torrent, and its roar can be heard for miles. The new railroad bridge just put in at this place has gone down in the floods and hundreds of yards of levee is washed out. . . . The Cedar Creek bridge is reported gone and Flower Creek is very angry and leaving her banks.
Libby Montanian, November 20, 1897

Libby camp, in its infancy, was too isolated to interest even the sporting women who swarmed to every new strike. It consisted solely of shacks and cabins and its chief diversions were found in its several saloons or in poker games which the "boys" played with the Chinese miners. Although Orientals were not permitted to own claims, they could lease them from whites and many did so, paying from $1,200-$1,700 for this privilege. At one time, as many as twenty-five Chinese held claims on Libby Creek and worked peaceably beside the white miners. As a rule, they were honest and industrious.

In 1890, M. V. Field, the Ross Brothers, and Thomas Bryant opened up ground that tested high in gold, yet when they made periodic cleanups, the amount of dust recovered was small. There was but one conclusion — someone was robbing the sluiceboxes and the men were determined to catch the thief at work. One dark night, Bryant saw a yellow-skinned miner, with a candle, cleaning the amalgam from the riffles of the sluiceboxes and pouring the dust into a flour sack. Bryant fired at the candle; aided by the sudden blackness, the thief escaped. Within a day or two, the angry miners held a meeting and decreed that all Chinese leave Libby Creek at once, giving them one hour to be on their way. Their estimated thefts were believed to total $5,000.

In addition to placer mines, lode mines were discovered by men who followed traces of color up the mountainsides searching for the vein. The biggest strike was made in the Snowshoe. This silver mine whose "great lode was traceable for miles," was situated in a rugged part of the Cabinet Range, on the south side of Snowshoe Creek, three miles above its junction with Big Cherry Creek. The mine, which became the leading producer in the Libby region and could be reached by wagon road from that town, was located in 1887 by Bregg Parmenter, A. F. Dunlap, and J. G. Abbett (Abbott). According to Libby's *Silver Standard* (July 13, 1895), about the middle of September, 1887, these three men met J. W. Leigh on the trail running up Libby Creek, and Leigh showed them some ore from a recent strike he had made, called the Alpine, and suggested they prospect for an extension. It was two weeks before they got started, but on October 6, the Snowshoe was located. Parmenter is said to have named it from Snowshoe Gulch, where he had broken a snowshoe while hunting mountain goats, or because a broken snowshoe added to their difficulty in staking claims in several feet of snow.

The three discoverers developed the property by open cuts and found the quality of the ore improved with depth. In 1890, they sold a quarter interest, sight unseen, for $300, to H. G. Lougee. Three years later the Chicago & Montana Mining Company bought the property for $125,000 and promptly built a road to the mine. By September, 1895, the company reported 2,000 tons of high grade on the dumps. A concentrator was also erected, which, according to company plans, was located "where there would be no possible chance of its damage by snowslides." When this company ceased operations, the manager, D. P. Bowers, leased the mine and continued to take out ore.

English investors, represented by Howard Walters, negotiated with the original owners and obtained a contract deed in 1895 for $200,000, although it took nearly three years to complete the deal. During this interim, Bowers continued to remove as much ore as possible from the mine. Early in July, 1898, a carload of concentrates was hauled to Libby by four- and six-horse teams. Late that month the English syndicate — the Pacific Northwest Mining Corporation, Ltd. — took over. Walters, as manager, immediately began to improve the property. Before winter he installed a compressor, the first in the region, built a new road, and brought in more than twenty-four draft horses to haul out ore. Within a year the mine employed one hundred men and had a monthly payroll of $10,000.

In the fall of 1899, a mineral collection, which included specimens of ore from the Snowshoe mine, was sent to Spokane.

L. H. Faust, who had charge of the Mineral Exhibit from Libby district at the Spokane Industrial Exposition is in receipt of a bronze medal. . . . On one side is the inscription: Sixth Annual Spokane Industrial Exposition. On the other: Washington, Idaho, Oregon, Montana, British Columbia. Awarded to Snowshoe mine, Libby, Montana, for Second place in Silver-lead ore exhibit.
Libby News, November 2, 1899

The manager of the Snowshoe, H. E. West, seems to have been both popular and competent:

Christmas 1899
Mr. West . . . arranged that we should give a banquet and entertainment at which should be present all the employees of the company and anyone else found within the confines of the gulch. . . .
Promptly at 6:30 everyone was in place, and after grace by Mr. West, they all fell to and attacked the good things. . . . Mr. West had prepared a program which consisted of toasts, songs and recitations . . . the first toast was to the Pres. of the United States and the Queen of Great Britain. . . . Then came a toast "The Mining Industry our Corporation." . . . Then came a song by the Snow Shoe Carol Club . . . which sang Auld Lang Syne. . . . Mr. West then declared a holiday of one week and then they all dispersed to their respective abodes.
Harry Jones
Libby Montanian, January 6, 1900

Until the wagon road was built up to the Snowshoe, horses or mules packed everything in to the mine. The hardiest of the pack string was "a little brown donkey," who on one trip carried a "good-sized cooking range up the steep, rocky trail." After the road was made, he was turned loose to wander around Libby, where he delighted the children and pestered the housewives, until one family took pity on him and kept him at their ranch as a pet for their children. Come spring, he ambled back to Libby. According to one tale, at the end of his life-span he roamed out to the cemetery, lay down, and died. He even made the *Libby News:*

"Mascot" Has Returned
The frisky little Jack, once the property of the Snowshoe Co., has returned from a barn-storming tour on the road with the McPhee Comedy Co. and is now placidly browsing about on his old feeding grounds. . . .
When repurchased and turned loose "Mascot" made his way to the schoolhouse to see his friends the children and at recess time all had a ride on his back. "Mascot" will continue to make his home in Libby and will star no more on the road.
Libby News, March 21, 1901

For three or four years the English syndicate operated the Snowshoe successfully, even proposing that a nineteen-mile railroad spur be built to the mine; then its money ran out. The Snowshoe was leased to Boardman and Bowers, until falling prices for lead and silver forced a shutdown. The Pacific Coast Company reopened the property and, by 1911, employed fifty to seventy-five men. During this period the concentrator handled 100 tons of ore per day. Total production figures for the Snowshoe, as of 1929-1930, estimate 130,000 tons of ore processed with a yield of $1,086,000 in net smelter returns for lead, silver, and gold, even though inefficient milling sometimes lost forty per cent of the concentrates.

While no lode mine near Libby equalled the Snowshoe, a number of properties contributed to the area's reputation as a mining region. One of the oldest of the deep mines was the Silver Crown, on the south side of Granite Creek, located in 1887 by George Blackwell and his party. Another early property was the Silver Butte, twenty miles southeast of the Snowshoe, near the headwaters of the Fisher River, and reached by wagon road from Trout Creek on the south by way of Vermilion Creek, or from Libby on the north by going up the Fisher River. This mine, discovered by William Criderman, was developed by the Kentucky & Montana Mining Company, who, after spending $200,000, lost it in 1899 through a sheriff's sale demanded by the creditors who held $30,000 in unpaid bills! Its $150,000 concentrating plant burned in 1905. Another mine located by Criderman, E. Hackett, John L. Hartt, and others in the early 1890's, was the Silver Cable, which lay on the Snowshoe fault on the south side of Cable Creek. A wagon road was built to it and a small concentrator erected in 1895, which, because of "internal trouble and litigation," was never even tested. By 1900, the mine was idle.

The lode mines on Shaughnessy Hill, six to eight miles south of Libby, were located about 1889 by Tom Shaughnessy and W. A. Hillis. One group of claims, patented under the name Buzz Saw, was bonded and leased by one promoter after another, with each withdrawing when only low-grade ore was found. John Town and A. J. McCorkle, who took a bond on the property, with an option to buy, interested C. Ed Lukens in the mine. The three men did considerable development, driving a series of tunnels on the vein and building a concentrator, and in 1911-1912, shipped several carloads of silver-lead ore.

The Glacier-Silver-Lead mine, six miles southwest of Libby, on Granite Creek, near its junction with Shaughnessy Creek, was originally called the "Hazel T." It, too, seems to have had many owners. One of them, aware that the mine was losing money, secretly removed all the new machinery and installed it in another property so that it could not be attached. This mine, later known as the Lukens-Hazel and still later as the Glacier-Silver-Lead, was active during the summer of 1930. Not long afterwards the mine was closed and its 300-ton mill, built at a time when the price of metals was falling, is now in ruins.

When word reached the miners at Libby Creek, early in 1889, that the Great Northern Railroad was planning to build west, across the Flathead Valley through Haskell Pass to the Fisher River, and down it to the Kootenai, the Howards, J. H. Horton, Oliver Woodcoe, and John Rouse hustled down Libby Creek to stake claims at its mouth, so as to be close to the proposed road. Here a small but thriving settlement, which in time contained the railroad construction camp, sprouted on the edge of the forest, at a point not far from the present J. Neils lumber mill in Libby. The railroad right of way crossed the Howard claims, and the brothers are said to have exchanged their land for three passes to the World's Fair in Chicago and the right to name the new town Libby Creek.

The Great Northern, the first railroad in the lower Kootenai country, reached the mouth of the Fisher River in 1891. Along its route, camps sprang up, some, like Jennings, Libby, and Troy, to become permanent towns. Since there was no settlement on the Kootenai at the Canadian border, Jennings became the U. S. Customs station.

During the construction of the Great Northern . . . deer were so plentiful that the camps along the line were supplied with venison and the price of meat was so cheap that it scarcely paid anyone to hunt and bring the meat to the camps.

When the men were making the ties for the road and would fell a tree, the deer would come and eat the moss and twigs off the top while a man with an axe would be polishing off the other end. . . . At first the deer were a little shy but gradually they seemed to get acquainted in a way with the men, and would stay with them all the time eating only at the tenderest parts of the trees which they would chop down. But if a stranger came into camp and joined the men at work, the deer would not show up for a few days and they would return in a very cautious way.

Following the advent of the R.R., and the possibility of transporting hides of animals to markets on the outside, a large number of hunters made it a regular business to hunt them for their hides, the shipping of deer skins being a large revenue producer for this section of the state.

Libby Western News, January 8, 1903

All business houses in the bustling town of Libby Creek were built of logs or were canvas tents. Mercantile establishments were opened by John P. Wall, who arrived from Demersville in June, 1891, and by Jesse B. Neff and Fred M. Plummer, from Great Falls, who brought in two wagonloads of goods. Neff managed the store and Plummer did all the freighting. On these trips, he carried thousands of dollars, as well as dust, yet he was never robbed. When asked how he escaped, he replied that since he carried money for everyone — the hold-up men, as well as the railroad workers and merchants — the rough element saw no sense in stealing their own loot.

LIBBY

In the spring of 1892, a sawmill was erected half a mile west of the camp, and lots were offered for sale along newly cleared streets. At the same time, the residents of Libby Creek were upset to discover that the Great Northern's right of way kept so close to the Kootenai River that it bypassed Libby Creek by half a mile. To make matters worse, the station was built by the riverside, some distance from the town. Refusing to be left off the railroad, the entire town quickly moved to the new site, leaving behind it a ghost camp whose fifty buildings had been constructed only two years before. By May, when the rails were laid as far as the station, and the first construction train rolled in from the east, the new townsite was well established. It was hewed from the forest which stretched fifty miles in all directions, and residents had to carry a lantern at night for fear of falling over stumps. The land was so densely timbered that lots had to be cleared before a house could be built. Often the same trees that were felled were sawed into lumber and used in its construction.

According to the government survey, made in 1894, the Libby townsite lay on Northern Pacific land. Efforts to have this area classified as mineral land, so that mining claims might be filed on it, were unsuccessful. Thus, when newcomers were unable to obtain clear deeds to lots, they bought sites on the A. B. Johnston homestead in South Libby, through

MINERAL AVE., LIBBY

which Flower Creek flowed. This became a residential section about a half-mile distant from the rest of the town and separated from it by dense woods. Through this forest corridor ran a trail, bordered on one side by a raised wooden footpath.

By 1897, both the placers and some lode mines were flourishing and the town possessed two sawmills, a ferry boat across the Kootenai River, and, in addition to previously established businesses, one drug store, one livery stable, a postoffice, one blacksmith and wagon shop, and three hotels. When T. C. Cummings wrote to the Sturgis, Michigan, *Journal,* describing conditions in Libby, his letter was reprinted in the *Libby Montanian* on October 23, 1897. Excerpts from it tell that the

Mining payroll during the present summer is $15,000 a month and as yet but one of the mines is producing. Hay has retailed up to the present time at $25.00 a ton until just now it is being shipped in for $18.00. Eggs never get lower than 25 cents a dozen and butter 24 cents a pound.

In winter tie makers get all the work they want at 10 cents a tie for the making . . . some make as high as 100 ties a day. The average is 65 ties. There are no tramps in this country. They meet with too many insults in the offers of jobs.

The railroad through Libby was finished in 1898. The right of way west from Libby was difficult to lay out, as in places it cut through a canyon of the Kootenai, where the roadbed was hacked from the base of cliffs and pinched between them and the swirling waters. It was, therefore, several years before all work on this section of the Great Northern was completed.

The Kootenai River was a constant threat to the roadbed, especially during spring freshets. The *Libby News* gives a grisly account of a wreck at Kootenai Falls in 1894. Conductor Mathews of the ill-fated freight train tells the story:

During high water in 1894, there was a wreck at a point not far above the falls and the water was nearly up to the rails. A freight train and three of eight box cars were thrown into the water. On three of the cars were two brakemen and inside of the cars were a lot of hoboes. The cars and men floated down the stream and just before the falls were reached, one of the brakemen tried to swim ashore but the other one and the hoboes went over the falls and that was the last seen of them. The water was ice cold. . . . It is thought that the brakeman who attempted to swim was taken with cramps, for he went under and was carried over the falls with the others. . . . Attempts made to find the cars and bodies have been unsuccessful.

Some years later a section foreman . . . had a passion for fishing, just below the falls. Fish came that far but could get no farther. He thought he had a bite, (but couldn't pull it out) . . . instead of a 60-pound sturgeon, he had snagged a stiff, which had probably been floating in the eddy. He caught the dead man under the chin and drew him up head first . . . when he came out of the water he was staring right at the man at the other end of the pole. With a yell he dropped the pole, ran to the section house. . . . Men went back with him and pulled the man out of the water. An inquest was held . . . the man had no relatives so they buried him.

Mathews believes the man was the brakeman who tried to swim ashore and was carried with the rest over the falls. . . . This one caught in the eddy . . . and had been going round and round in the cold water ever since. His preservation was due to the coldness of the water. The dead man had long whiskers and the brakeman in '94 was a young man but hair grows on dead bodies.

Libby News, May 17, 1900

In the spring of 1898, John Berry, who "was determined to get to Libby in spite of heat and high water," arrived from Missoula

having driven in a single buggy all the way. He came across the Flathead reservation from Jocko and had easy sailing after leaving Kalispell. He took the old tote road that follows the Great Northern right-of-way and a great part of the distance he traveled on the railroad itself. As streams are very much swollen and there are no bridges, he crossed them on railroad bridges. His horse got so used to it that he was able to walk the ties of a railroad bridge as easily as a cat, and where the ties were unusually far apart, he would balance himself on the rail and keep on coming. Mr. Berry has certainly shown more determination to get to Libby than anyone since the placer mining excitement of 1866 when people packed in here from Ogden.

The Libby News, May 19, 1898

With each year Libby's local pride increased:

James J. Hill, Pres. of the Great Northern railroad, passes through Libby today on his way west on a special train. If he will slow his train down to about thirty miles an hour and blow the frost off the plateglass of his observation window, he will behold the most promising little town on his entire railroad system.

Libby News, February 23, 1899

That the president's train was not accustomed to slowing down is shown by this item:

Paul Pratt's horse, Peekaboo, met with violent death last week, having been spread over about two miles of the Great Northern right of way by Jim Hill's special, which passed through Libby without stopping last Thursday. The intelligent animal had expected the train to slow up at the switch and thus give him time to get safely across the track. . . . Peekaboo was a thoroughbred and his sanguinary demise will cost the president of the Great Northern a few pesetas.

Libby News, September 8, 1898

Even though Libby was now a town on the railroad, the placer mines on Libby Creek and its trbutaries and on West Fisher River were not abandoned. In fact, throughout most of the twentieth century, placer gold has been recovered on a larger scale than previously. The first miners could only sluice or drift the gold from the readily accessible stream gravels. Later on, men explored the ancient stream channels that lay far below the surface and from them dug or washed the golden particles with hydraulic washers and other modern machinery. The source of gold was attributed to a porphyry dike extending from the Slocum District of southern British Columbia to the Coeur d'Alene District of Idaho.

Between 1902 and 1909, most of the placer gold was recovered from the Libby Placer Mining Company's huge pit — 1,600 feet long and 400 feet wide — on the east side of Libby Creek and from the holdings of Vaughn-Greenwell on Howard Creek. This company, which installed a hydraulic plant, worked a bar fifty feet in depth, from which the gold ran "ten cents to $3.50 to the color." By 1905, the placers owned by the Howards on Libby Creek were worked out. These pioneer mining men then obtained 800 acres of ground on Big Cherry Creek and called it the Montana Placer. This they operated successfully for a number of years.

$25,000 Hydraulic Plant Completed at Libby
The flume is a thing of beauty, snaking around the hillsides for over 8000 feet from intake on Cherry creek to penstock. It is four feet by four feet and is made of surface lumber, grooved and matched.

ZONOLITE MILL, LIBBY

LIBBY, THE KOOTENAI RIVER AND THE
CABINET RANGE

The Pipe line is 2000 feet long. The company is now using a hydraulic elevator to handle the tailings. The capacity of the plant is 1400-1500 cubic yards in twenty-four hours.

Western News, June 13, 1907

During the 1930's renewed activity centered around Libby Creek and Fisher River properties. A Milwaukee syndicate, near Howard Lake, hydraulicked the creekbed; and the Nugget Placer Mining Company on Libby Creek, one mile below the mouth of Bear Creek, ran a dragline and a scraper bucket on its ground. The pit at this placer cut through thirty-five feet of gravel before reaching bedrock. The gravel recovered averaged thity-five cents a cubic yard.

Lode mines along West Fisher River were also developed in the early 1900's. One of the first was the Fisher Creek mine called the Brick & Branagan, named for its discoverers, a property whose ten-stamp mill produced many gold bricks. The mine was on the south side of Bramlet Creek, two miles above its junction with the West Fisher River road. Profits in 1900 averaged $100.00 a day. Between 1901 and 1903, the owners cleaned up $150,000, although milling saved but sixty per cent of the values.

The *Tip Top,* formerly the *Blacktail* lode, was near the Brick & Branagan, situated 26 miles south of Libby on Bramlet Creek. It was a gold property and had a stamp mill. . . .

American Kootenai, situated on the south side of West Fisher River, ¾ of a mile below Mill Creek, operated during the first decade of the 20th century. . . .

Golden West Mining Company held 2 properties on the West Fisher River, the *Little Annie* 1200 feet and the *New Mine,* 700 feet above the main camp, where several large cabins were built by the company.

Having described the growth of mining in the Libby District, let us see how the town developed after the advent of the railroad.

The *Libby Miner,* the camp's first newspaper, was published by John W. Pace and Edward S. Doyle, miners, from 1892 to 1897. It was succeeded by the *Libby News,* a paper "initiated by the Townsite Co." and printed at their building, north of the railroad tracks, with Leo H. Faust and Frank Leonard as publishers. It contained in its first issue the following sprightly item:

The *Libby News* wishes to call the earnest attention of just 21 marriageable ladies to an article published elsewhere in these columns and entitled "Libby's Surest Sign of Prosperity." To those who are not familiar with the circumstances, we will say that the list contains 21 dwellings to be erected the coming summer by 21 bachelors. And as the summer wears away and the chill autumn nights bring to mind the fact that the dreary winter months will come upon us, how sweet it would be to contemplate these 21 homes made happy by the gentle ministrations of woman. And this is not all. As the long winter will wear itself away and the verdure of spring is followed by the more mature months of summer, one does not have to stretch the imagination much to see the complacent smile of our merchants as they view a procession of 21 baby carriages. Followed to its logical conclusion it is a great proposition. It will bring joy to everyone.

Libby News, April 21, 1898

Other early papers were the *Libby Weekly Montanian,* which appeared in 1894, and the *Silver Standard,* whose first issue was run off on July 13, 1895. The *Western News,* which started July 17, 1902, has lasted until the present and is now called the *Western News and Libby Times.*

Religious services were first organized by the Presbyterians, with Reverend Edwin M. Ellis of Stevensville coming to Libby in the spring of 1893 to start a Sunday school. These gatherings, which were held in the schoolhouse, served all denominations and were the first to be instituted between Bonner's Ferry and Kalispell. In 1894 the Methodists organized. A year later, Reverend J. M. Eastland, who preached at Tobacco Plains, came regularly to conduct services at Libby and Troy. When the Methodists built a church, Neff & Plummer, Libby merchants, gave

two windows and a door . . . for the purpose of furnishing the lower part of the steeple, which is also the ante room of the church. A ceiling has been put in and the wainscoting is nearly finished and the new floor will probably be laid by Saturday night.

Libby News, November 10, 1898

The same year

The ladies of the Presbyterian church gave a ten-cent social at the schoolhouse Monday evening . . . playing games and listening to a literary program which had been arranged. A lunch of coffee and cake was served from 10-11 o'clock. Receipts for the evening were $19.25.

Libby News, November 3, 1898

For several years a Roman Catholic missionary priest came to Libby once a month to hold services. Yet as late as 1899:

Rev. Father Gallagher of Kalispell will hold Catholic services at Hensen's Hall at 10 o'clock Sunday morning. Owing to his other duties, he is only able to visit Libby every three months.

Libby News, October 26, 1899

A regular Sunday School was established in 1903 and a church built in 1910.

In 1903 the Right Reverend L. R. Brewer, Bishop of Montana, held the first Episcopal service in a store on the corner of Mineral Avenue and Fourth Street. Thereafter, Reverend Henry Green of Kalispell made the trip to Libby once a month. A frame church was built in 1920. The Christian Scientists organized in 1900 and in 1902 bought a building in South Libby, which served them until 1911, when a larger church was built.

Libby's first school building was a one-room affair built of upright green planks by voluntary labor. The session lasted three months with fifteen children in attendance. The pupils issued a weekly newspaper and on Friday mornings, when it was read aloud, townspeople visited the school and heard the news. By 1898 a large, two-story public school was under construction, partly through the financial aid given by the Libby Pastime club, a social organization, which met Saturday evenings for music, dancing, and games. "All proceeds of this club aside from the absolute necessary expenses" were voted to the public school fund.

The School Trustees have on hand $3500, the proceeds of a sale of bonds for the erection of a school. . . . The refusal of the Great Northern to pay the special school tax, left the public school here entirely without funds three months ago. [Proceeds from] a social club's [parties are] . . . devoted to the school fund. The result is that the stamps are still dropping in the educational works, and there is no immediate prospect of the knowledge mill shutting down.

Libby Montanian, April 2, 1898

Attendance on the opening day in September was 42.

A difference of opinion prevails as to the harmony of the colors used in painting the outside. The roof is bright green, the sides are brindle and there is a belt about the waist of the building about the color of fermented currant jam. The general effect is reminiscent of the impressionist school of painting.

Libby News, July 21, 1898

At first only the second story rooms were needed for classes and one downstairs for a gymnasium. The other was rented to the Presbyterians for Sunday School and church use. Occasionally the Catholics also held services in one of the first floor halls.

The forests surrounding Libby were full of wild life, and men hunted as much for food as for sport. Deer were abundant, and bear, both black and grizzly, came closer to town than was comfortable. Traps were set, and when caught, the animals were shot and skinned, for pelts brought $20.00 apiece. Game laws covered a variety of wild animals:

Open season for grouse, prairie chickens, fool hens, sage hens, pheasants and partridges is from Aug. 15 to Dec. 15. The open season for wild geese, ducks, brants and swans is from Sept. 1 to May 1 of the following year.

Catching, trapping or restraining buffalo, elk, moose or mountain sheep, for any purpose whatsoever is prohibited, under a penalty of not less than $100 nor more than $500 or by imprisonment not to exceed 6 months, or by both fine and imprisonment.

The taking of fish, except with a pole, line and hook is prohibited. Catching for sale, selling or offering to sell speckled trout or mountain trout is punishable by a fine of not less than $200 nor more than $500 or by imprisonment of not more than 5 years. Fishways must be constructed over every dam or any stream.

Libby Montanian, August 19, 1899

Perhaps the laws were not too strictly enforced; for when F. K. Robinson and his son, Frank, returned from a prospecting trip to the Cabinet Mountains in the summer of 1899, they brought with them a four-months-old mountain goat which they found asleep among the rocks. According to the *Libby News,* it became "quite domesticated, was taught to drink milk and eat grass and has a keen appetite for flowers."

The fact that the country belonged to the Indians until they were arbitrarily removed to reservations seemed to escape the settlers. When, therefore, the Kootenai and Flatheads continued their tribal practice of annual forays, they naturally returned to the hunting grounds that they knew better than the white intruders who had pushed them away from their streams and forests. The attitude of the white pioneer settlers and prospectors toward the Indian is clearly shown when they object to

Indians Hunting Deer With Dogs
Jake Teeters . . . made a trip to the Wolf Creek country to get some Indians reported to be running deer with dogs. . . . He told them if they didn't get out of the country at once, he would take them to the countyseat and put them in jail. They agreed to leave. . . . There were ten lodges in all from the Flathead Reservation . . . all had come over for a

big hunt. . . . Officers are determined to stop the practice of the Indians coming into this section every fall and using dogs for the purpose of getting in a supply of meat for the winter. This section is noted all over the west for the excellence of its hunting grounds and these Indians have made regular pilgrimages here every fall for the purpose of hunting. . . . Hunting with dogs to run deer . . . drives all the game out of the country and spoils the grounds for legitimate hunting.

Libby News, November 30, 1899

A year later, when Jake Teeter found a party killing deer out of season, he arrested five of the bucks and brought them to Libby for trial. Judge Hoffman fined them $25.00 each, but remitted the fine and assessed them costs of $35.00 and their three ponies.

During the Spanish American War, news of victories were celebrated by setting off "firecrackers consisting of three sticks of giant powder tied together and thrown into the air." When the war was over and the Libby men who had served in Company "H" were due to return, a "Grand Ball and Supper" was tendered them at Neff & Plummer's hall.

Early in Libby's history a number of fraternal organizations secured charters. The "Modern Woodmen of America" organized in January, 1899, with forty members and immediately gave a "Woodchoppers' Hop"

to celebrate the installation of a new lodge. . . . Tickets 75c for the dance and 75c a couple for the supper which will be given by Miss Lewis. Kootenai Camp No. 6054 is the new camp of Modern Woodmen of America.

Libby News, February 2, 1899

In June 1899, the Masons were "taking steps" toward organizing a lodge with eleven charter members and the same spring the

Odd Fellows of Libby celebrated the eightieth anniversary of that order at the M.W.A. hall. . . . Neatly printed invitations had been issued and the hall was literally jammed. The members of the order and their families wore white satin badges.

Libby News, April 27, 1899

The next year an I. O. O. F. lodge was organized with eighteen charter members, and a meeting place was obtained over John P. Wall's store.

The Federation of Workingmen gave a ball after Christmas in 1899 in Neff & Plummer's Hall, which was attended by 150 masked guests "and as many more spectators." Awards for costumes were given. Charles Downing, "who represented a Chinaman," received a pipe for the "best sustained male character." To Jack

Weir, who appeared as a Spanish dandy, went a pair of silk suspenders; while the best dressed lady, Miss Mary Hodgson, who impersonated Queen Esther, received a "China tea set." Harry Fowler came as an owl. His was voted the "most ridiculous costume," and he received a jack-in-the-box.

When the Redmen gave a ball at Neff & Plummer's Hall "conveyances took all who desired to attend." According to the *Libby News* (Feb. 21, 1901) "After 1 a.m. each hour a team will convey the guests to their homes."

Winters in these northern woods were long.

A light snow fall, the first of the season, was visible on the summits on the morning of Sept. 4, and on the fifth frosts in the valley nipped Potato vines, Winter is in sight.

Libby Montanian, September 10, 1898

Each successive snow added depth to the packed surfaces left from earlier storms. Olga Johnson tells how the people complained when the narrow, shoveled paths, walled with snow higher than a man, were blocked with wandering hogs.

Harry Hamilton's trip to the Selkirk mine in early May, 1899, shows the extremes in weather that could be encountered at that season, within thirteen miles of the town. His experiences, as written in the *Libby News* of May 4, are headed "From Dusty Streets to Fifteen Feet of Snow in One Day." The article describes his departure from Libby at 6 a.m. He walked down the railroad track to Cedar Creek and then took the trail up the gulch to snowline, where he put on snowshoes. From there on the trail was much steeper, with the last mile so precipitous that "snow or anything else had to hang on with both feet." Even wearing snowshoes, he "sank to his middle at each step." By the time he reached the Selkirk shaft he was soaked through, and in order to dry out, decided to hike an additional three-quarters of a mile to a higher cabin where there was a stove. Not wanting to tote his grub any farther, he tied it to a tree near the shaft and started straight up the mountain to the shack. While clambering up this last stretch, an unexpected blizzard struck, which so numbed him that he "took off his sweater and wrapped it around his head so he could breathe." He had forgotten to bring gloves, so he took off one pair of socks and wore them on his hands. A fifteen-foot mound of snow showed him the location of the cabin, but to get into it was another matter. He had no shovel, so he broke a limb from a tree and with it dug through seven feet of snow to the roof. To

LIBBY PANORAMA FROM THE KOOTENAI BRIDGE

MASONIC HALL, LIBBY

enter, he had to tear away a portion of the roof. Here was the stove but his grub was down by the mine, so he decided to take the sheet-iron stove down there, carrying it and the stovepipe on his back. Arrived at the shaft-house cabin, he couldn't find the tree where he had cached his food and only discovered it at 2 a.m. He stayed at the mine cabin for three days. In Libby, the streets were still dusty.

With placer ground frozen and most lode mines shut down until spring, Libby settled down to sit out the winter. Dances helped to pass the time, and nothing was too much trouble to insure their success. Pioneers recall that on many an occasion, a piano was carried for blocks to the hall where the ball was to be held.

There is a project on foot to organize a brass band in Libby and nothing would kill the monotony of these long winter nights more readily than the sweet strains of music. . . . A brass band is a feature of a live town that should not be overlooked. . . . There is a carpenter in town who is able to lead on the "B" flat cornet; T. J. Hollinger is an adept on the trombone, Thos. Switzer plays well on the baritone, E. M. Brown can find music in the solo alto, Brockey is a rattler on bass, Lou Berger can buzz the clarionette to perfection, Ray Greeley can rattle the tenor drum to a finish and the editor can beat the bosom out of a bass drum. The Libby brass band will be a reality before long sure. Give it encouragement.
Libby Montanian, January 5, 1898

Snow did not hamper recreation; instead, it provided a variety of sports:

An Exhilarating Toboggan Slide.
Chas. Seifert, foreman of the Silver Cable mine, took a toboggan slide a short time ago, not in his calculations. He fell on the high trail near the mouth of the main tunnel and slid down the side of the mountain 1500 feet. [With] a hard crust of snow, angle 45 degrees, (and he weighs 200 pounds), . . . he was going pretty fast when he landed against a tree. No bones were broken. His face was badly scratched and his body bruised, but he was able to clmb back to the mine without assistance.
Libby News, January 12, 1899
* * *
Impromptu Straw Ride
An idea occurred to a couple of people Monday night to give a straw ride on the spur of the moment. Senator Geiger and F. M. Plummer hitched their teams up, and drove around town till their big bob sleds were full to overflowing. . . . The sleigh ride lasted for an hour or more when the party wound up at the store building at South Libby, where music was in attendance, and the pleasure of dancing was indulged in for several hours. The affair was entirely impromptu.
Libby News, January 4, 1900

Harry Johnston drives a novel sleigh. It is a small two-seated cutter and is drawn by two large mastiff dogs in harness. It is a neat rig and South Libby Townsite is engraved on the sides. Two can ride in the rig very comfortably.
Libby Montanian, January 20, 1900

Skating parties are now the order of the day. There are several stretches of ice along the river which afford the skaters plenty of room to disport themselves at this popular pastime. Below the big riffle is a long stretch of clear ice, that each afternoon has been the rendezvous for a crowd of merry skaters. This week the ice men are getting in their work and are storing a quantity of frozen fluid for use next summer.
Libby News, February 7, 1901

Will Hillis, Woody Williams and others put in last Friday morning in spearing fish down the river. The species caught were suckers, but at this season of year their meat is hard and firm and they are good eating.
Libby News, February 14, 1901

In summer, horseback riding and picnics were the pastimes enjoyed especially by the ladies. When Charles Ryder opened a bowling alley, he instituted a "Ladies Day" every Thursday afternoon with "suitable prizes for the best lady bowler." To further tempt them and to prove the respectability of his establishment, he provided soda water and lemonade for refreshments.

As early as 1902, Libby was startled with a motor vehicle:

Wm. Whiteside has received the first motorcycle to get this far west in Flathead county and started out on Tuesday afternoon for the placer mines at the head of Libby creek, at which place he is employed. The new machine excited a great deal of curiosity when it was brought out on the street and a large crowd of children followed it for a considerable distance after the start was made. How it will fare on the mountain roads is problematical.
Western News, August 7, 1902

In January 1898, a local dramatic company was organized to give entertainments during the long winter months. Occasionally traveling troupes found their way to the isolated settlements and played in halls and so-called "opera houses" to theatre-starved audiences.

Downie's Big Dramatic & Specialty Co. took the city by storm last evening. The opera house was crowded to suffocation . . . to witness a presentation of "My Uncle from Manila."
Libby Montanian, February 3, 1900

McPhee Comedy Co.
On the opening night the company presented a five-act drama "An Arkansaw Romance." Between acts specialties were introduced and after the drama there was a concert. The second night the program was "An American Abroad."

Libby News, January 24, 1901

In March, the McPhee Company played a return engagement, presenting the play "Peace Stricken Blind."

As soon as the Libby Baseball Club was organized in 1900, it gave a dance for the purpose of raising funds for suits for the players. On Sunday, April 5, the first practice was played on the Libby diamond so as to "get ready to skin all the teams withing hailing distance." The first game of the season, which was played on the Troy diamond, resulted in Libby beating Troy 25-20. Encouraged by this, the Libby team beat the Kalispell club 16-15 and made "preparations to wipe up the diamond with the Kalispell boys on the glorious Fourth." That baseball remained a popular sport is shown by the following item:

The Eureka fork swingers and the Libby gravel scratchers tied into each other last Sunday at the latter place in a friendly game of ball. After a most strenuous search all over the field, the hay diggers from up the line could find only 9 beautiful goose eggs, while the gravel scratchers, during the same period, dug up 6 nuggets, which looked mighty fine to them and made them feel and look as though they had done a good hard day's work.

Troy Herald, June 24, 1910

Like all timber towns Libby had its fires.

Olander & Best's hardware store on Second St., Libby, was entirely consumed by fire Monday morning about three o'clock. . . . It was the first fire of any note that ever occurred at Libby and caused the citizens to get together for the purpose of effecting a volunteer fire company with buckets sufficient for a good-sized bucket brigade.

There were not over 150 people at the fire; the balance slept. Six occupants of the Devine House in the same block never awoke which is surely a good recommendation for the quietness as well as the kind of beds furnished there.

Libby Montanian, May 5, 1900

One blaze which leveled portions of the business section on Front Street in July, 1906, caused the death of Michael Brick. Despite efforts of the townspeople who formed a bucket brigade, from the canal by the tracks, the entire block, with the exception of the Ross building, went up in flames. The most dreaded fires of all were those that started in the dense

timber, or in the slashed-over land which surrounded the town on all sides.

Fires in the West Fisher
Thousands of Dollars Worth of Valuable Timber
Being Consumed.
Brick & Branagan force of men are compelled to fight the fire to save the mill. The only way they can now be put out will be by the fall rains.

Libby News, August 9, 1900

Each year the town expanded. After the Libby Lumber and Development Company bought the townsite land from the Northern Pacific, Frank Leonard made certain changes in the original plat and added forty acres which formed West Libby. In 1909, when the town was incorporated, South Libby was also included in the total site.

Libby is Putting on Airs.
There has been a wonderful change in the city within the last twelve months. It has donned a new dress to replace the old rambling mining town with its unsightly dumps, unkempt streets and weather-stained buildings. There are probably 100 new buildings. Great piles of stumps in the squares show the work of the cleaning up now going on, preparatory to several miles of street grading and cement walks. Timber and brush between Oldtown and South Libby have been cleared away and the intervening space is being built upon, so that the two are practically one town.

Troy Herald, July 8, 1910

No bridge spanned the river at Libby until 1916, and until that date, persons wishing to cross took the ferry — a pontoon-supported raft with side railings, controlled by a cable and propelled by the current. One of the first ferrymen ran a bankside saloon as well, and it was often hard to attract his attention from the opposite shore. Passengers, tiring of shouting, would fire a gun to bring him across. But even a ferry ride had its perils:

Boat With Seven Capsizes in Midstream and Cable
Pulls Out Causing Further Horrors.
It was a new boat in service less than a week. The Kootenai river is always treacherous and all those on the boat were washed off by the swift current when the accident occurred except Mrs. Roderick, who obtained a firm hold and hung on . . . when the cable gave way it came down upon the crowd underneath, killing John Mullenix and Theo. Wall. . . . Mullenix had his face terribly smashed by the big iron rope.

Troy Herald, June 17, 1910

As years passed and Libby continued to grow, the emphasis on mining lessened and new industries developed. As early as 1899

Prof. J. M. Emery of the Montana Experiment Station at Bozeman arrived in Libby on the delayed train from the east and spent the afternoon in getting acquainted with those of the residents of the town who are interested in the growing of fruit. . . . In the evening there was a meeting of those who have set out fruit trees or expect to do so in Mr. Lonard's office. Thirty persons were present.

Libby News, April 20, 1899

Today, many farms and ranches are found in clearings and along streams, wherever thick forests do not cover the soil. Although a little hard rock mining is still carried on, Libby's chief sources of income in the 1950's were from cattle, Christmas trees, lumber, and vermiculite.

Upon entering Libby today, one is more aware of lumbering than of any other industry; for logging trucks rumble along the highway and the J. Neils Lumber Company's mill dominates the eastern end of the town. Not that this is a new industry; for the enveloping forests have provided timber for mills ever since the winter of 1891-1892, when machinery for the first sawmill was freighted in by wagon over the old tote road. This mill was supplied from trees that were cut from the streets and lots of the original townsite. Beginning in 1899, other sawmills were erected on the fringes of the settlement, one by the Libby Lumber & Development Company, which worked two shifts and employed forty men, and another by the Pacific-Northwest Mining Corporation, which operated on a large scale for two years until lack of capital and the reduced demand for lumber necessitated its shutdown. This company built pole roads into the forest equipped with "rails" made of tall slender trees. Flange-wheel trucks drawn by four- and six-horse teams hauled the logs on these improvised tracks. In addition to these two companies, Burlington & Sons built small mills near Libby.

In 1906, D. E. Dawson, a millwright from Wisconsin, and his partners, established the Dawson Lumber Company and procured a fifty-acre millsite beside Libby Creek. Here the company erected a mill and a logging railway into their timber lands south of the town. The lumberjacks lived in company camps in the forests near their work. This successful company enlarged its plant, only to sell out in 1911 to the Julius Neils Lumber Company. Within a year, the property was purchased by the Shevlin Clarke Lumber Company, which remodeled the mill. Next, the J. Neils Lumber Company repurchased the plant, and they still run it.

No sooner had Francis and I gotten settled in a motel on our first visit to Libby, in 1955, than I began looking for someone who could tell me where to find a few of its mines. Three people were most helpful. The first was Mr. H. B. Smith, a geologist from Salt Lake City, who had just returned from inspecting the Silver Butte mine.

"It's twelve miles up the Fisher River road," he told me, drawing a crude map as he talked. "Mr. Kurtz is the present owner, but he may be off logging. If you go up there, you'll find the last mile and a half pretty steep, the part over the Trout Creek divide. That's the lowest saddle in the Cabinets. You'll see the mill and the mine two miles before you reach them. You can't drive above the mill. When you reach the Kurtz ranch, go through the gate, turn back inside and go on to the mine."

Our second source of information was Mr. Len Olson, accountant at the Neils Lumber Company. Having phoned Mr. Olson and told him what I needed to know, I accepted his invitation to drop by for a chat. In a short time I was sitting in his big, tree-shaded home while he told me many things about the town which he knew so well.

"You've heard of the Brick and Branagan mine, haven't you?" he began. "It was one of the first properties to be opened. Branagan was an odd man. He always took the gold down from the mine by himself. He'd ride a horse right into town. It's a wonder he wasn't followed and hit over the head.

"I would't go up to the original site of Libby placer camp if I were you. There was nothing whatsoever left of it the last time I was up there. Too bad you weren't here when the Snowshoe was running. I was there fifteen years ago, and the buildings were about to fall down then. If you want to find some mines near town, drive up Granite Creek. They're not logging up that road right now, so you won't have to watch for trucks. The Glacier-Silver-Lead is up there. At one time it was owned by Mr. Lukens. He remarried and his wife's name was Hazel. That's when the mine was called the Lukens-Hazel.

"There's not much hard-rock mining any more. Zonolite's the new industry here now. There was a man living alone, up on the mountain, in a cabin some years ago. He had a fruit farm. No one knew anything about him. It was thought he might be a killer, keeping away from the law. He had money and he never did any work. He was pleasant enough. One time, when I was up there, he had a sample of vermiculite on the windowsill. He told me that he thought it might have some metal in it. Once a hunter started a campfire and put some of the stuff in the fire and it began to unroll and expand! When a few men finally learned how to handle it, one or two companies were formed to develop it commercially.

"The chief trouble was with the expansion. One carload raw equals fifteen carloads roasted. When it gets dark tonight, you'll see the lights of the mill. It's about seven miles northeast of Libby, and the mine is about 3,000 to 4,000 feet higher than the town. The Zonolite Company ships about fifteen to twenty carloads each day. The deposit as found is almost pure, except for some asbestos in it. Vermiculite rated tenth in the mineral production in Montana in 1952. That year nearly 155,000 tons were produced, valued at $1,973,387.

"You ask about the placers. Libby Creek is the only one that was worked for placer gold as late as 1947. Liberty Placer Mines were operating then, and used two hydraulic giants and bulldozers to wash out 15,000 cubic yards of bench gravels. As near as anyone knows, the total amount of placer gold washed out since 1902 was $95,000. No one knows how much was recovered before then. According to the Government Survey of 1948, a total of $4,500,000 has been recovered from placers and lode mines."

Next morning, following specific directions given us by Mr. Olson, we found ourselves on the Granite Creek road. The first signpost read "Old Snowshoe Mine," and pointed left. We kept to the right. At the next fork, the Flower Creek trail ran right. We kept left. We drove for several miles, climbing all the time through forests, with only occasional breaks where we could see the wide valley below covered with second or third growth trees, or cleared for ranches whose metal barn roofs shone in the sun. Beyond the valley loomed the Cabinet Range. At the foot of a hill stood a new cabin from which bounded three dogs as soon as the door was opened by a woman who peered out sleepily when I asked her if there were any mines nearby.

"Sure, there's lots of them around here," she said. "There's a big one about two miles ahead, but it doesn't work now. The road goes on beyond it quite a ways but mostly fishermen use it."

GLACIER-SILVER-LEAD MILL, GRANITE CREEK

Her directions were correct, for within two miles we reached an empty cabin, a barn across the road from it, and a trail leading uphill to the right. Just beyond it stood the ruins of a large mill. Leaving the car beside the road, we climbed to the top of a flat above the mill where there were more buildings, one of which was the mine office. Farther back on the meadow were covered pits, part of an old boiler, and a big dump. We followed a dry creek back toward the timber and discovered concrete foundations of a large building, a small shack, and piles of blackened lumber. Up the hillside in the trees were more cabins and a small concrete building. Tram ties led back from the dump to a foundation.

We were not sure what mine this was, and when we drove back toward Libby, there was no sign of life at the cabin where we had stopped as we came in. That afternoon, while I was scanning old newspapers in the Libby Public Library, I told the librarian, Mrs. Robert Herrig, where we had gone and asked her what mine we had seen. To answer my question, she rang up the county clerk.

"Hello," she said. "This is a test. What's the name of the mine with the ruined mill, six miles up Granite Creek?" After his reply she turned to me and said: "Its the Glacier-Silver-Lead Company. That's the property that made people around here lose their shirts."

"Since most of the old mines are inactive, let's go see what a modern mill looks like," I said to Francis after our search for the Granite Creek properties.

Before breakfast the next morning we started for the Zonolite plant, whose twinkling lights on Zonolite Mountain we had watched the previous evening. Crossing the Kootenai, we drove four miles along the north side of the river to the mouth of Rainy Creek. There a well-graded, but steep, road leads to the big plant. At the end of a six-mile pull, we saw ahead, and above, a shiny new building on top of the mountain. Passing an older mill and some settling ponds, we finally drew up beside a throbbing mill whose six stacks were belching smoke. Around it clustered smaller buildings, sheds, and tanks, connected by trails and catwalks.

While we were looking back toward the wooded Kootenai Valley, amazed at how high we had come, and impressed by the majestic mass of the Cabinet Range cutting the horizon to the south, three buses and several private cars drove up, filled with men ready to start the day's shift.

With a last look at the glittering plant, set in the midst of a sea of conifers, we drove back to the river. Large bins were built along the north bank, and piles of something — presumably vermiculite — covered with canvas, stood beside them. More storage bins and a string of freight cars on a siding stood on the far side of the Kootenai. Connecting the bins was a belt-conveyor, suspended over the river.

"Just what is vermiculite?" I asked Francis as we hurried back to Libby and breakfast.

"It's a mica-like material which swells and peels when heated. I believe it was discovered in 1824, but no commercial production was made until 1915, when a small amount was processed near Salida, Colorado. One of the men I was talking with last night told me a good deal about the plant here.

"Vermiculite was accidentally found in the Rainy Creek area after World War I, when some men were prospecting for vanadium. The deposite at Libby is very large, virtually a whole hill of the mineral, from which the top is being removed by open pit mining with power shovels. When E. N. Alley found this deposit in 1915, he realized its potential value and experimented with it in a small expanding plant which he built. The first commercial production was in 1925, when two tons of it were shipped. That year, the Zonolite Company was formed.

"The Mecalite Company and the Asbestos Company were organized next. In 1931, the Dominion Stucco Company of Manitoba bought an interest in the Zonolite Company. Three years later, the first concentrating plant was built near the mines. By 1939, the Zonolite Company and the Vermiculite and Asbestos Company combined to form Universal Zonolite Company, whose headquarters were in Chicago. The name was simplified, in 1948, to the Zonolite Company.

"When we were up by the mill, did you notice, high above us, another large building on the summit, at the edge of the deposit? That's where the twelve-ton trucks, which are filled by the big shovels, dump their loads. The ore is partly sorted there and the big chunks are run through the crusher. From there, the rock is brought by a 1,300-foot conveyor-belt to bins at the big mill. The chunks and flakes of ore that go into that mill are refined and cleaned, as well as graded. When they leave the mill, they are hauled by truck to the bins beside the river, ready to be loaded and shipped.

"Some of the crude ore is processed at the expanding plant and is then ready for use, but since it increases so greatly in size when heated, it is cheaper to ship it crude and exfoliate it near points of consumption. After roasting it is very light in weight also — a cubic foot weighing between six and fifteen pounds. It changes color, too — becoming a lustrous gold, bronze, reddish, even dark green and black."

"What it is used for?" I persisted.

"It is infusible up to 2,500 degree Fahrenheit and is such an excellent thermal insulator that it is used in fireproof roofing, electrical installations, refrigerator packing, bake ovens, refractory brick, and insulation for bank vaults and safes. It is also a sound deadener and is added to acoustical plaster. Small amounts are added to paint and wallboard and may be decorative elements in wallpaper. It has high tensile strength, is vermin proof, insoluble, lighter than cork and extremely cheap."

"If it can do all those things, no wonder the company is flourishing, and Libby, too," I replied as we drove up Mineral Avenue in search of a cup of coffee.

Before I left Libby, I wandered over the town looking for landmarks. The back streets with their dense shade gave some idea of what the place must have been like during its first two years. At the south end of Mineral Avenue, I looked into woods. This was approximately where the trail to Old Town began in the days when the two parts of town were separated by a dense stand of firs and tamaracks.

One of the larger buildings that I found is the hospital. Could it be the one erected by Dr. William M. Howsley, who arrived in 1899 and built a hospital on West Second Street, carrying on his practice in a large tent while construction was going on? Howsley was one of the doctors for the Snowshoe Mining Company, "which introduced hospital insurance for its workers in 1899."

In February, 1900, the first case of smallpox was reported "imported direct from Spokane," according to the *Libby News*; for the man had been in a smallpox hospital there, and had been discharged. He was immediately quarantined, and a notice was posted in the Lbiby postoffice, warning everyone to keep away from him.

As I stopped beside the Masonic Hall to sketch, three men came out of the front door and looked over my shoulder. When I asked them about the building, one said that it was one of the oldest in Libby and had served many purposes: first as courthouse, then as county jail, next as high school, and now as the Masonic Hall, A. F. & A. M. Libby Lodge No. 85. While I scribbled this information on the back of my drawing, the second man spoke up.

"Yes, it has been all those things and now it also has the office of the best lawyer in Libby."

"Who is that?" I asked.

"I am," he replied, and the three sauntered off. On the door was a sign: "Oliver Phillips, Lawyer."

One could spend weeks in Libby, especially in the library or newspaper office, where both the editor, Mr. Russell Littell, and Mrs. Olga Johnson kindly put at my disposal the old files; but Troy, another mining town, beckoned to me, and I headed west for new adventure.

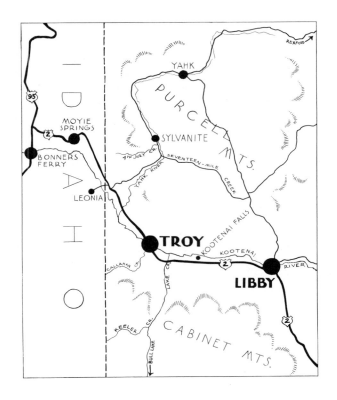

CHAPTER 18

TROY and the YAHK DISTRICT

The Kootenai River is within sight of the highway between Libby and Troy most of the way. In some places the road is close to the big, blue-green stream; in other stretches, it is high above it. Once or twice the railroad and the highway fight for a toe-hold on a rocky spit of land below towering cliffs. Just above Kootenai Falls, at China Rapids, rocks pile up in the turbulent stream, giving some idea of the constant dangers encountered by rivermen who navigated it. China Rapids were named, according to one legend, for the Chinese placer miners who were run off from Libby Creek after they were caught pilfering sluice boxes. In their flight down the river on a raft, they were drowned at this point. Yet some oldtimers claim that the China Rapids were near Jennings, and that the miners for whom they were named were run off from their placers on Gold Creek, below Rexford.

The rapids are dangerous, and many accidents have occurred in or near them. When Brag Parmenter decided to take several bales of dried deer hides to Bonner's Ferry to sell, he invited several of his cronies to accompany him. The party packed their guns and plenty of grub and camp duffle, looking upon the whole thing as an excursion. Taking two canoes, the expedition set out, with James Horton in charge of one boat and Parmenter handling the other. The boats floated easily downstream until they reached the rapids. There one of them hung on a rock, but Pat Dolan, an experienced boatman, guided it safely through the white water. Parmenter's canoe capsized when caught in an eddy, spilling him and the hides into the icy, swirling current. He and the hides were rescued, the boats reloaded, and the party pushed off, minus rifles and camp outfits. They made a portage around the falls and slid swiftly down to Bonner's Ferry.

Summer or winter, the river is a force beyond man's control.

High Water Causes Ice Jam in River
The high water carried a jam of ice into the Kootenai from the Fisher River Sunday and the rising water in the large river broke up the ice in the Kootenai and started it downstream. The mass of ice filled the river bank to bank and several miles in length. It arrived at Libby in midafternoon and a large crowd gathered on the bridge watching the unusual and pretty sight. . . . The larger chunks struck the bridge piers with great force shaking the entire structure.

310

At Kootenai Falls, large chunks of ice were shoved bodily out of the water and onto the rocks in the middle of the stream. The ice extended seven miles upstream from the falls. . . . Another jam reached Libby after midnight. The road supervisor spent the rest of the night at the bridge. It required five hours for the second jam to pass. Piles of ice ten feet high are resting on one of the big islands upstream.

Western News and Libby Times, March 3, 1932

At Kootenai Falls, a trail leads through woods to the brink of the cataract. Here the rushing water drops 200 feet in a series of cascades. Large rocks jut out of the river, causing the rapid current to break against or over them and swirl on to the next boulder. In the grove of big trees near the falls, the U.S. Forest Service maintains a campground. Below the falls, the river cuts through a gorge over which dangles a suspension bridge with a footpath. Originally, as the following item shows, the only trail along the riverside lay on the north bank. Mike Wallace wrote in the *Libby News* of January 6, 1899, that

Ten Horses Drowned at Kootenai Falls.
The last outfit of Indians that went out on the Bonner's Ferry trail met a dozen horses just above the Kootenai Falls on the other side of the river. The trail is very narrow and steep at this point and one of the Indians stampeded the horses so that they jumped into the water. Of the eleven horses that jumped, ten were swept over the falls, and only one succeeded in swimming the river. This one will probably starve to death as there is no feed on the south side of the river. The State ought to offer a bounty on these worthless Indians that infest this part of the country. They destroy more game and stock than the lions and coyotes.

The present highway between Libby and Troy is often close to the railroad, and seeing it brought to mind the story of J. F. Harris, who, in 1897, walked the track for fifty miles, carrying a turkey to his family for their Thanksgiving dinner. Harris, who lived in Jennings, some miles east of Libby, had been in Spokane on business and was ready to start home two days before the holiday. In the meantime, a slide had blocked the track along the Kootenai River, east of Bonner's Ferry, and no trains were running. Learning that a work train was going to the scene of the slide to clear the track, he bought a turkey, two cans of oysters, a dozen each of oranges and bananas, put them in a sack, and boarded the train. At Bonner's Ferry, a traveling man, Carl Greenhook, joined him, and the two rode to the barrier, which was fifteen miles east of the ferry. It was a big slide which would

necessitate several days' work to clear; so when Harris heard that the superintendent's car and engine were standing on the far side of the wreckage, he saw a chance to negotiate a ride as far as Libby. Confident of transportation, he and Greenhook scrambled over the debris, Harris with his turkey and fruit and the salesman with his grips. Unable to arrange the anticipated ride, they set out, up the tracks, covering the twenty miles to Troy by late evening. There was no train there, either, and the tired men turned in for the night. Early the next morning, Harris gave his oranges and bananas to the station agent and "shouldering his turkey and oysters," started alone up the track toward Jennings, thirty-one miles away. He got as far as Libby and still found no train. Doggedly, he plodded on, reaching Jennings at 2 a.m., having kept his vow to bring home a Thanksgiving bird.

TROY

Troy's early history is much like that of Libby's. It, too, had an "Old Town," situated at the mouth of Lake Creek, east of the present settlement. In 1890, when Robert Gregg, one of Troy's pioneers, camped where the business section now stands, he found only tepee poles on the flat; for Indians made this ground annual headquarters while getting their winter's supply of fish and deer meat. The following spring the Great Northern's construction crews were grading west from Libby, and to serve the workers, a rough camp sprang up at the mouth of the Heryakaha River, locally known as Lake Creek.

Lake City was a typical grader's camp, full of saloons and tough characters. Robert Gregg, in his reminiscences, mentions the Big Eight mining property on Callahan Creek as under bond to Marcus Daly at that time, and recalls that some miners who were developing it came down to the camp to celebrate. In the course of the evening's carousing, one or two lost their payrolls in a saloon and announced that they'd been robbed. A crowd of their friends produced a rope and threatened to hang one of the saloon men unless the money was restored. It was.

By the fall of 1891, when the grading was completed, the floating population moved on, leaving Lake City on the skids. In the meantime, E. L. Preston, surveyor for the Great Northern road, bought up several mining claims a short distance west of Lake City at a proposed location for a freight division point.

Here he laid out a townsite, which he called Troy, naming it for Troy Morrow, the son of the family with whom he was boarding in Bonner's Ferry.

All throughout 1892, people drifted into Lake City, waiting to see if it or Troy was to become the railroad town. By September, 1892, when the right of way was secured and the railroad began planning a ten-stall roundhouse, freight yards, and a coal chute at Troy, people poured into the new camp. Gregg remembers "one morning when I got up about fifty saloon men and half as many 'wild women' were jumping the townsite." During this moving process, Tom Dobson, who ran the grocery store at the dying camp, walked down the track to the new townsite, carrying a teakettle. "What you got there?" his cronies called out as he tramped by. "The Lake City post office," he replied. In the kettle were letters, cash, and stamps, all of which Dobson handled in his grocery in lieu of a proper office.

The D. T. Woods and their two small children were among the newcomers to arrive in October, 1892. Mr. Wood, a repair man for the raiload, met his family at the depot and led them through the gaudy camp whose fifteen saloons were crammed with boisterous patrons. Two dancehalls, one grocery store, several "beaneries," one drug store, and a sprinkling of shacks and tents made up the town. Troy was so notorious for lawlessness that railroad car doors were locked as the trains rolled through the settlement for fear of hold-ups.

Except for the river, which ran in front of the town, Troy was surrounded by thick forests filled with game. When high water flooded the tracks and left Troy without trains for forty days, the people lived off venison, fish, and wild strawberries. The huckleberry bushes that grew near the B. & B. mine were stripped, not only by the townspeople, but also by bears which roamed the woods. Coyotes slipped into Troy at night to steal food cached on back porches. Fish were so plentiful that train crews could throw their lines from a caboose into Lake Creek, whenever a freight stopped at the station, and hope for a catch.

Since Troy had no resident physician until 1910 and the nearest qualified medic was at Spokane, "Doc" Sailey, the druggist, and several women who gladly cared for the sick were called upon in emergencies.

As soon as the railroad completed its installations in 1893, most of the rougher element of the town drifted away and Troy became a mining and agricultural center. The hills west of the camp held ore deposits, while the climate proved favorable to the cultivation of fruits, vegetables, and grain. Only a few years later, in 1904, wheat from Troy received third prize at the San Francisco Exposition.

The first issue of the *Troy Times* appeared on September 28, 1894. Its advertisements called attention to B. Downer, notary public; Baggs & Aitken, milk dealers; Ed Riley, saloon-keeper; Henry Howell, proprietor of the Windsor Hotel, and Mrs. Linnie Wylie, manager of a restaurant; T. H. Dobson, merchant; D. T. Wood and F. B. Callow, grocers; R. Sailey, druggist; S. T. McGrath, butcher; T. J. McGrath, justice of the peace, and Thomas Baggs, constable.

In 1894, a meeting was called to organize a school district and arrange for a building which would serve both as school and general meeting place. All labor was donated: men hauled logs, Tom Dobson provided doors and windows, and the women raised money with which to furnish the interior by giving a variety of entertainments. The first teacher in the little log building on Yahk Avenue was a Miss Valentine. She had seven pupils.

The Methodists held the first religious gathering in Troy in 1894, with Rev. G. C. Stull presiding. He was followed by Rev. J. M. Eastland, whose circuit included Kalispell and Libby. From these three churches he received a modest salary; one year it was $81.25. During his pastorate, a parsonage was procured and a church completed by 1902. The Ladies Aid Society was started in 1898. Up until 1910, the Methodists had the only church building in town; the Episcopalians and Catholics built later.

The disappearance of Alexis Berk, the young Methodist preacher sent to Troy in November, 1896, troubled the community for more than two years. Soon after his arrival, he went alone into the hills back of Troy, to hunt mountain sheep, and never returned. Search parties found his tracks but lost them after a short distance. New storms prevented further search until the following spring. On November 5, 1898, an announcement in the *Libby Montanian* stated that:

The remains of the lost Rev. Berk were found last Sunday in the high ranges six miles southwest of Troy . . . by Wm. Keeler, a prospector. . . . Clothes, shoes and papers are fairly well preserved. . . . Judge D. P. Boyle has gone down to Troy to hold an inquest over the remains.

FRONT ST., TROY

TROY

On Nov. 10 the *Libby News* announced that Keeler had refused to disclose the place where the remains lay until he was paid the $200 reward.

Judge Boyle gave an order commanding him to accompany the jury. Keeler refused to obey the order and Judge Boyle then fined him $50 and 25 days in jail, for contempt. . . . The remains are still in the mountains, the jury discharged and Keeler in the hands of the Constable. Judge Boyle went back to Libby.

Tragedy struck the Frank Baggs family the following year, 1899.

Mr. Baggs and his wife started to his ranch to feed his stock. Owing to the fact that the Great Northern had given orders to have all persons attempting to cross Callahan creek on its bridges arrested, and the persistent refusal of the county commissioners to erect a proper bridge on the public highway over the stream, the public has been forced to ford the stream ever since November 1897.

Baggs knew that others had forded the stream a few hours prior to his crossing. Before starting, he examined his team and followed the usual track, but the wheels dropped into a hole recently washed out and the wagon box overturned. . . . They were both thrown into the stream and dashed against boulders. She was drowned. Her body was found near the railroad bridge, one-half mile below the ford. She left a husband and four daughters.

Libby News, June 22, 1899

As Troy grew, a variety of social organizations were established. As early as 1898, a baseball nine was formed. This team, attired in suits ordered from Chicago, was soon playing Libby, Kalispell, and other clubs in the region. That it was still flourishing in 1910 is shown by a newspaper notice which mentions a basket social which "netted the baseball boys $46 besides providing the large crowd present with a most enjoyable time." A lodge of the Modern Woodmen of America was organized in May, 1899, with 18 members. The 16 members of the Pinetree Whist Club, which met at members' homes in 1900, "served midnight lunches and arranged invitational dances" held at Town Hall. "Literary Evenings," held at the D. T. Wood home during the Russian-Japanese war, consisted of papers covering "all phases of life and letters" in those countries. They were written and presented by the members. An Athletic Club, with fifty members, was organized in 1911; a Woman's Club in 1921.

The year 1910 was a memorable one. On May 20, the *Troy Herald* made its appearance

and from its pages some idea of the sixteen-year old settlement can be had. The paper boosted the community, calling it the "Garden Spot of Montana, Surrounded by a World of Mineral Wealth and other Natural Resources." When J. H. Ehlers, promoter of the mining camp of Sylvanite, planned a two-story brick bank with offices on the second floor, the paper applauded his enterprise, explaining that it would be the "first brick structure in town and in all probability marks the era of the passing of the shack stage in the life of the town and will make it one of the most beautiful little cities in the northwest."

The County Ferryboat Goes on a Long Voyage.
The Troy ferryboat has gone hence, and it is very probable that it will never see these parts again. Tuesday evening a returning pedestrian from Sylvanite, whose intentions were probably all right but with a knowledge bordering on foolhardiness, arrived at the landing on the north shore where the boat was anchored. The ferryman was up in town upon an errand and the wayfarer must have been in an awful hurry, for he cast the boat adrift and jumped on for a run across. The swift water caught the boat broadwise, tore loose the cable fastenings on the Troy side and away went the navigator and boat down the Kootenai. He yelled . . . as he was swept along. . . . Fortunately the boat caught on some branches and he clambered out. His craft went down the stream. . . . What became of the impromptu ferryman is not known but about an hour later a stranger was crossed in the Waters rowboat a mile up the river, who is believed to be the one. . . . It was an inopportune time for some heavy supplies were to be taken up the Yahk and this is the only means of transportation to the camp. A new boat can be built, it is more difficult to replace the cable.

Troy Herald, June 3, 1910

All throughout August forest fires raged in the mountains, destroying the camp of Sylvanite and threatening to wipe out Troy as well. Civic preparations are described in the paper:

The 900 feet of railroad company hose was laid from the yards to Front St. and Sunday evening a demonstration was made to test the service, a locomotive furnishing the pressure. The buildings on Front St. were thoroughly soaked and it would seem that the business part of town can be saved, and the depot and other RR property as well, even if the worst come.

Saturday and Sunday an engine was kept steamed up and a string of cars nearby, in case it should be necessary for town people to be carried away with such effects as they might be able to move. . . . Some . . . citizens buried valuable papers and treasures and others packed up valuable personal goods to be ready for the anticipated calamity.

Squads of men sent on the trains from nearby points throughout the day were re-inforced in the evening by a carload of 100 fire-fighters from Spokane. . . .

About 9 o'clock Saturday night the family of Miles Powell was brought to town, Mrs. Powell suffering a broken arm and a fracture of the skull, having been thrown from the wagon while en route. She had been taken up with her three children at the homestead on Lake Creek, 8 miles south of town by Archie Carr, as flames were approaching the home, and in the wild ride, the vehicle struck a stump, throwing her out. . . . Fortunately a physician from Bonner's Ferry was in town and he immediately waited upon her. Her husband followed her into town a few hours later.

Mr. Powell was on the fire line about 4 miles from his home. . . . he ascended a hill to look toward the little clearing only to see heavy clouds of smoke and a wall of flames sweeping toward the spot. Dropping everything, he hastened to the spot. His path lay down Keeler Creek and for 4 miles he made his way through the fire zone — at times in the creek and again along the banks. On the way he passed six bear and a blacktail deer in the bed of the creek, with their hair singed, all taking refuge in the waters of the small stream and not paying the least attention to the being who was rushing headlong by them. Arriving at the clearing . . . (he found that) everything was leveled, house and outbuildings, here a cow, there a pig, yonder a chicken — everything was in smoking, smoldering ruins — even the faithful dog and pussy cat were burned to a crisp. The garden was shriveled.

Troy Herald, August 26, 1910

When he saw shovels in the debris that were not his, he knew that they must have belonged to fire fighters who rescued his family. By fall, with fire hazards lessening, Troy began planning for its future:

The people of Troy are going about the boosting business in a business way . . . they have raised a fund for the erection of a building for a Chamber of Commerce where they can hold public meetings and where samples of their rich grain and vegetable fields and fruitful orchards may be shown. . . . Troy is the only town in the northwest that has had the enterprise to build a home for a boosters club. Kalispell has been talking about it for years, but they have never come to the scratch. . . . The town that builds its own commercial club headquarters has the stuff in it to do other things.

Troy Herald, September 9, 1910

Before looking for Troy's mines, I wandered up one street and down another, searching for the early buildings that had survived floods, fires, and twentieth-century restoration. I was especially curious to see Front Street, a broad avenue that parallels the railroad, for I

TROY AND CABINET RANGE

had read that a fire in 1906 destroyed most of its buildings. The blaze started from an overturned lamp in Allen's Hotel, and before it was extinguished, that hotel, as well as D. T. Wood's hotel, the post office, a store, and Whiting's saloon were burned to the ground; for the city had no fire department. The following day the post office was in operation again, and Wood was carrying on his business in a tent.

In 1956 Front Street presented a solid line of stores, and the side streets contained more modern homes and business blocks than old structures. A striking characteristic of both Libby and Troy are the immense evergreen trees that tower above the buildings, shading the streets as well as beautifying them. The Kootenai flows by the town, the railroad and highway cut lengthwise swaths through it, but back of Troy stand the mountains whose mineral deposits brought the first prospectors to the region.

Four men, Thomas Baggs, William Doyle, Robert Atkins, and James Freeman, cut a trail over the Cabinet Range for themselves and their pack horses from Hope, Idaho, in 1888. Finding Callahan Creek, they followed it to its mouth on the Kootenai. Shortly after this, James Stonechest, Robert Hulse, and Bart Downey discovered and located the Banner and Bangle mine, later known as the Snowstorm. This lead and silver prospect was the first steady producer of the district.

By the middle nineties, the mine was operated by E. J. Mervin Brothers and Maurice Downey (Mervin and Downey Brothers) and ore was packed to the Great Northern station at Troy at the rate of one carload a week.

With the completion of a wagon road to the mine, shipping costs dropped from $8.00 to $2.00 a ton and the amount of ore produced increased to a carload a day.

By 1910 the B. & B. was the biggest producer in the Troy area. A mill to handle its ore was built at Troy in 1916, as well as a large office and a company residence. To further facilitate the transportation of ore, a thirty-six-inch-gauge railroad was constructed from the mine to the mill. Ore mined in the higher levels was collected at the lowest adit and loaded on cars for transit. Between 1917 and 1928 over $4,000,000 was recovered from lead, zinc, silver, and gold. The company also reported 150,000 tons of reserve ore in sight. The 500-ton mill at Troy treated both Snowstorm and custom ores. After it burned in 1927, the mine shut down and has seen little activity since.

The second most important mine in the district was the Big Eight, whose property, north of the Snowstorm, was on both sides of Callahan Creek. The principal vein, eight feet wide, was "well exposed on the abrupt rocky banks of the stream." The mine was developed by crosscuts and tunnels, the lowest of which cut the vein at a depth of 600 feet.

The Big Eight, like the B. & B., was controlled by a stock company whose investors were chiefly from Spokane. The mine contained large bodies of silver, lead, and zinc. During its years of activity, it was developed by several companies. Like the B. & B., it was connected by rail with the mill at Troy.

"Since these two mines are on Callahan Creek, let's see if we can drive to them," I said when we stopped at a filling station in Troy.

"Take the North Callahan Creek road," the attendant directed. "You'll find it just beyond the shingle mill. Turn left at the mill and keep left all the way. Here comes someone who can tell you about it," he continued, hailing a big man in a truck who drove into the station.

"I've just been up there fishing," the newcomer said. "You'll know when you get there, because there's a padlocked gate across the road. I don't know how far it is, but it took me half an hour in my truck. The worst stretch of road is at the beginning. There's a hell of a hill. Cars make it, but don't let your wheels get spinning in the gravel. The road levels off on top. When you're nearly there, the road forks with an upper and a lower branch. Be sure to take the lower one."

We found the shingle mill and the road which led up a wooded hill. An extra spurt of power carried us up a steep pitch to the top where the road leveled out. The next few miles were through timber with only occasional glimpses into a deep wooded ravine with Callahan Creek in the bottom. Before long the road branched, the right fork — the much better roadbed — leading up, and the left dipping to the creek. A sign — "Big 8 Mine 2 Miles" — pointed down. There were no indications of mining even when we reached the bottom of the hill and drove ahead toward a log fence and the locked gate. On the flat beyond it were old buildings in a grove of trees near the stream.

Leaving the car by the gate, we squeezed between the logs and walked up the road toward a cabin with a neat garden in front of it. From behind the building came a man carrying wet towels, which he hung on a line. He was gracious and told us to go ahead and look around, adding that we were six miles from Troy on Big Eight property. Up the hill, beyond the creek, was the Snowstorm mine. If their mill in Troy hadn't burned in 1927, both properties would be active now, he assured us. The Snowstorm had been idle since 1931. The loss of the mill had affected all mining operations in the area and had cut production.

At his suggestion, we walked through the grove beyond battered cabins and a loading station and crossed the creek on a sturdy bridge. Higher up the stream was a sagging trestle, and on the far bank, two or three mine sheds. All this was Big Eight territory.

The road continued up a steep hill to the Snowstorm. On a meadow stood several red buildings, an ore chute, and a compressor house. Above this group, flanking the road at intervals, were ruined cabins and one store with a porch. Weathered shacks in varied states of dilapidation were nearly hidden from sight by rank thickets of bracken and underbrush. By the time we returned to the watchman's cabin, he had finished his washing and came to greet us. I showed him my sketches and he identified the buildings. As we drove away he called after us, "Don't be surprised if the Big Eight opens up soon. It's still a good property."

Prospecting in this whole area began in the early 1890's. Most of the mines were either on Callahan and Keeler Creeks or on Grouse Mountain, a spur of the Cabinet Range, about eight miles southwest of the town. Coarse gold in paying quantities was found in placer ground

BIG "8" MINE, TROY

SNOWSTORM PROPERTY, TROY

and small amounts of it were recovered from sluicing, as late as 1924, 1934, and 1942. In addition to the Big Eight and Snowstorm, the Heron, Key West, Tip Top, and Pathfinder mines lay along Callahan Creek. A few copper properties were discovered in the Bull Lake District.

SYLVANITE

The sign at the mouth of the road to Sylvanite is sobering to anyone who looks upon logging trucks as the juggernauts of back roads in timber country.

STOP. READ THIS SIGN
THIS ROAD IS BEING USED BY HEAVY LOG-
GING TRUCKS REMOVING BEETLE INFESTED
SPRUCE TIMBER.
DRIVING IS HAZARDOUS.
YOU SHOULD NOT TRAVEL THIS ROAD UN-
LESS IT IS NECESSARY.
PLEASE OBEY FOLLOWING INSTRUCTIONS.
1. DRIVE SLOWLY AND CAUTIOUSLY.
2. KEEP RIGHT AT ALL TIMES.
3. DO NOT PARK ON ROAD.
4. PASS ONLY WHERE ROAD IS CLEAR
   AHEAD.
5. USE EXTREME CAUTION ON CURVES AND
   NARROW SECTIONS OF ROAD.
U. S. FOREST SERVICE

The first time I read this, I decided that a drive to Sylvanite *was* unnecessary. But as I read more about this mushroom town, deep in the woods beside the Yahk River, my craving to see it overcame some of my fears. Choosing late afternoon, when loggers were through for the day, Francis and I turned north onto the gravel road ten miles west of Troy and headed for the townsite. It was a serpentine climb through the forest to the top of a hill, with underbrush on each side of the road coated with brown dust from the day's heavy traffic. On top, the country opened up and we passed a few ranches. Beyond a stretch marked "Narrow Road" was a series of switchbacks known as the Stonechest Grade. From its summit the rocky bed of the Yahk River, in the bottom of a deep gorge, looked very narrow. When we reached the foot of the grade, the river appeared wide but shallow and was filled with small rapids. Near a cluster of cabins was a bridge across the Yahk and a sign pointing east across the stream marking the "17 Mile Road." The next ranch that we passed had a gas pump near the road. A little farther on stood a Ranger Station. Another two miles brought us to a group of empty frame company houses, a big barn, and an old ore mill. Inside the barn a man was welding, and when he stopped work I asked the name of the mill and where Sylvanite was.

"This is the old Haywire mill," he replied. "It's called the Morning Glory now. The mine carried gold in lead. You passed Sylvanite down by the Ranger Station. Go talk to Mr. Grush. He lives in the ranchhouse with the tin roof where you saw the gas pump."

Back we went, discovering a schoolhouse and a few more cabins among the trees. We drove through a logging camp with company houses, many families, piles of logs and loaded trucks ready for the morning run to the sawmill.

"If we drove through Sylvanite, why didn't we see it?" Francis asked while we retraced our way, looking for the house and the gas pump.

"Because it burned up," I replied.

Ore was discovered in the Yahk (Yakt, Yaak) District in 1894 or 1895, when two trappers, Bill Lemley and Pete Berg — although some sources mention two Lemley brothers — found free gold the size of a pin head in quartz formations at the head of Crawford Creek on Friday Mountain, and called their discovery the Friday claim. This strike caused a stampede to the Yahk District, where many other claims were staked, including the Keystone.

The Friday Mining Company with headquarters in Spokane was organized, and at first assays from the mine ran as high as $300.00 a ton in wire gold. But when a shaft was sunk, the gold began to pinch out and the claim was abandoned.

The Keystone, on Fourth of July Creek, was discovered by William Johnson and S. J. Whitcomb, during the summer of 1895 and was bonded for $13,000 almost immediately by Finch and Campbell, mining men from Spokane, who proceeded, during the following winter, to develop it, packing in supplies on horses, sixteen miles over the snow.

It is a silverite ore, with a large ore body. . . . H. J. Jory, manager of the Keystone, is having a reservoir built on Fourth of July creek.

Several small sales and transfers have been made in the last week and loose change is plentiful among the boys.

Coeur d'Alene Press, February 22, 1896

By spring the owners were convinced that the Keystone warranted a ten-stamp mill, and, when construction on it began, people poured into the area. At the mouth of Fourth of July Creek, the camp of Sylvanite sprang up

HAYWIRE MILL, SYLVANITE

beside the Yahk River, a good twelve miles above its junction with the Kootenai. The forest from which the townsite was hacked was described as "a sunlight-proof stand of white pine and cedar timber."

Even though snow lay eighteen inches deep on the river flats, and three feet on the level among the trees, lots and streets were staked out "so that parties contemplating building will know where to put them." By late spring, 1896,

Jimmy Hayes an old Demersville hotel man, opened a hotel; Ed Riley of Troy a saloon; D. T. Wood of the same place a grocery store; T. H. Dobson of Hillyard, a feed stable; and a Seattle man rented a building and is bringing in general merchandise in a few days. Ten buildings are ready for occupancy and more are being constructed. Whip-sawed lumber sells for $60.00 a thousand. Quite a number of men are engaged in making shakes for sale.

Parties traveling the road from Troy to Sylvanite load their goods on pack animals in Troy and do not have the annoyance of having to unpack them until they arrive at Sylvanite, crossing the Kootenai river . . . on a free ferry, traveling a good county road, crossing a free bridge on the Yahk river and arriving in good shape at the journey's end.

Helena Weekly Herald, May 7, 1896

Sylvanie was nineteen miles by county road from Troy and only thirty-five miles from Canada. It was only six miles from the Idaho line, although at that time the state boundary was not definitely established. No one knew with certainty whether Sylvanite was in Idaho or Montana. Without waiting to find out, local officers were elected, and fortunately, when the boundary was settled, the camp was conceded to be within Montana.

Additional mining claims located in 1895 and 1896 were the Julietta and Yankee Girl, worked as one property and lying but 600 feet from the Keystone. Adjoining the Keystone on the south was the Jim Hill, bought, in 1899, by Senator S. H. West of Illinois, from the original locators. This ore body lay at grass roots and was reportedly "ten feet wide at the bottom of an eight-foot shaft." The Eberhart lay south of the Jim Hill. Next to the original Friday mine was the B. & M. and the Sixteen-to-One, owned by "Troy parties and others."

Five miles farther up the Yahk River was the Red Top District, where a number of claims and some development work was done on such mines as the Iron Mask and Iron Cap, copper properties. Four miles south of Sylvanite was the Paisley District, which contained "over 100 claims." The ore strata was believed to be a continuation of the Keystone vein. The only property east of the Yahk River was the Montana, one mile from Sylvanite, located and developed by William and Tony Lemley, the original prospectors of the district.

All during the first winter, forty pack animals freighted food and supplies to the isolated camp through four-foot drifts, using a trail that had to be continually broken for them. Rates of five cents a pound were charged until the snow melted, when the price was cut in half.

The camp reached its peak in 1897-1898 with an estimated population of 500 (although one writer insists that an "accurate census" did not exceed 411). It contained three hotels, two restaurants, six saloons with dancehalls and girls, a post office, three general merchandise stores, one meat market, one brewery, and one drugstore, one quartz mill and a sawmill. Because of the latter, many of the newer buildings were made of planed lumber instead of logs. Sylvanite was also said to be "very orderly" since only four men died with their boots on — the occasion being a dancehall brawl.

By May, 1898, the camp had its own paper, the *Sylvanite Miner,* owend by R. McLellan of Libby, who mentioned in the May 14 issue that Sylvanite "was the liveliest gold camp in the northwest." A visitor's opinion of the place is given in the *Coeur d'Alene Press* of April 2, 1898:

The town has grown from a village of tents about one year ago with a population of 100, to a substantial place of 600 inhabitants, with graded streets and better buildings than are usually found in mining camps of a year's growth. There are several good business blocks and five hotels, one of which is a three-story structure. There are two properties that are sufficiently developed to be called mines.

These two properties, the Keystone and the Gold Flint, which adjoined it, proved to be the most productive mines in the district. The Gold Flint was discovered shortly after the Keystone by C. H. Bartlett, who was prospecting on a grubstake provided by E. J. Merrin. Upon testing the ore, the two men decided to develop the property at once.

Machinery for both the Keystone and the Gold Flint was hauled, in 1896, over the newly built road from Leonia, Idaho — the nearest railroad station — and mills were erected — the

Gold Flint equipped with twenty stamps and the Keystone with ten. Both mills were some distance from the mines, so that each required trams to convey the ore to them. By 1897, each property was working to capacity, and by 1898, the combined payroll averaged $10,-000 a month. During this period the Keystone employed fifty men, exclusive of ore haulers and wood choppers, and the Gold Flint, sixty-five. The Keystone concentrator ran night and day, producing thirty tons of ore every twenty-four hours. Monthly cleanups produced bullion which was sent regularly to Spokane. In June, 1897, "seven gold bricks averaging $2000-$3000" were turned out by the Keystone. Its ore body was huge and so wide in one place that a four-horse team could be turned in one of the underground chambers. Had the deposit not been so large and the gold so easily extracted, returns would not have been so gratifying; for the ore was low-grade and ran between $4.00 and $12.00 per ton.

The Gold Flint vein was also large, thirty-feet wide in places. Seventy tons of $8.00 to $12.00 ore were handled each day, the base ore being run through the concentrator, and the oxides through the mill. In 1899 the Keystone and the Gold Flint properties were consolidated, and the following year

the Keystone Consolidated Mining Co. acquired a controlling interest in the Yankee Girl and Julietta properties. The Company has two stamp mills at Sylvanite, one at the Keystone and one on the Gold Flint. These will be torn down and a new one with 100 stamps built on the banks of the Yahk river. Work will commence within sixty days.
Libby News, August 2, 1900

With the exception of Troy, the railroad town of Leonia, just across the Idaho line on the Kootenai River, was the Yahk mining camp's only connection with the outside world. All during the boom, Al Sweesey and George Moore ran a stage between Troy and Sylvanite, and a second company ran a stage and wagon freight-line twice a day between Sylvanite and Leonia. After the four-horse stagecoach ride from Leonia, "passengers went to Bondanza's City Barber Shop and had a 25c bath." As a special attraction, "P. M. Bondanza . . . arranged to give baths on Wed., Sat. and Sunday of each week." During the summer of 1898, Libby talked of building a road to Sylvanite "up Pipe creek and down Seventeen mile." This and a new bridge across the Yahk were finally constructed. James Stonechest, who carried the mail to and from

Leonia on horseback, went to Libby in April, 1899, and purchased a team of horses, preparatory to putting on a stage "for the convenience of those going in and out of Sylvanite." It was a lonely road at best and occasionally the scene of a crime:

Pat Doran, well known citizen of *Leonia,* and formerly Great Northern Agent at this place, was shot by Andy Whitley on the road between Leonia and Sylvanite.
. . . . Whitley had previously been in the employ of Doran, who runs the freight and stage line between the two places mentioned, and there had been some difficulties between the two men about a settlement. Whitley was in a bad humor and took three shots at Doran with a revolver, only one of which took effect. This struck him in the right side of the back and passed through him. Doran was not armed. This took place three miles from Sylvanite and Doran was able to walk that far and have the wound dressed. He is resting comfortably and is expected to be out in two weeks. Whitley escaped.
Sylvanite Miner, September 1, 1898

By 1899 the easily worked ore at Sylvanite was mined out, and as the free-milling processes then in use failed to save values in the base deposits that remained, the mills closed down and the camp began slowly to die.

But two men are employed at the Keystone and Goldflint. Wm. and Tony Lemly have commenced work on the Montana claim and will do their assessment. . . . Mrs. Pat Doran has moved from the hotel into the old school building. Most everyone has put in a garden patch and considerable garden truck will be raised the present season.
Libby News, May 18, 1899

Sylvanite has been quite dead for the past eighteen months. . . . Messrs. Daigler and Epperson, of the Leonia Merc. Co. . . . have moved their main store to Libby during these dull times.
Libby News, August 2, 1900

In 1907 Sylvanite served as a hideout for two train robbers:

He's the Stayer of the Gold Camp.
Fritz Lang . . . has been the lone inhabitant of Sylvanite for these dozen years past as watchman at the Keystone-Goldflint Consolidated Mining Co. mills and perhaps the most stirring diversion to break the monotony was the advent of the Rondo train bandits, McDonald and Frankhauser, who made their cache of the big roll of bank bills in one of the old tunnels in the gold camp, and whom Fritz entertained during their visit there. . . . Fritz says they looked and acted like well-to-do mining men, were well dressed and fitted the role well.
Troy Herald, May 20, 1910

With the revival of the district in 1910,

the Orphan Boy, located on the original Friday claim, the Blue Jay, Billy Sunday — an extension of the Woodrat — the Iron Mask, and other mines became active. A townsite company and a stock company, the Lincoln Gold Mining Company, which was backed by Spokane capital, pushed development and reopened the Keystone, whereupon a new shoot of ore was discovered that averaged $10.00 a ton. A new thirty-stamp mill was running early in August.

The *Troy Herald* publicized Sylvanite's reawakening by printing enthusiastic notices in its columns:

Sylvanite is going ahead. . . . Some of the old buildings have been disposed of to purchasers for business and residence purposes. The old Tremont House brought $700. . . .
Prospectors and claim holders are coming through Sylvanite daily to start on their claims again. A crew of men began work this week installing the telephone line from Troy to Sylvanite.
Troy Herald, May 20, 1910

Eight Feet of Ore in Blue Bell Showing Free Gold All Over It.
The Blue Bell is one mile from Sylvanite. The big mill started yesterday. At the mine two shifts are working. . . .
It looked like old times again on Monday evening to see four freight teams and the stage come in.
Troy Herald, June 24, 1910

And then, late in August, a forest fire destroyed Sylvanite. According to the *Troy Herald* of August 26th:

SETTLERS FLEE FROM FLAMES
SYLVANITE WIPED OUT
Saturday and Sunday were anxious days for the residents of the Troy district. With the first tinkling of the telephone ring from Sylvanite last Saturday morning telling the news that the town was threatened with destruction by fire; and that the women and children had been started for Troy, the telephones up Cabinet valley way, to the south, began to tell of fires getting away and that they were reaching the danger point; and our people were brought face to face with a situation which has confronted so many sections at more distant points for many weeks throughout the timbered areas.
The Sylvanite telephone line was in good working order up to the time that the town was swept away, and later the phone instrument was brought down from Sylvanite to the Yahk bridge and communication with Troy again established, the ranger station having been burned down.
The fire which destroyed Sylvanite started on Seventeen Mile and crossed the Yahk river at the old slaughter house and swept toward the town and engulfed it in a mass of flames. . . . Up the river

where the former Goldflint mill stood, a building used as a residence escaped.

The new stamp mill and tram company buildings are a total loss. The fire swept Keystone hill bare. The only insurance carried was $1,000 by the Western Mercantile Co. Ike Rouse, saloon and restaurant owner and Wood & Baggs, merchants, saved a portion of their goods, which they had buried. The merchandise and other personal property carried into the streets burned up in the general conflagration, and the town practically ceased to exist with the passing of the fire. The valley is swept clean on both sides of the river from a point above town two to three miles below.

The forest people established a camp at Yahk bridge to protect that structure from the fire, and Ranger Dennis telephoned in for 50 men as the fire, then about a mile away, was becoming threatening.

Frank Baggs, postmaster and merchant of Sylvanite arrived Sunday morning . . . firmly of the opinion that some of the Yahk fires were of incendiary origin, especially the one which was so destructive to the town. Earlier in the week, a fire was noticed on the Seventeen Mile trail, just across from Sylvanite, used by packers in carrying supplies to the fighters at the head of the stream. This was put out . . . but an acre of ground was burned. Along the same trail, a couple of days later another fire started and gained such headway that it got beyond control and crossed the Yahk with the results stated.

When the telephone line to Sylvanite ceased to work, Stanley Wood, started on horseback for the camp, but was stopped by the fire above the Yahk bridge. . . . This side of the bridge Stanley saw a broken telephone wire lying upon the ground . . . not an accidental break, but cut clean and smooth close to the insulation, like the work of some instrument. There was no fallen tree nearby.

The heaviest loser at Sylvanite is the Lincoln Gold Mining Co. which has had probably $40,000 worth of property destroyed. The Townsite Co. is also a loser.

Within a week plans were made to rebuild the gutted camp.

The (total) loss was about $75,000. More than one hundred people lost their homes. . . . Two weeks ago the owners of the townsite met and decided to install a waterworks. The incorporators will meet in a few days to decide whether to make improvements right away.

Troy Herald, September 2, 1910

In December a sawmill was freighted in from eastern Washington with a contract to cut "at least a million feet of lumber for the Lincoln Gold Mining Company from their timber land at Sylvanite." This company continued to operate the Keystone and Gold Flint mines for several years, building a 2,400-foot tram and a mill with a capacity of 200 tons.

Except for some lead and silver shipments from the Black Diamond in 1922, very little work was done in the district until 1932, when more than 300 tons of gold-silver-lead ore, valued at $1,806, were recovered "by one operator." The Keystone properties were also readied for work by the installation of a ten-stamp mill and a flotation plant, under the supervision of Frank McNees. Test holes, drilled by the Gold Basin Mining Company on the Yahk River, below Sylvanite, were preliminary to the company's installing hydraulic machinery on their ground.

It was almost dark when Francis and I spotted the gas pump and the ranchhouse for which we were looking, and found Mr. Gene Grush, a retired forest ranger who had been in the area since 1910, and his wife Ruth. They were very friendly and asked us to stay to supper. The couple told us they were married in 1918 and had been in Sylvanite ever since. Their present home was one that burned in 1910 and was rebuilt the following year.

"Tell me about the fire," I coaxed.

"It destroyed the whole town except the two story, frame, hotel which had a bar stocked with lots of whisky," said Mr. Grush. "The boys fought hard to save the building so as to have the whisky. That's why it didn't burn.

"Sylvanite was all around here and on down below too. Once it had a thousand people. Harry Cobbedeck's hotel was the best one in the county. If you look around through the trees and underbrush, you can still find cellar holes with old bedsprings in them. The post office was up behind our house. The old safe is still there, laying in the brush. There's a cookhouse, too, with an old stove crumbling away."

"I've seen a picture of Sylvanite, taken before the fire," said Mrs. Grush. "It stood in the midst of a white pine forest, just like a park."

When I mentioned the steep road down to the Yahk River, she said, "That used to be called 'the switchbacks.' It was rebuilt in 1914 and is called the Stonechest Grade. Bob Young used to run a jitney to Troy and when he got to the foot of the grade, he made the passengers get out and carry their suitcases to the top and then help push the machine up.

"Do you remember the bridge at Seventeen Mile road?" she asked me. "Mr. Grush is largely responsible for its having been built. He talked for that bridge to be moved there from the lower Yahk. Before it was built, you had to cross in a boat and hold on to a cable to pull yourself over. He finally put in a cable-car carrier with a rope, so you could pull it back to the other side when you wanted it. Mr. Grush homesteaded across the river; so he knew how much a bridge was needed."

"The buildings you saw up near the Haywire mill were built after the fire," Mr. Grush said. "They were company houses for the mill. Now they're used by state highway men. The Haywire claims were next to the Gold Flint, now called the Morning Glory. When the property was taken over by the company, a trade of seven shares of Haywire was made for one share of Morning Glory. The ten-stamp mill was later converted into a ball mill. It ran from 1907 to 1910. The mill you saw was the third one on the property. The Keystone mine was on Keystone Mountain. It was a gold property. Their third mill was further up, where the tailings are. The fourth mill was at the mine. The ore in this district is hard, blue, flinty quartz which doesn't look as if it had anything in it. Yet the best ore is sixty-per cent free-milling, and additional values are saved in concentrates.

"Do you recall the rock cut below town? It forms a natural gate. We used to turn the horses loose in Sylvanite, knowing that they wouldn't go beyond that gate. The fire started down there too. At the same time there was another fire on Seventeen-mile. After 1910 the town didn't rebuild like before. Frank Baggs had a store in a log building and there were a few other cabins and a sawmill, but nothing like boom days. It's all lumbering around here now and some ranching. The fire really finished Sylvanite and it never came back. This is home to us and we wouldn't want to leave here," he added, smiling, as we left.

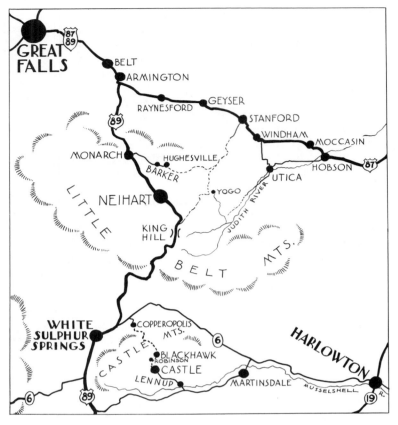

CHAPTER 19

THE LITTLE
BELT CAMPS and
CASTLE MOUNTAINS

As seen from Helena, the Big Belt Mountains form a solid barricade east of the Missouri River. Farther east and separated by a wide valley, through which runs the Smith River, is the Little Belt Range. In amongst its peaks are tucked several mining camps whose quiet streets attract tourists, fishermen, hunters, and an occasional leaser, and whose busy years are only memories stored in the keen minds of a few old-timers who live in the past.

Less than fifty miles southeast of the thriving smelter city of Great Falls, a drive through wheat country brings one to the northern end of the Little Belts where a wooded canyon road crosses a low saddle and drops down to Monarch.

MONARCH

Just outside the camp, two stone buildings and a circular stone kiln or furnace stand back from one side of the highway. The cemetery

with its fenced graves hides among trees and shrubs on the opposite side of the road.

The town is just off the pavement and the main street, which parallels the railroad, is dwarfed by the high white and brown limestone cliffs that hem in the canyon through which flows Belt Creek. The railroad station stands beside the tracks, and a small white church with a cross marks one end of the street. Two schoolhouses, one old and one new, guard the opposite end. A large, white house beyond the tracks and close to the depot is the most pretentious building in town. On the main thoroughfare stand a few stores — old false-fronted buildings, some of which hide behind modern facades. In the town garage we found a young woman, Mrs. Gwen Vaughn Rhys, waiting for her car to be fixed and from her learned something of Monarch and of Barker and Hughesville, the two camps which we planned to visit next.

Mrs. Rhys, a Welshwoman who lives in

MAIN STREET,
MONARCH

Barker, told us that there were few roads through the Little Belts even today, but that most of the range could be reached on horseback. The snow was deep in winter and drifted badly. Even as late as June it was often hard to get about in the hills. Monarch was the only settlement in the immediate area. After the railroad was built to Monarch from Great Falls, ore was packed down from the mines to the station and shipped to the big smelter quite easily and much more cheaply than formerly. Mrs. Rhys pointed out the road to Barker and promised us a cup of tea if she got home before we left that camp. Hughesville, she added, was a mile beyond Barker, and though it was quiet now, it had seen several mining revivals since 1905. We thanked her for the information and, after a further look around Monarch, drove back to the main road and turned south.

Within a short distance we turned off the highway and started toward Barker, and as we rode I read from my notes two items dated 1893 from the *Belt Mountain Miner*, the Barker newspaper, each of which dealt with Monarch:

Charley Martin has great hopes of the placer diggings located by himself and others in the neighborhood of Monarch. They have struck a quantity of black sand which is pretty rich. Mr. Martin has disposed of his interest in the Monarch Hotel and will devote all of his time to the new diggings. He will leave

for the east next week to procure a new gold-saving apparatus.

November 16, 1893

Last week a shooting scrape occurred in Monarch in which a saloon keeper named Cameron endeavored to bore daylight through J. Mickleson, also of Monarch. After a preliminary hearing, before Justice Schmidt, Cameron was taken to White Sulphur Springs for trial.

September 9, 1891

BARKER and HUGHESVILLE

A thirteen-mile drive up a wooded canyon took us past white granite outcroppings which protruded like great teeth through the forest walls. At one point we heard sheep bleating high above us on the mountain slopes and by peering through the trees we discovered

APPROACH TO MONARCH

the herder's tent and his horses tethered nearby. We broke out of the forest close to a large, terraced settling pond whose tailings were stained many colors and out of whose edges grew scrawny trees. Beyond the pond were the foundations of a smelter and debris from other buildings. Charcoal kilns alongside Galena Creek, below its fork, were also part of this once busy plant. Farther up the gulch were a number of cabins, many more foundations, and the vestiges of two or three streets. This settlement, according to Mrs. Rhys' description, was Barker, but to be sure, I consulted my notes; for on old maps, several camps were shown — Gold Run, Clendenin, Meagher City, and Hughesville. The following clippings were most illuminating:

Clendenin Townsite. The village of Barker is an anomaly in the line of names. All over the state the place is known as "Barker" whereever the camp is spoken of, and it's "Barker" in the newspaper, while really there is no village of Barker. The village is built on the Clendenin and Gold Run townsites and the post office is Clendenin. The Barker townsite, which was platted in June has not been accepted by the county commissioners and Barker's sister town, Hughesville, lies about one mile north. This variety of names, applied to the same place, is not only inconvenient, but is mystifying to the stranger. . . . If Buck Barker's spirit visits the valley it will find that his name has been fixed on this camp and will forever remain.

Belt Mountain Miner, October 28, 1891

The first discovery of metals in the Little Belts was made by Patrick H. Hughes and E. A. "Buck" Barker, who left the Yogo District, where they had been prospecting without success, and set out to find new placer fields. On October 20, 1879, they camped on Galena Creek, a tributary of the east fork of the Belt River. The following day, while Barker went hunting, Hughes searched for placer ground, and finding a location that he liked, started to run a drain to it. While digging, he noticed lumps of galena mixed with the earth. This encouraged him to look for the ledge from which they came, which he found and named the Barker. The Grey Eagle adjoined the Barker at the center of the creek, but from there the two claims ran "into the hills in opposite directions."

Soon after these initial discoveries, H. L. Wright and H. K. Edwards discovered the Wright & Edwards lode a "short half-mile from the Barker on the same mountain." Oscar Olinger, Pat Donahue, and August Oker-man located the Homestake lode, above the Barker, and the Hancock, Maggie, Summit, and the DeSoto. Placers were also discovered, but they were unimportant; it was the ledges and lodes that carried the most valuable deposits. By 1880 nearly one hundred men were working in the gulches of the area, and several hundred locations had been made. By the fall of 1881 a reporter from the *Benton Weekly Record,* having obtained directions at Baptiste's place, "fifteen miles outside the mines," went to see the new camp in November.

From the very mouth of the gulch up to Gold Run the way is very bad, yes, outrageously bad for over ten miles. Freighters who try it once declare that it is the last trip unless they are paid five cents a pound to compensate them for the risk.

There was a foot of snow in the gulch by the time we reached "Dog Eating Jack's" and still it was snowing when we arrived at the smelter. . . . There being no hay in the camp, nearly all the teams had been sent out to feed. . . . The sound of a steam whistle and the sight of mechanics going to labor with timed regularity conveys some idea of the changes in camp within the last six months. The smelter with its enormous brick chimney and iron pipes, loomed up immensely as I drove into Gold Run.

Four towns prosper — Gold Run, like villages of New England, is proud of its smoke stacks and the quiet of its people. It is the headquarters of the smelter.

Meagher City is noted for its beautiful avenue and is the kind of a town where a rich man would build a residence and take a wife to live. She would be two miles from the bustle of Gold Run and nearly a mile from the rougher element; perchance dominant at Hughes City.

Galena lies down in the gulch below the hill in front of Meagher. It looks like a part of Deadwood in having its houses dotted about on the mountain sides and in the gulch — irregular but picturesque. There is not much business in Galena as yet but its people are sanguine.

Hughes City is the town just now. It is at Hughes City that the old Colorado miner meets the Nevada pioneer and compares the prospects of Barker with the Georgetown or Eureka mines. . . . It is the place where gambling is indulged in and the black eyes come from. It is in Hughes City that a miners' meeting is held and it is agreed that if any man works for less than $2.00 a day he shall be run out of the camp.

During my stay I went up to the Wright & Edwards mine. . . . Ore is being taken out and a pile of over 200 tons beautifully built up under the ore shed, shows the wealth of the lead.

Mail facilities are badly lacking in the camp, and our Benton people should help this District as far as possible.

BARKER

My horse was at the foot of the trail at Allis' ranch so I had to get out of the District on foot. This was no easy job with a buffalocoat, a gun, some cartridges and two feet of snow to pull through, but I managed to get from Gold Run to Hughes City.

Another year will place the Barker District on a footing it surely is entitled to . . . a good road can be made over the trail for light teams. The estimated cost of this improvement is $2500. The present roundabout way of entering is needlessly long except for freighting. . . . It is discouraging to the Barker people to have to do every single thing without a particle of outside aid.

Benton Weekly Record, November 10, 1881

Two weeks later the correspondent's second letter was printed:

Barker mining district is taking a quiet little boom. . . . Most of the business is done in Hughes City at present. . . . There are two stores, [and] two saloons besides Capt. Foly's billiard parlor. . . .

Gold Run has a well-appointed store. There is also a saloon kept by Pete McDermot where the boys do congregate to while away the time in a friendly game of draw and to quench their thirst occasionally. Gold Run has also a law office. . . .

We had quite a nice dance here about two weeks ago and all enjoyed themselves hugely. Some of the boys wore loud neckties. Judging from the white spots on some of their heads, it's a long time since some of them were boys.

P. H. Hughes has built him a comfortable residence in Meagher City where himself and Mrs. Hughes are snugly domiciled.

Yours,
Endymion
Benton Weekly Record,
November 24, 1881

The Clendenin smelter, built during the summer of 1881, was blown in late in November. Built by George Clendenin of the Clendenin Mining & Smelting Company, it helped develop the district by producing many tons of bullion from the several large mines which fed it silver-lead ore between 1881 and 1883. According to James Arthur MacKnight, it operated for eighteen months.

Although a failure, it ran out in that time $375,000 worth of bullion. Whether a monument to folly or inexperience, it failed and buried Barker in obscurity for over seven years.

J. A. MacKnight, *Mines of Montana*,
National Mining Congress, July 12, 1892

With high transportation and smelter costs,

327

only the richest ore was freighted out and, after 1884, when the deposits at Neihart were discovered and men rushed across the mountains to be in on the new strike, the camp of Barker began to decline.

With the completion of a silver smelter at Great Falls in 1888, plans were made for the construction of the Belt Mountain branch of the Great Northern road as far as Barker. This road was completed on October 1, 1891, and "although few mines were in condition to ship ore and not sufficiently developed," the station agent's books showed 1,280 tons of ore shipped out during October. The Barker mine was operating in 1891, for "the Shriek of Steam Whistles, Hum of Wheels and Creaking of Cables at the Barker Hoist" was mentioned in the local newspaper. The Paragon was also active, with "200 tons of ore on its dump." The same year, T. A. Lusk, a mining expert from Milwaukee, visited several of the mines, and after conferring with the owners of the Moulton, "succeeded in bonding these properties for six months. The group consisted of the Bellefont, Harrison, Moulton and Pioneer."

The Belt Mountain branch of the railroad revived Barker. Even before the last construction crews pulled out, curious visitors from Great Falls tried out the road:

The Great Falls Bicycle Club Takes an Outing Among the Belt Mountains.
During the last week the Great Falls Bicycle Club organized a Sunday excursion to Barker. The train arrived at the Barker depot about 12 m. and most of the visitors immediately repaired to the hotel for refreshments, others being entertained at private homes.

Promptly at 1 o'clock teams were in readiness to transport passengers to the mines. Many however were unable to find seats in the carriages and were obliged to walk, a few members of the club mounted their wheels and successfully rode the hill between the lower camp and the mines.

The Barker being nearest the railroad terminus was visited first. Here T. W. Maloney, the gentlemanly foreman, received the sightseers and conducted them through the tunnel, explaining the workings. . . . All were interested in an examination of the ore dump, the ladies especially being anxious to obtain specimens of the ore. Here again Mr. Maloney had occasion to render assistance, as the ladies invariably selected the shining pyrites rejecting the less attractive but valuable galena. Continuing on the road up the canyon the party soon arrived at the Carter. . . . A chamber 14 feet square and from 8 to 12 feet high, cut in solid ore is a rare sight even for experienced mining men and for those not familiar with mineral bodies the contemplation of so many embryo silver dollars is pleasing in the extreme.

The train was due out at 4 p.m. . . . . Capt. Matteson and Mr. Mitchell of the bicycle club on their wheels, took the trail for Monarch, intending to board the train at that point. They left at a speed that should have caused the locomotive to blush with humiliation and though we have not since heard from them we have no doubt they reached their destination in safety.

The excursion party was made up of the elite of Great Falls, and represented the best class of society that Montana or the world affords.
Belt Mountain Miner, September 23, 1891

With the arrival of the railroad, the various camps on Galena Creek grew together into what the *Belt Mountain Miner* described as a "substantial town." The principal store was that of F. J. Henzlik. The lower floor was devoted to drygoods and groceries, while the upper floor was divided into "nine pleasant rooms all ceiled and sided with red wood." Probably Mrs. Minta Bolton, conducted her dressmaking establishment in her home. Her advertisement in the paper stated:

I desire to announce that I am prepared to make a limited number of fine dresses. Perfect fit and eastern prices guaranteed.

November 25, 1891

Even when the waterworks were completed, no organization was set up to cope with fire.

Last Sunday evening, while the paper hangers were at work on the second floor of Silver & Co.'s new building, a large Rochester lamp which they were using exploded, throwing the boiling oil over the room. The whole room was in a blaze.
Belt Mountain Miner, December 9, 1891

Destroyed by Flames.
About 8:30 Sat. evening Mike Sund . . . noticed smoke issuing from the rear of F. J. Henzlik's store and residence building. . . . The alarm was given and in a few minutes nearly all the people in the camp were on the ground fighting the flames and saving what they could. . . . Within an hour the stores of F. J. Henzlik, Thisted, Brosnan & Co., and Barker Meat Co. were burned to the ground.

That evening . . . for the first time in the history of Barker the fearful cry of fire rang out on the frosty air. . . . People seemed to be at a loss at first how to act, it being the first fire, and there being no organized fire apparatus. The dry pine building made the little water at hand practically useless, but nearly everyone carried a bucketful before they realized the fact.

The origin of the fire was obviously a lamp explosion.

For three years Barker has been going to organize a fire brigade, and now that there has been a fire, it may have a tendency to wake people up to the situation. . . . At this fire there were about 30 captains and 3 firemen and of the latter, John the Chinaman was one of the best.

Belt Mountain Miner, November 3, 1892

The praise given to John Chinaman as a fire fighter is unusual, for most mining camps were hostile to the Chinese within their boundaries and seldom singled them out for commendation. Two other items from the paper indicate Barker's attitude toward Orientals, possibly because the camp had but one such resident.

The Chinaman's Sign

A short time ago Ah Lee the inoffensive celestial who runs a laundry in Barker, left the camp for a visit elsewhere. . . . When he returned to camp he found everything as he left it except his sign.

Belt Mountain Miner, July 13, 1892

The article continues by stating that the stolen sign was returned.

Last Thursday was the Chinese New Years and John, the lone Chinaman of Barker, celebrated it in great style. He kept a good supply of Chinese and American liquors and other Chinese refreshments on tap and all his friends and customers were invited in to share in the good things.

Belt Mountain Miner, February 23, 1893

Like all new and isolated communities, the people of Barker and the nearby camps arranged their own amusements; which were duly recorded in the *Miner:*

Annual Ball

McHughes' hall was tested to its utmost to accommodate the gay throng of pleasure seekers. With a few exceptions the people of Hughesville and Barker joined and made this the most successful and pleasant occasion enjoyed for years. Waltz, quadrille, polka, schottische and newport followed in rapid succession until the musicians were glad when supper was announced. The tables of the Clendenin hotel were loaded with every delicacy of the season . . . to which all did ample justice. After supper, dancing continued until about 5 a.m.

Belt Mountain Miner, January 6, 1892

A masquerade ball was given at Monarch Wednesday night. A number of Barker people brushed up their old costumes and went down. Some of them went as God made them and appeared fittingly for the occasion.

Belt Mountain Miner, January 5, 1893

The Show That Didn't Come.

Many were on the street in front of the hall and a thermometer that registered 30 degrees below zero an hour before the time. When the disappointing news came that the "company" would not come, the pause that followed was so silent that one could hear

HUGHESVILLE MERCANTILE CO.

a pistol shot a rod away. . . . Then the crowd went away and we were glad, for we had been asked about thirty times in ten minutes what a 'soubrette' was, and having no more idea than the questioners, we told them to wait and we would show them.

Belt Mountain Miner, February 2, 1893

A description of the district's mines as of 1892 is given by James Arthur MacKnight:

When the passenger alights at the Great Northern depot at Barker he finds himself under the shadow of a towering mountain, lying to the south. This is Manitoba mountain, taking its name from the Manitoba mine, which one can see about 600 feet above. This mine was discovered three years ago (1889) and sold to E. J. Barker, who organized the Ontario Mining Company for the purpose of working it.

From the depot the road passes up Galena creek, through the camp of Barker for two and one-half miles to the Silver Bell mine . . . located October 13, 1880, by H. C. Foster. . . : On this mine are two sets of workings. The upper work consists of about 1400 feet of tunneling on a blanket load of lead carbonate ore in limestone. From these workings in 1883 were taken 2500 tons of ore which was worked at the Clendenin smelter. The lower workings consist of a shaft 180 feet deep, with several hundred feet of levels. From these workings were taken 420 tons of ore in 1883, but it was too base to be worked by the Clendenin smelter, though some of it carried 200 ounces of silver. It laid on the dump until the advent of the railroad in 1891. So far in 1892 it has yielded about twenty cars of ore.

A mile above is the Wright and Edwards mine, known as the "P" Mining Company, owned by U. S. Senator T. C. Power. This mine was located in 1880, and for the benefit of the Clendenin smelter put out 2700 tons of ore with an average value of forty-two ounces of silver and forty-eight percent lead.

Around the hill and up the creek a quarter of a mile, in the same granite belt, is the Barker mine, owned and operated by Paris Gibson, T. C. Power and C. X. Larrabie. This was the first mine discovered in Barker. . . . In 1883 it yielded 300 tons of ore that assayed sixty-five ounces of silver and forty percent of lead.

Across the creek from the Barker is the Queen Esther property, organized in June, 1891. . . . Next above the Barker is the Carter. . . . Up the east branch of Galena creek is the Tiger.

Mines of Montana, National Mining Congress, July 12, 1892

By January, 1893, the *Miner* stated that Barker was "becoming the great transportation point of the Judith Basin." Yet only a few months later business on the railroad fell off to such an extent that service was cut to one train a week. On December 21st, without warning, the

Railroad Station Closed

This means that after today there will be no regular trains run between Barker and Monarch. . . . This has been contemplated for some time. . . . We are in hope that it will not be long until the shipments of freight will be sufficient to warrant the re-opening of the station.

Trains between Great Falls, Monarch and Neihart will continue as heretofore.

Belt Mountain Miner, December 21, 1893

The loss of the railroad, coupled with the silver slump, nearly finished the Barker District. The editor of the *Miner* tried to rally the mine operators by taunting them:

What's the Trouble With Barker?

Neihart is fast coming to the front as a silver producing camp. . . . The Neihart ores are principally dry, and the smelters must have lead ore in order to successfully treat such ores. Barker is a silver-lead ore camp, (containing) large bodies of ore which can be treated at smelters at very small cost.

Belt Mountain Miner, January 6, 1894

His exhortings failed to save the situation, and three weeks later, he admitted himself licked:

J. E. Sheridan, Lessee
To the Public

As the business of the camp will not longer justify the publication of a newspaper, we have decided to temporarily suspend the publication . . . with this issue. We are hopeful that the price of silver will alvance sufficiently to warrant mine owners in the district in resuming operations in which event we will be "on deck" to keep the ball rolling and assist as far as we are able in showing to the world that the Barker district has as large and good paying bodies of ore as can be found in any camp in the West.

Adieu.

Belt Mountain Miner, January 27, 1894

That the district was fairly quiet no one could deny although some mining was carried on, especially in the Tiger and Moulton properties. Both were worked under lease, as were others in later years, for short intervals of time. Several million dollars worth of ore in all was produced by the camp, chiefly from the Wright & Edwards mine (later known as the "P" property). This mine was worked until 1930.

My only visit to Barker and Hughesville was in 1955. A mile above Barker, in Hughesville, I found both old and new houses near the road and across the creek as well as several false-fronted stores and one empty building with leaded glass windows. Mine dumps and mine buildings were not far away, and up ahead, where the road swung around the shoulder of a hill, was the big yellow dump of the "P" property, topped with a shafthouse.

On the return drive to Monarch, we met but one car — that of Mrs. Rhys. We waved as we drove by, disappointed that we could not stop for tea and hear more about the district's history.

NEIHART

Straight south from Monarch, a fine road (Highway No. 89) winds for miles, following Belt Creek through a forest canyon where private cabins, set among the trees, are the only signs of habitation. On the outskirts of the mining camp of Neihart are mills and dumps — the usual approaches to all such towns — while on either side of the main street stand many old buildings, some boarded up, and others which serve the small but permanent population.

Neihart is set in the bottom of a canyon and cut by a stream. High, timbered mountains rise on all sides of it, dwarfing its weathered frame buildings. We drew up at a store in front of which stood several cars and a truck. This place seemed to be the town rendezvous, and inside I hoped to find someone whom I could question about Neihart's past. Francis found a Mr. Sutton, a gentleman of seventy-six, who said he'd been in Neihart since he was six years old. Taking us outside, he pointed up and down the thoroughfare, whose weathered board sidewalks, flanked by vigorous weeds and tall grass, led from store to store or stretched in front of vacant lots, which were so overgrown with brush that stone foundations of former buildings were all but hidden.

"This street used to be solid with buildings and so did the side streets," he said. "There

HUGHESVILLE

was a railroad into the town, too. At one time, Neihart was bigger than Great Falls. This was a silver camp. The mills recovered only silver and let the zinc and lead go, until World War I. Then they reworked all the dumps. There was a lot going on around here between 1935 and 1937, and again in 1946, when a Canadian outfit came in and bought up sixteen properties. It planned to drain the lowest one and then work through a cross-cut tunnel. There's very little mining going on here now." With this briefing, he left us and went back into the store.

Prospectors have restless feet, so perhaps it was only natural for James L. Neihart, John C. O'Brien, Richard Harley, and a few others to leave the mining camp of Barker in the summer of 1881 and work their way across the intervening hills to a gulch which to them looked promising. There, on June 15 or July 6, 1881 — authorities differ as to the date — they located the Queen of the Hills, a silver-lead deposit and the first mine to be staked in the region. As soon as the news reached Barker, several parties of men equipped themselves and set out for the new location, where, upon arrival, they staked out many claims

within the next few weeks. The Homestake mine, 500 feet above the Belt River, contained "black and red sulphates, easily taken out and worked." The discovery shaft of the Queen of the Hills adjoined the Homestake. A horn silver ledge, the Montana Belle, was one of the best in the district.

Perhaps the most explicit description of the region in its infancy is given by O. G. Mortson. He mentions Canyon City. Since the miners held no official meeting until the following spring, this name was probably the first to be applied to the settlement that we know as Neihart.

At present the route from the Barker district to this place is by pack animal, and goes over the low pass on the left bank of the Dry Fork about three miles below the smelter, and then across a hilly trail to Belt Creek, crossing which we arrive at the Park with its picturesque scenery . . . proceeding almost to the head of the Park, and arriving at Harley creek, (we) arrive at the western limit of the mines, and descend into Belt creek which we follow upstream two miles to the future site of Canyon City.

The characteristic rocks in the camp are essentially granitic, at the eastern boundary changing to quartzite.

At Canyon City . . . nineteen distinct veins have been discovered on which are eighty locations. . . . Messrs. Neihart & Co.'s locations give an assay, I hear, of nearly $1,000.

Parties visiting the camp this fall pointed to the absence of live timber as a great draw-back to the camp. A stream flows through the center of the camp (and) six miles upstream exist untouched forests. One-and-a-half miles west of Canyon City, Fly or Carpenter's creek enters the Belt river from the northeast.

Belt Park District. This pioneer district on the main Belt, was discovered May 14, 1881, by Messrs. Carpenter and Aldrich. At present in its infancy, it has 33 locations.

Benton Weekly Record, November 17, 1881

"By April 7, 1882, most of the locations in the camp had been made," writes D. B. Mackintosh, in the Souvenir Edition of the *Neihart Herald* in 1895. "That day we held our first town meeting. . . . J. C. O'Brien, seated on a rock was the chairman of the meeting and I, as Secretary, lay at full length upon the ground. The Secretary moved that the town be called Farragut. . . . This motion did not receive a second. Hamilton moved that it be called Neihart." This was accepted.

The limits of the town (were set at) Harley's creek on the west and O'Brien creek on the east. . . . Two lots are all that any one man is entitled to take up in the same townsite. All persons taking up town lots shall fence and record them within 40 days. . . . Plans have been made to plat the town and survey it and keep a book of records. Main St. is to be 80 feet wide and cross streets 60 feet wide.

Rocky Mountain Husbandman, April 20, 1882

Mackintosh continues his reminiscences in the *Herald*:

The first log shack was built by Ed Tingal in what is now called Jericho. . . . In June, 1882, the business men of White Sulphur Springs employed M. L. Sohmers to cut a trail from Sheep creek into the camp. Later on these same men contributed $1100 toward building a wagon road from the Smith river to the head of O'Brien creek, which road was built by James Brewer, the men of Neihart building up that creek to join Mr. Brewer at his terminus.

Our supplies were brought from Barker over the trail on horseback. In October, James Chamberlain brought the first team and wagon over the range from White Sulphur Springs.

In August, 1882, Reverend W. W. Van Orsdel, superintendent of the North Montana Mission of the Methodist Episcopal Church, held two meetings in a log cabin.

Both services were free from tinsel, fuss or feather and there was no visible presence of the golden calf of jewish history. Saint Paul or Peter in their working clothes would have felt perfectly at home, and in either would have been given a front seat.

Neihart Herald, Souvenir Edition, 1895

The first woman to visit the camp was a Mrs. Leach. She rode horseback man fashion. Either this picturesque way of traveling or her husband's propensity for interfering with other men's claims, made Mr. and Mrs. Leach rather unpopular and their stay in camp was short.

Neihart Herald, Souvenir Edition, 1895

For the first year or two the camp had no regular mail service. Prior to the summer of 1884, when William Woolsey received the contract to carry it between White Sulphur Springs and Barker via Neihart, mail arrived whenever anyone bothered to bring it in from the nearest office. A sack was sometimes dropped off along the trail by some volunteer carrier, knowing that whoever found it would open it. If the contents was addressed to the destination to which he was going, he might tote it there, otherwise he would hang it in a tree to await the next passerby. One bag of mail, which left Neihart in November 1883, reached White Sulphur Springs, forty-two miles away, in June of 1884, "having spent the winter on the range."

Mackintosh opened the first store in a small log cabin with a dirt floor. "Poles served as shelves and a door did duty as a counter. The first stock of goods came from the firm of F. W. Reed & Co. of Barker. A few days after shipping the goods, the firm failed, and for several days thereafter, a brisk and lively trade went on at the log shack, the general fear being that the lawyers would take the goods from camp."

In 1885 the *Rocky Mountain Husbandman* described the camp's growth. The Fort Benton paper copied the article:

Neihart has 2 saloons, 2 eating houses, 1 private boarding house, a post office, 1 store, 1 blacksmith shop, 1 chinese wash house, 1 barber shop, 1 butcher shop, 2 stables, 24-25 houses with roofs and as many more without, and a number of tents. Dwellings are of a primitive nature, small log houses covered with poles and dirt, and the place looks for all the world like a new placer camp.

There is plenty of room for a town and the creek bottom is staked into town lots for a distance of five miles.

The Belt river rushes through town. . . . We feel confident that someday [Neihart] will eclipse Leadville, Virginia City, (Nev.) Butte or any mining camp of recent days.

Husbandman
The River Press, May 20, 1885

APPROACH TO NEIHART

NEIHART

The *River Press* urged more trade between Fort Benton and Neihart:

We hope our citizens will take some prompt action in regard to opening a road from Fort Benton to this most promising mining camp in the territory. Each day's delay is a positive loss of business to the city, and a loss of transportation to the river and a loss to the camp.

The citizens of Neihart and the entire length of Belt creek will perform their portion of work and with the aid of a few hundred dollars from Fort Benton, the road can be an accomplished fact inside of three months.

The River Press, April 22, 1885

From the start, the mines made the camp. Throughout 1884, the Queen, Galt, Belle, and Mountain Chief began shipping ore to Omaha; net returns averaging $200.00 a ton, after "deducting $100 a ton for freight and treatment." Carpenter and Aldrich, the discoverers of properties in the Belt Park district, developed the Dubuque and Mammoth No. 1 and No. 2 at the same time.

The whole camp waited impatiently for the completion of the Hudson Mining Company's $200,000 concentrator and smelter and mile-long flume, which were completed between 1885 and 1886. The company had bought the Mountain Chief group on Carpenter Creek in 1884 for $18,000 and spent $10,000 more in developing the mine. Around this property, two miles below Neihart, the camp of Jericho sprang up — an industrial village which was regarded not only as a suburb, but also as the inevitable site of future smelters.

In April, 1885, the St. Julian, Minnehaha, Maud S., Montana Belle, and Dickens properties — a group of mines on the west side of Baldy, about one-third of a mile from Neihart — were acquired by Colonel C. A. Broadwater, Longmaid, J. J. Hill, and others and worked by a crew of seventy-five men. As the rich surface became exhausted, refractory material hard to concentrate was encountered and, halted by this metallurgical problem, the promoters suspended work, according to some, "just when success was within easy reach."

The districts' other mines were experiencing the same setbacks, and, as property after property ceased to operate, most of the miners left to try their luck in more active camps. Between 1887 and 1890, Neihart was nearly deserted. Recalling this period of recession, a reporter for the *Great Falls Tribune* wrote:

This was a time that tried men's nerve and fortitude for often the cabins contained only flour, beans and bacon, and at one time it is said that in Neihart there was not a candle in the camp for more than a week.

Deserted cabins without doors or windows, stared on every hand, the advent of a stranger was a matter for village comment, saloons were practically deserted and the one general store was bearing a heavy burden of "jaw bone."

Great Falls Tribune, January 3, 1891

But mining camps have amazing recuperative powers, and the news, in 1890, that a railroad to Neihart was assured, brought the camp back to life. People flocked in, mines changed hands or were bonded to investors, and new buildings rose on vacant lots between weathered shacks, dating from the eighties.

Building Boom
On every hand may be heard the ringing of hammers and the merry whistle of the masons laying stone on stone and fast bringing great business blocks from the ground up.

Great Falls Tribune, June 19, 1891

The railroad, which was a branch of the Montana Central (later a part of the Great Northern), was completed to within fifteen miles of Neihart by June, 1891. The line was finished on November 15, and two days later, Neihart held a welcoming celebration. A special excursion train, filled with passengers from Great Falls and Helena, left Great Falls at 8 a.m. and reached the mining camp about noon. The visitors were met by the Neihart Free Coinage Brass Band, but as the temperature registered below zero, the musicians were unable to play. Blasts of powder and dynamite set off on the mountainside provided noisy salutes and prefaced the carefully prepared program, in which a silver spike, cast from Queen of the Hills ore, was driven symbolically to complete the road. Because of the weather, the rest of the program was shortened and each visitor was hastily given a souvenir badge, which entitled him to lunch at any hotel dining room or restaurant in the town.

The return trip was boisterous, for many of the passengers had found refreshment to their liking in Neihart's many saloons. Jew Jake, a gambler, was particularly pugnacious and resented the attempts of George Treat, the marshal of Great Falls, to quiet him down.

"Cut it out, Jake," said Treat. "There are women and kids on this train, and we don't want to make any trouble for them."

"You're not man enough to make me cut it out," said Jake, and shot his hand back to his gun pocket.

Treat looked him in the eye without moving.

"I'll settle with you when we get off the train," he said. Jake made the mistake of believing that he had Treat bluffed and he kept calling him names till the train approached the station. . . . People sensed tragedy ahead as they piled off the coach.

Treat waited in the car till all the crowd were on the ground and had time to get away. Through the window he saw Jew Jake standing on the platform waiting for him. As Marshal Treat stepped to the platform Jake began to shoot. His aim was wild and one bullet struck a bystander, injuring him. But when Treat's forty-five went into action no bullets were wasted. The lead flew at Jake in a stream and in a few minutes he lay on the platform with one of his legs practically shot off. It was amputated at the hospital a little later.

Jew Jake later ran a saloon at Landusky and often used a Winchester for a crutch.

Fairfield Times, February 18, 1918

With the revival of mining and the advent of the railroad, Neihart emerged from a "Deserted Village to a Bustling Mining Camp." The Belt Mountain Miner's Union, organized May 10, 1890, "bolstered up the standard of wages," and provided a library for its members "second to none in this part of Montana." Several hotels were built, the Neihart and Manitoba on Main Street and the National on Granite Street, but all three were eclipsed by the Frisco Hotel, George Roehl, proprietor, which opened October 1, 1890, with "water on every floor and electric lights" in each of its sixty rooms. On December 4, 1890, the *Neihart Herald* was born, edited by J. C. Wilson and A. L. Crosson.

Several secret societies were organized during this period: the Belt Mountain Lodge, No. 18 A. O. U. W. in October, 1891, with sixty-four members; Banner Lodge No. 49 I. O. O. F. on March 25, 1893, with twelve members; Local Assembly No. 864, K. of L., instituted in 1893 and reorganized as the Neihart Labor Union, with seventy-five members.

As soon as the Neihart Fire Department was established in 1891, the members gave a dance to raise funds for the buckets, ladders, and a bell. "The bell or pot as it might be more properly designated, was raised upon Henry Wilson's stable. Chas. Crawford was elected Chief." By 1893, a hose house had been built, 1,000 feet of hose and two hose carts purchased, and the volunteers divided into three companies — two hose and one hook and ladder. This caused rivalry between Hose No. 1 and Hose No. 2. "No public day is passed without a hose race for a keg of beer or some light refreshment. Co. No. 1 holds the belt

STORE, NEIHART

which No. 2 will certainly win in the next race." Yet four years later, civic interest in the fire department seems to have waned:

At a fire meeting held to organize a company, where was expected a majority, at least of Neihart's business men, only twelve were present to discuss plans or to do business. . . . Dick Brennan remarked that most of the citizens employed hoodlums and bums to watch their houses from fire while they sleep . . . and all were of the opinion that the public would take little interest in a fire company until the gulch is once burnt out from Jericho to Last Chance saloon.

Neihart Herald, February 5, 1897

The next week the *Herald* smugly reported the organization of a fire company.

Throughout 1891 development work in the several large mines readied them for steady production. Just as all seemed set, the price of silver tumbled and once more Neihart's boom collapsed. Fortunately for the camp, W. J. Clark and his associates purchased the Broadwater and Chamberlain properties for an estimated $165,000 and operated them steadily for two years, averaging a carload of ore a day. From this production, the company's net profits totaled $200,000-$300,000. The Benton and Big Seven mines also continued to work despite the low price of silver.

About 1908, Colonel Hubbard of Great Falls played a hunch which paid off. When Neihart's poplation dropped from several thousands to less than one hundred and property could be bought up for taxes, Hubbard bid for the townsite at a county sale and obtained thereby nearly 1,000 lots. Surveyors laid off the choicest sites, and within a year Hubbard sold enough to repay his investment and give him a margin of profit. When World War I broke out and the price of silver and lead increased, Neihart began to boom just as he had hoped. Since then, Neihart has had other revivals, the first between 1919 and 1929, when:

A crew of engineers and samplers, reported to be representing W. A. Clark interests of Butte, are making a survey of the Big 7 Silver-Lead mine near Neihart. . . .

Reports from Great Falls fix $325,000 as the price to be paid by the Clark interests if the deal is consummated.

Froid Tribune, April 3, 1925

The next was from 1935 to 1937 when several properties, including the Rochester, M. & I., Florence, and Silver Dyke, yielded zinc as well as silver-lead-gold ores. Total production for the district up to 1935 is estimated at $16,-000,000, mostly from silver.

In 1945 Neihart received another blow when rail service was canceled between it and Great Falls after fifty-four years of operation. The last train, drawn by Engine No. 511, with engineer George Doros at the throttle, and George Montgomery as fireman, left Neihart on a Saturday in November. Its one coach was crowded with nostalgic passengers who had often taken it on excursions and picnics and on trips to the big city. Its departure marked the end of an era. But even without rail connections, Neihart is still a mining camp and also a summer resort.

Until recent years when forest fires destroyed timber at the lower end of the canyon and the beauty of the clear mountain-born stream flowing through it had been ruined by the tailings of the concentrator near its source, Neihart canyon was said to rival Switzerland for scenic beauty.

Froid Tribune, September 12, 1924

Belt Creek runs clearer than it did in 1924 and the hills are greener. Who knows when Neihart will have its next revival?

Just before we left Neihart, I consulted the map to see where the Yogo-Running Wolf District lay, for I knew it was in the mineral strip of the Little Belt Mountains. Everyone to whom I talked said it was impossible to reach from Neihart, although it lay directly east of the town, and that even from the Judith Valley, it was difficult to reach by car. Since its fame lay in its gem deposits rather than in gold or silver, I decided to scratch it from an already crowded itinerary, but to learn as much as I could about it.

YOGO

Across the mountains east of Neihart lies the Yogo District. All that was needed in the

spring of 1879 to send hundreds of men stampeding to that portion of the Little Belt Mountains was a rumor that rich placers had been discovered in the alluvial gravels of Yogo Creek. Their concerted efforts produced miles of ditches and flumes and piles of gravel from which the elusive colors had been recovered. With tents and log houses strewn along the creek for fifteen miles, two embryo camps called Yogo City and Hoover City sprang up only a few hundred yards apart, each determined to become the metropolis of the gulch. While the excitement lasted, their peak population was reported as between 1,200 and 1,500. At the end of the first season the boom was over, for cleanups revealed so little gold that further work seemed useless and the disgruntled miners packed out as speedily as they had rushed in. By 1883, nearly everyone was gone; ten years later, only a dozen men remained in the vicinity.

Jake Hoover had a cattle ranch on the South Fork of the Judith River. He had come to the Judith Basin early in the 1870's and had taken part in the gold rush to Yogo Creek in 1879. In fact, he was made the first recorder of the district, and Hoover City was named for him. With prospecting in his blood, he spent his summers in the mountains and on one expedition he made an important discovery. There are at least two versions of his strike, but each ends identically. Jean Sutter relates that during 1894, Hoover and Frank Hobson, while gophering in the Little Belt Range, took refuge under a rocky ledge during a mountain storm. In a crevice they uncovered flake gold. Exploring the area more carefully, they sank "some forty holes between Yogo and Sage Creek divide," and then, confident that they had made a strike, interested S. S. Hobson in their discoveries, offering him a share in their claims in return for a much needed ditch to bring water to their ground. Hobson obtained the necessary money from Dr. J. A. Bouvet (Bovette, Bovett), a Chicagoan, and the doctor was included in the partnership. The ditch, which carried water from Yogo Creek to the benchlands east of Yogo Canyon, was completed in 1895 and cost $38,000. The partners could hardly wait for the cleanup, but when it was made, the gold totaled less than $1,000. This unexpected blow caused the gold operations to be dropped. To be sure, whenever the men cleaned their sluiceboxes, small blue pebbles were found caught in the riffles with the gold, but these were tossed out with the rest of the waste. Soon after this disappointment, Frank

Hobson went to Maine and while there told a friend, who was a teacher, about his mining experiences. She asked him to send her some specimens of gold ore to show to her pupils. Upon his return home, he packed some dust in a small box, as well as a few of the blue pebbles, and sent them to her. In her response, she said nothing about the gold but thanked him for the sapphires, which she had had appraised.

"What in hell is a sapphire?" asked Hobson. This was the first clue as to what the men had found.

The *Grass Mountain Review* (March 21, 1921) tells it differently. According to it, Hoover started alone on a long pack trip into the mountains to look for a lead that he had noticed years before. It was late afternoon when he crossed Yogo Creek, and since the weather was cold, he decided to spend the night in one of the old abandoned cabins. Before leaving in the morning, he could not resist washing some of the creek gravel. Since the first few pans revealed scarcely any colors, he was about to quit, when he noticed a few smooth blue pebbles in his pan. He tried again, only to find more of the transparent stones with each washing. His pack trip forgotten, he rode twenty miles to the S. S. Hobson ranch at Utica. Hobson and he were mining associates, and any strike that he made was developed with Hobson's money.

"What have I found?" asked Hoover, displaying the strange blue pebbles.

"They could be sapphires," Hobson replied. "I'm leaving for Helena. Let me take them along and show them to a jeweler." Upon his return he reported that, according to a Swiss gem cutter, the stones were high grade sapphires.

According to a third story, Mrs. James H. Connely of Brooks, Montana, believes that she found the first sapphire in the gulch:

My husband and myself went to Yogo in 1880 with the first big stampede. There was a position as cook there for me at the time and I remember that was one of the reasons for going. A sawmill went into Yogo district in March of that year, being freighted in by P. W. McAdow and Ben Dexter. Mr. Connely worked at the sawmill.

I found what I believe to be the first blue sapphire ever discovered in Montana. We were walking down the gulch and I saw the sapphire in the creek and picked it up. I looked at it and threw it away. Two or three years afterward a sheepherder found a sapphire and gave it to Jake Hoover and he in turn gave it to S. S. Hobson, who sent it to Helena.

In April, 1881, we started for what is now Maiden.
Richland County Leader, January 9, 1922

Jim (John) Ettien, a settler in the Judith Valley, was prospecting on a bench land east of Yogo Creek early in 1896 when he noticed in a limestone fissure a soft filling which resembled the outcrop of a vein. Close by were several gopher holes, dug in an almost straight line in the same soft earth. These also attracted his attention until he reasoned that the adjoining ground was too hard for the little animals to excavate. Ettien was looking for gold; so he filed two claims on the barren bench land, but his prospects yielded nothing but blue stones, which he didn't recognize as sapphires. (Later on, some of the best gems were picked from the fissure and the gopher holes he had discovered.) Hoover and Hobson were, at the time, working a placer claim nearby; for, by 1896, the two men and Dr. Bouvet had formed a partnership and were developing the mine which Hoover had located. Their engineer warned them not to run tailings on Ettien's claim for fear of a suit and urged them to buy up the ground if they could. The purchase price was $2,450. The men worked their sapphire mines until Dr. Bouvet died. Long before this, Hoover had sold his share of the property to Hobson and Matt Dunn for $5,000 and gone to Alaska.

In 1898 the New Mine Sapphire Syndicate, Inc., a company financed by English capital, operated the mines. This company worked their territory through open cuts and by hydraulicking the deposit from the sides of the hill. In 1901, the English company also sank a 250-foot shaft and ran drifts into the lead. The ore was hoisted to the surface and dumped on washing floors where it was left to weather and further disintegrate. This latter process took time — at least a year, sometimes four. The sapphires, held in chunks of hard clay, could not be recovered until the rock became pulverized. It was then washed in sluice boxes and the sapphires caught in the riffles. The larger stones were hand-sorted at the mine, but the most valuable stones were sent first to London and then to European centers for grading and cutting.

No attempt was made to find a mineral vein west of Jim Ettien's discoveries until in 1901, by accident, one showed up about three miles west of the English mine. An employee from the Burke sawmill, which stood at the mouth of Yogo Creek, left Utica one afternoon and started back to the mill. Perhaps he tried a shortcut; in any event, he got lost and spent the night on top of a hill. In the morning, to his surprise, he found himself lying on a sapphire vein, with several stones visible in the outcrop. His discovery was staked and recorded as the Lion lode on September 23, 1901. Early in January, 1902, Patrick T. Sweeney made a location on ground extending across Yogo Creek. John Burke and Sweeney worked these claims together, in a superficial way, by means of cuts from which they hauled the dirt to his sawmill and washed it.

The American Sapphire Company took over their holdings in 1904 and for ten years carried on extensive operations. The ore was handled in much the same way as at the English mine and then run through the company's mill, which was constructed in 1906. The American mine, as it was called, lay at the junction of Kelly Coulee and Yogo Canyon. Around it grew a company camp whose buildings lined the sides of the canyon, forming two streets which intersected at right angles. The mill and blacksmith shop stood opposite the mouth of the coulee, on the east wall of the canyon. Up Kelly Coulee was the "mess hall and a small private schoolhouse for the children of the president's sister, several houses . . . a recreation hall and a number of barns."

Interestingly enough, the American Sapphire Company introduced daylight saving time by setting the clocks one hour ahead, which gave the men long evenings in which to fish and pursue their individual hobbies. Any employee suspected of stealing gems, or caught with the stones, was immediately discharged and sent packing, on foot, to Utica, twelve miles away, the nearest point at which he could catch a stage and leave the district. The company sold the mine in 1914 to an English company which made no attempt to operate it.

Even during its most active years, the Yogo District was hard to reach. It was some distance from a railroad, and all supplies and ore had to be hauled over a wagon road between Utica and the mines. A horse trail led across the mountains to Neihart.

During the first stampede to the district, in 1879, a similar rush to Dry Wolf and Running Wolf Creeks, north of Yogo, took place, with prospectors staking hundreds of lode claims in anticipation of the silver and lead deposits they hoped to uncover. Sahinen, in his report (1935), mentions two shipments from the Mountain Side mine which "showed 59-90 oz. of silver and 10% lead and 20% zinc," and adds that a small amount of placer gold was recovered from the stream gravels of Running Wolf and Yogo Creeks. He concludes,

"A few small mines at the head of Dry Wolf and Running Wolf have been productive, — the Woodhurst, Montana, Yankee Girl and Sir Walter Scott."

The sapphire mines were closed in 1929 and were not reopened due to litigation, which prevented Charles T. Gadsen, who remained as caretaker after the shutdown and organized the Yogo Sapphire Mining Company, from developing them. Since then, the properties have deteriorated and their buildings, ditches, and flumes have been badly damaged by vandals, animals, and weather. The cabins of Yogo and Hoover were long since carried off by homesteaders for use on the treeless plains of the Judith Basin. Six empty and dilapidated cabins are the sole survivors of a district from which between $3,000,000 and $4,000,000 worth of sapphires have been mined. The stones were sold for gems, as well as for use in scientific instruments, watches, clocks, and as bearings in meters. Sapphires from Yogo ranged in color from pale to royal blue, with first quality stones bringing $6.00 a carat in London. According to the U. S. Geological Survey (1952), the Yogo deposit was the most important gem locality in the country.

In July, 1956:

Sidwell and Commercial Uranium Mines, a Denver corporation, bought up 145,000 of 150,000 shares in the British syndicate . . . (which) stopped working its claims because of currency difficulties involving the pound sterling and double taxation by U.S. and Great Britain.

Great Falls Tribune, July 11, 1956

Who knows what will happen next in the gulch?

COPPEROPOLIS

Three miles north of White Sulphur Springs, Highway No. 6 joins Highway No. 89. Had we driven east for several miles on Highway No. 6, and looked closely, we might have seen one cabin — all that remains of Copperopolis. In its early years, the place was primarily a stage station, about halfway between White Sulphur Springs and Martinsdale, but the discovery of copper veins in the area north of Castle Mountain, in 1866, by E. J. Hall and his partner, Hawkins, attracted attention to it as a mining center. These two men, who are credited with discovering the first copper ore in Montana, packed out five tons of the rich metal by jack train to the Missouri River, where it was shipped to Swansea, Wales, for smelting. Hall made a profit on his ore and held on to his claims, eventually selling them in 1900 for $1,800.

The discovery of copper brought prospectors to the region and customers to Elizabeth Scott's hotel and stage station. In July, 1884, Mary Holliday bought Scott's hotel for $2,000 and ran it successfully for a number of years, catering to miners and stockmen from the Judith Basin. During the eighties and nineties, little development work was done on the several properties that were located, and only small amounts of ore were shipped out; for hauling costs were exorbitant until a railroad was built into Martinsdale in 1896. Although John Blewitt's strike, in the nineties, uncovered rich ore, it was not until Marcus Daly bought up the copper prospects just before his death in 1900 that Copperopolis flourished.

With such backing, W. W. McDowell lost no time in locating a townsite and offering a lot to anyone who would build immediately. All was confusion, but before the end of October, twenty-five structures stood on land bordering what would become the two main business streets, although men with teams were still grading them. By the time that sewers were laid and sidewalks built, five and six-horse teams were hauling ore from the mines for shipment on the railroad.

Copperopolis, a company town to which the miners brought their families, was equipped with a general store, livery stable, blacksmith shop, barber shop, boardinghouse, restaurant, and bunkhouses. It was self-sufficient, and the men were expected to trade in its stores. On November 12, 1900, Daly died, but even without his vision and guidance, Copperopolis carried on for a time.

Two patented claims in the camp were the Northern Pacific, originally opened in 1867, and the Darling Fraction, located on the slopes north of the Musselshell River and northeast of the stage station. Other properties included the Copper Duke (also known as the Virginia), Ohio, Hecla, East Hecla, and Calumet. The deepest shaft was 550 feet; much of the ore, however, was recovered close to grass roots, some running as high as eighty per cent copper.

During the first nine months of big-scale operation, a quarter of a million dollars was recovered from the mines. No doubt this was a mere start, but the economic depression in Germany, in 1901, which cut copper exports in half, caused copper prices to fall. Under these circumstances, the mines were forced to close in 1903, and the miners and their families left camp. From then on except for two men — George Dinsmore and Jack Norris — Copperopolis, the boom town one-quarter of a mile from the highway, was deserted. These two, who hated each other, stayed for years in the empty settlement, each living his own life and avoiding meeting by going at different hours to the town spring. Occasionally leasers opened one or more of the old properties, but other than their brief explorations, the camp was quiet. When the "dry-landers" in the valley attempted to homestead the area in 1915, they tore down the buildings for lumber and hauled them away.

Copperopolis is a true ghost town, with pitted hillsides dotted with stained dumps. Some years ago, the Northern Pacific hoist was still standing and, below it, a log cabin on ground once occupied by the stage station. The site of the company town, now a swampy meadow, may be seen by looking through a gap in the hills to the south of the highway.

CASTLE

The hills and rolling lands around Castle Mountain were known only to a few cattle and sheep men until early in the 1880's. These open ranges and forested hillsides were fairly accessible; for wagon roads connected Livingston, on the south, with White Sulphur Springs, on the west, and with Martinsdale, on the east. Except for a few ranches, the land was untouched.

Hanson H. Barnes, a veteran miner who came around the Horn, was probably the first prospector to wander into the area. Having settled first at Diamond City, he moved on to White Sulphur Springs, where, by 1881, he was postmaster; but these duties did not prevent him from tramping over the mountains in search of ore. He found outcroppings in 1882, but did nothing about them, and it is generally conceded that his first real strike was made in 1884. Authorities differ as to whether his initial discovery was the Bluebell, near Robinson, or the Princess, near Castle. He also staked the Maverick, Alaska, and Bassom.

Early in 1883, F. Lafe Hensley, an experienced miner and assayer, went hunting in the valley of the Musselshell River, fifty miles below Castle Mountain. While on this trip, he found a small piece of carbonate iron float, and with a miner's compulsion, started searching for the lead from which it came, working his way up the Musselshell and following all its tributaries. For two years he prospected first one gulch and then another, until in June, 1885, he found the outcrop and staked the Yellowstone mine on a mountain near the present town of Castle. It was the following season before he had enough money to return to his claim and locate it, and when he did start back to the hills, his three brothers, Ike, Joe, and John accompanied him. The Yellowstone, which became one of the largest producers in the district, was situated high on a mountain spur between Hensley and Hamilton Creeks, at 7,200 feet elevation. The brothers worked it until the spring of 1887, when they bonded it to Messrs. Crounse, Hauser and others for $75,000. When fully developed, the mine ranked third in the district.

The Hensleys were fortunate in opening other mines — the Morning Star, Belle of the Castles, Lamar, and Chollar in 1885, and in bonding them, in 1887, to Messrs. Kindred and others for $40,000. In 1886, they discovered the Great Western and American, and in 1887, the California, Iron Chief, Golden, and Gem.

At about the same time, Lafe and Ike Hensley discovered, close to their Yellowstone lead, the Cumberland, which became the bonanza of the camp, producing, before its final shutdown in 1894, between $750,000 and $1,000,000 of ore. This mine, situated in the canyon, three-quarters of a mile above Castle, the brothers worked during the winter of 1886. In the spring they bonded it to Messrs. J. R. King and Thomas Ash of Billings and Helena, for $50,000. Word of its huge ore body attracted other men to the region, and many more properties were opened.

During the winter of 1885-1886, George K. Robertson found samples of lead and silver float near Yellowstone Ridge, while prospecting with Lafe Hensley. When specimens were sent to Riley Lewis and C. F. Chapin, assayers at Wickes, the men not only returned a favorable report on the ore, but also hurried to the mountainside to look at the prospect.

Lewis and Chapin and George H. Higgins were successful that same year in locating the Great Eastern and in bonding it, in 1887, to Messrs. Woolsten and Hamilton of Helena, for $60,000. The Great Eastern, which became the second biggest producer in the camp, was also on Yellowstone Ridge. By 1888, the Castle Mountain Mining & Smelting Company had been organized at Helena to operate the mine with a capital stock totaling $1,000,000. In time, the American, Chollar, Potosi, and Great Western properties also came under the jurisdiction of the Castle Mining Company.

The Hidden Treasure, discovered in 1887 by Dunn and Donovan, was bonded to Hauser & Company for $40,000; the Princess, owned by H. H. Barnes, was bonded for $10,000. Most of the 1,500 mining claims were discovered between 1886 and 1890.

ROBINSON and BLACKHAWK

While this rush was going on, certain of the prospectors pushed several miles up the canyon to search for lodes. At two points, small camps developed — Robinson, four miles beyond Castle, and Blackhawk, seven miles distant from it.

George P. Robinson, for whom the camp was named, and who was one of the first prospectors to reach the district, located the Top (later called the Eclipse) in 1885. Paul Grande (Grade or Grandy) and N. A. Nelson, who ran the Pioneer House in the new camp, found the Silver Star and North Star in 1887. The camp never exceeded 300 in population.

Smith's Camp, soon renamed Blackhawk, was three miles beyond Robinson. The Smith brothers were the sole owners of the Blackhawk mine, as well as part-owners of virtually every other mine in the camp. These included the Alice, Altha, Legal Tender, Little Casino, and Iron Chief.

In 1891, the town had a building boom and its population reached 200. The following year the Castle newspaper devoted a column to "News from Blackhawk."

There was a pleasant surprise party at the home of E. S. Pardee one night last week; dancing was kept up till after 3 a.m. . . . a scarcity of men was the only thing that prevented the party from being a complete success.
Castle Reporter, October 15, 1892

Blackhawk's prosperity, however, was short-lived, even though low-grade ore and small quantities of zinc and lead were shipped after the camp declined.

CASTLE (Continued)

As a result of all these discoveries, a town named Castle, because of the turreted peaks above it, came into existence in April, 1887. Lafe Hensley and George H. Higgins built the first cabin in June and were joined before Christmas by 200 other settlers who had gathered in this embryo camp at the southern end of the mining district, at the foot of the mountains. Its buildings straggled along Allabaugh Creek, named for Sam Allabaugh, a stage driver and prospector, following the rough wagon road that cut through the narrow gulch to the mines. As Castle grew, the high mountains to the north prevented expansion in that direction, so it sprawled over the rolling meadowland south of the gorge.

Prior to the stampede, James Keen and John N. Reynolds of Townsend drove to Castle Mountain in a buggy and camped where the town now stands. While there, Reynolds said, "I'm going to own a town lot in this place." Cutting and labeling location stakes, he drove them into the ground. Two years later, when he was making the town survey, he ran across his markers in the middle of what was designated as Main Street. Worse still, his claim had been jumped, although, according to another version of the story, he sold the lot to Ash & King for $25.00, only to learn that some time later, the same ground brought $5,000.

The Castle Land Company platted eighty acres for the townsite and, according to a news item, "so popular is this beautiful tract that during the first sixty days, when it was placed on the market, over $100,000 worth of lots were sold. Water from Allabaugh Creek is pure and wholesome."

Dr. J. P. Rhoads and two of the Hensley brothers opened the first store, which handled merchandise. Before long, there were "80 dwellings, a score of business houses . . . a hotel, post office . . . resturants, lodging houses . . . carpenters, blacksmiths, wagon shops and two sawmills."

By the time the camp population reached several hundred, lot jumping was a common practice. A man, upon reaching his property some morning, would find it occupied by rough, armed men who drove him off and told him the ground had changed hands during the night. To stop this, a Vigilance Committee, composed of most of the solid citizens, was formed, headed by postmaster H. H. Barnes. The toughs hung out in a log cabin on a slope of the gulch. The Vigilantes rushed it one night, but a guard, stationed by the jumpers, warned the men of the posse's approach, and one of the desperados called out that the first man at the door would be shot down. The Vigilantes seized a log from a woodpile and battered at the door. After the first blow, there was a commotion at a

CASTLE TOWNSITE

side window, and when the attackers entered the cabin, it was empty. The toughs were gone for good.

Bill Gay and Gross, his brother-in-law, caused considerable excitement in the town during 1890. Gay and his brother Al had taken part in the Black Hills gold rush — Gayville is named for them — but after Bill killed a young fellow and was sentenced to the penitentiary, he spent all his money getting his term reduced to three years. When he and his quarter-breed daughter arrived in Castle, he was stone broke. The G. K. Robertsons were good to them, giving Gay odd jobs and befriending the girl.

Gay discovered a coal lead at the edge of town and dug a twenty-five foot shaft. One day he found a Mr. Benson, the editor of the newspaper and owner of a print shop, not only on his ground, but also in the shaft, having jumped the mine. Gay ran off Benson's hoist man and threw the windlass rope down the shaft. Benson's shouts soon brought help, but as a result of this incident, a lawsuit developed over the mine. When the case was tried in Helena, fifty witnesses from Castle were summoned to appear. The bi-partisan group drove to the court in "buckboards and buggies," stopping for lunch at a stage station east of Townsend. While there, the opposing teams of witnesses got into a fight and reached Helena with black eyes and bloody knuckles.

After the trial was over, Gay, assisted by Gross, took revenge by burning Benson's print shop and setting fire to other buildings in Castle. The pair were seen behind Fowlie's saloon just as they were about to set it afire, but in the dark, they made their escape. Since Gross was also suspected of several burglaries, sheriff William Rader of White Sulphur Springs, accompanied by a group of deputized citizens from Castle, followed the man to his cabin in the hills. When the posse reached the stronghold that was built against a sheer cliff and protected by breastworks, Gross called out that he would shoot to kill any man who tried to enter. Sheriff Rader replied that they only wanted to search the place. Gross then came out and was handcuffed while the deputies rooted through the shack but found nothing. Since the arson charge was not conclusive, he was released and promptly left Castle. A second visit to the cabin by the sheriff revealed a cache of stolen goods under the floor. Again a posse set out to capture Gross, who, by then, had joined Gay somewhere in the nearby hills. When found, the two were "forted up," and in the ensuing gunfight, sheriff Rader was killed by Gross. In the subsequent manhunt, the two were spotted in a thicket of willows on the bank of the Musselshell River. There, Gross killed Jim Mackay and aimed at Robertson, but Gay, remembering the blacksmith's kindnesses to him, threatened to shoot Gross if he killed his friend. In the general melee, the two criminals escaped.

Castle reached its peak in 1891, the year it was incorporated. At its height, it contained nine stores, one bank, two barber shops, two butcher shops, two livery barns, two hotels, a photo gallery, dancehall, church, $5,000 schoolhouse, jail, fourteen saloons, as well as a justice of the peace, a deputy sheriff, and a brass band. Most of its development was with home capital from the farms and ranches in the vicinity. The camp was supplied with milk from More Brothers' dairy and with butter from Lincoln's and Potter's ranches. "Two-hundred and fifty goats were kept at Hill's ranch, the dinner station between Castle and White Sulphur Springs." Three four-horse stage lines provided daily service between Castle and Martinsdale, White Sulphur Springs, Townsend, and Livingston. So great was the traffic that Castle's streets were jammed with freight wagons and bull teams hauling in mining machinery and coke for the smelters. Any delay in delivery threw the town off balance.

During its brief life, Castle was furnished with four newspapers. The *News* appeared in 1888, followed by the *Reporter* in 1889. Next came the *Tribune,* and last the *Whole Truth,* which published during the nineties.

Congregational church services were held regularly at the Odd Fellows' Hall twice on Sundays, under the direction of Reverend Alice Barnes. Mrs. Barnes also held a Bible Study class at which "attendance was not small." As a licensed Congregational minister, she preached at Castle and later at other towns. The Methodists also met in the Odd Fellows' Hall, where they heard Reverend John Hoskins of White Sulphur Springs preach. St. Andrew's Episcopal Church met the first and fourth Sundays at 11 a.m. and 7:30 p.m. in Sharp's Hall with the Reverend Charles H. Reinsberg conducting services. The Presbyterians also held services and were hoping to build, but as far as I know, did not realize their ambition.

Besides the church services, there was the W. C. T. U. This organization met the first and third Saturdays of each month and had a regular column in the newspaper "edited by the Local Union 'For God and Home and Native Land.'" In addition, Castle was not lacking in secret societies, to which many of the citizens belonged. The Castle Mountain Miners' Union was considered the "strongest order existing" in the camp. Other organizations included Carbonate Lodge No. 39 I. O. O. F.; Loyal Lodge No. 27, K. of P.; and A. O. U. W.

With its mines active during 1892, Castle continued to thrive. A few topics of local interest that appeared in the paper show what the people were doing:

The flag purchased for the school last summer now floats over the schoolhouse daily. The Republicans of Castle will hold a primary tonight at 8 o'clock in the room under the Castle Mercantile Company's store, formerly occupied by Reed & Scott's drug store, to nominate two candidates for justice of the peace, and two candidates for constable.
Castle Reporter, October 8, 1892

Some fifteen or twenty of the town people have organized a coasting club for recreation and pleasure, the coming winter. The "Flexible Flyer," a new kind of sled, will be used.
Castle Reporter, November 5, 1892

The ranchmen are not bringing in vegetables enough to supply the demand here. A good market can be found here for potatoes, turnips and cabbages.
Castle Reporter, November 12, 1892

Grand Leap Year Ball
The ladies of Castle did the gallant this week and gave a grand ball at Odd Fellows' Hall. About forty couples were in attendance and all had a nice time. The girls made all the arrangements, paid the bills, etc. and every one agreed that they made things hum as they usually do when they try.
Castle Reporter, December 3, 1892

The town seems to have been concerned with the importance of fire protection, for on

EMPTY STORE, CASTLE

CASTLE

January 21, 1893, the *Reporter* stated that

The fire boys were supplied this week with two heavy grappling hooks, chains and ropes, and a half dozen axes. These with the long ladders and 24 fire buckets puts them in pretty good shape to fight fires.

The winter of 1893 seems to have been unusually severe for

A number of frostbitten ears and noses are the result of the present cold snap. At 2 p.m. Monday the thermometer registered 11 above zero; two hours later it was 11 below; sometime Monday night 41 below; at 8 a.m. Tuesday 39 below; at noon 30 below. About 18 inches of snow has fallen which is somewhat drifted.

Castle Reporter, February 4, 1893

A number of ice houses in Castle are being filled this week. The ice is about 12 inches thick and of good quality.

A. R. Frame shoveled his way through the snow from Robinson one day this week on his way to Lucas' ranch from which place he is hauling hay.

Castle Reporter, February 11, 1893

Castle's three smelters, which were built between 1889 and 1891, were kept busy refining the district's ore. The Cumberland and Hensley plants produced, in 1889, $16,550 in gold and $36,355 in silver. Bars of bullion, weighing 100 pounds, were hauled by ox-teams to Livingston, to the railroad. Freight teams, consisting of 6-8 head of horses or mules, also pulled ore wagons with unusually heavy loads, for the trip was all downgrade. Each year the output of the Cumberland mine increased until, during 1890, it produced 500,000 pounds of argentiferous lead and over 20,000 ounces of silver; by 1891, it was the largest single producer of lead ore in the state.

In 1892, however, the output fell to 300,-000 pounds of silver, and jittery stockholders of the Cumberland Mining & Smelting Company became dissatisfied and suspicious of each other. When J. Kennedy Tod of New York City obtained control of the property, he arranged for W. P. Parsons, a mining expert, to investigate the mine and its reserves. After considerable expenditure of funds and further exploration, operations were suspended early in 1893.

The district needed a railroad to move its ore and cut shipping costs and, had it not been for the financial panic of 1893, a road would undoubtedly have been laid into Castle by that date. When it did not materialize, the Cumberland and other properties closed to await its arrival.

With the mines inactive, the miners melted away. The Cumberland boardinghouse, which had served 135 meals on the last night, served six men three days later, and these were the crew kept by the owners to dismantle the machinery. The last group to operate the mine were Len Lewis, B. R. Sherman, and Charles E. Severance, who formed a stock company and worked the Cumberland until 1894.

Even after the slump, some $500,000 of ore was shipped out, work continuing as long as the mines showed a profit. The few families that remained — about twenty in all — made a living by "pecking around and raising small crops."

The demand for a railroad was not new. Ever since the town of Castle had been built, the people had been clamoring for one.

Richard Austin Harlow, a promoter of vision and shrewd business sense, together with a knowledge of human nature, was aware of the people's need and set out to satisfy it. During the summer of 1890, he first conceived of building such a road. The Cumberland smelter had already reduced 6,000 tons of silver-lead bullion from its great mine, but had not attempted to ship the ore; for it was too low-grade to warrant the cost of a long haul. Conferences with citizens of Helena, Livingston, and Bozeman resulted in offers of $250,000 in money and real estate as bonuses to anyone who would build a road to the mines. Three companies were formed, but Harlow's was the only one to progress beyond the "paper stage." Although the Montana Railroad, which he built, reached Castle too late to save the camp, it provided a link between the Missouri River and the Judith Basin and, in time, paid off. The road was called the "Jaw Bone" because of Harlow's reputation of cementing a deal with persuasive talk instead of funds, yet, as he explained more than once, of the $2,950,-000 invested in it, only 3½% of the capital was covered by notes held by the various contractors.

Mrs. William T. Hart, of Harlowtown, writes of her interview with Richard Harlow in the *Richland County Leader* of January 9, 1922, and tells the story in his own words. Excerpts from her article are included in the following description.

During the summer of 1890, Harlow got in touch with J. P. Whitney, a friend from New Jersey who had some money to invest. Harlow interested him in the project, but Whitney's loan was only enough to start things moving. Just as work got underway, the panic of 1893 struck and Helena's promised support was withdrawn. With many men out of work, Harlow went into Helena's saloons and put the following proposition to any laborer who wanted work, saying, "If you'll work on my Montana Railroad grade between here and Canyon Ferry, I'll provide you with board, work clothes, shoes, and tobacco. Anything due you over that amount I'll pay in warrants, redeemable as soon as the grade is completed." The grade was built, but by the time it reached Canyon Ferry, Harlow's $25,000 capital was all spent. A hurried trip east failed to raise additional funds. This and other delays prevented further construction until May, 1895.

The right of way as planned ran from Lombard, on the Missouri River (south of Toston), up Sixteen-mile Creek, past Ringling to a point near Lennep, and thence up Allabaugh Creek to Castle, a total distance of sixty miles.

Work began and we thought our troubles were over. . . . We had a frightful time getting supplies up Sixteen-mile creek. A team and wagon had to travel sixty miles to get from the lower to the upper end of a box canyon which was scarcely half-a-mile long. A four-horse team with oats was sent to a camp from Toston and landed without a pound of oats in the wagon. It was caught in a snowstorm and the driver had to feed all the oats to the horses. The owners of little ranches we crossed held us up with shotguns. Ranchmen hesitated to sell us supplies, fearing they wouldn't get their money.

The line was finally built to Summit, with a branch completed in the fall of 1897 to Leadboro, two miles below Castle.

The day before Thanksgiving the last construction train left Leadboro for Lombard, loaded with passengers. It was caught in a snowstorm at Dorsey and lay there seventy-two hours without fuel or supplies. We finally got the train through without serious damage to the passengers.

With the completion of the railroad, the contracted 7,000 tons of ore from the Cumberland smelter were delivered to the American Smelting & Refining Company's plant in East Helena.

All during construction, the price of silver and lead was steadily declining. When the ore was finally delivered, both commodities were at the lowest point reached for years. Lead was 2½ cents and silver down in the forties. We got something like $78,000 for the ore. But our road was finished.

In the spring of 1898, an early thaw flooded Sixteen-mile Creek and washed out the roadbed so that it had to be completely rebuilt. By the time trains were running, traffic began to taper off. The only way to capitalize on what had been accomplished was to build a twenty-four mile extension east to Martinsdale. Next, an extension to Harlowtown was constructed with assistance from the Northern Pacific Railroad. The final lap to Lewistown was begun in 1902 and completed in 1903. "This extension," said Mr. Harlow, "justified the expense."

Now that the Northern Pacific was interested in the road, an official told Harlow that

the company was issuing a new folder and wanted to put our train table in it. He needed to know the name of towns and their distance from Lombard. There were no towns on the line, so I made up some, and strangely a number are on the map today. I was put to it for names. . . . There were two ladies visiting (us) named Fan and Lulu. On the road you will see the name Fanalulu, just below the town of Ringling.

Some years later, the "Jaw Bone" was sold to the Milwaukee & St. Paul Railroad. Harlow paid all his debts before he died and redeemed every warrant as soon as he sold out to the Milwaukee. Although the new owner tore up the road, it retained the route through Sixteen-mile Canyon to Lombard. The closest to Castle that the main line of the Milwaukee runs is through Lennep.

As the town quieted down, the residents made every effort to boost the morale to wait out the lull in production that they believed was temporary. To pass the time, a variety of entertainments were planned:

Free Reading Room
We desire to call the attention to the reading room. There are some things on our table that the readers of Castle cannot afford to pass by. There is an article in the March number of the Ladies Home Journal 'A Day with the President at his Desk' by the Hon. Benjamin Harrison, that is well worth reading. . . . Ladies are welcome in the afternoon.
J. A. Smith — Pastor
The Whole Truth, March 27, 1897

Mr. & Mrs. Jas. J. Fisher had a phonographic party at their residence Monday evening and invited a number of their young friends. . . . The guests were regaled by listening to the dulcet and melodious strains of the phonograph.
The Whole Truth, October 9, 1897

A Grand Success
The pop-corn festival on Friday evening was a grand success. . . . This was the first of a series of festivals in this city under the auspices of the ladies of the

Missionary Society. . . . Net proceeds . . . were the handsome sum of $25.00.

The Whole Truth, January 29, 1898

War hysteria and sentimentality mark this reference to the

Gallant Castle Boys in Blue

Harry McKee, Roy Sherman and Nug Corduro the gallant and brave boys of Castle who enlisted as volunteers in the First Montana regiment to fight the vile Spanish are by this time clothed in their blue uniforms. . . . Now boys, may God bless every one of you, for your cause is just, and after the war is over and the smoke of battle clears away, may you all return home with well earned honors to receive homage and ovation by friends and a kiss of hearty welcome and blessing by fond and loving parents.

The Whole Truth, May 21, 1898

By 1927, most of the abandoned mining claims were sold at a county tax sale to J. F. Brophy of Red Lodge. By 1936, only two men remained in Castle, "Mayor" Joseph Hooker Kidd and constable Joseph Martino. That winter the snow lay four feet on the level and in places piled up in forty-foot drifts. This isolated the elderly residents until their provisions got so low that Kidd, who was seventy-five, took his team and cutter and set out for Lennep, eight miles away. He made but three miles the first day and spent the night at a sheep camp. The next day he got to Lennep, stocked up on food, and with difficulty, reached a ranch by nightfall. Leaving early in the morning, he "shoveled snow and fought drifts all day." When within a mile of Castle, his exhausted team gave out. Turning the animals loose, he covered the rest of the way on foot. At nine o'clock that night, he reached Martino's place, drank some hot coffee, and started for his cabin, 500 yards away. Martino watched him go and held a lantern to light his way. Before Kidd reached his door, he collapsed, and when Martino reached him, he was dead. Martino was seventy years of age and too frail to move the body; so the best he could do was cover it with a blanket. Next day he skied to the sheep camp and told the herder what had happened. Three days later, the sheriff and coroner skied over from White Sulphur Springs and dragged Kidd's body out on a toboggan.

On the afternoon in 1955 when we drove south from Neihart, over King's Hill, a pass through the Little Belt Mountains, and dropped down into White Sulphur Springs, we debated whether to stay there and start for Castle in the morning, or to try to reach it before sunset.

"Let's start right now," said Francis, "and if we can't make it, we can go on to Helena." After we left Highway No. 89, some fifteen miles south of White Sulphur Springs, we were on a graded road. From it, the map showed two approaches to Castle. We found the first, an unmarked trail that took us across the Milwaukee tracks, through a gate and deposited us, after a mile's drive, in a ranchyard. Since no one was about from whom to inquire directions, we returned to the highway and drove east to Lennep, a drab little village consisting of one store, which was closed, a church, and three or four houses and sheds near a thicket of willows along the Musselshell River. By now it was late afternoon, and dark clouds hung over the mountains where Castle lay. As we left Lennep, a car, driven by a young ranch boy, came along, and we asked if it was going to rain.

"Yep," he replied. "The Castle road is gumbo when it's wet, but it's only seven miles." We drove on for a mile, watching the clouds. Where the road split, the Castle fork was deep, soft dirt, hard to manage even while dry. As soon as we could turn, we hurried back to Lennep and drove west over the Big Belt Mountains to Townsend, and on to Helena.

Our second attempt to reach Castle, in 1956, was successful. This time we left Harlowton early in the morning and drove to Martinsdale, where we stopped to ask directions. A truck pulled up ahead of us and eight men got out. They assured Francis that we could get to Castle even though the road wasn't kept up; for some boys were up there hunting uranium and they'd taken machinery in over it. With that, they disappeared into a tavern for a morning beer.

From Martinsdale, we drove west through ranch country, close to the Musselshell River and the Milwaukee railroad tracks. Before we knew it, there were the familiar buildings of Lennep in front of us, and, leaving the highway, we started for the mining camp.

The road beyond the fork was even worse than it had been before, and Francis drove carefully, straddling ruts, and measuring the width of a culvert which served as a bridge over a draw from whose surface dirt and boards were missing. After scraping between clusters of alders and willows, we crossed Allabaugh Creek on a few rattling planks and pulled up the bank to rejoin the good road, just beyond a fine ranch. The rest of the way was relatively easy, for the road had been dragged as far as a second ranch, which was only a mile from the Castle townsite.

At the end of our eight-mile climb, we saw buildings dotting the hillsides on both sides of the creek. Most of the houses were in ruins, although a few two-story frame residences looked sturdy enough, even though their windows and doors were missing. The sides of the road were lined with bushes which hid many foundations where business houses once stood. In some the whole cellar was filled with rotting debris and vigorous young saplings. In one lay an old trunk. Which broken walls, I wondered, had supported the Hensley-Rhoads building with its leaded glass windows, and where had James M. Addle and L. Peavy, Castle's two attorneys, had their offices? Which foundations marked the sites of the ten licensed saloons and seven brothels? When had the two-story schoolhouse, with its cupola and bell, been razed? Only from photographs had I any idea at which end of town it stood.

To investigate the camp more thoroughly, we left the car and wandered up and down the grass-grown but discernible streets. Which of the two frame sentinels with their bay windows and papered walls had belonged to Warren C. King, and which to Mrs. Smith? Just beyond them was a one-story house hidden among aspen and cedar trees. This, I had been told, was the home of Isaac M. Hensley, one of the four brothers who opened the Cumberland and other important mines.

The town was empty, but through the high thin air we could hear a gasoline engine and the sound of hammering. The noises must have been from the camp of the uranium boys.

On the way back to Lennep, I tried unsuccessfully to locate the site of the charcoal camp below Castle that was maintained by Italian wood burners as long as the smelters operated. When we reached the big ranch, we took the better of the two roads — the one which ran between its many sheds and buildings and through its barnyard. As we neared Lennep, we saw, across the creek, a new low-slung car rocking from side to side as it crawled over the miserable trail we had taken earlier in the day.

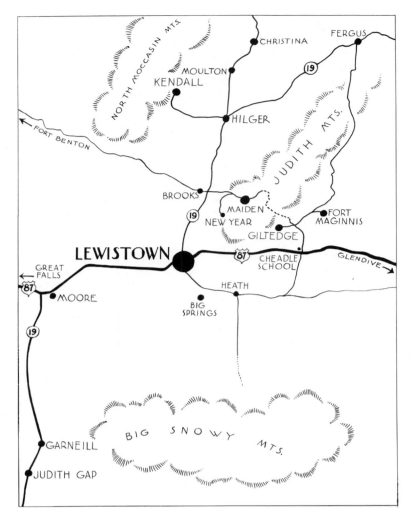

CHAPTER 20

THE JUDITH MOUNTAINS and the NORTH MOCCASINS

The wheat was ripe the first time we drove north from Big Timber on our way to Lewistown. The wide, rolling valley was a sea of gold, ruffled by wind into streamers of motion that came and went or traveled erratically like dust devils. By the time we reached Harlowton, with its grain elevators and the railroad, the Crazy Mountains to the west had been left behind and the Little Belts were piling up on the left. At Harlowton we crossed the Musselshell River and pulled away from its banks to drive through the wide-streeted town to its north edge. There, in front of us, lay another unbroken sea of quivering wheat, reaching to the horizon. As we drove on, glistening elevators cut its surface, indicating the location of the railroad and the tiny settlements that clustered around each station.

JUDITH GAP, GARNEILL, MOORE

The first of these, Judith Gap, is built on a hill on whose summit stands a church, a school, and a watertank. Many of its buildings are empty and others have been hauled away; for the Gap is no longer a busy grain-shipping center and important division point on the Great Northern Railroad. The terrain which forms Judith Gap provides a pass between the Big Snowy Mountains on the east and the Little Belts on the west. Over this trail numberless Indians, hunters, freighters, and stockmen traveled between the Yellowstone and Musselshell Valleys to the south and the Judith Basin to the north. The town's location, along this trail, was a strategic one.

Garneill, six miles north, has but one store,

a church, a school, and a scattering of occupied and empty buildings. Yet Garneill includes three townsites. When the Central Montana Railroad built a station there, in 1903, it was designated as Ubet, in honor of an old stage stop, three miles west of the present town. All that is left of the original historic site are one or two old log buildings; but long before the advent of the railroad, Ubet had a two-story, log hotel, a blacksmith shop, ice house, saloon, stage barn and stable, and a post office. A. R. Barrows, who ran the hotel in 1880, is credited with naming the place. When asked if he could think of a good name for the post office, he replied without hesitation, "You bet!" Ubet flourished until the arrival of the railroad; then its usefulness was over. In addition to the townsite called Ubet, there were also North Garneill and South Garneill, the latter laid out because of local friction over liquor. North Garneill was "dry" and has survived. South Garneill was "wet" and had a fine saloon, blacksmith shop, and several stores, all of which burned a number of years ago.

Moore, twenty miles farther north on Highway No. 87, is another grain center. Lewistown, sixteen miles from Moore, lies in a hollow which makes it invisible until one is nearly within its limits.

LEWISTOWN and REED'S FORT

Fergus County was not carved from Meagher County until 1885; but even before the legalities were completed, Lewistown, a small trading center, and Maiden, a flourishing mining camp in the Judith Mountains, were each sparring to corner the county seat.

Lewistown evolved from the small trading post on the ranch of Francis Janeaux, a Frenchman who had located in the valley in 1882 or 1883, and through whose land ran the Carroll Trail between Helena and Crow Island, which was at the mouth of the Musselshell River. In 1884, T. C. Power and his brother bought the post from Janeaux and enlarged it. By 1885, a saloon run by Kemp and Crowley, another owned by Henry Simons, a livery barn, a log hotel, and some cabins were grouped around Power's store and comprised this new town, which stood where the main business portion of Lewistown is today. That it was not widely known is shown by the story of the eastern stranger in Billings who asked how to reach it. "Never heard of it," replied one man. "You'd better ask one of these miners."

"Lewistown?" said the prospector. "That's the little trading post this side of Maiden."

One mile south of the new settlement was Reed's Fort, named for Major A. S. Reed, who, with a partner named Bowles, built a stockade and a fort and traded with the Indians for several years before Janeaux's arrival. In 1881 the Reed's Fort post office, housed in a log cabin which is still one of Lewistown's most treasured landmarks, was the only one in Central Montana. Until Lewistown's birth, Reed's Fort was also the only white settlement in the Judith Valley, except Fort Maginnis and Maiden.

Lewistown — named for Major Lewis, who in 1876 established Fort Lewis, two miles south of it — grew into a trading and freighting center for the miners, cattlemen, homesteaders, and ranchers who settled in the valley, especially after the Central Montana (Jaw Bone) Railroad was extended to Lewistown in 1903. Since then, it has continued to grow until today, when it is served by two railroads — the Milwaukee and the Great Northern — it has become a prosperous shipping center for the wheat and registered cattle that are raised in the surrounding country.

We made Lewistown our headquarters from which to explore the several old mining camps in the nearby mountains.

ANDERSONVILLE

Right after lunch, we set out for Andersonville, Maiden, and New Year, driving north from Lewistown eleven miles to Brooks and turning east toward the Judith Mountains. Somewhere along this gravel road, which climbed up the valley past several ranches and a few old cabins, we passed the site of Andersonville. This forgotten camp was named for a half-breed Indian, "Skookum" Joe Anderson, one of the original discoverers of gold, who in 1880 made a strike in this area. A year later Andersonville was founded. The town had but one street, a quarter of a mile long, on which stood two stores — one belonging to P. W. McAdow — one meat market, two saloons run by Jeremiah Thornton and John Campbell, one hotel conducted by R. R. Millet, one restaurant, one blacksmith shop, one feed stable, one steam sawmill, a post office, and an express office managed by A. M. Thomson. Its peak population was 200. When the camp of Maiden sprang up, Andersonville ceased to grow and ultimately disappeared.

The original discovery was placer gold,

found in the spring of 1880 by Joe Anderson and David Jones, who had left the Black Hills in 1879 for Yogo Gulch and from it had wandered to the Judith Mountains. They were joined in June, 1880, by C. C. Snow and F. T. McPartlan who also found colors and, as soon as the news spread, by others who hurried to the diggings. The first strike that paid off was found in Alpine Gulch, where several claims were located by June 10. The next discoveries were made in Warm Spring Gulch, and, a few days later, Frank McPartlan located ground in Maiden Gulch. Another successful prospector, J. R. Kemper, opened up ground that paid "$115 to each sluice box of twelve feet." Thereafter, Alpine and Maiden Gulches were worked each season for a number of years.

Oh, Maiden, beautifully fair,
  Couched between those mountain hollows,
Charming thy form and golden hair
  And eyes bright as silver dollars.
Maiden of wealth on paper told,
  Breast of pearls, ribbed with silver,
Awaiting ready to unfold
  And give up her rarest treasure.

Maiden whom many anxious sought,
  Fondly courted, strived to woo;
Who to empty words heeded not,
  Smiled while heart broken they withdrew.
  Rocky Mountain Husbandman, July 27, 1882

To the irritation of my husband, who likes real poetry, I repeated this ditty as we drove six or more miles east from Brooks until the gravel road became the main street of the once active camp of Maiden. Only a handful of old buildings remain, scattered among a few newer cabins and frame houses. Two stores and the stone foundations of a large warehouse mark the center of town. There the street divides, the righthand lane leading up toward the Maginnis mill, and the lefthand branch winding up the mountain out of sight. According to the one resident whom we talked to, most of the mines and mills were on that road, near the summit of the range. Prospect holes and dumps were yellow accents on the timbered hillsides.

It is said that the population of Maiden in 1881 was 6,000, most of the miners living in tents along the gulch. Mrs. James H. Connely who arrived by bull team from Billings (then called Coulson), tells how the camp received its name:

In April 1881, we started for what is now Maiden.

Snow and Kemper, prospectors, intended to establish a townsite there. I asked them what they were going to call the town and they said Grovenire after Grovon, a squaw. I said, "Give a white woman a chance." They laughed and asked me what I would name it. By my side was standing my daughter, whom the prospectors called "Little Maiden." I said, "Name the town after your little maiden." They did.
  Richland County Leader, January 9, 1922

Maidenville.
Col. J. J. Donnelly, who returned from Maidenville and vicinity yesterday, says that pending the development of the leading quartz mines, the camp is somewhat dull. The placers are, however, turning out well. The Col. saw one placer claim where the owner was washing out nuggets without the aid of quicksilver, and about eighteen dollars per day is the average cleanup. There is no question but that Maidenville will yet prove a great mining camp.
  Benton Weekly Record, July 20, 1882

The Judith Mountains were packed with minerals, and, as subsequent discoveries revealed, the greater part of the ore, which was free-milling quartz carrying both gold and silver as well as some galena leads, was centered in the portion of the range close to Maiden. Since no accurate records were kept, no one knows the amount of gold that was taken from the hillsides. Maiden was considered a "high grade" camp, because of the many small but rich veins of ore that were located in the several properties and from which an estimated $5,000,000 was produced.

The War Eagle, the first quartz lode to be uncovered, was located by the initial prospectors in the region — Jones and Anderson. It ran eighty ounces in silver and a few dollars in gold per ton. The Black Bull was next, discovered by the same men, who by then had taken Perry W. McAdow in with them as a partner. It was a gold-bearing lode and lay near the War Eagle. The Alpine, a galena lode found by these three prospectors and a man named Dexter, was reported "to be second to none in the camp." Following these discoveries, other mines were staked.

The Collar mine, one and a half miles from the camp, was a silver prospect discovered in 1880. An item in the *Rocky Mountain Husbandman* of October 26, 1882, reports not only on the mine, but also on its chief owner and the politics of the town.

Maiden Frills.
The Collar mine, of which so much has been expected, has fulfilled all its expectations. Gen. Mead of Omaha Smelting Works has purchased a half-inter-

MAIDEN

est for $50,000 and a 20-stamp mill is to be erected. Johnny Kemper, the largest owner, goes east to-morrow, and the report says he is to be hitched up and will in future trot in double harness.

Prospects never looked better for Maiden than at present. We believe Maiden will be the banner Republican town of the county.

The years 1882 to 1885 saw the greatest activity in the region. The Maginnis mine, one-third of a mile up the gulch from the town, dominated Maginnis Hill from which the forest was stripped to provide cordwood for engine fuel and mine timbers. The mill, below the big dumps, ran steadily and reported a cleanup of $300.00 per day "with only half of the crushing capacity at work."

Half a mile farther up the gulch than the Maginnis mine was the famous Spotted Horse. When "Skookum" Joe Anderson discovered the outcrop on the north side of the Judith Range in 1880, he uncovered a lead from which hundreds of thousands of dollars were recovered. After removing a quantity of high-grade ore from the discovery shaft, Anderson sold the mine for $5,500 to Perry McAdow, a veteran miner who came to Montana in July, 1861.

McAdow's entry into Montana was violent; for he came up the Missouri River from St. Louis on the steamer *Chippewa*, which blew up in Disaster Bend. From there McAdow made his way to Fort Benton and, by December, reached Gold Creek in the Deer Lodge Valley. From Pioneer Gulch, he dug some of the first gold to be recovered in Montana. By the time he reached Maiden, he was paralyzed and bound to a wheel chair, but his knowledge of mining enabled him to direct procedures and to assay the ore with a horn spoon. His wife assumed active charge of mining operations, and under the combined management a ten-stamp mill was built. According to reports from old timers, "somewhere in the neighborhood of a million dollars was taken from the property."

In 1892 the mine was sold for $300,000 to the Jay Gould Company, "which did not understand it and wanted to take out $1,000,-000 without putting anything in." Their operation of it was unsuccessful, and after they encumbered it with a considerable debt, it reverted to McAdow, who again put it in the black and "took out another million or so."

It is proposed to furnish a gold brick from the Spotted Horse, of a value of $100,000 to head the Montana exhibit at the World's Fair.

Copied from *New Northwest*
Belt County Miner, August 3, 1892

For a time the mine produced steadily and the owners received good returns until, in 1894, a crooked manager skipped with the profits. Its creditors — the Bank of Fergus County, the Power Mercantile Company of Lewistown, and M. L. Poland — then took it over and retained it until 1896.

The Spotted Horse has been sold to J. L. Bright of Columbus, Ohio . . . who also gets the Kentucky Favorite and other mines belonging to the late Double Eagle Mining Co. . . . The history of the Spotted Horse during the last twenty years has been one of ups and downs. . . . It has made some people rich while it has impoverished others. Bus McAdow, the original owner probably made more out of it than any one else. . . . It is a peculiar sort of mine, there is no lead. . . . Wherever a pocket can be found it will sometimes yield as much as $10,000 in gold. That much or twice that amount is then spent in the endeavor to locate another pocket.

The Double Eagle Mining Co. did very well for awhile and but for the rascality of the manager, might have scored a success. He feathered his own nest and left the United States to escape prosecution. . . . The mine was sold for $25,000 face value of attachments two years ago. The pumps have been worked to keep it clear of water.

Helena Weekly Herald, October 8, 1896

The property continued to change hands until it was purchased by the St. Paul Montana Company. These new owners were primarily interested in their purchase of Whiskey Gulch and the New Year properties, and when the Spotted Horse was "thrown in to complete the deal," they made no attempt to work it.

But under various other operators, the mine was active until 1919, when a combination of events forced it to close down. First, wages rose to $6.00 a day; then it was found that the high-grade ore was almost worked out. Plans to deepen the shaft were suspended when some of the owners died, and finally, the leasor quit mining to enter the oil business.

When C. C. Snow and J. R. Kemper planned the Maiden townsite, the land had not been surveyed, and no titles or deeds could be given for the lots. Each buyer registered possession by immediately fencing his property; for otherwise the lot could be jumped. Mrs. Otto Anderson owned two lots, and when her fence needed repairing, she got big Pat Skinner to mend it for her. Pat was so busy with the repairs that he didn't see "Hungry Wolf" approach until the man pointed a shotgun at him and ordered him off the ground, Pat's temper saved the day, for he grabbed the man's gun and broke it, throwing the pieces into the bushes. The jumper left.

A good account of Maiden, as it appeared in 1882, is given by a correspondent to the *Rocky Mountain Husbandman.*

Five miles of travel along a sparsely inhabited gulch road took me to Maiden. . . . The Main street follows along the creek, and upon each side steep mountains stand, leaving only room for the narrow street and a row of houses on the east side of it.
. . . . The majority of houses are of logs and lumber finish. There are 8 saloons, 2 clothing stores, 5 general merchandise, 1 dry-goods, 1 butcher shop, 1 blacksmith, 2 barbers with 2 chairs each, 1 feed stable, 1 lawyer's office, 1 doctor, 1 hotel and 1 restaurant.
Bollanger and Boissoneault have the largest store on Main St. Eating & Pompany . . . have not yet undertaken the work of building a store, but have a very large canvas house, in which their goods are displayed to advantage.
. . . . The hotel, kept by Joe Dennison, is located at the forks of Montana and Maiden streets. The only attorney is S. C. Edgerton, a son of Montana's ex-governor. He is a genial fellow and is here at the right time to grow up with the town, camp and business.
J. W. Caldwell is the assayer. . . . Dr. W. E. Turner of Benton, buys ore . . . and ships it to the Omaha Smelter Co., paying charges himself and giving the owner of the lead one-half gross assay value of the same. Of course he only buys the best rock.

July 27, 1882

Up until the summer of 1883, the townsite was inside the Fort Maginnis military reservation. On August 8, Captain Cass Durham, the commanding officer of the cavalry battalion stationed at the Fort, had posted at Maiden the following notice which both startled and infuriated the residents:

Order No. 134, . . . dated Washington, D. C., April 13, 1883, . . . all persons now residing on the military reservation of Fort Maginnis, M. T., or working any mines or prospecting for mines, or carrying on any other kind of business, . . . I hereby warn that they must leave the reservation and remove therefrom all property that they may have brought with them or acquired since coming on the reservation. Sixty days from this date will be granted for the completion of this removal herein ordered, at the end of which time those remaining without proper authority will be forcibly ejected.

By order of Captain Cass Durham,
F. W. Kingsbury, post adjutant.

A meeting was hastily called with John Beck, the recorder of the Warm Spring Mining District, as chairman, at which a committee was appointed to draft a petition and present it to Captain Durham. The protest was written and given to him by August 13. After careful consideration of their case, he agreed to approve a request to reduce the size of the military reservation so as to exclude Maiden and its surrounding mines. Such a petition was drawn up by the committee and approved by the citizens of Maiden; and thus the matter was adjusted.

In March of the following year, the settlers in the Judith Basin persuaded the Territorial Legislature to create Fergus County out of Meagher County. The next question was the location of a new county seat. The stockmen and ranchers lobbied for the new settlement of Lewistown. The citizens of Maiden were equally determined that their camp was the logical location and sent a committee to Helena to present their case. According to Leeson's *History of Montana*

Maiden presents a strong claim for the county seat, and urges as reasons why it should be located there that four-fifths of the criminal business and three-fourths of the civil will originate there. A petition was largely signed in April 1885 by the citizens, requesting the county commissions not to build a jail at Lewistown until the county is organized.

Despite their pleading, Lewistown won out, although Maiden was still the principal settlement in the county with a newspaper, the *Mineral Argus,* a Cornet Band, thirteen saloons, and several hundred population. As of November 4, 1885, the Fort Benton *River Press* wrote: Maiden. . . . is built principally on three streets, one across the gulch forming the resident portion of the town, while the business is carried on on Main and Montana streets. The town shows evidence of great prosperity by the number and variety of its business interests.

The *Mineral Argus* has a neat and convenient office. The Argus has a large circulation throughout the Judith country.

On my return from Maiden I passed through Andersonville. Only two or three buildings bore any evidence of being inhabited.

Amusements in the camp took various forms:

The Maiden Club Dance

Mr. Herring, an experienced caller, being absent, several members volunteered their services and there was calling in A minor and B flat, and dancing in all the octaves. It was an evening of pleasure however

to the round-dancers if not to others. The next party is Feb. 25. . . . Gentlemen accompanied by one or more ladies are exempt from financial obligations.
Mineral Argus, February 19, 1885

Last Friday morning some parties turned loose their guns in the street. Constable Washburn took their trail and captured the offenders of the law. They were arraigned before Justice Sharpless and made to pay their fines.
Mineral Argus, January 1, 1885

Although the troops at Fort Maginnis were for the protection of the settlers, Indians continued to harrass the ranchers and cattlemen and pilfer from them.

The Indians, on their recent raid, took five horses from Wm. Fergus — all he had. Hon. James Fergus says the thieves had their cache within three miles of Maiden and eight miles of Ft. Maginnis.
Mineral Argus, July 9, 1885

While the settlers had some reason for their feeling toward Indians, their attitude toward Orientals seems less justified.

Good Bye John!
The Departure of Maiden Chinamen Hastened by
the Appearance of a Band of Masked Men.
The weeks past have held forebodings of evil to the few Chinamen living in Maiden. The first intimation . . . was the appearance of a skull and crossbones posted in several conspicuous places, containing a few words of warning.

One or two meetings were held last week at which the programme of procedure was discussed and decided upon. There was little attempt at secrecy. However much we deprecate or disapprove of such proceedings, it must be admitted that the Chinamen were duly warned of the action of the meeting and given time to gather up their personal effects and depart in peace to more congenial climes. They did not heed the warning but tarried with their pipes and "hop" until Monday night, when about 11 o'clock a party of some 30 men, wearing masks, came from a rendezvous on the hillside south of Montana St., marching in singlefile and proceeded to carry into effect the decree that had already gone forth.

Gee R. Joe, Montana St. laundryman, was first visited and apprised of the fact that the hour of his departure had arrived and any unnecessary delay would not be conducive to longevity. Joe started for Lewistown accompanied by four other Chinamen who had been alike admonished by the klan to go hence.

They were escorted down the gulch some distance and told to keep right on going. On Tuesday teams were secured and the effects of the Chinamen taken, as we suppose to Lewistown. There was no violence used, no weapons fired or vicious passions aroused, which in a measure paliates the unlawful proceedings.
Mineral Argus, January 14, 1886

As the years passed by, mining dwindled until only a few properties like the Spotted Horse continued to produce. As the mines closed down or were worked intermittently by small crews of lessees, the population began to drift away, leaving buildings vacant. A photo taken in 1888 shows a solidly built up settlement. A fire which swept through the quiet streets in 1905 leveled the town and there was no need to rebuild.

NEW YEAR

About halfway between Maiden and Brooks, we found the road which led to New Year. It was narrower and less traveled and looked as if it would be slippery if wet, but since the clouds were only lowering, we started out, climbing over a saddle and around the edge of a hill into the next valley where there were several ranchhouses. As we proceeded, the rain began to fall and the valley ahead became obscured by a white curtain of drifting mist.

The road became muddy and slick, and we almost slid into a ditch. We were now more than three miles from the main road and there were still no signs of mining that I could detect. We started back but just as we neared the first ranch, I saw, toward the east, about a quarter of a mile away, a blackened, empty mill . In the nearby farmyard was a boy feeding bums (motherless lambs) milk from beer bottles. When I asked him the whereabouts of New Year, he pointed to the blackened skeleton. The big mill, we were told, had been torn down by the ranchers. The miners' cabins had stood in the gulch below the mill. On top of the distant mountain were mine dumps. Since everything in the lush valley, where New Year had once stood, was dripping wet, I took one long look and we drove away. A few yards beyond the ranch was the road that led to the mining properties. A signpost listed the Finley Ranch and a mine whose name was illegible.

Fortunately I had seen a picture of the New Year Cyanide Plant in a Pictorial Edition of the *Fergus County Argus*. The photograph showed a large mill and surrounding buildings, and the caption underneath read: "New Year Gold Mines Co. The New Year Cyanide Plant is considered one of the best properties in the Judith Mountains and one of the largest."

As we drove back toward Lewistown, I opened my Fergus County notebook and read from the notes about New Year. "It says," I told Francis, when we were back on the graded road, "that gold was discovered there in 1880, that New Year is five miles from Maiden and that the mines and mill are situated in a picturesque gulch. The owners of the mine in 1896 were W. G. Harmon and Adolph Harmon. I wish this article had been dated, for it continues, 'Only three years ago the first experimental plant was built on the New Year group of mines. When it was found that the cyanide process was successful, a large company took hold of it and began to enlarge the capacity of the mill.'

"The group contains eighteen and a half claims and 2,000 acres of land. The ore is hauled two miles by teams from the mines to the mill. The mill is at the bottom of the gulch. The mines are diagonally up the mountainside. An aerial tram is to be built next summer, more than a mile in length, at a cost of $15,000. There has been a shortage of water for the mill. A mile and a quarter ditch has been built from a spring at a higher elevation. The ditch cost $2,000, in addition to the piping. Fifty men are employed in the mine and mill; the capacity of the mill is 200 tons of ore and the tank capacity is 729 tons. The company also owns and operates its own coal mine. Above and back of the mill, on the side of the mountain, is the mouth of the tunnel which taps the coal vein. Tram cars run to the top of the mill and the coal is dumped down a chute and deposited in front of the furnace doors.

"A crystal cave opens off the main shaft of the New Year mine. The main chamber is 300 feet across and 100 feet high and water saturated with calcites and minerals make a sparkling showroom."

"Well," said Francis, "I'm glad to know what it was we didn't see."

GILT EDGE

The camp of Gilt Edge is just across the range from Maiden. The road that connected the two places is now impassable, and the only way to reach Gilt Edge is by driving east from Lewistown ten or eleven miles to Cheadles schoolhouse and then northwest to the townsite. We had no trouble in finding the turn-off and were traveling easily along the dirt road toward the Judith Mountains when we came to two cars parked beside the road so that their women drivers might visit. "It's

GILTEDGE

GILTEDGE AND THE JUDITH MOUNTAINS

six miles from here to Gilt Edge," one of them told us. "You can't miss the place. Go on to where there's men working on the road and then turn west."

Even before we had covered six miles, we saw mine dumps and mine roads on the distant hillside, and, by the time we caught up with the grader, we were close to the lefthand fork which ran straight toward the mountains.

Gilt Edge lies on a flat at the mouth of a gulch. Its scattered houses are old or moderately so. A few log cabins, a couple of good-sized residences, one big store, ruined stone buildings, and many foundations lined its several streets. On the hillside, close to the town, were the ruins of a cyanide mill with three tanks and, behind it, a big yellow dump. As we drove past a field, a man who was plowing left his tractor and came up to the fence to talk.

"Sure, there's lots of mines in these mountains," he began, leaning against a fencepost. "That high road on the hill goes over the hump to Maiden, but it washed out ten or twelve years ago and it's never been fixed. You can't get through any more."

Eager to get started on sketches, I started down the road toward the main street. The man watched me go and turning to Francis, said, "She ain't hobbled, is she?"

The same rush that brought prospectors to the west side of the Judith Mountains in 1880 found a few of the men looking for placers on the eastern side of the range and discovering some colors in the creekbed. Lode mining began in 1881, but the real development of the eastern slope of the Judiths did not start until 1893, by which time cyanidation had proved an effective process to save the gold that had evaded recovery by other methods. As soon as a group of Great Falls capitalists secured control of the Gilt Edge mines in the spring of 1893, they put up a cyanide mill at the foot of the mountains. Even before its completion, a town began to shape up around it and, as always, the local papers played up the new enterprise.

The Gilt Edge Mining Co, have now got their new mining machinery in operation and are treating 100 tons of ore per day. The new plant cost $35,000 and they have about 50 men at work. . . . The Gilt Edge ore assays about $20 per ton and its owners feel sure that they have a bonanza.
Belt Mountain Miner, August 3, 1893

Gilt Edge City
The New Gold Camp Rapidly coming to the Front

The Gilt Edge Co. has paid out in the neighborhood of $18,000 in the past ten days, and the larger portion of this amount went to the miners and other employees.

Gilt Edge now has 3 hotels, 2 restaurants, 1 general store, 1 drug store, 5 saloons, 1 butcher shop and a livery stable, in course of construction.
Copied from Lewiston *Argus,*
Belt Mountain Miner, November 30, 1893

The first output of the new refinery of the Gilt Edge Co. is on exhibition at the Cascade bank at Great Falls. It consists of two bars of bullion, estimated to be worth $2700. The larger bar is 9 inches long, 2 inches square and weighs about 10 pounds. The two bars are the result of a four-days' run of the new mill. So far, about $60,000 in bullion has been taken out of the mines.
Belt Mountain Miner, December 14, 1893

Despite these press notices, conditions were not so rosy as pictured. A few months after starting operations, the company failed to meet a payday, but, as the men were promised their wages at a later date, most of them stayed on. When successive paydays were skipped, the manager, H. S. Sherard, talked to the discontented miners and finally, when twenty-five of them demanded their money, raised the needed cash. As soon as he paid them, he discharged them. This action kept most of the remaining force at work.

The company then issued worthless "Gilt Edge" checks and flooded the county with them, until the Lewistown merchants demanded payment. In the meantime, Colonel Robert A. Ammon, a "Tammany Hall lawyer from New York," who had replaced Sherard as manager of the property, paid a few of the men part of their back wages in an effort to pacify the others and renew their confidence in the company.

Finally, the Fergus County sheriff seized the entire plant and closed down both mine and mill. This threw all of the men out of work and left their families facing virtual starvation. To increase their discomfort, the winter of 1893-1894 was unusually severe, and with no money forthcoming for food and fuel, thefts became so common that nothing was safe. One man who had a pot of beans simmering on his stove, returned after a few minutes' absence from his cabin to find both pot and beans gone. Some of the desperate men turned to cattle rustling and, although this gave them meat, they had nothing to eat with it.

While the former employees were unsuccessfully trying to scrounge enough food to feed their families, manager Ammon was tipped off by Frank Moshner, who also had a claim against the company, that he feared the property would be attached by the sheriff the next day. Ammon, with the help of an employee, Jack Parr, took all the bullion in the mill, which amounted to $25,000 and, giving it to Parr to carry, made his getaway. Parr left Gilt Edge at five o'clock the morning of January 24, 1894, in a wagon whose bed was weighted down with the stolen gold. A description of the chase to recover the stolen bullion is given in the Fergus County *Argus* (Pictorial Edition). In it, Ammon is described as "a tricky piece of human furniture . . . who could smile on a creditor like one of those bright days in June that you read about." Excerpts from the *Argus* article state that

Parr went through Lewistown at 7:15 A.M. headed for Great Falls. It was ten o'clock before the chase for Ammon and Parr began. Three hours behind them, four deputies started on their trail by as many different routes, each with assignment papers. An attachment was made against the plant at Gilt Edge and was served before noon.

The chase for the fugitives crossed their trail at Stanford, 50 miles from Lewistown on the road to Great Falls. Parr and his wagon were not seen but were believed to be in the neighborhood. Ammon talked his way out of the situation. The sheriff only caught up with the treasure after it was across the county line and in Moshner's possession. At Great Falls the treasure was sold to the Cascade National Bank for $25,000 and Moshner got his money.

Ammon was rash enough to return to Gilt Edge once more and to attempt to pry money from some of its residents. Appraised of his visit, angry employees rushed to the mill, intending to hang him, but again, he eluded them and slipped safely out of town. It is pleasant to report that some time later he did a five-year stretch at Sing Sing Prison in New York State. "Many Gilt Edgers believe he should have been there since 1893."

When the sheriff attached the Gilt Edge property, he found several hundred dollars worth of provisions in the warehouse, and these he distributed to the desperate miners. Through the efforts of the women of Lewistown, two large wagonloads of supplies were also sent to the "famine-stricken" camp.

Calamity Jane was known in Gilt Edge and is even said to have called it her favorite camp. Henry Parrent, who went to Gilt Edge in October, 1898, told Marcella Rawe, a writer for the *Great Falls Tribune* how he met Calamity.

At Gilt Edge I met two remarkable women — my wife and Calamity Jane. She won me a lot of money . . . and that's more than anybody else has ever done. I was sitting in a poker game one night and a tin horn gambler was taking my money away from me right and left.

Realizing that the game was crooked, Parrent pushed back his chair and was ready to leave when

a deep bass voice spoke from behind me, 'stay right where you are young fellow. I'll see that you get fair play.' It was Calamity Jane and she had a nice little gun poking right into the middle of the card game. . . . I stayed where I was and somehow or other my luck began to change and I came out the winner by a whole lot.

She always sat up on the box with the driver whenever she rode the stage and she smoked big black cigars. Once her cigar was pretty nearly smoked up and the driver had just lighted a fresh one. She borrowed his to relight her own and when the driver got it back he had the stub. The last time I saw her she had two tents side by side in Utica and was living in one and washing clothes in the other for the shearers and freighters.
Great Falls Tribune, November 22, 1936

By 1900-1901, Gilt Edge, with a population of "350 people who get direct mail at the post office," was considered one of the best towns in the county. Old photographs show wooden sidewalks in front of stores with false fronts and porches, such as the Gilt Edge Mercantile Company and the Silver Dollar Saloon.

It was during these two years that Dr. Frederick F. Attix, who opened an office at Gilt Edge, served as physician for the Whiskey Gulch, Spotted Horse, and New Year mines. Certain of his experiences are found in an article in the *Lewistown Daily News* of December 21, 1947. His first call was to New Year. This meant a fifteen mile trip in January, 1901, during a blinding blizzard. After

GILTEDGE RUIN

treating the man, who had pneumonia, Attix was asked to carry back with him the first run of gold bricks from the New Year mine. With these in his custody, he returned to Gilt Edge, complaining only that the bricks got pretty heavy before he arrived. Commenting on this case, the doctor recalls that

After a week or two, the patient, Judge Nelson of St. Paul, the treasurer of the New Year Mining Co., wanted to come into Lewistown. We hauled him to the city limits on a sled. Then he wanted to ride into town in style, so we went ahead and came back with a fancy cutter and brought him in.

Mining camps had no infirmaries in those days, nor medical facilities, and the sick were cared for at home or in rough bunkhouses. "All doctoring was done by lamplight." Dr. Attix had but one nurse to assist him — a negress from Fort Maginnis who was "known throughout the Judith Mountains as Old Aunt Fannie." When he finally succeeded in installing a steam shower at Whiskey Gulch, it was an event, for even Gilt Edge had but one tin bathtub, housed in I. M. Beatty's barber shop. Baths were a luxury, especially at the mines where "the miners worked three shifts and as one shift rolled out of bed, the men coming off duty crawled in the other side." According to the doctor,

the cook at one of the camps . . . believed in buying whiskey instead of overcoats. Whenever he got cold he bought another suit of long underwear, until by spring, he was wearing seven suits. Then he would go to Beatty's barber shop, stand his underwear up in a corner like a suit of armor, and take his annual bath.

Gilt Edge reached its peak between 1908 and 1909, and although its mines continued to produce gold for several more years, the quantity tapered off, and in time, the properties were abandoned, as was most of the town.

FORT MAGINNIS

As we left Gilt Edge, I looked to the north and east, searching for the approximate site of Fort Maginnis, the military post which, during the earliest years of mining activity in the Judith Mountains, was situated close to both Maiden and Gilt Edge.

The fort was established in July, 1880, by Captain Dangerfield Park to protect the settlers and stockmen from Indian attacks, and was laid out on ground that was part of Granville Stuart's ranch. The soldiers lived in tents and the officers and their families in log cabins. The fort, which was named for Major Martin Maginnis, a territorial delegate to Congress, was abandoned in 1890, and its buildings carried off by ranchers and people from Lewistown. On the whole, the miners and stockmen found that the fort offered them scant protection from thieving Indians; for stolen horses and cattle were seldom recovered by the soldiers, due, as some of the ranchers said, to "indolence, ignorance or official delay." Of greater service was the Montana Stock Growers' association, which, under the leadership of Granville Stuart, dealt with rustlers, prairie fires, stampeding cattle, stock diseases, and other problems of the range.

While we drove back to Lewistown, I told Francis about Mose Latray, a French Canadian who was the undertaker at Gilt Edge. There were a good many killings in the camp and business was good. The only embalming fluid available was whiskey and Latray disliked wasting it on his cases. So he put charcoal into the bodies instead, which preserved them sufficiently for their long journeys by stagecoach or train.

KENDALL

After our morning visit to Gilt Edge, we had a hasty lunch in Lewistown and directly afterwards set out for Kendall, a mining camp at the foot of the North Moccasin Mountains. What appeared to be dumps and the silhouettes of several large buildings were faintly discernible against the distant hills toward which we were traveling. We drove north out of Lewistown, through Brooks and on to Hilger, where we stopped at the railroad depot to talk to Joe Jost, the station agent, and to admire his fine mineral collection. Mr. Jost pointed beyond the tracks to a gravel road that ran west toward the Moccasin Mountains. "It's a good four miles," he said. "Keep right when you reach the fork to a ranch."

The first part of the trip was across open country. Then the road cut in behind a low ridge of hills, where we found the ranch turn-off that we were to ignore. By now, we were climbing up a shallow gulch, where shrubs and trees were dense enough to shut out any vista ahead. We had come over five miles. From the time we left Hilger until we started up this draw, I had watched the shiny roofs of the mine buildings on the mountainside grow bigger with each mile. Now that we were getting closer, they had disappeared in the folds of the hills.

I had read a good deal about Kendall and had seen photographs of the camp in its prime, when its streets were solidly built up and its several large mining properties equipped with mills and auxiliary buildings. Kendall was not as old as Maiden or Gilt Edge. Surely much of it would have survived.

The strike that produced the new mining camp got under way in the early 1890's. Years before a townsite was laid out, gold had been found in the North Moccasin Mountains and claims staked by a few experienced prospectors. The best placers were found in Iron Gulch, where nuggets weighing up to four ounces were uncovered. Bed Rock and Plum Creeks also yielded colors. These early placer discoveries, as well as the lode mines that were soon found, are described in the initial issue of the *Kendall Miner* (December 8, 1905), in an article called "The Story of Our Famous Mines." Written when they were in active operation, it is perhaps the most accurate account of their start:

Many years before a town in the North Moccasin Mountains was ever dreamed of, the Buchanan brothers and Messrs. Waldorf and Draper and a few others were working over in Iron Gulch in some placer diggings. Their work was fairly successful but there was a lack of sufficient water for sluicing, and after a few seasons, this work was practically abandoned.

W. C. Draper commenced at that time to work on a silver and lead proposition over in Iron Creek vicinity and together with his partner, W. C. Waldorf, still owns some good ground on that side of the mountain.

In 1896, Adolf Harmon located the Horse Shoe and Mule Shoe claims, located at the north end of the present Barnes-King group. J. P. Barnes purchased a half-interest in these claims a year or so later, and Harmon soon afterwards disposed of his other half-interest in them to C. E. Barnes. Little more than the ten-foot hole and assessment work for one or two years had been done up to this time. J. T. Wunderlin and M. L. Woodman located the Discovery claim in 1898 and a few months later in the same year, located the Passaic upon which the mill now stands.

In the same year, Messrs. Draper and Waldorf located a lot of ground now comprising a portion of the Santiago and Kendall group of claims. When they came to stake it off they decided to let the Kendall ground go. Thus for the first time was this property, now worth millions, cast aside.

Shortly after this, in 1898, Charlie Allen located some claims now among the most valuable of the Kendall group and gave Tom Riser a half-interest for digging a ten-foot hole on one of them.

Harry T. Kendall, who had cleaned up a neat stake by working over some tailings in the Judith Mountains bought out Tom Riser's half interest for $150.00 cash and took a six-month's bond on Allen's half-interest for $500.00. He took up this bond in the spring of 1900, having had two men working on the property during the life of the bond. Shortly after the bond was taken up, a small cyanide mill was erected and Kendall commenced to work some of the ore. The process was a success from the start and the proceeds more than paid for further development of the ground. That fall the property was bonded by Kendall to Finch and Campbell of Spokane for $50,000, Kendall retaining a one-tenth interest, valued at that time at $50,000.

In March of 1901, Henry Parrent (who had been in the Gilt Edge excitement) struggled through a blizzard to reach the new camp which was just beginning to sprout, and found a number of miners already at work. Joe Wunderlin, one of the original discoverers, and a few others had log cabins, but the majority of the men were living in tents. Parrent, who was sent there to put up a new mill at the Kendall mine, found that a number of claims had already been staked near Wunderlin and Kendall properties and several placers had been located farther back in the hills. On July 4, the *Great Falls Tribune* printed a description of the camp:

Real estate is changing hands and forty lots have been sold from $75-$200. . . . Thirty men are employed at the Kendall . . . and the hills are full of prospectors who are looking for 'cyanide ore.'

Three mills are now running and two more nearing completion. . . . The production of gold will be this year in excess of $1,000,000 of which the Kendall will produce one-half. . . . There are some copper and lead properties of promise that would be working in any other county where there is railroad transportation. . . .

In the same belt to the east are the Draper and Waldorf properties. . . . Ten men have been working here. . . . Still farther east and about one-half mile from Kendall is the Barnes-King property, where the same character of ore is opened up. A 100-ton mill is under construction and the woodwork is mostly completed, and the machinery is due, with one carload at Fort Benton and one at Harlow.

Stage service meets the Montana Railroad at that point and fifty-five miles brings one to Lewistown.

Western Mining World
Great Falls Tribune, July 4, 1901

From 1901 to the final shut down in the 1920's, the four most productive properties were the Kendall, Santiago, Barnes- King, and Horse Shoe, each of which included a group of claims.

Harry T. Kendall, one of the most successful mining men in the county, came to Montana in 1878 at the age of eighteen and settled on a ranch near Ubet in 1880. He gave up ranching for prospecting and was soon working in the Spotted Horse and Maginnis mines at Maiden. He also ran a small smelter in Alpine Gulch, but it was soon abandoned. From it, he went to the North Moccasins and bought a prospect that was "little more than a discovery hole," although it had been found ten years before by Ira Knapp, George Mason, and others. A certain amount of assessment work had been completed on it; still it failed to show ore. A few hundred feet from it was another prospect called the Leaking claim, which interested Kendall even more; for in it, he recognized a "cyanide prospect." This he bought for $500 or $650 from Charles Allen in November, 1899, as well as the adjoining Klondike claim, for which he paid $1,500. Within a year he had erected a small cyanide mill, a residence, a boardinghouse for his forty employees, and a stable on the property; and by 1901, when he bonded it, an estimated 150,000 tons of ore were in sight. The *Helena Semi-Weekly Herald* of June 14, 1901, describes the next development:

A new corporation known as the Kendall Gold Mining Co. has been organized with a capital stock of $2,500,000 in $5.00 shares. The trustees are: A. B. Campbell, John A. Finch and R. K. Neill of Spokane; Henry Wick of New York and H. T. Kendall of Lewistown. The property . . . has been a dividend payer from the grass roots.
Great Falls Tribune, July 4, 1901

By July the plant was running smoothly, cyaniding 100 tons of ore per day which averaged $8.00 a ton. The efficacy of this mill is described by the *Fergus County Argus:*

The ore is not sorted. Everything goes, except the cookstove and the family Bible, and they would go too if they were as highly mineralized as the rest of the stuff. Kendall says he never found a piece of waste. The ore lies from the grass roots and the grass roots go in to.
Pictorial Edition, *Fergus County Argus*

Early in 1901 the big Kendall mill was erected and immediately began to grind out gold bricks. This profitable process continued for over four years with the results given below:

In the five years of its operation, the output of the Kendall mine in bullion is $2,500,000 paying $1,000,-000 in dividends, besides creating a substantial sink-

ing fund and paying for all plant installations and improvements, including an electric plant. This property would pay double the present amount of dividends were it worked to full capacity.
Kendall Miner, December 8, 1905

Part of the Kendall Mining Company's development included the purchase of water rights to Big Warm Spring, which was located on the Horseshoe Bar ranch of Oscar Stephens. A large ditch was constructed to connect the spring with a power plant, built five miles downstream for the purpose of supplying electricity to the Kendall and Barnes-King properties. The Kendall mine continued to be worked until 1913. An estimated 700,000 tons of ore were removed from it and dividends amounting to $1,450,000 were paid its investors.

In 1915 the Barnes-King Development Company bought the Kendall mine and mill and the 400-horse power hydroelectric plant on Warm Spring Creek, as well as a controlling interest in the North Moccasin Gold Mining Company's holdings. The Barnes-King company did not work the Kendall mine, but leased it. Up until 1921, operations were largely confined to excavations in an open pit and to further exploration of the upper levels of the Kendall shaft, which was sunk an additional 63 feet.

Ore was discovered in the Santiago group of claims in 1898, but it was not until June of 1907 that they and the Barnes-King properties were combined. In 1908, after the collapse of the Barnes-King company, the six Santiago claims which lay between the Kendall and the Barnes-King holdings, were sold to the North Moccasin Gold Mining Company, which already owned ground in the same area and had erected the third mill in the district as early as April, 1902. Prior to 1909, 27,500 tons of ore had been mined with a yield of $127,000 in gold bullion.

In 1912, the property was reopened and worked through the Barnes-King mine. When, by July, 1920, even the $3.00 ore was believed to be exhausted, the company shut down. Lessees then proceeded to operate the mine and mill "on a sliding scale of royalties." In 1923, all work ceased.

The Barnes-King ore body was discovered in 1893, but little was done with the prospect until 1901. In the spring of 1900, E. M. King obtained a bond to the property, valued at $75,000, and although he worked a force of several men at the mine, when the bond expired, he did not take it up, but offered to

KENDALL MAIN STREET

VAULT IN RUINED BUILDING, KENDALL

build a 100-ton cyanide mill in return for a half-interest in the group of claims. This was agreeable to the several owners — J. T. Wunderlin, John P. Barnes, M. L. Woodman, and C. E. Barnes; whereupon "Mr. King succeeding in interesting Messrs. A. D. Ledeaux (Ledoux) and W. B. Devereaux (Devereux), two Colorado mining men and capitalists, in the proposition." With the consolidation of these several interests, the Barnes-King Mining Company was organized in 1901, under the control of E. W. King.

Just what the bullion output has been is known only to the management as the figures have never been made public. It is safe to put the yield at $700 or $800 a day. The cost of mining and milling is about $2.00 a ton, (so) a large margin of profit is left to the Company.

Kendall Chronicle, March 25, 1902

At the close of 1905, the *Kendall Miner* reported favorably that

The Barnes-King output, since the plant first went into operation four years ago, is $1,800,000 and half--a-million has been returned in dividends to shareholders besides the payment of large amounts of development work of all kinds.

December 8, 1905

From time to time the owners of the bonanza received offers to buy the mine, but these were consistently refused, until the middle of 1906, when Butte and New York capitalists were permitted to send experts to examine the property. Their report was so glowing that an offer of $1,200,000 was made and accepted, with negotiations concluded in August. The first payment was made in September; the final amount was due on March 1, 1907. According to the *Kendall Miner* (April 5, 1907), "Three Lewistown men," John P. Barnes, M. L. Woodman, and J. T. Wunderlin, received "close to one-half million dollars" from the final payment for the property.

The new company of eastern capitalists immediately reorganized and incorporated as the Barnes-King Development Company, with a capital stock of $2,000,000. According to report, "this stock was oversubscribed by half a million within eight hours," of its listing on the market. The company made further developments of its property and hired 200 additional men. All seemed prosperous until fall, when an unfavorable report caused the stock to tumble.

The Barnes-King Development Co. bubble has burst and several thousand stock holders in Butte and else-where . . . have been brought to realize that they are victims one and all.

Kendall Miner, October 11, 1907

Not only the stockholders, but also the promoters were caught in the crash; so it is not surprising that by November, the mill shut down, although the reason given was "a shortage of cyanide." The company later resumed operations and is reported to have mined 237,-195 tons of ore which yielded $828,110 in gold bullion between 1907-1910. It worked intermittently on its own and additional acquired properties until about 1920. In December, 1925, the Barnes-King Development Company was legally dissolved and trustees were appointed to supervise the property.

The Horseshoe group was the most northerly of the gold mines and was worked chiefly through open cuts and small stopes. In 1905, work was begun on a 6,000-foot tunnel, which was planned to tap existent ore bodies in the Horse Shoe and Mule Shoe claims.

From 1901, when the town of Kendall began to emerge as a settlement instead of a colony of tents and stray cabins, its growth was sure and rapid.

Things are Lively on the Avenue
(On) McKinley Ave. . . . from end to end graders and carpenters are at work. Kendall is but one year old, yet it is the brightest and snappiest camp in the state.

Kendall Chronicle, April 15, 1902

Ranchers and business people from nearby towns moved in with their families. A small school grew so rapidly that before the first white child born in Kendall was old enough to attend school, several teachers were employed and the large school building was too small.

Great Falls Tribune, July 14, 1935

Jealous of Kendall
There are a few people in Lewistown who feel some alarm lest the growth of Kendall may injure the business and future prospects of the former place. On occasion they display a spirit of envy.

Kendall Chronicle, May 20, 1902

Much building went on during 1902 and 1903, with several of the new structures made of stone. One of these, the R. C. Cook building, contained a banking house and provided a hall for lodge gatherings. Another stone structure was the H. V. Turner block, which was devoted to merchandise. Probably the most pretentious building was the wedge-shaped Shaules Hotel at the junction of King Mill Road, Teddy Street, and McKinley Avenue.

VIEW FROM KENDALL ACROSS VALLEY TO JUDITH MOUNTAINS

This handsome, fireproof, two-story stone hostelry, which was built by W. A. Shaules and cost $12,000, contained twenty-six bedrooms, a ladies' parlor, hot and cold baths, and was heated by hot air and lighted by electricity. The hotel was opened in February, 1903, with a ball at which "the attendance was so large that sometimes the dance floor was taxed to its utmost."

Early in 1902, the Kendall Stage Company began to run four-horse coaches daily (except Sundays) between Lewistown and the camp. The stages left Lewistown at 9 a.m. and reached Kendall two and a half hours later. On March 25, 1902, the initial issue of the *Kendall Chronicle* announced additional transportation facilities:

Locomobile for Kendall
Space to be Literally Annihilated by Rapidly Moving
Vehicles
Within a few weeks passengers can travel between here and Harlowton on a locomobile, and the time of the journey will be but a few hours. John R. Cook, the hustler for Kendall is to solve the transportation problem. . . . It is his intention to introduce an locomobile just as soon as it can be built, and construction is now in progress in Spokane. . . . The locomobile is to be operated by steam, and gasoline will be the fuel consumed. . . . It . . . shall have a carrying capacity of 4000 pounds, and as many as 16 passengers will find accommodations. The front car, (there will be two), will carry the propelling apparatus along with baggage and express matter. The rear car will carry the human freight. The wheels are to have four-inch solid rubber tires. This breadth of tire will help to solve the problem of traveling over roads in muddy condition. It is estimated that not over two gallons of gasoline will be used in making the trip. It is expected that 12 miles an hour will be made with ease. This will put Kendall within easy distance of the railroad.

June 13 was celebrated in all the camps where the Miners' Union was established. Kendall's program in 1902 was "pulled off according to schedule."

The first event was the Miners' Union march headed by the Lewistown band, to the pavilion, where the Hon. J. H. Calderhead, Auditor of state, delivered the address. The speaker was of the opinion that the interests of the people of the United States would be best served by the government owning the railroads and other public utilities, and that a socialistic system should supplant the present order of things. This sentiment met with the approval of the audience. The festivities closed with a double-hand rock drilling contest for a purse of $150.

Kendall Chronicle, June 17, 1902

363

Other celebrations during 1902 such as the Fourth of July and Christmas were described in the *Chronicle*:

The cold wave somewhat chilled the ardor for outdoor sports and games but many visitors came and all enjoyed themselves to their full capacity.

At 10 o'clock a.m., aa large crowd had assembled on the platform where the dance was to take place later in the day, to hear Miss Alma Meyers of Deerfield read the Declaration of Independence and afterwards Judge Cheadle, the orator of the day, commanded the attention of a most appreciative audience. Miss Meyers done herself well in the reading and her fine clear voice carried each word distinctly to the farthest limits of the audience.

Kendall Chronicle, July 8, 1902

Christmas Entertainment
Last Wednesday evening (Christmas eve) the spacious hall on the first floor of the bank building was comfortably filled with parents and friends of the children of the Kendall public school.

At the close of the program Miss Ella McLain came forward and after reciting the following stanza composed by Mrs. O. F. Wasmansdorf, presented to Mrs. Henry a ring with an opal setting:

Santa Claus is here on Christmas eve to treat the
        children of Kendall town;
He's watched us sing and speak and drill,
But he hasn't forgotten the patient skill
Of the teacher who taught us without a frown;
And he brought a ring, a little thing, a token of
        the days of Yule;
We ask you to take with the love of all the children
        who go to school.

The presentation came as a surprise to Mrs. Henry. Santa Claus then entered and distributed bags of nuts and candies.

Kendall Chronicle, December 30, 1902

By 1905, the *Butte Evening News*, in its Christmas supplement, described Kendall as having a population of 1,300, and 700 lots platted by the Townsite Company for sale at prices ranging from $50-$500. The town, which was lighted with electricity, generated by the Kendall Mining Company's power plant, had two banks and the Jones Opera House, a two-story, dressed stone edifice, in which reserved seats cost $1.00, with the balance of the main floor 75 cents, and the balcony 50 cents. Each year the camp increased.

The number of people who go over to Kendall every day tax the capacity of the coaches, three of which leave Lewistown every day with an occasional extra thrown in when passenger traffic becomes congested. On the road one meets dozens of two, four and six horse teams hauling merchandise, mining supplies and coal in to camp.

The two big producers — Kendall & Barnes-King are running full blast.

Kendall Miner, April 13, 1906

In May "property owners and public spirited citizens" met to consider the construction of waterworks "to cost not over $2000 . . . the water to be used for fire protection only." As Labor Day approached, the town arranged for a rousing celebration, to include a ball game and a contest between members of the Gun Club and the "Lewistown shotgun artists."

Farmers for miles around suspended operations in hay fields. Mines and mills were practically deserted . . . and a constant stream of vehicles arrived from Maiden, Gilt Edge, Lewistown, etc.
The parade was led by the famous K. P. band . . . the line of march was down McKinley Ave. and then to the bandstand . . . where the oration of the day was delivered by T. E. Latimer of Seattle. Mr. Latimer in a masterful manner depicted the labor conditions in various parts of the country. . . . When the multitude had been fed with sumptuous chicken dinners provided by the several hotels and restaurants, they gathered around the block of granite at the head of McKinley Ave. (the band was there) in anticipation of the drilling contest (and the) tug of war near the Kendall Hotel.

Kendall Miner, September 7, 1906

Rock drilling contests were a standard event in all mining celebrations. One that was held in Hilger, in 1907, is described by E. B. Coolidge in the *Lewistown Daily News* of December 21, 1947. On this occasion, his team from the Spotted Horse mine at Maiden competed against those from the Kendall and the Barnes-King mines. At that time, each of the Kendall properties employed over 200 men, while the Spotted Horse had a crew of but 25 or 30. The boulder to be drilled weighed five tons. The two Kendall teams participated first, the Barnes-King men drilling a hole 39½ inches deep, a record for the county at that time. Coolidge was so sure of his boys that he "could easily have wagered $10,000" on the outcome, as the Barnes-King employees had plenty of money with which to place bets and were positive their team would win. The Spotted Horse contestants — Chris Carstensen and Fred Sherman — were the last to compete. Both were experts and Carstensen "struck 36 blows in 30 seconds the last half-minute he was on the rock, using an eight-pound hammer." According to Coolidge, "He had given his all, as he fainted when crawling down off the rock. A steel tape was run in the hole and it was found to be 41⅛ inches deep. So," concludes

Mr. Coolidge, "my boys won the prize money and I was only too glad to buy them each gold medals with their names engraved thereon describing the event."

Kendall and Lewistown were kept in a dither during 1907 as survey crews and inspection parties looked into the feasibility of running a railroad to the mines.

Walter J. Hill and retinue were in Lewistown on Wednesday after a tour of inspection of their new line now being built. While there he settled the question as to who would get the new road and said "We will build to Kendall and leave Lewistown for the Milwaukee people." Operations will begin immediately following the finishing of the Stanford tunnel.

Kendall Miner, May 17, 1907

Plans to erect a Presbyterian church were also well under way by summer.

While the miner has very little to say regarding church matters in Kendall, still we do not wish people to think that we are infidelic. It is true that we go fishin' on Sunday and do other things too numerous to mention that are not orthodox, yet we want to put ourselves on record as believing in Christianity. . . . We want to see a church building go up, in Kendall, this summer and we are willing to donate fifty percent of all money paid in during the month of August for subscriptions to the *Miner*, either as part or paid in advance.

Kendall Miner, August 2, 1907

Corner Stone is Laid

The cornerstone was laid Monday at 3:30 p.m. in the presence of a large crowd. School children marched in a body from the schoolhouse to Jones' Opera House and from there to the church lot. . . . The Trustees of the church had the honor of placing the stone in position and a tin box containing a Bible, a list of church members, trustees, Ladies Aid, workmen, a copy of the *Kendall Miner* etc. were sealed into the stone, to be opened many generations hence. The new church will cost $3500.

Kendall Miner, November 1, 1907

As long as Kendall's mines produced, Kendall flourished, and as long as the town boomed, the freighters kept busy. By 1913, Fergus County, in which Kendall lay, was the foremost gold-producing section of the state. Henry Parrent in his reminiscences mentions that no provision was made for guarding the gold that was shipped out. Mine office safes were much too small to hold the accumulation of bricks that were sent from time to time to the Lewistown banks. One day, when Parrent's wife rode to Lewistown with the mine secretary, her feet rested on $30,000 worth of gold bricks, each of which was valued at $2,000.

"It was better to disguise the gold or send it another way than to risk a shooting and having good men killed," said Mr. Parrent. "No one knew when the gold would be taken out. A stage driver brought two kegs of nails from Great Falls to Lewistown one day and nobody ever knew it was money until he stopped at the bank."

Great Falls Tribune, November 22, 1936

Kendall's peak population is said to have been 1,500, and its mines are credited with having produced a certain nine million and a rumored thirteen to fifteen million in gold. Placers yielded between $10,000 and $50,000. In 1920, when the Barnes-King Development Company ceased to operate, the town collapsed.

Down from the canyon where the noise of a thriving town had been came wagons loaded with everything from children to building materials. The houses were drawn on skids to become dwelling or hen houses of ranchers in the valley. Silence descended upon the mountains.

Great Falls Tribune, July 14, 1935

From 1920 on, what little production was carried on was done intermittently by leasers. For a time during the middle 1930's, Mrs. J. H. McLean successfully managed certain mining operations, using surface and open cut methods; but since then, the district has been neglected, although it is believed that there are still 150,000 tons of ore in the abandoned properties.

Realizing that most of Kendall's buildings had been razed or trundled away in the 1920's, I was disappointed, but not too surprised, as we drove out of the trees onto a sloping meadow, to find only three or four sizable ruins still standing, although the foundations and excavation holes that flanked the roadway revealed the numbers of structures that once stood upon them. We drove past the broken stone walls and rubble piles, up to the head of the street, where the mines were. The mills were gone, but huge mounds of tawny, gouged-out earth laid bare the surface of the mountain and formed a rust-colored backdrop to the townsite. As the road climbed in among these dumps, we passed vestiges of loading stations and more foundations and, when we were close to the biggest cut, we could see trench-like fissures extending into the mountain.

Beyond, on the right side of the road, was a huge tailings dump and the splintered remains of a building. The road continued to climb and then forked, one branch turning down the mountain and the other rising to the left, in among open-pit workings. We tried it, although its surface was much the rougher. More broken-down wooden debris from small mine buildings was visible and more dumps, with vestiges beside them of ladders, steps, and flattened buildings; but not the long, shiny roofs that we had seen from Hilger.

Back again at the forks we took the lower road, which curved around the shoulder of the hill and brought us to workings on the front of the mountain and to a group of mine buildings of a later date than the other properties we had seen. These were covered with tar paper and had metal roofs. At last we discovered the gleaming structures that had lured us from Hilger! On a flat below the workings were several large cabins, probably bunkhouses. In exploring this area, we crossed an earth bridge, above and below which a great cut in the yellowish earth had been made. Beyond this cut was a flat bench and there the drivable road ended. On the edges of the flat and below it were a number of buildings, long sheds, a mill and a gas pump. In front of us was the valley, stretching for miles across the plains to Hilger and beyond as far as the Judith Mountains. We could only see their base; for low clouds sliced off their summits.

As we retraced our way to the head of the sloping meadow and looked down on the site of Kendall, we noticed faint, grass-grown tracks that had once been streets, leading off from the main road. When we reached the few stone sentinels that remain as evidence of the once active camp, we stopped to investigate them.

Of the two that stood on the east side of the street, one had a swaybacked roof or perhaps it was a ceiling, for a few feet above it rose the walls of a second story, part of which was still intact. This portion was entered from a back street that was gouged out of the hillside, several feet above the main road.

Farther down, on the west side of the main thoroughfare, was a large stone building with three distinct divisions. The left hand unit was two stories high and its inside walls were covered with lath, to which clung large patches of plaster. The level of the second floor and the location of a staircase were visible on the righthand wall. Also on this wall, at the first floor level, was an archway that led to the middle section of the building. A rear door and window openings pierced the first floor and basement walls. What little was left of the façade was made of dressed stone. The building had a full basement from the middle of which rose an oblong unit. This sturdy stone pedestal, reaching to above the level of the second floor, contained a door. It must have been a vault and the building a bank, hotel, or store. From old photos, the location appeared to be at the corner of McKinley Avenue and Teddy Street. Some distance back from the ruin, on the opposite side of McKinley Avenue (which runs east and west), was another two-story stone shell with a full basement and windows on each floor. Could this have been the Presbyterian church about which I had read? There was no one to ask, for the only life that we saw in Kendall were grazing cattle.

Just before we left Lewistown, we stopped at the Fergus County Courthouse to see if they had a plat of Kendall. In answer to my request, Miss Dorothy R. Woods, in the Recorder's Office, took the plat from a large bin of maps at one side of the room and gave me paper on which to copy it. In addition to the diagram of the streets, the hand-lettered document contained the following description:

O. F. Wasmandorff, civil engineer and surveyor, made the survey of the Kendall Townsite, . . . the streets of said Townsite (excepting McKinley St. and Main St.) are 60'0" wide. McKinley St. being 80'0" wide; that the alleys thereof are all 20'0" wide, that all rectangular lots are 100'0" long and of a width as shown on the plat.

(signed by Shaules 31st day of May 1902
Kendall Investment Co.
by Jno. R. Cook. Pres't.
William A. Shaules (seal)
Mary A. Shaules (seal)

On the drawing I noticed that three thoroughfares — McKinley Avenue, Teddy Street, and King Mill Road — met at angles to form the hub of the plan. The other streets, which were arranged in gridiron fashion, bore proper names such as Garfield and Lincoln Avenues, Astor and Clark Streets, or those of trees — Elm, Spruce, Cedar, Pine, and Wood. In addition, there were Beacon and Center Streets, Prospect Avenue, and Kendall Mill Road. A second plat, dated March, 1903, showed the Draper Addition.

All the way south to Harlowton, we were enveloped in sheets of rain that turned the windshield into an opaque screen through which the fenceposts beside the road appeared distorted into grimacing shapes.

"I meant to tell you about the man who liked to stay in jail," I told Francis as we drove cautiously through the downpour. "His name was Livingston, but everyone called him 'Libby.' He lived at Maiden at the time that the citizens were taking up a collection with which to build a jail, and Libby gave five dollars. When the building was completed, the people decided to name it after the first person who was locked up in it. Libby was not only the first occupant, but also a frequent tenant, and folks said it was because he wanted to get a return on his investment. By the time he drifted to Kendall, they already had a jail. But by then, he had a pattern established. He never waited to be arrested; whenever he got drunk, he went weaving down the street to the jail and stayed there until he sobered up."

By the time we reached Harlowton, the rain stopped, but the clouds were down and the mountains on all sides were hidden. As this was no day to explore old towns, we drew into a motel by mid-afternoon, thankful for a place in which to be warm and dry. On the wall of our unit was a cupboard with a sign:

There is enough coffee in the percolator for 4 cups.

Fill coffee pot with water before plugging in.

On the shelf were two china mugs. Never did coffee taste so good to a pair of wet and draggled wanderers.

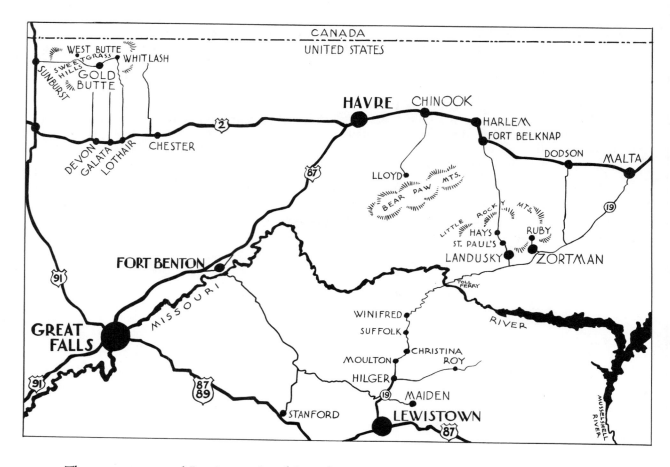

CHAPTER 21

THE LITTLE ROCKIES and the SWEETGRASS HILLS

The country around Lewistown is cultivated wheatland, but farther north the terrain is less productive and the grasslands are replaced by alkali-strewn, sagebrush prairie, where dryland farmers periodically homestead barren acres only to abandon them when prolonged drought blights their crops and kills their cattle. Through this arid stretch flows the Missouri River, whose eroded badland brakes served as hideouts for outlaws during Montana's cattle wars. Some distance north of the river, rise the Little Rockies, an isolated range of mountains, called by the Indians the Island Mountains, since they thrust themselves out of the high, dusty plain that stretches to the horizon. When gold was found in them, two mining camps sprang up, and it was these semi-ghost towns that I was eager to investigate.

When we inquired in Lewistown about the roads to the mining camps of Landusky and Zortman, and about the ferry across the Missouri, everyone cautioned us against making the trip. "It's a dry weather road," said one. "If you get stuck, you're stuck." "I had to sit in my car all night till the gumbo dried

out," said another. "Be sure to call the D. Y. garage man at Winifred before you start," said a filling station agent in Lewistown. "He can tell you if it's slick." We took his advice and called up. The road was dry; it hadn't rained in four days.

Leaving Lewistown, we drove straight north, between wheatfields and prosperous ranches, through the grain-elevator towns of Hilger, Moulton, Christina, and Suffolk to Winifred. At the D. Y. Garage, we asked more specifically about the road. "It's a dirt road," the agent said, "but it's all right. You won't have any trouble and you can't get off it."

From the time we left Winifred until we slid down a gumbo-covered hill to the banks of the Missouri River, we were on our own. The road, if it might be so-called, was no more than two rutted tracks stretching thirty-five miles across a dry, dusty plain. Every few miles it made a right-angled turn, as it skirted some dryland farmer's property — the farm buildings as bleached as the landscape. Parched, cracked earth, white with alkali deposits, stretched as far as one could see on either side of the road; or the alkali lay in caked sloughs in the middle of fields and arid pastures. I think we passed six ranches four of which were deserted, and but three cars, in the thirty-five miles to the river.

Some distance ahead, a deep gorge, rimmed with chalk-colored bluffs, indicated that we were nearing the Missouri. As we approached this gash, the land became more rolling and vegetation increased slightly. Within the next few miles, we caught a glimpse of the river, far below, winding between high, sandy bluffs and edged with thickets of willow.

Finally, the road swung into a narrow canyon and corkscrewed down from the rim to the water's edge. It was hot in the canyon and the roadbed, to our surprise, was slick red mud, making it necessary to guide the car with extreme care to avoid slewing into the gully beside us. At the last blind curve was a crude sign — "River 200 feet." The road ended abruptly in the water, where car tracks disappeared into the swirling current. There was no dock, no parking area — just muddy ruts, washed by the water. A steel cable was anchored on shore and spanned the river, which at this place was several hundred yards wide. The chain ferry was docked on the far side, close to a farmhouse, hidden in a thicket of willows and brush. It took several blasts of our horn to rouse the ferryman, but in time we saw him walk slowly down the bank, board the boat, and adjust the rudder. The flat scow, which was chained to the overhead cable, was propelled across the river by the push of the current. It was just large enough for one car or truck, and the only guard rails were on the sides. As it bumped the shore, the ferryman jumped off and hooked it to a ring, secured to a post. We drove aboard and the man

loosed the hook and with a long pole, which was kept on the shore, pushed us off and then jumped on. With a windlass attached to the cable, he wound or unwound the steel drum as needed, thus controlling the course of the craft. All too soon, we bumped the far bank, and Francis drove off into more mud. He paid the man the $2.00 ferrage and offered him a tip, which he refused, saying that the fare went to the rancher who owned the ferry and that he was paid wages.

"Where does all this mud come from?" asked Francis as we pulled up the bank to the road. "We were told it hadn't rained for days."

"We had an inch of rain last night," replied the ferryman. "Watch out for mud holes as you go. To get to Landusky, you follow the road down the river about a mile. Then it climbs out of the brakes back from the river."

The narrow trail hugged the shore at first and then wound up a gully between chalky, eroded cliffs to the top of a hill and the open prairie. In the next eighteen miles we passed a few ramshackle, empty ranches, and we saw some cattle. One truck approached us in a cloud of alkali dust, and everyone waved as it passed. The roadbed was so rutted that it was impossible to go faster than thirty miles an hour. In three places on this lonely stretch were almost obliterated signs marked "Ferry," pointing back toward the river.

With each mile the Little Rockies loomed larger. Finally, when a dirt road branched north and ran straight toward them, we took it. Before long we entered the Lewis and Clark National Forest, and the roadbed improved. Now we were close enough to see mine dumps on the mountainsides. About six miles from the roadfork, we rounded a corner and found ourselves on the main street of Landusky.

LANDUSKY

No one seems certain who found the first gold in the Little Rockies. That the Indians knew of it seems likely, for they are believed to have shown samples of the yellow metal to two French priests who visited them in the middle 1860's. The priests were warned not to mention the gold lest the Whites come to the mountains and overrun the Indians' lands. In 1867, a priest was killed by the Indians, presumably because he knew the whereabouts of the treasure. To protect their land further, the Indians posted scouts to keep out intruders. As late as 1875, the few white men who passed through the country reported having seen sentries in the Little Rockies.

According to Al J. Noyes' book *In the Land of the Chinook, a Story of Blaine County*, the first settlement in the Little Rockies was set up by fur traders on Rock Creek, one mile east of Landusky. The four men who made up the party left Fort Benton on October 1, 1865, in a mackinaw loaded with goods for trade with the Indians. By the middle of the month, they beached near a number of lodges belonging to Gros Ventres and River Crows, whose encampment was at the mouth of a creek. Here the men obtained horses from the Indians and planned to build their post, but they were advised by the redskins to move upstream, toward the mountains, so as to avoid trouble with the warlike Sioux. The men took this advice and built four log cabins and a stockade on Rock Creek, where they remained four months trading for fur robes with the Indians and encountering no trouble. The Indian encampment contained about five hundred lodges with "five people to a lodge."

Another account concerns Chris Kies, who disappeared in the same area at about the same time and whose entry into the region has certain similarities. In the middle 1860's, Kies and his partner, John Lepley, mined and ranched near Silver Creek in Lewis and Clark country. Kies became discontented with this life and left for Fort Benton, where he bought an outfit and a mackinaw and set off alone on an exploring trip downstream. The next winter he reappeared in Fort Benton with a poke of dust and sent a message to Lepley, urging him to sell out his holdings and join him in a new venture — a rich gold strike. After waiting some time for Lepley, who failed to appear, Kies confided his secret to three other men and the party started down the river, each man accompanied by an Indian squaw. Their trust in Kies must have been implicit, for he refused to divulge their destination. On the way to the diggings, the party was attacked by Indians, and all were killed except one of the squaws. The location of Kies' lost mine is thought to be in the Little Rockies.

One other incident proves the Indians' awareness of gold in their isolated mountains. On Thanksgiving Day, 1868, at Fort Browning, on the Milk River, fifty miles below the site of Fort Belknap, an officers' dinner was in progress, when an Indian, known as Nepee, came to the fort and displayed a small pouch of gold dust and nuggets to Major John Sim-

mons, Capt. D. W. Buck, James Stuart, and Major Culberton. Nepee, who was on good terms with the officers, gave the sack to Major Simmons, but no amount of questioning induced him to reveal the source of the gold. If he told, he assured the officers, he would be killed by his own people.

Perhaps Nepee did tell Joe Hontus, for the two were close friends and had "slept together and been on the prairie together for weeks and months at a time." If so, his information probably led to Hontus' death. A few years later, Hontus boasted, while drunk, that he knew where the mines were and that he was going to find them. He evidently started out and was discovered by some members of Nepee's tribe, for his bullet-riddled body was found sometime later. Nepee died in 1876.

Some say that William Hamilton's party made the first strike in 1868. Frank Aldrich, Powell Landusky, and "Dutch" Louie Meyers, who found gold in the region in 1884, say that they stumbled upon a pit 100 by 150 feet, near the mouth of Beauchamp's Creek, that had been sluiced out years before. Harry Rash, who also prospected with Landusky and Dutch Louie, told of camping on Alder Gulch and finding the above-mentioned pit, some tools, and possibly the remains of the prospectors who had worked it.

During the eighties, rustlers, road agents, and gunmen hid out in the badlands along the banks of the Missouri. When Wyoming ran its desperadoes out, they headed for Montana and the unmapped brakes of the river. These "wolfers" and toughs used Dutch Louie's ranch at Crooked River as a stopping place as they traveled to and from their lairs in the cottonwood thickets and eroded canyons that led back from the river. Fearing that he would be identified with them and would be hunted down by the Vigilantes, Dutch quit the ranch and, with Powell Landusky and Frank Aldrich, went to the Little Rockies to prospect.

Powell Landusky, or "Pike" as he was called, was a native Missourian of French and Polish descent, who drifted west to Montana in 1864, coming up the Missouri by steamboat to Fort Benton, bound for Last Chance Gulch. He was only fourteen at the time, a rangy, quarrelsome six-footer, who became known as one of the best shots in the West and one of the toughest fighters. His generosity to friends was as well known as his hatred of enemies, especially Indians. His uncontrolled temper and his complete fearlessness made him a dangerous

LANDUSKY, LOOKING WEST

LANDUSKY'S MAIN STREET

antagonist. In Last Chance Gulch he received his nickname of Pike. When teased and asked where he came from, he knocked his tormentor down and replied with an oath, "From Pike County, Missouri."

He left Last Chance in 1868 to trap and hunt with John Wirt, whose headquarters on the Missouri River were at the mouth of the Musselshell. From then until he discovered gold in the Little Rockies, the stories of his savage fights and vengeful retaliations were common talk. One writer in describing him says that "he never killed a white man, just beat them with his hands so they didn't fight any more." His hatred for Indians included all tribes.

When he was captured by a war party of Brules, he hammered one of them with a frying pan and then tore off the brave's breech clout and beat him with it. The Indians, believing Pike to be crazy and therefore to be feared, withdrew, leaving two ponies to propitiate the evil spirit which so obviously possessed him.

371

Once when Pike and Wirt were on the Musselshell, a party of twenty-two Sioux visited their camp while Pike was cooking meat over the fire. One of the Sioux snatched one of the hot steaks. Pike angrily threw the man into the fire and, seizing his gun, beat the rest of the Indians with it, kicking them until they scattered. They, too, thought him crazy.

One winter, Pike and Flopping Bill had a camp twenty miles down the river from Rocky Point, where they traded whiskey to the Indians. When three Sioux came to trade, Pike recognized two of them as part of the band that had stolen his horses, pelts, and traps the preceding winter, and had beaten him up. Pike warned the "Flopper" that he was going to kill all three. After two were disposed of, he ran after the third with an ax, and chased him onto the river ice where he hacked him to pieces. He then scalped the bodies and pushed them through a hole in the ice to destroy any evidence. This was too much for Flopping Bill, who promptly dissolved the partnership.

Up until 1880, Pike trapped and hunted and maintained a woodpile for river steamers. In 1880, he built a trading post on Flatwillow Creek, seventy miles southeast of Lewistown, and took as partners, John J. Healy and a man named Hamilton. Another Indian fight ended this enterprise. While drunk, Pike fired his rifle into an Indian lodge and shot White Calf's squaw. A Blackfeet brave fired his buffalo gun at Pike, tearing away part of his jaw. Pike yanked out the loose flesh and bone containing four teeth, and threw them on the ground. It took his partners a week to get him to Lewistown and Dr. LaPalme, during which time and for ten days thereafter, he lived exclusively on whisky. After his recovery, in the spring of 1881, he and Hamilton opened in Maiden a saloon which he operated for three years. While there, he married a widow, Mrs. Descry (Dessery), who had several children. Their marriage by "Pony" McPartlan, justice of the peace, is said to have been the first in the mining camp. In 1884, he took his family to the Little Rockies, to a ranch near the mouth of Alder Gulch.

The placer gold that was found at the mouth of Alder Gulch in 1884 caused a brief boom and brought many prospectors to the gulches. No one is certain, but several old-timers agree that Dutch Louie Meyers made the first discovery. At any rate, Louie, Landusky, and Aldrich seem to have been in at the start of things; for as Aldrich related later on, he and Charles Brown, while prospecting in the same gulch, came upon Dutch Louie at work on June 15, 1884. He had found colors but had not examined the ground thoroughly. Aldrich seems to have been associated with Louie and Landusky from then on; for as soon as the discovery was made, Landusky left to take the news to friends at Maiden, and Aldrich was sent to Fort Assiniboine for grub. During the two weeks and two days that Aldrich was away, Louie panned $109.00 in dust. Before long, Bob Man, Charlie Smith, Dutch Louie, and Frank Aldrich were sluicing for gold and taking out $20.00 per day to the man.

Landusky's news of the strike brought swarms of men to the gulches, where they dug feverishly in Little Alder, Rock Creek, Camp Creek, Grouse Creek, and the other stream-beds in the mountains. The heaviest gold deposit was found at the mouth of the gulch "on a high rim by 'Nigger' Eli Shelby." A nugget worth $83.00 was found by William Skillen. A mining district was organized and Willard Duncan made recorder. Although the pay streaks were lean and the boom short-lived, by fall 2,000 men roamed the district.

George A. Ottowa, early day prospector, tells of the wild rush out of Fort Benton to the Little Rockies in the fall of 1884, when men were looking for placer gold:

Bob Orman, Sam Cook and myself bought four broncs, harness and a wagon and loaded the wagon with supplies. We blindfolded the broncs, and harnessed and hitched them to the wagon, four men holding to the green, blindfolded broncs until I mounted the high seat and took the lines. The blinders were pulled off, and left free to go, they started running and bucking up hill toward the government coulee over which we passed down to Bill Embertson's ranch. . . . (We intended to stay at Mose Solomon's) . . . but so many teams and wagons were ahead of us that we halted only long enough for the horses to feed out of nose bags and the men to snatch some lunch. . . people were passing us with light wagons, buggies and wheelbarrows. Many were afoot with only what was in their pack to support them.

At Twenty-eight-mile Springs, we decided to leave the caravan and pass south of Bear Paw mountains by Antelope Springs. . . . It was trackless country . . . no signs of teams that had gone before us . . . nor any following.

It soon began to rain and the soil was of a silty alkaline . . . gumbo, clinging to anything that hit it. It began to roll up with the wheels and lodge against the brake beams, making progress impossible. The horses were too tired and couldn't pull the load against the resistance of heavy gumbo. We were stalled, the broncs with their heads drooping and panting. We unhitched and tied the broncs to the sagebrush, unloaded the wagon, took it apart and carried every part and our belongings, as well as the supplies to the summit, a distance of 600 yards. Then we brought up the weary horses, hitched them and went on, one man driving and the other two with shovels clearing the wheels of gumbo. Eventually we were out of the gumbo into gravel and made it over to Slippery Ann Hot Springs where we fed the horses and connected with the old road to Rocky Point. We found there dozens of teams, pack and saddle horses all headed for the new Eldorado. After eating, we hitched up and followed the base of the Little Rocky Mountains around to the Little Alder flat and to Murray Nicholson's, a squaw man. His place was a mile from the diggings. We moved on and got to the end of the rainbow, or where Zortman stands. We turned the horses loose for a much needed rest (they hadn't had their harness off since leaving Benton).

Pike Landusky and Dutch Louie Meyers held Little Alder gulch so we started prospecting up Ruby gulch, at the head of which we found gold in small quantity.

It froze up the night we struck bedrock and we hired Ben Johnston and Charlie Walker, each with a 12-mule and 3-wagon outfit to go to Fort Benton for our supplies. The weather being cold, they brought no vegetables as they did not return until a few days before Christmas, but an abundance of tobacco, sowbelly, flour and Arbuckle coffee. . . . We were frozen in, then, till next spring.

I met a man named Curtis who suggested that I go with him into Little Alder gulch. . . . I was a boy of seventeen and . . . accepted. We started up the gulch with Curtis in the lead. We came to a flat, probably half a mile from where Zortman stands. Curtis suggested that we locate the ground, one to stand guard and the other to work. I stood guard while Curtis shoveled. Shortly after this I saw Pike Landusky coming down the trail, his big 45-six shooter strapped to his waist. I pulled a bead on him and told him to throw up his hands, which he did, as he had not seen us. He said he wanted to talk to us and I told him to unbuckle his six-shooter and drop it in the trail. He did, and came to where we were standing. He said we could keep our ground, that it was the other gang he did not want up there.

So we located our claim. . . . In the meantime Landusky and Dutch Louie cleaned up from bedrock above us $5000 in gold nuggets which caused a greater stampede than the first. We cleaned bedrock every Saturday afternoon. The smallest pay for the two of us for five days was $150 and often doubled that amount. Immediately after dinner on Saturday, we saddled our horses and went to Rocky Point to get supplies. F. M. Marsh and a man, Ritchie, had stores and saloons and a hotel at the "Point" where we left our gold.

Little Rockies Miner, July 1, 1935

The excitement of digging was linked with the fear of ejection; for the area in which the pay streak lay was within the Fort Belknap Indian Reservation, and white men were debarred by law from entering it. As soon as the strike was made, a detachment of soldiers from Fort Maginnis, under Captain Scott, was sent to Rocky Point (Wilder's Landing on the south side of the Missouri) to supervise the reservation. Soldiers of the Eighteenth Infantry, under Captain Potter, were also ordered from Fort Assiniboine to investigate conditions and to report on the situation. Although soldiers periodically drove the miners out, the men would slip back and go to work until the next military raid. Finally, Captain Potter told the miners that they could remain until a report was made on existing conditions, but that no liquor could be brought into the Reservation.

As soon as the placer gold was exhausted, the boom was over and the men left the area. The gulches were deserted until Powell Landusky, who had been riding range for Granville Stuart and the Pioneer Cattle Company from 1886 to the spring of 1887, returned to the Little Rockies to mine and in his gophering discovered the first lode mine, the Julia. This and the Gold Bug were located in January, 1890. For some time he worked alone, developing his claims, especially the Gold Bug in which he uncovered ore at grass roots.

In August, 1893, Landusky and Robert Orman, his son-in-law, while prospecting, were overcome by heat and thirst and scrambled down the mountain in search of water. Having drunk from a stream, they started back up the slope. About ten feet up the hillside, one of them picked up an odd specimen of rock and took it home to examine. There they crushed and washed it and found a "string of gold three inches long" in the pan. The men worked their claim, which they called the August, and packed out the quartz at night, believing that their prospect was within the Fort Belknap Reservation and that they might be run off by government troops.

As they continued to prospect, they discovered an ore shoot with a vein thirteen feet wide, which yielded $400-$500 a ton in free-milling gold. Gradually their secret leaked out, and, when it was known that their profits ran as high as $13,000 a ton on picked ore and $500 on unsorted lots and that it was rumored that they had obtained $100,000 from a hole less than 100 feet deep, a second stampede to the Little Rockies began. This was all hard-rock mining; the deposits lay in porphyry, granite, and lime stratas, and the indefatigable prospectors trudged over the mountains, even crossing their summits to uncover leads on the eastern slopes.

Warren A. Berry was one of many who started for the new strike, packing his bed on one horse and riding another to Alder Gulch, where he found two men digging a shaft. The one above ground was Pike Landusky; the one in the shaft was Tom Carter. Pike hired him to assist with the digging. On the divide between Alder and Ruby Gulches lay the Hawk-eye claim; the Alabama was located on the eastern side of the mountains. Rich deposits of free-milling gold were also found in Ruby Gulch by McKenzie and Carter and pay streaks were uncovered in Montana Creek. Pike Landusky, not content with his August and Gold Bug properties, scrambled over the ridges to stake thirty claims "in or near Ruby Gulch." The Gold Bug already had a stamp mill, but the ore was not free-milling, and the plant was a failure despite assay reports that showed the presence of considerable gold. In the midst of all this gold, George Manning uncovered a "rich lead of free silver which averaged 300 ounces to the ton." On his property he erected and operated a three-stamp mill.

In June, 1894, a settlement called Landusky was organized by the miners and stockmen. Like all such camps, it grew with each new strike until, before the summer was over, it had a postoffice and several saloons, as well as stage service to the nearest town.

Not till last spring was much information about the rich ores known. Then came the rush. . . . The camp there now is known as Landusky, whose future greatness may out-rival Cripple Creek. The town is only started, and as yet has only a dozen houses, but others are building and before snow flies . . . the population of Landusky (may) be four times as much as at present. The town is sixty miles from Harlem in a gulch near where Pike Landusky made his discovery.
Helena Independent, September 17, 1894

A more detailed account of its start it given in the *Havre Advertiser* of July 19, 1894:

Hurrah for Landusky for Capital.
Helena or Anaconda are not in it!
Ever since the 5th of July, it has been one continual strike of the richest quartz you ever heard of. I send you some samples which you do not have to take a glass to, to see gold in.
The sample . . . is from the . . . Hawkeye. The

boys have enough to pay the national debt after making themselves rich. . . a score of others have made good locations in the past few days. All that we need is, a stamp to make $20 gold pieces.

At a meeting held here on the 9th of June the following resolutions were passed without a dissenting vote:
the town organized to be known as Landusky, J. T. Throop to be recorder.
every bona fide citizen be allowed 2 lots 50 feet front by 150 feet deep.
That (said citizen) erect a building 16 by 18 feet with 10 foot ceiling inside within 90 days.
That he pay the recorder $1.50 as a recording fee for each and every claim; on the completion of the house, he pay $2.50 for deed of same 2 lots.

Outside of the new locations, P. Landusky, R. Orman, Geo. Manning, John Manning and a host of others have locations which would make Vanderbilt jealous of himself. We are sure of it; Landusky for the Capital? . . .

Clarke and Cochrane furnish liquid refreshments at reasonable prices. J. T. Throop is the dispensing agent at the same place and he sure gets there. R. Curry is in the same business and he is sure a rusher. Chas. Chamberlain can furnish you with the best meat in Montana. J. H. Peck is contractor and builder. Jake Harris, better known as "Jew Jake" is about to embark in the saloon business.

We have some swift men here. Messrs. Blackwell & Co. made the trip to Fort Benton and return in three days. But Duncan takes the cake; having a record of 48 hours.

Keno.

Warren A. Berry, who was in at the start of the new camp and constructed many of its original buildings, recalls that the panic of 1893 left a good many of his patrons without cash, so that he received little money at first for his work. Trade and barter and gold dust were the usual mediums of exchange. A man in Chinook, named O'Hanlon, also befriended the miners by issuing orders on himself, which the men used as specie. Groceries, supplies, poker chips, and drinks were paid for with O'Hanlon drafts. These circulated so constantly that they frequently became illegible. When this occurred, they were returned to O'Hanlon, who replaced them with fresh copies.

No sooner did the camp materialize than it became the rendezvous for the bad men of the region, whose chief diversion was to shoot up the place. The story is told of a gambler who, in describing such a raid, said, "I could a gone out in the street anywhere and swung a pint cup around and caught a quart of bullets in it." The rough element was made up largely of rustlers who were wanted by the ranchers and stockmen. To protect their property, these cattle owners, led by Granville Stuart and Reece Anderson, organized a Vigilance Committee, whose members were called "Stranglers" by the wolfers.

Among these outlaws were three brothers, Harvey, John, and Lonnie Logan, who constituted the Curry gang. Harvey, the leader, was called "Kid." Associated with them was a cowman, Jim Thornhill, who rode the ranges south of the river. The Currys owned one ranch five miles south of Landusky, where they raised cattle and horses. They also had other ranches, as well as some mining property adjoining that of Pike Landusky. For nine years the Currys and Pike were friends as well as neighbors. Then, in 1892, a feud developed, some say over a borrowed plow, and others because of Lonnie's attentions to one of Pike's four step-daughters. Pike knew of Lonnie's reputation with women and objected to the suit. Before long, the Currys and Pike, each supported by their respective friends, were lined up in opposite camps and were threatening each other with bodily violence. A showdown was imminent.

When the Kid and his brother John were arrested on some minor charge, such as changing a brand, Pike, as deputy sheriff, was ordered to take them to Fort Benton for trial. This gave him the chance for which he was looking. While the men were in his custody, he is said to have secured them to the wall of the jail with a logging chain and then beaten them up, in a roundabout attempt to show his disgust for Lonnie. Upon their release, the Currys claimed that their arrest was trumped up by Pike as part of a plan to disgrace them and force them out of the country, so that he could take over their land and claims. The Kid swore that he would get Pike for this; but before he succeeded, Landusky held a celebration.

At a town meeting, the camp voted to get together at Christmas for a big feed and a dance. John Curry lent his new barn for the dance, and Lonnie, who played the fiddle, conducted the impromptu orchestra. When someone mentioned a Hamlin organ that belonged to a rancher ten miles away, a "dead-ax" wagon was sent for the instrument. For the preparation and serving of the food, John B. Ritch donated his new bungalow. Warren Berry insisted that the menu include some specialty that everyone could talk about afterwards; so the committee decided to get four dozen quarts of big, juicy, Baltimore oysters. "Lousy," the stage driver, was instructed to wire the order the next time he went to the railroad. Lousy's familiarity with oysters was slight, and all he had ever heard of was the canned "Cove" variety; so he telegraphed to Minneapolis for canned ones. They arrived in good time, although the express charges were greater than their cost.

When the news got around that Landusky was putting on a feed, over a hundred men from ranches and hideouts miles away converged on the mining camp, many of them bringing food with them, to be used at the feast. "Tie Up George," a round-up cook, prepared two wash boilers full of oyster stew, having been warned not to get drunk until the guests left. During the two days and nights of the spree, great quantities of food and drink were consumed, and, as the hours passed, the participants grew happier and noisier. The gunmen, as soon as they arrived, cached their weapons and did not re-arm until the evening of December 26th.

When the celebration was over, the men picked up their guns and the tension of the crowd increased. Instead of returning home, the men loitered in the saloons and stores that lined Landusky's main street, waiting for something to happen. Some of them drifted into Jew Jake's place, which had been built for its owner by Pike Landusky. Jake Harris came to Landusky from Great Falls when the camp was young. He was lame for he had lost a leg in a gunfight with the city marshal of Great Falls as the result of an argument that had started earlier that day in Neihart. Jake was a gunman, as was his partner, Hogan. He was also a friend of Pike, and the latter often came into his combination saloon and store, which carried overalls, gloves, boots, etc., displayed at the back of the building. Jake used crutches except when he substituted a sawed-off shotgun for support.

The morning of December 27, 1894, was cold, and the ground was white with snow. Few people were on the street. About 10:30 a.m., Pike and a friend stopped by Jake's for a drink. A half dozen men were inside, and the gunman Hogan was in the back room. Lonnie Curry and Jim Thornhill were in the saloon when Pike entered, but both were at the trade counter in the back talking to Hogan. As Pike was filling his glass with whisky, Kid Curry came in, walked up to him, and slapped him on the back. Pike whirled around and Curry struck him a heavy blow on the jaw which threw him to the floor. At the commotion, Lonnie and Thornhill entered the room with drawn sixguns, and while one ordered Hogan to keep out of it, the other covered the customers and warned them not to interfere.

When Pike fell, Curry pounced on top of him, pinning him to the floor and beating him mercilessly. Pike was hampered in returning the blows by his heavy fur-lined overcoat and to some extent by his age; for he was over fifty and older than Curry. He fought back, however, until Curry's punishing blows were more than he could take and he called out for help. Tom Carter, a prospector and a friend of his, attempted to get Lonnie and Thornhill to stop the fight, but they refused. Meanwhile, the Kid was pounding and smashing Pike's head and face into a pulp. When he finished, Pike staggered up, drawing the gun from his overcoat pocket and firing before Curry could draw; but the gun jammed, and the Kid shot Pike twice with his .45. Within a few minutes Pike was dead. The Curry brothers and Thornhill made a getaway in a spring wagon and presumably headed for the Missouri badlands; for nothing more was seen or heard of them for some time. Pike was buried on his ranch, one mile down the valley from the town of Landusky.

With Pike laid away, the town resumed its daily rough and tumble round of activities. Frank Kirkaldie hauled a printing press into Landusky in 1895 and for nearly a year, before removing his plant to Harlem, published a four-column, four-page paper, *The Miner and Prospector*. The Gold Bug group of mines promised a prosperous future for the camp, until it was found that the refractory ore refused to respond to the methods of extraction that existed. When the Gold Bug mill shut down, Landusky, which had been booming, slowly died. After cyanidation provided a successful means of recovering gold deposits, Landusky's mines were reopened and the camp began to come back. Its prosperity was also linked with Charles Whitcomb's development of Zortman's mines.

Ruel Horner, who reached Landusky in 1904 and drove stage for seven years, remembers when he hauled 1,200 pounds of bullion a month from its mines and brought in $10,000 in cash each month for the payrolls. On the hot summer afternoon that we drove up Landusky's long and nearly deserted street, past old cabins, remodeled cabins, a freshly painted schoolhouse with swings in the playground, a small stuccoed house marked "Grace Chapel," which was closed, and a few boarded-up stores, we were looking for refreshment. In the dark interior of a bar, we found an elderly man, who I believe was Ruel Horner. He served us beer and told us about the mines and the two mills that were up on the mountain. He pointed out the ruins of a concentrator almost across the street from his place, that used to process 300 tons of ore a day. He also pointed out the narrow road that ran north through People's Canyon to Belknap. Two miles north on that road, he assured us, we would find the August mine with its abandoned tram — the dangling buckets leading down the mountain to the ruined mill.

SAINT PAUL'S MISSION

I was tempted to explore this mountain trail, for it led through wild and picturesque People's Canyon and passed St. Paul's Indian mission, which was founded in 1886 by Father Frederick Hugo Eberschweiler, a Jesuit priest whose knowledge of the Gros Ventres language won the Indians' respect. His request for help to build his mission went unheeded by the men in Fort Benton; they were afraid to go to the Little Rockies while the Gros Ventres and Canadian Bloods were at war with each other. The priest then turned to the prospectors who were swarming to the Landusky diggings and from them obtained the services of a volunteer crew, which put up the necessary buildings. The Mission, which serves the Gros Ventres and Assiniboine Indians, is still administered by the Jesuit fathers. Except for one log house which is still standing, the mission buildings are of stone.

To reach Zortman, our next objective, we retraced five miles of road to the dusty highway that had brought us from the banks of the Missouri. With each mile, the roadbed improved, and after traveling some ten or more, we swung into the second mining camp on our itinerary. On this lonely stretch between the towns, I told Francis two stories about Pike Landusky.

A business friend of Pike grubstaked a prospector, who found a good prospect and sent word for the man to hurry over and stake his claim, the most valuable one so far uncovered, with the exception of the initial strike; but the man did not appear. Pike knew that anyone who set stakes on the land had a legal right to it. Ignoring the arguments and threats of those who wanted to jump the ground, Pike sat on the claim, fingering his rifle and daring anyone to run him off. His reputation as a dead shot was known, and he succeeded in holding the claim until his tardy friend arrived.

The second story was about Warren A. Berry, perhaps the only man who won an argument with Pike and lived to tell about it. Berry contracted to put up a log building for Pike, and when it stood six or seven logs high on a set of blocks, Pike came to look it over.

"Where's the foundation? It should have been built first," complained Pike.

"Foundation?" Berry replied. "I've got nothing to do with the foundation."

"What good is a house without one?" asked Pike irritably.

"If you want one, put it in yourself," said Berry.

"It's in the contract," stormed Pike; but the agreement had been verbal, and Berry as vehemently insisted that it was not. The heated argument continued until Berry asked, "Do you want this house or don't you?"

"Yes, but you've got to put the foundation under it," insisted Pike.

"Like hell I do," said Berry, seizing a cant-hook and tearing down the building, log by log, as he raged. Pike was unable to stop him, and as the logs were falling, rolling, and bouncing toward him, all he could do was yell and curse. Since he needed the building, he grudgingly agreed to do the foundation himself.

"Go ahead," said Berry. "I won't work for you."

"If you don't you might as well leave the Little Rockies, for you'll never get another job here," taunted Pike.

"The hell you say," retorted Berry, "I'll be around here when you're in hell." Pike was killed in 1894. Warren Berry was still alive in 1935.

ZORTMAN

In the fall of 1866, the government hired men from Fort Benton to build Fort Browning on People's Creek in the Milk River country. Upon its completion, the men were discharged, and they scattered in search of other work. According to the reminiscences of William Bent, a party consisting of Bill Hamilton, a trapper, Joe Wye, Fred Merchant, John Thomas, Bent, and three others was formed in the fall of 1868 to go into the Little Rockies to look for gold. Hamilton, the leader, led the group around to the east side of the mountains, where, in Dry Beaver Gulch, they found small quantities of gold. They had little time to dig before the ground froze; whereupon the disgusted men threw away their tools and turned to hunting. With a number of elk skins for trade, they packed out and returned to Fort Benton. The diggings were abandoned until the 1890's, when Pete Zortman reached the Little Rockies. After intensive exploration of the area, Zortman is credited with locating the Alabama mine on the eastern side of the range; although, according to the *Little Rockies Miner*, (July 4, 1907)

The Alabama was sold by the original locator for $40 to Spaulding who later interested Pete Zortman and Putnam, both of Chinook. They did development work and got some ore yielding as high as $2800 per ton at the Great Falls smelter and one lot of 1600 pounds returned $6000.

There is no doubt that by 1893, Zortman and George P. Putnam owned the mine and that they succeeded in interesting E. W. King (the promoter of the Barnes-King Company at Kendall) in joining them to form the Alder Gulch Mining Company. By 1899-1900, this company was also working the Pole Gulch group of mines in the high valley above the site of Zortman. A 100-ton cyanide mill, erected in Alder Gulch in 1903 for the reduction of Alabama and Pole Creek ore, was the next improvement. The distance of the mill from the mines made operation costs excessive and it was forced to close after running for several seasons. The Little Rockies Exploration Company, organized in 1906 as a holding company, immediately took over operation of the Alder Gulch Company's mine and mill, as well as several other productive claims. After further improvements in the plant, the mill reopened January 24, 1907. An aerial tramway connecting the Alabama mine with the mill did away with ore hauling by wagon.

Back in the nineties, Tom Carter and John Throop prospected and worked claims in nearby Ruby Gulch. These did not seem particularly promising but in later years proved among the richest of all. The Independent mine at the head of Ruby Gulch was another active property in 1895-1896.

In the late 1890's, or perhaps it was not until 1903, Charles Whitcomb came to the district and, after gophering around, found a large deposit of pay rock at grass roots. This he bonded, as well as several other claims at the head of Ruby Gulch. Whitcomb was both a prospector and a professional footracer. In fact, is was said that he secured his mines with the stakes he had won in a race. The newspaper of the day described him as a man with vision, a "pusher," and one who would "stake a thousand on the high card as quickly as a dollar."

The region owes its development to Whitcomb and to B. D. Phillips, a wealthy sheep man, more than to any other individuals. As soon as Whitcomb had obtained his claims, he approached Phillips and got him to back the development of the several properties by building a 100-ton cyanide mill. One of his bonded claims, the Carter (named for Tom Carter, who located it) contained quantities of low grade ore. By accident Whitcomb fell through a schist wall and "came out with his pocket full of $80 rock." Whenever this rock slid, as it sometimes did when very wet, the mass of earth and rock was sent through the mill and ran $4.00 a ton.

This Ruby Gulch property lay south of the Alder Gulch Company's holdings and contained a lead 600-feet long and 75-127 feet wide. The large ore body, which was said to contain millions of tons of pay rock, was worked by open cut and tunnel. Much of the ore extracted milled at a little more than $10.00 a ton. Whitcomb and Phillips proceeded to develop the property and, in 1904, organized the Ruby Gulch Mining Company with Phillips owning slightly more than two-thirds of the shares. From time to time the two bought other properties until they owned a group of thirty patented claims. In 1905 they enlarged their mill.

The Ruby Gulch Mining Co. . . . made a record run for a cyanide plant. . . . Last week Mr. Whitcomb, . . . deposited in the U.S. Assay Office 6000 ounces of gold worth $60,000 as the result of an eighteen day's run. . . . This is the first from the enlarged mill and cyanide plant. . . .

The 4200 tons of ore were taken from the open cut of the mine, the deposit is eighty feet wide and the pit at no place over 35 feet below the surface. . . . It is worked from grass roots or better than that for "dirt, ore and everything that was found were run through the mill, this being cheaper than to strip the surface dirt." The ore averaged $15 a ton for 4200 tons. Some of the tanks ran as high as $23 a ton. There is a mountain of this ore which can be mined with a steam shovel.

Helena Daily Independent, September 2, 1906

During 1906, the mine was bonded to a New York syndicate for $7,500,000. By the time the bond expired, Whitcomb and Phillips were bursting with new plans for improving the property.

A Big Mine.

The Ruby mine was purely a piece of luck handed out by a kind providence to a party of tenderfeet so far as mining was concerned.

B. D. Phillips, the principal owner says: "When I built this mill as a 100-ton plant, the only ore we had was that exposed in a little 30-foot open cut in the Independent. . . . It turned out all right but it was a mighty long chance to take but the open cut happened to be on a true fissure vein and a little later another was discovered. . . . When the tunnel is completed a plant of 1000 tons capacity will send up its smoke from the Lodge Pole side. This means employment of fully 1000 men and a population of 5000 for Zortman.

Excavation has started for a new boarding house three stories high to contain 41 rooms. In addition, ten to fifteen cottages are to be built for the use of employees having families and it is the policy of the company to employ men with families whenever they are found competent.

The company stands capitalized at $100,000. Mr. Phillips owns 65% of the stock and has spent so far on buildings, claims, etc., $550,000 and when the cleanup is made this coming week, the mine will have paid it all and still leave a little velvet in the treasury. . . . There is enough ore in sight to warrant that. None of this generation will live to see it exhausted.

Little Rockies Miner, August 29, 1907

By 1908 the Ruby mine was the "largest cyanide proposition in Montana," placing the Little Rockies in second place among the gold-producing districts in the state. A new mile-and-a-half long tram and an enlarged mill, equipped to handle 300 tons of ore a day, provided work for a force of more than 100 men. Even with this mine working to capacity, Whitcomb and Phillips continued to increase their holdings, until they included the Independent and the Beaver Creek mine, the latter several miles north of Ruby Gulch. This property, with development, became the third largest producer in the district. The August property near Landusky was also procured. No wonder that the *Hi-Line Weekly* wrote in later years:

Landusky, Zortman and his successors had mines. Whitcomb had the vision and daring and Phillips had the capital. This . . . with partners such as Louis Goslin, Coburn Bros. and the Helena bankers Marlow & Smith, finally brought the August mine

ZORTMAN LOOKING TOWARD THE MISSOURI RIVER

ZORTMAN AND MOUTH OF RUBY GULCH

at Landusky and the Ruby Gulch mine at Zortman into successful and profitable production.

Hi-Line Weekly, December 16, 1935

Another property to come under their management was an old mine, the Little Ben, two miles north of Landusky, on the Harlem road. Originally worked only on a small scale by prospectors, it was operated early in the twentieth century by the August Mining Company, under whose management a tunnel was driven "to tap the central part of the properties," but before any rich ore was discovered, the company went broke and asked the Ruby Gulch Company for financial aid, which Whitcomb agreed to furnish.

Whitcomb, who had his eye for some time on the Little Ben, welcomed this opportunity to get an option on the property. After a thorough investigation of the mine, the Ruby Gulch Company put up the money for further development in return for fifty per cent of the company's stock. While working the northern end of the mine, Whitcomb struck a bonanza from which sufficient ore was recovered to pay off the option and repay the investors. To handle the bulk of this rich deposit, a coarse-crushing cyanide leaching plant was hastily built near Landusky and was operated successfully for a number of years, with Whitcomb in charge of all operations. The very first carload of ore shipped brought $14,000 and the second car $11,000. As work progressed, a shaft several hundred feet deep was sunk below the tunnel. It cut into a silver lead, but this ore the leaching plant was unable to extract. Because of this, it shut down, but not until it had paid $600,000 in dividends to the investors. As recently as 1932, when the Little Ben Mining Company (which had been organized by Whitcomb) was incorporated, its output necessitated a crew of seventy-two men. Between January 1, 1935, and November 21, 1939, it produced $1,500,000 and paid dividends.

All this time the Ruby Gulch mine continued to yield quantities of ore. It was worked efficiently through a large glory hole with an electrically lighted haulage tunnel 500 feet below the surface, through which an electric trolley line ran ore trains to the mill. The mine was in good financial condition; dividends amounting to over $1,000,000 were paid from the seemingly inexhaustable deposit. The enlarged mill burned in 1910 and was immediately replaced by a coarse-crushing cyanide leaching plant of 600 tons capacity, which

operated for six years. Not until the 1920's did the high cost of labor and machinery cause the mill to shut down. While it was closed, two catastrophies occurred — the mill burned and Phillips died.

Soon afterwards, his sixty-nine per cent interest in the company was sold to Mose Zimmerman of St. Paul and to Siems Brothers-Helmers, Incorporated of the same city. Whitcomb retained the rest of the shares of stock. The new owners, however, made no effort to resume operations, and when Zimmerman died, the First National Bank and Trust Company of Minneapolis became one of his executors. Finally, Carl J. Trauerman obtained an eighteen-month option on Zimmerman's estate and reopened the mining property in January, 1935. Trauerman soon found such high-grade ore that the option was paid off in five months. In June of the same year, Trauerman was elected president of the company, with Charles Whitcomb vice-president and general manager. By the fall of 1935, Whitcomb and Trauerman owned ninety-eight per cent of the shares, with Whitcomb the largest stockholder. A newspaper item hints at the owners' future plans for the mine:

The Ruby Gulch Co. is now completing a mill of 300 tons daily capacity, later it will be enlarged to 1,000 tons. . . .

The mill is so placed that there is room for millions of tons of tailings in two gulches on two sides of the plant. Zinc dust precipitation will be used and gold bullion will be produced at the plant. . . . The new mill should be in operation in January, 1936.

With the money obtained from the August, Little Ben and Ruby Gulch properties, Charles Whitcomb developed the Beaver Creek property, three miles north of Ruby Gulch. The ore is low grade gold. A test mill produced around $100,000 a few years ago but was destroyed by fire. The property is now controlled by the Little Rockies Mining Co. of which Charles Whitcomb is head.

Hi-Line Weekly, December 16, 1935

Fire not only destroyed mills but also on more than one occasion threatened the town itself. The most disastrous blaze started near Landusky on July 25, 1936, and whipped across the mountains to lick the edges of the helpless settlement, which was saved only by the concerted efforts of its residents. Actually, there were two fires, the first caused by a cigarette tossed away by a miner who was smoking in bed. This fire took three lives with a fourth victim succumbing later as a result of his burns. The three casualties were Dr. S. H. Brockunier of Lowell, Massachusetts, Cameron Baker of

Havre, a member of the U.S. Geological Survey crew, and John Rowles, a Landusky miner.

When it was seen that the fire was spreading, Otis Pewitt of Zortman, a fire guard who had been on duty for twenty-four hours, drove to the nearest telephone, which was at Harlem, forty-five miles away, to call for help from the district office. In response to his request, several members of a geological party left their camp at three a.m. to join the crew of three hundred Indian firefighters already at the scene. These new arrivals were trapped in a narrow canyon when the wind changed, and the fire crowned the treetops, creating a ground vacuum. Nine of the suffocating men managed to reach a shallow cave and dug into the earth floor in an attempt to find air, but the shelter was much too small to hold all of them, so Brockunier, Baker, and Rowles, with Pewitt to guide them, made a break for other protection. Unfortunately, just as they dashed out of the cave, a downdraft of blistering air struck them and tossed them helplessly about. They died where they fell. Pewitt, who knew fires, rushed through the flames and rolled to the bottom of the gully, to an old forest trail, along which he staggered until he collapsed. With his clothing gone and his entire body seared, except the soles of his feet, he was rescued by a party of firefighters. His death from cancer, sometime later, was attributed to the damage suffered by his lungs and throat during his escape. This fire, which raced through a forest of lodgepoles and burned 23,000 acres, between Landusky and Zortman, was brought under control on July 27.

The second fire started two days later near the Little Ben mill, five miles away from the first blaze. The flames almost caught the mill and the miners' shacks, but the wind shifted and swept eastward, over the mountains, toward the Ruby Gulch mill and the town of Zortman. As each fire crept close, the terrified people in Landusky and Zortman carried their belongings out to the prairie. Miners, ranchers, C.C.C. camp workers, Indians, and Forest Service personnel pitched in to save the settlements. At St. Paul's Mission, priests and nuns filled sandbags to form a barricade around the church and school buildings. The fire burned for a week and when it died out, only blackened, ash-covered slopes remained. The Forest Service replanted 500 acres of the charred area, but trees grow slowly in high, dry Montana, and as yet only the lodgepoles have caught hold.

It was mid-afternoon when we reached

ZORTMAN CLIFFS

Zortman. The last couple of miles the road wound between young trees until it reached a clearing at the mouth of a canyon. There stood the mining camp!

Most of the settlement was south of the creek that meandered through town and some distance from the two-story frame schoolhouse, whose bright blue roof was the only gay note among many drab buildings. The upper part of the camp lay on a gently sloping meadow which ended abruptly against rocky cliffs and big, gray, boulders. More of these rocky projections formed a wall on the far side of the stream. On one low hill, stood a church. Cabins were tucked in among trees on back streets, but it was the main street that contained the core of the town — homes, a stone jail with barred windows, and several small, false-fronted stores, most of which were boarded up.

Periodic fires have destroyed many of Zortman's original buildings. One in 1929 did considerable damage and a fairly recent blaze in September, 1944, wiped out most of the north side of the main street. Wind racing down the gulch fanned the flames, which spread to a building in which the winter's supply of coal was stored. Fed by this unexpected fuel, the fire leaped forward and was only prevented from sweeping down the canyon and out onto the dry prairie by the persistent efforts of all the townspeople — a meager number; for mining had ceased at the Ruby Gulch mill in 1943, and many of Zortman's residents were already far away.

Zortman came into its prime at the beginning of the twentieth century, after Charles Whitcomb began to develop its mines. By 1907, when the *Little Rockies Miner* made its appearance, it was an established and flourishing camp.

After many unforeseen delays, the *Little Rockies Miner*, . . . makes its appearance and bid for recognition in the field of local journalism. . . .

Politically, its editor has always been a republican though, it may be confessed, somewhat of the independent order, and may be expected to voice such sentiments during political campaigns.

Zortman is the metropolis of the Little Rockies. . . . It is a typical mining town with all lines of business well represented and a village of probably 200 houses and a population of 400.

July 4, 1907

Of one of Zortman's prominent citizens the *Miner* writes:

L. S. Goslin came to Zortman in 1903. His first venture was to buy a weekly stage line between Malta and Phillips. . . . He then extended it to Zortman. Through these efforts he got a post office here. He built the first house on Main St. having purchased the ground of Brown who held it as a placer. He has since improved it with a livery and feed barn, stage barn, residence, office and blacksmith shop. He is the best posted man on mining in the district.

He is a bachelor but not beyond the marriageable age.

Little Rockies Miner, July 18, 1907

On our visit to Zortman we found two stores, two or three bars, and a restaurant, all doing business. In one of the general stores called "Kellerman's," we bought crackers and soda pop for a belated lunch, and talked to Mr. Kellerman and his daughter, who run the store. Miss Kellerman told us she had always lived in Zortman.

"You ought to be here Saturday night when there's a dance," she said as she waited on us. "It lasts all night. One week it's in one of the bars and the next week, it's held in the other one. While you're here, you should drive two miles up the gulch to Ruby, or Whitcomb, as they cometimes called it, and see what's left of the Ruby Gulch property. The company took out over three and a half million dollars from the mine and their mill that burned was the second largest cyanide mill in the world. The old stage road up the mountain is narrow, but it's in good shape. If you go to the top of the mountain, you'll see the huge glory hole from which the ore came. If you keep on going down the far side of the hill, you'll be in Beaver Creek and you'll see another ruined cyanide mill."

We thanked her and started up the gulch. The road that was said to be in "good shape"

turned out to be very rough. It hugged the edge of the mountain and climbed rapidly toward a big black mill that was silhouetted against the sky. The whole bed of the stream, below us, was a huge settling pond filled with fine, reddish gravel, so deep that in places the tailings covered standing timber. As we approached the mill, we could see that this tremendous mass of tailings came from two distinct gulches which joined just below the mill.

Cabins and frame homes of all sorts and sizes perched on several levels among the underbrush and trees, which covered the mountainside opposite the mill. These comprised the camp known as Ruby or Whitcomb. The Kellermans had told us that when the mill closed, because of high production costs, the people pulled out, leaving everything behind them, for they expected the shutdown to be temporary and were sure that before long, they would be back. But as late as 1956, the mill was still silent and most of the cabins were closed up.

On the return to Zortman, the car nearly slid down the steep mountain grade. As we neared the town, we could see how snugly it was held between the canyon walls. Beyond the townsite, the cliffs fanned out toward the wide prairie, which extended to the horizon. This tremendous area of flat land was broken only by the trench cut into it by the Missouri River.

In Zortman we took a last look around and talked to several people about the early days. One of them spoke of Joe Mallette, a freighter whose ingenuity was equal to any emergency and who, therefore, was given the toughest assignments. On mountain trails he rigged a boom on the uphill side of his wagon and rode it to steady his load. Once the slant was too great for his weight to offset it, and his load upset, tossing him down the mountainside in a shower of broken glass and foaming beer. On another occasion he was hauling a boiler over the alkali flats to the Ruby Gulch mine and his wagon wheels sank to the hubs. Mallette rigged a rolling hitch and rolled the boiler, a few feet at a time, across three miles of mud.

From another resident I learned about the mine manager who drove down the mountain one winter day in a bobsled loaded with gold bricks. His wife was with him, and when she complained of the cold, he stopped, gathered some wood, built a fire, and heated the bricks. They made a fine foot-warmer.

An old lady to whom we talked mentioned

RUBY GULCH MINE AND MILL WITH ACRES OF TAILINGS

the power plants that once serviced the big mines. "Did you see the swimming hole, four miles from Landusky, and not far below the Zortman road?" she asked. "It was made by the dam that the Ruby Gulch Mining Company built to hold water that was carried through wooden pipes to the old power plant, a mile below it. At the plant the water ran over a big wheel to help generate electricity for the mill and the mine in Ruby Gulch. When the new plant was built at the river, the old one became a sub-station. Later on, the water was carried through ditches and a flume, across Rock Creek, to a reservoir below the Gill ranch.

"The new plant at the river was built in 1914 by Phillips and cost a quarter of a million dollars. When the mining company was operating full blast, that plant burned seventy tons of coal a day. You can imagine what it meant to haul in those heavy boilers and generators when they were building the plant. Joe Hartman brought in two of them with two twelve-horse teams. He freighted them all the way from Winifred through snow, with the temperature forty below. A third boiler came up the river from Bismarck by steamboat. The rest were dragged in from Malta."

While in town, we met a man who had returned to Zortman after an absence of forty-two years. He had with him many old photographs which he kindly showed us, and it was especially helpful to see what the big mills looked like when they were running. Had it not been for him, we would have missed the painting in the bar, which showed Zortman at its peak, prior to the first fire. I left Zortman reluctantly. After a few miles of dirt road, we struck pavement and skimmed along at what seemed an indecent rate after traveling so many miles over dusty, rutted road-beds. At Malta, we turned west and headed for Havre, where we spent the night.

BEAR PAW MOUNTAINS

The Bear Paw Mountains, another isolated range like the Little Rockies, rise some thirty-five miles south of the towns of Harlem and Chinook, and as we drove through each of these communities on Highway No. 2, on our way to Havre, I remembered reading of the gold rush to the Bear Paws that took place in the later 1870's. The deposits were not extensive, but to a prospector each gold strike is a potential bonanza, and only participation in it can prove its merit.

Stampede to the Bear Paw Mountains
Among the old residents of Benton, there has been for years a strong belief in the existence of good paying placer mines in the Bear Paw Mountains. Prospects were made as far back as 1860 and of late years "colors" have been repeatedly found by parties traveling through the mountains; on hunting or fur trading expeditions.

There is a suspicion that something rich has been discovered . . . and that the men are trying to keep the matter a secret. . . . They [finally] admitted they had found gold and said the field was very extensive and that there was a probability of better pay yet to be found.

At present writing, nearly all the male residents of Benton who can possibly leave their occupations are preparing for a trip to the new gold fields, it is likely that in a few days the town will be almost deserted. . . . A stampede from Benton is a dead certainty.

Benton Record, June 14, 1878

Those who rushed to the new placer field recovered some coarse gold by panning or sluicing the gravel beds, but the strike was not rich enough

to warrant such an influx of population as to overcome danger from roving bands of Indians from across the British line and the opposition of our own Indians, who were then adverse to having the country opened up in that way.

"Old Man Lloyd," as he was called in Fort Benton, an experienced prospector who was one of the earliest explorers of the area,

uncovered a splendid vein of argentiferous galena and recorded his lead in this county . . . calling it Black Diamond. Assays made at various times proved that the ore ran 56-69% lead and many ounces of silver. The old man stuck to it and sank a shaft 60 feet deep in the vein, which grew wider and richer as developments progressed. He came into Benton during the summer of 1879 for provisions and left his assistant at the mine. When he returned, he found Indians in possession. They had just driven his hired man away and he came upon them unexpectedly.

A fight followed, and the old man by dextrous use of his needle gun, succeeded in saving his scalp and escaping. He afterwards sold his interest in the mine to certain citizens in Benton and then left for New Mexico to try his luck among the Apaches where he had a hair-raising escape.

The River Press, May 16, 1888

All through the 1880's, whatever mining was carried on was illegal, since the claims lay within Indian reservation land. But in 1888, at least the portion which contained the mines was opened to Whites and after that, according to the *River Press,*

everything has assumed a different aspect. Old and experienced miners have quickly slipped in from Butte and Helena and other mining camps of the territory and prospecting is going on at a lively rate.

Some fine veins of argentiferous galena as well as silver carbonate ore have been uncovered and numerous records and leads have already been filed with the recorders of Choteau County. . . .

A company of twelve men have staked off twenty acres each of 240 acres of placer mining ground, which they propose to work by means of ditches and hydraulic appliances. The ground is said to yield $2-$3 a day to the hand by use of ordinary sluice boxes. There are several other streams putting out of the Bear Paw Mountains, the bars of which prospect well.

June 6, 1888

The 1888 rush to the Bear Paw Mountains attracted Lewis V. Bogy and other Chinook business men who developed an argentiferous galena vein three miles southeast of the Lloyd post office. At that time, Lloyd's abandoned Black Diamond claim was relocated and recorded as the Bear Paw lode by L. V. Bogy and Charles Smith.

Chinook Items.
A new mail and stage route has just been established, between Chinook and P. Murphy's ranch in the Bear Paw Mountains, twenty-five miles distant. . . . Murphy has made fine improvements and is now engaged preparing a fine, commodious hotel for . . . tourists, home seekers and prospectors, who undoubtedly will come in rapidly as soon as spring opens, as there is rich silver quartz in Silver Peak Mt. and placer mines near the head of Snake creek. Some miners are reported to have taken out $4-$6 per day.

The River Press, February 5, 1890

The mines in this district were worked for about four years, with only seven tons of sorted ore being shipped to Great Falls for treatment. After the property was patented in 1892, little if anything was done with it, and the Bear Paw excitement died down.

An early morning start from Havre took us southwest through miles of wheat fields, toward Great Falls. "Let's go to Fort Benton," I said when road signs showed that the Missouri River town was only about five miles off the highway. "So much of Montana's early history centered around it that I'd like to see the place that was for so long the head of navigation."

The town of Benton was surveyed in 1859 by Colonel DeLacy and incorporated in 1865. Five years later, with a population of 180, it contained four Indian trading posts, one brewery, one bakery, two blacksmith shops, twelve saloons, a courthouse, a jail, and a school. Mails arrived tri-weekly. The adobe fort for which the town was named stood 120-feet back from the river and twelve feet above the low-water line. Its storehouses and the commandant's office were of hewn logs and roofed with shingles, whereas the other buildings were made of unhewn logs.

Nearly everyone traveling to the frontier settlements or heading back to the States passed through Fort Benton, and, although this made a large transient population of miners, freighters, and adventurers, it provided business for the merchants, traders, and transportation agents, who made the river port their headquarters. As early as 1878, the banking house of I. G. Baker ran a freight line and owned the Baker line of steamers, while T. C. Power and Brothers were both freighters and proprietors of the Benton line of steamers.

Arrival by stage is described in *The Glendale Atlantis* (November 24, 1880) under the heading:

A Trip to Benton.

All of a sudden the stage puts on the brakes at the brow of a high bench land and looking down, one sees a flat one mile wide and two miles long with the Missouri cutting its eastern side, and near the middle of this flat and immediately facing the river is the old adobe Fort and the town just above it. Above, below and opposite, are bluffs several hundred feet in height and these are stained by dark colored slate and shale.

As we came in sight of this memorable old trading post a scene reviving memories of bygone days was being enacted. The Chief White Calf, with a large village of Piegans was crossing the river. They camped over night, traded some and passed eastward to the buffalo country, climbing the bluffs, not by the white man's graded wagon road but by the steep travois trail of the red man, which, though not so easy, was more direct.

TAILINGS BELOW MILL, RUBY GULCH

The town itself appeared to be

a thrifty river town, regularly laid out, with broad streets running at right angles, and the Missouri River running along the Eastern or Southeastern side, a bold, clean, mountain stream between 200 and 300 yards in width.

Glendale Atlantis, December 1, 1880

The three-story Grand Union Hotel, considered the "leading hotel of Montana Territory," opened its doors on November 2, 1882, with Hunsberger and Travers, proprietors. The hostelry was built by Tweedy & Coombs at a cost of $50,000 and is still standing. Frank Coombs, who had a brick yard and provided building material for many of Benton's more pretentious buildings, estimated that 550,000 brick were used for the Grand Union hotel alone, with an additional 350,000 for the Masonic Hall and 300,000 for the Odd Fellows Hall. The Grand Union was not the only hotel in town during the eighties; for the Choteau House, with Jere Sullivan, proprietor, announced, "Terms, $2.00 per day," and the Overland Hotel, whose "beds have all been renovated and are first class," advertised a reduction in rates to $1.50 per day.

What must Fort Benton have been like

during the sixties and seventies when many tall-stacked steamboats tied up along the shore and deckhands carried inconceivable amounts and varieties of freight up the sloping banks from the river's edge to the broad street where the log and adobe warehouses stood? The trip up river was a constant struggle. Treacherous and shifting currents, shallow water and hidden snags, were ever ready to ground the boat unexpectedly, or slam it against a bank or other obstruction while threading a rapid. In certain places, the crew actually propelled the boat by dragging it upstream with ropes snubbed to trees along the shore, while a full head of steam, which was intended to provide momentum to buck the current, might, instead, cause the boilers to blow up and the craft to burn.

The fuel burned was wood, necessitating frequent stops to replenish the woodpile. On the lower river, woodyards were established near cottonwood breaks, and when the boat tied up alongside, the deckhands loaded as many cords as needed. Farther upstream, however, each crew had to cut and load its own wood, sometimes having to go a mile inland to find suitable timber which then had to be dragged back to the riverside. Great rivalry existed between individual boats, and often, when one overtook another, races were run to test the speed and maneuverability of the competing vessels. Such races sometimes ended abruptly with the wood-crammed boilers of one of the craft exploding and scattering passengers and freight into the river. Years after steamboating was over, it was determined that 295 boats had sunk in the Missouri, and that cargoes worth millions of dollars lay in the riverbed. Of these wrecks, eighty per cent were attributed to the boat's hitting a snag and the rest to "boiler explosions, fire, rapids and falling banks."

The *Chippewa*, loaded with trade goods and thirty kegs of powder and whiskey, lay off Poplar Creek in 1861, when a thirsty deckhand went below decks to tap one of the kegs. His lighted candle fell into some spilled whiskey, which ignited. The flames licked through the boxes and bales to the powder, which exploded and wrecked the vessel. On one run, the *Nellie Peck*, while tied up, broke its anchor cable during a severe thunderstorm and drifted downstream until it grounded on a bar. There she was boarded by a Sioux war party, which locked the crew and passengers in the cabin. While they were debating how to kill their captives, lightning struck the boat and the Indians scattered. The crew repaired engine damage and other breakage, and the trip was resumed. This same boat later raced the *Far East* and set a river record between St. Louis and Fort Benton of seventeen days and twenty hours.

By the 1880's, steamboating on the river was nearly ended. Since then, the once famous head of navigation on the Missouri has gradually settled down into a quiet town, much like others, with comfortable homes surrounded with gardens and shaded by trees. Front Street has brick buildings which date from the eighties and a few false-fronts and frame stores facing the river bank. A big steel bridge spans the wide, brown, swift stream. No smoke-belching steamboats cut its surface or breast its current nowadays, and herds of buffalo no longer swim across it.

SWEET GRASS HILLS and GOLD BUTTE

"The only other mining area in this part of the state is in the Sweet Grass Hills, due north of here and close to the Canadian border," I told Francis, as we approached the outskirts of Great Falls and got our first glimpse of the smelter, surrounded by grain fields.

The real discoverers of gold in this section were the Indians, who, as early as the 1860's, found traces of color in a gulch on the western slope of the Sweet Grass Hills. Some twenty years later this gulch held the mining camp of Gold Butte. With the exception of occasional fur trappers, the Sweet Grass Hills were first seen by white men in the 1870's when members of the boundary survey explored the area. In 1874, Captain Twining, who was a member of the survey party, had a road built to the Hills, and at this time, a little prospecting was done by "parties in the permanent supply camp," who found some quartz but no placers. These officers and men were unfamiliar with mining and their scratching of the surface was most superficial.

In the fall of 1884, a party of four men, Marion Carey, Fred Derwent, George Walters, and John Des Champ, discovered gold in the Hills, and although it was too late in the season to carry on any systematic work, the party made camp and wintered in the mountains. Early in the spring they prospected the east side of Middle Butte and found placer ground in "all of the side gulches to the west," but nothing in the gulches running into East Butte.

No sooner had they started work, than another party, consisting of Joe Kipp, Charles Thomas, Hi Upham, and ten others, arrived and proceeded to locate claims. A meeting was held and a mining district formed with Hi Upham as recorder. In May, Fort Benton learned of the strike when Marion Carey appeared with five ounces of gold with which to purchase supplies. On May 27, the *River Press* reported the arrival of a man from the Sweet Grass Hills:

Chas. Thomas was in the city Sunday. . . . The mines are on the west side of the middle butte and near the top, a place where no one with any experience in mining matters would look for placer mines. The gold is found from the grass roots down, and in many places the bedrock, which is a black slate, crops to the surface.

Fifteen men are there engaged in sluicing, but water is scarce and it is feared that work will have to be abandoned for the summer. All the coarse gold has quartz mixed with it. If water was plenty, it is thought that the placers would pay at least $10 a day to the man.

The Hills were remote, and no one bothered to find out whether they were within Indian reservation land or not. All summer, prospectors slipped into the gulches, staked claims and worked them, eager to recover as much as possible before government interference. As soon as it was known that the miners were prospecting on the Blackfeet Reservation, John D. C. Atkins, commissioner of Indian Affairs, wrote to the U.S. Indian agent at the Blackfeet agency:

The law provides how tresspassers shall be removed. . . the law is mandatory. . . you are hereby directed to notify the miners and prospectors in the Sweet Grass Hills, within the reservation limits. . . and warn them to remove from the reservation. If they refuse to comply with such warning, you will at once report the fact to this office.

The *River Press* of June 17, 1885, printed the Commissioner's letter under the headlines:

This is Too Bad!
The Miners and Prospectors of the Sweet
Grass and Little Rockies Will Probably
Have to Go.

By fall, a company of infantry was stationed at the Sweet Grass Hills camp, seemingly to protect rather than eject the miners, for a letter, written to the editor of the *River Press* (November 4, 1885), states that the company was

performing good service for the government in endeavoring to put a stop to the incursions of marauding Indians. Camp life is not all that fancy has painted. It is review at sunrise, inspection at sunset, taps and lights out at 8 P.M., no one allowed to leave camp without permission. Our bill of fare is as follows: breakfast, bacon, dinner hog meat, supper bacon. It is very good for a few meals, but for a steady diet it gets monotonous. . . . There are two prisoners in one guard tent. We are not allowed to go out fishing in sight of the camp without permission. There are several more candidates for the guard house. We regard the restrictions of the camp insupportable, and it is important that the rations should be increased and improved.

Rex
Camp of Sweet Grass Hills
October 23, 1885

When gold mining ceased, about 1890, Gold Butte became a ghost camp. A more recent effort to recover gold was made in the 1930's by a "gold-mining dragline outfit," which attempted to wash and save the flour gold that had eluded earlier methods; but even this enterprise ran but a season or two and shut down.

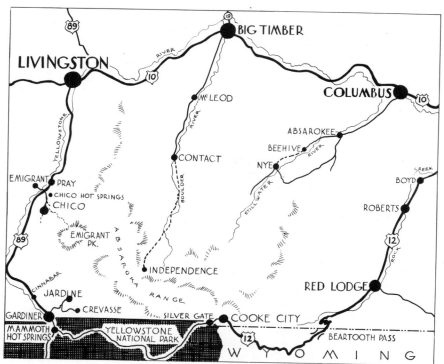

CHAPTER 22

YELLOWSTONE
COUNTRY

The portion of Montana that lies directly north of Yellowstone Park is cut by few trails and fewer roads. Even today, craggy peaks and deep canyons are locked within the boundaries of the Absaroka Primitive Area and the Beartooth Wilderness. Roads that enter the area from the north are river trails that skirt the Yellowstone, Boulder, and Stillwater, good for a few miles, but useless when a steep pitch or a rock slide blocks further progress. High in the mountains, these trails become grass-grown tracks. The best of the three follows the Yellowstone through a wide valley between the Absaroka and Gallatin Ranges.

This was Indian country, unknown to Whites until the 1860's, although an occasional trapper penetrated its virgin forests. It was also trackless, except for scattered Indian trails. The first white men who ventured into it were promptly run out or killed. Between 1868 and 1882, a large section was withdrawn from public domain and set aside for the Crow Reservation. Its intangible boundaries hampered, but did not prevent, those who were searching for gold from continuing their work until they were ejected. That mining camps materialized in several portions of this unexplored area just goes to show what stuff prospectors were made of and the risks which they would take to develop a strike.

Most of the camps they built had a brief and gaudy life and are enjoying a long sleep. One or two have prospered, more from tourists than from minerals. The rest are almost forgotten sites, known only to hunters and sheepherders.

Late in July of 1956, my husband and I drove from Colorado into Wyoming, to Cody and north through Powell and Elk Basin, into Montana. Winding roads through wide valleys and over high ridges brought us to Red Lodge, where the sixty-eight mile scenic highdrive into Yellowstone Park, across Beartooth Pass, begins. This $3,000,000 highway, begun in 1932, and completed four years later, rises for sixteen miles from Rock Creek Canyon to the 10,940 foot pass by a series of curves and switchbacks, appropriately named Big Thrill Turn, Mae West Curve, Deadwood Switchback, and Dead Man's Curve. The views on the ascent are breathtaking and cannot be described.

Once a year, the Red Lodge Chamber of Commerce selects a snowbank beside the road, carves out an icy counter, stocks it with beverages, and serves all who pass from its "Top O' the World Bar." The date is a secret, but the event has become an annual celebration. Our drive over the highway did not coincide with it.

From the summit of the pass, Pilot and Index Peaks rise above the lesser crags of the Absaroka Range to the west. As the highway loops down to the Beartooth Plateau, from the eighteen miles of tundra into spruce and balsam forests, it passes a number of small but beautiful lakes. Back on the valley floor, six miles south of the Wyoming border, the road crosses the Clark Fork of the Yellowstone and follows it into Montana. Eight thousand-foot Cook Pass was nothing after Beartooth, and the gentle descent on the far side, through dense stands of timber and past clumps of brilliant wildflowers, brought us to the outskirts of Cooke City, the oldest existing town in Park County. In among the trees, I saw the first evidence of mining — empty buildings of the McLaren Gold Mines Company, and a big settling pond.

For the ghost town hunter, the place is a disappointment. Ever since 1921, when the first tourist campground was set up, old cabins have been restored or hidden behind newer buildings. Some shacks with moss-covered roofs stand among the trees and a few false-fronted stores, well camouflaged with corrugated metal roofs and fronts, mingle with new homes and roadside stands. Shiny, peeled log façades support neon signs to lure tourists and fishermen off the road for a coffee break, souvenirs, or a night's lodging. Cooke, as it is now called, is a wide-awake resort town with gas pumps and juke boxes.

Its setting is magnificent, for although the valley widens at this point, high wooded mountains hem in the sides and block any northern exit. Mine dumps and prospect holes cover their slopes, and in a few places dim trails lead up to empty shacks and sheds. Far up the side of Republic Mountain, but below its rocky crest, is the shafthouse of the Brooks mine. A clear stream runs behind the main street, and beyond it is another mine and a dilapidated mill. One well-kept, two-story frame house, painted white, seems to date from Cooke City's prime and must have been a boardinghouse or a hotel. Could it have been the Allen which was built in 1883 by J. P. Allen and which contained mahogany furniture brought across the plains in a covered wagon? It was not the Cosmopolitan Hotel of which I had seen a photograph, for the architecture was quite different. No one to whom we spoke seemed to know its past. In fact, the storekeepers whom I questioned were either newcomers or were too busy with customers to tell me anything of Cooke's history.

George Houston (Huston), who left Virginia City in 1864 with Peter Moore and a small party of adventurers, was, in all probability, the first to explore the mountainous area near present Cooke City, but apparently no discoveries resulted from the trip. Few other expeditions were undertaken until 1869, or the early seventies, when four trappers — Adam or "Horn" Miller, Bart Henderson, J. H. Moore, and James Gourley (Gowsley) — outfitted for a prospecting trip and left Crow Agency for the mountains. Accounts vary or overlap, but apparently, near the head of Clark Fork of the Yellowstone and/or on upper Soda Butte Creek, they found float in the gravel as well as galena deposits in three or four places. Further prospecting was cut short when Indians rode into their camp and ran off all their horses. Helpless without their mounts, the men cached their equipment and supplies near a stream, now known as Cache Creek, and backtracked across the divide, making as good time as possible on foot back to the Agency. There they described their adventures and discoveries and announced their determination to return and continue their search for the gold that they were certain the area held. According to one account, this group discovered the stained outcrop that with development became the Republic mine at Cooke City.

When the return expedition was organized in 1874, it contained the original party (with the exception of Bart Henderson), and in addition, Sam Shively, Pat O'Hare, "Dutch Bill," and men named Banks and Parker. From the Agency, the group traveled up the Boulder River to the divide and back to their prospects. Horn Miller went to work on a vein of argentiferous galena which he uncovered, and the others struck out for new prospects. Before snow drove them out of the high country, in the fall of 1874, several more mines were discovered and staked. The following summer, placer claims were located on both Republic and Miller Mountains and a Mexican furnace was constructed to smelt lead ore from the Miller Mountain lodes.

The miners called this area the New World District. When glowing reports of its deposits were published in a Bozeman newspaper, men rushed in. A smelter, built in 1876 by the Eastern Montana Mining & Smelting Company, successfully reduced eighty tons of silver-lead ore to thirty tons of bullion early in 1877.

Joseph, chief of the Nez Percé Indians, who

during the summer of 1877 led his people in a strategic and desperate retreat across Montana in a vain attempt to reach Canada and freedom, passed through Cooke City to the annoyance of the miners. His warriors burned the gold mills and took with them the silver bullion that was ready to be packed out of the area. This they cast into bullets to use against their pursurers. After this episode, new smelters were built and mining resumed, although the men had to admit that their crude equipment was inadequate to process any but high-grade ore. Even sluiceboxes could not save flour gold from the placers. Some of the miners left, but about twenty stayed in the district though they had no right there. The ground lay within the Crow Reservation and was not opened to settlement until 1882.

Two years before that date, George Houston bonded his Republic group of claims to Jay Cooke, Jr., and his associates. Cooke, a Northern Pacific contractor, and his party reached the district, intent upon examining their property, to find that eight to ten feet of snow covered the dumps where several hundred tons of $100 ore were stacked. So eager were the prospectors to interest eastern capital in the mines, that they shoveled the snow from the dumps and away from the tunnel mouth and cleared the ground to show the veins. While the party was on an inspection tour, the miners held a meeting and voted unanimously to name their camp Cooke City in honor of the new investor. In return, Cooke promised to do what he could to bring a railroad to the town and to develop the settlement into an important center. Everything seemed set, until Cooke found himself in financial straits. After an initial payment of $5,000, Cooke forfeited the bond and the property reverted to its original owners.

Since all the mines were on Indian land, outside capital refused to invest in them until the government returned the territory to public domain in 1882. Men immediately poured in on horseback, on foot, and on Norwegian snowshoes (or skiis), so that before long, 1,450 locations were made and recorded in the New World District. To be sure, the majority of these were not developed—nearly a thousand were allowed to lapse—but Cooke City grew during the summer until the 135 dirt-roofed log huts and the scattering of tents barely held the swelling population.

John P. Allen first heard of the area in the seventies, when news of the discovery of float near Soda Butte Creek was printed in eastern papers. Allen at that time was twenty years old and lived in Rhode Island. In 1876, he went to the Black Hills, where he prospected for five years. Next, he tried Cooke City, which he reached in May, 1882. The journey from Bozeman was unusually trying, for he was the first to drive a four-horse team and loaded wagon into Cooke. Between Soda Butte and his destination he even broke the first road, digging out the mountainside and leveling ledges which were formerly barren, precarious pack trails. Near Cooke City, he located several mines — the O'Hara, War Eagle, and McKinley. On the town's main street he built the Allen Hotel in 1883, an hostelry which could serve 150 guests a day. Some idea of the appearance of the camp is indicated by the following:

The houses are dirt-covered log shacks, that indicate the lack of building material instead of poverty of purse and mild architectural ambitions rather than indifference to comfort.

From being few, the present buildings are numerous and stretch out to make a street as long as the main street of Livingston, though the population of the camp will not number above two-hundred, exclusive of the prospectors scattered through the mountains.

Livingston Enterprise, October 17, 1883

That Cooke City was without a jail is shown by this account of a crime:

At Cooke City on the 10th inst., Frank Young shot and killed Daniel McCarthy. The former was intoxicated and the latter in some way procured Young's money. Young insisted that McCarthy intended to rob him and procuring a gun shot McCarthy, inflicting a fatal wound. Young was arrested and is in jail in Bozeman.

Avant Courier, July 19, 1883

By the fall of 1883, the residents of Cooke City were eager to see the townsite platted so that title to lots could be obtained. Sigmund Deutsch was employed to make the survey, which included forty-one acres. All would have been well had not this area contained several millsites, previously filed on by different companies and to which title could not be obtained. Settlement on such lots was not concluded for eight years. While the survey was progressing, there was considerable lot jumping. There were also those who favored a change in the camp's name. At a meeting to discuss the subject, Major George O. Eaton suggested Eidelweiss, but when put to a vote, the majority of the miners favored the old name and the townsite was recorded as Cooke.

As the mines in the area were developed, the

COOKE CITY AND REPUBLIC MOUNTAIN

SIDE STREET, COOKE CITY

need for cheap haulage became evident, and as soon as the Northern Pacific's branch line through the Yellowstone Valley to Cinnabar was completed, in 1883, the mine operators began to clamor for an extension of the road to Cooke. Access to the region was admittedly difficult from every direction. The only feasible route was from Gardiner, which entailed passing through the northern part of Yellowstone Park, and this the government refused to allow. Meetings were held to devise ways to raise capital for the construction of the road, and for a number of years, every Congress was bombarded with petitions and bills requesting permission for a right of way.

In 1885, the first bill to remove the needed area from the Park was presented to Congress. All interested persons in Cooke, Gardiner, and Livingston tensely awaited news from Washington. When a telegram reached Livingston that the bill had passed the House, the operator interpreted it to mean that everything was favorably settled. He therefore broadcast the good news. This was exactly what the speculators and prospectors had been waiting for, and although it was winter, a rush into the Soda Butte region commenced. The first waves of stampeders reached the diggings before the miners of Cooke City learned of the wire. Although they hurriedly packed in by night, by the time they reached the ground, all the best locations had been staked. Then came the apologetic announcement from the operator that he had made a mistake and that nothing was decided.

The Park Bill
Congress expired without doing anything more with the bill. . . . Congress objected to allowing a railroad in the park and it was then asked that the Park boundaries be changed to allow the railroad to pass over public domain. But suspicions of jobbery entered the minds of the senators and they would not agree upon the amendment to that end made by the House.

Livingston Enterprise, March 7, 1885

Disappointment gave way to a determination to try again. The most concerted effort came in 1891, when Cooke City prospectors and Livingston businessmen raised $1,500 and sent a delegation, headed by Sigmund Deutsch, to Washington to lobby for a railroad. The first night there, Deutsch threw a wet party to further the cause of the road, and the next day wired for additional funds. That ended that.

Snow slowed down the development of the mines as much as did the lack of transportation facilities. For more than half of every year, the area was isolated and little could be accomplished except to get ore out to the mouths of the tunnels from which it could be hauled in summer to the mills or sent outside to smelters.

The *Park County News,* reporting on conditions during the one severe winter, comments that "Cooke City is full of idle men . . . . There are two general stores and thirteen saloons." In one of the latter, two miners played

A Big Game of Crib
Cooke City Miners Stake Their Lodes on a Game of Cards.
A highly excitable cribbage match was played here last night. The stakes were 100-feet of the Snowslide lode against 100 feet of the Elevator lode — both rich properties. The conditions were that 100 games of cribbage were to be played, and the man winning the most games was to take the stakes. The game began about 3 p.m. and ended about 3 a.m. with the Elevator ahead and winner. The deeds to the 100 feet of the Snowslide were made out and given him and he was immediately offered $1500 for them.

Livingston Enterprise, August 2, 1885

In winter, all travel was by snowshoes, and the danger from slides was constant. Martin Ramnael, a packer, accepted a contract to deliver a ton of supplies to a mining camp ten miles northeast of Cooke City, where twelve men were at work driving two tunnels into the mountain. The snow was so deep at the high camp that the men had to cut passageways between the buildings and burn lamps and candles day and night for light. Ramnael found that by carrying 75-120 pounds at a time, he could make one round trip a day, but each time he had to break a new trail through the snow to prevent starting a slide.

Once, when he had a case of coal oil in a harness on his back, and was carrying a pick and sledge hammer in his hands, the snow on a high ridge gave way. He successfully rode the avalanche to the bottom and landed, buried in deep snow. Hampered by his skis, which were strapped on, and by the heavy case of coal oil, it took him fifteen minutes to work himself loose.

Ramnael was in the valley on New Year's Day, when a snowslide killed two of the miners and nearly wiped out the camp. That morning, a small slide came down and buried the mouths of both tunnels. The men shoveled them clear and went to the bunkhouse for dinner. Several of them returned in the afternoon to finish clearing the entranceway. Tredennick, the foreman, was standing on a timbered ridge, seventy-five yards from where the men were working, when, as W. H. Banfill tells it in the *Park County News,* "the whole side of the mountain broke loose and swept everything before it. Spruce trees two feet through were broken down." The avalanche crashed to the bottom with such force that it swept across the valley, covering an area one-third of a mile wide, and pushed a wall of snow up the opposite side of the draw.

When Tredennick heard the roar, he instinctively grabbed a tree, but it was snapped off by the impact of the snow. He was lifted into the air but managed to grab the limb of a big spruce to which he clung as long as he was able. When he let go, the main run of snow had passed by, but he was carried down the mountain for fifty feet, until stopped by another tree. Rescuers were unable to find the miners Clarence Martin and Tony Wise, in the mass of hard-packed snow. The body of Wise was uncovered the following June, with a shovel still in his hand. Martin's body was not found until the fourth of July. He had been carried halfway across the narrow valley and nearly everyone of his bones was broken. The bunkhouse escaped the avalanche by twenty-five feet. The surviving miners were so unnerved by the experience that most of them quit.

Beginning with 1882, mining development in the district was steady. The Eastern Montana Mining & Smelting Company, which built its smelter after the Indian raid of 1877, had already been in operation for five years. At first the company bought charcoal from Pennsylvania, but the expense of hauling it in by wagon or pack train from Bozeman or Livingston was too great. From 1882 on, the company manufactured its own, hiring woodchoppers to cut and stack green timber, of which there was an abundance, and cover it with wet branches. The piles were then set on fire and allowed to smolder until the charcoal was ready for use.

In the same year, George O. Eaton bought the Great Republic, Greely, Houston, and New World mining claims and organized the Republic Mining Company. By 1883, the company had spent $300,000 in developing the property and building the Cooke City or Republic smelter, which operated somewhat unsuccessfully throughout 1884 on the complex lead, silver-zinc ores of the district. Reuben Rickard, superintendent of the Republic mine, was in charge of the smelter and ran various tests as soon as he found that the amount of antimony and zinc in the ore prevented reduction by usual methods. Heap roasting was tried, but it, too, was a failure; so a roasting furnace was added in 1885.

That fall, 440 tons of silver-lead bullion were produced and sold for $95,000, but the profits were canceled by the costs of coke and transportation. If only a railroad were closeby, the district's troubles would be over, but Cinnabar, the Northern Pacific's railhead, was fifty-one miles away.

Rickard had an idea. Build a desilverizing plant, so that silver could be recovered and shipped out and the lead held back and allowed to accumulate until the sheer mass of it would so impress railroad officials that they would want to build the long-sought line. When funds for the plant were not forthcoming, Rickard resigned. The smelter and mine closed down and were not reopened for twenty years.

Although the Republic, the best mine in the district, was closed other properties were active.

In 1888, new gold deposits were opened on Henderson Mountain in both the Homestake and the Daisy, and several carloads of ore shipped out. The oxidized ores were exhausted before the drop in silver prices struck Cooke City in 1894 and resulted in further shutdowns.

The camp revived in 1905 when several companies reopened old properties or made large-scale plans for the development of new discoveries. One of the latter was a copper lode four miles north of Cooke City, at Goose Lake. The Copper King Mining & Development Company, which opened the mine, built a road between it and Cooke and continued to operate the property until the financial panic of 1907 forced it to close. The Precious Metals Company, formed in 1904, built a lead smelter one-half mile east of Cooke City. When no suitable ore was found in the vicinity of the plant, copper ore was purchased from claims on Henderson Mountain, but since the smelter was built for lead reduction, attempts to process copper ore were not successful, and the plant shut down. By 1912, the property was idle.

The biggest project was that of the Montana Company (later affiliated with the New World Smelting Company), which acquired nearly one hundred claims northeast of Cooke City and by energetic and skillful promotion launched a large scale development program. The company properties included the National Park mines on Henderson Mountain, the Treadwell Group on Scotch Bonnet Mountain, as well as the Silver Fraction, Money King, Dalhousie, Sampson group, and North Star mines. The company's holdings covered "lumbering, electric power and smelting plants" valued at $100,000 on the Clark Fork of the Yellowstone River and a townsite called Falls City, half a mile below the smelters and four miles above the Big Falls. When completed, their 100-ton silver-lead furnace and copper matting smelter was expected to yield a "net profit to the company of $750.00 a day."

During the summer of 1907, the Montana Company sought to attract capital to the isolated area. Their brochure announced:

The Montana Co. will conduct a special excursion to the wonders of Yellowstone Park and points of interest in the New World Mining Camp, leaving Union Station, Chicago via the Chicago, Milwaukee & St. Paul and Northern Pacific Railways on Wed., July 17, 1907.

The excursion is for men, women and children, and in charge of a polite corps of men and women. It will cover all the main points of interest in the Park by special carriages.

The mines of the plants of the Montana Co. are situated within seven miles of the border of the Park. Those of the excursion may visit the great New World Mining Camp and examine our vast plants, mines and business prospects, while their families are doing the Park. The terms of the excursion, which covers two weeks in the Park, are very tempting. Join and bring your wife.

Charles A. Hart,
Vice-Pres. of the Montana Co.,
Hartford, Conn.

In 1908, the New World Smelting Company replaced the Montana Company as the leading force in the district. Its most ambitious dream was an electric railroad, to be built from Columbus (on the Northern Pacific), up the Stillwater Valley to the mines, a distance of eighty miles. Both the Stillwater and Boulder River Routes were surveyed in anticipation of its construction with the former selected as the more practical.

Cooke City was entirely dependent upon the mines for its prosperity, and its population fluctuated from "a few dozen to a few hundred, according to mining and smelting operations." By now, the town had two smelters, two steam sawmills, three general stores, and two hotels.

The winter of 1921 found six companies at work in the district, producing so much tonnage that the old question of a railroad was again raised. Operators began to say that "connection by rail with the outside world was only a matter of time" and that "within two years the engine whistle will be heard in Cooke City." In the meantime, auto trucks hauled lead-silver ore to Gardiner, sixty miles away, where the railroad ended. Again, the railroad to Cooke failed to materialize, and by the middle 1920's, first one and then another property closed down or became involved in litigation.

Up until 1925, the estimated production of the district was $215,000 in gold, silver, copper and lead. Since then, some properties have been leased from time to time and ore from them trucked out to the railroad; but Cooke City is no longer a mining camp, but a resort town, and the ore in its encircling mountains awaits a future boom.

Cooke City has its legend of buried treasure —a prospector's boot full of gold which is thought to be hidden two and a half miles east of the town and 150 yards from the highway. The boot belonged to one of two prospectors who made their pile in Virginia City around 1880 and then started back to the States. Fearing that road agents might steal the treasure they were packing out, they stuck to trails through Indian country rather than traveled roads, and, after many hardships, drove their heavily-loaded mule into Cooke City.

Despite all precautions, they were followed by thieves who attacked them in the mountains shortly after their departure from the camp. One of the men was killed and the other, frantic with fear, jerked off his partner's warm boot, stuffed it with as much of their fortune as it would hold, and buried it. Scrambling out of sight, he hid in the mountains until the robbers left. He was afraid to carry the treasure with him; so he left it in the boot and carved a cryptogram on a nearby tree, which was intended to guide him to the cache upon his return from the East. He never returned. Some years later, three nephews arrived in Cooke City with a map and a guide and spent several months in a vain search for the heavy boot. They found the tree stump, as others have since, and they studied the cryptogram which supposedly holds the key to the valuable location. The weathered carving consists of an eight-inch circle inside of which is a three-inch cross. Below is the date 1880 and beneath that a triangle, resembling a tepee. Under it are two numerals, six and five.

GARDINER

Steam was rising from the soda terraces at Mammoth Hot Springs as we left Yellowstone Park the next morning. Just beyond the massive, stone arch which marks the park's northern entrance is the railroad town of Gardiner, named for Johnston Gardiner, a trapper who worked this upper Yellowstone country in the 1830's. The hostile attitude of the Crow Indians, who resisted white encroachment on their hunting grounds, deferred the founding of the town until 1883, just after the land was opened for

MINE OFFICE, JARDINE

JARDINE

development. Gardiner immediately became the freighting center for the Cooke City mining area, and when, in the same year, the Northern Pacific road talked of extending a branch line through the Yellowstone Valley and establishing a terminal near the Park, Gardiner naturally expected to be the railhead. Disputes over the location of the terminal resulted in the selection of Cinnabar, four miles north of Gardiner. In spite of this snub, Gardiner held its own and, twenty years later, watched with satisfaction as Northern Pacific crews laid rails within its boundaries. Since 1902, it has been the road's terminus, and Cinnabar has shriveled in size.

Old-timers recall that in 1886 almost every building, except the two general stores, was a saloon. George Colpitts, the blacksmith, was the town's champion spitter, taking on opponents at $1.00 a spit. One such contest was held in Charley Scott's Corner Saloon, after Neal Gillis had won all of Colpitt's money at poker. George won it all back by spitting at a mark.

The Fourth of July, 1886, was celebrated with gusto. The day began when explosions of black powder, that had been touched off on anvils, broke the glass in nearby buildings. Horse races and foot races went on all day, and the saloon doors were never still.

It's a stiff five-mile climb from Gardiner to Jardine on a road which skirts the deep green valley of Bear Gulch. The camp lies in a high meadow on Bear Creek, named by the Austin party in 1863 when, according to the *Bozeman Avant Courier* of February 12, 1880, the men caught on its banks "a cub bear so young it was still furless."

Placer gold was discovered at the mouth of Bear Gulch by "Uncle" Joe Brown and two others during the winter of 1865-66. In May, after a few weeks' work, they recovered $1,800 in gold. From then until 1884, Brown and Vilas, his partner, worked their property in a small way, sluicing surface gravel and constantly searching for the ancient channel of the creek, which was certain to hold rich deposits. Between 1875 and 1877, Brown and the other placer miners constructed a system of ditches to the several bars. These drains, which cost several thousand dollars, were used long after their builders abandoned them.

Some say that the first quartz deposits were uncovered in 1870, and others contend that it was 1874; but all sources agree that the discoverers were James Graham and "Uncle" Joe

Brown, and that the lodes were on the slope known as Mineral Hill. They were not developed until 1877, when Graham, Brown, and Heffner built an arrastra at the Legal Tender claim but found the ore too refractory to yield to that method of extraction. Within a year or two, the Graham and other lodes were discovered; but, again, little was done with them until 1884, after Brown sold his claims to Major Eaton and Sturgess. The new owners spent large amounts of money in exploring the placer claims by tunnels and drifts and uncovered "an ancient channel 206 feet wide." Their corporation, the Bear Gulch Placer Company, also installed powerful hydraulic equipment which consisted of a giant "served by 1200 feet of 12-inch pipe." The force of water that burst from the six-inch nozzle of the giant was "sufficient to bend an ordinary iron bar double."

In 1885, a reporter from the *Livingston Enterprise* visited the property:

The water used in the hydraulic has a fall of 410 feet and passes through the little giant with a tremendous velocity, striking the bank with a roar and force that is wonderful. We enjoyed the Colonel's hospitality at supper and for the first time broke bread with the sturdy miners.

August 22, 1885

Major Eaton also erected a combination five-stamp mill and sawmill on Bear Creek to handle the oxidized surface ores from the lode claims. This was a success and ran nearly two years, but disagreements among the stockholders and the difficulty of hauling the ore to the railroad at Cinnabar forced a shutdown in 1886.

Edgerton & Jewell of Helena, who reopened the Eaton mill and added five stamps in 1890, made other improvements in the property and were operating it successfully when the panic of 1893 brought another shutdown. The next few years saw only desultory prospecting and staking of claims. Then, in July, 1898, Harry Bush arrived and the district came alive!

Bush, an Englishman, was a natural leader and promoter and he thought big. He was not a crook, but a visionary speculator who believed in taking a long chance and then seeing that it paid off. When he reached the gulch, the mining camp consisted of four log cabins belonging to Mr. and Mrs. George Welcome and two other residents. His first act was to negotiate a three-year lease with E. F. Wilson, the receiver for the First National Bank of Helena, which held the Edgerton-Jewell properties on Mineral Hill, including the Legal Tender. His second was to organize the Bear Gulch Mining Company and to

secure $5,000 from New Brunswick investors with which to begin operations. Ten days after his arrival, he enlarged the Eaton mill to twenty stamps and, after installing new vanners and tables, successfully milled the oxidized ores. His next move was to lay out a townsite.

Shortly after his arrival he watched the start of the first of the new buildings—a large hotel for the laborers. In rapid succession, three hotels, three general stores, one of them owned by Bush and Welcome, three saloons, a barber shop, a school large enough for 200 pupils, company office buildings, and an "elegantly furnished" guest house "without a peer in the state," took shape. Within the year, 130 new buildings were erected, some of which, such as the mine office and guest house, are still in use. A post office was established with J. B. McCarthy, postmaster, and telephone service was provided. Upon the completion and operation of the company's mill, in the spring of 1899, Jardine's monthly payroll reached $20,000.

While the town was growing, Bush organized the Revenue Mining Company to take over the property of the Bear Gulch Mining Company and to acquire additional claims. These, in addition to the Revenue, which belonged to George Phelps, included the Sowash, the Keets (an extension of the Sowash), the West Point, North Star, Norse, and W. W. Dixon, as well as Brown's forty-acre placer and 3,000-foot ditch.

Just before Bush left for Chicago to sell stock in the new company, the mine superintendent, A. C. Jardine, asked him how he could afford to run the mill at a loss, on ore that averaged only $1.50 a ton.

"There's nothing else to do," replied Bush crisply. "If Daugherty and his gang hadn't jumped the Legal Tender, we'd have good ore to mill. We'll get rid of them when I get back. In the meantime, keep the mill going day and night even if you have to feed it pine stumps. We can't sell stock with an idle mill, can we?"

With claim jumper Daugherty and his crowd in control of the Legal Tender, the best of the company's mines, Bush was really in trouble. He had hoped that deposits from the Sowash would tide things over until he could regain control of the paying property, but Sowash ore was the disappointing "dead rock" that the mill was grinding. All winter the mill operated and the company met its payroll, although the men knew the ore was worthless. Early one morning, while it was still dark, a blast woke everyone in camp. Upon investigation, it was found that the Daugherty cabin had been dynamited. Knots

REVENUE MILL, JARDINE MINING CO.

of men gathered to discuss the incident and describe how the roof had a hole in it big enough for a horse to fall through. Inside, one of the logs had fallen across Daugherty's bed, which was empty at the time. Daugherty and his partners escaped unharmed and, realizing that their game was up, made a hasty getaway. With their departure, claim jumping ceased.

A few days later, a shift boss brought a dinner pail full of rich quartz samples from the Sowash into the mine office. They were from a pocket of ore found during the night in a drift tunnel. When assayed, they showed values up to $50,000 a ton in gold. This strike and the repossession of the Legal Tender claim started the period of development and steady production that Bush had anticipated. The Sowash ore was too rich for the mill to handle; so it was sent to the East Helena smelter. Bush, by then, was in Helena rather than Chicago, with a bank credit of $40,000 made, as he explained, by selling stock by wire. Upon his return to Jardine, he outlined plans for the company's future and began to spend money recklessly. When the new forty-stamp Revenue mill was completed in the

spring of 1900, Bush celebrated the event by providing a ball and a "feast of buffalo meat and liquor," which cost $3,000. The successful operation of the mines by the Revenue Mining & Milling Company was short-lived, for inadequate mine development, insufficient funds, and Bush's extravagances brought the company into receivership. Work was suspended because of the resulting litigation.

At this point, "Cabbage Ryan" enters the scene, and although he was interested in the properties, he and Bush soon disagreed. Ryan, who appears to have been sharper than Bush, was assisted by Peter L. Kimberly, the owner of another defunct mining company at Jardine. These two men forced Bush out of the deal in 1901, and, after more litigation, obtained control of both the Revenue Company and the Bear Gulch Mining Company. In the spring of 1903, Ryan and Kimberly consolidated these properties with the inactive Kimberly Mining Company and organized the Kimberly-Montana Gold Mining & Milling Company.

Under Ryan's supervision, a hydro-electric plant was built in Bear Gulch, not far from the

Yellowstone River, and a large, 150-ton cyanide plant was erected near the mines. Company plans called for another forty-stamp mill and a future plant equipped with 500 stamps. Underground drilling was done with the aid of a new air compressor. These improvements, while useful, cost more than the company could afford.

Ryan and the new company were most unpopular in Jardine, as this item in the *Gardiner Wonderland* shows:

Kimberly-Montana Shuts down on Sunday Evening. H. M. Ryan, the man who does the blowing for the company, has been the cause of a great deal of dissension among the men and if the mines have not paid in the past, he alone is probably at fault due to the fact he has absolute control. . . . he has ordered respectable citizens from camp because their views were not in line with his. The manager of the company believes there has been something wrong with the mill . . . [it is] hinted that the plates have been tampered with by putting grease upon them, to make the gold slip off and go with refuse into the creek. . . . [this] cannot be verified.

April 23, 1904

Despite financial crises and animosity, the company is credited with the discovery of scheelite, a tungsten deposit of commercial importance. The credit belongs to Wortenweiler, the mine superintendent, who recognized the presence of the mineral in the ore in 1904. The following year, he made private shipments of the rock without the knowledge of the management. After Wortenweiler left the company, Ryan learned of his actions and traced his shipments all the way to Germany. Curious as to the ore, Ryan had tests run at the East Helena smelter which showed the presence of tungsten. Scheelite was also found on the dumps, where it had been discarded by the early miners, who did not know how to separate the gold from this heavy, unknown rock. Following this discovery, the Kimberly-Montana Company shipped several hundreds tons of scheelite in 1906.

But even scheelite could not save the company, and it failed in 1906 from "financial difficulties and internal friction." Legal entanglements which harrassed the property were not settled until 1917. During this period, the mines changed hands three times.

The Jardine Gold Mining & Milling Company acquired the property and equipment in 1914 through a bondholders' foreclosure sale. In 1916, Harry C. Bacorn of Butte and W. S. Hunnewell, leased the mines. Bacorn, as president and general manager, assisted by his brother, F. W. Bacorn, the treasurer of the

company, overhauled the property so as to start operations as soon as possible.

By this settlement, the Jardine Gold Mine & Milling Company owned just about everything in Bear Gulch — a large group of developed mines, twenty-three patented claims, a townsite, hydro-electric plant, and 350 additional acres. Mining and milling of gold and low-grade scheelite ores commenced within the year and continued until 1921, when the properties were purchased by the Jardine Mining Company and refinanced. Harry Bacorn remained and served as general manager and president until 1936. During this period, the mines were reasonably productive and paid modest dividends.

Ore rich in arsenopyrite was discovered; and concentrates which were shipped to Tacoma in 1922 averaged thirty-eight per cent arsenic trioxide (commony known as white arsenic). A complete arsenic plant which cost $125,000 was built in 1923 to produce both crude and refined arsenic trioxide from arsenical gold concentrates. The plant operated almost continuously from 1923 to 1926 and again from 1932 to 1936.

In January, 1942, due to war-time restrictions, the Jardine Mining Company, the only operator in the district, closed its 225-ton amalgamation-concentration mill. The continued need for arsenic resulted in a Federal government contract to rehabilitate the plant and install new equipment. White arsenic was then delivered to Metals Reserve Company over the two-year period from January, 1944, through the year 1945. On May 8, 1948, fire destroyed the cyanide plant, and on July 15, the Jardine Mining Company closed the mine. During its years of operation, the mill treated 33,416 tons of gold ore.

The town of Jardine, referred to in 1900 as the most prominent and wide awake gold camp in the state, is rather quiet nowadays, yet in many ways it has retained its original appearance. An early photograph shows many buildings on the main street, a group of cabins just beyond the mill, more mine structures higher on the mountain, a flume and mine dumps. Even before swinging into the main street, we noticed signs of placering and hydraulicking in the creekbed and of prospect holes riddling the sagebrush-covered hills. Most of the mining claims are 800 or more feet above the townsite, on the timbered slopes. The Revenue mill dominates the settlement; individual houses are smothered in trees.

The majority of the homes are one story

and are built of logs or boards. Painted fences, neat gardens, and parked cars or trucks indicated those that were occupied. Since no mining was going on at the time of our visit, the cars and trucks, or the washing on a line, were our only clues as to the number of people living in Jardine in 1956. The older buildings — one of which was a two-story boardinghouse that teeters on the bank of the creek which runs through the town — were made of chinked, squared logs. A Pepsi-Cola cooler rested on the porch of an abandoned cabin. One long, low, chinked log house in the middle of a fenced garden plot bore a sign, "Post Office." The firehouse was a small, open shed just big enough to hold the hand-drawn hose cart.

To reach the mine office and the big mill on the hillside, I crossed the creek on a wooden bridge that was covered with signs: "Antler Guide Service, 1 blk.," "Load Limit 10 tons." The two which fascinated me most were:

Positively no Sleighriding	Danger
Across Bridge	Drive Slow
Jardine Mining Co.	Children Coasting
	Jardine Mining Co.

On my way to the silent mill, I passed the schoolhouse and the office of the Jardine Mining Company, a two-story frame building with a porch. The mill seemed in good repair and was larger than I had expected. Beyond it were more cabins and behind it were eroded dumps and sheds. As I walked back to the car, down a different street, a woman called from the doorway of a log building to tell me that it used to be a boardinghouse. Parked beside another home was a yellow school bus marked "Rosebud Consolidated School District." At the upper end of town, close to the sagebrush hills, was a two-story "chalet" with a rustic porch made of unpeeled poles. Could this have been the company guest house?

I did not see many people on my stroll through town, although voices from within the houses carried through the high, thin air. Children stopped playing to stare at me as I passed, and an old man, sunning himself in front of his cabin, spoke. "Have you been over to the Revenue mill?" he asked. "Lots of ore went through it before the shutdown. This camp was never unionized. The company ran three eight-hour shifts and paid $4.25 a day for outdoor work and $4.75 for underground. Timbermen got $5.00. The foreman made $200 a month. Placer mining went on long after Uncle Joe Brown sold his ground in the

1880's. Alex McDonald worked placers through a tunnel up until he died in 1939. Then W. L. Kearns came in from Livingston and carried on underground mining for a spell. If you're looking for old camps, you'd ought to go to Crevice," he told me. "It's five miles farther up and around the mountain back of Jardine. There's a few cabins left and lots of prospect holes."

CREVASSE (CREVICE)

The Crevasse Mountain District, which includes Bear Gulch, is in the northern part of the Absarokas, just outside Yellowstone Park, where the mountains are known as the Snowy Range. The mines in Crevasse (or Crevice) Gulch and on the mountain were discovered and worked simultaneously with those in nearby Bear Gulch. The placers date from 1863, and the lode mines from 1879, when someone named Stoner located the Pilot on Crevasse Mountain, and with his partner worked the gold quartz deposit in an arrastra which the two built. The same year, Neil Gillis and Charles H. Wyman discovered the Highland Chief on the south side of the ridge. They held the property until about 1891, when they disposed of it to Edgerton and Jewell of Helena, who promptly formed the Crevasse Mining Company. This new company owned, in addition to the Highland Chief, the Mizpah, Summit, and Granite lodes, and, to handle the volume of ore, moved the machinery of the ten-stamp mill that they had previously operated in Bear Gulch to a location on Highland Creek. Here the mill, which was finally enlarged to twenty stamps, operated successfully for a number of years.

Although the main development of claims at Crevasse was by organized companies, the initial strikes were made by individuals like Thomas Lewis, Adolph Hageman, and Frank Watson, who had lived in the region most of their lives. Little mining went on for the ten years after 1911, except during World War I, when Hageman and Watson processed and shipped small amounts of scheelite from their diggings.

Don Davenport revived the district in 1921 by leasing the Hulse and Hageman groups of claims and organizing the American Gold Mines Company.

Edgar Weld, James Reardon, and Norman Bongard leased the Snowshoe mine from the Treloar interests in 1931, installed a pebble mill on the property the following year, and worked the lode through an open cut, recovering more than 800 tons of oxidized ore.

We did not try to reach Crevasse. From Jardine, we could look south for miles, right into Yellowstone Park. On the horizon was Electric Peak and almost below us was Mammoth Hot Springs.

CINNABAR

"Look at that red mountain across the river," I said, as we drove north from Gardiner down the Yellowstone Valley. "That must be Cinnabar Mountain, and those vertical dikes down the face of it are the Devil's Slide. The early settlers and the Soule brothers, who were prospectors, thought the red rock was valuable cinnabar and contained quicksilver.

"Charles and James Soule were disappointed miners. Their attempts to reach bedrock in the Curry District of Emigrant Gulch were unsuccessful, and in disgust they left their cabin in Yellowstone City and struck out across the hills toward what is now the northern boundary of the Park. On a mountainside not far from the river was a quantity of reddish rock which they believed was cinnabar ore. They staked claims and worked their prospect throughout the summer and then, loaded with samples, rode to Virginia City to announce their quartz strike. So confident were they of their good fortune that they offered to stake claims for any one who would pay them $100.00 or its equivalent in dust, grub, or tools.

"That November, a string of pack animals laden with provisions, tools, and powder jingled into Yellowstone City. The Soule brothers were back, bringing mail from Virginia City and eager to talk about their mine. The lode of Cinnabar ore which they had uncovered lay on the west side of the Yellowstone Valley, and in order to get money with which to develop their property, they had sold seven claims to Virginia City people who were glad to get in on the bonanza. Now, the brothers were ready to drive a tunnel into the mountain. They displayed samples of ore and offered to locate more claims if paid to do so. Davis Weaver and others who examined the specimens were unimpressed; for the ore resembled the reddish rock that underlies hard coal formations, rather than cinnabar. One miner jeered at their plan, saying, 'They plan to tap the vein where it is rich so that the quicksilver will seep through the rock and form a pool in the bottom of the tunnel. Then they can dip it out with a cup.'

"When none of the men at Yellowstone City bought claims, the Soules rode back to their mountain and began to drive the tunnel. Before long, they were in trouble and called on Richard Owens, an experienced miner, to come over from Emigrant and dig out some fuses that had not fired. It was dangerous work, but Owens used a stick of wood instead of a steel pick and removed the duds, at the same time showing them how to set future powder charges. While at the mine, he investigated the area and found outcroppings of coal not far away. When he reported this discovery, the brothers were delighted, for coal would roast out the quicksilver even better than wood. The Soules worked on their tunnel until the spring of 1866 without finding any quicksilver. Finally convinced that the ground was barren, they set out for the diggings at Last Chance. In 1872, Professor F. V. Hayden, while making a geological survey of the region, visited the mine and identified the deposit as part of a coal formation. Yet, despite this, he named the red-stained upthrust Cinnabar Mountain.

"The small town we are approaching is also called Cinnabar," I continued. "Back in the eighties, it had several hundred population and was a lively place. I believe it started in 1883 and for twenty years was the terminus of the Yellowstone Park branch of the Northern Pacific Railroad. The first coal mined in Montana was near here, too; and there should be some ruined coke ovens left. Cinnabar served as railhead for both the coal and the hard-rock mining camps of the vicinity until 1902.

"In the spring of 1903, Cinnabar had its big moment. The railroad station and other facilities at Gardiner were not ready for occupancy when President Theodore Roosevelt came to the area to dedicate the stone arch at the northern entrance to the Park. He and his party, therefore, used the private Presidential train, which was drawn up at the Cinnabar station, as headquarters. During their sixteen-day stay, which included a tour of the Park, the train was the temporary White House from which Secretary William Loeb, Jr. conducted official business, with telegraph facilities provided by the Cinnabar railroad station."

EMIGRANT GULCH

Emigrant Gulch, in which placer gold had been found in the 1860's, lay on the east side of the Yellowstone River Valley. To get our bearings, we drove over the bridge across the

CHICO AND EMIGRANT GULCH

Yellowstone River to the town of Emigrant, on the railroad. In the combined store and post office, I inquired as to the whereabouts of Chico and Yellowstone City. According to the postmistress, we could drive to the old Chico townsite, where there were still a few cabins and one of the oldest schoolhouses in the state. The site of Yellowstone City was inaccessible, since a dredge had worked over the ground. As we were about to leave, a customer entered and the postmistress told the man about her daughter who was driving a car when a buffalo jumped over the radiator and put his foot through the windshield!

We recrossed the river and took the highway north, watching for the turnoff to Chico Hot Springs Hotel and Plunge, whose green lawn and well-kept cabins tempted us to stop for a swim. As we continued up the gravel road into the mouth of Emigrant Canyon, we passed a big ranchhouse and a little more than a mile beyond it, entered the Chico townsite. Here we found rotting log foundations buried in deep grass, as well as new cabins surrounded by trees and flowerbeds. The schoolhouse, if

old, had certainly been remodeled. A short distance above it stood Conlin's Confectionery, a two-story frame building that was boarded up. Emigrant Creek flowed by the townsite and cut a channel between dredge dumps, both above and below it, to enter the Yellowstone River, a few miles above the town of Emigrant. Upstream, the creek disappeared among interlocked folds of mountains. The head of the gulch was framed by snow-capped Emigrant Peak.

At one of the cabins, I talked to a woman who knew the place well. She spoke of Whitetown or White City, a group of cabins painted white, situated two miles above Chico. They were built by a Mr. Carr, who came into the gulch twenty years before, to highgrade. "You won't find anything left of Yellowstone City," she said. "It's around the hill, down on the flat in the dredge pond."

Emigrant Gulch Mining District is the oldest in Park County. When Thomas B. Curry and his two companions discovered the placers, in the summer of 1863, they were the first to visit the area except the Crow Indians, who

401

claimed all the land east of the Yellowstone River as theirs. The three white men, who had left Virginia City on a prospecting trip, were excitedly preparing to start work in the gulch, when they were interrupted by a party of Crows who dashed into their camp, stole their food and supplies, and ordered them off the land. Curry and his partners had no choice but to return to Virginia City and spend the winter. By spring, they were back again and were soon joined by thirty men from a wagon train that Jim Bridger was guiding up the Yellowstone. Early in the same year, Sam Word and N. P. Langford obtained a charter for a stage and telegraph line between Virginia City and Emigrant Gulch, and when this news got abroad, more men stampeded to the diggings. Their efforts at mining, however, produced little gold.

That same spring, in far away Pennsylvania, five men started west. David R. Shorthill, George Travis, Alexander Norris, Davis B. Weaver, and Richard Owens outfitted at Omaha for their long journey across the plains by buying a wagon, four oxen and two cows. For safety, they joined an emigrant train of sixty-eight wagons that was heading west. At one place they saw the fresh scalp of a white man dangling from the branch of a tree and realized that the train ahead of them had been attacked. Their train got through safely. When it reached Yellowstone Canyon, the big party separated, and the main train forded the river and went across the divide toward the Gallatin Valley. Those who withdrew included Shorthill, Weaver, and Norris. These three took as their share of the original outfit, two of the oxen, one cow, and the wagon. They reached the mouth of Emigrant Gulch on August 27, 1864.

YELLOWSTONE CITY

Somewhat to their surprise, they found thirty-six men hard at work, preparing to placer the streambed. The group was well organized; it had whip-sawed lumber and built sluice-boxes, and was constructing a drain ditch so as to be able to reach bedrock. At a meeting, it had organized the Curry Mining District and elected a justice of the peace. It had also drawn up laws. Three crimes were punishable by hanging — murder, theft, and insulting a woman. The camp, which consisted of tents, dugouts, and a few cabins, was called Yellowstone City. The gulch was named because it

was settled by "emigrants" from the States. Some men averaged $2.00 a day from the placers, but others, discontented with such paltry returns, left in disgust. Thus the population began to dwindle — the number of new arrivals being less than the number of departures.

Shorthill and Weaver, accompanied by Frank Garrett, decided to try their luck farther up the canyon and to investigate any side gulches that they passed. They worked their way upstream for several miles and found one place where bedrock was exposed. By probing under a rocky shelf, Shorthill dug out sand that yielded $1.00 to the pan. News of this strike, which was made on August 30, 1864, was immediately sent to Yellowstone City, and in no time, many surface claims were staked adjacent to those of the three discoverers. A messenger, provided with several ounces of gold as proof, was also sent to overtake a wagon train bound for Virginia City. His news caused some to turn back. A miners' meeting at the new location was held on September 12, at which the area was named the Shorthill District and Shorthill made recorder.

It was October 19 when the water froze in the sluices and the miners packed down to Yellowstone City for the winter. Most of them built log cabins, "roofed with pine poles, then grass," and topped with a layer of earth. The dirt floors were covered with "fresh elk skins." Over three hundred persons, fifteen of whom were women, waited out the winter at the mouth of the gulch as best they could. It was a hard season for all, and supplies ran short; for the men had been too absorbed with mining to think about restocking their larders. Fortunately, late in the fall, two French-Canadian freighters reached the Yellowstone with four or five wagons of Indian trade goods, and instead of going on to the lodges of the Crows, changed their plans and built a log store in Yellowstone City. Even their supplies of food were soon exhausted. Flour, packed in from Virginia City, cost $100 a sack with ten cents a pound extra for freight charges. Tea brought $2.00 a pound, tobacco $5.00 a pound, and bacon $1.00. Had the country not been full of elk, deer, and antelope, many of the prospectors would have starved. By spring, they were glad to eat gum from the pine and fir trees that lined the gulch. As early as possible in 1865, Shorthill went to Virginia City for provisions and found the city in the midst of flour riots. Hearing that freighters from Salt Lake City, who were bound for the mining camp, were delaying their arrival lest their flour be seized, Shorthill rode to meet them and bought what he needed directly from them.

All winter the men did road work along the gulch and even made a trail to the upper district so that Gage, the packer, could run his string of seven jacks to the mines, carrying freight for $3.00 a hundred pounds. Mining was resumed in the spring and carried on all summer. A miner's wife, Mrs. Moore, proudly planted some seeds she had brought with her from the States. Her vegetable patch, which lay on a slope, back from the placer claims, flourished under her regular weeding. Someone saw paydirt clinging to the roots of the weeds, and away went her garden, into the sluiceboxes.

By the fall of 1865, the placers at the mouth of the gulch were nearly worked out and men began to drift away. The camp's vulnerability to attack also contributed to its abandonment; for, although the Indians rarely came close, men in the open valley, or miners working alone, were easy targets. Late in the fall of 1864, six miners went into the valley to hunt in the vicinity of Mission Creek. While there, they were joined by a man named Hughes and by another, whose name is unknown. None of the party had seen any Indians, but as they sensed that they were being watched, they prudently broke camp and returned to the Yellowstone country. Hughes and the other man, however, remained behind. Several months later, Hughes staggered into Yellowstone City in bad shape with bullet and arrow wounds; his companion was dead. During 1866, five men left by boat to go to the States. They were attacked and one was killed. When this news was delivered, more men hurried away. By August, 1866, the place was deserted. In its cemetery is the grave of Donald L. Bynum, judge of the miners' court that met at Nevada City and convicted George Ives.

CHICO

The exodus from Yellowstone City began as early as the spring of 1865, when men started to pull out for richer camps. Others moved farther up the canyon so as to be better protected from the Indians. At the new location, which was called Chico, the miners built cabins and then went prospecting higher up the gulch. Shortly after the founding of the town, Albert Hall, who preferred farming to placering, took a ranch in the valley

CHICO STORE

on Giesdorf Creek and raised wheat and other crops to sell to the settlers. Even in its new location, the mining camp was open to attack. E. S. Topping, in his *Chronicles of the Yellowstone* (1883), describes a raid by a party of Crows in the spring of 1868. Two women and a child were alone in a cabin at the mouth of the gulch when they were warned that Indians were approaching. Although they managed to escape up the canyon, the raiders looted the home and destroyed what they did not want. When they left, they took all the miners' cattle and drove them down the river. The miners, who were working claims farther up the gulch, fortunately had their horses with them. When they returned and found what had happened, they started after the thieves and overtook them twelve miles down the valley. The Indians and miners exchanged shots before the Crows rode off, leaving the stock behind. Four of the cattle were dead and others had arrow wounds, but the miners drove the remnant of the herd back to the gulch and returned to their sluices.

During the sixties and seventies, many of the miners and their families left the region during the winter months. The most feasible method of transportation was by boat, until roads and rails were laid through the fertile valley. To convey the impatient travelers back to civilization, a number of enterprising men, like W. J. Davies, who ran the ferry across the Yellowstone River, built pirogues, mackinaws, and flat boats in Emigrant Gulch from timber that covered the hillsides. Some idea of the hazards and difficulties that were part of every trip is found in an account written in 1865 by J. Allen Hosmer. He left Virginia

City and drove to the valley of the Yellowstone, where the boats were launched.

Sept. 26

We arose very early, and harnessed up the horses and started without breakfast, after driving a few miles we came in sight of the lofty peaks of Immigrant Gulch, and the green trees that border on the Yellowstone. . . .

We could not start on account of all the boats not being built, we spent most of the day in and around the camp, and in the evening formed an assembly and made some rules. One of which was as follows: That they should not fire a gun in the Indian country.

Sept. 27

Early this morning the boats were finished being 36 in number and divided into four different fleets. . . . No. 1-Knox & Bradbury's fleet of ten boats, these boats were sharp at the bow, 32 feet long, 3 feet high, 8 feet wide in the centre and 4 feet at the stern.

The second fleet was Bivens' of nine boats, these were common flat boats and were of different length, they had small cabins at the stern. . . . The third, was the German Flats of 19 boats common flats or mud scows, the family boats had cabins but the others were plain scows used in the states for hauling mud.

The boats were all built of pine lumber. Fleet No. 4 belonging to Van Cleave S. Hanson, consisted of four boats built of cottonwood lumber and sharp at each end, like the original mackinaw boat. . . . This morning we hurried about and got our things from the wagon into the boat and at ten o'clock our boat got its crew on board.

We started . . . and sailed down one mile and camped for the rest of the boats to come up, in going that mile we passed through five rapids. . . . we loafed about until about three o'clock when most of the boats arrived and we all set sail for America . . . there were about twenty boats with us at this time. . . . After four miles we ran on a gravel bar, our men jumped into the water to get the boat off, some of them jumped a little too far and went into the water above their waists . . . we finally got off and sailed down eight miles and hauled up to an island. When we arrived a large Elk with immense antlers crossed the river . . . an old hunter told us we had chosen a very good spot for fighting Indians . . . we had the advantage because the island was covered with willows and furnished ambush for us as well as red skins.

Oct. 1,

Four buffaloes crossed the river right in front of our boat. . . . we slept on the bank until midnight, when waking, my ears were assailed with the intermingled cries and howlings of wolves, coyotes, night hawks and other creatures. . . . Among other noises was a peculiar whistle, long, trilling and frequent, which came from several directions. . . . I roused the family and we changed our quarters to the boat, with

the intention as a last resort, to push out into the stream . . . just as we got fairly located in the boat, one of the guards came in, and on making known to him our apprehensions, (about Indians) he, on hearing the marvelous whistle, informed us that it was the call of the male to the female Elk, and was very common, in the rutting season with those animals — We slept soundly after this.

Messrs. Cone and Trout struck paydirt at bedrock at the mouth of Emigrant Gulch in 1870 or 1871, and following their discovery, a placer strip, 400 feet wide and nine miles long, was gradually opened up in which several new leads were uncovered. Throughout the 1870's, mining continued in the gulch with a number of companies working placers by drifting or with hydraulics. Letters written to the *Bozeman Times* in 1876 and 1877, describe visits to the district by its reporters:

June 8, 1876

On Monday morning we made a successful crossing of the Yellowstone river which was up to the high water mark of last year. We arrived at Emigrant about noon. . . . In the evening we started for the Upper District, about eight miles, over one of the roughest trails in the mountains.

The season is very backward and the miners were just getting started to work. . . .

Tuesday, May 30, a tremendous snow and rain storm set in, and continued almost unceasingly for three days and nights. Friday the sun came out and the snow disappeared from the Yellowstone valley, but this proved very unfortunate, for that night a heavy frost fell and nipped nearly all the vegetables the grasshoppers had left.

The road over the range was in terrible condition — almost impassable, with snow two-feet deep and in places where it had drifted — and there were many — four to five feet deep.

As we were wending our way leisurely home last Saturday, on the eastern slope of the range, endeavoring to shade our eyes from the scorching rays of sun reflected from that world of glistening snow, we beheld a large animal making toward us, which we took to be a horse or an ox, and so went on; but what was our astonishment on coming to the verge of a little hollow to see a huge grizzly bear rise up on its hind feet not fifteen paces distant. We rose up in our stirrups, Whee-OO! and gave one terrible yell, . . . our cayuse turned a double somersault; we landed in a snowbank, and, — to cut it short — the last we saw of bruin he was making 2:40 time over the brow of the mountain about two miles away.

R.O.L.

June 28, 1877

Last Sunday we . . . started for the mines of Emigrant. . . . The ferry for the accommodation of teams has not yet been constructed. . . . We crossed over in a small boat rowed by Mr. Reese, and our horse followed after — at the end of a rope.

Chico is a quiet little mining town, and is entirely different from the ordinary camp on account of the total absence of drinking saloons, gambling, etc. The town affords one store, run by Mr. Aylesworth, who keeps a general miners' supply; 2 boarding houses, kept by Swan & Mulheron, and numerous dwellings on the flat, which present a very cosy and comfortable appearance. . . . All the companies are running steadily ahead and taking advantage of the abundance of water which rushes down the gulch like a very torrent.

In the Upper District more work is being done this season than at any other time for a number of years. . . . Clifford is running a hydraulic and flume on a bar on the left of the gulch. . . . One mile farther up some parties are working the top gravel and are taking out from $4-5 a day.

Chico in 1880 is described by the Bozeman *Avant Courier* (February 12) as follows:

The mining now done is principally in deep ground. The past season John Cone took out about $8000. The gulch is ten miles in length and supports a post office . . . at Chico, a hotel, meat market, store, blacksmith shop and a schoolhouse. Sixty to seventy men are located there and in all there are about sixty cabins.

Around 1900, an optimistic estimate of the gulch's potential wealth was set at 150,000,000 cubic yards of undeveloped dirt which lay between the falls of Emigrant Creek and its mouth, and which was believed to contain $50,000,000 in gold; but no such bonanza has as yet been recovered.

While the placers of Emigrant Gulch, from which half a million dollars were washed, were without doubt the most profitable properties, several quartz leads — the Great Eastern, St. Julian, and North Star — were also productive. These were discovered slightly later than the placers, on Mineral Mountain, some miles above the mouth of the canyon. The St. Julian, which was discovered in 1887 by D. C. Lilly, contained ore that assayed as high as $368.00 in gold and $40.00 in silver, per ton; but the mine's development was slow due to lack of capital. A ten-stamp gravity concentration mill operated as late as 1902.

A copy of the *Park County News*, dated August 16, 1934, contains an article written by Don C. Evans about his trip to the head of the gulch. He begins by saying:

Few go to the end of the road where the Yellowstone Gold Mining Co. has its intake water pipe at the residence and mine of Judd Hossfeld, three miles above old Chico. Just above Hossfeld's the trail is very steep. It is no auto road.

After reading his article, I could almost see the gulch and its mines.

Two miles above Chico is the group of painted cabins known as White City. Close by are the claims of the Yellowstone Gold Mining Company, which extend along the river for a mile. For many years this company, under the management of W. F. Carr, cut down the hillsides with hydraulic hoses, obtaining water for the "giants" from a source near Judd Hossfeld's cabin, one mile above the company's property. The gravel washed down by hydraulicking was run through sluiceboxes and the gold recovered at periodic cleanups. Carr died in 1933, and little has been done with his property since then.

One mile above the Yellowstone Gold Mining Company's claims is Judd Hossfeld's cabin and mine. A little more than two miles beyond them are the remains of extensive workings left when W. F. Carr drove two tunnels into the ground in a vain attempt to locate the old river bed.

Just beyond the tunnels (three miles above Hossfeld's), is the Great Eastern lead and copper mine. Half a mile above the Great Eastern, opposite Slide Rock Hill, Henry Billman did considerable "tunneling and sluicing along the old river bed, which at this place is high above the present creek."

One mile farther, on the left side of the gulch, 350-feet above the creek, is an old molybdenum mine, unsuccessfully operated by the company which built a mill and a small camp at the junction of the north and south forks of the stream. Its ruined concentrator and weathered buildings were standing in 1934, and its cabins were occupied by the men employed by W. L. Kearns, who operated a gold mine nearby.

One mile up the north fork is the cabin of an old-timer — William Cameron. Three miles above Kearns' camp, on the right side of the gulch, at an elevation of 7,900 feet, are the ruins of the St. Julian concentrator. The *Livingston Enterprise* (1900) mentions eleven quartz claims in the St. Julian District, all of which were located a short distance below the mine.

Before we left Chico, I walked out onto the mounds of waste rock that border the stream. Gravel dumps and dredge ponds cover acres of ground in this vicinity, both above and below the townsite; and within this worked-out area, Yellowstone City once stood. Much of this earth was turned over with a steam-shovel years ago by the Pinkerton Construction Company. More recently, Allen A. Floyd and Wilson T. Herron of Reno, operators of a dredging outfit, leased the ground, which included the Hefferlin, Keystone, and Empire placer claims. The returns obtained by the company did not warrant further operations, and work ceased in 1933.

Emigrant Gulch, like many other districts, has its lost mine. It was discovered by Davis B. Weaver and a party of prospectors in 1866, two years after he struck placer gold in the creekbed. The lode, which was extremely rich and from which Weaver took samples which assayed $5,000 to the ton, lay in the mountains near Emigrant Peak, but winter cold and the constant threat of Indian ambush forced the party to leave the strike before any work was done. Two years later, a couple of the men who had accompanied Weaver returned in the spring and tried to locate the lode, but the country looked different and their search, which lasted for months, was fruitless.

BIG TIMBER

From Chico, we followed the Yellowstone River down the valley to Livingston, a railroad center founded in 1882 when surveyors for the Northern Pacific camped on the site. Called Clark City, for William Clark, the explorer, it was later renamed in honor of a director of the railroad — Crawford Livingston of St. Paul.

From Livingston, we drove on to Big Timber, a livestock and ranch center, named for a creek that flows into the Yellowstone from the north, opposite the town. The settlement, which started as a stage station, had a law officer in its early days who was both ingenious and efficient. A town character, called Bad Swede, was a nuisance and was always in trouble. Finally, he was arrested and sentenced to three days in jail; but there was no cell nearer than Bozeman, sixty miles away. The simplest solution was to drop the prisoner in a thirty-foot prospect hole to serve his time.

CRAZY MOUNTAINS

Big Timber Creek, along whose banks cottonwoods grow, rises northwest of the town of Big Timber in the Crazy Mountains, thirty-five miles away. Henry Ellingson, in gophering in the Crazies in June, 1892, found evidence of free-milling silver, lead, and gold ores and staked out several claims, including the Bonanza. He even made plans for a mill and an access road which reached to within four miles of the diggings. By September, the rush began.

A few weeks ago a prospecting party started out from Castle, prospected the Crazies and were rewarded by making good locations near the head of Sweetgrass. . . . Upon their return to Castle for supplies, tools, etc., they exhibited some of their rock, with the result that a number of miners have left Castle to make locations in the new camp.
Big Timber Pioneer, September 20, 1892

Nothing came of these discoveries, and mining was forgotten until 1922, when the Granite Mountain and Stemwinder mines were discovered. The ore blocked out in these properties assayed 55% lead, fifty-five ounces of silver and some gold, but again nothing further was developed.

INDEPENDENCE

South of Big Timber lies the Boulder Mining District, so isolated in high country near the summit of the Absaroka Range that it is still inaccessible. In these rugged mountains, many mineral veins were located and developed during the 1890's. Access to this remote area is by road and trail and starts at the south edge of Big Timber, where McLeod Street becomes the highway which skirts the Boulder River for over fifty miles, through its valley and up into the mountains, toward its source. Seventeen miles south of Big Timber is McLeod Hot Springs. Ten miles farther south is Contact, an early stage station and gamblers' hangout. The Contact District was named because of its position "at the point of contact between a limestone formation and quartz lodes."

From Contact to the ghost mining camp of Independence, thirty-five miles farther up in the mountains, the entire country is wild and rugged. Even now, prospect holes and dumps throughout the hills are monuments to the brief mining boom which flourished in this vicinity. At Hicks Park, twenty miles south of Contact, high-grade copper leads were located, ten or more of which were patented; but the major placer and quartz mines were nearer the source of the Boulder River.

The Independence or Boulder Mining District was only a short distance by airline from the Cooke City Mining District, but mountain peaks and high passes of the Yellowstone or Snowy Range Mountains separated the two. Enthusiastic prospectors were positive that once ore was uncovered, a railroad would be built up the Boulder River and over the mountains to Cooke City. But first, a good wagon road was needed, over which ore, supplies, and machinery could be toted. The building and maintenance of such a road became an acute issue between the miners and homesteaders and the county road authorities.

F. F. Baker, the supervisor of the Road district from Yellowstone to Boulder basin and thence down the Boulder river to Big Timber, is in town . . . soliciting subscriptions to put that road in condition for travel. Mr. Baker wished to raise the sum of $200 . . . and when we last saw his paper was in a fair way to be successful. . . . $600 will make a good road from here to the Boulder. . . .

The county appropriated the munificent sum of $50 for that district . . . about one dollar a mile for the whole stretch of road. If the citizens of Livingston will contribute $200, the residents of the district will feel encouraged to supplement the sum by their own labor and that of their teams . . . and complete a good road. . . . The greater part of the labor is needed beyond Mission creek on the divide between that and Boulder basin. A very long and steep hill at that point renders it almost impossible to haul a load out of town. . . . The settlers of the Boulder valley . . . do most of their trading at Big Timber but would prefer to come to Livingston where they can make better trades.

Livingston Enterprise, April 25, 1885

Although the mining boom took place in the 1890's, the first discoveries were the Boulder River placers, found in 1866. When heavy snow fell that October, work was stopped and claims were abandoned. The first gold lodes were discovered in 1872 by Professor Hayden and his party on Basin Creek, a tributary of the Boulder River; but no locations were made until 1879, when William Langford, Seth Porter, and Albert Schmidt, learning of the prospects, opened some of the gold and silver quartz leads. Since the deposits were on Indian land, prospecting was both dangerous and illegal, and little was done until 1882, when the Crow Reservation was opened up. Even then, little more than assessment work was done until 1889.

Between 1889 and 1891, several properties, the Poorman, Hidden Treasure, and Independence mines were opened. In 1890, when only a "promising prospect," the Independence was purchased by H. E. Leveaux of Cleveland, who put up a one-stamp mill to treat its ore. When Leveaux went east to buy "a complete

saw mill and stamp mill with a daily capacity of twenty tons," the *Big Timber Pioneer* reported this and added an extra fillup:

The first pieces of jewelry made from the product of the camp are a watch and chain worn by H. E. Leveaux, made from Independence gold, 18 karat fine and weighs 7 ounces.

May 31, 1892

All throughout 1892, men fought their way up the rugged trail to the mines.

With the going out of the snow, a large number of men are making for the Boulder camp to make locations and work properties already located. . . .

There are now sixty men in the main camp, about thirty at Hick's Park and fifty to sixty scattered throughout the hills. John Anderson, the Superintendent at the Independence, recently uncovered a 16-inch vein. There is much development on the Hidden Hand.

Big Timbr Pioneer, June 21, 1892

In July, a contract was signed with the Thompson-Huston Electric Company for the construction of an eighty-five horsepower plant. At this same time, the townsite was laid out.

The location is on the east fork of the Boulder, three miles from the Poorman mine. Wires will be connected with all the mines and mills using the power. The plant is expected in Big Timber and will be freighted at once into the camp.

Geo. P. Urner returned Saturday night from the camp where he had gone to survey a townsite. . . . The location of what is called the upper town, or properly speaking, Independence, is between the Independence mill site and the mine. One main street and four blocks of lots were laid off. . . . On coming out, Mr. Urner had no difficulty in crossing the river and reports the teams pulling directly into the camp. The Boulder Mines Stage line has been purchased by H. E. Leveaux who intends putting on additional stock, new coaches and will run on a regular time and business basis. H. J. Dixon has been appointed agent and will look after all express and passengers for the mines and intermediate points.

Big Timber Pioneer, July 5, 1892

By the end of the summer, the camp had a population of 400-500 men.

As Independence continued to grow, its mineral properties were also developed. The three owners of the Independence mine — H. E. Leveaux, J. B. Hooper, and John Anderson — soon organized a stock company, which enabled them to develop the mine by driving three tunnels and by enlarging their mill. They next built a 1,000-foot tramway "to shute ore from the upper tunnel into their ore house at the lower mill."

The Poorman, owned by Billings and Big

Timber capitalists, was also well equipped. The Hidden Treasure mine ran rich in free gold. Under the management of William Townsend and Maurice Roth of Livingston, between 4,000 and 5,000 tons of ore were handled in a ten-stamp mill. Adjoining the mine and owned by the same company was the Daisy.

During 1893, the camp hit its stride. Even deep snow failed to retard work or to discourage the miners.

Snow in abundance has enabled freighters to haul heavier loads by sled than by wagon, by smoothing over some irregularities in Hell's Canyon and on the road up the mountain from the town. The road was kept open from the Independence to the Poorman mine on one side and up to Solomon City on the other, as long as they were needed, and another winter will see them kept open all the time.

At present there is a tri-weekly stage from Big Timber carrying mail, express and passengers. The trip now is made in one day, the stage leaving Big Timber at 6 a.m. and arriving at its destination at 6 p.m. Telephone poles are up and wire stretched to within ten miles of Independence. . . . It will be a few days before the "hello" of the hills comes dancing into the valley.

TEDERICUS.
Big Timber Pioneer, May 18, 1893

The parties who have bonded the *Accident* were in camp a few days ago and let a contract to Larry Ryson to extend their present 50-foot tunnel another 100 feet. To a pilgrim it would seem impracticable to even think of working a mine where it required a 15-foot bar of steel to locate the roof of its blacksmith shop, under the snow, on the first day of June, but to the Boulder miner, such trifles as that, prove no obstacles.

Big Timber Pioneer, June 5, 1893

No one could foresee that this would be the camp's last year of prosperity, and that the stock-promotion schemes, which had thus far provided capital for its mineral development, would burst in the silver crash. As late as May 11, the *Pioneer* hinted that $1,000,000 would be invested that year in the Boulder camp. Everyone welcomed

The Opening of a New Era by the Starting of the Electric Plant.
No more smoke, soot, grease, warning of fire or hissing of steam. . . . The company is an independent one, and controlled by no particular mine. The Line thus far stretched, covers a distance of two-and-a-half miles, and used 20,000 pounds of copper wire. For the present it has been extended only to the Poorman and Daisy mines.

TEDERICUS.
Big Timber Pioneer, May 18, 1893

By fall, the crash struck without warning. One by one the properties closed or were sold and the five hundred dazed miners and merchants drifted away.

The electric power plant in the Boulder district, sold last week under a chattel mortgage, was bid in by J. R. Wetmore, representative for Montana for the Northwestern Electric Co. of St. Paul, who held the mortgage.
Big Timber Pioneer, September 1, 1893

The Poorman mine will be sold at sheriff's sale tomorrow, to satisfy a judgment, obtained in district court in favor of J. J. Mickey et al, for the sum of $9,773.28, $23.00 costs and $800 attorney fees.
Big Timber Pioneer, November 2, 1893

From time to time since then, certain properties have been reworked, but in general, the district is quiet. In 1940, the Independence Consolidated Mining Company was in control of the old properties at Independence.

Nothing is left at the Independence townsite (below the Independence mill), except a few rotting log cabins and some rusting mining machinery. Of the mill itself, part of the boiler, one stamp, and a portion of the mill-frame remained in 1951. The only people who see these ruins are hunters or sheepherders who graze their flocks on the high mountain meadows. In the library of the State Historical Society, at Helena, are several photographs of Independence taken in 1951 by Dudley White. One showed three log cabins without roofs, beside a grass-grown road which cut through a lush, sloping meadow, below jagged barren peaks. Another included a trail marker which indicated that Solomon City lay two-and-a-half miles higher up the mountain. Mr. White had scribbled on the back that he had tried to reach the place, but that his car couldn't make the climb. Solomon City must have been a camp that grew up around the King Solomon claims of J. W. Nelson & Company, which were located about 1897. At any rate, Independence is a true ghost town.

NYE

At Columbus, forty miles east of Big Timber, the Stillwater River joins the Yellowstone. Thirty miles up the Stillwater is Nye, a small trading center. This is not the old mining camp of Nye of which only the site remains. It was situated five or six miles farther upstream and, like Independence, had a brief and even stormier life.

The first prospectors in the area are thought to have discovered gold in the mountains in the late 1860's. Joseph Anderson states, in his diary, that he was in the neighborhood of the mines as early as 1870; but since this land was within the Crow Reservation, the miners could not develop their prospects. A survey of the reservation, made in 1882, showed the mining area to be several miles outside its boundaries, and as soon as this was known, prospectors streamed into the section where indications of ore had previously been found. By the fall and winter of 1883, a number of men had staked claims and built shelters near their prospects.

When Henry J. Armstrong, the Crow Indian Agent, learned of this, he sought to drive them out, claiming that they were within the limits of the reservation. In his zeal to defend the rights of the Indians against white intrusion, he had already antagonized most of his neighbors, first by insisting that all squaw men who were not supporting their families leave the reservation; and second, by refusing to allow Horace Countryman to run a ferry across the Yellowstone River at Columbus, knowing that it would encourage traders to smuggle whiskey to the Agency, which was fifteen miles up the Stillwater, at Rosebud Creek. Now, he had miners to contend with, so he sent Indian police to arrest them and bring them to the Agency. When the Indians failed to find the men, they burned one of the cabins instead.

This incident, which occurred in March, 1884, brought the issue to a head, with each side claiming to be in the right. The dispute concerned the western boundary of the reservation which, according to the 1882 survey made by Major Blake, placed the mineral land well outside the reserve. Shortly after the burning, the *Billings Herald* (March 8, 1884) ran a letter of explanation, written by William T. Hamilton, a mountain man who had spent forty years in the West and was the recognized leader of the miners. In his letter, he stated that he had been working his claim since the preceding September and had "passed openly through the reservation at all times," traveling in daylight between his mines and the mouth of the Stillwater, and even improving the trail between the two points. He insisted, furthermore, that the harrassed miners had, before working their claims, obtained a map from Major Blake, which showed conclusively that the claims were three miles outside the boundary. His letter concludes:

I desire to say . . . that these mines were discovered and worked more than twenty years ago by Mr. Hubbell and others before the Reservation was ceded to the Indians by the government and fourteen years ago by Anderson and myself, the present occupants. By false testimony, addressed before the Sherman commissioners at Fort Laramie in 1868 to the effect that there were no mines or miners working in that section, it was included in the Crow Reservation and Mr. Hubbell and others were compelled to leave their property and remained absent until the recent recession of this part of the Reservation to the United States. We did not return until the line had been surveyed and were assured our property was off the Reservation. Firmly convinced that we are right, we will defend our rights until legally convinced that we are wrong, any orders emanating from the Crow agency to the contrary, notwithstanding.

The following week, Armstrong wrote to the paper. His letter reiterated his stand that the men were trespassing on the land. He said he was sorry they were not home when the police arrived and offered to rebuild the cabin and "forfeit $100 if the claims were not five to eight miles" within the boundary. Armstrong made no more trouble and the men went back to work.

Among these miners were Jack V. Nye, Joseph Anderson's partner, said by some to be the original discoverer of the properties, although Hamilton contended that Hubbell preceded Nye by some years. Anderson's mines had already attracted Billings men who were willing to finance them. In January, 1887, he sold his interests for $3,000. In 1886, the real development of the district began with three eastern corporations — the Minneapolis Mining & Smelting Company, Stillwater Mining Company, and Nicollet & Hennepin Mining Company — acquiring and controlling the major mines, millsites, placer claims, and even the townsite.

Nye City, whose original locators are said to have been Jack Nye, H. A. Thompson, E. R. Nichols, and E. S. Case, was built in a wooded basin at the base of a granite bluff. Prior to 1887, it consisted of but four log cabins, a boardinghouse, and a saloon. With the boom, it mushroomed, within months, from a canvas town to a log city, which contained 500 people, most of whom were busy building houses, stores, and a smelter which the Minneapolis company hastened to erect. The company also laid out a wagon road all the way to the camp, with a gentle grade over which both freighters and the tri-weekly stages rolled with comparative ease.

At its peak, the town contained forty to fifty buildings. Six of its seven saloons, which were built of wood and canvas, were demolished by a gusty wind which ripped through the camp one New Years Day. They were immediately rebuilt, more solidly, with logs. James Toohey was proprietor of the largest saloon and gambling establishment. Mont Sylvester ran a boardinghouse, and Cavanaugh, the hotel. In addition, there were five or six restaurants and a laundry where Lee Lute washed clothes in a dirt cellar near the river. Mr. and Mrs. J. E. Mushback had the post office, and Mushback was also the Minneapolis Company assayer. Jim Hedges ran the company commissary and sometimes doubled as head cook. Dan Countryman carried the mail between Columbus and Nye City. The twenty-mile route over the mountains from Nye to Cooke City was handled by Albert Bowman and Oliver Kelseth, who used pack horses in summer and in winter mushed over the range on snowshoes. Few men brought their wives to the camp. The first three women were Mrs. Toohey, Mrs. Mushback, and Mrs. Seeley. The town was crescent-shaped and extended from the river bank to the big mill. Lots were sold as placer claims, and owners were required to do annual assessment work. Nye never had a school or a church; its sole purpose was mining and smelting, and nothing else mattered.

Just to haul machinery and mining equipment from Columbus to the smelter site took skillful handling; but Buford and his ox-teams were equal to it, and in record time the smelter was blown in. In the meantime the company had tapped several good veins of ore. As Nye City continued to grow, N. J. Trodinick (Tredennick), the "official boss of the camp," and his brother Steve, who was timekeeper and bookkeeper, viewed the boom with satisfaction. Then, without warning, the legality of the location of the mines was questioned for the second time by the government. The uncertainty of the outcome of this issue, coupled with discouraging tests, which showed that anticipated values from the ore were not justified, stopped further expenditures by the Minneapolis Company investors and others. On July 17, 1888, Joseph Anderson wrote in his diary: "[I] Go to Nye on a visit. See Bill Hamilton and a few other men. It is one of the most dead towns I ever saw."

The end came swiftly. In November, 1889, the Secretary of the Interior sent word that Nye City and the surrounding mining property were within the Crow Reservation, and ordered the evacuation of the place. Work stopped, and within a few days, the three hundred or more residents pulled out, leaving tools and heavy equipment behind. The Minneapolis Mining Company was the hardest hit by the decision, for it had opened up the region and had spent $200,000 in developing it.

A few die-hards hung on for a year or two, with Mr. and Mrs. John Turco the last to leave. Toward the end, homesteaders and settlers from the valley invaded Nye City, tore down the old buildings, and hauled them away. The mining companies employed a watchman to protect their property, but the man could only protest when machinery and valuable equipment were carried off. Since then, all cabins have disappeared.

That mining has revived is shown by an item in the *Mining World* for May, 1960. This mentions a ferrochrome plant of the American Chrome Company at Nye, which produced 2,-100 tons of ferrochrome during 1959. The article continues: "When the present government contract ends in 1961, the company will own and have under lease all the facilities to continue a mining and smelting operation." This just goes to prove that mining camps come and go and that the term "ghost town" is merely relative.

SELECTED BIBLIOGRAPHY

Sources consulted in the State Historical Library, Helena; State School of Mines, Butte; and Public Library, Libby

Abbott, Newton Carl, *Montana in the Making.* 8th ed. 1943, Gazette Printing Co., Billings, 1943.

Allen, William R., *The Chequemegon.* William-Frederick Press, New York, 1949.

Anaconda, Diamond Jubilee 1883-1958. Leach, Donovan L., and Howard, A. C., (eds.). McKee Printing Co., Butte, 1958.

Anaconda Standard Almanac 1893.

Anderson, C. R., and Martinson, M. P., *Helena Earthquakes, A Story of the Earthquakes that Rocked Helena, Mont., and Vicinity in the Fall of 1935, Together With Attempts of Science to Explain it all, and a Short History of the City.* Pub. by authors, Helena, 1936.

Athearn, Robert G., *Westward the Briton.* Scribner's, New York, 1953.

Bancroft, Hubert Howe, *History of Washington, Idaho and Montana.* Vol. 31, San Francisco, 1890.

Barker, Sam, Jr., *History of Mining in Montana. Seven Talks About Mines.* Chamber of Commerce, Butte, 1939.

Barrows, John R., *Ubet.* Caxton Printers, Ltd., Caldwell, Ida., 1934.

Billings Business Directory 1883.

Billings Geological Society Guidebook, Second Annual Field Conference, Sept. 7, 8, 9, 1951.

Billings Geological Society Guidebook, Fourth Annual Field Conference, Sept. 10, 11, 12, 1953.

Bogert, John R., "Will This 75-Ton Electric Truck Revolutionize Open Pit Haulage?" *Mining World,* vol. 23, March 1961.

Browne, J. Ross, *Report on the Mineral Resources of the States and Territories West of the Rocky Mountains.* U. S. Government Printing Office, Washington, 1868.

Burlingame, Merrill G., *The Montana Frontier.* State Publishing Co., Helena, 1942.

Burlingame, Merrill G., and Toole, K. Ross, *A History of Montana.* 3 vols. Lewis Historical Pub. Co. Inc., New York, 1957.

Campbell, William C., *From the Quarries of Last Chance Gulch.* Pub. by author, Helena, 1951.

"The Castle Mining Region," *The Northwest Magazine,* Vol. IX, January 1891, St. Paul, Minn.

Clark, A. L., "Revolution in Butte," *Rocky Mountain Life,* December, 1948.

Cope, George F., *Statistical Descriptive Report of Mines, Madison County, Montana, compiled September, 1888.* Montana School of Mines, Butte, 1936.

Copper Camp, Marsh, George D. (ed.), compiled by Workers of the Writers Program of the Works Projects Administration in the State of Montana, Hastings House, New York, 1943.

Dayton, Stanley, "Anaconda Maps Greatest Expansion Program in the History of Butte!" *Mining World,* vol. 18, November 1956.

Dimsdale, Prof. Thomas J., *The Vigilantes of Montana,* 12th rev. ed. McKee Printing Co., Butte, 1950.

Duffy, Joe H., *Butte Was Like That.* Pub. by author, 243 East Broadway, Butte, 1941.

"Early History of Glacier Park," Madison Grant, 1919, Department of the Interior, Government Printing Service.

Economic Geology and the American Geologist, Vol. VIII, 1913.

Eggleston, Charles H., *The City of Anaconda, Its First 25 Years. 1883-1908. Souvenir of Anaconda's Silver Jubilee, July 4, 1908.* Standard Pub. Co., Anaconda, 1908.

Engineering and Mining Journal Press, passim.

Fletcher, Robert H., *Montana Historical Markers.* Naegele Printing Co., Helena, 1938.

Florian, Rev. Martin, *The Story of St. Mary's Mission.* 1959.

Florin, Lambert, *Western Ghost Towns.* Superior Publishing Co., Seattle, Wash., 1961.

Fowlie, George, "Reminiscenses regarding Castle Mining Camp." MS in Helena library.

Freeman, Harry C., *A Brief History of Butte, Montana, World's Greatest Mining Camp.* Henry O. Shepard Co., Chicago, 1900.

Fuller, George W., *A History of the Pacific Northwest.* Alfred A. Knopf, New York, 1949.

Gibson, R., "Metalliferous Deposits Near Libby and Troy, Montana." Memorandum for the Press, Release for June 8, 1931, U. S. Department of the Interior, Washington.

Glasscock, Carl B., *The War of the Copper Kings.* Grosset & Dunlap, New York, 1935.

Goodale, Charles W., "The Apex Law in the Drumlummon Controversy," *Transactions of the American Institute of Mining Engineers,* vol. XLVIII, 1915.

———————, "The Drumlummon Mine, Marysville, Montana," *Transactions of the American Institute of Mining Engineers,* vol. XLIX, 1915.

Greenfield, Marguerite, "Old Fire Bell on Tower Hill," Helena, 1935.

Hamilton, James McClellan, *From Wilderness to Statehood, a History of Montana 1805-1900.* Binford & Mort, Portland, Oregon, 1957.

Hanks, Jay W., "History of Ghost Town (Nye)," July 28, 1952, MS in Helena library.

Helena, as the Capital City, 1894. (Helena).

Helena Board of Trade Report for 1887. **Helena,** 1887.

Helena Board of Trade Report for 1889. **Helena,** 1889.

Hill, James M., *The Mining Districts of the Western United States.* Washington, 1912.

Historical Sketch and Essay on the Resources of Montana, Including a Business Directory of the Metropolis. Helena Herald Book & Job Printing Office, Helena, 1868.

Historical Society of Montana. Vol. I, 1876; vol. II, 1896; vol. III, 1900; vol. V, 1904, Rocky Mountain Pub. Co., Helena.

"History of Jefferson Valley." Written and compiled by the History class of 1928, Whitehall High School. MS in Helena library.

"History of Libby, Montana." By request of Montana Federation Woman's Club, compiled by Hillis, Maie; Herbst, Anna G.; Wall, Mrs. John P. MS in Libby library.

History of Yellowstone Valley, Park, Sweet Grass, Carbon, Yellowstone, Rosebud, Custer, Dawson Counties. Western Historical Pub. Co., Spokane, Wash., c. 1907.

Howard, Helen A., and McGrath, Dan L., *War Chief Joseph.* Caxton Printers, Ltd., 1941.

Howard, Joseph Kinsey, *Montana, High, Wide and Handsome.* Yale University Press, New Haven, 1943.

------------------- (ed.), *Montana Margins, A State Anthology.* Yale University Press, New Haven, 1946.

Johnson, Dorothy M., "Durable Desperado Kid Curry," *Montana the magazine of western history,* vol. 6, April 1956.

Johnson, Olga W., *Early Libby and Troy, Montana.* Kootenai-Craft Productions, Fortine, 1958.

Johnson, Olga W., (ed.) *The Story of the Tobacco Plains Country.* Pub. by "Pioneers of the Tobacco Plains Country," Caxton Printers, Ltd., Caldwell, 1950.

Jones, Vernon, "Spring Hill Gold Deposit," *Economic Geology,* vol. XXLX, Sept.-Oct. 1934.

Kennedy, J. M., *The Resources and Opportunities of Montana,* 1914 ed., compiled by Dept. of Agriculture and Publicity, Independent Pub. Co., State Printers, Helena, 1914.

Kennedy, Michael S., Paladin, Vivian A., Dempsey, Mary K., (eds.) "Glacier Park's Lost Place Names," *Montana the magazine of western history,* vol. 10, October 1960.

Knopf, Adolph, "A Magmatic Sulphide Ore Body at Elkhorn, Montana." Economic Geology Pub. Co.

Lavendar, David, *The Big Divide.* Doubleday & Co., Inc., Garden City, 1948.

Leeson, Michael A. (ed.), *History of Montana 1739-1885.* Warner Beers Co., Chicago, 1885.

Life in the Mining Camps. Great Northern Railroad, n.d. (Helena).

Lott, Mrs. (M. H.) Melvina J. (ed.), "The History of Madison County, Montana," Madison County Federated Woman's Club, n.d. (Helena).

MacKnight, James Arthur, *The Mines of Montana. Their History and Development to Date, prepared for the National Mining Congress held at Helena, July 12, 1892.* C. K. Wells Co., Helena, 1892.

Madison County, Montana, Its Resources, Opportunities and Possibilities. Madison County Publicity Club and County Commissioners, n.d., c.1911. (Loaned by Mrs. Leah Morris Mendenhall, Bozeman.)

Majestic Montana. Chase, W. H.; Remington, C. L. E.; and Cross, Frank, (eds.). Reporter Printing & Supply Co., Inc., Billings.

Mangam, William D., *The Clarks, An American Phenomenon.* Silver Bow Press, 289 Fourth Ave., New York, 1941.

Marcosson, Isaac, *Anaconda.* Dodd Mead & Co., New York, 1957.

Mathews, A. E., *Pencil Sketches of Montana.* Pub. by author, 925 Broadway, New York, 1868.

McClure, A. K., *Three Thousand Miles Through the Rocky Mountains.* J. B. Lippincott & Co., Philadelphia, 1869.

McPherren, Ida, *Imprints on Pioneer Trails.* Christopher Publishing House, Boston, 1950.

Mendenhall, W. T., *Going West? History of Gold and Silver Mining in Montana.* Collins Press, 15 Milton Place, Boston, 1890.

Millard, J. H., "Wagon Road — Virginia City to Summit." MS (Helena).

Mineral Yearbook 1948. "Gold, silver, copper, lead and zinc in Montana," by C. E. Needham and Paul Luff, U. S. Dept. of the Interior, Washington.

Mining Review of Greater Helena Region, July 1935. (Helena.)

Montana. American Guide Series, Hastings House, New York, 1939.

Montana Bureau of Mines and Geology. Bulletins and Memoirs, Butte.

Bulletins.

No. 6. Geology and ore deposits of Bannack and Argenta, Montana, by Philip J. Shenon, 1931.

No. 8. Mines and Mineral Deposits, Missoula and Ravalli Counties, Montana, by Uuno M. Sahinen, 1957.

Memoirs.

No. 4. Geology of a portion of the Rocky Mountains of northwestern Montana, by C. H. Clapp, 1932.

No. 5. Placer mining possibilities in Montana, by Oscar A. Dingman, 1932.

No. 8. Geology and gold deposits of the North Moccasin Mountains, Fergus County, Montana, by John E. Blixt, 1933.

No. 9. A geological reconnaissance of the Tobacco Root Mountains, Madison County, Montana, by Wilfred Tansley, Paul A. Schafer, and Lyman H. Hart, 1933.

No. 10. Some gold deposits of Broadwater, Beaverhead, Phillips, and Fergus Counties, Montana, by Andrew V. Corry, 1933.

No. 13. Geology and ore deposits of the Neihart mining district, Cascade County, Montana, by Paul A. Schafer, 1935.

No. 17. Geology and ore occurrence of the Hog Heaven mining district, Flathead County, Montana, by Philip J. Shenon, and A. V. Taylor, Jr., 1936.

No. 19. Geology and ore deposits of the Rochester and adjacent mining districts, Madison County, Montana, by Uuno M. Sahinen, 1939.

No. 20. Directory of Montana mining properties, compiled by W.P.A., Mineral Resources Survey, Carl J. Trauerman, and Cecil R. Waldron, 1940.

No. 23. Gold, arsenic, and tungsten deposits of the Jardine-Crevasse Mountain district, Park County, Montana, by George F. Seager, 1944.

No. 25. Geology and ore deposits of the Hecla mining district, Beaverhead County, Montana, by Thor N. V. Karlstrom, 1948.

No. 26. The gold placers of Montana, by C. J. Lyden, 1948.

No. 31. Directory of Montana mining properties, 1949, by Millard C. Reyner, 1950.

No. 32. Geology and ore deposits of the Highland Mountains, southwestern Montana, by Uuno M. Sahinen, 1950.

No. 34. Geology and mineral deposits of the Zosell (Emery) mining district, Powell County, Montana, by Forbes Robertson, 1952.

Montana Institute of the Arts Quarterly, "Al Lucke Plans a History Group Field Trip." (Zortman) by Rita McDonald, vol. 8, No. 1, Fall 1955, Montana State College, Bozeman, 1955.

Montana, the magazine of western history, Historical Society of Montana, Helena, passim.

Montana History — Term papers written for Merrill G. Burlingame, Montana State College, Bozeman. MSS in Helena library.

Anders, Clayborn J., "Lincoln, Long Forgotten Gold Camp," 1953.

Bing, George R., "History of the Smith River Valley," 1952.

Gilbert, Jane, "Brandon, Montana," 1946.

Ronning, Anna, "Vermiculite Deposits in Libby," 1952.

Schulz, Rose, "History of Mining in the Vicinity of the Ruby Valley."

Setter, Jean, "Yogo, Sapphire Mines."

Speck, Virginia Lee, "History of Deer Lodge Valley in 1870," 1933.

Montana Territory History and Business Directory, 1879. Fisk Bros., Helena, 1879.

Montana Mining. Northern Pacific Railroad, n.d. (c. 1901), Helena.

Morley, James H., "Diary of James Henry Morley in Montana, 1862-1865." MS in Helena library.

Mouat, M. W., "Early Surveys of the Country in the region of Nye, Mont.," Feb. 4, 1923. MS in Helena library.

Mullan, Capt. John, *Mineral and Travelers Guide to Oregon, Washington, Idaho, Montana, Wyoming and Colorado via the Missouri and Columbia River.* Wm. N. Franklin, 24 Vesey St., New York, 1865.

Northwest History, Sources of, Paul C. Phillips (ed.), reprinted from *The Frontier, a Magazine of the Northwest,* pub. at State University of Montana, Missoula.

No. 16. Stuart, Granville, "Montana As It Is, written in 1865," vol. XII, November, 1931.

No. 17. Hosmer, J. Allen, "A Trip to the States in 1865," vol. XII, January 1932.

No. 19. Phillips, Paul C. (ed.), "Upham Letters from the Upper Missouri, 1865," vol. XIII, May 1933.

No. 22. Housman, Robert L., "The Beginnings of Journalism in Frontier Montana," vol. XV, Summer 1935.

No. 24. Meredith, Mrs. Emily R., "Bannack and Gallatin City in 1862-63," vol. XVII, Summer 1937.

Noyes, Al J. (Ajax), *In the Land of the Chinook or the Story of Blaine County.* 1917.

Nyland, Waino, "Western Mining Town," *Scribner's Magazine,* vol. XCV, May 1934.

Our Neighborhood (Avon, Ophir, etc.). Compiled by the Get Together Club, 1949.

Parker, William. Letter to Howard Parker from Murray, Idaho, Feb. 11, 1885. MS loaned by Richard G. Magnuson, Wallace, Idaho.

Peck, Loretta B., "Early Mining Activity in the Glacier Park Area." MS in Butte library.

Quiett, Glen Chesney, *Pay Dirt.* D. Appleton-Century Co., New York, 1936.

Rand McNally, *Pioneer Atlas of the American West.* Text by Dale L. Morgan, facsimilie reproductions of maps and indexes from Rand McNally Atlas of 1876. 1956.

Raymond, Rossiter W., *Statistics of Mines and Mining in States and Territories West of the Rocky Mountains.* 2nd Annual Report, 1869; 4th Annual Report, 1871; 5th Annual Report, 1873; 6th Annual Report, 1874.

Residence and Business Directory of Billings, Montana 1883.

Robie, Edward Hodges, "Producing Gold and Arsenic at Jardine, Montana," reprinted from *Engineering and Mining Journal-Press,* Nov. 14, 1925.

Ronan, Margaret, "Memoirs of a Frontier Woman, Mary C. Ronan," Master's Thesis, State University of Montana, Missoula, 1932. MS in Helena library.

Rolle, Andrew F. (ed.), *The Road to Virginia City, the Diary of James Knox Polk Miller.* Univ. of Oklahoma Press, Norman, 1960.

Sahinen, Uuno Mathias, "Mining Districts of Montana," Thesis, Montana School of Mines, Butte, 1935. MS in Butte library.

Sanders, Helen F., *History of Montana*, 1913.

Sassman, Oren, "Metal Mining in Historic Beaverhead (1862-1940)," Thesis, Montana State University, Missoula, 1941. MS in Butte library.

Shinn, Charles Howard, *Mining Camps, A Study in American Frontier Government*. New York, 1885, reprinted by Alfred A. Knopf, New York, 1948.

Smurr, J. W., and Toole, K. Ross (eds.), *Historical Essays on Montana and the Northwest*. Western Press, Historical Society of Montana, Helena, 1957.

Sterling, Rt. Rev. Chandler W., "Frontier Bishop on the Loose," *Montana, magazine of western history,* vol. XI, No. 3, July 1961.

Struble, John Linton, "The People's Bishop," *Montana, the magazine of western history,* vol. VI, January 1956.

Targ, William (ed.), *The American West*. World Publishing Co., New York, 1946.

Tenth Census 1880, Lewis and Clark County. Vol. I, 1880.

Thane, Eric, *High Border Country*. Duell, Sloan and Pearce, New York, 1942.

——————————, *The Majestic Land.*

Toole, K. Ross, *Montana, an Uncommon Land*. University of Oklahoma Press, Norman, 1959.

Topping, E. S., *Chronicles of the Yellowstone*. Pioneer Press Co., St. Paul, 1883.

Trimble, William J., *The Mining Advance into the Inland Empire*. Bulletin No. 638, History Series, University of Wisconsin, Madison, 1914.

Turnley, Lilbourn G., "Turnley Quartz Mill (Park City)." MS, Helena.

Tuttle, Daniel S., *Early History of the Episcopal Church in Montana.*

U. S. Geological Survey, Reports, Bulletins, etc., Washington.

  Reports

  Eighteenth Annual Report 1896-97; 1897. Part III, d. Geology and mineral resources of the Judith Mountains of Montana, by W. H. Weed and L. V. Pirsson.

  Twentieth Annual Report 1898-99; 1899. Part III, c. Geology of the Little Belt Mountains, Montana, with notes on the mineral deposits of the Neihart, Barker, Yogo, and other districts, by W. H. Weed.

  Twenty-second Annual Report 1900-1901; 1901. Part II, d. Geology and ore deposits of the Elkhorn mining district, Jefferson County, Mont., by W. H. Weed.

  Bulletins.

  No. 139. Geology of the Castle Mountain mining district, Mont., by W. H. Weed and L. V. Pirsson, 1896.

  No. 213. Contributions to economic geology, 1902. Mineral deposits of the Bitterroot Range and Clearwater Mountains, Mont., by Waldemar Lindgren, 1902; Gold mines of the Marysville district, Mont., by W. H. Weed; Ore deposits at Butte, Mont., by W. H. Weed.

  No. 315. Contributions to economic geology, 1906. Part I, a. The Granite-Bimetallic and Cable mines, Philipsburg quadrangle, Mont., by W. H. Emmons.

  No. 340. Contributions to economic geology, 1907. Part I, a. Gold deposits of the Little Rocky Mountains, Mont., by W. H. Emmons.

  No. 384. A geological reconnaissance in northwestern Montana, by F. C. Calkins, with notes on the economic geology by D. F. MacDonald, 1909.

  No. 430. Contributions to economic geology, 1909. Part I, c. *Lead and Zinc,* Notes on the mineral deposits of the Bearpaw Mountains, Mont., by L. J. Pepperberg.

  No. 470. Contributions to economic geology, 1910. Part I, b. Gold-bearing ground moraine in northwestern Montana, by F. C. Schrader; b, Geologic relation of ore deposits in the Elkhorn Mountains, Mont., by R. W. Stone.

  No. 507. The mining districts of the Western United States, by J. M. Hill, with a geologic introduction by Waldemar Lindgren, 1912.

  No. 527. Ore deposits of the Helena mining region, Mont., by Adolph Knopf, 1913.

  No. 540. Contributions to economic geology, 1912. Part I, e. Economic geology of the region around Mullan, Idaho and Saltese, Mont., by F. C. Calkins and E. L. Jones, Jr.

  No. 574. The mining districts of the Dillon quadrangle, Mont., and adjacent areas, by A. N. Winchell, 1914.

  No. 580. Contributions to economic geology, 1913. Part I, n. The Elliston phosphate field, Mont., by R. W. Stone and C. A. Bonine.

  No. 660. Contribution to economic geology, 1917. Part I, f. Ore deposits of the northwestern part of the Garnet Range, Mont., by J. T. Pardee; g, The Dunkleberg mining district, Granite County, Mont., by J. T. Pardee.

  No. 805. Contributions to economic geology, 1928. Part I, b. Deposits of vermiculite and other minerals in the Rainy Creek district, near Libby, Mont., by J. T. Pardee and E. S. Larsen.

  No. 811. Contributions to economic geology, 1929. Part I, a. The New World or Cooke City mining district, Park County, Mont., by T. S. Lovering.

  No. 842. Metalliferous deposits of the greater Helena mining region, Mont., by J. T. Pardee and F. C. Schrader, 1933.

414

No. 847. Contributions to economic geology, 1934-1936. f, Geology and mineral resources of north-central Chouteau, western Hill, and eastern Liberty Counties, Mont., by W. G. Pierce and C. B. Hunt, 1937.

No. 956. Geology and ore deposits of the Libby quadrangle, Mont., by Russell Gibson, 1948.

No. 969. Contributions to economic geology, 1949-50. c. A geologic reconnaissance of parts of Beaverhead and Madison Counties, Mont., by M. R. Klepper, 1950. [1951.]

No. 974. Contributions to general geology, 1950. e. The eastern front of the Bitterroot Range, Montana, by C. P. Ross, 1952.

No. 1021. Contributions to general geology, 1955. 1. Geology of the area east and southeast of Livingston, Park County, Mont., by P. W. Richards, 1957.

No. 1027. Contributions to economic geology, 1955. m. Reconnaissance geology of western Mineral County, Mont., by R. E. Wallace and J. W. Hosterman, 1956.

Professional Papers

No. 27. A geological reconnaissance across the Bitterroot Range and Clearwater Mountains in Montana and Idaho, by Waldemar Lindgren, 1904.

No. 57. Geology of the Marysville mining district, Mont., a study of igneous intrusion and contact metamorphism, by Joseph Barrell, 1907.

No. 74. Geology and ore deposits of the Butte district, Mont., by W. H. Weed, 1912.

No. 78. Geology and ore deposits of the Philipsburg quadrangle, Mont., by W. H. Emmons and F. C. Calkins, 1913.

No. 147. Shorter contributions to general geology, 1926; b. The Montana earthquake of June 27, 1925, by J. T. Pardee, 1926.

No. 292. Geology of the southern Elkhorn Mountains, Jefferson and Broadwater Counties, Mont., by M. R. Klepper, R. A. Weeks, and E. T. Ruppel, 1957. [1958]

Circulars

No. 7. Gold-quartz veins south of Libby, Montana, by Russell Gibson, 1934.

The Production of Gold, Silver, Copper, Lead and Zinc in the Western States and Territories, in 1907. Mine Production, by A. V. Brooks, V. C. Heikes, C. T. Kirk, H. D. McCaskey, Chester Naramore, and C. G. Yale, Washington, 1908.

Walsh, William, *Biennial Report Inspector of Mines, States of Montana for years 1905-6; 1909-1910; 1911-12.*

Weisel, George F. (ed.), *Men and Trade on the Northwest Frontier as shown by the Fort Owen Ledger.* Montana State University Press, 1955.

The West Shore, an illustrated paper devoted to the Resources of the Pacific Northwest, vol. IX, No. 89, April 1883. Portland, Oregon. (Issue devoted to Montana.)

White, Dale, *The Johnny Cake Mine.* Viking Press, New York, 1954.

Williams, Addison, "Discovery of Confederate Gulch," *Wide World Magazine,* International News Co., New York, n.d. (c. 1899).

Wilson, Neill C., *Treasure Express.* Macmillan Co., New York, 1936.

Wood, D. T. (Mrs.), "Early History of Troy, 1888-1909." MS, Libby.

Zellick, Anna, "A History of Fergus County 1879-1915." Sept. 1943.

NEWSPAPERS

Anaconda Standard
Atlantis (Glendale)
Avant Courier (Bozeman)
Belknap Sun
Belt Mountain Miner (Barker)
Benton Weekly Record
Big Hole Breezes
Big Timber Pioneer
Billings Gazette
Bozeman Times
Brady Citizen
Butte Advocate
Butte Daily Miner
Butte Evening News
Bynum Herald
Cascade Courier
Castle News
Castle Reporter
Castle Tribune
Coeur d'Alene Press (Idaho)
Columbus News
Dillon Examiner
Dillon Tribune
Dutton Sentinel
Fairfield Times
Fallon County Times
Fergus County Argus (Lewistown)
Flaxville Democrat
Fromberg Herald
Froid Tribune
Glasgow Courier
Granite Star
Grass Range Review
Great Falls Tribune
Havre Advertiser
Helena Weekly Herald

Helena Independent
  Record
Helena Journal
Hi-Line Weekly
Hysham Echo
Weekly Independent
  (Deer Lodge)
Intermountain (Butte)
Ismay Journal
Jefferson Valley Zephyr
Joliet Independent
Judith Basin Star
Judith Basin County
  Press
Judith Valley News
Kalispell Bee
Kalispell Times
Kendall Chronicle
Kendall Miner
Lewistown Daily News
Lewistown Democrat
  News
Libby Montanian
Libby News
Little Rockies Miner
  (Zortman)
Livingston Enterprise
Lump City Miner
Madison County Moni-
  tor (Pony)
Madisonian (Virginia
  City)
Madisonian Times
Meagher County News
Medicine Lake Wave
Mineral Argus (Maiden)
Missoulian
Montana Post (Virginia
  City, Helena)
Montana Daily Record
Montana Sunlight
  (Whitehall)
Mountaineer
Neihart Herald
New North-West
  (Deer Lodge)
Northwest Tribune
Opheim Observer
Park County News

Philipsburg Mail
Plains Plainsman
Pony Sentinel
Powell County Post
Prospector (Helena)
Red Lodge Picket
Richland County
  Leader
River Press (Fort
  Benton)
Rocky Mountain Gazette
  (Helena)
Rocky Mountain
  Husbandman
  (Diamond City,
  White Sulphur
  Springs)
Roosevelt County
  Independent
Roundup Record
  Tribune
Roy Enterprise
Saco Independent
Scobey Sentinel
Silver Occident
  (Missoula)
Silver Standard (Libby)
Spokane Spokesman-
  Review (Washing-
  ton)
Swift Current Courier
  (Altyn)
Sylvanite Miner
Three Forks Herald
Townsend Messenger
Townsend Star
Troy Echo
Troy Herald
Troy Tribune
Twin City Advocate
Wallace Miner (Idaho)
Western Mining World
  (Butte)
Western News and Libby
  Times
Whitefish Pilot
Whole Truth (Castle)
Winnett Times
Wonderland (Gardiner)

INDEX

417

419

431